Interventions is produced on the land of the Wurundjeri people of the Kulin Nation. We acknowledge the Traditional Owners of country throughout Australia and recognise their continuing connection to land, waters and culture. We pay our respects to their Elders past, present and emerging. Their land was stolen, never ceded.

It always was and always will be Aboriginal land.

THE NEW THEATRE

The people, plays and politics behind Australia's radical theatre

Edited by Lisa Milner

INTERVENTIONS

Dedicated to Norma Disher Hawkins: New Theatre Life Member, Waterside Workers Federation Film Unit member, political activist, music lover, beloved Glebe community member. Norma has been my inspiration for research and writing on the Australian left cultural scene for decades.

First published 2022 by Interventions Inc

Interventions Inc is a not-for-profit, independent, radical book publisher. For further information:
    www.interventions.org.au
    info@interventions.org.au
    PO Box 963
    Coffs Harbour, NSW 2450

Cover and interior design and layout by Viktoria Ivanova.
Front cover image based on photo of New Theatre League at May Day march, Sydney, 1942.
Back cover image: Freda Lewis as Manuela, with Frank Callanan and Vic Arnold in *Remember Pedrocito* (Boynton), 1938.
Photographers unknown. Images courtesy New Theatre Sydney.

Editor: Lisa Milner

Title: The New Theatre: The people, plays and politics behind Australia's radical theatre
ISBN: 978-0-6451839-0-0: Paperback
ISBN: 978-0-6452534-3-6: ebook

© Lisa Milner
Individual chapters remain the property of their respective authors.

The moral rights of the author have been asserted.
All rights reserved. Except as permitted under the Australian Copyright Act 1968 (for example, a fair dealing for the purposes of study, research, criticism or review), no part of this book may be reproduced, stored in a retrieval system, communicated or transmitted in any form or by any means without prior written permission.

All inquiries should be made to the publisher.

 A catalogue record for this work is available from the National Library of Australia

Content

Introduction – Lisa Milner ... 1

Act 1: Setting the stage ... 11

1. The International Context ... 13
   Angela O'Brien
2. Communism Stage Left: the Political Influences ... 61
   Gabriela Zabala

Act 2: A tour around the branches ... 91

3. Purpose and Passion: Melbourne New Theatre 1935–2000 ... 93
   Angela O'Brien
4. Sydney New Theatre ... 127
   Lyn Collingwood
5. Rural Radical Theatre: the Newcastle NTL 1937–40 ... 155
   Laura Ginters
6. Red Hot Up North: The Brisbane New Theatre ... 179
   Connie Healy
7. Fomenting Revolution in Perth ... 211
   Charlie Fox
8. Adelaide New Theatre ... 235
   Peter D Douglas

Act 3: Plays with a purpose ... 259

9. Political Theatre and the State ... 261
   Phillip Deery and Lisa Milner
10. 'Them Songs are Dangerous': Anti-fascism, Antisemitism and Jewish Connections ... 285
    Max Kaiser and Lisa Milner
11. Sydney New Theatre: Give Peace a Chance ... 317
    Lyn Collingwood
12. Sydney New Theatre: The Fight for Equality ... 337
    Lyn Collingwood
13. No Handmaidens Here: Women, Volunteering and Gender Dynamics ... 367
    Lisa Milner and Cathy Brigden

14	Brave Red Witches: Communist Women and Identity *Susan Bradley-Smith*	399
15	Radical Theatre on the Move in the UK and Australia *Cathy Brigden and Lisa Milner*	429
16	Workers' Struggles on Stage *Cathy Brigden and Lisa Milner*	451
17	The Glen Davis 'Stay-In' Strike: 'Sydney Actors Make History' *Lisa Milner and Cathy Brigden*	469
18	A 'Great Antiwar Play' *Lisa Milner*	489

Encore: A Musical as Warm as a Handshake — **513**

Acronyms and Abbreviations — 539
Image Credits — 541
Index — 547

NT cast arriving at Glen Davis, 1952.

Introduction

Lisa Milner

The New Theatre is one of Australia's oldest continuously performing theatres. Its birth drew on inspiration from British and US early radical theatre groups, including the British Unity Theatre and the American New Theatre League. Workers' Art Clubs (WAC), starting in Sydney and Melbourne, soon adopted the New Theatre League (NTL) name. Brisbane, Perth, Newcastle and Adelaide followed. Over the decades, some theatres disbanded and reformed; only the Sydney New Theatre remains active, with an unbroken record of performances from 1932 to today.

The Sydney WAC formed in 1931. Initially, visual art and writing – including the first exhibition of Soviet art in Australia – featured heavily in its activities. After a few years, the main activity became theatre: 'the drama took over full control'. In Melbourne, the Workers' Theatre Group (WTG) emerged in 1935 from both the Pioneer Players and the WAC. In 1937, it affiliated with the American New Theatre and became the New Theatre. Brisbane, Perth and Newcastle opened their theatres in 1936. Also in 1936, the Sydney WAC became the NTL, and other locales followed. Few of these theatres survived longer than 40 years; but, during that time, they produced over 400 plays by Australian and overseas dramatists. The international productions highlighted the New Theatre's transnational connections. Studies of America's New Theatre League and Britain's Unity Theatre have demonstrated that radical theatre sought to embody the broader aims and aspirations of an international working-class theatre movement, as well as developing cultural activism locally. New Theatre in Australia was no exception.

For much of the 20th century, Australia's New Theatre staged works with a highly conscious, explicit, democratic working-class orientation. The Theatre's strong tradition of performing socially and politically relevant work made it crucial in developing a long-lasting, left-wing cultural activist impulse in Australia. Programs featured classical and experimental theatre (including both Shakespeare and Bertolt Brecht) and works inspired by current industrial and political situations, local or international. Antiwar and anti-oppression themes and plays in support of marginalised groups were most common. The theatre's strong tradition of performing socially and politically relevant work attracted a predominantly working-class following – both artists and audience. Antiwar and pro-peace works have been always important in New Theatre repertoires, and works such as *Bury the Dead*, *Till the Day I Die* and *On Stage Vietnam* have been popular with audiences. As an amateur theatre, the New Theatre relied on volunteers for both front and back of stage. There were few paid roles. Non-professional actors were the mainstay of productions, although many well-known performers emerged from the New Theatre family. Perhaps more significant were its writers, who contributed immensely to Australian literature.

The theatre combined stage-based productions, in a variety of venues, with 'mobile' or 'contact' work – taking performances out to audiences. The significance of mobile work was its reach at workplaces, on picket lines and in working-class communities: to audiences who might otherwise not attend the theatre because of cost, distance or unfamiliarity. On a street corner in working-class Fitzroy in Melbourne, on the banks of the muddy Brisbane River or on the Port Kembla wharves, the New Theatre appeared. Some chapters detail the highlights of this mobile work, including Chapter 15: 'Radical Theatre on the Move'.

The New Theatre was possibly the most well-known Australian artistic organisation made up of left cultural activists in the mid-20th century. People with strong opinions on the nature of social justice and with faith in the utility of collective action drove these groups. They mobilised their own creative resources to establish and sustain their groups, relying on formal as well as informal networks of communication. Their aim was to provide not just artistic, but political, training. They used the technologies and forms of existing cultures for oppositional purposes, and their activities inspired and supported the upsurge in cultural production of the period. Many individuals were active in several areas, so cross fertilisation of groups was common. This created a network of left cultural activists in Australia and across the world, supported by the New Theatre. O'Brien's first chapter of this volume illustrates the strong inspiration the international workers' and theatre movements have offered for the development of theatres throughout the country.

CONSTITUTION.

The name of the organisation shall be New Theatre.

The Theatre shall consist of all persons agreeing to the objects and principles of the Theatre, once admitted to membership in accordance with the rules.

Objects and Principles.

The objects of the New Theatre are:—

1. To express through drama, based on the Australian tradition of freedom and democracy, the progressive aspirations of the Australian people.

2. To cultivate a theatre free from commercialism, capable of developing a native drama, and of educating all sections of the people to appreciate a high standard of contemporary and classical drama.

3. To secure the widest possible co-operation with all associations aiming at social justice.

Life Membership.

£10. A reserved seat for every New Theatre play season, and for every experimental production for life. Full membership rights as set out in next clause.

Membership.

£1/1/- per year, or 2/- per month.

Classes available, for small fee, on various aspects of theatre work.

Training in experimental productions.

First page of Sydney NT's founding constitution.

The New Theatre's commitment to broadly socialist ideas extended to their performative style and its unique range of performance sites. Theatre members would perform at parks and beaches, next to dole queues and from trucks. During the 1949 coal strike, a concert party travelled from the Sydney New Theatre to the Newcastle area to entertain the strikebound workers and their families. Requests for performances came from factories, rural and regional localities and country towns. Audiences remembered their presentations on street corners, in union and trades halls, in large factories and in workplaces such as railway yards and wharves long after the applause died away.

The highlight of the New Theatre's popularity was the season of the Dick Diamond musical *Reedy River* in 1953. It became very well known through its championing of Australian folk music, and this proved to be a critical factor in the ongoing success of each of the New Theatre outposts around Australia. Many thousands of Australians have seen *Reedy River* over the years. Its popularity, with music performed by the Bushwhackers Band, was the crest of a wave of nationalist interest in folk and bush music, among the most lyrical manifestations of a radical nationalist movement.

As the New Theatre pursued its ideological and political objectives in advancing working-class culture and activism, relationships with trade unions and union members were key. New Theatre members would often produce plays or short sketches for unions or other left organisations. There were strong connections between the New Theatre and communist-led trade unions, especially the Waterside Workers Federation (WWF); it is no accident that New Theatres have flourished in port cities. In particular, the Sydney New Theatre and the Sydney branch of the WWF enjoyed a longstanding alliance. New Theatre member Betty Roland wrote *War on the Waterfront* in response to the 1938 pig iron dispute; it played in Sydney to appreciative audiences – and to police, who stopped performances and arrested actors. Artists from WWF art groups worked in the Theatre. From 1954 to 1968, after the New Theatre lost its permanent premises in Sydney's central business district, it operated within the WWF Federal offices in Phillip Street and performed regularly at the Sussex Street hall, under the auspices of the WWF Cultural Committee. The wharfies offered their Sussex Street premises to the New Theatre on the Friday, Saturday and Sunday of each week, for a number of years. Writer Mona Brand recalled:

it was a two-way relationship with the WWF and the New – the New Theatre giving something of itself whenever possible, from handing out strikers' leaflets to performing daytime fundraising sketches and on one occasion writing the 20-minute operetta, *Butcher's Hook*, for members of the WWF Women's Committee to perform.

In Chapter 2, Zabala details the Communist Party of Australia's (CPA) relationship with the New Theatre. New Theatre member Jock Levy has addressed:

the role the Communists played within the Theatre. They gave it vigour, a commitment and undoubtedly played a vital role in the development of the Theatre presenting a working-class perspective.

There were 'fraction' meetings of CPA members within the larger New Theatre arms. In the 1950s, when party membership was at its peak of 23,000, a leading member of the CPA's Cultural Committee described the New Theatre as 'the party's main and foremost enterprise in that area of cultural activity.' The committee hosted many discussions and arguments about the role of culture and the arts within a progressive movement and the New Theatre's responses.

Censorship and surveillance have been a consistent part of the New Theatre history. Like the CPA and other left cultural groups, the New Theatre attracted the attention of governments and security services anxious about the influence of left-wing workers' theatre. The Australian Security Intelligence Organisation (ASIO) carried out extensive surveillance of the New Theatre's so-called 'insidious propaganda', especially during the Cold War. ASIO's dozens of files on the New Theatre – tens of thousands of pages, recorded from 1936 to 1970 – provide a rich history of the various locales, including production committee notes; overheard comments; pen-portraits of people of interest; and detailed reports on meetings, National Conferences and summer schools, including the names of everyone who attended or spoke. They kept lists of the members of the cast and crew of productions. They raided New Theatre premises, arrested thespians and confiscated scripts on more than one occasion. And, for some periods in its history, the mainstream press rarely reviewed New Theatre performances because of their political content, dismissing the organisation as a communist propaganda front. In Chapter 9, Deery and Milner focus on the larger Melbourne and Sydney New Theatres, which attracted the particular attention of governments and security services. They explore the various attempts to monitor, censor and silence those organisations from 1936 to 1953 and suggest that the state circumscribed, but did not cripple, the groups' contribution to the development of a radical cultural activist tradition in Australia.

One of the most appealing aspects of the New Theatre movement in Australia was the participation of women right from the start, with the establishing work of Jean Devanny and Nelle Rickie in the Sydney WAC. Women wrote, directed and staged pieces that were among the first public performances. In all locales of the Australian New Theatre, women contributed strongly in every aspect of the organisation – as playwrights, actors, musicians, dancers, singers, artists and administrators. A particular strand of Australian women writers was an important New Theatre legacy: Oriel Gray, Mona Brand, Dymphna Cusack and other women writing for the New are now considered some of Australia's most important playwrights of the period.

In contrast to other gendered spaces found in the theatrical, industrial and political spheres, women held together the New Theatre. Not only did the theatre give opportunities to women as performers; women also embraced roles as directors, stage managers, writers and designers. They held elected offices. With the theatre relying on voluntary labour, many of its women combined these roles, sometimes for decades. In reconfiguring traditional female roles, these women provided both creative and organisational leadership to the Theatre, in contrast to mainstream theatre. The voluntary nature of the work, the longevity of their involvement, their political commitment and the theatre's democratic structure shaped their pattern of involvement. The blending of organisational and creative leadership created spaces for women's voices in ways that were crucial to the long-term success of the Theatre, at a time when women were generally expected to focus on the domestic sphere.

Existing histories of the New Theatre, this extraordinary case of art flourishing at the margins, are scattered, incomplete and disparate. The New itself is the most prolific producer of its history, which is to be found in the writings of Mona Brand, Dot Thompson, Marie Armstrong and others within its own archives. Each year since its inception, the Sydney New Theatre has celebrated its anniversary with a recounting of its history, activities and performances, and has always been very determined to keep its history alive. Lyn Collingwood's Sydney New Theatre wiki collection is an excellent addition to these historical documents; other versions of the Theatre's history appear in doctoral dissertations and articles.

This volume aims to expand on these earlier efforts. Some of these essays have been commissioned for this publication; others have been previously published, and these have been revised for consistency and readability within the context of this collection. There is, nonetheless, a certain degree of overlap. These works come from theatre practitioners, historians, academics and political ratbags to reveal a rich vein of Australia's cultural history, gathering together past and present researchers' works. It reclaims stories of creativity, protest and ingenuity, filling a vital space in Australian cultural history. This volume plays with the classic three-act structure of theatre. Act One provides historical trajectories of New Theatre branches; Act Two gives accounts of the New Theatre locations in Australia. The essays in Act Three consider particularly active members, productions, and political preoccupations. A pictorial chapter on the most popular of the New's works, *Reedy River*, provides an encore.

I would like to thank the authors of these chapters for their scholarship, generosity and willingness to be involved in this labour of love. Importantly, I acknowledge those authors whose early research on the New Theatre has contributed much to later findings. Thanks to the Interventions team for their superb work in publishing this volume, particularly, project manager Janey Stone, copy editor Eris Harrison, layout maestro and cover designer Vik Ivanova, and editorial assistant Sara Runciman. My thanks also go to the teams at the Sydney New Theatre and the Search Foundation for their support. Some of the chapters have been previously published, and I thank the publishers and others for their permission to reproduce that material:

- Chapter 4 'Sydney New Theatre' by Lyn Collingwood. The information in this chapter draws heavily on the New Theatre wiki compiled by Lyn Collingwood, http://newtheatrehistory.org.au/wiki/index.php/New_Theatre_History_Wiki:Home, with the author's permission. The adaptation here presented is by Lisa Milner.
- Chapter 6 'Red Hot Up North: the Brisbane New Theatre' by Connie Healy. This was originally published in Healy, Connie. *Defiance: Political Theatre in Brisbane 1930–1962*. Brisbane, Boombana Publications, 2000, pp. 109-188. Published here with kind permission of Boombana Publications, Rosemary Lacherez and John Healy.
- Chapter 9 'Political Theatre and the State', by Phillip Deery and Lisa Milner. This was originally published as Deery, P. and Milner,

- L. (2015), 'Political Theatre and the State, Melbourne and Sydney, 1936–1953', *History Australia*, vol. 12, no. 3, December, pp. 113–136. Published here with kind permission of Taylor and Francis and *History Australia*.
- Chapter 10 '"Them Songs are Dangerous": Antifascism, Antisemitism and Jewish Connections', by Max Kaiser and Lisa Milner. This was originally published as Kaiser, M. and Milner, L. (2021), '"Part of What We Thought and Felt": Antifascism, Antisemitism and Jewish Connections with the New Theatre', *Labour History: A Journal of Labour and Social History*, vol. 120, 2021, pp. 95–116. Published here with kind permission of *Labour History*.
- Chapter 13 'No Handmaidens Here: women, volunteering and gender dynamics', by Lisa Milner & Cathy Brigden. This was originally published as Milner, L. and Brigden, C. (2017), 'No Handmaidens Here: women, volunteering and gender dynamics in the Sydney New Theatre', *Women's History Review*, vol. 27, no. 2, pp. 266–287. Published here with kind permission of Taylor and Francis and *Women's History Review*.
- Chapter 14: 'Brave Red Witches: Communist Women and Identity', by Susan Bradley-Smith. This was originally published as Pfisterer, S, 'Brave Red Witches: Communist Women Playwrights and the Sydney New Theatre' in Pfisterer, S. and Pickett, C., *Playing with Ideas: Australian Women Playwrights from the Suffragettes to the Sixties*, Currency Press, 1998, pp. 167-174. Published here with kind permission of Currency Press.
- Chapter 15, 'Radical Theatre on the Move in the UK and Australia', by Cathy Brigden and Lisa Milner. This was originally published as Brigden, C. and Milner, L. (2015), 'Radical Theatre Mobility: Unity Theatre, UK, and the New Theatre, Australia', *New Theatre Quarterly*, vol. 31, no. 4, pp. 328–342. Published here with kind permission of Cambridge University Press and *New Theatre Quarterly*.
- Chapter 18 'A "Great Anti-War Play"' by Lisa Milner. This was originally published as Milner, L, (2018), 'A "Great Antiwar Play": *Bury the Dead* on the World Stage', *Australasian Drama Studies*, Issue 72, April, pp. 31–65. Published here with kind permission of *Australasian Drama Studies*.

FURTHER READING

Arrow, Michelle, *Upstaged: Australian Women Dramatists in the Limelight at Last*, Sydney, Pluto Press & Currency Press, 2002.

Arrow, Michelle, 'Written out of history? The disappearance of Australia's women playwrights', *Overland*, no. 155, 1999, pp. 46–50.

ASIO, New Theatre files, Series no. A6122 and A467. National Archives of Australia, Canberra.

Capp, Fiona, *Writers Defiled: Security Surveillance of Australian Authors and Intellectuals 1920–1960*. South Yarra, McPhee Gribble, 1993, pp. 155–175; specifically, see chapter 'Acting the Part: The New Theatre'.

Fotheringham, Richard, *The Politics of Theatre and Drama*, London, Palgrave Macmillan, 1992, pp. 66–83; specifically, see chapter 'The Politics of Theatre and Political Theatre in Australia'.

Harper, Ken, 'The Useful Theatre: The New Theatre Movement in Sydney and Melbourne 1935–1983', *Meanjin*, vol. 43, no. 1, 1984, pp. 60–1.

Harper, Ken, 'The new theatre: Roots of radical theatre in Australia.' *Mask*, vol. 1, 2009, pp. 6–11.

O'Brien, Angela, 'Theatre of the Old Wave: Mona Brand's *On Stage Vietnam*', *Double Dialogues*, issue 11, Winter, 2009, http://www.doubledialogues.com/article/theatre-of-the-old-wave-mona-brands-on-stage-vietnam/

Zabala, Gabriela, 'New Theatre – Unacknowledged and Out of the Mainstream: the Life of "a theatre with a purpose"', *Southerly*, vol. 69, no. 2, 2009, pp. 187–200.

Zabala, Gabriela, *The Politics of Drama: The Relationship between the Communist Party of Australia and New Theatre Writers 1932–1980*', Ph.D. diss., University of NSW, 2012.

Act 1

Setting the Stage

Scene from London Unity Theatre's first production Aristocrats (1937).

CHAPTER 1

The International Context

Angela O'Brien

Critics accuse Australians of a lack of passionate commitment to revolutionary politics. Whenever revolutionary zeal has appeared, either in direct political action or, particularly, through the arts, it has invariably been dismissed as `ratbaggery' or received with concerned disapproval; examples include the more politically directed writings of Communist Party members Jean Devanny and Katharine Susannah Prichard.

Although theatrical and literary artists in Australia have seldom become rich, most have been both urban and educated. Drusilla Modjeska points out:

> the connection between class and writing is
> endorsed by the availability of education and leisure
> and by access to intellectual and literary circles as
> well as to publishing.

The dominant political stance of the middle-class artistic elite in Australia has been a form of liberal, with an attendant conviction that social justice can be attained through class negotiation rather than class war.

The view of Australia as a democratic egalitarian society, complicated by a romantic mythology that the honest, rugged bushman was the idealised national character, supported this stance. The suburban class of city dweller appeared 'wowserish', commercial and tainted by the influences of cheap popular culture – and, therefore, beyond redemption. 'In the suburbs', said Louis Esson, 'all is repression, stagnation and a moral morgue'.

Paradoxically, although Australian culture extolled the virtues of bush life, stories emerged from high culture, which is the antithesis of political theatre. John Romeril points out that political theatre is rough theatre, quoting Peter Brook:

> Style needs leisure: putting over something in rough conditions is like a revolution, for anything that comes to hand can be turned into a weapon. The rough theatre doesn't pick and choose: if the audience is restive, then it is obviously more important to holler at the troublemakers or to improvise a gag than to try to preserve the unity of style of a scene.

Romeril argues that protest must be, by its very nature, spontaneous. When protest becomes too professional, it 'feels' wrong, perhaps because it is playing by the rules of the class that is the object of the protest. In the light of this, it is useful to recall that, in Europe, agitational theatre characteristically involved the urban, rather than rural, worker.

Because the creation and evaluation of literature and drama in Australia has been the province of the urban educated, neither revolutionary theatre nor working-class theatre has found a substantial voice; nor has that voice been evaluated. Until recently, this has been true of the international workers' theatre as well, so there has not been appropriate research for comparison with the Australian achievement. Richard Stourac and Kathleen McCreery write:

> Just as women have been ignored by historians, so revolutionary working-class artists are swept under the carpet by the chroniclers of culture. They are members of a dominated class and subject to cultural domination, however subtle, which expresses and reinforces the rule of capital.

The few evaluations have focused on the new wave theatre of the 1960s and 1970s and on the street theatre and political student drama which accompanied the Vietnam moratoriums. Unfortunately, there has been little recognition of the connection between such theatre productions and the theatre of the 1930s. Romeril points out that they have much in common in terms of their broad motivation, including:

> the desire to create a theatre of persuasion for example, to make political drama, to give the left

wing a set of cultural symbols and myths, to espouse socialist values, disseminate information and propaganda.

New Theatre performed political drama, and not just in the sense of the catch-all proposition that all theatre is political. The New Theatre was, and partly still is, political. Playwright John McGrath speaks of 'the theatre that exists somewhere within the shadow of the idea of Marx and the Marxists':

> Theatre that has as its base a recognition of capitalism as an economic system which produces classes; that sees that this can happen only through the rise to state power of the current underclass, the working class, and through a democratisation – economic as well as political – of society and its decision-making processes. A theatre that sees the establishment of socialism, not as the creation of a utopia or the end of the dialect of history, but as another step towards the realisation of the full potential of every individual life during the time that every individual has to live.

But how broadly can we interpret New Theatre as Marxist or socialist? Although it was a response to the world situation, it was less specifically focused on events than the anti-Vietnam movement. It was also more homogeneous in its political charter. Was the New Theatre in Australia little more than a revolutionary weapon for the CPA? If so, did the New Theatre offer political theatre, or did performance merely serve political intent? Certainly, the New Theatre repertoire, in terms of both form and content, was most often an artistic response to social and political events of an immediate or longer-term nature. It was unashamedly 'theatre with a purpose' and rejected art that was purely entertainment or that existed for its own sake.

Many of the liberal writers of the period were associated directly or indirectly with the various states' New Theatres. New Theatre, similarly, was concerned with the development of a national drama performed within a national theatre context, strongly rejecting the anti-cultural effects of imported films and commercial 'pulp' literature. It represents a striking example of the paradox of a revolutionary theatre, which sought to maintain what were essentially educated middle-class aesthetic 'standards' while also taking on some of the traditions of the agitational propagandist (agitprop) theatre of the previous decade. The international shift in left-wing theatre to a more 'professional' indoors theatre, as opposed to agitational street theatre – influenced by the shift in Stalinist Soviet cultural policy in 1935 to a popular front approach and a growing emphasis on social realism – further complicated this tension.

During the 'left turn' in Communist International (Comintern) cultural policy (1928–34), the Communist Party supported art forms that rejected any engagement with, or recognition of, professional bourgeois art (indeed, the whole history of Western art). The art of the working classes, *Proletkult*, should be a newly forged movement, with revolutionary form and content, tied inextricably to the Marxist workers' revolution. This position changed with the Depression and the rise of fascism in Western Europe, particularly Germany. The Comintern, seeing the fight against fascism as the most significant political war, not just for communists but for the broad left, redirected its energies.

The Comintern officially accepted a new policy at the Seventh Congress in Moscow in August 1935. The keynote speaker at the Congress was Bulgarian George Dimitrov, best known for his heroic defence at the Leipzig trial of those accused of burning the German Reichstag. Dimitrov's long speech, 'The United Front Against Fascism', laid down the ideological line: that of the struggle against fascism. More importantly, it set the thinking of a generation of communists who joined during this period; their involvement in the party was consistently characterised by united front and nationalist sentiments, even after those ceased to be official policy. Dimitrov described fascism as:

> the most ferocious attack by capital on the toiling masses; unbridled chauvinism and annexationist war; rabid reaction and counter-revolution; the most vicious enemy of the working class and all the toilers.

He argued:

> The first thing that must be done is to form a united front, to establish unity of action of workers in every factory, in every district, in every region, in every country, all over the world. Unity of action of the proletariat on a national and international scale is the mighty weapon which renders the working class

> capable not only of successful defence, but also of successful counter offensive against fascism, against the class enemy.

Along with the development of a united proletarian front, he advocated the development of an anti-fascist People's Front – a 'Popular Front'. The popular front opened the way for unity of action with the labour movement and with socialists. The 'third period' had seen the denunciation of bourgeois art; now, the popular front supported arts workers to engage with like-minded professional artists from theatre, film, literature and other arts.

Because there is little doubt that the political nature of New Theatre in Australia continued to be a response to contemporary social and political pressures, it is important to provide some understanding of the broader social and political environment from which it sprang. The combined economic, social and political rigours of the 1930s fuelled the creative output of the period.

The Depression changed the lives and political preoccupations of a generation. After the stock market collapse of 1929, it became increasingly difficult to trust the security of capitalism. The growth of fascism, especially its attacks on personal liberty and use of censorship, shocked Australian artists, as they observed book burning and the exile and imprisonment of Italian and German artists. The Australian Government's attempts to exclude the Czech writer, Egon Kisch, from entering Australia to speak at a Movement Against War and Fascism (MAWF) conference boosted a concerted fight against censorship. David Walker notes that Kisch's visit 'emerged as a test of Popular Front policies aimed at broadening the appeal of the Communist Party, especially in its opposition to fascism'.

Drusilla Modjeska has written that the Kisch affair had the longer-term dramatic effect of bringing the Fellowship of Australian writers under the control of the left. For the first time, communist writers joined the Fellowship. It provided a popular front focus for writers in the years before World War II. Jean Devanny, a dedicated communist writer, had set about establishing a broad front artists' group, the forerunner of Sydney New Theatre, before it became Comintern policy. Non-communist artists and intellectuals became involved in a variety of popular front organisations, which members of the Communist Party often dominated. The New Theatre Melbourne was a significant popular front organisation. Members included committed communists, liberals and many middle-class intellectuals and artists whose membership of the CPA was limited to the prewar and war years. Nonetheless, for many of those members who stayed loyal to the New Theatre from 1947, the idealistic principles of a broad-based struggle against war and the erosion of civil liberties continued in the Peace movement and in their theatrical attacks on McCarthyism and Menzies.

Both David Walker and Drusilla Modjeska argue a case for the nationalistic thrust of the literary and theatrical movements of the 1920s. With the advent of fascism, the notion of nationalism became politically suspect; the New Theatre response to this situation was to walk a fine line between its aim of supporting the development of a national culture and its need to respond to international issues. Throughout its history, Australian New Theatre drew the content and style of its repertoire less from the existing Australian theatre than from the New Theatre League in the USA and Unity Theatre in England – which, in turn, were influenced by similar movements in Europe and Russia.

Its commitment to Australian drama – and it was a significant commitment – was to encourage contemporary Australian drama. Rather than providing continuity with earlier dramatic achievements, it drew on certain literary and artistic traditions established in Australia towards the end of the 19th century, which the CPA later adopted within its cultural policy from the mid-1930s.

To understand and interpret the effect of international theatrical influences on the Australian left-wing theatre, it is useful to consider the development of workers' theatres in both Britain and the USA. The shift in left-wing theatre away from agitprop during the 1930s influenced the direction the Australian New Theatre took. The international plays New Theatre included in its repertoire were often as influential, in terms of both content and origin, in determining the direction of the Australian plays being written as were their Australian predecessors.

While the tradition of revolutionary theatre was strongest in Germany and Russia during the 1920s, this chapter focuses on Britain and the USA. These English-speaking theatres affiliated with and inspired the Australian New Theatre.

EARLY SOCIALIST THEATRE IN BRITAIN

Raphael Samuel points out that socialism always had an appeal for those who were 'artistic'. In the broadest sense of the word, this included craftspeople, artisans and anyone considered bohemian or unconventional. One of the most famous 19th century socialists in Britain was William Morris, an artist and 'bohemian' rather than a politician, economist or unionist. Morris' associates, the pre-Raphaelites, a group inspired by the philosopher Ruskin, provided a way of interpreting the relationship between aesthetics and the new order:

> Socialism was the talismanic term for the beautiful; it represented, in the moving terms of Oscar Wilde's *Soul of Man Under Socialism*, all that was potentially fine; capitalism, by contrast, was an incarnation of the 'base', the 'mean', the 'sordid'.

Significant socialist influences on English theatre at the turn of the century included the sociological dramas of George Bernard Shaw and the experimental productions of Ibsen, whose psychological realism and modern ideas exposed the superficial naturalism and social anachronism of the well-made play. Also part of a broad socialist drama were the later 'social problem' plays of Fabian Society members – Granville-Barker, Galsworthy and Drinkwater – and regional plays like Harold Brighouse's *The Price of Coal*, which were to find a place much later in the Workers' Theatre movements. Shaw was a popular playwright for the socialist and progressively minded theatres from 1905 for 30 years. It is pertinent to recall that *Mrs Warren's Profession*, written in 1893, was the subject of public censorship until the 1920s. From 1933 to 1935, the Sydney Workers' Art Club performed five Shaw plays: *How He Lied to Her Husband*; *Man of Destiny*; *Pygmalion*; *On the Rocks*; and *Mrs Warren's Profession*.

In England, performance entered the broad socialist movement through the 'lecture-recital', which could include dramatic readings and recitations by 'elocutionists'. Singing and dancing featured in the campaigns and in most meetings of the British Socialist Parties. Angela Tuckett remembers the Stacy family in Bristol – particularly the eldest daughter, Enid, whom the Fabians' Hutchinson's Trust sent touring up north:

> Few could compete with her in holding a crowd of several thousand miners or engineers at mass open air meetings; her powerful and beautiful speaking voice needed no amplification. In the studio gatherings to which everyone flocked after political meetings she would lead the singing to close each evening with Morris's *Message of the March Wind* sung to an Irish folk air.

The earliest organisation of socialist players in England appears to have been the groups associated with the left-wing *Clarion* newspaper. In 1912, a National Association for Clarion Dramatic Clubs formed, to develop a library of labour and socialist plays and to encourage local authors. Raphael Samuel describes one Clarion member group: The Newcastle People's Theatre (which began in 1911 and is still operating today) drew its early repertoire from the plays of Shaw, with propaganda sketches provided by the Clarion League, and later the plays of Ernst Toller and the brothers Capek.

In the 1920s, the Independent Labour Party (ILP) sponsored plays as part of their weekly meetings, often forming companies; again, Shaw was staple fare for these groups. The ILP formed the Masses Stage and Film Guild in support of Socialist Drama at a national level, winning support from actors Lewis Casson, Sybil Thorndike and Elsa Manchester. Miles Malleson, whose *Six Men of Dorset* was to become a popular workers' theatre vehicle, became Director. The Guild staged Toller's *Masses and Man*; Upton Sinclair's *The Singing Jailbirds* (1928) – a play about the International Workers of the World (IWW or 'Wobblies') martyrs, written for the first left-wing professional company in the USA, the New Playwrights' Theatre; the expressionist play *Gas*; and Elmer Rice's *Adding Machine* (1923, Theatre Guild). Bob Mathews, foundation member of the Melbourne Workers' Theatre, remembers *Gas* as one of the earliest plays that the Melbourne group staged, although there is no recorded evidence for this. The Labour Party, although less ambitious, set up a London Labour Dramatic Federation, which organised 15 groups to put on Capek's *Insect Play*. Samuel points out that the most sustained of the Labour initiatives were the Labour Co-operative Societies, providing social and cultural life for working people; their charter was primarily an educational one, and drama was an important element. Samuel indicates that the propaganda was 'ethical rather than directly political in character'. Shakespeare was popular for his 'wonderful knowledge of humanity'; Sybil Thorndike was a 'great spiritual actress'; Galsworthy wrote 'drama with a purpose'.

THE BRITISH WORKERS' THEATRE MOVEMENT

The Workers' Theatre Movement (WTM; 1926–35) belonged to the Communist, as opposed to Labour, wing of the Socialist Theatre Movement and was 'concerned with agitation rather than moral uplift or entertainment'. Where the earlier movement had been committed to the naturalistic/realistic forms of the 'discussion plays' and problem dramas, the WTM turned to agitprop, cabaret and revue, inspired by the Russian left-wing theatre the 'Blue Blouse'.

Its first production, a reading of *Singing Jailbirds*, toured with support from the Plebs League and the National Council of Labour Colleges, which offered working-class education in great rivalry with the more conservative Workers' Educational Association (WEA). As we shall see, there is a parallel for this in the early Australian movement, with Samuel noting:

> one unifying thread which connected the WTM in its early years with the broad Labour movement was a kind of free-floating 'proletarianism' – the belief that workers were the 'coming class' and that the future would be made in their image.

Samuel describes the earliest leaders of the movement, Christina Walshe and Huntley Carter, as 'a kind of upper-middle class bohemian, passionate advocates of modernism in the arts and "advanced ways" of living as of revolutionary socialism'.

The rise of the WTM was associated with the 'left' turn in the Communist International (1928–1934). It saw the revolution in terms of a struggle of class against class, in which the workers needed to seize power, as opposed to the subsequent popular front policy that allowed for a more evolutionary movement towards a workers' state. The 'Third Period' policy called for a rejection of the notion of educating the worker through contact with art that was essentially bourgeois or 'reformist': 'the task of the WTM is the conduct of mass working-class propaganda through the particular method of dramatic interpretation'.

They dismissed the 'reformist' social problem plays of the earlier period; irrespective of the good intentions of their authors, they were too pessimistic and defeatist, not sufficiently inspiring or positive about the inevitable replacement of the present system with the workers' state. Significantly, Tom Thomas' stage adaptation of *The Ragged Trousered Philanthropists* omitted the final scene, where Owen vomits up blood and decides to kill his family rather than let them suffer a life of hunger and misery, because:

> after the abounding confidence in the socialist future of mankind in Owen's great oration, it would have been wrong for the audience to be plunged into Owen's final tragedy.

The form was to be episodic, with 'punch rapid and exciting actions, satirical revues'. The WTM saw itself as experimental, turning from realistic to symbolic presentation and abolishing the stage curtain. The agitprop style offered satiric cartoons instead of characters. The actors spoke directly to the audience and called on the audience to participate in the show. It reflected the influence of Piscator and postwar German expressionism, with montage, mass spectacle and a rejection of naturalistic forms. With this came the influences of a drama that reflected the machine age, drawing from the Russian forms of bio-mechanics, modernism, cubism and constructivism which Meyerhold, Eisenstein, and the group of left artists around Mayakovsky developed.

The WTM's fortunes declined in 1928, until Tom Thomas, adaptor of *The Ragged Trousered Philanthropists* and a member of the Hackney People's Players, stimulated the second movement of workers' theatres in England. In 1931, the German branch of the International Workers' Theatre Movement invited the Hackney group to Germany, where the agitprop style of *Arbeitertheaterbund*, which incorporated the tradition of the German cabaret, strongly influenced them. When the group returned to England, they adopted a similar idea:

> Instead of a theatre of illusion, ours was to be a theatre of ideas, with people dressed up in ordinary working clothes. No costumes, no props, no special stage. 'A propertyless theatre for a propertyless class' we called it.

From this point the movement grew exponentially, with the development of 10 groups in London and many others throughout England and Scotland. The groups called themselves the Dundee Red Front Troupe, Greenwich Red Blouses, Hackney Red Radio and the like, in the style of the Russian workers' theatres.

In Bristol, the visit of Tom Thomas' Red Troupe on 23 January 1932 led to the formation of a Workers' Theatre, with members from the Communist Party, the ILP, the Young Communist League and the National Unemployed Workers Movement.

By 1932, the overwhelming issue was the Depression and its attendant unemployment. The Bristol group fizzled out because the Bristol unemployed had succeeded in cancelling threatened cuts in relief, highlighting the

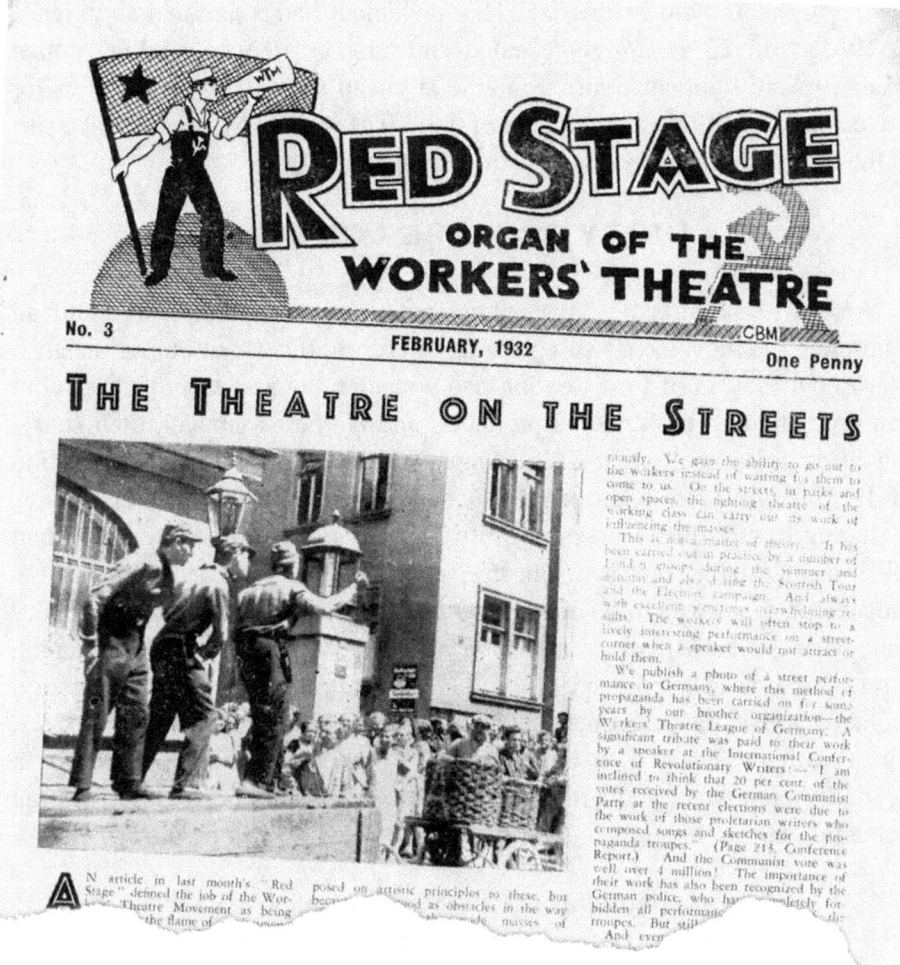

Early issue of *The Red Stage*, a bulletin of the Workers' Theatre Movement.

significance of immediate political concerns for these short-lived groups. The companies of the subsequent period, including the Australian New Theatre movement, had a greater theatrical energy and broader sociopolitical concerns, ensuring their survival after the collapse or achievement of particular political ambitions.

The WTM organisation established a publication, *Red Stage*, and rented a room. Groups wearing workers' overalls, the unofficial uniform of the movement, performed sketches like *Meerut*. The chief target of sketches was the Tory government of the day. The movement had a national conference in 1932, with 22 groups represented and another 10 who couldn't come; sketches were duplicated and available at cheap rates, with no royalties for performance. In 1933, a contingent of the WTM went to Moscow to take part in the International Workers' Theatre Olympiad.

UNITY THEATRE LONDON

Around 1934, after the Moscow delegation returned, there was a shift in opinion in the movement, with growing interest in the use of indoor theatres. The Rebel Players of East London had considerable assistance from André van Gyseghem, a professional producer, and Herbert Marshall, then studying filmmaking in Russia. This group gained notoriety with a production of *Waiting for Lefty* (October 1935) and joined with the smaller groups, including Red Radio, to become Unity Theatre. By this time, the WTM had taken a new name, the New Theatre, and become associated with the US movement, from which they drew the greater part of their repertoire. Unity split with the New Theatre and then acquired premises, first in Britannia Street and later (September 1937) in Goldington Street. The first production included songs, dances, a mass recitation and Albert Maltz's *Private Hicks*. The theatre was run as a club, to avoid censorship and the need for a licence. Actors were anonymous until 1943. A contemporary described the bohemian atmosphere:

> There are satirical cartoons on the wall, bare boards on the floor. There are wet mackintoshes, roll-necked pullovers, sandals, beards, open necks. Actors take curtain calls with right fists clenched in salute.

Unity's objectives were:

> (a) to foster and further the art of drama in accordance with the principle that true art, by effectively presenting and truthfully interpreting life as experienced by the majority of people, can move the people to work for the betterment of society

> (b) to train and encourage actors, producers and playwrights in accordance with the above ideals
>
> (c) to devise, import and experiment with new forms of dramatic art.

Unity declared itself:

> a people's theatre, built to serve as a means of dramatising their life and struggles, and as an aid in making them conscious of their strength and of the need for united action.

The earliest Unity plays were short pieces, a legacy from the WTM sketches staged at meetings, social functions and the like. These were strengthened by mass recitations, such as *On Guard for Spain*, a long poem about the Spanish Civil War by expatriate Australian Jack Lindsay, and, of course, longer plays. *Waiting for Lefty*, discussed below, was the most popular of the plays performed, followed closely by a comedy, *Where's That Bomb?* (November 1936), by London taxi drivers Herbert Hodge and Buckley Roberts. This latter play concerns a young worker poet, sacked for publishing a socialist poem, who agrees to write a commissioned piece for the British Patriots' Propaganda association. After he writes the story, the characters come to life and reject their stereotyped roles; the `Bolshie', the owner of the bomb in the title, becomes the hero of the play. Both *Where's That Bomb?* and a second play by Herbert Hodge, *Cannibal Carnival* (June 1937), became popular pieces in the early Australian New Theatre repertoires.

Vernon Beste suggests that the staging of *Where's That Bomb?* was quite elaborate:

> Mechanical stage effects, much lighting play, careful use of make-up and specially designed costumes made their appearance. The angry rebellion of the pioneer street groups against these trappings of theatrical illusion as 'symbols of a bourgeois decadence' was dead.

Malcolm Page describes how the indoor performances of *On Guard for Spain* used relatively sophisticated lighting effects, with shadows of peasants and soldiers on a backcloth. Beste explains that the changes incurred by the move into indoor theatres might have been of the:

> crudest but for one important factor... The group was recruiting a new type of member. Its early members had all been workers, but now, attracted by the immense vitality and sincerity of these untrained actors, many middle-class theatre enthusiasts, accustomed to the skill of the bourgeois theatre, but disgusted by its narrow commercialism, began to join.

This was certainly evident in Unity's General Council, which included Victor Gollancz, publisher of the Left Book Club; Sean O'Casey; Paul Robeson; four politicians; directors Michel St Denis and Tyrone Guthrie; and actors Miles Malleson and Lewis Casson.

The Left Book Club supported the growth of Unity by forming the Left Book Club Theatre Guild in April 1937, operating from the Unity offices. The intent of the Guild was largely to supply speakers to the groups and to publish suitable plays. Central Unity now employed six staff with 80 actors, some working at Britannia Street, some on tour and some doing mobile work. Unity and the Guild jointly operated a one-penny monthly publication, *New Theatre*, and a summer school for actors. The summer school became an annual event, under the direction of Herbert Marshall and with an emphasis on Stanislavski-based techniques. They conducted evening classes for members.

Unity Theatre London gained considerable notoriety when Paul Robeson agreed to take the lead role in Ben Bengal's *Plant in the Sun*, winner in 1937 of an American New Theatre League contest for plays about youth. *Plant in the Sun* is about a group of five teenage boys, working in a candy factory, who stage a sit-down strike when one of their group is fired; the strike subsequently spreads to the whole factory. The play included some opportunities for the boys of various ethnic backgrounds to engage in some 'low comedy clowning', unusual because the US workers' theatres, unlike the British, had tended to take their political mission very seriously. In this instance, the Unity production 'treated the play as a serious dramatisation of a poignant and stirring moment of working-class struggle', adapting it to suit their purposes: 'the skeleton characters were given flesh and blood by the actors bringing to them their own bitter experiences'. (Of the five leading actors, three were unemployed.) Unity added business and movement to the script, and:

[character] points were brought in with extra dialogue. It is true that the final characters were in so many respects different from what their author had conceived them to be, but they had a reality rarely if ever equalled on the English Stage.

The play was a great success, essentially because of the involvement of Robeson – although most histories of the play suggest that Robeson's fellow actors matched his standards. *Everybody's Magazine* noted: 'Although solid working-class folk form the bulk of the audience, the West Enders are almost falling over themselves to get inside.' Malcolm Page quotes Bram Bootman, an early member of Unity:

> At the time of *Plant in the Sun* so many things were going on and we were getting so successful, it was going to people's heads. We played to packed houses and tickets were being offered on the black market, though prices were only one shilling and sixpence to five shillings and we never put the prices up: this was a theatre for the workers. Personally I still felt our real function was touring, and that the theatre was a white elephant. It was nothing but committees.

A year later, *Plant in the Sun* (without Paul Robeson) won the National Drama League Festival in a field of 600. André van Gyseghem directed another US New Theatre League import, *Bury the Dead*.

Unity introduced the living newspaper technique (discussed below) to London audiences with *Busmen*, which dealt with the London Busmen's strike of May 1937. A group effort devised the script, and John Allen edited it. Reviews were mixed, ranging from *Reynolds News*: 'A play possessing the essential qualities of outstanding theatre… It will live as people's drama' to the *London Times*: 'Inexcusably dull.'

Unity broke all theatre records in these early years with a political pantomime, another form that was to be translated into Australian idiom. *Babes in the Wood* (November 1938) ran for six months; it featured two 'babes', Austria and Czechoslovakia, deprived of their rights by robbers Hitler and Mussolini, who were supported by the babes' wicked uncle, Chancellor Chamber Music. The year 1939 offered Hodson's *Harvest in the*

North, performed four years earlier by a professional company, and Geoffrey Trease's *Colony*, a play in which a Black strike leader exposes the villainy of the colonial governor. The production committee meeting which decided to tackle O'Casey's *The Star Turns Red* lasted seven hours. Because Unity felt itself to be lacking in resources, it staged this play in cooperation with other amateur groups in London. The earlier WTM would not have countenanced such an action.

By 1938, Unity Theatre groups had been established throughout the country; by mid-1938, they apparently numbered over 200. Many of these were long lived. An undated, short 'official' history of Unity (probably written about 1946) puts the membership at 10,000, with 2,000 of them active in 50 branches. A further 300 organisations, including labour Co-operative Societies, Trade Councils and unions, affiliated with the Unity Theatre Society. The stories of two of these groups, short-lived compared with London Unity, give some indication of the variety within the British New Theatre movement.

BRISTOL UNITY THEATRE

The early days of Bristol Unity give a clear indication of the association of the Unity Movement with popular front attitudes and the striking departure from the WTG style of performance. The earlier agitational movement had rejected involvement with bourgeois professional theatre workers; Unity, as we have seen, welcomed it. The founder of Bristol Unity, Joan Tuckett, was a performer and teacher of dramatics and elocution. Angela Tuckett recounts her sister's attitudes in establishing Unity:

> She was unresponsive to the often crude material then passing for agit-prop... She found it intellectually unconvincing and dramatically ineffective...agit-prop all too easily deteriorated into a decadent and pessimistic expression. What was needed was a return to realism and representation on a straightforward but new basis, to lead on anti-fascist, antiwar and socialist ideas which people could feel as answering their own problems as they themselves saw them.

Joan Tuckett assembled 'grouplets' of players, including women workers from Fry's Chocolate Company, Imperial Tobacco and Robertson's Golden Shred Factory (the last had employed Joan to produce plays for its dramatic club); student groups; teachers; housewives; and Young Communist League members. For each grouplet, Joan wrote a tailor-made sketch. For one group, she adapted Tolstoy's *The Wisdom of Children*. The groups presented their own pieces at women's clubs, churches or schools, by invitation. By mid-1936, the groups had come together as Bristol Unity Players (BUP), with an addendum to the rules describing members as:

> from many walks of life – workers in industry, shop assistants, clerks, workers in education, workers in the distributive trades; the average income is below £200 per annum.

The group chose plays 'portraying real situations having a bearing on modern problems' and reflecting:

> those of similar people and will concern our life at home, our life at work, our life at leisure, our life as citizens, our life as people of England and our life as inhabitants of the modern world as internationalists.

Bristol Unity wanted to return to a tradition of theatre as a 'social voice and a social force', seeking 'intimate contact and participation and criticism from every audience' by performing at public meetings, halls, trade union gatherings and the like. The first joint production was in June 1936. It consisted of two BUP-written plays and a mock adaptation: *The Mock Beggar*, *The Bulls See Red*, *Smash and Grab* and *The Wisdom of Children*.

Bristol was an industrial town that had suffered enormously during the Depression. Labour anxieties were high in Bristol, and the trade unions had been weakened. Sir Stafford Cripps, who held Bristol East for the Labour Party, founded the Socialist League and led a united front approach; Cripps was subsequently expelled by the political party which had earlier banned united front activities. The BUP had some difficulty building an audience. It drew for its repertoire on London Unity – *Waiting for Lefty* and *On Guard for Spain* were popular – but, more often, the BUP wrote their own material or adapted heavily. Angela Tuckett spent 1937 to 1939 in New York and wrote to Joan weekly, sending her material from the US New Theatre League. Angela records: 'Much of this American material was adapted or entirely re-written in British – not to say Bristolian – terms'. By summer 1938, the group had put on 150 shows, finally tackling a serious full-length play, Irwin Shaw's *Bury the Dead*, on 26 November 1938. After the outbreak of war, the group struggled on despite enormous problems, taking a children's anti-fascist play, *The Revolt of the Beavers* (4 April 1940), around to guilds and co-op groups. The children involved played it in Bristol parks during the summer holidays.

As the war continued, a 'housewives section' grew, performing mainly in the daytime. After the Bristol Aid to Russia Council formed in 1941, the 'evening section' performed a Russian play, *The People's Court*, during Aid to Russia Week; following the success of this work, Joan Tuckett produced *Distant Point* (July 1942) as a joint effort with the WEA. The proceeds went to the Bristol Royal Theatre Appeal. The housewives section worked with five other groups, including co-op youth clubs, to produce *Landmarks of Liberty*. While some factions within the BUP found it difficult to work with members from other groups, Joan Tuckett quashed any sectarian dissension in her producer's report in 1942 by arguing that it was important to 'avoid a tendency to want to keep ourselves to ourselves, often a sign of being rather superior about nothing':

> We cannot have a people's theatre or a people's anything if we miss the opportunity of making allies and friends with any people or peoples who are willing to push the job forward.

Towards the end of the war years, the group continued with pageant-style extravaganzas with combined groups, often for presentation at May Day celebrations, adapting *Over to You* from *An Agreement of the Peoples*, by Montagu Slater (June 1943) and dramatising, in pageant form, Samuel Bale's *An Account of the Labour and Socialist Movement in Bristol* for 7,000 people in Queen's Square on Sunday 6 May 1944. The pageant, entitled *Now is the Day*, concluded in acceptably optimistic vein:

> Awaiting stands a world at bay
> Dearest comrades, now is the day.

Although BUP kept in touch with London Unity, the group seldom produced a script without substantial rewriting. This was not the case with Ted Willis' *Buster*, which Joan produced. It toured army camps, hostels and factories throughout 1944. After the tour, Ted Willis, then President of London Unity, came to Bristol. He outlined a grand scheme to build Unity into a professional company, with an academy, and to establish a national scheme with travelling producers and a Unity library of pamphlets on acting and production. Willis intended to launch the scheme at a People's Theatre Building Conference in March 1945. He sought Bristol's support. BUP joined London Unity but never established their own premises – as Willis and Bill Ramsay, Unity's national organiser, had recommended. For the May Day celebrations in 1945, Joan Tuckett tracked down a lost script of a William Morris play, *Nupkins Awakened or the Tables Turned*, which the original Socialist League had performed in 1887 to celebrate the battle for free speech in London. Lacking Joan's vision, the May Day committee turned down the play. Shortly afterwards, unwell with rheumatoid arthritis, Joan Tuckett resigned. A few stalwarts tried to keep the movement going, but members rapidly fell away, and BUP folded.

The history of Bristol Unity is the history of the contribution of one woman, Joan Tuckett, to the development of a socially committed theatre in Bristol. For this reason, as we shall see, Bristol Unity is analogous to the development of New Theatre in Melbourne, except that the longevity of the Melbourne company demanded a succession of Joan Tucketts.

GLASGOW UNITY

A different story again is in the rise and fall of Glasgow Unity, a group which began after the outbreak of war (24 January 1941) with a production of Odets' *Awake and Sing*. Glasgow Unity was an amalgamation of five earlier groups: the Clarion players, the Glasgow players, the Transport Players, the Jewish Institute Players and the Workers' Theatre Group. The short-lived Glasgow Workers' Theatre Group was more like the early London Unity Theatre than the British WTM. It operated between 1937 and 1940. Opening with *Waiting for Lefty*, it drew its repertoire almost exclusively from Unity Theatre, playing *On Guard for Spain*, *Where's That Bomb?*, *Till the Day I Die*, *Rehearsal* and *Plant in the Sun*. Although the group undertook short plays, sketches and living newspaper activities, Glasgow Workers' Theatre Group was more reformist than agitational in style.

In its early years, Glasgow Unity produced two Odets plays, *Golden Boy* and *Till the Day I Die*; two Russian plays, *Distant Point* and Vishnevsky's *Optimistic Tragedy*; O'Casey's *Juno and the Paycock*; and three Scottish plays: *Major Operation* and *The Night of the Big Blitz*, by John Barker, Unity's first chairman; and John Kincaid's *Song of Tomorrow*. In 1945, Glasgow Unity rented a theatre. From this more permanent status, the theatre began to develop an artistic policy, with the aim of creating a national Scottish People's Theatre:

> Unity aims at a theatre indigenous to the people of Glasgow in particular, and Scotland in general... What we try to create is a native theatre, something which is essentially reflecting the lives of the ordinary people of Scotland.

The artistic style of the Scottish group was that of group theatre, relying on the US experience as a model:

> there are no stars – only co-workers co-operating towards the idea of the production worked out as a collective of which the producer is the leader.

After the success of the 1945–46 season, Glasgow Unity rode a wave of success and confidence; perhaps also partly disillusioned by the professional theatre in Scotland, it turned professional on 9 April 1946, drawing its company of 12 exclusively from members of the group. It also maintained an amateur wing, although it preferred the terms full-time and part-time, and instituted a full-scale touring policy. Glasgow Unity's greatest success came with *The Gorbals Story*, by Unity member Robert McCleish (2 September 1946) – an episodic play, set in a slum kitchen, about squatting, the postwar housing shortage and the miseries of Glaswegian poverty. By April 1947, estimates were that 100,000 people had seen the play. Other signature Scottish plays Unity performed were those of housewife Ena Lamont Stewart: *Starched Aprons* (1945–46), about hospital life, and *Men Should Weep* (circa 1947).

With the advent of the first Edinburgh Festival in 1947, Glasgow Unity called for the inclusion of Scottish representation in drama. When the official position suggested that there was no Scottish company of sufficient standard, Unity decided to attend. The Arts Council subsequently withdrew support from Unity's planned three-week season at the Little Theatre. Unity later acquired alternative financial backing and took themselves to the Festival, receiving excellent reviews for their productions of Gorky's *Lower Depths* (adapted into local idiom) and *The Laird o' Torwatletie*, a broad comedy set in 1716 and played in dialect. But, as John Hill points out, one of the more significant aspects of Glasgow Unity's presence at this first festival was the establishment of the notion of the 'fringe'. After the Festival success, the permanent company toured extensively, relying on its tried successes, leaving the part-timers to premiere new Scottish plays.

In 1948, on the strength of a tryout of *The Gorbals Story* in West Hartlepool, Glasgow Unity was offered a West End season at the Garrick. After a six-week run at the Garrick, Unity moved to Swiss Cottage, following this play with a production of *Starched Aprons* touring from that venue. With a longer stay in London, the situation became paradoxical – a Scottish native theatre was virtually working from London. Touring and professional work took their toll, and members began to leave. Only a handful returned to Scotland to join the part-timers in another production of *The Gorbals Story*; eventually, both aspects of the theatre collapsed.

UNITY THEATRE AFTER THE WAR

Glasgow's decline sprang partly from its decision to become a professional company and the demands that imposed on the group. London Unity inspired the change, having turned professional in 1946 with a production of O'Neill's *All God's Chillun Got Wings*. Throughout the war and after it, Unity presented a mix of plays, both from the USA and locally written, and added a repertoire of classical plays, including *Spanish Village* and plays by Molière. This policy, advocated by Ted Willis, was to have a marked effect on production policy at the Melbourne New Theatre. Writer Ted Willis became Unity's most prolific playwright, producing *Buster*, *All Change Here*, *God Bless the Guv'nor* and *What Happens to Love*, all of which found their way to New Theatres in Australia. In 1947, Unity accepted a commission from the Ministry of Fuel to create a living newspaper, *Black Magic*, as part of a publicity campaign. After the war, Unity's united front policy was particularly broad:

> Unity exists to be of service to the people and especially to be of service to the labour movement

which embraces the great majority of 'workers by hand and brain', and which today is the strongest single progressive force in the country with power in many hundreds of local authorities and in the Government.

Unity maintained its production principle, begun a decade earlier: 'Unity believes in the Group Ideal. There are no stars in our theatre. There are teams.' The group extended distribution of plays and its magazine *New Theatre*, both of which were to have international, as well as national, circulation.

U.S. THEATRE OF THE LEFT

The evolution of a US theatre of the left has similarities to the British movement, but with a difference of approach determined by the different sociocultural characteristics of the working classes in both countries. In the USA, a working-class theatre was associated with the Communist Party and drew its inspiration from the workers' theatres in Germany and the Soviet Union. As with the British experience, leftist US theatre in the period 1928-34 was quite different in intent and style from the ideas that characterised the popular front. But the composition of both the workers' and the broader front movements differed significantly from those in Britain, predictably leading to differences in content and style. Stuart Cosgrove points outs out:

> The American working class was, and to a lesser extent still is, composed of indigenous white workers, European migrants and disinherited black workers... It is understandable therefore that the politics of racialism concerned the American worker more directly than it did the British working class and predictably this concern is reflected in the American Workers Theatre [which] produced a potent and effective anti-racialist theatre.

Cosgrove identified a second major difference: 'there seems to be a higher level of involvement by intellectuals and theatre workers than has ever been the case in Britain'.

The significant occasion for this alliance of the organised working class and New York's intellectual 'bohemians' was the *Paterson Strike Pageant*

THE INTERNATIONAL CONTEXT

Cover of the *Manchester Unity Theatre Bulletin*, October/November 1956.

(7 June 1913). The IWW organised this during the strike of silk workers, and Jack Reed directed around 1,000 performers. The left wing in the USA during the 1920s was diverse. It included anarchists, communists, socialists, and idealists. The Communist Party began in 1919, but the IWW continued to attract strong support, and one of the earliest plays of the left theatre, *The Singing Jailbirds*, celebrated its martyrs. During the 1920s, there were hundreds of small theatre groups attached to immigrant groups, but these relied on the European theatre, rather than developing a new US immigrant genre. Two early movements characterised the style of the burgeoning left theatre. John Howard Lawson, Emjo Basshe, John Dos Passos and Michael Gold established the New Playwrights Theatre in 1927 under the financial protection of Otto Kahn, in an 'attempt to buck the tide and put on plays dealing with the industrial life around us in a novel experimenting manner'. It included works by these writers, along with Upton Sinclair and Paul Sifton. The attempt failed, and the group folded after two seasons; but it represents an early instance of the union of radical political and theatrical ideologies in its experimentation with expressionism and constructivism. A second group – also involving the communist writers Gold and Lawson, along with a Russian visitor, Artokov – was the Workers' Drama League (WDL), an amateur troupe founded in 1926 with the aim of reaching a working-class audience. Its first production was Gold's short revolutionary sketch *Strike*, modelled on plays he had seen performed in Europe.

Not until the crash of the stock market in 1929, however, did the proletarian art movement really establish itself as a vital literary and revolutionary force. The communist journal *New Masses* carried new literature and reports on workers' art, including information about workers' theatre groups. About 12 of these companies, led by the Workers' Laboratory Theatre (WLT) – a regrouped section of the old WDL – formed the Workers Dramatic Council, promoting classes in playwriting to extend their repertoire. They were open supporters of the Communist Party. Malcolm Goldstein notes:

> It was the [Communist] party's burst of trade-unionist activity in the late twenties that brought the proletarian theatrical societies into being, and the crash of the market that kept them alive.

Also prominent in the Council was the Prolet Buehne, a German speaking group headed by John E. Bonn; like the WLT, it was modelled on the Russian 'Blue Blouse'. Ben Blake, the earliest chronicler of the US left theatre, described them:

> In the fall of 1930, word began to spread from mouth to mouth in radical circles of the New York labour movement of a German speaking theatre group that gave exciting performances of a new chanted type of play which the group called `agit-prop'... No theatre housed them. They would turn up at labour meetings, rallies of the unemployed and the like, and give one or two of their agit-prop plays on the stage if there was one, or on the speaker's platform or even on the floor... the plays themselves...were crude in plot and characterisation and full of revolutionary labour clichés. Yet they had a hard-hitting directness of statement that would often strike off flaming sparks of emotion in the beholder.

The agitprop form involved considerable unison work, chanted dialogue and mass movement, with plots so rapid fire that there was little time for reflection. The agitprop reflected worker solidarity and the extremes of third period Stalinism. The acting was far removed from the style that was to characterise the post popular front period:

> It is to be remembered that it is not necessary to portray a particular character but rather a class angle or conception of that character, which should not be difficult for a class conscious worker. The leading comrade, therefore must be careful not to force his or her conception of the character upon the actor, but rather the class angle – our angle through the actors' own person.

THE DEVELOPMENT OF THE NEW THEATRE LEAGUE

In 1931, the WLT began publication of a monthly, *Workers' Theatre*, which exhibited a hard line against cooperation with the bourgeois theatre. In 1932, the magazine's editors called for a National Conference and *Spartakiade* (international theatre event) of agitprop productions to be held in New York. After the artistic failure of the *Spartakiade*, their hard line softened in the period between 1932 and 1935. The League of Workers' Theatres, a forerunner to the New Theatre movement, formed in 1932. By 1933, there was growing evidence of a willingness to cooperate with a broader section of the labour movement, and the issue of anti-fascism gained in importance. By this time, there were more than 250 Workers' Theatre Groups in the USA, and that rose to 400 in the following year. In July–August 1933, *Workers' Theatre* suspended publication, beginning again in 1934 with another name: *New Theatre*. In January 1935, the League of Workers' Theatres became NTL; it dropped all dogmatic pro-Soviet slogans and called for 'a united front against war, fascism and censorship.' By the time the popular front became official Comintern policy, the NTL had established a new theatre school and had affiliated across the country.

In the USA, in contrast to the British experience, there was considerable interest in finding a new voice for the left theatre that would address a broader audience in the professional theatres and among intellectuals; this influenced the movement's popular front phase between 1935 and 1940. But Stuart Cosgrove notes that the professional groups working in left sociopolitical theatre 'varied enormously and often only had one thing in common, a general dissatisfaction with Broadway's soporific and escapist naturalism.' The League itself recruited several professional organisations. The Theatre Collective was a producing unit set up as a branch of the WLT. By 1935, it had become less active except for maintaining a studio school and a film unit. The Shock Troupe was a faction of the WLT, a professional group of about 13 members who based their style on Soviet revolutionary theatre. The group was 'a special emergency theatre group' formed in 1931; its members lived collectively and operated as a mobile theatre, performing agitprop, mass recitations and similar political revue at strike meetings, in neighbourhoods and at party gatherings, pickets and similar occasions. The group developed a large repertoire, much of which was collectively written – including *Newsboy*, an elaborate 12-minute agitational play about a newsboy for a capitalist paper who becomes a convert to the left. At a Festival and Conference of Workers' Theatres held in 1934, *Newsboy* won first prize. The Shock Troupe was also heavily involved in anti-racist material, writing a version of the agitprop *Scottsboro* about Black youth wrongly accused of rape and including Black workers in their productions.

THE GROUP THEATRE

Perhaps the most influential of the professional companies of the 1930s, the one that was to change the directions of radical political theatre through one of its members, was the Group Theatre. A socially committed company with collectivist ideals, it was essentially a Broadway organisation and ran from 1931 to 1941. Lee Strasberg, Harold Clurman and Cheryl Crawford led the Group Theatre; Goldstein points out that 'they were more interested in revolutionising the stage than in revolutionising the national political structure'. The Group is most memorable for its commitment to the Stanislavski technique of acting (discussed in more detail in chapter 3), brought to the US theatre by two actors from the Moscow company; they stayed on to work at the American Laboratory Theatre with which Strasberg was associated. It was the Group Theatre's popularisation (and Americanisation) of the technique that was to influence its use in popular front left-wing theatres. The New Theatre magazine and other leftist theatre journals to which the Australian branches of New Theatre and Unity subscribed carried articles about Russian and German theatre techniques:

> The aim of the system is to enable the actor to use himself more consciously as an instrument for the attainment of truth on the stage. If we had been satisfied that such truth was achieved in most productions, there would have been little purpose in troubling ourselves over the system, for it was not something taught novices, but rather a method employed in all our productions with experienced actors... It seemed to us that without such true experience plays in the theatre were lacking in all creative justification. In short, the system, was not an end in itself, but a means employed for the true interpretation of plays.

Cover of *New Theatre*, journal of the US New Theatre League, February 1935.

WAITING FOR LEFTY

The Group Theatre was a professional collective, but many of its members assisted in other theatre projects. The communist cell of the Group were supporters of the workers' theatre groups around New York. In 1934, the League set about finding appropriate new scripts and began a series of New Theatre nights on Sundays at the Civic Repertory Theatre in 14th Street. The most famous of these was *Waiting for Lefty*, the play that became a signature piece for workers' theatre groups around the world. Clifford Odets presented the play to the League in 1934 and won a prize for the best Labour play. *Waiting for Lefty* subsequently played on 6 January 1935 and received such audience acclaim that the evening has become legendary.

Waiting for Lefty was based on the New York taxi drivers' strike of February 1934. The play is composed of six scenes set on a bare stage at a workers' strike meeting. One of the men, Fatt, the head of the Union, is a 'stool' for the capitalists and opposes the strike. While the members wait for Lefty, the radical chairman, five of the worker protagonists act out their reasons for supporting the strike. These scenes all present victims of capitalist pressure or racism: Joe, a driver who is convinced to strike by his wife Edna; the Young Hack, too poor to marry his girl; and three drivers from other walks of life: the Young Actor, the Jewish doctor in the Intern Episode, and the Lab Assistant. At the end of the play, Agate, a union agitator, stands up to call for a vote; we learn that Lefty has been found 'behind the car barns with a bullet in his head'. Agate's final rising cry was:

> Hear it, boys, hear it? Hell, listen to me! Coast to coast! Hello, America! Hello. We're stormbirds of the working class. Workers of the world...our bones and blood! And when we die they'll know what we did to make a new world! Christ, cut us up to little pieces. We'll die for what is right! put fruit trees where our ashes are! (TO AUDIENCE): Well, what's the answer?

Actor-plants in the audience called out Strike! – echoed by Agate from the stage until the audience is moved to join in. Harold Clurman records the first production of *Lefty*:

> The first scene of *Lefty* had not played two minutes when a shock of delighted recognition struck the audience like a tidal wave... The actors no longer performed; they were being carried along as if by an exultancy of communication such as I have never witnessed in the theatre before. Audience and actors became one. Line after line brought applause, whistles, bravos and heartfelt shouts of kinship... When the audience at the end of the play responded to the militant question from the stage: Well what's the answer? with a spontaneous roar 'Strike! Strike!' it was something more than a tribute to the play's effectiveness, more even than a testimony of the audience's hunger for constructive social action. It was the birth cry of the thirties. Our youth had found its voice. It was a call to join in the good fight for a greater measure of life in a world free of economic fear, falsehood and craven servitude to stupidity and greed.

Hundreds of New Theatre League groups across the USA joined in 'the good fight', using *Lefty* as their voice; the play became equally popular in Britain, as we have seen, and in Australia. *Lefty* is an interesting meeting point between the agitation of the third period drama and popular front social realism. It is vigorously pro-Soviet and owes a good deal to the agitprop drama for its construction. The Notes for Production in the 1937 Left Book Club Edition of the play suggest that:

> the strike committee on the platform during the play should be used as a chorus. Emotional, political, musical, they have in them possibilities of various comments on the scenes... In the climaxes of each scene slogans might very effectively be used – a voice coming out of the dark. Such a voice might announce at the appropriate moments in the Young Intern scene that the USSR is the only country in the world where Anti-Semitism is a crime against the state.

On the other hand, the internal scenes give a clear insight into an aspect of the lives of the strikers, which are revealed in a naturalistic idiom that was to influence the writing of later plays which came to be described as socialist realism.

THE LIVING NEWSPAPER

One of the other important US influences on British and Australian popular front theatres was the Living Newspaper Unit, which grew out of the government-sponsored Federal Theatre Project. As part of the New Deal, Franklin Delano Roosevelt employed millions through the Works Progress Administration, a Depression federal relief agency. The Federal Theatre was a national theatre project which began in 1935 as a division of the Work Projects Administration. Hallie Flanagan, previously director of Vasser Experimental Theatre, directed the project from Washington. Though an academic, she had an interest in the workers' theatre movement. She wrote one of the first articles on the movement in 1931 and wrote and directed an agitprop piece, *Can You Hear Their Voices?* which became a popular performance piece for radical amateur and student groups. Elmer Rice, a playwright who had explored non-naturalistic techniques taken from German expressionism in his work for the Theatre Guild, became the New York Regional Director. The Federal Theatre project employed 10,000 people at its peak, giving impetus to an African-American theatre. Admission to Federal Theatre productions was cheap, allowing for popular access; many of the performances allowed free entry. The most successful way of employing the enormous numbers of actors on relief, and of creating a true labour theatre which considered the real problems of the day, was in the Project's Living Newspaper Unit under Arthur Arent. Rice had organised for the Newspaper Guild to sponsor the unit, and playwrights worked with unemployed Guild members to develop the scripts. Goldstein suggests that the origins of the living newspaper form were not clear, but that the US living newspaper evolved out of the work of the unit, and was:

> [a] narrative method [which] combined historical documents and the latest news flashes with invented dialogue and brought together real figures of the past and present alongside invented characters, all presided over by the disembodied Voice of the Living Newspaper that rang across the

stage by means of a loudspeaker. Projections, films, charts, graphs, the novel use of light, and scenery of both naturalistic and expressionist varieties were part of the technique. Music, both orchestral and vocal was used.

It is significant that, while the US theatre adapted the living newspaper format to its needs, the term was first used in relation to the Soviet 'Blue Blouse' movement, when:

> Three students from the Institute of Journalism... made an appearance at the third anniversary evening of the Institute (October 1923)...where they put on a then quite new amateur living newspaper.

The 'Blue Blouse' actually defined itself as a 'dramatic living newspaper'.

DECLINE OF THE NEW THEATRE LEAGUE

The New Theatre magazine was to last only three years, from January 1934 to April 1937. The organisation it represented continued some five years longer. Herbert Kline recalls those involved in the magazine (himself included) as:

> impassioned participants in the theatre renaissance that New Theatre helped generate from 1934 through 1936. Three rebellious creative challenging years of dramatising the harsh realities of American life and the imminent dangers of fascist triggered wars.

While the New Theatre League was to be the most successful and long lived of the US organisations for the development of the left-wing stage, there was nothing especially revolutionary or experimental about the dramatic form it fostered. From 1934, socialist realism had become the official cultural policy in the Soviet Union, and the League, with its Communist hardcore, followed this policy. Mark Marvin wrote in *New Masses* in 1935 that the new theatre:

> must present a drama which reflects the immediate personal and collective problems of both the past and present...such a theatre naturally fights along with the masses for an extension of democratic rights, for the right to organise trade unions, against war, against fascism...in brief for a better and richer life.

The intent was to get rid of sectarianism and promote a 'People's Theatre', presenting a drama with 'love, ambition, fear and hope'. The movement also had a stronger nationalist sentiment: 'Our beliefs were a kind of all-embracing humanism stemming from the American Revolutionary Ideals of Democracy, but strongly and openly leftist.'

The League became a play distribution outlet, controlling the rights for plays by many of the USA's most talented writers, including Albert Maltz, Irwin Shaw, Paul and Clair Sifton, Philip Stevenson, Ben Bengal and Clifford Odets, and translations of European and Soviet texts such as Brecht's *Señora Carrar's Rifles*. Affiliate groups of the League would extend overseas, including Australia. The League developed a school outside New York and, by 1941, had decentralised to include offices in a variety of regional centres. The USA's involvement in the war made it difficult for the League to continue. The *New Theatre News* stopped, and the groups began to disband. In 1942, Toby Cole, the League Secretary, handed over materials to the New York Library and shut the office – not with a bang, as it had begun, and with scarcely a whimper. Goldstein says in his summation of the movement:

> It is a measure of the passion generated by the period's events that with virtually no material gain so much talent should have been given over to the service of a single organisation.

It is notable that the New Theatre League was crippled by the USA's wartime mobilisation, which diverted the energies of its (mostly male) leaders. As we have seen, this was not true of the female-led Bristol Unity Theatre, which developed the activities of housewives, female workers and children. And, as we shall see, the active involvement of women as directors, writers and organisers was to sustain New Theatres in Melbourne and Sydney throughout the war and well beyond.

Members of the United Auto Workers District 65 Drama Club kicking up their heels at the annual Hudson River boat trip of the warehouse workers' union, 1940. The photo was taken by a rank-and-file camera club member.

EARLY AUSTRALIAN 'LEFT' THEATRE

The Australian workers' theatre movement has little of the sociopolitical tradition evident in the formation of the British and US movements. The CPA formed in 1920 in Australia, but its earliest literary expressions tended to be in poetry or narrative, rather than dramatic, form. Any national Australian dramatic form in the 19th century was primarily melodramatic, if Australian in character: high-spirited currency lads and lasses, congenial bush types and buffoonish new chums. The theme of these pieces was essentially Australia as an egalitarian society, the 'great leveller'. This attitude pervaded all the literature of the 19th century, particularly that of the *Bulletin* school of writers, but it found a more developed expression in the prose of Joseph Furphy and Henry Lawson than it did in the drama. It was this tradition which the New Theatre movement would recognise as its literary ancestor in the quest for an Australian voice.

The non-commercial and 'little' theatre movement in Australia was essentially conservative and drew its repertoire from lightweight British comedies. At the Melbourne Repertory Club (1911–17) and, later, the Sydney Repertory Theatre Society (1920–27), Gregan McMahon was somewhat more adventurous with productions of Ibsen, Chekhov, Shaw and Galsworthy and occasional Australian plays; but he was, essentially, a professional actor–producer with commercial training. Although McMahon was dedicated to developing an innovative theatre, his professional orientation and the fact that he was 'consumed in the immediate service of a conservatively inclined and superficially mannered minority group' exclude his work from being seen as dramatically or theatrically radical.

THE PIONEER PLAYERS

Perhaps the closest Australia came to an early leftist theatre movement, or at least a national folk theatre, was the development of the short-lived Pioneer Players in Melbourne, which Stewart Macky, Vance Palmer and Louis Esson founded in 1922. The Pioneer Players, however, was essentially an authors' theatre; while sympathetic to the broader socialist issues, it owed more to Yeats' notion of 'naturalism' and the Abbey Theatre than to the working-class theatre of the day. Nonetheless, Esson's plays have an influence on the later New Theatre movement, just as the Fabian plays of Shaw were to provide an impetus for a pre-Comintern 'third period' labour theatre in England. William Moore produced two Esson plays, *The Woman Tamer* and *The Sacred Place*, at his 'Australian Drama Nights' (1910, 1912), and Gregan McMahon performed *Dead Timber* and *The Time is not yet Ripe* at the Repertory Theatre in 1911 and 1912. Esson had contacts with members of the nascent Australian Communist Party, most notably Katharine Susannah Prichard. Prichard was a girlhood friend of Hilda Bull, who later married Esson and, subsequently, became one of the more influential figures in the Melbourne New Theatre movement. Hilda Esson describes the dramatic aims of Esson and those who surrounded him in the early days of William Moore's Australian Drama nights (1909):

> Even then we dreamed of the new Australian drama, and the foundation of a theatre which would present something more than the imitative and second-hand productions of the commercial stage, a theatre that would show our own problems, as Shaw and Galsworthy were trying to do in England.

Despite its significance for Australian theatre, the Pioneer Players was extraordinarily short-lived. It had four short seasons in 1922, three in 1923, none in 1924 and 1925, and a final one-night showing of Esson's *The Bride of Gospel Place* in June 1926. Walker notes: 'Esson's vision of a popular movement in the theatre which might perform in any country, in small towns etc.' was far grander than the achievements of the Pioneer Players. Apart from the limited nature of performance, Esson's comments on the production of *The Bride of Gospel Place* give some sense of the crudeness of the productions:

> The house was almost full, except the balcony, and the show went over not so badly. It was a slow start as usual, not a laugh coming until page 5. We had only two breaks, Joe going out for a plate and not returning, but Frank as Smithy covered it up cleverly, and even Rowe didn't notice it. The second was that the curtain in Act III fell on the screen.

Louis Esson blamed the failure of the Pioneers on the cultural receptivity of Melbourne, which he described as 'a wowser, bourgeois town, without an idea of any kind, and intensely bored with its respectability and stupidity'. The

Pioneers had little chance of survival, given the coldness of local audiences, the transient lifestyles of the leading proponents and Esson's impractical idealism. Hilda Esson wrote to Vance Palmer:

> I admit that what we have actually done is not anything to be elated about either in spirit or performance. It was something so much less than what we dreamt it would be.

Reading Louis Esson's letters to Vance Palmer about the Pioneers, one senses that it was Hilda who maintained any organisational calm: 'Hilda managed everything in the most marvellous way'. Ironically, despite Hilda Esson's deep suspicion of the Communist Party, the New Theatre benefited from her experiences with the Pioneers, her hard-won theatrical efficiency and the Pioneers' vision of a community-based Australian theatre, all of which created a spirit of cooperation, with a number of people 'uniting in a common creative purpose'.

WORKERS' ART GROUPS IN MELBOURNE AND SYDNEY

The earliest records of politically radical groups appear in both Sydney and Melbourne in 1931–32. The Sydney movement was the WAC; the theatre wing of the group was to become NTL, Sydney (1936). Jean Devanny, one of the founders of the WAC, tells of its beginnings:

> In 1931, I, as National secretary of the Workers International Relief [WIR], with headquarters in Berlin, was invited to Berlin as Australian delegate to the International Congress of the WIR. Therefore I found that the German section had a splendid art and theatre section. So on my return to Sydney I immediately set about organising a like group in the Australian WIR. No difficulty in collecting round me a sufficient number of suitable types; the artistic fraternity, equally with the industrial workers, were sunk in the doldrums of the crises of that time.

The early plays of the WAC included *The Ragged Trousered Philanthropists* and plays by Shaw, Upton Sinclair and Eugene O'Neill. Drusilla Modjeska notes that Jean Devanny's interest in a broad front organisation of leftist artists predated official party policy by some years and became an early source of conflict between Devanny and the CPA.

A WAC was also established in Melbourne, around 1931–32, largely comprising artists and radicals from the University Labour Club. In April 1932, Guido Barrachi, a leading intellectual communist of the day, opened an exhibition of drawings by Jack Maugham, described as 'Proletarian Art'. Jack Maugham had also designed the cover for the *Proletariat*, publication outlet for the Melbourne University radical left. He was subsequently actively involved in the later New Theatre Club. The first theatrical production of the group, and the only one of which there appears to be any surviving evidence, was a production of Ernst Toller's *Masses and Man*. The participants' names were not listed on the program, but it is worth recording the WAC rationale printed therein:

> The current art of capitalism, the art of the lap dogs and flunkies of the boss-class, is, equally with the pulpit and the press, 'the opium of the people'. Cinema, theatre, novelist, artist, poet, all serve, wittingly or not to divert the attention of the toiling masses away from the real solution to the problem of their impoverishment and degradation. By treating them to carefully doctored versions of the class struggle, they seek to prevent them from coming to grips with realities. This imposition is worked in ways that are various and subtle. Booze, sex-suppression, and money grubbing are the main themes about which the capitalist futilities of bourgeois art revolve. While Capitalism in its last dying hours gurgles forth a last hymn of frustration, the growing vitality of proletarian or workers' art manifests itself. Born out of the living stuff of reality, out of the day to day struggles and aspirations of class-conscious workers, fighting towards emancipation, proletarian art necessarily makes its chief appeal to workers. No longer need workers bow to the patronage of bourgeois art. All over the world workers' theatres and art groups spring into being.

The *Smith's Weekly* review of Kylie Tennant's *Ride on Stranger* suggests that her description of the Proletarian Club in Sydney is, in fact, a description of the Melbourne WAC, a movement the writer goes on to describe as:

> a typical Leftist association which had a brief but cheery life in a grubby attic near the Tivoli theatre. It had little or nothing to do with workers of any kind, but included in its membership a collection of young men and women of pink political views and somewhat bohemian manners.

A review of a WAC theatrical production noted:

> Many of the ladies in the audience wore red blouses and the men's neckties and the programmes were of the same sanguine colour. An atmosphere of intense seriousness pervaded the house.

A much more robust proletarian theatre company, and one that took itself less seriously, was to develop in Brisbane in about 1933–34. Called the Roving Red Revue Company, it is the only company whose name reflects identification with the earlier agitational and solely mobile theatres of the pre-united front period. Jim Crawford, the most radically left writer to emerge out of the New Theatre movement, first recalled the history of this short-lived group at the Twelfth National New Theatre Conference in Brisbane in 1959. Crawford dates the Roving Red Revue from the period of the eviction of unemployed workers from Mackay; most of the Roving Reds were there:

> It operated on what could be called an arbitrary basis without any refinements whatsoever in such things as playwrighting [sic], casting, production and so on. It worked on a strictly utilitarian basis...it was organised to raise funds for the Unemployed Workers' Movement and other militant bodies. The main base was the bagmen's camp in Victoria Park. When some sort of program had been decided on the committee cast the sketches by the simple expedient of going along to the bagman's tent, humpy, semi-cave or sleeper shelter and telling the particular inmate 'Hey Boofhead, you're

playing this'... None of the cast wanted to be in the program at all of course. They turned out purely and simply in the interests of solidarity. They evolved a technique of assessing their parts in terms of rum, to give them both verve and nerve... A walk-on was rated as a two rummer, while a lead part rated anything up to eight or 10 rums, according to a player's purse.

The Roving Reds were three and four strap men in the tradition of:

One strap – never been on the track before.

Two straps – looking for work.

Three straps – don't give a damn if you find work or not.

Four straps – a travelling delegate of the Transcontinental and International Union of Bums, Stiffs and Hoboes.

In a letter to a Miss Murnane (later Pat Crawford, his wife), Jim Crawford describes the Roving Reds as an 'endemic' type of theatre, which played on only three or four occasions. The theatrical forms of the group were 'those of the music hall and vaudeville'. While the Reds used Australian vernacular (and a specific vernacular developed in the bagmen's camps), 'international questions were handled'. Crawford recalled, on different occasions, two particular Red Roving Revue productions which are worth repeating at length. The first of these, as Crawford himself points out in a letter, has some similarities with Unity's *Cannibal Carnival*, which the early Brisbane New Theatre would perform before the war:

> The bagmen in the hobo's camp at Victoria Park are eating each other. This fact comes to the knowledge of the local Labour member. The member and his secretary both agree that the cannibalism at Victoria Park is obviously a Red-inspired plot to smear the Labor image (Labor was in power in Qld) and cause the party to lose the next election. The loyalty of the bagmen to the Fighters of the Nineties, who founded the Labour Party, must be invoked. The secretary

must down to the Park and appeal to the bagmen to reject Communism and Cannibalism and stop eating each other...at least until after the election. The secretary who is very sleek and plump speaks to the bagmen, who after studying his plumpness, drag him away to be boiled in a bathtub over a fire made of old railway sleepers.

Evidence of cartoons from popular papers and magazines of the 1930s, like *The Australasian Post* – and indeed, continuing right into the 1950s – indicate that cannibalism was a recurring theme in popular humour. Jim Crawford records the second of the plots, both in his speech to the New Conference and in a later letter to Miss Murnane. Crawford calls this play *The Metro-Vickers Trial*, and there is little doubt that this show bore some relationship to *The Moscow Trial of the Metro-Vickers Workers*, attributed to Bert Thompson and the Workers' Art Theatre (WAT), which the Sydney WAC performed on 14 August 1933. How the play found its way from Sydney to Brisbane is unclear, although the CPA largely organised the United Worker's Movement (UWM) and the WAC. The aim of the production was to ridicule contemporary press attacks on the Soviet Union, including characters such as 'Bullkof, the Executioner and Nina Nincompoopsky, a beautiful double agent'. Crawford's notes for his speech provide a sense of the Roving Reds theatre and offer an excellent example of his delightful storytelling skills. Playwright Jim Crawford will feature elsewhere in the Melbourne New Theatre story:

> I remember the opening lines of the play, because I had to speak one of them. The Judge says 'damn those dogs! They're always fighting under the courtroom windows.' The prosecutor replies 'That's not a dog fight, Y'Honor...that's the prisoners being prepared for cross-examination.' The stage directions for this were: 'Blows, shrieks, curses, scuffles, bumps and exclamations.' The backstage boys really swung into this stage direction. The whole cast, which was backstage at this time, bogged in to give them a hand. They thumped the walls, kerosene tins and each other and cursed and groaned and shrieked until they had half the audience glancing at the exits. After a couple of minutes of this (during which any dialogue or action

on stage was impossible), the first prisoner made his entrance. We had picked the ugliest hairiest militant bagman we could dig up in Brisbane and cast him as Nina Nincompoopsky, the female teenage spy who had sold her country for a pair of jazz garters and a deener [shilling] bottle of scent. The character who was press ganged as Nina had been doing a bit of dilldoll dropping (or back door hawking). He had a few bob in his pocket, he was scared about the 'yack' and rude remarks he'd cop after playing Nina, and he was extra nervous in any case. He'd rated his part at about 12 or 14 rums, and it took a long argument and three strong men to hoy him on to the stage. But he must have been a born actor, after all, for after we'd got him on to the stage, we couldn't get him off it. After he'd warmed up a bit, and the rum had reached boiling point, he minced around as long as the show lasted, flashing his garters, sniffing his scent and chucking his arms around anybody he could get next to. The show had gone to the pack with the opening uproar, of course, but after Nina got on stage there wasn't a sign of a cue line, timing or any sort of organisation whatever. The cast wandered on and off at will, and said whatever lines they'd remembered where and when they liked. The Judge made things worse. He'd rated his part pretty highly, and he was as full as a goog before the show started. He had a string of saveloys around his neck, as a sort of chain of office and he growled and chewed at these, with appropriate savagery, while he was 'playing' – quote and unquote, his part. Every now and then he'd throw a sav, or a piece of sav, at some guard or witness to speed up the action.

There seems little doubt that this early workers' theatre had little interest in either scripting or theatrical innovation, but their work is evidence of a militant theatre that, for some reason or other, never really found a developed expression in this country. Jim Crawford's description of the origins and of the differences between the terms 'bagman' and 'swagman' offers some insight into how this group, defiantly Australian, fitted in with the developing national culture:

> The swagmen (long hallowed by Lawson and the moleskin school) was relatively respectable. The coves who called themselves 'bagmen' belonged to the younger generation. They had no pretensions to any kind of respectability (romantic or otherwise) and like all younger generations were obviously monsters of subversive delinquency. They were more apt to quote Marx than Banjo Paterson.

EARLY WORKERS' THEATRE GROUPS IN OTHER STATES

The groups that developed in the various capital cities after 1935 were committed to the notion of the popular front. They were more organised, less sectarian, and had a greater concern for artistic quality than the early Workers' Art Groups – certainly the Roving Reds. In Perth, Katharine Susannah Prichard and Keith George formed the Workers' Art Guild (WAG). George became its first theatre group director. The Guild's early performances included *Waiting for Lefty* (1937), *Till the Day I Die* (1936), *Bury the Dead* (1936) and *Where's That Bomb?* (1937). In October 1937, at the West Australian Drama Festival, the group presented Ernst Toller's *Hinkemann* (with a cast of 32) to an audience of 1,000. The *West Australian* reviewer commented: 'In its tragic intensity, its rage and command, it has seldom been equalled on the Perth Stage'. The group presented Betty Roland's *Are You Ready Comrade?* to open the Festival the following year. Katharine Susannah Prichard remained an inspirational figure in the movement, although she does not appear to have been closely involved for any substantial period of time. As one of the founders of the MAWF, she attended the antiwar Congress in Melbourne in 1934, when Kisch was invited to be the guest speaker. Her involvement in this movement led to a deep involvement with the Spanish Relief Committee in Western Australia (WA), for which she wrote the agitprop-style play, *Women of Spain*, first performed by the Guild in 1937 for the Spanish Relief Fund.

The Adelaide radical theatre group seems to have developed as the Left Book Club Theatre Group, with early meetings in November and December

1938. It presented its first production, *Vote No*, on the Billy Hughes' WWI referendum, at a picnic in the Adelaide Hills in January 1939. The prewar group was short lived, and there is little record of its activities. *Remember Pedrocito* played twice in 1939 in various indoor venues, and it is likely that there were other productions. In 1941, Vic Arnold, New Theatre director from Sydney, assisted the Labour Youth Theatre with a production of *Waiting for Lefty*. This group continued into 1942.

In Brisbane, the Student Theatre Group presented their first production, Soviet comedy *Squaring the Circle*, on 19 November 1936. Another group in Brisbane, calling themselves the Workers' Art Theatre Group (WATG), had presented *The Ragged Trousered Philanthropists* a fortnight earlier (7 November 1936); however, WATG appears to have been an ad hoc collection from other groups, brought together for that particular production. It was the Student Theatre Group, made up of full-time and evening students, public servants and others, which subsequently went on to become Unity Theatre (October 1937). While *Squaring the Circle* is the first Brisbane Student Theatre production of which there is evidence, John Callaghan remembers early productions of *Slickers Ltd*, performed by Sydney in July 1935, and *Who's Who in the Berlin Zoo*, agitprop pieces from the British and US movements. The group's second production, *Waiting for Lefty* (19 May 1937), played successfully to a full house at the Princess Theatre, Brisbane's largest theatrical venue. Accounts of later productions of the Student Theatre suggest that it included a radical element, but this did not invite open press censorship. 'HTH', the *Courier-Mail* reviewer, who included discussions of the worldwide development of left-wing theatre in his weekly column, gave it good coverage in its early years. Early in 1937, 'HTH' noted:

> The `left' theatre is reported to be growing in influence and activity in Australia. When plays like Odets' *Till the Day I Die* and *Waiting for Lefty* come to Australia in manuscript form, they are practically assured of performances in Sydney, Melbourne and Perth.

It is hard to know how radical the early New Theatre was in Australia at this time. In Queensland, other groups were tackling plays on new and daring themes; for example, the Brisbane Repertory Theatre first performed *In Beauty It Is Finished* in 1931. The plays of Lilian Hellman and Odets' less politically pointed plays, like *Awake and Sing*, received early productions by little theatres in Australia. The WEA maintained Drama Societies in most states and collaborated with the Unity Theatre Brisbane in 1939 in a production of Capek's *Insect Play*. The WEA described itself as:

> a federation of working class and educational bodies, together with individuals interested in Education, formed to co-ordinate a working-class educational effort, and to enable working men and women to determine and control the education organised for their benefit.

Jim Crawford describes the WEA as:

> a liberal leavening in a society whose ruling class was heading for fascism, but, in the fight against this tendency, the WEA lacked both grip and bite.

It is interesting that the Queensland Government withdrew its subsidy from the WEA in December 1939, suggesting that some activities 'had not maintained strict neutrality', and because letters in the press had suggested that the library was used for 'subversive propaganda'.

The stories of the state-based companies will address the extent to which the development of the New Theatre movement throughout the next 60 years reflected the aims and aspirations of the international workers' theatre movement, and also how it established a specific national identity and contribution to Australian culture. The many questions raised earlier in this chapter are likely to have different answers at different times for any theatre company considered over more than five decades of operation; the shifting emphases are often related to changes in the wider political situation and the way the theatre responded.

Did the New Theatre see its prime focus as providing cultural propaganda for the Communist Party? Often, the group or its factions were at odds with the party line. Essentially, it was a theatrical movement rather than a political one, even if it debated political issues as vigorously as aesthetic principles. At certain times, because of current political chauvinism, those who knew little of its operations conveniently pigeonholed and scapegoated the theatre. A love of the stage, artistic liberalism and a heightened social conscience motivated New Theatre members more than the fires of revolutionary zeal.

While Esson's views of Melbourne as 'a wowser, bourgeois town' are extremist, there is little doubt that the city, until modified by postwar immigration, was homogeneously conservative and inclined to favour imported culture, whether popular or highbrow, over the local product. In such a small city, isolated by its geographical distance from the cultural maelstrom of Europe, it is not entirely surprising that a liberal radical group such as New Theatre could be so successfully marginalised. And the same might be said for left-wing companies in the other states.

FURTHER READING

Goldstein, Malcolm, *The Political Stage*, New York, Oxford University Press, 1974.

Himelstein, Morgan Yale, *Drama was a Weapon: the Left-Wing Theatre in New York 1929–1941*, New Brunswick, Rutgers University Press, 1963.

Kisch, Egon, *Australian Landfall*, Melbourne, Macmillan, 1969.

Modjeska, Drusilla, *Exiles at Home: Australian Women Writers 1925–1945*, Sydney, Angus & Robertson, 1981.

Samuel, Raphael, McColl, Ewan and Cosgrove, Stuart, *Theatres of the Left 1880–1935*, London, Routledge & Kegan Paul, 1985.

Stourac, Richard and McCreery, Kathleen, *Theatre as a Weapon: Workers' Theatres in Soviet Union, Germany and Great Britain 1917–1934*, London, Routledge & Kegan Paul, 1986.

Williams, Margaret, *Australia on the Popular Stage, 1829–1929*, Melbourne, Oxford University Press, 1983.

Jean Devanny, a founder of the WAC in Australia.

CHAPTER 2

Communism Stage Left: the Political Influences

Gabriela Zabala

New Theatre is one of the longest running theatre companies in Australia. Jean Devanny, a writer and member of the CPA, initiated it. Beginning life as the WAC in Sydney in 1932, it was one of the first theatres in Australia with an orientation to working-class audiences. By 1936, it had become the New Theatre. By the 1950s, there were also New Theatres in Adelaide, Melbourne, Perth, Newcastle and Brisbane. New Theatre was particularly interested in the innovations in theatre, such as agitprop and dramatic reportage, typical of workers' theatre in the Soviet Union and the USA.

The New Theatre movement's social mission was inextricably linked to the political perspectives of the CPA, which adopted ideas and theories of socialist realism and proletarian culture which Zhdanov decreed in 1934 in the former Soviet Union. Matters of culture did not preoccupy the CPA very much in its formative years; this changed almost immediately after the Moscow Stalinist bureaucracy commenced a concerted campaign among the world's intelligentsia to harness culture and direct it towards serving the USSR bureaucracy's interests through the formation of cultural fronts. In August 1931, the world congress of the WIR met in Berlin; it had begun there in 1921 as an adjunct of the Communist International (Comintern) to organise international relief for the victims of drought and famine in the Volga in the Soviet Union. The WIR also provided relief to workers internationally who were on strike and to victims of other social and political ills by distributing necessities such as clothes, food and funds. Its activities from 1922 onwards included cinematic propaganda, screening Soviet films in Germany for the first time.

The WIR had many adherents, including writers Upton Sinclair, Maxim Gorki, George Bernard Shaw and Henri Barbusse and painter and sculptor Kathe Kollwitz. The WIR dissolved in 1935 after the Nazi takeover in Germany. Renowned international figures who attended the 1931 Congress included Clara Zetkin, advocate for women's rights and member of the German Communist Party (KPD), and Albert Einstein. Jean Devanny, a CPA member, attended as the Australian delegate. Devanny brought back to Australia the idea of forming a WIR art and theatre group, which the CPA leadership approved. However, according to Devanny, members of the Australian WIR were 'out of sympathy with the artistic temperament', and she sought to separate the art and theatre group from the WIR. She persuaded artists to put a proposal to the WIR committee; she supported it and was able to command a majority of votes. Devanny was elected director of the new art and theatre organisation, which she named the Workers' Art Club. Its premises were in Pitt Street, Sydney, near Circular Quay.

The ostensible purpose of WAC, according to Devanny, was to:

> activise progressive artists, and to win to such policies the politically backward – to which end, I and my fellow colleagues had tried to maintain the kind of balance between party educational work and what might have been termed neutral, that would hold the non-progressives to us.

In Devanny's absence, 'undesirables' (usually those the CPA considered bohemian) were admitted to the WAC, but she maintained that 'the influence of my fraction and their supporters was strong enough to keep the general line in correct perspective'. The WAC functioned in the same manner as other cultural organisations affiliated to the CPA: it was subordinate to CPA dictates and political expediency in the interests of promoting the USSR bureaucracy and its decrees on cultural methods and themes. Central Committee member Bob Bessant passed on a reprimand from the party hierarchy, instructing Devanny that George Finey (the Australian artist who had volunteered his services to the artists at WAC) was to 'be brought under proper control, the undesirables thrown out, the drama section was to confine its productions to leftist plays'. The sectarianism became intolerable, and Devanny and Finey left the WAC. With their departure, the literature and art sections petered out, the theatre section assumed full control over the WAC, and it continued on this basis for a number of years. The CPA's decision to order Devanny to keep away from it demonstrates the extent of the political function of the WAC. A tersely worded letter to Devanny in 1932 from the CPA Central Committee articulates the political ambitions of the CPA for the WAC:

> Comrade, the decision of the C.C. Secretariat that you withdraw from the W.A.C. fraction still stands and under no circumstances must you interfere with their work. The reasons for your withdrawal are – we consider that your lack of stability and failure to strictly adhere to discipline would seriously hamper the work of the fraction – particularly in its present weak stage. Until further instructed you must confine yourself to unit work and remain a member of the W.I.R. fraction, making yourself available for lecture and other work determined on by the fraction.

This characteristic letter indicates how the CPA exercised control over the WAC, which proved to be both energetic and influential on wider Australian cultural movements. By the end of 1935, the WAC had presented around 30 plays. Of these, seven new plays were by Australians; others were by George Bernard Shaw, Sergei Tretyakov from Russia, Ernst Toller from Germany and the USA's Eugene O'Neill. CPA members, claims Devanny, gradually 'took more and more the power of flexibility into their own hands'. In 1936, the WAC renamed itself the New Theatre. The name originated in the USA; the political theatre developed there was linked to increased trade union activity in the 1920s, passing through a series of stages before becoming the NTL in 1935. The New Theatre in Sydney was established as the most 'vital and provocative' theatre in Australia's history when it produced Clifford Odets' *Waiting for Lefty*.

New Theatres soon appeared in every other state except Tasmania. The level of activity at New Theatre resembled that of worker bees in a hive: Sydney New Theatre alone produced over 100 full-length plays or acts from plays between 1936 and 1946. The CPA's enthusiasm for art, however, was a relatively new phenomenon. There is no indication, either in historical accounts of the CPA or in its own records and archives, of any inclination towards the arts, let alone a firm policy on cultural matters, before the 1930s. In fact, the CPA regarded art and literature as weapons for propaganda rather than an autonomous field of activity.

It was an auspicious beginning for the WAC. It was able to muster support from artists, including financial support, as this correspondence from the Melbourne branch of the CPA in 1932 on the function of fraternal organisations demonstrates; the unnamed writer says of the WAC:

> As far as I could gather the club has about 100 members some of whom can give it good financial support. It is proposed to publish the first number of an official organ about the middle of August. The proposed name is *Masses* to be published monthly at 6d. One of the two editors is a Party member and the District Agitprop will be able to see the material. The plan is to have it well illustrated, the club has a number of fairly good artists and I was able to see some of the drawings which may appear.

It was difficult to convince the CPA leadership, who considered art and literature a fanciful pastime of the petty bourgeoisie, of the supposed necessity and potential of art as an ideological weapon for its political program. One year later, a Political Bureau letter to the District Committee of 30 May 1933 from the Central Commission of the CPA discusses the methods of work among the fraternal organisations and fractions and the necessity of

A 1932 article from The Labor Daily outlining the aims of the WAC.

Workers' Art Club

Progressive Step

To give the worker an opportunity of intellectual and cultural development free from financial embarrassment is the object of the newly formed Workers' Art Club, presided over by Mr. George Finey.

The club will pursue the study of art in its various channels of music, drawing, painting, literature, drama and craftsmanship, embracing practically every profession and trade in the community.

It desires to place knowledge and expression within the grasp of every person interested, and, through individual and collective exhibitions, to encourage and propagate new ideas in the evolution of modern art.

Where the average working man is excluded from an academic education by economic adversity, the club aims to promote learning and ability in an atmosphere of comradeship.

Musical evenings, entertainments, and debates will be held, in addition to exhibitions. A library is being installed for the benefit of members, and the club rooms will be complete with all domestic conveniences.

The address is 273 Pitt Street, next to the School of Arts, and Miss Sloane, secretary, will be glad to enrol members any time during the day, the fee being 1/- a month.

There will be a recital or gramophone records on Sunday night, and on Monday evening Mr. Norman Nelson, of Sydney University, will speak on present day writers of his acquaintance.

'political guidance' to develop these organisations along the correct party line, noting: 'The mass fraternals are avenues to the factories, the unions and are reservoirs of recruits – if we organise the fraction work'.

In an organisation report of the Fourth Plenary Session on 31 March and 1–3 April in 1934, George Bessant discusses the problems associated with the running of the WAC and the development of a correct party attitude towards it:

> Other organisations which have developed during the year are the Workers' Sports Federation and the W.A.C. here and in Melbourne. In regard to the W.A.C, here again we see an under-estimation in this district in this important field of work, we generally discovered that the W.A.C was considered a joke by some comrades, used to sneer at it, and talk about it as a booze club. It may have been, but W.A.C is an important channel which we have to work through. How can we make this an organisation to be of use to the working class? Some attempt has been made to correct the work of this organisation, owing to inability from artistic viewpoint to give correct political guidance in this work we are handicapped, but with correct work we are hopeful of overcoming the right opportunist tendencies. Make an attempt to set up every kind of organisation possible which we can work through and which will assist us in our work.

The forming of the WAC corresponded with the development of cultural fronts by all communist parties affiliated with the Comintern; the WAC magazine's editorial of 1933 reinforces this. It provides an elaboration of the tasks and program of the WAC and the decision to subscribe 'wholeheartedly' to the 1930 Kharkov Resolutions, which are:

> Fight against Imperialist War: defend the Soviet Union against Capitalist aggression. Fight against Fascism, whether open or concealed, like Social Fascism.
> Fight for the developing and strengthening of the revolutionary labour movement. Fight against race discrimination and the persecution of the foreign born. Fight against the influence of middle-class ideas

in the work of revolutionary artists and writers. Fight against the imprisonment of revolutionary writers and artists, as well as other class-war prisoners, throughout the world.

The Kharkov Congress was an initiative of the international left to 'formulate a unified program for revolutionary artists and writers. International Bureau of Revolutionary Writers delegates from around the world attended, but the Soviet Union articulated policies and criticism of various capitalist countries; Germany and the USA were particularly singled out for censure. Max Eastman claimed in the mid-1930s that Soviet control in art and culture over left-wing and communist writers was established at Kharkov. He asserted that Soviet cultural policy over the previous 10 years should be seen as:

> a systematic effort of the bureaucratic political machine set up in Soviet Russia after Lenin died to whip all forms of human expression into line behind its Organisational plans and its dictatorship.

According to Angela Kershaw, 'Kharkov demonstrated the dominance of the dogmatic RAPP [Russian Association of Proletarian Writers] in the Soviet debate on revolutionary literature'.

Corresponding with the Kharkov resolutions, the WAC magazine exhorts all those who are interested in 'working class art' or 'working class literature' to attend WAC classes and invites them to the accompanying lecture. As a supposed added inducement for those undeterred by the club's program, they included a reminder for a forthcoming lecture, ominously titled: 'Cultural Progress under the Five-Year Plan.' The Melbourne group of the WAC published *Masses* in 1932; they dedicated the magazine to promoting art and literature that was 'National in form, proletarian in content'.

As an offshoot of the WAC, New Theatre was more trenchant in its political orientation and aims. The CPA's paper, the *Communist Review*, promoted New Theatre productions, which sometimes included agitprop sketches by Betty Roland, a playwright who wrote for New Theatre, and stories by Australian writer Allan Marshall among others. It published short stories and poetry by contributors. These contributions were usually laudatory, featuring communist leaders as heroes; most were politically themed, with the Spanish Civil War featuring prominently during the mid-1930s.

Victor Arnold was director of Sydney New Theatre. In the *Australian Left News* of January 1939, he called on aspiring playwrights from all walks of life to contribute to New Theatre's playlist. Referring to Roland's agitprop sketch *War on the Waterfront* as an example of the politically utilitarian function of New Theatre, he says:

> Much more can be done in this direction when the Australian theatre and its playwrights become more positive and social in their outlook. We will be glad to receive any suggestions in connection with developing a campaign around these questions and the possibility of organising a play-writing group associated with the ideals of the Left Book Club and the New Theatre Movement, who will be prepared to dramatise any progressive action or ideas held by the Australian people.

Behind the scenes, the discussions about the political ideology of New Theatre were more explicit. Correspondence between the CPA District Committee and the New Theatre Secretary in January 1939, acquired by ASIO, reveals the objectives of New Theatre as a CPA organisation. A New Theatre member, Barbara Boles, asked the Secretary to submit 'a rough report concerning our attitude towards the establishment of a Party branch within New Theatre, Melbourne'. The reply, which does not bear the writer's name, serves to demonstrate the relationship between the CPA and the functioning of New Theatre:

> We strongly support the idea. Since this was done in Sydney two years ago much better work has been done by both the comrades and the New Theatre Group, with the result that we have been of far greater value to the Communist Party. The formation of a Branch would enable Party comrades within the Theatre to concentrate and specialise on specific tasks in which they are vitally interested.
>
> It enables the Party to organise members and potential contacts on their fundamental interest, which is that of the theatre.

> The Left Theatre can only function correctly along these lines, and the establishment of a Unit within the framework of the Group will give birth to greater creative activities.
>
> The work of the New Theatre movement urgently demands consolidation, and this can only be achieved by a well organised highly trained and politically developed Branch, unfettered by any other obligations.
>
> In addition to this, a Party Branch could act as a stimulus and a link between the Theatre, the Communist Party and all fraternal and progressive organisations.
>
> The immediate task at the New Theatre, Melbourne, should be to throw more emphasis on Trade Union work and performances, and the encouragement of a mobile Group, which would get out and about, and prepare the way towards mass influence.
>
> We have no doubt that this form of specialisation is highly desirable and will give theatrically minded Party comrades more scope and expression to their particular interest.

Victoria's New Theatre constitution 'Objects and Principles' makes no mention of socialism but includes the vague formulation: 'To express through drama, based on the tradition of freedom and democracy, the progressive aspirations of the Australian people'. However, those attending a performance in 1939 would have held few illusions about New Theatre's political orientation, as the Sane Democracy League (an anti-communist, right-wing organisation founded in 1925 by Aubrey Barclay) noted. A redacted extract from the Sane Democracy League Notes held by ASIO notes that the League for Peace and Democracy (previously MAWF and considered a communist front organisation) staged two sketches in conjunction with New Theatre. The writer describes a performance where:

> blasphemy and vulgarisms, as well as highly immoral references, were freely used by those taking part. Derogatory and calumnious references were gibingly made to Britain and Chamberlain at every opportunity. At the conclusion of the performance the clenched fist salute of the Communist Party was given by all present.

This observer also found it disturbing that 'a notable feature of the audience was the presence of well-dressed young men and women'.

The extent of the priority given to political work in the New Theatre sections varied across the states. The contents of another letter held in ASIO files reveal some of the tensions between the New Theatre artists and the CPA's perception of their lack of commitment to active political work in different states. Extracts from a letter by 'Lil' refer cryptically to party members as 'PMs' whose political level she describes as 'very poor' because they are too liberal in outlook. Conversely, referring to the Sydney branch, the interceptor of the letter writes that 'Lil' considers Sydney too sectarian. 'Lil' claims that Melbourne New Theatre members find it impossible to attend their branches and classes regularly 'which means they're not getting any stronger politically'.

The question of literary style was of paramount concern, and discussion of it became more pronounced during the 1950s within the CPA. Jack Beasley, a CPA member, novelist and critic, recalls that socialist realism only became party policy in 1952 when J. D. Blake, a leading member of the CPA from the 1930s to the 1950s, addressed a meeting of 'communist cultural workers'. He condemned trends in formalism and experimentation and reaffirmed the slogan 'Art is a weapon'. Emphasising the responsibilities of politically committed writers, Blake declared that the essence of socialist realism lay in its 'ideology and party spirit' and advanced the view that the essential tasks for artists and writers were:

> to publicise the Party's policies; to portray our Australian reality, our working people and the ideas of Communism in realistic, artistic imagery and to build a mass movement of cultural workers.

Beasley makes his assertion based on his recollection, or assumption, that the calls for a socialist realist method before 1952 were merely personal opinions of certain people and leaders, such as J. B. Miles, within the CPA. However, as far back as the 1930s, Jean Devanny recalls Central Committee member Bob Bessant admonishing her for permitting the WAC to produce 'non-leftist plays' such as G. B. Shaw's *Pygmalion*, thereby 'kowtowing to the right [wing] element' of 'undesirables' who were allowed membership of the WAC.

Socialist realism had the CPA's approval long before it became official policy. It was the vital element in the choice of New Theatre repertory, even in its formative years. Seeking approval from the CPA hierarchy for a 'correct' attitude to the cultural groups affiliated with the CPA dated from 1933, as a CPA report to the District Committee in September 1933 demonstrates. The WAC was floundering, according to this report, because:

> Practically no activities are carried on despite attempts to rebuild, a short time ago. The chief reasons for present weaknesses is [sic] lack of energetic leadership and lack of attention by the D.C. [District Committee]. The D.C. is faced with the responsibility of ensuring that the W.A.C. is revived and placed upon a sound footing.

If a policy emanating from the upper echelons of the CPA was not officially forthcoming until 1952, the fact remains that what the leadership suggested was, in effect, to be interpreted as a command. According to Jean Devanny, who was a published novelist, the 'suggestions' made in relation to cultural production in Australia within the CPA before 1952 came from J. B. Miles. Miles' anti-intellectualism characterised his entire approach to artistic matters. Devanny offers one example from her experience. She had conducted a longstanding romance with Miles, who was self-taught and with scant knowledge about matters aesthetic or literary. Devanny recalls asking him to comment on her book *Cindie*. Miles returned to her three foolscap pages of commentary, half of which, according to Devanny, had a 'sneering hostile tone' and was barbed with 'personal jibes' aimed at her.

A more regimented approach to the work of New Theatre developed in the 1950s during the Cold War. Another ASIO report contains information from an informant, possibly a government infiltrator, noting that CPA members within the theatre determined the policy of New Theatre and its methods of operation. As soon as New Theatre members join the CPA, the informant noted, they are:

> automatically elected to the governing committee of the theatre. The committee is restricted to CPA members and when they hold a meeting, no other members are permitted into the area around the office or in the foyer.

According to the report, the New Theatre committee, consisting of CPA members:

> not only decides the policy of the theatre and what is to be done in the theatre, but also what Party duties are to be done by the theatre, just as an actual Party Branch would perform, such as lectures, classes, pasting up, etc.

Simon Bracegirdle and other former CPA members confirm these claims.

The Melbourne and Sydney New Theatre groups adopted the NTL name in 1936 and shortened it to New Theatre in 1945.

To discourage political dissent on the cultural front, Miriam Hampson, aunt of leading CPA members Laurence and Eric Aarons, replaced Pat Bullen as Secretary of NTL – 'following a Party decision to clean up the NTL'. In Adelaide, a heavily redacted ASIO report reflects the growing Cold War tensions and the intense surveillance of the CPA and its organisations such as New Theatre. Menacingly titled *A.S.I.O. War Book – Preparation for an Emergency – The Adelaide New Theatre,* it reports on the election of New Theatre officers in April 1952, when CPA members were elected as a provisional committee at Adelaide New Theatre. It reports that the CPA exercises influence in Adelaide New Theatre through their New Theatre CPA fraction.

ASIO reports, on their own, cannot be considered evidence of the relationship of the CPA to New Theatre. Nevertheless, while ASIO found little that could be used against the CPA and New Theatre –the purpose of their surveillance and infiltration – their reports of the connection between the CPA and New Theatre have been subsequently confirmed in the writings of former CPA and New Theatre members. The influence of the CPA over New

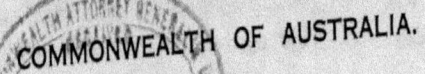

COMMONWEALTH OF AUSTRALIA.   D/772

COMMONWEALTH INVESTIGATION BRANCH,

CANBERRA,
(A.C.T)

TELEPHONE:
B. 098.

TELEGRAPH:
SUBSIDED, CANBERRA.
WW/MM

SECRET

1st October 1941.

W 3779

MEMORANDUM for -

The Secretary,
Attorney-General's Department,
CANBERRA.

NEW THEATRE LEAGUE.

With reference to your memorandum W.3779 of 26th September 1941, the propaganda put out at the New Theatre League has not materially altered since Germany invaded Russia. It appears to be particularly active in Adelaide at the present moment and, early in September, staged two plays: "Waiting for Lefty" and "Soak the People". Another play was staged at the Labour Ring at Botanic Park by the Youth Theatre group on Sunday afternoon, 31st August 1941, and Police Report which was submitted on this play is enclosed.

I also forward herewith a leaflet called "Forward to a Peoples Theatre", giving a resumé of the future intentions of this organization. The leaflet is the only one in our possession.

H.E. Jones
DIRECTOR.

Theatre is evident in the minutes of New Theatre meetings, which became more stridently regimented than in the past. One example is a discussion about the nature of the plays in 1950. It makes clear the political objectives behind the choice of play:

> While we will continue to criticise Labour [sic] leaders we must never allow such criticisms to act as fetters on development of the mass movement. To be more explicit the Sydney revue *Pot of Message* was a very fine contribution to the general fight; but it did contain certain sectarianism which if repeated in the present period would be far more serious. Therefore in Sydney we are doing a revue this year – great care will have to be taken to see that our satire does not drive away potential allies.

The political situation greatly affected New Theatre's artistic fortunes. During the Cold War, left-wing theatre was no longer popular, being regarded with suspicion. This prompted discussion within management and production committees about the future direction of New Theatre. The minutes of a production committee meeting during the National Conference of New Theatres in 1952 reveal these tensions. Norma Disher apparently said that the theatre should 'definitely teach audiences more art of theatre and not politics' and that 'people don't bring their friends because the propaganda is too prominent and not enough entertainment'. Miriam (presumably Miriam Hampson) disagrees, reportedly saying that New Theatre 'has certain traditions' and arguing that altering the choice of plays may alienate their established audiences. Hampson notes that other theatres are experiencing similar problems and puts New Theatre's plight down to a lack of publicity, noting that they don't 'even "sell" our theatre to the Communist Party where a great deal of our support comes'.

The small audiences may have been the result of a media boycott in Sydney between 1948 and 1963, but the Cold War era and the corresponding ideas about communism also contributed to the working class' alienation from the theatre – or their reluctance to attend or to be associated with a left-wing theatre. Another New Theatre member at the conference, Keith Gow, stated that he did not advocate changing New Theatre's policy; however, during the war years they had put on better plays. Since then, 'our choice has been declining'.

He reiterated that New Theatre chooses 'too many plays on a political basis and not artistic merit and this is the main cause of lack of audiences'.

Another New Theatre management and general meeting report confirms Gow's contention that New Theatre chose plays on the basis of political imperatives. The play in dispute is Frank Hardy's *Nail on the Wall*, which they considered for production but ultimately rejected. The reasons for not staging the play are entirely political, as the minutes of the General and Management Committee demonstrate:

> Firstly, although an imaginary situation set at some time in the future, it envisages a situation in which the CP is smashed, denuded of all form of organisation and its leaders all in gaol or in panicked flight. The whole premise is one of utter defeat wherein the forces of reaction have proved too strong for the working-class movement and yet at this time the working class is more militant, better organised and more capable of battling fascist legislation than ever before. Furthermore, a Communist leader, who shows such a lack of knowledge of illegal work as to seek refuge in his own home, immediately endangering his own liberty and the fate of the Party, is hardly an inspiration to the people.

New Theatre writers were often at risk of falling foul of the party line for one reason or another. Consequently, their plays were either amended, to ensure political orthodoxy, or not produced at all. A writer who broke acrimoniously from the CPA would never see their plays produced again. This was Betty Roland's experience. She had achieved critical acclaim for her play *The Touch of Silk* in 1928, had fallen in love with Guido Baracchi, a founder of the CPA, and had left an unhappy marriage to travel with him to the USSR in 1933. She returned to Australia in 1934; but, instead of becoming Australia's Eugene O'Neill, as she'd hoped, she devoted her talent to writing topical political propaganda for New Theatre. One of the first tasks imposed on her upon arriving in Melbourne in 1935 and becoming a member of the CPA was to establish a New Theatre there.

Roland says of her plays written in the 1930s for New Theatre: 'I was writing propaganda – articles and playlets – political agitprop. No art. Well, there's a certain skill in them, but they had no artistic merit'. Roland, romantic in temperament and with aspirations to become a great playwright, had to work twice as hard as a CPA and New Theatre member to overcome party prejudices about her middle-class background. Her efforts to prove herself worthy of Communist Party respect included smuggling documents from the Communist Party of Great Britain (CPGB) through Nazi Germany, back to the Soviet Union in 1934. She writes of this mission in *Caviar for Breakfast*:

> member of the despised petty bourgeoisie though I might be, no party member could have carried out the mission more successfully. I felt that I had won my spurs and was entitled to respect.

Roland's agitprop pieces were mainly on topical issues and were invariably calls for political action or syndicalist solidarity. New Theatre performers presented agitprop plays titled *War on the Waterfront*, *The Miners Speak*, *Vote No!* and *Are You Ready, Comrade?* from the back of trucks on the street, in parks and at factories, and *Communist Review* published them.

Roland claims that these plays 'were fun to do', and she enjoyed writing them. However, when she broke from the CPA, citing her opposition to the Stalin–Hitler pact as the reason, she claimed that her:

> only sign of political life has been the agitprop plays I have written from time to time which dealt with immediate working-class issues and in which I refrained, in every case, from making any mention whatever of the CP or its members.

Politically, Roland became *persona non grata*; her New Theatre plays suffered the same fate. Simon Bracegirdle, a CPA member from the 1930s until 1991, recalled in an interview with Wendy Lowenstein that they were rehearsing a Roland play at the time when Baracchi was questioning the party line over the Stalin–Hitler pact in 1939 and had voiced his opposition to it. Because Baracchi was Roland's partner, the theatre dropped her play in the spirit of CPA solidarity. Bracegirdle claims that they managed to stack the meeting to ensure that every loyal member voted to drop the play. In her later writing, Roland clearly seeks to downplay her work written for New Theatre in this period, referring to it as 'literary cartooning'; she stated that the New Theatre 'withdrew from me when I was expelled from the Communist Party in 1940'.

Oriel Gray also wrote for New Theatre as a CPA member from 1938 to 1950. Although she, too, broke from the CPA, she did not publicly politically denounce the Party. New Theatre continued to perform her plays, therefore – except those considered to be ideologically at odds with the party. In addition to writing for New Theatre, Gray also wrote scripts once a week for three years for New Theatre's radio plays on 2KY in the 1930s and 1940s. Current Book Distributors, 'another face of the Communist Party', sponsored this program. Gray won the Playwrights Advisory Board Competition in 1955, jointly with Ray Lawler's *Summer of the Seventeenth Doll*, for her play *The Torrents*. Unfortunately, it was not picked up for professional production at the time. In the 1960s, Gray wrote scripts for the popular television series *Bellbird* for 10 years. Oriel Gray's literary output with New Theatre began with a production of *Marx of Time* (1942), a comic musical revue. Gray has the distinction – paradoxical though it is, given her exclusion from the canon of Australian theatre historiography – of being the first 'resident writer in Australian theatre'. She claims this as 'another record for the left theatre'.

New Theatre's promotion of *Marx of Time* made grand claims, drawing on satire's predecessors in ancient Greece and Rome, where:

> it was a weapon in the hands of the dramatist to direct attention at the anomalies in their civilisation, and played a potent part as [a] factor in impending change.

Impressing upon the reader this historical analogy, New Theatre explained how they used satire:

> That is our aim in employing this form. Our aim, as always, is not mere entertainment, but the arousing of our audiences to action. We take the musical comedy and imbue it with a new content, so that when your laughter dies away there is left a deep-rooted determination to add your effort to secure change.

The anti-fascist line of the popular front remained a major and constant animating factor in New Theatre and the CPA throughout the 1930s until the 1939 Hitler–Stalin non-aggression pact. This event hit the party and New

1942 cast of *Marx of Time*, written by Oriel Gray.

Theatre members like a thunderbolt, disorienting many, including Gray, and compelling them to resign from the CPA. Adherents to the policy of the popular front within the CPA and those on the periphery and other sympathisers of the CPA were also outraged. New Theatre immediately faced a dilemma as a result of this new policy: Odets' anti-Nazi play, which had offended the German Consul, was to be staged that night. Gray recalls her bewilderment at the time: 'Out there in the theatre tonight we'll be playing *Till the Day I Die*!' Victor Arnold, CPA member and New Theatre Secretary (and subsequent Victorian State secretary of the Actors' and Announcers' Equity Association of Australia) responded that they would have to call a management committee meeting about it. According to Gray, New Theatre's season of *Till the Day I Die* ended abruptly; New Theatre began staging antiwar plays instead (although few referred directly to World War II), such as *Angels of War*, which was about women ambulance drivers in World War I.

The party line soon changed again. No criticism came from the Comintern or the CPA about the Nazi invasion of Czechoslovakia, Poland or France as a result of the Soviet–German pact. It was not until Germany invaded the Soviet Union in 1941 that the Kremlin declared it the 'people's war'. Once again, Moscow issued a new line and policy; CPA forces were mobilised and galvanised in support of the war; and New Theatre again fell into lockstep.

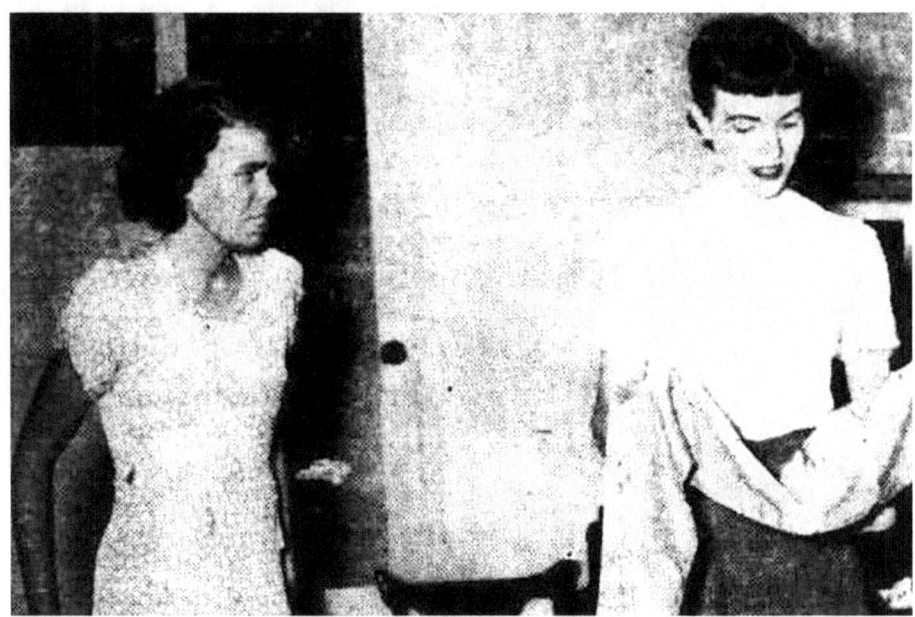

Loretta Boutmy and Pat Hill as pupil and teacher in *Had We but World Enough and Time*, 1950.

This is evident from a letter, dated 15 September 1941, which came to the attention of the Commonwealth Investigation Branch (CIB: ASIO's forerunner) – from 'D' in Melbourne to Victor Arnold at Adelaide New Theatre about preparations for agitprop plays:

> Re *Till the Day* Alterations are simple. References to Germany are brought up to date. Popular Front position in France (recall where Ernst welcomes news?) changed to Pledge of America and Britain to support S.U. Also call to action in present position. Well [sic] send you a script with other as soon as typed. Best of luck and keep up good work.

Dusted off and revived as an anti-fascist play, *Till the Day I Die* is altered to reflect the CPA's new-found opposition to the Nazis. The CPA's control over New Theatre productions was also bound up with their suspicions about the supposedly inherent bohemianism of artists, who are apparently less amenable to authority and therefore required stricter ideological vigilance by the party. 'An open schism' erupted between the CPA and New Theatre when the CPA removed New Theatre Secretary Pat Flower from her position. It was a decision, Gray recalls, made by someone in the party who was conversant with political theory but knew nothing about the theatre.

If any New Theatre writers laboured under the illusion that New Theatre existed only to provide a medium for aspiring Australian playwrights, they were mistaken. McKernan comments that, above all, the theatre and other CPA-affiliated cultural groups 'were an important focus for the energies of young communist supporters and a public platform for a socialist message'. The purpose of New Theatre was no secret from either its dramatists or performers. Ken Harper notes that New Theatre held 'ideological commitment' as a fundamental tenet and expected every writer to bear this in mind. By the end of the 1940s, according to McKernan, 'ideological problems loomed larger than artistic ones'.

One example of the 'ideological problems' is New Theatre's management committee's criticisms of Gray's play *Had We but World Enough*. Unlike Leslie Rees' critique that, despite some weaknesses, the play had 'one of the best-written scenes in Australian drama, so free from melodramatics', the New Theatre Management Committee's criticisms of the play were political in character. The minutes of the meeting record a summary of the discussion of *Had We but World Enough* and suggestions for a revision of the play. Although substantial in length, the criticism is cited in full, to provide an example of the magnitude and the extent of the political considerations that were paramount in their appraisal of the play:

> (a) The bringing of the school master into the forefront and allowing him and his emotional problems to dominate the end. It was agreed that his character is a true one and that he is an important middle-class type with his typical fear of positive action which would put him in opposition to the ruling class. However, the emphasis in the end on him is misplaced, for he has not been a key character and his soul searchings are not as important as what the reaction of the main people are – Nan, Phyllis and Nick and what is more important, what action they were going to take.

(b) Members felt that we, as a left-wing theatre, should point to a more positive solution to the problem and situation, that the three main characters should work out a positive attitude at the end, clearly cut and stated, which would send audiences away with some positive feeling on the subject. Otherwise it became a matter of posing a problem and then leaving up in the air, with the emphasis on purely personal relations.

The criticism takes the form of an attack on Gray and suggests alternative scenarios to provide the required optimistic resolution:

> The writer gives too much importance to martyrdom and too little to the winning of allies and to practical achievement. Martyrdom in itself is useless and the yearning for it reveals a Tolstoyan individualism, a secret wish for self-perfection rather than for the winning of some actual gains for the whole of humanity. I would suggest that after the failure to state the position about racial prejudice to Lily, and Lily's consequent suicide, Nan should redeem herself by putting it clearly and comprehensibly to some other aborigines – say Lily's mother – and that she should come to see the necessity of winning allies, say among the aborigines themselves, who by the way, are depicted as mere passive victims in the struggle. Phyllis is not the only one capable of being won over. Are there no workers or small farmers in the community? Is there no effective opposition to Whalen? The struggle is too much confined to a detached group of intellectuals who are by themselves obviously too weak ever to gain victory and must be crushed unless they can find effective support somewhere.

Gray's later works from the 1950s, such as *The Torrents*, *Sky Without Birds* and *Burst of Summer*, are less concerned with the 'positive hero' and are therefore less contentious. However, *Burst of Summer* was considered antithetical to party doctrine. It was, therefore, the only one of Gray's plays not to be produced by New Theatre. Gray intimates that the New Theatre's prescriptive methods circumscribed her own writing and possibly explain her lack of commercial theatre success:

> The unions were our basic audience and they were very conventional. Some people have said what stopped me being a good writer was my devotion to the Theatre and the Party. I was too narrow.

Mona Brand wrote for New Theatre from 1954, after having joined the CPA in 1948. Brand also comments on party narrowness and the sectarian dogma imposed on New Theatre, but she accepts this as a by-product of the struggle for a greater good:

> At its best it has been able to generate a spirit of excitement and collective enthusiasm, especially in times of crisis when a play's social or political importance has called for all-out efforts from the whole membership. On the other hand, elements of narrowness and sectarianism sometimes alienated either temporarily or permanently some of its devoted followers. There was sometimes a failure to listen to other people's points of view, especially if any actual or supposed aspect of the Party 'line' was questioned.

New Theatre reprimanded Brand for her emphasis on the prejudices of the upper-class characters, rather than on the struggles of the Malayan resistance fighters, in her 1954 play *Strangers in the Land*. In 1953, New Theatre's production committee protested in a letter to Brand:

> [the character] Giff is politically bad, a man of ideas who is prepared to do nothing about them [other] than slowly drink himself to death in some outpost of the empire. At no time is there any contact made with the Malayan people, who, presumably, must depend on liberal minded whites to state their case for them. Herein, incidentally, lies the strength of Nance McMillan's *Christmas Bridge* – the exploited people's

> problems [in this play] are solved by themselves by action in conjunction with other exploited people, and not by the altruistic intervention of some kind member of the petit bourgeoisie.

Brand defended herself against the criticisms of the play at a New Theatre National Conference; she argued that, as a:

> working-class theatre we needed to keep our minds broad. We should be broad in our attitude towards plays that show that workers come from everywhere.

The political criticism of her play is recorded in a conversation tapped by ASIO, where Brand is admonished for 'not writing good material' and told that she 'should pull her socks up'. The source's comment on the conversation is that '[name deleted] was voicing [Communist] Party criticism of Mona Brand'.

The results of suppressing the creative process in favour of political dogma and doctrine become increasingly apparent in Brand's case. She was criticised for lack of depiction of working-class solidarity and collective action in *Strangers in the Land*, and her response testifies to the narrowness that she has wittingly or unwittingly adapted to: 'a play can have Menzies as the central character but it still could be moulded as [a] play for the working class'. She argues for *Strangers in the Land*'s proletarian orientation, claiming that it:

> was a working-class play because it is a working-class judgement on a working-class situation, and could only have been written by a member of the working class.

Despite Brand's efforts at appeasement, the criticism continued. In an address to a CPA cultural conference, she claims to have been called a 'revisionist' and a 'carrier of right-wing ideas' for her defence of Patrick White. This situation was not a new one at New Theatre: decades before, Alan Marshall, who collaborated with Catherine Duncan and Kim Keane at Melbourne New Theatre on *Thirteen Dead* (about the 1937 Wonthaggi mine disaster in which 13 men died), experienced a similar situation. L. H. Gould, a CPA member involved in cultural aspects of party work, recalls the incident and makes an impassioned plea to the CPA for freedom of artistic expression in New

Theatre in a letter entitled 'Suggestions to Party re Literary, etc., Artists: On the need for self-restraint in dealing with them'. Gould writes of knowing at least one leading CPA member who advised artist friends against joining the party because of its interventions; in the case of Alan Marshall, he writes that the party in Melbourne wanted him to 'write differently'. CPA member Alan Watt discussed the matter with Marshall and, as a result:

> Marshall has not written as well since; he writes much less and for us hardly at all. Watt himself said he was afraid we had 'killed' Marshall. Marshall said that after the discussions, whenever he started to write he thought of Watt's words – and couldn't write a line of his own.

Of party attitudes and approach to New Theatre, CPA Central Committee member Jack Hughes says:

> Along similar lines, Party interventions in respect of New Theatre League productions also disturb me. I felt that if the author of *Cannibal Carnival* for instance were a member of the Party here, or close to us, we would either kill him stone dead as a writer or drive him away from us.

New Theatre's production committee's criticism of Brand's *Strangers* reflects the changes New Theatre underwent during the late 1940s and early 1950s. The CPA's isolation at the height of the Cold War compelled it to undertake closer scrutiny of New Theatre's repertoire. Information contained in ASIO files discloses vital details about certain leading individuals within New Theatre and their relationship to the CPA, also suggesting an intensified intervention into New Theatre programming. For example, the file dated 1955 states that Paul Mortier is a CPA member who has been 'mainly associated with the League [NTL] as party supervisor to keep the theatre on the right ideological path'. Of Miriam Hampson, it says:

> Member of the CPA. Took over the position of Secretary from Pat Bullen following a Party decision to clean up the N.T.L. Jerold Wells and Victor Arnold were 'banished.' Assisted in this activity by Paul Mortier.

> Hampson and Mortier 'got rid of a number of arty hangers on who were not considered good prospects by the Party' and otherwise reorganised the League. She is a sister of June Mills, an active and leading member of the CPA.

For writers, New Theatre was a 'vehicle for plays of social critique', but it also 'played an important recruiting role for the CPA.' Alluding to the difficulty for women of being taken seriously as playwrights in Australia, women New Theatre writers who were also CPA, such as Brand, Gray and Roland, believed that it 'was a blessing and curse' for their careers; although New Theatre provided immediate audiences for their plays, they were nevertheless 'exposed to swifter and more obtuse censorship from within and without the party'.

The postwar period was particularly difficult for all New Theatre writers as a result of anti-communist Cold War propaganda. The New Theatre sought to recover its dwindling audiences by clinging to the trade unions. Its management committee sent letters to the Federated Clerks Union, the Seamen's Union, Painters and Dockers Union, Telegraph Union and even the Soviet Embassy in Canberra. The letters sought permission from union secretaries for New Theatre members to address the union members, to promote upcoming New Theatre productions and invite them to attend. Bill Hill's recollections confirm the relationship between the CPA, New Theatre and other amateur theatres and the trade union movement, noting:

> Well, yes, the Communist Party did play a significant role in the theatre. In many ways it played a role in the establishment of the theatre...and in ensuring that the audience was there – the theatre was very well publicised by party organisations at that time and a lot of the sales went through that area and through the union movement.

Audiences also expressed opposition to the propaganda of New Theatre productions in this Cold War period. In 1949, New Theatre audiences were critical of the heavily 'political' plays being presented, so New Theatre decided to offer lighter fare in the form of Ted Willis' *God Bless the Guv'nor*. A modernised version of a Victorian melodrama, it was given an ironic proletarian twist suitable for a workers' theatre. Despite New Theatre's self-deprecating attempt to shake off its reputation as a serious theatre lacking in humour, the *Australian Quarterly* critic commented:

> the New Theatre boys and girls show they can take a laugh at themselves but it seemed to me there was a certain amount of risk in it, looking at the matter propagandistically.

Although the play was meant to be humorous, the left wing, presumably specifically the hardliners in the CPA (although Healy does not explicitly state or allude to this), were not impressed. Syd Davis provides an explanation:

> *God Bless the Guv'nor* was a light-hearted sort of thing...and some people in the left-wing movement decided that it was too critical of the working class. It pointed out certain of the failings that the working class is capable of...from time to time. And there was a bit of heavy criticism – if it was not strictly on the 'correct political line' it shouldn't be played. And there were various plays which were read and then tossed out for that reason.

By the 1960s, the CPA had begun to disintegrate because of the crisis within the Communist Party of the Soviet Union; as a result, in 1964, the CPA splintered into two separate entities: the pro-Moscow stalwarts and those adopting the Maoist-China line (Marxist–Leninist). The attitudes between the warring factions towards art and culture in general reflected the polarisation within the CPA. Moscow hardliners, such as Jack Beasley, maintained a doctrinaire socialist realist line; others adopted a more liberal attitude, which New Theatre in this period reflects. However, the CPA's disintegration left the New Theatre without the party's 'strong advice' upon which it had relied in its early years and during the Cold War. Ken Harper notes that this, coupled with the resumption of mainstream reviews of New Theatre productions, unsurprisingly led to 'a freer feeling in the group'.

Now that its plays were receiving mainstream media reviews once again, New Theatre's management recognised the need to reappraise their approach to art and literature – posing a challenge to the authority of the CPA in matters of culture. These tensions manifested themselves in a major disagreement about Arthur Miller's adaptation of Ibsen's *An Enemy of the People*, which Sydney New Theatre produced in 1962. The hardliners protested against the play's lack of proper political perspective, arguing that the work promoted 'individualism' rather than collective action; others argued for its artistic integrity. Mona Brand claims that, despite the many rewarding aspects of working in New Theatre – such as collaboration and dedication to shared ideals – the imposition of political dictates proved an impediment which 'sometimes alienated either temporarily or permanently some of its most devoted members'. This is how she recalls the Miller incident:

> I recall a major dispute around Arthur Miller's adaptation of Ibsen's *An Enemy of the People* in which Stockman declares in a speech that the majority is not always right. Communists in the theatre were split on the issue until it was resolved by the theatre membership as a whole deciding in a vote that the play should go on. (Although I was on Miller's side in the argument, I have to say that so far as this vote was concerned I thought the majority was right.)

If I understand Brand correctly, although she agrees with Miller's point that the majority is not always right, in the case of New Theatre the majority decided that Miller was indeed right, and she concurred.

While New Theatre's stated objective was to bring culture to the working class, there is little question that the New Theatre was also a means of recruiting to the CPA. Joyce Batterham demonstrates this, saying that she:

> was interested in amateur dramatics and a group of us in Newcastle formed a branch of the New Theatre League. This was quite successful and involved me a lot.

Through New Theatre, she became closely associated with political people and trade unions, and those links influenced her decision to join the CPA in 1937. Wendy Lowenstein confirms that the New Theatre was usually a route to CPA membership: 'they became communists in the course of working with New Theatre'.

It is not clear whether New Theatre plays were always altered to conform to the critiques of the production and management committees, but there is ample evidence to indicate that a thread of 'obtuse censorship' impacted on the playwrights' work. The prescriptive ideological demands imposed on artists ran counter to the freedom of artistic expression so necessary for them.

The history of New Theatre and its relationship with the CPA is, therefore, complex and contradictory. The innovations and activity of New Theatre, however constrained or limited by the underlying political imperatives of the CPA, nevertheless constitute an integral part of Australia's theatrical development. Moreover, New Theatre also provided the training ground for future professional work for many aspiring playwrights, directors and actors (although that is beyond the scope of this discussion). It gave many women the opportunity to have their plays produced. It was one of the first theatres to encourage and produce plays by Australian playwrights.

New Theatre continued to stage plays with political themes and satires and to promote Australian writers well into the 1990s. It still continues production in Sydney, making it one of the longest continuously operating theatres in Australia. Its influence over the development of Australian theatre is yet to be examined in full within the context of its political and cultural heritage. In that sense, the New Theatre is as much a political phenomenon, originating as it did in Kharkov out of an international left-wing movement, as it is an important aspect of Australian theatre history.

FURTHER READING

Beasley, Jack, *Red Letter Days: Notes from Inside an Era*, Sydney, Australasian Book Society, 1979.

Bracegirdle, Simon and Lowenstein, Wendy, 'Simon Bracegirdle interviewed by Wendy Lowenstein' in *The Communists and the Left in the Arts and Community Oral History Project* [sound recording],1992.

Brand, Mona, 'A Writer's 36 Years in Radical Theatre: New Theatre's Formative Years 1932–1955 and their Influence on Australian Drama', in *Australian drama 1920–1955: papers presented to a Conference at the University of New England, Armidale, September 1–4, 1984*, Armidale, NSW, University of New England, Department of Continuing Education, 1986, pp. 1–8.

Giuffre, Giulia, *A Writing Life: Interviews with Australian Women Writers*, Sydney, Allen & Unwin, 1990.

Harper, Ken, 'The Useful Theatre: The New Theatre Movement in Sydney and Melbourne 1935–1983', *Meanjin*, vol. 43, no. 1, 1984, pp. 57–71.

Kilner, Kerry and Tweg, Sue (eds.), *Playing the Past: Three Plays by Australian Women*, Sydney, Currency Press, 1995.

'Michelle Rayner interviews Oriel Gray' on *Verbatim*, ABC Radio National, 13 December 2003.

Milner, Lisa and Brigden, Cathy, 'Staging International Communism: British–Australian Radical Theatre Connections', *Contemporary British History*, Special Issue: 'The Politics of Popular Cultural Production and Performance in Britain since the Great War', vol. 33, no. 4, 2018, pp. 507–523.

Rees, Leslie, *The Making of Australian Drama: A Historical and Critical Survey from the 1830s to the 1970s*, Sydney, Angus & Robertson, 1973.

Roland, Betty, *Caviar for Breakfast*, Melbourne, Quartet Books, 1979.

Stevens, Joyce, *Taking the Revolution Home: Work Among Women in the Communist Party of Australia, 1920–1945*, Melbourne, Sybylla Co-operative Press and Publications, 1987.

Tilley, Christine, 'A Writer's Thirty-Six years in Radical Theatre: Perspectives on Mona Brand's Isolation from Mainstream Australian Theatre', in *Australian drama 1920–1955: papers presented to a Conference at the University of New England, Armidale, September 1–4, 1984*, Armidale, NSW, University of New England, Department of Continuing Education, 1986, pp. 7, 9–16.

Act 2

A Tour Around the Branches

CHAPTER 3

Purpose and Passion: Melbourne New Theatre 1935–2000

Angela O'Brien

This chapter is dedicated to Dorothy (Dot) Thompson, 1914–2001.

I first came into contact with New Theatre Melbourne some time in late 1978. In its fifth decade of operation, New Theatre had established its final permanent theatre in The Organ Factory in Clifton Hill, Melbourne, a former factory now used as a community centre. I recall walking up the steep narrow stairs at the back of the downstairs hall, to emerge into the compact upstairs theatre space on the right, which would have held about 50 seats with an end-stage. Behind the stage were the change-room, the green room and storage spaces. Not long after that first visit, I learnt more about its long history, mainly through Dorothy (Dot) Thompson, a Melbourne New Theatre luminary who became my mentor and good friend. I joined the theatre and asked whether I might do some research on the theatre, with the aim of undertaking a doctoral thesis. Dot and Don Munro, one of the theatre's longest serving actors, gave me two boxes of documents – programs, magazines, scrapbooks, set designs and letters – and my New Theatre story began. Over the next decade, New Theatre members generously shared their stories with me and gave me their memorabilia. I added to, and sorted, the growing archive. By 1989, I had produced not only a doctoral thesis but also two children. The archive, which formed the basis of the research, is now in the Victorian Arts Centre Performing Arts Museum; the children are grown up; and many of my Melbourne New Theatre subjects have passed on. It is in a different world that I write this chapter, based on that research, but it has been my aim to recreate

Waiting for Lefty being performed to Melbourne taxi drivers from a truck, 1936.

the stories of New Theatre as I heard them and experienced it – as a work of collective memory and homage to an extraordinary theatre movement.

The earliest years of the Melbourne WAC (circa 1931–32) have been discussed elsewhere in this volume. This chapter takes up the story from the time when the Melbourne New Theatre, then the WTG (1935–36) established itself as part of the wider International New Theatre Movement. Betty Roland, celebrated Melbourne actor, journalist and playwright, became the first 'artistic director'. Betty's left-wing credentials included a two-year stay in the Soviet Union; she had eloped to Russia in 1933 with Guido Barrachi, Australian Communist Party luminary and popular speaker on life in Russia. Betty Roland's middle-class background and previous life in commercial theatre might have disqualified her for this role, despite her connections, had it not been for the softline popular front policies which tolerated more liberal affiliations in the interests of broadening the political base of the party in the fight against war and fascism. The task of ensuring that the dramatic art of the WTG would be used as a political weapon fell to Frank Huelin, then Organiser–Secretary for the International Labour Defense. He had first proposed the group and seen it established under the auspices of the Friends of the Soviet Union. Despite initial Communist Party concerns, Huelin was given 'six months freedom' from his other responsibilities, on the recommendation of Ralph Gibson, 'to see how the WTG might operate'. The burgeoning group experimented with short plays, locally written by Betty Roland and Frank Huelin or 'which have come from Russia, America or England intended to "show a new light on the use of drama as a political and class weapon"'.

From 1935, American Group Theatre member and communist Clifford Odets' plays were beginning to find a stage in international leftist theatres, including in Australia. The first public production of the Melbourne WTG was Odets' *Waiting for Lefty*, presented on 11 August 1936. New Theatre attempted its second Odets play, *Till the Day I Die*, just three months later on 18 November 1936. Melbourne actress Catherine Duncan directed, taking over from Betty Roland, who was then seriously ill. Famously, police stopped the production on opening night. Deery and Milner (Chapter 9) tell the story of the political furore that surrounded attempts to stage this eponymous play in Australia.

In Melbourne, the WTG had officially affiliated with the International New Theatre Movement to become the New Theatre Club. It successfully staged *Till the Day I Die* in a double bill with *Waiting for Lefty* on 16 February 1937. This production not only gave a notoriety to the burgeoning company, it also attracted considerable new membership – including Lilian and Dick Diamond, who 'graduated' to New Theatre from the leftist Youth Theatre of Action and adopted key roles in New Theatre for the next two decades. Hilda Esson and her son Hugh also joined the theatre around this time. Hilda had been a founding member of the Melbourne University Dramatic Society; later, with husband and playwright Louis Esson, she was involved in the development of the Pioneer Players. Although Hilda Esson trained as a medical practitioner, she maintained a deep interest and involvement in the theatre and was one of New Theatre's most active directors and theorists. Her earliest involvement came by way of her friendship with Catherine Duncan, who invited Hilda and Hugh to a rehearsal. Unlike many members of the group, the Essons were not members of the CPA; but they were liberal left-wing intellectuals and strongly aligned with MAWF. The Essons' commitment to the artistic and social aims of the group exemplifies the broad base of the movement and illustrates the fact that there was little other opportunity for visual and performing artists to find an outlet for alternative or avant-garde artistic expression.

After the success of the double Odets bill, the New Theatre Club created a locally written piece, *Thirteen Dead*, based on the Wonthaggi mine disaster of 15 February 1937: number 20 shaft blew up, killing all 13 men in the mine. Almost immediately, a group of writers and actors led by Catherine Duncan, her husband, journalist Kim Keane and Alan Marshall began developing a play they described as 'dramatic reportage'. They researched the history of Wonthaggi mining disputes, examined the findings of the disaster enquiry, interviewed miners and their wives and went down into the mines. They invited miners to rehearsals to give advice on mining terms, tools and clothing. With the development of the first living newspaper, New Theatre redefined and restated its purpose as 'not the box office, nor the manufacture of dramatic drugs'. *Workers Voice* reported:

> The aim is the restoration of the theatre for its historic right of social criticism. This will mean that the theatre will become what is meant to be a communal institution and a weapon in the hands of the masses for fashioning a sound society.

New Theatre saw itself as a 'real people's theatre...formed to sponsor plays of social realism and help link together all forces making for cultural and social progress.'

Workers' Voice discussed the writing of *Thirteen Dead* at length, in the hope that it would 'prove to be the beginning of a new period of dramatic power and freedom in the Workers' Theatre of Victoria'. The play is structured into five sequences, balancing the views and experience of the miners, the capitalist owners of the mine and politicians who supported them. The play opens with a symbolic action where a miner, by the light of his cap lamp, finds the 13 dead; it concludes as the figure of a miner appears in silhouette. *Thirteen Dead* played on 5 July 1937 at the Kings Theatre, with *Private Hicks*, by Albert Maltz, as the curtain-raiser. The 'reality and sincerity' of the cast and production team, rather than the strength of performance, characterised the production. The innovative lighting effects were lost 'by lack of adequate trial'. Reviewers recognised that *Thirteen Dead* had broken ground in the history of Melbourne theatre. The *Argus* described it as 'a daring experiment', adding:

> The play is frankly propaganda, tinged with satire of the bitterest order, but with sincerity. **Thirteen Dead** is probably too near to reality to be a successful stage piece. The crude strength of much of the dialogue was marred by resort to expressions which are not and never will be acceptable to the ears of most theatregoers.

In 1937, Melbourne New Theatre opened its first theatre in Flanigan Lane off Sutherland Alley, at the rear of the Duke of Kent Hotel. Lilian Diamond described the space in her short history, *New Theatre's First Decade*:

> The Club's first theatre was built in a disused loft above a garage... It was as modest a place as its name implied. Somebody donated a bolt of hessian, from which all the stage drapes were made – sets weren't even thought of. The audience sat on hard wooden forms.

From 20 November until the end of the year, *Till the Day I Die* and *Waiting for Lefty* played there alternately on Sunday nights. The Flanigan Lane Theatre continued to operate until March 1939, when the premises were condemned as 'unsafe'. During these 18 months of occupancy, New Theatre performed weekly on Sunday, and later Saturday, nights, adding to its repertoire: *Song of Spain*, by Langston Hughes; *Vanzetti in the Death Cell*; *Where's That Bomb?*; *The Eternal Song*, by Marc Arnstein; radio play *China*; *Transit*, a drama by Philip Stevenson from the novelette *Season of Celebration*, by Albert Maltz; *Women of Spain*, by Katharine Susannah Prichard; *Bring Me My Bow*, 'a satire on re-armament' by Sydney Box; and *Rehearsal*, by Albert Maltz. These plays were all imports from left-wing theatre in England and the USA, except for *Women of Spain*, written for the Perth WAG. Both left-wing and mainstream press reviewed the plays fairly widely, and the response was generally favourable.

During this period, a dual commitment to artistic form and political content continued. For New Theatre, the dilemma was to ensure that political and artistic radicalism was supported sufficiently by artistic quality. There was constant concern for artistic experiment and quality and a good deal of discussion about, and development of, artistic theory. Frank Huelin recalls:

> We were regular students of the *International Theatre Magazine*. We ran a Wall Newspaper on such themes as propaganda in Art, Gorky plays and social realist theatre and similar subjects such as Stanislavsky's 'Method Acting'. We also corresponded regularly with the London Unity Theatre and Ted Willis.

The group of people who gathered around New Theatre included a number of left-wing or bohemian artists of the period. Many of them carried through their relationships from the days of the WAC, experiences at the Working Men's College (RMIT), the National Gallery Art School or the Melbourne University Labour Club, as well as the left-wing bookshops and pubs in central Melbourne. This group included unionists, workers, the unemployed and intellectuals, leavened and often supported by socialists like Guido Baracchi, who had an independent income, and Russian and East European Jews who had fled to Australia to escape the pogroms. For some artists, the involvement was peripheral; Noel Counihan remembers being asked to paint the backdrop for *Thirteen Dead*, but the reviews give little evidence of there being substantial scenic artwork in this production. Bob Mathews and Jack Maugham, whose involvement in left-wing theatre went back to the WAC days, were among the more active of the New Theatre artists, directors and producers. The New Theatre became an important training ground for theatre artists of the period.

From New Theatre's earliest days, its directors found inspiration in the acting methods developed by Soviet theatre practitioner Konstantin Stanislavski, published in his books *An Actor Prepares* (1936) and *Building a Character* (1948). Later, this became a political commitment. The Stanislavski 'method of physical action' became linked to the Comintern aesthetic dictate of social realism. Stanislavski's system – or the 'method', as it came to be known – sought 'truth' in acting and inspired the work of the American Group Theatre and the associated method school of acting. Maugham, Hilda Esson and, later, Dot Thompson were to write extensively about their interpretations of the system and their use of system-inspired exercises to train actors. It is difficult to ascertain who was the first to introduce these methods into the theatre – whether they came with those emissaries returning from the Soviets, expatriate Russians like Dolia Ribush, or through literature filtering through from Russia or publications such as *New Masses* and the US *New Theatre* magazine.

New Theatre saw its production of *Bury the Dead* (November 1938) as sufficiently important and possibly commercially viable enough to justify hiring the Apollo Theatre in Melbourne. New Theatre had considered the play for some time, following its first publication in the April 1936 edition of *New Theatre* – the American League's publication output – after the considerable success of its first production in New York. *Bury the Dead* is an antiwar expressionist play by the US writer Irwin Shaw. Members, including Dot Thompson, remembered it as the theatre's most compelling performance of the period. The *Argus* reviewer described it as:

> A play of macabre horror, of such power and dramatic intensity that it drives a message of peace into the most complacent members of the audience... The play is so much more important than the players that it is difficult to analyse individual performances.

In the 1938 Sydney New Theatre playwriting competition, judges Frank D. Clewlow of the Australian Broadcasting Commission (ABC) and Dr Lloyd Ross awarded first prize to Catherine Duncan for her play *The Sword Sung*, which opened in Melbourne at the Central Hall on Saturday 29 July 1939, for a season of seven nights. The support play was *A Plant in the Sun*, by Ben Bengal, which had achieved theatrical credibility when performed by Unity Theatre England, starring Paul Robeson in the leading role. *The Sword Sung* is a one-act antiwar play, constructed in seven scenes and written in abstract free-form verse. It was particularly noteworthy for its set design by William Constable. Constable was one of the pre-eminent designers of the period. He trained initially at the Melbourne National Gallery School (as did fellow designer Noel Counihan), later studying and working as a graphic designer in London. The New Theatre provided an outlet for radically alternative creative work, and Constable, well aware of European avant-garde trends, took the opportunity to develop his skills with the group. The play is of further interest historically because of a claim made in the *Guardian* that:

> For the first time in the history of the Australian Theatre, an Australian aboriginal – in a leading role – will depict the life of his people as they really live it. The actor will be Mr George Patten, a leader of the Aborigines movement and a strong fighter for aboriginal rights... One episode in this interesting and thought-provoking play presents a cross section of aboriginal life. In this particular scene Mr George Patten will take the leading part.

In 1939, world events moved quickly. On 3 September 1939, Britain declared that it was at war with Germany, and Australia immediately followed. Some months earlier, Russia had signed the German–Soviet non-aggression treaty. In the early years of the war, the withdrawal of communist support had a significant effect on the general involvement of the labour movement. The communist line was at odds with the Australian Labor Party (ALP), and the communist bloc inevitably became isolated within the labour movement. The *National Security Act*, passed on 8 September 1939, empowered the government to make regulations 'on almost any subject which might plausibly be linked with the defence of the Commonwealth or the efficient prosecution of the war'. By May 1940, there were strict limitations upon what could be printed in communist and trade union papers. On 15 June, the Communist Party, the League for Peace and Democracy and a few other associated bodies were banned, and police carried out raids on the homes and offices of communists and party sympathisers.

There were repercussions for the New Theatre. Immediately before the declaration of war, it was critically acclaimed and enjoyed relatively broad-based support. The early years of the war were difficult ones for the New Theatre

Club, and it battled to survive. There were ongoing problems associated with acquiring scripts, finding money for properties and settings, and attracting audiences. The declaration of war put an end to the united front hopes for peace, towards which the group had directed most of its theatrically purposeful energy. And now there was a conflict between government action and the CPA line. Flanigan Lane had been condemned as unsafe in March 1939, a police decision which changing political attitudes may have influenced. The fact that the theatre was unable to find suitable replacement premises for 12 months further exacerbated its problems. Nonetheless, it did survive; successes in the prewar years assured a continuing and diverse core membership and a small measure of general good will. For political expediency, non-communist members like Hugh Esson assumed leadership roles in the organisation.

Whatever the legislated political pressures against the left, there did not appear to be continuing government pressure on all those involved in the Melbourne New Theatre. Its early sponsorship by the party and the Friends of the Soviet Union had now become more informal connections, generally maintained through those members who were also active members of the party. At the time, the *Argus* described the New Theatre Club as 'a non-professional theatre which would not be adequately described as amateur'. It is useful to consider the New Theatre Club as an organisation with a common prime object, that is, the production of plays which were 'purposeful', but which contained a membership with some disparate purposes relating to politics, theatre, artistic outlet, education and social commitment and involvement.

Dot Thompson, who was the most influential of the New Theatre directors, joined the theatre after seeing *Bury the Dead* in 1938. Her memories of this period give some sense of both the theatrical reputation of the Club and of how non-party people were becoming politicised during the years immediately before and during the war. For many of the members, these years were memorable simply for the camaraderie and friendship that were associated with an idealistic dedication to strive for a better political and economic system. The membership of the New Theatre Club was relatively youthful, in a less affluent society which provided limited organised social outlets. In our conversations, Dot Thompson remembered a lively social activity:

> There were a lot of activities and, once a month on a Sunday night, we used to run a dance. Sort of various things like a hayseed dance or a country dance, pyjama party or something to raise funds for the show.

The early part of 1940 was devoted to the establishment of the theatre in a room at 48 Queen Street. The Queen Street theatre opened with *Cannibal Carnival*, a slapstick satire on capitalism, which most New Theatre groups around the country played with great success. Herbert Hodge, one of the authors of *Where's That Bomb?* was the writer. *Colony*, a play about striking sugar cane plantation workers in the West Indies, followed *Cannibal Carnival* in July – one of a sequence of plays attacking imperialism. Three one-act plays followed *Colony*: *Renegade*, about antisemitism in the USA (the 'most interesting' for the *Argus* reviewer) and two Australian plays, *On the Skids* and *Workhorse*. The review indicated that the New Theatre Club 'prefers to hide the identity of its players' and notes that the local plays were by anonymous playwrights. *On the Skids* concerned the plight of Victorian farmers facing bankruptcy during the Depression. The reviewer described *Workhorse* as 'an exceedingly bitter discourse on the tragic bushfires of last year' and further noted: 'the worthwhile themes of both could have been improved by a slight leavening of humour.'

The following years saw the theatre continue to voice its social criticism through the production of political reviews. A living newspaper by Dick Diamond called *Soak the Rich*, a satire on Fadden's *Soak the Poor Budget*, began 1941. The Sydney written revue *I'd Rather be Left* followed in June 1941. It was this production which improved the theatre's audience numbers and its general public profile. Lilian Diamond wrote in *Ten Years of New Theatre*:

> During all this time [the period at Flanigan Lane and Queen Street], we had been giving a great deal of attention to the problem of building a mass audience – without which, obviously, no theatre can be a people's theatre.

To this end, speakers went out to address trade union meetings; more importantly, the group presented short agitprop sketches at factory gates, street meetings and, as Hugh Esson remembers, at shopping centres on a Friday night. The sketches were short, witty and more politically hard hitting than the political revues. The political revues by New Theatre writers, which became a regular feature of the yearly repertoire, were a pastiche of sketch, song and dance, usually parody, and on a topical theme.

From 1941 until 1946, all sectors of the community were committed to the war, and the labour movement was involved in either active or support services. Lilian Diamond records the effect on the theatre:

Dot Thompson (second from left) and other Melbourne members, 1942.

Lawson by Oriel Gray, Melbourne, 1944.

Within two months our membership shrank to a mere handful – and those who remained were soon tied up with shift work, overtime and long hours. Scripts from America, our main source of supply, ceased to arrive, and it became increasingly difficult to carry on. The loss of our experienced actors and technicians resulted in a lowering of our standard of production. This in turn led to a falling off in our audiences. New Theatre entered upon the leanest phase of its existence.

Despite limited membership and small audiences during these years, New Theatre remained comparatively active, continuing to import and produce plays 'of social significance' from overseas – particularly with anti-fascist and war-related themes. It also maintained its relationship with Unity Theatre's

artistic director Ted Willis, producing British plays in the postwar period.

In late 1942, New Theatre member Bob Mathews located the premises which were to be the theatre's venue for the next 17 years. Until then, the group had been operating as a Club, working from unlicensed premises and charging a Club membership fee, as opposed to ticket entry. The new venue at 92 Flinders Street had an on-street entrance and the necessary exits and entrances required by the Health Department for a public theatre. Lilian Diamond described the building as a 'dingy café with a big bare factory at the rear'. Theatre members organised a campaign for funds, and the trade union movement gave practical assistance in building. They constructed a theatre entrance on Flinders Street, and the café became the theatre foyer. The far end of the factory housed a new end-stage, and 100 tip-up chairs supplemented those from the Queen Street theatre. The building was still being completed on the evening of 6 February 1943 when *Sabotage* opened.

Melbourne NT production of *Let's be Offensive*, 1943.

For the next five years, New Theatre continued to develop artistic standards and audiences. It became a viable force in the theatrical scene in Melbourne, seen as an artistic outlet for professional performers and artists and as a group with an innovative production policy in terms of play selection. During this period, the theatre developed its constitution. The primary objectives included: 'the establishment of a People's Theatre'; the presentation of 'social drama'; and 'development of a national drama and the encouragement of Australian Playwrights'. They certainly placed theatrical aims higher than political ones, and it is notable that those political aims are broadly non-sectarian, in the tradition of the popular front.

New Theatre Melbourne was one of the very few outlets for Australian playwrights in a period dominated by commercial theatre and imported shows and artists. The first production of 1944 was a solely Australian double

White Justice, a ballet from the Melbourne NT revue *Coming Our Way* (1946) performed by NT actors and members of the Aborigines' League. This group-devised dance drama was based on the then current strike of Aboriginal workers in the Pilbara in northwest Australia.

bill: *The Drovers*, by Louis Esson, and *Lawson*, an adaptation of the stories of Henry Lawson, written by Sydney New Theatre writer Oriel Gray. As a further impetus to the development of Australian writing, New Theatre mounted a one-act play competition in the February–March edition of the *New Theatre Review* the following year.

The most interesting program for 1946 was another Australian double bill, featuring *Fountains Beyond*, by George Landen Dann, with a curtain-raiser *Welcome Home*, a one-act play by Jim Crawford. *Fountains Beyond* is about a town's appropriation of an Aboriginal sacred site and has an Aboriginal community leader, Vic Filmer, as one of its central characters. New Theatre's decision to perform *Fountains Beyond* was part of a continuing concern with Indigenous issues – which had been dramatically presented in a ballet, *White Justice,* earlier in the year. *Welcome Home* is of similar interest in terms of topicality, and of historical interest in that it was the first play of New Theatre writer Jim Crawford. Of all the writers associated with the New Theatre Movement, Crawford is the one who can most clearly be described as a proletarian playwright, a writer solely dedicated to advancing the political ideologies of the left, workers' rights and union solidarity. In a writing career spanning 40 years, Crawford wrote eight full-length plays, 12 substantial one-act plays, at least three radio plays, many short stories and innumerable dramatic sketches and adaptations, all while working as a journalist for the left press.

New Theatre Melbourne had always taken its charter of education quite seriously, in terms of its mobile, or contact, group, and also in terms of its education of members, particularly in theatre craft and writing. During the summer of 1943–44, the first of the New Theatre Summer schools was held at Koornang School, Warrandyte; it would become a regular annual highlight for New Theatre members. The nine-day course promised:

> To cover both theory and practical work, including lectures on various aspects of theatre work such as production, lighting, criticism, history of drama, Soviet Theatre, voice production, movement and mime and preparation for the next play.

For the 10 years following its first public performance, the work of Hilda Esson significantly influenced theatre production theories. For a decade, she was a member and, generally, leader of the theatre's production committee.

She worked with younger directors, designers and stage management personnel to evolve a theory of theatrical production largely based on the writings of Stanislavski and the importance of the actor as a play's artistic determinant. In 1946, the New Theatre set up an Actors' Group, to coordinate discussion and develop continuing classes in acting. Hilda set down the necessary combination of technique and artistic sensibility:

> Acting is not only a matter of technique: it is an attitude to life, which has to be maintained and continually refreshed if any success is to be achieved.

Partly because of Hilda Esson's influence and partly because of the challenges of finding scripts, New Theatre produced a cluster of classics in the immediate postwar period, beginning with Lope de Vega's *Spanish Village* as the first production for 1946. In many ways, it was the theatre's most ambitious undertaking, because of the complexity of the production: it included dance, music, detailed period costumes and a variety of weapons and stage effects.

A significant development in 1946 was the appointment of Victor Arnold as a paid Artistic Director of Melbourne New Theatre. Earlier in the year, Unity Theatre announced the development of a cooperatively run, professional repertory company. This, along with New Theatre Sydney's successes, led the Melbourne group to recognise the need to move beyond the purely amateur. Vic Arnold was one of the founding members of Sydney New Theatre and, while his primary involvement was as an actor, he was also Secretary of the group for a number of years. His work with the theatre was to run classes in acting and to work on the production committee. When director Bob Mathews diverted his energies to the Realist Film Unit, and Hilda Esson became ill and subsequently went overseas, Vic Arnold became the leading figure in the continuing formation of a production policy for the Melbourne theatre.

One of the most ambitious ventures of New Theatre Melbourne during this period of prosperity was the publication of an eight-page magazine, the *New Theatre Review*. The *Review* was first published in May 1943 and then issued six times each year, every second month, until it ceased publication in July 1949 at the height of the Cold War period. Many of the articles in the *New Theatre Review* were of local interest only, dealing with the theatre's current productions, social jottings such as reports of summer schools, and lightweight articles about how various actors learnt their lines. The articles with a broader appeal are more interesting, and these fall into two categories:

those about Australian theatre, plays, writers or social issues, and those about international sociopolitical issues and literary or theatrical concerns.

Theatre design was integral to the New Theatre production process, valued as highly as the performance. Bill Constable contributed significantly to design for early productions. Later Melbourne artists involved in theatre design included John Bainbridge, 'Jeb' Bucklow, Vane 'Blue' Lindesay, Eve Harris and Erica Rathgeber. Vane was the artist who contributed most to the development of Melbourne New Theatre design; he worked for the theatre from 1944 (*The Ayes Have It*), designing for 26 productions, until the theatre finally closed its Flinders Street premises. Eve Harris was another active designer in the war years, as was John Bainbridge, the pseudonym of John Littlewood, a member of the Contemporary Artists group in Melbourne. The many woodcuts he designed for the *New Theatre Review* covers best exemplify his work.

Central to the production of *Spanish Village*, the Molière plays and the political revue work of New Theatre during this period was the Unity Dance Group, which Margaret Frey established under the auspices of the Theatre. New Theatre's interest in developing a ballet group was part of a broader renewed interest in locally produced ballet in Melbourne. Margaret Frey notes, in an article in the *New Theatre Review*, that the chief cause of this revival in interest was the work of the Borovansky Ballet Company. The New Theatre Singers had also formed during the later war years, under the direction of Bill Juliffe. Singing groups were an important part of early socialist meetings and rallies; accordingly, New Theatre Singers performed at a variety of venues, as well as at the theatre. New Theatre Singers and Unity dancers continued into the 1950s, when the Theatre embarked upon the production of a series of musical theatre productions.

A developing interest in film and in the significant impact of the film medium during the war years contributed to the formation of the Realist Film Unit. The group used New Theatre for its screenings but had no formal affiliations with it. Bob Mathews, one of New Theatre's most active members since its inception, was, along with Ken Coldicutt, the motivating force behind the development of Realist Film.

By 1947, many of the New Theatre members who had seen active service returned. In the immediate postwar period, optimism was high, and members threw themselves into the activities of the theatre. There was also renewed interest in trade union concerns, despite – or perhaps because of – the threat to left-wing dominated unionism by the Catholic Church-backed right-wing

Industrial Groups. During the war, New Theatre's activities at Union meetings, at factory gates and in the community had been curtailed. The April–May 1946 issue of the *New Theatre Review* announced the organisation of an Outside Group, for which purpose half a dozen actors and technicians were 'released' to perform topical sketches on prices, wages and other current problems at hall, street and factory meetings. In 1948, the Theatre launched a drive for funds to build a mobile stage. Unions assisted in providing these funds: for example, building workers on a Housing Commission job collected 18 shillings after having seen extracts from *Waiting for Lefty* and some short skits.

During the postwar period, New Theatre was particularly interested in the issue of supporting the growth of an Australian culture, especially an Australian drama. *New Theatre Review* covered the issue extensively. Along with many members of the acting and writing professions, New Theatre believed that the best way to achieve this was through the establishment of a national theatre. From as early as 1943, they put considerable effort into this campaign. The February–March 1944 issue of the *New Theatre Review* was devoted to Australian culture, including a long article: 'What's Wrong with Australian Theatre', in which Vance Palmer, Clive Turnbull, Leslie Rees and George Farwell all provide commentary. All writers agreed that there was no Australian theatre, particularly not a theatre that was prepared to take Australian drama seriously. Both Farwell and Rees argued that this is not because of a lack of Australian plays; while little theatres are prepared to take risks, they draw only 'a special minority audience'. Both Turnbull and Farwell deplore commercial theatres as 'purveyors of jam and treacle', presenting 'moth-eaten musical comedies'.

The New Theatre Movement, at the forefront of the national theatre movement and inspired by the London Unity Theatre's establishment of a professional company, moved to organise left-wing groups in the various states into a National New Theatre movement. In Easter 1948, Sydney and Melbourne New Theatres held a conference 'to draw up a plan of common action'. They affirmed that:

> art must have its roots in the very life of the people, drawing its sustenance from the political and social truths all of us sense.

Particularly concerning were 'the grave threats which our national culture now has to face'. The policy established at the meeting began:

> The Theatre identifies itself with the people, aiming to participate fully in their life and struggles, working among them, and attracting them to our Theatre.

It went on to acknowledge that the choice and presentation of plays 'must be determined by the needs of the people for a fuller and freer life'. Subsequently, groups in the other states joined what became known as New Theatre Australia.

By 1949, the political tide was turning in Australia. New Theatre had boldly maintained its positive attitude to the USSR, producing three Russian plays, *The Ordinary Man*, by Leonard Leonov, and *The Russian Question* and *The Whole World Over*, both by Konstantin Siminov. It had maintained an informal liaison with the Communist Party through those theatre members who belonged to the party. In March 1949, the theatre's annual review of the past 12 months noticed a 'marked decline in audiences' and 'some falling off and unevenness in our standards of production' and noted a need to recruit more personnel. July 1949 saw the last issue of the *New Theatre Review*. With the beginning of the Korean War, the Cold War ramping up, and Prime Minister Menzies' attempt at the Communist Party Dissolution Bill, World War III seemed a close possibility. At the 1950 Australian Peace Congress, Melbourne New Theatre lent its support with a season of peace plays which included a revival of Irwin Shaw's *Bury the Dead* and *Peace on Earth*, by Albert Maltz and George Sklar. The rest of the decade continued to prove challenging for the New Theatre movement. The membership base of New Theatre continued to be broad left; but, during the 1950s, social attitudes towards the left marginalised the New Theatre even more. An increasing use of stage names, or no actor listings at all, gives some indication that New Theatre artists felt a need to protect themselves against possible blacklisting.

By the end of 1952, the theatre was actively engaged on working towards its most famous production, the folk musical *Reedy River* about the shearers' strike of 1891. The program notes for *Reedy River* record how dozens of traditional Australian songs were collected and restored. The producers chose around 10 which were sufficiently linked in content and atmosphere to provide the basis for a musical. Dot Thompson, then Secretary of Melbourne New Theatre, called a meeting with representatives from Unity Dance Group,

Unity Singers, John Gray and musician Vera Bonner to organise the arrangements for songs. Dick Diamond was approached to produce a script for *Reedy River* (the name had already been decided) which linked the songs. In the next three days, he prepared a plot synopsis and wrote the first scene. The show opened in early March 1953. Reviews of the musical were overwhelmingly enthusiastic. Raymond Bowers, in a full-page article in *The Australasian Post*, described the play as 'uniquely Australian and comradely entertainment...a homegrown ambling, casually charming musical play based on Australian songs'. An estimated 3,000 people saw *Reedy River* in its first season at Melbourne New Theatre. It was to dominate the New Theatre scene for the next few years, including touring extensively to country areas.

While *Reedy River* was the theatre's most popular success, the most significant Australian drama performed in this period was *Strangers in the Land*, which opened in Melbourne on 16 October 1953, playing simultaneously with the Sydney New Theatre production (October 10, 1953). Mona Brand wrote *Strangers in the Land* while she was living in London (1948–53). Unity Theatre first produced it on 21 November 1952. *Strangers in the Land* tackles the issue of British exploitation in Malaya; the program notes that it 'was written as answer to the film *The Planter's Wife*, and the B.B.C. broadcast extolling the virtues of warfare in Malaya'.

The events of 1954 brought some improvements for New Theatre Melbourne, in terms of both audience attendance and, on the evidence of critical review, quality of performance. It was not a year of ease for the members and associates of the Communist Party. On 13 April 1954, Menzies announced the defection of Vladimir Petrov, Third Secretary at the Soviet Embassy, and his wife. Just before the 29 May federal election, Menzies informed the house that Petrov had named Australian citizens involved in a spy ring, and proposed the establishment of the Royal Commission into Soviet Espionage. It was in this social and political milieu that New Theatre presented its first two productions for 1954, *Trial by Falsehood* (5 March) and *Mother Riba* (2 July). *Trial by Falsehood,* by Eric Paise and William Bland, tells the story of Ethel and Julius Rosenberg, indicted for treason in the USA and electrocuted in June 1953. The *Guardian* newspaper threw itself into the campaign to publicise this play. Audience response was good; the *Guardian* reported that, from 57 on the opening night, the audience went up to 150 on the following Saturday.

Both *Trial by Falsehood* and *Mother Riba* were good examples of socialist realism, at a time when this was the prevailing literary influence on the left wing. Andrei Zhdanov's criticism of a number of writers in the *Communist Review* 1947 was to polarise artists associated with the Communist Party and those left-wing intellectuals with whom they had formerly been in accord. It heralded a period of artistic conformity which, together with the Hungarian Revolution of 1956, was largely the cause of an exodus of intellectuals and academics from the party in the latter half of the 1950s. For the next few years, there was considerable debate about art and literature in communist journals and papers. The gist of the communist line was that art should be national, positive and heroic; that it should be directed towards the evolution of society towards communism. New Theatre debated the issue of socialist realism at length. Many of the plays the theatre produced conformed to its tenets; but, for many of the pundits, the theatre was not always sufficiently hard line.

The Theatre's two most significant concerns were a commitment to, and promotion of, a socially conscious national drama; and a cooperative production style based on Stanislavski, rather than a dogmatic adherence to the tenets of socialist realism. Dot Thompson engaged in the debate in New Theatre's *Spotlight*. She argued the need for a simple approach to the theory, an approach which saw 'the relation of art to ourselves'. She used *Reedy River* to illustrate what might be seen as a broad interpretation of directional realism:

> It [*Reedy River*] has been successful because it is Australian in character, is entertaining and expresses a struggle easily recognised through typical characters. The way in which Joe shows his mates how to build the union after the 1891 strike is an object lesson for many people today.

Although New Theatre found the means of maintaining its place in Melbourne's theatre scene through the success of its folk musicals, it did not escape censure in other ventures. Sydney New Theatre experienced a mainstream newspaper media boycott which was not lifted until 1960. Reviews of New Theatre Melbourne did continue, as we have noted, although without the frequency and generosity that it had enjoyed in earlier days. Even *Reedy River* received some attacks, evidenced by a poster held in the New Theatre archives which has a large sticker pasted across it accusing the show of being 'Communist propaganda'.

The difficulties New Theatre experienced with its tenancy of 92 Flinders Street might also be interpreted as an attack on the theatre. On 7 October 1948, the Department of Health requested the removal of inflammable material from under the stage. The next decade saw increasing pressure on New Theatre, with tightening health and safety regulations and increasing demands for renovations. When the rent doubled in 1956, New Theatre recognised the difficulties of finding other premises and signed the new lease, increasing financial pressures on the company.

New Theatres in Melbourne, Sydney, Brisbane, Adelaide and Perth continued to meet, holding a national conference each Easter to establish policy and to exchange plays and information. Each Christmas, one or other of the state groups hosted a national drama school. New Theatre Australia published a *National Spotlight* journal which included information from each of the states. The relative popularity of New Theatre throughout this period mainly resulted from the enormous popular success of *Reedy River*. That success, in the main, enabled the theatre to overcome what might have been a crippling public association with the Communist Party, in a period when the party was under extreme duress. By the end of 1955, membership of the Communist Party had declined to between 5,000 and 6,000, an enormous drop of 10,000 from 16,280 a decade earlier, before the effects of the Cold War. Those who remained in the party were experienced political tacticians, with a focus on trade unions and the labour movement rather than on broader societal revolution. This trend continued into the next decade, as international and national events, particularly Khrushchev's denunciation of Stalin and the Soviet invasion of Hungary, further weakened or splintered the left.

The other development with marked implications for the New Theatre, and especially the Melbourne company, was the establishment of the Australian Elizabethan Theatre Trust, sometimes interpreted as the long-awaited beginning of a national theatre and a truly Australian form of playwriting. In November 1955, the Trust fulfilled its object of establishing 'a native drama which will give professional employment to Australian actors and those whose creative work is related to the theatre' by presenting an Australian play with an all-Australian company (the Union Theatre Repertory Company). That play, Ray Lawler's *Summer of the Seventeenth Doll*, had shared first prize with New Theatre writer Oriel Gray's *The Torrents* in the 1955 Playwrights' Advisory Board's annual full-length play competition. These concomitant and interwoven steps in Australian political and theatrical history further ensured that the New Theatre movement, and the Australian plays it fostered, would slip further from the mainstream.

It is interesting to speculate on the reasons why *The Doll* became a phenomenal success, not only in theatres in Australia, but in London, where it began a season on 30 April 1957; and, as a corollary, why it was that many other Australian plays, many of which had been Advisory Board winners (including *The Torrents*) failed to take off. The advent of the Trust's sponsorship of *The Doll* was not only significant in terms of the fate of Australian drama; it was the beginning of the decline in importance of the little theatres, a time when professional and amateur became polarised, largely because of subsidy, which must include the Trust's sponsorship of the first actor training school (NIDA). Further, in Melbourne, John Sumner, who was determined to develop the Union Theatre Repertory Company as Melbourne's foremost company, rapidly consolidated it. Its increasing professionalism and territorialism had direct repercussions on New Theatre, which was unsubsidised and weakened by the struggles of the Cold War. In a highly conservative society, plays dealing with public political issues, however cautiously, carried the taint of left-wing dissidence.

In this political and theatrical watershed, New Theatre Melbourne had its third decade of production. After the success of the *Reedy River* tour and its short return season in Melbourne, New Theatre presented Dymphna Cusack's *Pacific Paradise*, which Sydney New Theatre had produced towards the end of the previous year. The political event that inspired this play was the testing of a super-hydrogen bomb at Bikini Atoll. The theme of *Pacific Paradise* was timely for New Theatres, with a National New Theatre emphasis on plays about peace, and the play had seen some measure of success as the 1955 Playwrights' Advisory Board competition runner-up. Don Munro directed the Melbourne production, and it opened to fairly good reviews. The *Age* critic commented: 'never does the play's message sink to the level of propaganda'. Sadly, despite the considerable exposure the New Theatre movement gave to *Pacific Paradise*, public acceptance of New Theatre – or rather, lack of it – meant that the play did not attract the audiences it deserved.

Although international events had once again pushed the right and left political poles further apart, there was a significant local cultural event that could serve as a focus for a united front. That was, of course, the holding of the Olympic Games in Melbourne towards the end of 1956. Melbourne New Theatre celebrated the Games with the production of another locally written folk musical, *Under the Coolibah Tree*, by *Reedy River* author Dick Diamond.

There is little doubt that New Theatre hoped that the production would assist in restoring its diminished resources. The lease on Flinders Street had expired and, with the rent doubled in the new lease, it was imperative to attract greater audiences. The Communist Party was focusing attention on industrial struggles; with artists under pressure to devote themselves to finding professional work, the New Theatre found itself struggling for broad-based support. It continued its policy of presenting plays which were broadly, rather than specifically, left.

New Theatre commenced its 1959 season with *Fission Chips*, 'a topical revue with an atomic punch', and followed it with a new production of *The Biggest Thief in Town*, by famous American writer Dalton Trumbo, and a revival of *Reedy River*. The correspondence for the year indicates that New Theatre was having some difficulty finding appropriate scripts. The theatre considered a number of plays and eventually chose *The Night of the Ding Dong*, by Ralph Peterson. *The Night of the Ding Dong* opened in Melbourne on 9 September, and Sydney New Theatre's production opened a little over a month later, on 17 October. *Night of the Ding Dong* has a goonish quality, with a lot of very silly business. The conservative critics were not very enthusiastic about the play; the *Age* described it as 'overwritten and repetitive'. New Theatre had more success with the play when it won the Katharine Susannah Prichard award for the best Australian play at the 1959 Victorian Drama League One Act Play Festival (November 1959) and came fifth overall in a field of 38.

New Theatre's final production for 1959 was *The Six Men of Dorset*, by Miles Malleson and H. Brooks. It was the last show performed at the Flinders Street Theatre. New Theatre fought to retain the premises, even while having difficulty with the demands of the Health Department, rent increases, spiralling costs and dwindling audience numbers. When it was announced that 92 Flinders Street would be auctioned in 1959, New Theatre made plans to purchase the building and to improve its facilities, hoping to raise a good deal of the money from within the labour movement. They were unable to raise the money, and the new owners did not renew the lease. An article in the *Guardian* announced that New Theatre planned to 'move into the suburbs', noting that, given the population shift outward and the problem of costly and inefficient transport, 'it is appropriate and valuable that the theatre should go to the people rather than the people going to the theatre'. The first mobile production was *Writing on the Wall*, put together by John Hepworth in the 'form of a living newspaper'. The play previewed at The Catherina in St Kilda on Wednesday 11 May 1960 and is a collection of 'the best of New

Theatre plays', strung together by a backstage theatre narrative.

New Theatre set up its administration in the Eureka Youth League rooms in Queensberry Street, North Melbourne, playing a few performances in that venue. A set of stage rostrums came from Wal Cherry's Union Repertory Theatre. The group arranged some performances, but sympathetic organisations such as peace groups, community groups, unions and party branches arranged most venues and audiences.

The CPA never really recovered from the events of 1956–57. By the mid-1960s, an even more disparate socialist group emerged. The old guard communists treated this new group with considerable suspicion. A declaration published in September 1970, signed by 300 CPA members in five states, criticised the CPA Central Committee's:

> vacillating opportunist position...the direct result of the substitution of a mixture of right opportunist and so-called New Left or petty bourgeois radical trends in place of its formerly sound scientific socialist position.

The issue that united the old and the New Left, along with many other groups not necessarily on the left but nonetheless committed to progressive causes for various reasons, was the growing movement against the Vietnam War.

Throughout the 1960s, Melbourne New Theatre could not maintain its role as a working-class theatre because it became increasingly difficult to achieve reconciliation between the community the theatre wished to serve and the group interested in continuing to give support to a 'workers' theatre'. Between 1960 and 1963, the period before events in the Victorian State Executive developed into a national split, New Theatre continued to tour and eventually bought a truck. During that time, the theatre produced only seven plays, two of which it had mounted before. And, while the theatre survived financially, and those stalwarts involved learnt considerably from the touring experience, it was virtually impossible to maintain an audience and a sizeable membership with two productions a year.

In 1963, New Theatre found premises in the city, off Latrobe Street, at the corner of Sutherland Street and Guildford Lane. They named the new venue Centre 63, intending it to become an Arts Centre, a place where the many artists allied to the theatre could meet. The space was a long, narrow room with nothing in it. Without the resources to rebuild a theatre, the group used its portable stage, moving it around to suit each production. New Theatre brought its most recent touring show, *The Long and the Short and the Tall*, into Centre 63 for its first season.

It is significant that, between 1960 and 1974, New Theatre produced only nine Australian programs out of a total of 47, and these included a number of re-stagings. The only new work they presented was *The Rocket That Jack Built*, by Len Dowdle, the author of *Song of '54*. This significant dearth of Australian material in Melbourne New Theatre during the period reflects the poor output of Australian plays in the 1960s, competition with subsidised professional companies and, just as significantly, a changing style in Melbourne New Theatre play selection policies. It drew its plays from the New Left theatres off Broadway and their parallel movements in Britain and Europe, rather than from sources which appeared to be workers' theatres.

In 1967, Dick Diamond, then working in North Vietnam, sent a few pages of an exciting new US satire in an airmail letter; the rest of the script arrived with further letters. The play was Barbara Garson's *Macbird*, a youthfully exuberant Shakespearean spoof about the Kennedy assassination – with John Ken O'Dunc being liquidated by Macbird. As they had done for *Reedy River*, audiences queued for blocks to see this notorious but playful satire, which offended critics and politicians alike but was an unprecedented success with audiences. Next was a thematically related living newspaper-style play, *On Stage Vietnam*, by Mona Brand and Pat Garnett, a musically enhanced satire on the war in Vietnam. Brand continued to produce prolifically throughout this period, with all of her plays getting their first public airing in Sydney.

Towards the end of the 1960s, the older amateur theatre companies became increasingly marginalised as the New Left assumed a dominance of the culture. The movement of the late 1960s began as both highly experimental and political, insofar as its politics were associated with the Vietnam moratorium; but, by the mid-1970s, the new wave of theatre had become, in the main, aggressively naturalistic. The impetus for this new theatre movement came from the New Left youth culture, generally emanating from the university dramatic groups.

The 1970s saw an explosion of playwriting in Melbourne, and the Whitlam government's policies allowed for more generous subsidies for the less commercially styled companies. But, although New Theatre included a greater proportion of Australian plays in its offerings from the mid-1960s onwards, no playwright of significance or success emerged from its ranks. With its input of membership from the New Left and recent notoriety, New

Theatre seemed poised to provide some theatrical leadership in Melbourne; it failed to do so because younger and more vigorous theatres, most notably the Australian Performing Group (APG), filled the gaps. Moreover, New Theatre's amateur status rendered it ineligible for the subsidisation that the younger theatres attracted and made it virtually impossible to compete for publicity, and therefore for audiences. The New Theatre membership also included an often uneasy mix of the old guard and the new, which gave its repertoire a 'mixed bag' quality and confused its political direction.

All New Theatres other than Sydney and Melbourne closed before or during the early 1960s, when the political line seemed no longer clear and as the old guard membership aged. From the 1970s, New Theatre no longer had a voice as a national movement – whereas union structures had become increasingly centralised on a national basis, with a professional and bureaucratic management framework which no longer related to the rank and file as it had in the past. Because of the development of professional unionists, the political life of unions changed. In the main, union support, while it remained generally sympathetic, became spasmodic, especially as the theatre tended to rely on the links developed during the earlier decades. Increasingly, the unions no longer saw New Theatre as a theatrical voice for workers, largely because its politics and aims had become too diverse.

Following the successes and notoriety of *America Hurrah*, *Macbird* and *On Stage Vietnam*, the Melbourne New Theatre drew good audiences and needed larger premises. In 1970, Dot Thompson located the Pram Factory in Carlton. New Theatre negotiated with the APG to form the Community Arts Foundation, as an integral part of the Carlton Community, to provide a venue for a variety of theatrical expressions which covered the aims of both companies. The Community Arts Foundation took over the 1,000 square metre Pram Factory building, intending it as a centre for the arts.

Towards the end of 1970, New Theatre produced *Blood Knot,* the first play by South Africa's Athol Fugard to be staged in Melbourne, with Aboriginal actor Jack Charles in the lead. The production was a considerable success. Inspired by it, Dot Thompson developed an Aboriginal ensemble around Jack, as an offshoot of the theatre, and succeeded in obtaining an Arts Council Grant to present Jim Crawford's *Rocket Range*. The show did not eventuate, so the group redeployed the grant in 1972 for the development of a revue-style show, *Jack Charles is Up and Fighting, or It's tough for us Boongs in Australia Today*. The New Theatre was no longer able to develop and hold a strong company; it increasingly became a catalyst for the development of professional companies or a stepping-stone for those with specific political or theatrical agenda and those wishing to enter the subsidised theatre.

New Theatre built the front theatre upstairs in the Pram Factory, opening there with *Bloodknot*. It assumed that its next show, *If There Weren't any Blacks You'd Have to Invent Them* (1971), would be performed there as well, but the APG took over the space for *Marvellous Melbourne*. New Theatre then developed the back upstairs theatre, finally moving downstairs into a converted storeroom after the APG's continuing success. By 1973, New Theatre was again performing peripatetically, with varying success. There were only two productions in each of the years 1972 to 1974, primarily classics by Brecht, Chekhov and Shakespeare, along with Edward Bond's *Narrow Road to the Deep North* (1973). Back to back revues, *The Rocky Rogue Show* and *All Live Colour Revue* and a production of *One Flew Over the Cuckoo's Nest* filled 1975. In 1976, New Theatre converted the upstairs of a new factory building, The Organ Factory in Clifton Hill, and opened there with Steve Gooch's *The Motor Show* in 1976. It operated from these premises until its closure around 2000.

In the last 20 years of its existence at the Organ Factory, New Theatre performed very few plays which could be seen as new working-class plays, although its repertoire included some works from the new wave workers' movement in Britain. Dot Thompson, mindful of the theatre's policy to encourage and promote Australian plays, instituted playwriting 'competitions', and most of the new Australian plays arrived as a result of that initiative. Because of its essentially amateur or non-funded status, New Theatre had been unable to attract new plays by established writers, particularly after the establishment of a wide range of professional fringe companies and venues. There was no ongoing writers' group, and very few writers had maintained an interest in the company beyond the production of one or two plays. Efforts to develop a collaboratively written political revue during that time were fruitless. Nonetheless, mainly through the efforts of Dot Thompson, the company still identified and produced some significant politically relevant contemporary plays which the mainstream ignored, including *Savages*, by Christopher Hampton (1982–3); *Magnificence*, by Howard Brenton (1984); *Sandanista*, by the Great American Theatre Company (1985); *Sarcophagus*, by Vladimir Gubaryev (1989); and *Sink the Belgrano*, by Steven Berkoff (1989). Like so many of the New Theatre women throughout Australia, Dot continued to be a driving force in New Theatre Melbourne until she was no longer well enough to continue the work.

New Theatre Melbourne always interpreted itself within an international context, in terms not only of political and social issues, but also theatrical issues. It was a part of the broader network of workers' theatre movements which included the US New Theatre League and Unity Theatre – through membership and a constant cross fertilisation of ideas, scripts, articles, reviews and, sometimes, personnel. Throughout its existence, however, its other major concern was to promote an Australian drama and, in doing so, to develop a uniquely Australian culture. The two aims were not always compatible. While the theatre happily drew from the plays of the US and British left-wing theatres, it eschewed the control British theatre had on the theatrical styles of acting and directing and on the notion of drama as 'high culture'. It also rejected frivolous theatre and Hollywood escapism. The theatre purported to be about real people and real issues; to some extent, this meant the working class, but the theatre also operated within the broader context of a people's theatre. There was always a concern with ideas and theory, both political and cultural, and the theatre membership always included intellectuals and artists as well as unionists and working people.

Throughout its history, Melbourne New Theatre was often dismissed as little more than a cultural arm of the CPA – an organisation whose aims were primarily political, as opposed to theatrical, where art existed as a weapon in the class war. This was a simplistic assessment, and its development and achievements were far more complex. Melbourne New Theatre was part of a broader left-wing cultural movement which found a cohesion and direction because of the organisational work associated with the communist movement and associated organisations and because of the importance that these organisations, and earlier socialist movements, placed on aesthetics. This was no longer an issue from the late 1960s onwards, when the communist movement became weak and fragmented; doctrine did not dictate what being left meant.

It is difficult to draw simple conclusions from the history of the New Theatre in Melbourne. It made many contributions, in many diverse ways, and it was several movements within the one. Because it drew from so many sources and collaborated with so many other organisations and individuals, its threads are often barely distinguishable in the fabric of Australia's cultural development. Nonetheless, its contribution was significant. It provided a production outlet for Australian plays during a period when little else was available. It fostered and maintained a theatrical tradition in Melbourne which not only emphasised the cooperative nature of theatre, but assisted in ensuring that Australian drama could take its place as a performance, rather than purely a literary, art form. It provided a focus for dialogue between artists and for the development of cultural aesthetic theories in drama, theatre, literature, music, dance and the visual arts. Until its closure, New Theatre Melbourne continued to present 'theatre with a purpose'. However, many of the younger theatre members who joined New Theatre in its last two decades were politically and artistically transient, seeking experience rather than commitment, often aspiring to find employment in the professional theatre. By the end of the 20th century, it no longer seemed realistic to expect that social change might be shaped by activities on the theatrical fringe.

FURTHER READING

Diamond, Lillian, 'New Theatre's First Decade', *Ten Years of New Theatre. New Theatre Review 1947–1948*, Melbourne, New Theatre Melbourne, 1948.

Gardiner, Allan, *Ralph de Boissiere and Communist Cultural Discourse in Cold War Australia*, Ph.D. diss., Brisbane, University of Queensland, 1993.

Harant, Gerry, 'We Laid 'em in the Aisles: Some Reminiscences of the Realist Film Unit', *Overland*, no. 156, Spring, 1999, pp. 35–39.

Hillel (O'Brien), Angela, *Against the Stream: Melbourne New Theatre 1936–1986*, Melbourne, New Theatre Melbourne, 1986.

Hughes, John, *The Archive Project: the Realist Film Unit in Cold War Australia*, Melbourne, John Hughes, Early Works and The Teachers of the Media Inc., 2013.

O'Brien, Angela, *The Road Not Taken: Political and Performance Ideologies at Melbourne New Theatre 1935–1960*, Ph.D. diss., Melbourne, Monash University, 1989.

Thompson, Dot, *From My Direction*, Clifton Hill, New Theatre Publication, 1991.

Thompson, Dot, *My Method and a Little Madness: Stanislavsky Revisited*, Melbourne, New Theatre Publications, 2000.

CHAPTER 4

Sydney New Theatre

Lyn Collingwood

The Workers' Art Club premises formerly occupied by the Australian Seamen's Union above Nicolas Fatouros' wine saloon at 36 Pitt Street.

Sydney's New Theatre is one of Australia's oldest theatre companies in continuous production, despite receiving no ongoing funding and relying for its survival on the work of volunteers.

Sydney New Theatre began life during the Depression as the Sydney Workers' Art Club. It changed its name twice: to the New Theatre League in 1936, and to New Theatre in 1945. Its first known address was 273 Pitt Street, where a small clubroom opened in August 1932, offering lectures, music recitals, art classes, exhibitions and tuition in Russian, French and German. By October, the club had moved to 36 Pitt Street, premises formerly occupied by the Australian Seamen's Union. In 1943, the NTL shifted to 167 Castlereagh Street. From 1954 to 1962, NT performed at 60 Sussex Street under the auspices of the Cultural Committee of the WWF. In 1963, 'The New' moved to St Peters Lane and, 10 years later, took possession of its own building at 542 King Street Newtown, where it still operates.

THE 1930S: THE WORKERS' ART CLUB

Novelist and CPA member Jean Devanny took credit for founding the WAC, modelling it on clubs she had visited while attending a Workers' International Relief Conference in Berlin in November 1931. Back in Sydney by February 1932, she lectured widely on her experiences and was in Broken Hill on 23 October 1932 when English actress Dame Sybil Thorndike, a pacifist and socialist then touring Australasia with the theatre production *Saint Joan,* officially opened the Sydney WAC.

The WAC's biggest competitor for audiences was the Friends of the Soviet Union (FSU) Dramatic Society, also established in 1932. The FSU and WAC often staged the same Soviet plays, and WAC resented the richer organisation from which it sometimes had to hire chairs and a piano. The FSU was well heeled; it had a wide support base and its own hall. Until the journal was banned in 1940, it published *Soviets Today*, generously illustrated with photos from the USSR. FSU encouraged members of its drama group to write for weekly agitprop nights.

Entrance to the 36 Pitt Street location was by an external rickety, wooden staircase above Nicolas Fatouros' wine bar – which sold cheap plonk. The building's caretaker lived in a dark hole under the stairs, and drunks sometimes managed the steep climb to wander into the club. The main room had a red entry curtain, bare boards, a makeshift stage, an old wood-burning heater and wooden forms to seat up to 100 people. It also served as a workroom for building sets and May Day floats, which needed to be manoeuvred awkwardly down the narrow staircase.

Formal WAC activities were spread over four areas: art, drama, writing and music. A planned orchestra did not eventuate, and the music section soon folded. Art classes were popular under the tuition of WAC President George Finey. He organised an exhibition of Soviet posters in October 1932, a showing of his own sardonically bitter cartoons the next month, and an exhibition of students' and tutors' linocuts at an antiwar rally in April 1933. The literature section encouraged writing about proletarian life. *Sixty Miler*, performed in June 1935, about dirty colliers carrying coal on the Newcastle–Sydney 60-mile run, concerned worker safety. Authors of the one-act play were Sydney University Labour Club law students Jock Smail, Wally Weeks and John Cameron Foster.

Often behind in the rent, the WAC survived mainly through its Saturday dances and monthly fancy-dress parties with themes such as *Hooting, Looting and Shooting* (a burlesque on war), *Poets and Plumbers*, *Palettes and Picks*, *A Night with Conan Doyle* and *A Night in Araby*. The last featured murals of desert moons, minarets and palm trees, and a muezzin called the faithful to supper of tea and a biscuit.

The unemployed sought refuge in the clubroom. As did the underemployed whose jobs included door-to-door sales of 'the economical gas saver': a metal plate for two saucepans which fitted over a single gas burner (but took twice as long to heat up). Others posed as repairmen, who would declare a vacuum cleaner faulty, take it to the WAC, clean it up with Brasso, and return it to the housewife the next day for a 'nominal fee' – having performed an agitprop play the night before on the evils of the exploitative capitalist class. Others became 'shit shooters': illegal street photographers armed with Leica cameras, dodging the police and selling postcard-size prints for two shillings each from their booths in city arcades.

Not long after the WAC opened, key founders George Finey and Jean Devanny, both New Zealand-born pacifists, left the theatre after clashing with the CPA's Central Committee – for choosing popular plays such as *Pygmalion* over Soviet propagandist pieces and granting membership to 'artistic freaks'. Finey also drew criticism from the pro-Trotsky *Militant,* which described the WAC as a Stalinist-inspired outfit that 'has degenerated so rapidly that even the degenerates now shun it'. Finey then set up a short-lived People's Art Club above a speakeasy in King Street in the city.

Following the departure of Devanny, Finey and the WAC's first Secretary, Honey Sloane, Vic Arnold served as Secretary from 1933 to 1940, with Jerry Wells as President. Both acted in and directed a string of productions. In 1957, 'Casting Couch' Wells migrated to England, where he shared an Earls Court flat with New Theatre actor Reg Lye and worked in film and television; his last roles were in *The Two Ronnies* and *The Benny Hill Show* (usually as a pincher of female dancers' bottoms).

After the Writers' League drifted away from the WAC to form the Writers' Association, the drama group became the club's most successful section,

Backstage at 36A Pitt St. Jerold Wells at right helping Russel Ward make up for *Fountains Beyond*, 1942.

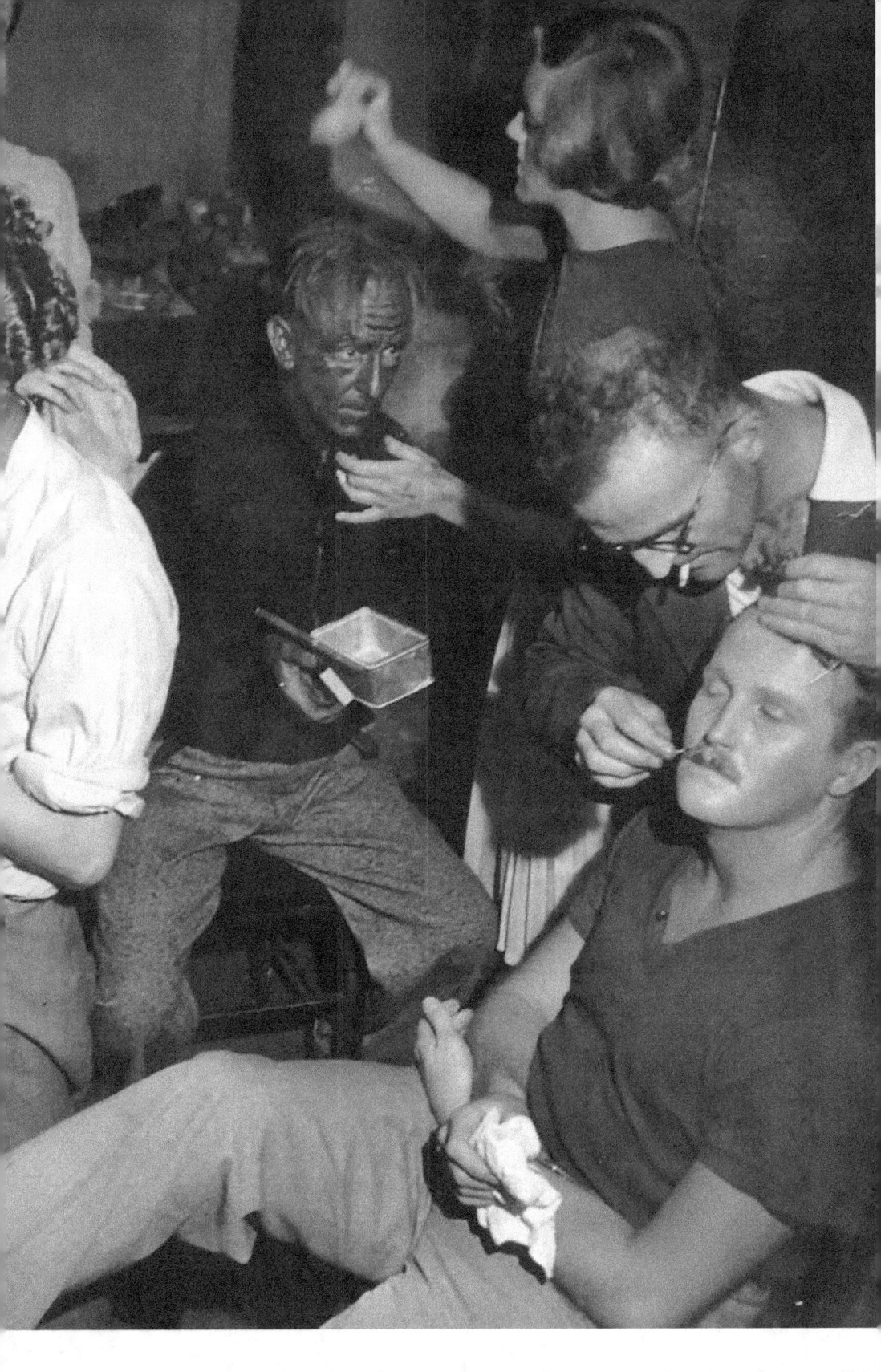

although Sydney's commercial theatres had shrunk from 10 to two with the popularity of cinema. Beginning with Tuesday night play readings, the New hired outside venues when casts or audiences grew too big for the clubroom. The normal club performance night was Sunday, when most Sydney citizens were expected to be in church. A 'donation' was extracted at the door because it was illegal for the unlicensed venue to charge admission.

The major writer in English dealing with social issues was George Bernard Shaw, a favourite with communist theatres because of his wholehearted support for the Russian experiment. His *Pygmalion* and *Mrs Warren's Profession* were popular successes, with Eileen Robinson and Vic Arnold as Eliza and Higgins in the former, and Cleo Grant in the latter's title role. Although the CPA Central Committee denounced *Pygmalion* as non-leftist, the NTL revived it in 1936. Other Shaw productions were *On the Rocks* in 1934 and *Major Barbara*, *Arms and the Man* and *How He Lied to her Husband* in 1936. Reviewers commented on uneven acting ability and the paucity of resources.

In April 1933, the WAC staged its second production: Nelle Rickie's *The Emissary*. At a time when the New Guard was active, it warned against the danger of fascism in Australia. Antiwar pieces included: *Slickers Ltd*, a London Unity Theatre one-act slapstick satire on armaments manufacturer Vickers and the arms race, 'a frenzied gambling orgy during a threatened war period in Europe'; the prologue of German expressionist poet Ernst Toller's *Hoppla! We Live*; and *Twelve Thousand*, by Bruno Frank, who fled Nazi Germany. John Drinkwater's *X=0*, a four-hander written in 1917 but set during the Trojan War, was revived several times. *Who's Who in the Berlin Zoo*, a sketch developed by the English agitprop group the Red Megaphones, was part of a double bill in 1935. In 1938, Freda Lewis directed *The Home of the Brave*, a burlesque on US fascism.

The NTL supported the Republican cause during the Spanish Civil War through fundraising, agitprop and mainstage productions and invitations to the Spanish Consul to address audiences. Ramón Sender's *The Secret* played in the clubrooms and at a Spanish Relief Committee rally. Michael Blankfort's *The Brave and the Blind* concerned the 1936 siege of the Alcázar by Spanish Government forces, 'a particularly searing episode from the grim struggle in Spain'. Although the subject was serious, the cast was undisciplined, making their noisy and leisurely way onstage from the dressing room. *Remember Pedrocito* was restaged several times and toured to Wollongong.

WAC regulars Edward Janshewsky, Harry Haddy, Cliff Mossop and Tim O'Sullivan appeared in the WATG's *The Ragged Trousered Philanthropists*,

The Brave and the Blind poster, Sydney, 1938

which opened to a packed house in the Rationalist Society's Ingersoll Hall at Easter 1933. Most of the cast were unemployed and had no theatrical experience, but they did well enough to start promoting themselves as the RTP Players. In March 1935, the work played to big houses at 36 Pitt Street, and a new version was staged at Newtown in 1987. An examination of the life and conditions of building workers in the fictional English town of Mugsborough, *The Ragged Trousered Philanthropists* was a dramatisation of the popular novel by Robert Tressall, who had worked as a house painter. Promising 'Love, Pathos, Humour, and a Message' and written 'in lurid, blood-red language of men on the job' with an abundance of 'bloodys', its ironic title refers to labourers who work as slaves for their capitalist masters but vote for them at election time. The gulf between the classes is highlighted when, after a worker falls from a ladder, his headgear is picked up by the house's new mistress – who comments: 'What a filthy cap'.

In 1927, Italian-born US immigrants Nicola Sacco and Bartolomeo Vanzetti were executed by electric chair in Massachusetts. Despite the fact that another person confessed to the killings, they were convicted of the 1921 murder of a paymaster and his guard. The execution was delayed for years because of an international outcry – that the men were being tried for their anarchist beliefs rather than the crime. Edward Janshewsky recited the monologue *Vanzetti in the Death House* several times at the WAC and other venues, and Robert Noah's play *The Advocate* examined the subject in 1965.

NT frequently revived London Unity's pantomime satire *Where's That Bomb?* Its unemployed hero writes propaganda on toilet rolls, telling workers of their duty to their bosses and country.

Geoffrey Trease's *Colony* is set in 1936 West Indies, where there was an economic recession and unrest among indentured labourers working for the minority planter class. The 1940 production predated the Moyne Report, not published in full until 1945, which found appalling economic and social conditions among sugar workers: poverty, child mortality, malnutrition, venereal disease and general ill health. In the play, trouble among the sugar workers expands to a strike of taxi drivers, then to power station workers.

THE 1940S: WAR AND COAL STRIKE

When conditions became cramped at 36 Pitt Street, the International Seamen's Club moved there and the League took out a three-year lease in 167 Castlereagh Street, a three-storey building owned by the Grand United

Order of Oddfellows. Close by were a telegraph office, a chemist where 'Mark' helped actresses find the right shade of lipstick, and the Masonic Club whose male members sang loudly in competition with those rehearsing in the theatre. The local watering hole was the Castlereagh Hotel; at a time when women were not allowed in public bars, both genders drank together at a big round table in an upstairs back room: 'Ask the waitress – they know us'. The Sydney committees were egalitarian, in contrast to Melbourne New Theatre, where men and women had to drink in separate areas in their pub.

The theatre was on the first floor, reached by wide concrete steps. The space felt vast in comparison to the old premises, and echoing wooden floorboards added to the familiar noise of trams rattling past. Below was Phillips Café, with its smelly garbage bins. Above was a clothing factory run by two Austrians who had escaped from Vienna the day Hitler marched in. They and their children sat in the front row every opening night.

In preparation for the first show in 1943, *Let's Be Offensive*, members pitched in to transform the big, empty rooms. Jack Bickerdike and his team built a Louis XIV-style stage, painted cream with gold decoration and a plush red curtain. But Council workers forced their way in, wrecked the stage, pulled down the lights and curtain and ripped out the switchboard. Theatre members hastily built a new stage, covered in hessian, and the opening was delayed by only one night.

The New managed to stay on at 167 Castlereagh Street for over a decade, although the City Council, the Fire Brigade and the building's owners regularly attempted to close it down for breaching the *Theatres and Public Halls Act*. Finally, the theatre was served with an eviction notice. A special meeting decided not to fight a court case and voted to find other premises. This was in November 1953, when the theatre's finances and committee were both exhausted. A month later, the smash hit *Reedy River* turned everything around.

War became a reality on 3 September 1939. That night, Miles Franklin and Leslie Rees were overwhelmed by 'sadness and despair' after leaving a reading of Rees' *Lalor of Eureka* to hear newsboys crying: 'Britain declares war on Germany!' The NTL had its allegiances to the Communist Party tested, because Soviet Russia had signed a non-aggression pact less than a fortnight earlier with the communists' archenemy – Nazi Germany.

In June 1940, after the Menzies government banned the CPA under the *National Security Act*, police raided the NTL office, confiscating scripts and Boer War rifles used as props. Oriel and John Gray burnt their copies of the *Communist Review*, and Len Fox put his left-wing books in an outside lavatory. In the city, carrying a case full of typed material for the CPA printer, Fox saw two big plainclothes police running towards him. 'Grab him!' one yelled. 'This is it', he thought; but they rushed past to hop into a taxi. One CPA member convinced police that a portrait of Karl Marx was his grandfather, but another was arrested when her picture of Beethoven was mistaken for Mussolini.

Authorities banned Australian journalist Rupert Lockwood's *No Conscription* after a couple of performances at Transport House and 36 Pitt Street. Set during the heated debates of World War I, the documentary had actors planted in the audience, newspaper boys running up and down the aisles shouting headlines, and the audience exhorted to fight conscription. *Colony* was hastily substituted for *No Conscription* when a CIB officer and a censor turned up in the audience.

Things suddenly changed in June 1941, when Germany attacked Russia. The NTL flipped allegiance and supported the war effort, marching at War Loan rallies and staging patriotic agitprop. Some members worked in munitions factories. Many enlisted, including Vic Arnold, who reduced his age by seven years to join the Australian Imperial Force. An English army officer with riding crop and moustache lectured a bored League audience on how to survive the war, escape to the mountains or out west and make Molotov cocktails. Because of this change of attitude towards the war, the Attorney-General's Department did not proceed with some planned prosecutions.

After reviewing the 1948 production of Sean O'Casey's *The Star Turns Red* as 'magnificent theatre', the *Sydney Morning Herald* boycotted NT plays and refused to accept paid advertising. Mona Brand described this act:

> In retrospect, this withdrawal of *Herald* coverage was the first icy blast of the Cold War that was to breathe on the Australian New Theatre movement for the next 12 years.

Ironically, the New itself was guilty of self-censorship when it turned down Sumner Locke Elliott's offer of *Rusty Bugles* because of its use of 'the great Australian adjective'. The subsequent Independent Theatre production was a smash hit after the Chief Secretary banned it, and the New then found itself opposing the ban in company with others – including the Public Librarian, who said that the word was not an oath from 'by Our Lady' but a Dutch word meaning 'very' and used for emphasis. Not until 1979 did the New stage *Rusty Bugles* – long after the furore had died down.

Because of power cuts, kerosene pressure lamps lit the auditorium and stage during the run of *Birthday of a Miner* in 1949, when coal miners struck over wages and conditions. Union leaders were jailed, there were major blackouts, and thousands of workers were stood down. The strike collapsed when the Chifley government brought in troops to operate the mines. Commissioned by the Miners' Federation of Great Britain, *Birthday of a Miner*, like many NT plays, had a big cast. Twenty-two performers played 30 characters, with the author supplying a doubling list that would work as long as 'no actor is required to play two parts in the same scene'.

THE 1950S: PEACE AND PETROV

City rentals were in short supply in April 1954 when a court order forced the theatre to vacate 167 Castlereagh Street. The New had trouble finding other accommodation and ran the office from Secretary Miriam Hampson's flat. A rented garage stored stage furniture and props. Leasing several different addresses was a major strain on finances; lack of proper premises led to the interruption of classes and workshops; and rehearsals took place in church halls and members' homes.

As a 'temporary' measure, the theatre moved into the hall in the WWF building at 60 Sussex Street. It remained there until 1963, under the auspices of the WWF Cultural Committee.

It was an imperfect solution for both landlord and lessee. The WWF put up with overdue payments of its nominal rent. Extra rehearsal times and late finishes meant that the caretaker had to stay beyond the 10.30 pm curfew. New Theatre could play there only on Saturday and Sunday nights; audiences had trouble finding the venue, identified by an outside banner at performance times. The stage was small and the wing space minimal. After the Sunday show, cast and crew had to strike sets, props and furniture and store them in a tiny loft, and clear the makeshift dressing room. In summer, the hall was like an oven, and cigarette smoke added to the discomfort. The committee decided to ban smoking during performances and put up a no smoking sign (with limited effect).

The biggest disadvantage was that the hall was regularly needed for other purposes. Performances were cancelled, sometimes at short notice, after ads had already been placed. This meant loss of income, audience loyalty and block bookings, and playing only one night a week did not help actors' performances. The number of productions dwindled, and theatre membership fell.

Agitprop protestors including Jean Blue at far left and Oriel Gray's sister Grayce at right.

There was one upside. The relationship between the theatre and waterfront workers was strengthened with the move back to the harbour end of town, and several maritime workers became NT members. Lionel Parker created a piece of agitprop in protest against *Daily Telegraph* allegations that wharfies were drunk, lazy and strike-prone, while others supported the Seamen's Union by performing sketches on wharves and at pay depots in lunch breaks.

Fear of nuclear war increased when the USA dropped atomic bombs in 1945. At the height of McCarthyism in 1951, NT staged Herb Tank's *Longitude 49*, based on a World War II incident when an African-American seaman was shot dead by a white 'liberty' ship officer who said that the seaman was a communist and a troublemaker.

Dymphna Cusack's *Pacific Paradise*, staged in 1955, had casting problems but struck a chord with the public. The author set the play on a South Pacific island affected by atomic testing, after seeing *Children of Hiroshima* and a newspaper placard: 'Hydrogen bomb test at Bikini kills Japanese fishermen 80 miles away'. Despite criticism of its many long speeches, *Pacific Paradise* proved popular, probably because it dealt with issues close to home. The *ABC Weekly* called it:

a plea from the little people of the world who wish to be allowed to live in peace and happiness – indeed, to be allowed to survive.

Oriel Gray wrote *Had We but World Enough* while she was living in a Housing Commission Nissen hut at Herne Bay with her two young sons. Her inspiration was her time in Lismore, where she witnessed injustice to Aboriginal people. Lily, a 12-year-old Aboriginal girl chosen by a country town schoolteacher to play Mary at Easter, suicides. The play had mixed reviews. The *ABC Weekly* considered it 'a superbly lively study of the colour problem in our country', but Oriel Gray thought, on reflection, that it was overwritten and sentimental.

Mona Brand's *Better a Millstone*, set in a London council flat, examines the effect of a young man's execution on a postal worker and his family. It deals with the broader issues of child abuse, criminalisation of the young and the influence on them of comic strip sagas of violence and sex. The stimulus for the play was the hanging of illiterate, 19-year-old Derek Bentley in England in coronation year 1953. After he and 16-year-old Christopher Craig broke into a sweets factory, a policeman confronted them and ordered Craig to drop his gun. Bentley called out: 'Let him have it, Chris', and Craig fired. On the day before the execution, the House of Lords disallowed an appeal for mercy, concentrating instead on preparations for the forthcoming coronation. A film called *Let Him Have It* was released in 1991; and, in 1998, Bentley's conviction was quashed.

In the 1950s, the New supported the Australian Culture Defence Movement (ACDM). Its key founders included composer Raymond Hanson, actor Leonard Teale and poet Roland Robinson. The ACDM promoted Australian cinema, music, literature and radio programs which were being displaced by imports from the USA: offensive, sex-filled, shoddy films, magazines, comics, 'unmusical groans, grunts and howls, and juke box rubbish'. In 1952, the New sent delegates and entertainers to an ACDM conference in Sydney's Lower Town Hall, where Australian books, films, music, theatre and art were on display. In 1953, the New hosted a night for Raymond Hanson, who believed that his association with the ACDM and his later involvement with the Australian–Soviet Friendship Society were detrimental to his professional career and his salaried position at the Sydney Conservatorium. After the ACDM folded under the weight of anti-communist criticism, Hanson reflected that 'culture' had become a dirty word, 'associated principally with strong left ideas and more principally with communism'.

Out of Commission was Mona Brand's Gilbert and Sullivan-style satire on the Petrov Royal Commission. Its leaflet and poster took the form of a legal summons. A popular show, its season was extended and included a performance in the Newcastle Stadium. During the rehearsal period, its author dived fully clothed into Lake Macquarie to rescue the script, which had fallen into the water. No cast or crew names appeared in the printed program. ASIO agent F. G. Murray attended the opening night, a full house where most seats were reserved – witnesses at the Royal Commission had received special invitations. The satire included the 'Security boys' number, sung by dark-hatted, sunglassed, trenchcoated stereotypes. The real-life agents (conspicuous in their suits and oversize hats) reported that the show was of a professional standard; 'at no time did the cast falter in their parts'; and some players wore 'a type of rainproof coat issued to members of this Service'.

Another financial success was US author Howard Fast's *Thirty Pieces of Silver*, staged in 1951. Washington DC statistician David Graham betrays his wartime friend, a Russian-born Jew. Unlike Judas, Graham does not receive 30 pieces of silver but loses his government job in Treasury. Fast wrote to the New:

> We were most cheered to read of the struggle being put up in Australia...we are part of a great peace movement whose victory is inevitable.

One of the political targets in the 1950 revue *Press the Point* was Foreign Affairs Minister Sir Percy Spender, a key figure in developing the USA-backed Colombo Plan, its goal to raise Asian living standards in the hope that participating countries would battle communist movements. His counterpart sang, to the tune of 'I've Got a Lovely Bunch of Coconuts':

> *I've got a luvverly Suspender plan*
>
> *I wrote it myself in luvverly pen and ink*
>
> *I'll nip in the bud the red roaring flood*
>
> *Singing rolla and bowl the commos into the clink.*

Also parodied was Sydney's ALP Lord Mayor Ernie O'Dea, who received bodyguard protection after demonstrations against the City Council's refusal to let Sydney Town Hall to the Democratic Rights Council, declared a 'Red' organisation. The Dean of Canterbury, the Australian Peace Council and the Australian Carnival of Youth for Peace and Friendship were also denied use of the venue. In real life, O'Dea had been created an honorary chief of the Suquamish tribe by the visiting Mayor of Vancouver, who presented O'Dea with a five-foot totem pole and full headdress. This provided the sketch writer with excellent comic material; the Lord Mayor's only line was: 'How'.

THE 1960S: CAUSES AND POLITICS

The search for a new home continued into the 1960s, driven by the limited availability of the WWF hall, the discomfort of the occasional flea plague and the birth of a local alley cat's litter under the stage. In 1963, the New moved to the rear of a car salesroom at 151 William Street Darlinghurst, where it remained until 1973. The entrance to the theatre, converted from a motor garage housing two Rolls Royces, was on St Peters Lane. Some female theatre members became friendly with prostitutes who frequented the area. The NT watering hole was the Lord Roberts Hotel in Stanley Street.

The auditorium was at ground level, with administration offices, a meeting area and dressing rooms constructed above. After a plea went out for help, trade unionists joined working bees at night and on weekends, and NT supporters donated items such as a refrigerator and a vacuum cleaner. NT bought second-hand carpet and 114 cinema seats from the Prince Edward 'Theatre Beautiful', which was slated for demolition. Work was still happening on the St Peters Lane building when the first show was about to open. During the dress rehearsal, auditorium floorboards were hammered down and walls painted. As the opening night audience gathered in the foyer, the front row seats were being screwed into place.

There were ongoing problems with fleas and cockroaches and regular thefts from the theatre (including the Tasmanian bush fire appeal box in 1967) and nearby parked cars. The wide, shallow stage was not high enough to accommodate fly rigging, and the sound equipment sometimes picked up local police and taxi messages. Allocated seating made extra work for front of house volunteers; they had to act as ushers in addition to their regular box-office and cleaning duties (including sifting cigarette butts out of the audience ashtray, so the sand could be reused), and they often failed to turn up. But the auditorium's excellent sightlines and acoustics were in marked contrast to earlier venues, and, during its decade at St Peters Lane, NT broadened its audience and its program. It revived acting classes, workshops and children's theatre and staged more shows, with shorter seasons.

After a long search for material opposing the Vietnam War, the theatre devised its own. Mona Brand, Patrick Barnett and Roger Milliss were the key creators of *On Stage Vietnam*, a stylistic mix of stage, slides, mime and dance drama requiring split-second timing of special effects. The 1967 show drew audiences and added an extra weekly performance. It toured locally to Gordon and Sydney University. Security was improved after the theft of 22 slides, which were remade courtesy of *Tribune*. The NSW Education Minister attacked the New for charging half-price admission for children and for publicising the show in the Teachers Federation journal – where children might see it. The New regularly sent petitions, telegrams and letters opposing the Vietnam War to the US Consul and Prime Ministers Menzies and Holt.

During the 1960s, NT consistently opposed apartheid, supporting The Friends of Africa and urging South African Prime Minister Hendrik Verwoerd to end the policy. The theatre also pressured Menzies to push for the expulsion of South Africa from the Commonwealth of Nations and NSW Premier Heffron to drop charges against local protesters.

NT was also a consistent supporter of Australian Aboriginal and Torres Strait Islander people. Activists Faith and Hans Bandler were regulars in the audience and at social events. Tranby Co-operative College invited NT to its official opening, and the New held fundraisers for the Aboriginal-Australian Fellowship, the Aborigine Progressive Association, the Northern Territory Council for Aboriginal Rights and the Federal Council for Aboriginal Advancement. Members called for equal citizenship rights and, during the Gurindji dispute (the 1966 strike by Wave Hill stockmen), sent money to the strikers and urged the Australian Council of Trade Unions to black ban station owners, the Vestey Brothers. (The Vesteys featured in a Street Theatre item, David Young's *The Born Loser*.)

The children's musical *Mumba Jumba and the Bunyip* intertwined Aboriginal legends with a plea for the protection of the bush. In the 1970s, the New raised money for Muraweena pre-school and the Free Kevin Gilbert campaign, and in 1988–9 it donated $1 from each ticket sold and $5 from each member's dues to the Aboriginal National Theatre Trust.

Sandhog, an Australian premiere in 1962, is a US folk opera about the compressed air tunnellers who built the Manhattan Hoboken Tunnel under the Hudson River in the 1880s. Such public works were built on the sweat of workers who were often carried out dead or incapacitated; 'Song of the

Bends' dramatised the danger. If the pressure in the tunnel was high enough to dry out the quicksand at the bottom, the roof was likely to blow off; if the pressure was too low, the shield sank into the quicksand. Staging was simple: a bare stage with black curtains, the tunnel evoked by projections of slides across the actors.

In Frank Hardy's *The Ringbolter*, an escaped convict on the run after killing a warder (an amalgam of the Dugan–Mears/Simmonds–Newcombe manhunts) stows away on a coastal steamer whose crew are deliberating whether to go on strike. The ringbolter (a stowaway hidden below a hatch opened by a ringbolt) is the catalyst who complicates the situation. The unpublished script was staged in 1967; the previous year, a ringbolter had shot a seaman at Darling Harbour.

In 1960, the *Sydney Morning Herald* boycott of NT suddenly ended when critic Lindsey Browne turned up at *All My Sons*. The change in editorial policy apparently arose from a meeting between WWF General Secretary Jim Healy and a *Herald* executive. In 1973, after hearing that the *Herald* would no longer review non-professional productions, WWF official Norm Docker reminded Warwick Fairfax that all Sydney newsprint passed through the hands of wharfies.

The decade's biggest sensation was John Tasker's 1968 production of Jean-Claude van Itallie's *America Hurrah!* – satirising the worst aspects of the US way of life and concluding with giant dolls scrawling obscenities on the walls of a motel room. After the play had been running five weeks, a grandmother who took her grandson to see it complained about *Motel*, one of the three one-act plays comprising *America Hurrah*. NSW Chief Secretary Eric Willis banned the segment as going 'beyond boundaries of decency and decorum'. Rather than risk massive fines, Mona Brand wrote, and Betty Lucas narrated, a new version, *Hotel*, as a comment on Australian censorship laws: 'It's hard to keep things clean these days but where there's a Willis there's a way,' and the scribbled four-letter word became 'F111'. Meanwhile, a broad committee called Friends of America Hurrah circumvented the *Theatres and Public Halls Act* with a free one-night performance of the unaltered version at the Teachers Federation Hall. Harry Kippax, holding up a note 'SMH must review', managed to get in, and he and Katharine Brisbane watched the show from the stage manager's box.

In the end, there were no prosecutions; but the *America Hurrah!* furore paved the way for *The Boys in the Band* and *Hair* to be staged uncut. It was John Tasker who had urged the New to apply for the rights to *America*

Hurrah! which he predicted no other Australian theatre would touch: 'It could be a bombshell on the Sydney scene'. The production received huge press and television publicity and toured to Hobart and the University of New England; but, even with this success, the theatre was soon broke again. The *America Hurrah!* rights were the highest ever paid to that date, past royalties and old debts were settled, the following show *War and Peace* lost money, and there was no carry-over of interest in van Itallie's *The Serpent*, staged the next year.

In 1960, the year the *Telephonic Communications (Interception) Act* was passed – supposedly to protect the privacy of the individual – NT staged Mona Brand's *Hold the Line or The Land of Teletap*, a parody of *The Mikado* satirising ASIO's phone tapping in its hunt for 'Reds under the beds'. Lavishly costumed and reviewed as good-humoured and smoothly directed, it was also seen as propagandist. One audience member agreed that the original *Crimes Act* was too sweeping, but:

> Surely in this electronic age you do not seriously imagine that there is a land in the world that isn't a land of teletap. Or do you naively believe that Holy Mother Russia is all-pure?

The cartoon-like *Macbird!* had a long run in 1967. The Shakespearean parody plays out the power struggle following the assassination of John F. Kennedy; its main characters are Lyndon B. Johnson as Macbird and Robert Kennedy as the Macduff figure. US author Barbara Garson wrote it for a student protest demonstration at Berkeley and said that her intention was not to accuse LBJ of having anything to do with JFK's assassination but to expose the hypocrisy of political leaders. Rather than trust them, she worked from the premise that 'those guys don't know at all what they're doing'. J. Edgar Hoover condemned the work as 'unbridled vulgarity, obscenity, blasphemy, perversion and public desecration of every sacred and just symbol'. English actor John Barnard, who came to Australia with Laurence Olivier and the Old Vic Company in 1948 and joined NT soon after, directed the Sydney production.

THE 1970S: A PERMANENT SPACE

Another rent increase in 1969 initiated another hunt for new premises. Solicitor Sid Conway was among those recommending the purchase of a building, with a separate legal entity to administer it. NT set up a Premises Fund and increased fundraising activities. Money also came from members' loans, and trade unions, other theatres and left-wing political parties offered support.

In August 1972, New Theatre paid the 10 percent deposit on 542 King Street, at the St Peters end of Newtown. Its last occupier, the Sure Brite television picture tube factory, left behind a cavernous space covered with broken glass. NT had to completely re-lay the drainage, remove part of the roof on the King Street side, build a new mezzanine floor and extensively reshape the rear of the building on Iredale Street.

Miriam Hampson and Jack Mundey were the driving force in getting support from unions. Construction company Civil and Civic secured a bank loan, supplied bricks and second-hand timber and provided a full-time leading hand. At a time when there was a shortage of skilled labour because of the amount of building work happening in Sydney, the New was able to engage a bricklayer, two carpenters and three labourers. Trade union boilermakers built the steel framework for the raked auditorium, and a volunteer plumber installed the guttering.

In April 1973, amid piles of bricks, mortar and timber, the theatre staged *Newtown Prom*, a fundraiser featuring singers Jeannie Lewis and Marian Henderson and offering wine with supper instead of the customary keg of beer. Minister for Media Doug McClelland formally opened the Newtown building on 15 September 1973, on the opening night of the revue *What's New*, before an audience that included trade unionists and South Sydney Councillors.

Settling in at King Street coincided with the period in office of the Whitlam government, which was supportive of the arts. A federal grant secured the building, and Australia Council grants financed children's workshops and freelance directors. Keen to justify such financial support, the New promoted itself as a community space, with children's arts and crafts, workshops and productions; puppetry; folk dancing; karate; street theatre; and activities involving migrant groups. Despite these efforts, local and general audiences were hard to find for the mainstage shows, and the exhausted committees met in a sometimes 'poisonous' atmosphere. The theatre struggled on until financial salvation came in March 1975 with the Australian premiere of *One Flew Over the Cuckoo's Nest*, a work that combined theatricality with a political message.

The Newtown New Theatre premises, 1972 and 2006

Jules Feiffer's antiwar dark comedy *The White House Murder Case* was originally a commentary on Vietnam. NT staged it in 1974 when it was publicised as relevant to Watergate.

In 1977, Street Theatre's *The Great International Uranium Show* played at Lucas Heights, the University of NSW, Macquarie University and the Mascot Fair. Discussions with guest speakers on the nuclear issue and uranium mining followed John Romeril's *The Radioactive Horror Show* in 1978.

Events While Guarding the Bofors Gun, set in an army camp in the British sector of occupied Berlin in 1954, played in 1979 with a strong ensemble cast. The play's author, John McGrath, founded the 7:84 Theatre Company; its title came from a 1966 statistic showing that 7 percent of the population of Great Britain owned 84 percent of the wealth. That company, which aimed to present the realities of working-class life and history to working-class audiences, survived from 1971 to 2008.

The New staged several plays on historical figures in the 1970s. In *Hair*-like style, *Tom Paine*, by New York's La Mama playwright Paul Foster, is rough Brechtian theatre about the 18th century philosopher who wrote *The Rights of Man* and inspired the US War of Independence.

Friday the Thirteenth, set during NSW Premier J. T. Lang's last day in office, was a world premiere in 1978. Its author, Kevin Barry Morgan, an ex-Labor parliamentarian, also acted in it and was convincing and amusing as an ALP Speaker. Jack Lang was played by Stan Ashmore-Smith, then

Secretary of the Kings Cross branch of the ALP and, later, a City of Sydney alderman and deputy Lord Mayor who organised public meetings on disarmament. The play attracted good houses, including school students studying Australian history. Laurie Brereton was in the first night audience.

In exuberant circus style, Barry Oakley's *The Feet of Daniel Mannix* satirises the Melbourne Roman Catholic archbishop's influence on Australian politics in the period 1912–63 in areas including conscription, unemployment and the formation of the Democratic Labor Party. Combat sequences featured Mannix and Scullin wrestling over Catholic education, Mannix and Hughes fighting with thunderbolts over conscription, and H. V. Evatt strangled by a red octopus. Bill Charlton played the title role.

The Disorderly Women, adapted from *The Bacchae* and updated with references to Women's Liberation (plus hallucinogenic drugs and the Charles Manson murders), played in 1971. It was a gory show: a big budget item was a bottle of 'blood' a week. A stylised blend of dance and drama, its most moving piece was *Four Women*, with words by Jean-Claude van Itallie. Costumes ranged from topless to long-john leotards with rumpled underwear showing through.

Steve Gooch's *Female Transport* focused on the hardships women convicts endured during their six-month journey to Australia. Props included leg irons fashioned by the blacksmith at Old Sydney Town, where it played on Australia Day 1976.

THE 1980S: MORE AUSTRALIAN WORKS

By the 1980s, NT was producing more Australian works, although there was increasing competition – especially from the Nimrod Theatre Company – for their performing rights.

The theatre financially supported Australians' participation in the 1980 Moscow Olympic Games and continued its overt support of the Soviet Union until Miriam Hampson's retirement as Secretary in 1982. A play script competition commemorating the New's 50th birthday that year attracted 92 entries. Also marking the anniversary was '50 New Years', an exhibition mounted in the Opera House. Speakers at its opening included ex-New Theatre President Maurie Keane, who also attended Hampson's retirement testimonial in Sydney Town Hall with fellow ALP politicians Bob Tickner, Tom Uren, Senator Arthur Gietzelt and Lord Mayor Doug Sutherland.

Oh What a Lovely War, Mate was a popular success in 1980. The script, by Joan Littlewood with additional Australian material by Nick Enright, used a pastiche of World War I songs, music, dance, comedy skits and political spin, juxtaposed with a visual montage of newspaper reports, casualty lists, recruiting posters and battlefield photographs to expose the hoopla that concealed the grim realities of the conflict. A troupe of music hall entertainers entice young men to embark on an adventure with appeals to patriotism and promises of exotic lands, sex on tap and 'the King's shilling', but with no mention of them becoming cannon fodder.

In *Ron Raygun in the Antipodes*, a musical play by Stafford Sanders and Tom Bridges, President Raygun comes to Australia to safeguard US interests after the sacking of a Labor government. Targets include Pine Gap, Three Mile Island, Northwest Cape, Omega, Esso, Utah, Pan-Continental, F111, Watergate, Agent Orange, Australian conservative politicians and press baron Mudrock cutting his ties with Australia to concentrate on London and New York operations.

Publicity for George Sklar's *Brown Pelican*, a play about pollution and conservation staged in 1980, referenced Agent Orange and the birth defects it caused.

The 1984 presentation of Mona Brand's *Here Comes Kisch!* marked the 50th anniversary of the declaration of Egon Kisch as an illegal immigrant. A Czech journalist and anti-fascist communist, Kisch (who had been a fellow student of Franz Kafka) was invited to Melbourne for an antiwar congress. When the ship docked, Kisch jumped onto the wharf, breaking his leg.

Because of a court application, he was able to get to Sydney; he was rearrested and subjected to a dictation test. Fluent in many languages, he failed Scottish Gaelic and was given six months' jail, a sentence quashed by the High Court. His public appearances attracted big crowds, including Jean Devanny, who kissed him in Sydney's Domain. Kisch, whose counsel was left-wing lawyer Christian Jollie Smith, left Australia in March 1935 after reimbursement of his legal costs. Reviewers of Mona Brand's play called it a 'wonderful political romp', 'fast, funny and very enjoyable'; the season was extended.

Sandinista! in agitprop style portrayed the politics behind the scenes and the extent of US involvement in Nicaragua; after the revolutionary Sandinistas won power from dictator Somoza in 1979, the USA had begun destabilising the new regime, withdrawing foreign aid and funding anti-government rebels.

John Summons' *The Savage Heart,* short-listed in the 50th anniversary competition, was presented as a rehearsed reading in 1984. Its subject matter was the Myall Creek massacre of Aborigines and the murder trials that followed. Theatre member Roger Milliss examined the same incident in his epic work *Waterloo Creek,* co-winner of the 1992 CUB Non-Fiction Award.

The Death of Phillip Robertson: the true story of a black death in custody played in 1988. The Fannie Bay Gaol prisoner had been asphyxiated by vomit after being struck on the back of the neck; a charge of manslaughter against a prison officer was dropped. The play's author, John Tomlinson, Secretary of the Northern Territory Council for Civil Liberties, sat through the inquest and believed that a miscarriage of justice had occurred. He constructed his play from transcripts of the inquest and added his own prologue.

During an industrial dispute in 1980, the New bought copies of the strikers' paper *The Journalists' Clarion* and gave them out gratis in the foyer. That year's revue, *And I Still Call Home Australia,* included a press baron's takeover bid. *Waiting for Rupert Murdoch,* joint winner of the 1982 NT playwriting competition, was staged in 1983. Set in the office of a suburban newspaper, the play examines the ethics of modern journalism, where profits are put ahead of keeping the public informed. Its author, John Upton – who edited the theatre's *Spotlight!* newsletter, handled publicity for a while and had several of his plays workshopped – went on to a long career as a professional stage and television dramatist.

First in a women's season in 1981, John McGrath's *Yobbo Nowt* focuses on bureaucratic absurdities, the downgrading of working-class women and the liberating effect of political awareness. In comic book style, the play tracks the journey of a naïve Liverpool housewife who learns about the workings of the capitalist system as she tries to get a job. There were Sunday post-show discussions on issues raised. Guest speakers included NT member and UNSW School of Psychology academic Bill Hopes and Justice Staples of the Arbitration Commission, whose topic was the strain of living on a weekly wage of less than $160. *Yobbo Nowt* received a second production in 1985.

First Class Women, written by Nick Enright for the New, deals with the exploitation and repression of female convicts in the Parramatta Female Factory, where life on the inside is possibly worse than outside the institution.

THE 1990S: WAR AND IMPERIALISM

Competition with other companies for performance rights of left-wing plays continued during the 1990s. NT actors and directors also worked regularly at other venues: the Zenith at Chatswood, Ensemble, Iron Cove Theatre, Crossroads Theatre, Belvoir Downstairs, Voices in Dickson Street, Harold Park Hotel, Shakespeare by the Sea and the Genesians in Kent Street. There were more productions of Shakespeare and Australian works. A world premiere in 1994 was Alan Kelley's *Portrait of An Artist*, an account of the controversy surrounding the awarding of the 1943 Archibald Prize to William Dobell for his painting of fellow artist Joshua Smith.

Maintenance on the King Street building and changing fire regulations were a constant financial drain. Fundraising, particularly activities organised by Sandra Campbell, kept the New afloat: raffles, jumble sales, picnics, fashion parades, harbour cruises, theatre parties and restaurant get-togethers. Marie Armstrong's dinner–dance at City Tattersalls (no denim, no thongs) pulled a good crowd. In 1995, the theatre hosted a party for Mona Brand's 80th birthday and the launch of her autobiography, *Enough Blue Sky*. Mona wrote a letter of thanks: 'It was good to feel New Theatre's long history of mateship still alive and well'. That mateship was apparent the next year, when money from a *Cherry Orchard* performance was donated to James Warner after fire gutted his costume hire rooms.

The decade began with NT's affiliation with the Bring the Frigates Home Coalition, opposed to a Gulf War. The New raised funds for the Care Australia Rwanda Appeal and East Timor; and, in 1999, refugees from Kosovo attended a performance of *A Midsummer Night's Dream*. Diane Samuels' *Kindertransport*, about the British Government's prewar program of taking unaccompanied Jewish children out of Austria and Germany, was workshopped in 1997.

Alex Buzo's *Pacific Union* concerns the first conference of the United Nations in 1945 in San Francisco, where Australia's independent foreign policy was created in a hotel room.

Workshopped in 1991, Pieter-Dirk Uys' *Panorama* juxtaposes anti-apartheid campaigners in jail and white middle-class women shackled by their ignorance and fear. Using comedy to expose the absurdities of the South African Government's racial policies, Uys developed the character of Tannie Evita, an Afrikaner socialite inspired by Australia's Dame Edna Everage.

THE 2000S: HITTING TARGETS AND EXPOSING BIG BUSINESS

In the noughties, NT remained a membership-based organisation. Volunteers, under the guidance of a management committee, carried out most work other than office administration, publicity and bookings. After the Sydney Olympics adversely affected box office takings, the New in 2001 embarked on a massive fundraising campaign to keep its doors open. Major support came from members, the NSW Government and the estate of Stefan Kruger. Another drive in 2008 paid for major fire safety upgrading and disabled access. Improvements in 2014–15 included repainting the foyer, installing glass entrance doors, reupholstering audience chairs and commissioning a mural on the King Street façade. Crowdfunding and donations from NT members and supporters, particularly the Australia-Russia & Affiliates Friendship Society, financed the upgrades.

The New continued to produce Australian plays, notably world premieres such as *A Nasty Piece of Work*, *Mad Before Midday*, *Pandora's Garden* and works in the *New Directions* series. Dorothy Hewett's *The Man from Mukinupin*, a musical celebration of rural life, was radical and confronting when commissioned in 1979. Set in a mythical Western Australian wheat-belt town during World War I, its daytime comfortable middle-class sequences contrast with excluded or disadvantaged night-time characters on the fringes. The massacre of the local Aboriginal population is a repressed collective memory. Mary-Anne Gifford directed the 2007 production.

Large-scale musicals proved popular: *Assassins*, *Into the Woods*, *Little Shop of Horrors*, *Cabaret*, *The Venetian Twins* and *Sweeney Todd*. *The Diary of Anne Frank* had sell-out seasons in 2001 and 2015. Its climax had many in the audience reaching for their tissues.

The *All Ordinaries* revue marked federal election night in 2001. The 2002 cast of *Stop Laughing, This is Serious! 70 Years of Revue at the New* included Bartholomew Rose, who played Prime Minister John Howard and, for some years afterwards, took that persona into the real world – including the Bennelong electorate and the City to Surf marathon. He reappeared in *Australia's Most Wanted*, a trivia night fundraiser in 2005, and in *Howard's End*, an election night revue in 2007.

Jez Butterworth's *Jerusalem* comments on the state of 21st century England, lamenting lost freedom, community and innocence – leaving in its place a manufactured, corporate landscape of shopping malls and food chains, a nanny state of concrete, warning signs and closed-circuit television cameras. An anarchic vision has replaced William Blake's 'green and pleasant land'. The action of the play takes place on local county fair day, St George's Day. Central character 'Rooster' Byron, a local wastrel and modern-day Pied Piper, lives in a caravan in the woods and surrounds himself with hangers-on he plies with drugs and alcohol. A frenetic chain of events follows when Rooster receives an eviction notice. Sydney critics voted *Jerusalem* one of the city's best shows in 2013.

The Angry Brigade, staged in 2019, takes its title from a cell of anti-elitist young urban guerrillas who carried out a series of bombings in Britain in the 1970s, at a time of global political and cultural upheaval and high unemployment, austerity measures and deregulation at home. James Graham's play raises questions about the fine line between freedom fighter and terrorist and the point at which anger tips into armed protest.

Harley Granville-Barker's *The Voysey Inheritance*, directed by Kevin Jackson in 2006, concerns financial fraud. When young Edward Voysey becomes a partner in the family legal business, he discovers that his solicitor father has been defrauding clients for years and that family members knew this but feared scandal.

Part of the 2013 season, Lucy Prebble's *Enron* charts the rise and fall of the US energy giant whose corrupt practices lead to its collapse and its executives' imprisonment. The play is set inside the bubble before it burst, exposing a world of glamour, hubris, risk-taking and spin. In 2001, the world discovered that Enron executives had hidden from its board and shareholders the corporation's debt of millions of dollars from failed deals and projects, by means of accounting loopholes and misleading financial reporting. At the time, it was the largest corporate bankruptcy in US history.

Glengarry Glen Ross, David Mamet's satire on the cut-throat world of real estate sales, played in 2021, as a reminder that the wealth of the USA's 45th President was built on his father's real estate business.

From its humble origins in 1932 until the present day, Sydney's New Theatre continues to perform an important role in the left-wing theatre community. Its influence ripples out into broader society. The theatre often struggled to remain solvent but stood firm against sustained political pressure, especially during the Cold War. Although it has become more mainstream, the New has continued to tell stories about marginalised and disenfranchised groups and individuals that might otherwise have stayed untold and forgotten.

FURTHER READING

The information in this chapter draws heavily on the New Theatre wiki compiled by Lyn Collingwood, http://newtheatrehistory.org.au/wiki/index.php/ New_Theatre_History_Wiki:Home, with the author's permission, but the format has been adapted.

Arrow, Michelle, 'The New Theatre', in Terry Irving and Rowan Cahill (eds.), *Radical Sydney: Places, Portraits and Unruly Episodes*, Sydney, UNSW Press, 2010, pp. 210–215.

Barrett, Kathleen, 'Sydney New Theatre 1950–1959: Committed Commies, Parlour Pinks or Radical Reactionaries?' M.A. diss., University of Sydney, 1988.

Brand, Mona, 'New Theatre Movement Part 1: 1932–1948', *Theatre Australia*, October, 1978, pp. 13–15.

Brand, Mona, 'New Theatre Movement Part 2: Cold War and After', *Theatre Australia*, November, 1978, pp. 19–20.

Herlinger, Paul, 'New Theatre – The Pre-War Years 1932–1939', M.A. diss., University of Sydney, 1981.

New Theatre, *15 Years of Production*, Sydney, New Theatre, 1948.

New Theatre, *50 new years 1932–1982: an exhibition of the plays, people and events of fifty years of Sydney's radical New Theatre, Thursday 10 June–Sunday 4 July 1982*, ed. David Milliss, Sydney, New Theatre, 1983.

New Theatre, *The New Years, 1932–: The Plays, People and Events of 75 Years of Sydney's New Theatre*, Sydney, New Theatre, 2007.

Noakes, Frank, 'New Theatre', *SNOOP: A Magazine of UTS Journalism*, no. 5, Winter, 1996, p. 21.

Roland, Betty, 'War on the Waterfront – a Banned Play', *Illawarra Unity – Journal of the Illawarra Branch of the Australian Society for the Study of Labour History*, vol. 7, no. 1, 2007, pp. 49–55.

ONE OF THE PRIZE-WINNING FLOATS in the May Day procession to-day.—Arranged by the New Theatre League, the tableau protested against war, Fascism and exploitation.

CHAPTER 5

Rural Radical Theatre: the Newcastle NTL 1937-40

Laura Ginters

Today, the work of the first Newcastle NTL in the late 1930s has almost entirely disappeared from memory and the public record. But it was a vibrant and active contributor to the national and international project of the NTLs – changing the world through theatre. From early 1937, it ran for nearly four years.

EARLY HISTORY 1933-36

In 1932 in Sydney, the Sydney Workers' Art Club (later renamed the NTL) had set itself up under the slogan 'Art is a Weapon', and drama activities in Newcastle, by and for working-class participants, followed quickly. Newcastle was Australia's first industrial city, centred on mining, a steel works and its port, and has had a long and strong union tradition: the Newcastle Trades Hall Council is the oldest continuous peak union organisation in Australia.

From the 1930s, the trade union movement was active in promoting adult education; it played a significant role in the eventual establishment of the university in Newcastle. It was also involved in theatre and the arts more generally. On his appointment to the Newcastle WEA in 1933, 'tutor-organiser' Lloyd Ross conducted lunchtime classes with railworkers at the Broadmeadow Workshops and established a 'Dramatic Club' to read and present plays:

> with a view to instructing members in practical spheres of the theatre, and also to give facilities for the presentation of plays written by members.

Lloyd Ross, whose work established the Newcastle New Theatre.

Ross quite explicitly sought to forge an alliance between left-wing cultural activism and pro-labour politics. He himself penned several dramatic historical re-enactments, including *The Second Congress of Soviets* – drawing on John Reed's *Ten Days that Shook the World* – and *The League of Nations at Geneva* in mid-1933. The Dramatic Club produced his play, *Labour's Cavalcade*, in December that year, with assistance from the Australian Railways Union (ARU).

Ross had developed connections with the ARU; the ARU sub-branch Secretary in Newcastle, Tom Hickey – one of his lunchtime students – became a strong supporter of his work. They worked together on several of Ross' productions, including *May Day Through the Ages* in 1934. Ross' incumbency was short-lived; he left Newcastle for a WEA-related position at the

University of Sydney in May 1934. The following year, he was elected NSW ARU Secretary. However, his work through the WEA with railway workers and his close association with the ARU set the scene for the establishment of a new branch of the NTL in Newcastle.

Acknowledging the mostly overlooked connections between the Sydney and Newcastle branches, especially through trade unions and individual workers and the WEA, adds detail to our understanding of how the NTL functioned in Australia in the 1930s and its widespread geographic and cultural influence. This relationship was a reciprocal one: the earlier established, metropolitan NTL group did not simply 'export' ideas, plays and skills to the regional NTL (although this did occur). Rather, like-minded individuals and overarching umbrella organisations with a presence in each place developed this work more broadly.

So, for example, before the Newcastle NTL formed, Ross toured *Labour's Cavalcade*, 'performed by men and women unionists from Newcastle', to Sydney in late May 1934. Sydney audiences welcomed it warmly as 'a valuable piece of proletarian dramatisation', according to the *Australian Worker*. There are several examples of the Newcastle NTL contributing the first Australian production of a particular play, before the Sydney branch. It is clear that collaboration, rather than competition, characterised the relationship between these two branches of the NTL.

Interestingly, the editorial of the first issue (November 1938) of the monthly *Australian Left News*, the journal of the Left Book Club movement, opened with the comment:

> In Australia one of the most difficult things to achieve is practical unity in national problems. The reason is to be found not only in the distances which separate great centres of population from one another, but also in certain almost fundamental differences of outlook.

Difficult but possible: indeed, the NTL is a model for addressing 'practical unity in national problems'. By the following issue of the journal, in fact, Vic Arnold of the Sydney NTL had reached out to the *Australian Left News* to align the NTL to their purpose.

One example of this 'practical unity' is the way the NTL branches shared plays: their repertoires overlapped to a significant extent. Clifford Odets' play, *Waiting for Lefty*, is one example. It was very significant for, and widely produced by, progressive theatre companies around the world in the 1930s. Sonya Langelaar reports that the Unity Theatre in Brisbane, as well as the New Theatres in Adelaide, Perth, Melbourne, Newcastle and Sydney, all opened with this play (while *Waiting for Lefty* was its first great success, the Sydney NTL had actually begun work four years earlier).

Another of Odets' plays was also particularly important to the history of the New Theatre, both in Sydney and in Newcastle: *Till the Day I Die* is an anti-Nazi play set in Berlin in 1935, written as a curtain-raiser for *Waiting for Lefty*. The New Theatre in Sydney had programmed it in 1936, but the German Ambassador to Australia complained to the Prime Minister that the play was 'hostile to a friendly power'. The NSW State Censor promptly banned the play, amid considerable public uproar. The theatre nonetheless went ahead with the production; a police raid and a fine resulted. Ultimately, the Sydney New Theatre successfully circumvented this prohibition by organising a series of private, 'invitation only' performances. The production also toured to Newcastle.

The Secretary of the Newcastle sub-branch of the Australian Railways Union attended and declared the play: 'of great educational value to workers'. He proclaimed his desire to 'see an ARU art club established in Newcastle'; a meeting of the sub-branch 'decided to give all assistance possible', which ultimately included making their hall available for performances.

BIRTH OF THE NEWCASTLE NTL

The Newcastle NTL formed six months later, in February 1937, at a 'well attended inaugural meeting in the Newcastle WEA Rooms'. It adopted the constitution of the Sydney NTL with only slight variations. It immediately began rehearsals for its first production – Odets' *Waiting for Lefty* – which opened on 10 April 1937.

By the time of this inaugural meeting, more than 40 members from all over Newcastle had already signed up. This was partly due to what Lisa Milner has described as an early instance of crowdsourcing; the energetic Joyce Deans (later Batterham) wrote to unions offering deals for group subscribers: '£2 entitled you to two tickets to each production'. Individual membership fees were one shilling per month, and a person could become a subscriber by paying ten shillings and sixpence per year. This entitled the subscriber to two free tickets for each performance and the right to participate in play readings. Deans later recalled that 'union support was good with most unions subscribing'. That brought other practical benefits for the fledgling company: '[t]wo blokes from the carpenters and joiners union signed up straight away which was excellent as they could make sets and props'.

The inaugural committee shows how actively women were involved in the Newcastle NTL. Women held the three main offices: Mrs Barbara Roberts, the longstanding Secretary of the WEA, became President; Treasurer was Miss Lily Wilson, who performed in many of their productions and later, as Secretary, represented the Newcastle NTL at the 1940 National Conference; Miss Joyce Deans, the Secretary, had also been a WEA student and acted for the NTL. Deans' recollections of her time in Newcastle offer valuable first-person insights into the organisation.

Joseph Smith joined the committee as Publicity Officer. Smith acted in many of their plays, had acclaimed makeup skills and directed several plays, including the Australian premiere of a Brecht play. Norman Clark took the role of 'producer' – the common designation for 'director' in the 1930s. Clark, 'from the railways', was 'not only an actor of high standing, but has produced many plays'; indeed, he directed the NTL's inaugural production, *Waiting for Lefty*, and went on to direct all but one of their full-length plays and a good number of the one-act plays they regularly presented. The exception was George Bernard Shaw's comedy about the futility of war, *Arms and the Man*, which Joseph Smith directed in 1939.

The NTL also established a play-reading and producing committee, comprising Tom Hornibrook, Doris Britten, Ken Barnard and Norman Clark. The NTL members met monthly to progress the work of the NTL, in addition to rehearsing their plays. The group met initially at the WEA, and the ARU made the hall at their premises in the Longworth Institute available for productions. This would become the NTL's permanent home: in late 1938, the ARU moved out and sub-let to the NTL, which was then able to have both venue and club rooms in the same location.

The NTL successfully attracted many, mainly young, people as active participants; however, not all were universally welcomed into the fold. Joyce Deans remembered that the times were full of suspicion. She recalls an occasion when:

> Union members wanted to get rid of a young electrician who was interested in stage lighting because he was a cadet engineer with BHP and so a staff member. They thought he was a provocateur. But he stayed and came in very handy.

We learn a little more about the makeup and members of the Newcastle NTL from Jerold Wells, a director for the Sydney New Theatre. Wells spent several months in Newcastle in 1938, directing *Bury the Dead*; directing and performing in a repeat performance of *Waiting for Lefty*; and performing in *Private Hicks*. He reported back to the Sydney branch:

> [t]he members are essentially working class and most of them are in the fortunate position of being regularly employed. This tends to bring an air of quiet prosperity and confidence right into the heart of the League. Among the women members a surprising number are married and this, too, seems to make the League more mature and steady.

Cast lists confirm Wells' observations; they feature married couples, such as Ken and Eileen Barnard, Tom and Dorothy Hornibrook, Harry and Doris Hales, Charles and Elsie Mellords and Melba and Bob Middleby.

Melba Middleby appeared in a number of productions over the life of the NTL, beginning with *Waiting for Lefty*. She won a good review for her contribution to *Angels of War* in 1937 ('maintained the action of the play with sincerity and dramatic ability'); played a female Cabinet member in Sidney Box's *The Government Regrets* (1937); scored a role in the first Brecht play to be produced in Australia (*The Ragged Cap*, 1938); performed in Friedrich Wolf's *Professor Mamlock* (1939); and finished with a role (Mrs Stockmann) in a warmly received production of *An Enemy of the People* (1940).

An active member of the Clerks Union, Melba Middleby was the first woman to be elected to the Committee of the Newcastle Workers' Club in 1949, making her one of the first women to be elected to any club-governing committee in NSW. Many decades later, her interests would converge. She contributed her story to the highly successful verbatim theatre play, *Aftershocks*, about the 1989 Newcastle earthquake which destroyed the Workers' Club; and she went on to perform in the subsequent film of *Aftershocks* in 1998 – 61 years after joining the Newcastle NTL. Paul Brown, one of the co-creators of *Aftershocks*, remarked that the film demonstrates the role of local stories in shaping national culture; we might well say that the same applies to the Newcastle NTL's contribution to the larger New Theatre movement across Australia.

On the Newcastle NTL's formation, President Barbara Roberts declared:

> We are living in the midst of a most important epoch of the world's history... Problems of the day are reflected in many of the plays that are written, and it is our purpose to perform those that have not only literary merit, but are socially important.

One of the NTL's objectives was 'to sponsor plays of social realism'; it stated clearly that '[t]he aim of the group is to produce plays offering a true interpretation of social forces'. The NTL was active from the start in carrying out its mission of being 'opposed to all forms of injustice and oppression and the exploitation of human life and labour'. This extended from the everyday struggles of working people to support themselves, through to issues of global significance. The NTL gave their support – by arranging a float – to the International Labour Party's procession and demonstration in 1938 to protest against the increased price of bread. Their productions benefited both local causes, such as striking miners and the unemployed, and national causes and celebrations. While most plays were by international authors, they also produced some Australian writers, and those plays drew attention to contemporary social issues, such as housing slums in Newcastle and the issue of child labour. In 1938, the NTL staged a one-act play by a Newcastle engineer, Arthur Searle, *Two Hoots*; it is 'a brief episode in a strike situation, and is a play of psychological reactions'.

The NTL members also had a clear sense of themselves as being part of an international community of workers and artists. They took an active part in international celebrations and campaigns. They were enthusiastic participants in the annual Newcastle May Day parade, which celebrates International Workers' Day; their first, prize-winning May Day float in 1937 declared their 'antiwar, anti-fascist, anti-capitalist' commitment, and this public appearance won them new members. The NTL condemned international acts of aggression. The theatre carried a motion at their October 1937 meeting to:

> express its horror at the unprovoked attacks being made on the Chinese populace by the Japanese militants, and call on all members to boycott Japanese goods.

They endorsed significant international events, such as the celebration of the 20th anniversary of the establishment of the Soviet Union, for which they arranged a play and agreed that 'a resolution conveying greetings from the workers of Newcastle would be sent overseas'.

At this critical moment in the late 1930s, the NTL worked actively for the International Peace Campaign. It assisted the International Peace League to put together a tableau for May Day in 1937; the following year, it participated in *Men Who Marched Away*, a Peace Pageant staged by the International Peace Campaign at the Newcastle City Hall. The NTL contributed a verse chorus, 'Work', which 'stressed the economic chaos and the misery which follows war'.

The Spanish Civil War (1936–39) was also raging at this time. Australia did not officially participate, but around 70 Australians had volunteered to fight for the Republicans against the fascist Nationalist forces. Despite the small size of this local contingent, there was high awareness and deep concern among leftist groups in Australia (and internationally) about this far distant conflict – which has subsequently been widely considered to be a dress rehearsal for World War II. *Workers' Weekly* notes that the Newcastle NTL contributed £1 to the Spanish Relief Fund collection, which in 1937 collected the substantial sum of £2,671 from many individuals and organisations from across the country to donate to the cause. At the 1938 May Day Parade, which included a Spanish Relief Fund float, a minute's silence was offered for those who had 'shed their blood for democracy', and 'three cheers for the workers of Spain' followed. Like many other New Theatre groups, the Newcastle NTL also performed topical plays relating to this conflict, such as *The Secret* (1937), Brecht's *Señora Carrar's Rifles* (1938), discussed further below, and *Remembering Pedrocito* (1939), to raise awareness.

This was only one strand of the Newcastle NTL's accomplishments in its relatively short existence. The NTL programmed works advocating pacificism; condemning the armaments trade and war; highlighting industrial issues; detailing the miseries, dangers and inequities facing working-class people, including miners; criticising fascism, antisemitism and Nazism; and, both implicitly and explicitly, championing equality for women. These were often plays which had only recently premiered internationally, pointing to the vibrant paths of exchange and rapid circulation of these contemporary works among this network of left-leaning companies around the world.

In 1938, the editor of the *Australian Left News*, in welcoming the cooperation of the New Theatres, wrote of the significance of these organisations, which can 'broadcast our views and increase our funds', acknowledging that the 'importance of dramatic presentations needs no emphasis here, most people being more easily influenced through their emotions than through their intellect'. The Newcastle NTL walked an interesting line in this respect: while they did not shy away from challenging and, sometimes, confronting works, they also wanted and needed to fill their sizeable venue, which could seat around 300 audience members. To that end, as well as the very occasional lighthearted and non-political play (like Shaw's *The Village Wooing*), many of the plays they produced were farces and satires: serious topics could be canvassed and a 'message' delivered, but through humorous genres. Ross Edmonds has noted that the NTL reached large audiences, not all of whom were supporters of the left; nonetheless, the NTL 'could convey some of the ideas and ideals of the Left to a broader public' through their work.

Another notable aspect of the Newcastle NTL's work is how the plays they selected also drew attention to their own extra-theatrical reality – an unusual strategy for playwriting of the time, as several reviews noted. Quite apart from the themes of the plays, which often resonated with the audience's experiences and lives, the NTL programmed a number of works which drew audience attention to the artifice of their activities, such as breaking the fourth wall. (Brecht, we imagine, would have approved.) In *Waiting for Lefty*, for example, the audience becomes part of the action and – one reviewer noted – 'unusual effects are gained by the players rising in the middle of the audience with interjections and speeches'.

The conceit of two further plays over the following two years, James Wallace Bell's *Symphony in Illusion: An Allegory in One Act* and Albert Maltz's *Rehearsal*, is that the actors are rehearsing a play. In the former, described as 'a very unusual type of play', an all-woman cast in the aftermath of war prepares to stage a play about the difficulties of making peace. Written after World War I, when there was a wave of amateur plays for women because so many men had been killed in the war, the play reflects on some of the difficulties that women specifically faced in and after war, with one character reviled for bearing the child of an 'enemy'.

Maltz's *Rehearsal* (previously produced by the Sydney NTL and winner of the City of Sydney Eisteddfod), depicted a group of amateur actors 'similar to the New Theatre League' rehearsing a play; as such, the reviewer noted, the NTL were 'really depicting their own problems'. The fictional play being rehearsed centred on the real 1932 Detroit strike, in which police shot a number of strikers. It emerges that one of the actors struggling in the staged rehearsal had a brother who was badly and permanently injured by the police during that struggle. This sense of reality and fiction coinciding in these plays may well have contributed to the solidarity between performers and audiences in their shared experiences, whether in the theatre or in their wider community.

INAUGURAL SEASON: 1937

From the Newcastle NTL's formation, there was interest and reciprocal exchange between it and Sydney. The Sydney-based *Workers' Weekly* offered congratulations and cheerily suggested: 'What about writing and telling us about yourselves?' Joyce Deans recalled: 'We had no professional help apart from advice on how to proceed from the Sydney group'. Following her election as the President of the NTL, Barbara Roberts promptly visited Sydney and 'investigated the possibilities of new plays being performed there', concluding that 'great scope exists for dramatic work in Newcastle'. Jerold Wells came up from Sydney to attend their second full-length production, *Judgment Day* (December 1937), and 'expressed his appreciation of the players' efforts'. He was apparently 'particularly impressed with their enunciation'!

Pamphlet for Angels of War, 1937.

NEWCASTLE NEW THEATRE LEAGUE
will present
"ANGELS OF WAR"
A.R.U. HALL, Longworth Institute
SCOTT STREET. NEWCASTLE
WEDNESDAY, 18th AUGUST, at 8 p.m.
SUNDAY, 22nd AUGUST, at 8 p.m.
WEDNESDAY, 25th AUGUST, at 8 p.m.
:: SUITABLE FOR ADULTS ONLY. ::
'Phone New. 1369 for Reservations.

Leaflet courtesy of Vera Deacon.

Waiting for Lefty, the by now well-known play depicting a meeting of taxi drivers who are planning a strike, opened the NTL's first year. It had been a great success for the Sydney NTL, winning first prize at the City of Sydney Eisteddfod in 1936. Audiences would have been familiar with it through reports in the local newspapers. Audiences received the production warmly. A reviewer asserted that this was:

> an example of what can be done with young players to whom the play is more important than the glory of appearing on the stage.

We can imagine that the members of the NTL, dedicated to the greater cause of changing the world through theatre, would have been happy with this endorsement. The reviewer continued: 'It is a tribute to the producer, Mr Norman Clark, that the standard of the performance was so high'. The play was reprised in Newcastle in 1938, this time directed (and acted in) by Jerold Wells, director of the Sydney production.

Angels of War, by Muriel Box, was their next major production. This was an adaptation of Australian Helen Z. Smith's popular novel, *Not So Quiet*, which depicted the experiences of a female World War I ambulance driver. Muriel Box wrote prolifically, often with husband Sydney Box (whose plays *Bring Me My Bow* and *The Government Regrets* also played at the NTL). Many of their plays were for all-female casts.

Angels of War was a great success for the NTL: 'The play scored an instant success, was well acted and produced and the lighting and off stage effects were cleverly designed'. It was popular with audiences and had several seasons in Newcastle in 1937 and 1939. It toured to Cessnock in 1937, Cardiff in 1938 and Wallsend in 1939. The flier for the production warned that it was: 'Suitable for Adults Only', but Joyce Deans later recalled that, when they toured the play to Cessnock to raise money for the miners during a strike:

> Everybody came because many of the people would have never seen live theatre before, but we were severely criticised by the miners, who brought their wives and children, because the characters used 'bloody' a few times!

Perhaps some of the good citizens of the Cessnock district had more delicate sensibilities than their Newcastle counterparts; when the NTL toured their very successful production of Gow and Greenwood's *Love on the Dole* to Kurri Kurri (about 10km distant from Cessnock) in 1939, it provoked a highly indignant letter to the editor of the *Cessnock Eagle and South Maitland Recorder*, protesting against this 'most ignorant and degrading play' where the themes of the play were 'of the lowest nature' and the language used was 'the most shocking…the foulest kind I have every heard in my whole life uttered from a public platform'. The irate letter writer, Pat Harrington, warned the actors that 'if you keep on using the language you do, you will certainly never go to Heaven when you die'. *Love on the Dole*, an adaptation of Greenwood's novel about a poor, working class family in Northern England, destroyed by the consequences of mass, intergenerational unemployment and despair, did depict grim outcomes for its protagonists – but also struck a chord with British audiences: a million people had seen the play by the end of 1935 after it opened in 1934. Actor Joseph Smith took it upon himself to answer Mr Harrington. His response is worth quoting at length for the insight it gives us into the NTL's endeavours at this time. Smith writes:

> I have performed in this play on eight occasions and have not heard the foul language that Mr Harrington complains of, so must conclude that it was a figment of his imagination.
>
> The truth, in itself, cannot be degrading or immoral. The conditions which the truth reveals may be. If the searchlight of truth reveals conditions which are rotten, degrading and immoral, don't blame the searchlight, don't blame the New Theatre League as its bearer, but blame the system, which makes the conditions possible.
>
> Do Mr Harrington and the 'other respectable people' who viewed *Love on the Dole* doubt that the conditions portrayed exist? Or is theirs the type of mentality which recoils from the truth when it happens to be shocking?

If Mr Harrington is sincere in his protestations of sympathy for the unemployed, he should join the New Theatre League in the job of exposing the evils which unemployment brings in its train. This would be a more effective method than taking the easy course of laying the responsibility at the door of the Almighty, which, to say the least, is almost blasphemous.

We are told to go to the rich and the politicians. For the New Theatre League to go to them alone, however, would be futile. We need the masses, even those of Kurri and perhaps Mr Harrington to go along with us. To shake the people out of their apathy is the mission of such plays as *Love on the Dole*.

The final play in 1937 was Elmer Rice's *Judgment Day*, a courtroom drama based on the events of the Reichstag fire trial. This was the first Australian production of the play. A reviewer called it the 'Theatre League's Best Effort' and praised the group for reaching a high standard after little more than a year. A second reviewer was also enthusiastic, although more forthright in their assessment of it as a 'propaganda play'. The NTL advertised this production in the *Workers' Weekly* with the sensational headline: 'Damned in Amsterdam, News in Newcastle'. We could read this as the NTL further positioning themselves as progressive, internationally aware and ready to take its place on the world stage; it certainly attracted the attention of the Sydney NTL, with Jerold Wells travelling up to Newcastle to see the production. Following its second performance, the group noted the keen public interest in the play and considered extending the season – actually staging a new production in 1939.

THE HIGH POINT: 1938

The high point of this organisation's relatively short life was the year 1938, when the NTL acquired its own premises, expanded its membership, produced 15 plays (two full-length and nine short plays, along with touring productions), increased its visibility in the local community and 'became more widely known...through broadcasts'. NTL toured to several other coal mining towns in the Hunter Valley, with the proceeds of the performances

Newcastle cast of *Bring Me My Bow*, 1938.

A scene from the New Theatre League production, "Bring Me My Bow."

donated to the Lysaght's Strike Fund in Cessnock (raising over £50 for the 1,400 steelworkers who struck for three months) and the 'Wallsend No. 2 Miners Lodge'.

One of most popular plays in that year was *Bring Me My Bow*, by Sydney Box. Norman Clark, the director, in summing up the year's work, also judged it to be of 'outstanding artistry'. This is the only production for which we have a surviving image of the NTL's theatrical work.

This antiwar fantasy is set at a girls' school prize-giving. A bright, working-class girl whose father was killed in the war has been denied the opportunity to study at university, because the government has diverted funds away from education grants into a massive program of re-armament. A second chance at a scholarship to Oxford – sponsored by the Minister for War – comes at the price of writing an essay on the topic 'A Britain armed means a world at peace'. This she refuses to do, declaring that she will instead work in her mother's laundry; this, at least, would be a 'clean job'. The somewhat bizarre-looking image may come from the dream sequence of the play, but the raised fist – a well-established gesture of leftist resistance – of the woman in white is unmistakeable.

Bring Me My Bow was part of a triple bill with Odets' *Waiting for Lefty* and Albert Maltz's *Private Hicks* – a pacifist play about a national guardsman who refuses to shoot at strikers and is subsequently court-martialled – which had won the American New Theatre League's play competition in 1936.

The following production was Irwin Shaw's *Bury the Dead*. Shaw was a young writer who was also part of the American New Theatre League. This play was 'dedicated to the millions who love peace' and featured 'six dead soldiers who rise from their common grave on the battlefield to protest against the barbarism that has cut short their lives'. Publicity noted that it had been produced 'on three continents' – in the UK, the USA and now Australia. We can again see here the NTL's determination to be considered as part of an international radical theatre movement. *Bury the Dead* played at the Lyric Theatre instead of their usual venue at the Longworth Institute; the NTL was clearly anticipating expanding and reaching larger audiences – and its large cast also required the larger stage. *Bury the Dead* had done very well in Sydney, and reports of the success of that production spread to Newcastle: Norman Clark travelled to Sydney to see it. The Sydney NTL also supported the Newcastle production, not only through Wells' input as director, but also with technical expertise (Sydney NTL member Des Rowan travelled to Newcastle to work on the lighting) and audiences. The Sydney NTL noted in one of their 'wallpaper' newsletters that 'a bunch of N.T.L. members intend to be present on Saturday night at the Coaly City – best wishes from "Backstage" to Jerry and the cast'.

Joyce Deans recalled this as 'our most successful play'. At the NTL's AGM for 1938, the production was singled out as their 'most ambitious'. Perhaps unsurprisingly, it therefore attracted criticism from more conservative quarters. Catholic priest Father Leo Dalton launched a spirited attack on both the NTL and the WEA in a lecture he delivered on the topic of 'Communism, Capitalism and Catholicism' in late July 1938, because those organisations were 'being used to spread Communism'. 'Such plays', he said, 'as *Bury the Dead*, were meant for one reason – to broadcast Communistic views'. He qualified this, stating that he 'did not mean that everybody in the New Theatre Leagues was a Communist, but the inspiration of the league was'. Joyce Deans, an avowed communist, would probably have agreed with him.

His views did not go unquestioned. In an instance of great irony, D. R. Young of Moore Street, Cessnock wrote to the local newspaper on 1 September 1939 (the day that World War II was declared), defending democracy, the NTL and the WEA:

> Reviewing recent criticism of the activities of the New Theatre League and the Workers' Educational Association, I recall that every branch or movement promoting enlightenment on questions either national or international, of social problems or artistic advancement, are in the minds of some people 'Red'.
>
> Democracy is established on intellectual freedom. All who desire to maintain this status must give service either by word of mouth or pen to the greatest cause in human progress. Australians must jealously retain the vital foundation of their fathers' sacrifices. In recent years we have experienced several movements to establish dictatorships, and censorships on books and literature for the advancement of human thought has aroused strong resentment of those who would starve our minds of information essential for cultural development.

Father Dalton's views certainly did not give the NTL pause. They moved straight into rehearsal for their next season of four short plays: Australian Phyllis Harnett's play, *I Am Angry*, about child labour practices (mentioned above) and three topical international plays – *The Devil's Business*, by the British socialist politician and antiwar activist A. Fenner Brockway, which was critical of the international armaments trade; Frank Gabrielson and David Lesan's *The Home of the Brave*, a farce mocking Hitler's advocacy of racial purity by positing what would happen if North Americans tried to become 'pure' North Americans (that is, Native Americans); and a play named *The Ragged Cap*, which was written in support of, and to draw attention to, the Spanish Civil War.

The Ragged Cap is one of the Newcastle NTL's especially notable achievements, because it is, in fact, the very first production of a play by Bertolt Brecht outside Europe and North America. This significant contribution to Brecht's reception has remained unknown until now, because the NTL changed the play's name from *Señora Carrar's Rifles* to *The Ragged Cap* for their production, and Brecht himself is only credited as author in a single report in one of the local newspapers. I surmise that the members of the NTL may have, in this instance, adopted this new title to evoke empathy among their audience members for the plight of ordinary people affected by the war: the ragged cap belongs to Señora Carrar's son, who has been killed fighting with the Republicans, and the cap is emblematic of the sacrifice she, and others like her, make. The Newcastle production opened a year to the day after the play's world premiere in Paris with Brecht's wife, Helene Weigel, in the title role (and just a month after its first production in the UK); it is unclear whether this was intentional, but it does suggest that it may have been the Newcastle NTL's conscious decision to align itself as part of an international movement of progressive writers and theatre-makers.

ON THE NATIONAL STAGE: 1939

In the last issue of the *Australian Left News* in June 1939, Vic Arnold of the Sydney NTL reported on the National Conference of Left Theatre Groups which had taken place during the Easter holidays. The rapid growth of the movement, and Newcastle's now established position within it, is apparent in representation at this conference from Sydney, Melbourne, Brisbane, Newcastle and Lithgow ('and reports were received from Adelaide and Perth'). Arnold observed:

> Our past experiences conclusively demonstrated one fact above all else, namely, 'People's Theatre', which is our ultimate aim, is a mere phrase that will mean little or nothing at all if that theatre is not rooted directly and deeply in the progressive Labor Movement. Millions within and outside the Movement urgently need the information and education which the New Theatre can provide. These people form a national and profoundly important anchor for the artistically developed plays that further the cause of peace, democracy and progress.

With hindsight, we can observe how vain such valiant hopes were, when, just over two months later, the outbreak of World War II so thoroughly put a stop to 'peace, democracy and progress'.

It is difficult to read in retrospect of activities taking place in 1939 without leaping ahead to what that year inevitably marks for us today: the beginning of World War II. But it is also clear that there was a growing local concern about the ongoing rise of fascism. Just a week after the Nationalists won the Spanish Civil War in April 1939, the retiring President of the Newcastle WEA, Ken Barnard (also a member of the NTL) warned at their AGM:

> The chance of a Fascist invasion from overseas may be remote, but there is a definite fear of an insurgence of Fascist propaganda into this city unless we can combat it with a full and lasting cultural education.

In 1939, along with several antiwar plays dealing with earlier conflicts, the first full-length new production was Friedrich Wolf's 1933 play, *Professor Mamlock* – one of the earliest plays dealing with Nazi antisemitism. The ALP Women's Auxiliary were keen to have the NTL tour to Cessnock with this production, noting approvingly that it: 'is an excellent piece of anti-Nazi propaganda'. Another production of *Judgment Day*, with Doris Hales directing, finished the year, repeating its run of two years earlier with Norman Clark directing. At that point, one reviewer suggested that it might just as easily be describing the totalitarian situation in Russia; but, by late 1939, the play was clearly identifiable as an 'anti-Nazi play' – so perhaps audiences and actors alike were able to enjoy even more the vicarious thrill of the 'happy ending', when the tyrannical fascist dictator is shot and killed in the third and final act!

The NTL was again very active in 1939. They had hoped to be able to offer weekly performances in 1939. Membership had grown, and there was now a larger repertoire of productions to draw on for repeat performances and for touring to other centres, including Cessnock, Wallsend and Kurri Kurri that year. In the end, they did manage performances nearly every month that year.

A particularly striking feature of their work at this time was an unwitting anticipation of the war years, where women assumed roles previously undertaken by men. As well as the NTL plays with all-female casts (*Angels of War*, *Bring Me My Bow*) in 1937 and 1938, 1939 saw women direct some of the NTL's productions for the first time. In the previous two years, resident director Norman Clark had directed two-thirds of the productions and other men the remaining third; in 1939, women directed six of the 10 confirmed new productions for 1939. Five were one-act plays, and the sixth, the final production of the year, was *Judgment Day*, where Doris Hales replaced Norman Clark, the director of the earlier production.

Women had continued to play a significant role in the NTL: in office bearing roles (outlined earlier), in productions and in representing the NTL in various forums (e.g. delegates to the Peace Council and representatives at the National Conference of New Theatres). Some of the women involved were working women, like Barbara Roberts and Joyce Deans. Some were actively involved in political and social struggles, both local – such as campaigns to improve working conditions – and more widely, such as the Women's Auxiliary of the Miners' Federation support for Spanish refugees. Women educated local communities about international issues through bringing NTL productions to their communities. It was, perhaps, inevitable that, along with the growth and development of the organisation, women also began to take their place in leadership roles in the artistic outputs of the organisation; Barbara Roberts, Chris Logan and Doris Hales each directed two plays in 1939.

A bill of three one-act plays opened the 1939 season. Norman Clark directed *Remembering Pedrocito* (a Spanish Civil War play); Barbara Roberts directed *Hewers of Coal*, Joe Corrie's play about a mining disaster; and Chris Logan directed and starred as Queen Elizabeth I in George Bernard Shaw's *Dark Lady of the Sonnets*. Chris Logan had been involved from the beginning of the organisation, acting in a play reading in 1937. She was part of the 1938 play-reading committee and, in 1939, became Vice-President of the League, performed in four plays and directed two.

Following Clark's production of the full-length *Professor Mamlock*, the NTL offered another triple bill. Barbara Roberts directed James Wallace Bell's *Symphony in Illusion* (discussed above). Chris Logan followed with *The Little Green Bundle* (inaccurately, and rather bizarrely, attributed to Tolstoy in the local newspapers), which was an adaptation of a scene from Brecht's *The Mother*. In this 'playlet', writer Ben Irwin replaces Brecht's Revolutionary Workers distributing pro-communist leaflets with the German underground distributing anti-Nazi leaflets. Doris Hales rounded out the evening with another of Shaw's lighter works, *The Village Wooing*. Perhaps this was intended as a 'warming up' of their audiences for their next full-length production, Shaw's *Arms and the Man* (directed by Joseph Smith). Certainly, the two short Shaw plays previously produced by the NTL had been 'very enthusiastically received', so the NTL was confident of a good reception. This 1894 anti-romantic comedy, set in a 19th century Balkan War, still had 'a freshness and topicality in some situations that make [it] surprisingly modern'. Even when offering its audiences the pure fun of a Shaw comedy, the NTL's work still managed to resonate with contemporary relevance.

THE DEMISE: 1940

At the end of March 1940, the NTL produced Albert Maltz's *Rehearsal* in a double bill with Percy Corry's *Cupid Rampant*, a 'clever satire on totalitarian organisation'. A production of the Ibsen's *Enemy of the People*, directed by Norman Clark, followed in April. The *Newcastle Morning Herald & Miners' Advocate* drily noted: 'Germany's invasion of Norway has lent to the league unexpected topicality' in its production of this play. 'Epistemon' in the *NMH&MA* reported that they received notice of the NTL's production just an hour after hearing the news from Norway and suggested that, apart from introducing the people of Newcastle to this significant playwright, this:

> marks the first step to be taken in Australia since Norway became involved in the war to strengthen the cultural bonds between us and those who are now fighting beside us.

In early June, Eileen Barnard directed Somerset Maugham's play, *For Services Rendered*. This 1932 play examined the longstanding effects of World War I on the members of an English family. The antiwar message was not well received at the time of its first production in England; and, although the *NMH&MA* review described it as 'a grim drama of the after-effects of war', it must, like so many of the NTL's productions, have served as a (vain) warning to its audiences. This would be the last full production by the Newcastle NTL.

On 15 June 1940, Australian Prime Minister Robert Menzies banned the CPA – a ban that would last for two years. Police had intermittently harassed communist members of the Newcastle NTL in previous years, and those members would periodically leave Newcastle for a short break at a 'hideout' on the coast; but this declaration of illegality made it difficult for the group – and indeed the other Australian New Theatres – to continue their work. In Newcastle, the NTL also lost their venue very soon after the ban. According to a plaque still located on the front of the building in Scott Street (just opposite Newcastle's railway station), Longworth Hall had been 'presented to the Australasian Society of Patriots' by William Longworth in 1928. Although it was subsequently leased by the Australian Railways Union and then the NTL from 1938, it seems that the owners had reclaimed it for its original purposes as World War II continued. The *NMH&MA* reported that the Longworth Institute was 'taken over by the Victoria League for patriotic purposes'; the hall was converted to a dining room for soldiers who were being housed in a hostel built at the Lyric Theatre (scene of the NTL's great success with *Bury the Dead*).

It must have dismayed the peace-loving members of the NTL to see both their venues now being coopted as part of the war effort, but the NTL was clearly aware that the evolving circumstances of the war years meant that they had to be careful 'within the limits imposed by conditions', as they said, that their activities did not attract negative public attention. In early August, they declared that they intended 'to approach a patriotic organisation with an offer to produce a play'; otherwise, they would restrict their own activities for the rest of that year to a play-reading group which would present lighthearted and less provocative fare.

It seems that the Newcastle NTL was effectively defunct by the end of 1940. Somewhat ironically, perhaps, given the local antipathy towards communism and the difficulties this had caused the Australian New Theatres, Russia became an ally in June 1941. Two 'Aid for Russia' events were staged in Newcastle in August and September. The Sydney NTL contributed, travelling to Newcastle with their portable stage. The short play they offered at this second event, however, may well have been upstaged by the final feature event of the day – 'the burning of effigies of Hitler and Mussolini'! The Sydney NTL continued to visit and perform in Newcastle sporadically in the following years, and the New Theatre was re-established in Newcastle in 1956, enriching cultural life in that city for over two decades.

CODA: THE LATER NEWCASTLE NEW THEATRE

Lisa Milner

The second incarnation of the Newcastle New Theatre ran from 1956 until 1979. Dawn Allen, Mavis Savage, Olga Fairbairn and John and Phyllis Robson were among its executives. One of their first actions was to ask for the support of the Workers' Club. Their performances began with the acclaimed *Reedy River* in March 1957 at the Roxy Theatre in Hamilton. Sydney New

Theatre had already imported this play for the 1954 May Day festival, but it was still very popular: An estimated 450,000 Australians have seen the New Theatre's *Reedy River* productions over the years. Two years later, such was *Reedy River*'s reputation that when 'this new lively body announced its intention of staging the musical, many tickets were sold in Newcastle before rehearsals commenced'. Mark Gregory writes: 'in *Reedy River* can be found the interconnectedness of the folk revival, theatre and union culture and militancy'. One theatre member believed:

> to work in a theatre like the Newcastle New Theatre affords not only great pleasure in the many new friends we meet, but leaves us with the full feeling that it is a job indeed well worth doing and, in the case of **Reedy River**, a job well done.

For over two decades, they continued to stage plays of political and cultural interest by such writers as Arthur Miller, Sean O'Casey, Brendan Behan and Max Frisch. Millard Lampell – a US writer and musician, blacklisted in the House Committee on Un-American Activities trials because he had worked with Woody Guthrie – wrote *The Wall*, a drama about Jews in the Warsaw ghetto, which the Newcastle New Theatre performed in 1964. They also performed works by Australian writers Mona Brand (who wrote almost exclusively for the New Theatre), Oriel Gray and Tom Keneally, as well as local playwrights, including Joseph Costello of Maitland.

They presented plays at the Roxy Theatre in Hamilton and at the Dungeon, the basement theatre at the Trades Hall building in Union Street, where they had their club rooms. Sometimes, they rehearsed and performed in the Tech High School in Hunter Street or at the Newcastle Stadium Theatre. They also took their performances offsite: to the university (where, from the 1970s, New Theatre and Newcastle University drama students and staff worked together) and further afield. The NT team had a ten-by-six trailer for touring, taking their shows on the road from Newcastle. Venues included Toronto, Stockton, Kurri Kurri and Cessnock. Well-known Newcastle thespian Vic Rooney reflected on the early days of his acting career, when he took culture with New Theatre 'right out to the backblocks of Warner's Bay'.

Like their counterparts in other cities, the Newcastle New Theatre did not just stage performances. Many of their activities supported the development of literary and theatrical life in Australia and were designed to enable and strengthen connections to other cultural activist individuals and groups, particularly through trade unions and workers' associations. John Robson, Elin O'Connell and Dawn Allen ran classes in Movement, Speech and Acting. The NT regularly held drama school workshops and conferences, picnics, film nights and working bees. They always contributed to the Newcastle May Day festivals (with performances and floats in the parade), and they often donated part of their ticket takings to the May Day appeal and local charities. A great deal of interaction with other New Theatre groups proved to be very positive: in December 1958, the Newcastle group, who were strong advocates for a national theatre, hosted the National School of the New Theatre. In reaching out and working with other groups, they were a vital part of the Trades Hall Committees for May Day, International Women's Day, the Peace Committee and many unions.

FURTHER READING

Edmonds, Ross, *In Storm and Struggle. A History of the Communist Party in Newcastle 1920–1940*, Newcastle, Ross Edmonds, 1991.

Langelaar, Sonya, 'Theatre with a Purpose: Newcastle New Theatre 1937–1940 and 1957–1976', *Hunter Regional Journal of Labour and Industrial History*, no. 4, 1998, pp. 16–25.

Milner, Lisa, 'Theatre of Radicalism: Newcastle's Post-War Cultural Activists', in James Bennett, Nancy Cushing and Erik Eklund (eds.), *Radical Newcastle*, Sydney, NewSouth, 2015, pp. 152–161.

Stevens, Joyce, *Taking the Revolution Home. Work Among Women in the Communist Party of Australia: 1920–1945*, Melbourne, Sybylla Co-operative Press and Publications, 1987, pp. 200–212. This chapter on Joyce Batterham is a unique first person account of the work of the first Newcastle NTL.

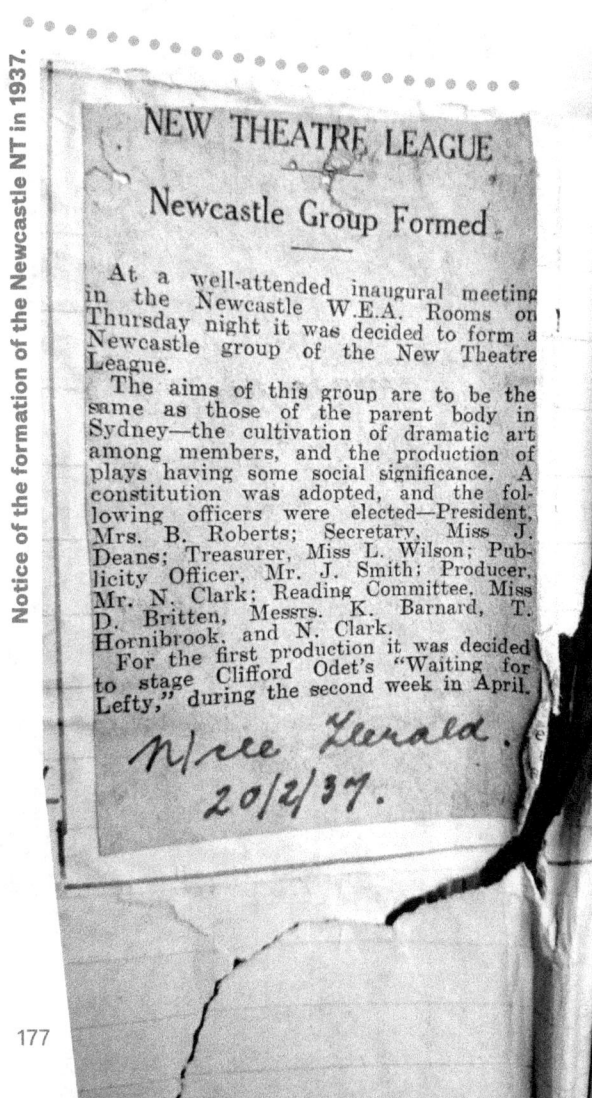

Notice of the formation of the Newcastle NT in 1937.

Ron Fraser and Gwen Mackay in *Night of the Ding Dong*, 1959

CHAPTER 6

Red Hot Up North: The Brisbane New Theatre

Connie Healy

Queensland has a long, thriving tradition of radical theatre. Unemployed workers from the bagman's camp at Victoria Park formed a dramatic group, the Roving Reds Revue Company, in the early 1930s. It later became the Proletarian Players. They staged their best-known work, *The Ragged Trousered Philanthropists*, in the Albert Hall in 1936. It proposed socialism as the remedy for unemployment and poverty – important issues in the Depression era. The Student Theatre formed in 1936 was an offshoot of the University of Queensland Radical Club, forerunner of Unity Theatre, and emerged as New Theatre after the war's end.

Unity Theatre's final production was in 1941. It then went into recess, because it lost members to the armed forces, and the demands of the national war effort took precedence over theatrical activity. It resumed at the end of 1947. On 17 May 1949, Unity Theatre was renamed the New Theatre and became part of a national theatre. Until its demise in 1962, it continued its role as a radical political theatre: promoting plays critical of capitalism, colonialism, racism and the insidious effects of conservative, right-wing Australian government attacks on left-liberal viewpoints and, in this Cold War period, any plays dealing with the dangers of war. By producing drama which dealt with Australia's working-class struggles and democratic traditions in a historical context, it also furthered a revival of Australian nationalism.

BRISBANE NEW THEATRE

Some of Unity's leading actors and stage-hands died during the war, and others were scattered throughout Australia at the war's end. In 1947, a few of the old members who had survived the battlefields, and some still in Brisbane, called a public meeting at the Rationalist Hall and revived Unity Theatre. In May 1949, Brisbane New Theatre Club was officially constituted to work for 'cultural progress and world peace and cooperate with other organisations with similar aims'.

Most of the themes the political theatres of the 1930s favoured carried forward into the 1940s. But there are some identifiable, broad trends specific to the postwar era. With a buoyant economy in the reconstruction period, a stronger trade union movement shifted markedly towards industrial militancy for a time, and New Theatre lent support to this struggle with several plays in defence of workers' rights. A remarkable development of working-class themes was a revival of the radical nationalist movement of the 1890s, which was partly due to the new sense of national identity encouraged during the war years to unite Australians behind the armed forces.

New Theatre gave expression to this left-wing nationalism in the 1950s by presenting plays and musicals emphasising the folk tradition. But, as the euphoria of anti-fascist victory gave way to Cold War hysteria, a whole range of issues related to postwar international politics also became a focus for the radical theatres. Finally, after long years of neglect – which we now find difficult to understand – New Theatre gave the problem of racism, and especially the inhuman treatment of Australian Aboriginal and Torres Strait Islander people, the attention it deserves.

WORKERS' STRUGGLES

An Australian historical drama by George Farwell, *Sons of the South*, based on the shearers' strike of 1891, was a fitting choice for New Theatre's first production in 1948. Brisbane workers were involved in major industrial disputes, including two of the longest and most acrimonious strikes in Queensland history: the meatworkers' strike in 1946, which ran for 14 weeks; and the railway strike, which commenced in February 1948 and lasted about nine weeks.

Sons of the South, set mainly in a shearers' camp outside Barcaldine, depicts the struggle in 1891 of Queensland shearers, organised in the Queensland Shearers' Union, against the terms of employment that the squatters had tried to impose. Under the deceptive slogan of 'Freedom of Contract', the squatters campaigned to substitute station agreements for union agreements in the pastoral industry. Troops intervened, union solidarity broke as 'scabs' came in, the strike was defeated, and the leadership went to jail. The premiere took place in the old Centennial Hall, the very platform from which the 1891 strike leaders had addressed Brisbane workers after they had been released from their infamous prison sentences.

From the theatre's prewar repertoire came four more plays dealing with workers' struggles, strikes and anti-worker propaganda. The ever-popular comedy *Where's That Bomb?* – a satire on anti-worker propaganda – and the strike play *Waiting for Lefty*, in which some of the 1937 cast appeared, had revivals and an extended season. *Rehearsal* and *Private Hicks* played in 1950, at a time when Albert Maltz, their author, was still serving a jail sentence in the USA. *Rehearsal*:

> tells of the 'American way of life' during the depression conditions of the early thirties – poverty, hunger, unemployment, militant unionism, strike-breaking and terrorisation by company police.

Private Hicks had 'strong topical interest at a time when the use of armed force to put down workers on strike [was] increasing throughout the world'.

New Theatre had a stated policy of encouraging the work of progressive Australian writers. Jim Crawford, who settled in Queensland in 1949, was to be a steady supplier of pointed plays in defence of the workers. He wrote his three-act play *Miner's Right* during the biggest coal strike in Australia's postwar history. It played on several occasions in Brisbane and was warmly received. New Theatre also performed it at the Miners' Hall in Booval in the Ipswich coalfields during the period of the national coal strike. An audience of 4,000 coal miners, their wives and friends gave it an enthusiastic reception and requested a repeat performance.

Ossie Nash, who lived in Ipswich, organised the Booval production. Gwen McKay, who acted in *Miner's Right*, recalls that he arranged for the cast to go down Box Flat mine near Darra so that the players would 'get the feel for what it was like'. Staged in Melbourne and other parts of the country, this play also proved popular with the public.

Officials of the Miners' Federation praised its depiction of the human effects of silicosis, which was prevalent in some Australian coalfields. Statistics showed that 30 Australian coal miners died in the pits each year; and, in the northern district of NSW, one miner in five was 'dusted'. Mr Len Boardman, rank and file miners' speaker from NSW, said in an interview after the show in Booval:

> This play is a real inspiration in the miners' fight against silicosis and other evils in this industry. It is a pity it is not being shown at present in the 'dustbowl' centres of NSW, where mining audiences would eat it up.

Hewers of Coal, by Australian playwright Oriel Gray, was another play written to win sympathy and understanding for the miners' cause and produced in later years. This was a one-act play in prose-poem form. It told, through flashbacks, the history of mining in Australia, exposing the hardships and hazards of the miners' life: the high incidence of lung disease; the dangers inherent to the mining industry; and the inadequate provisions for compensation for injury or ill health. Barbara Colley, who acted in all Brisbane New Theatre productions from 1956 to 1961, recalls that the troupe 'travelled round some of the mines with this production and actually performed it underground once.'

New Theatre also staged Dutch playwright Herman Heijermans' *The Good Hope*, which chronicles the lives of the inhabitants of a fishing village. Most of the action takes place in the cottage of Kniertje, the dour mother of two sons, Barend and Geert, whose father and two brothers drowned at sea. Despite misgivings about sea life and the seaworthiness of the old schooner, the *Good Hope*, the two boys join the crew. The ship fails to return. Six weeks later, a hatch cover and Barend's body wash ashore, evidence that all hands have been lost. The vessel's owner denies responsibility for the disaster and refuses to pay compensation to the relatives. When this play was first produced in Holland in 1901, it caused such public anger that the government had to hold a Royal Commission into the fishing industry.

In 1959, Queensland celebrated its centenary. With the help of Jim Crawford, Brisbane New Theatre was able to celebrate the centenary in fitting fashion by commemorating the story of a workers' struggle that had paved the way for the 1915 return of a Labor government. Crawford's new play, *Billets or Badges*, dealt with the 1912 tramways strike, which became a general strike involving 20,000 trade unionists in Brisbane and thousands of others outside the city, bringing Brisbane almost to a standstill.

The strike began when Joseph Badger, the US Manager of the English-owned Brisbane Tramway Company, refused to allow employees to join a union, sacked any employees who wore a union badge and introduced a company union. On Black Friday, a large procession of workers, including a women's contingent of 600, demonstrated in a two-mile long march. Repeated, brutal special police attacks eventually broke up the march. Although the strike collapsed after five weeks, Mr Justice Higgins' ruling in the Arbitration Court in favour of trade union rights vindicated the unions, and the militancy engendered by this struggle resulted in the defeat of the conservative Queensland Government.

Crawford's musical, containing some fine songs and dances as well as humorous and clever dialogue, traced these events and showed typical attitudes towards the tram strike and the movement for women's rights, exemplified by the main characters – Albert Plumper, a business-man; his wife, Amelia; their daughter, Phyllis; her wharfie friend, Frank; and some other workers and trade unionists. The title came from Mr Justice Higgins' remark that the men had been faced with the choice of their billets (jobs) or their badges.

AUSTRALIAN FOLKLORE AND THE DEMOCRATIC TRADITION

Speaking to the press on a visit to Australia in 1954, Dame Sybil Thorndike showed her theatrical vision when she suggested that Australian dramatists should take advantage of the opportunities Australia's 'colourful and unique outback' offered. Australian playwright Dick Diamond did that. With acknowledgements to Joseph Furphy and George Farwell, he wrote *Reedy River*, first shown in Melbourne in 1953. Brisbane produced it in 1954 to capacity audiences. This was a new type of musical comedy which aimed to highlight Australian democratic traditions.

The production of *Reedy River* signalled the revival of the old bush ballad, the bush poem set to music, and became a milestone in Australian culture. The musical's name, *Reedy River*, came from Henry Lawson's very lovely and poignant poem of the same name.

The plot concerns the shearers' defeat in the 1890–1891 strikes, which led to the virtual collapse of the union, the employment of blacklegs at squatter Brodie's sheds, and the eventual restoration of union conditions and full employment of all unionists under the leadership of shearer Joe Collins. The song *The Ballad of 1891*, by Helen Palmer, daughter of Vance and Nettie Palmer, outlines the events as the cast sing it enthusiastically.

The play emerged as 'the greatest success in the history of the Australian amateur theatre'. Brisbane and Queensland audiences greeted it with the same enthusiasm shown in southern states. London's Unity Theatre hailed it as 'the perfect people's musical'. With its focus on the life of ordinary people, its

NEW THEATRE CELEBRATES QLD'S CENTENERY IN 1959...

With the play *Billets or Badges* about the 1912 tramways strike. This play commemorated a workers' struggle which paved the way for the return in 1915 of a Labor government pledged to a socialist objective.

The Brisbane branch of the BWIU contributed to help the NT stage Billets or Badges in 1959.

TRIBUNE 5/8/1959

Play on Brisbane strike

THE great Brisbane tramways strike of 1912 for the right to wear the union badge — and hence, for free unionism — will be the subject of a new Brisbane New Theatre play by Jim Crawford.

It will be given a centenary presentation in October when the Queensland Trade Union Congress will be held.

The strike began on January 21, 1912, when "Bully" Badger American manager of the Brisbane Tramways Co. sacked every tramwayman who turned up for work wearing a union badge.

Badger had banned the union, replacing it with a company "union". By such methods he had lifted profits from £47,000 to £77,000 in a year.

Next morning a workers' procession of protest eight abreast and two miles long, marched from the Trades Hall to the Valley and back. Among the marchers was a women's contingent of 600 led by the famous "Granny" Miller.

A general strike by the worke was met, on February 2 (Bla Friday), by a general lockout.

Press advertisements warne that shops and businesses wou be closed while Police Commissio er Cahill put 3000 police into t streets, backed by "specials" d scribed by the Worker as "whi per-snapper sons of the wealth

This huge force was launch against the demonstrating wor ers on Black Friday.

Repeated sword and bat charges were made. Bayone were used to threaten any point resistance.

Unionists were prosecuted using threatening words to th who took their jobs. One unioni asked in court whether he h called a man a scab, replied: " you think I would call that sc a man?"

Harry ("King") Coyne, MLA Warrego, and other Labor poli cians, marched with the strike and wore the Red Ribbon of sol arity.

Labor politicians' support of t strike did not stop, but actua led to Labor's landslide electi win in 1915.

The strike was won on Febr ary 27 when Federal Arbitrati Judge Higgins awarded unioni the right to wear badges. T worker's had stated that otherw there would be no return to wo

BILLETS OR BADGES, 1959 (Brisbane New Theatre)
Playwright Jim Crawford. Principal players: Val Mald and Eddie Clarke

historical setting, its tale of humble heroism and solidarity, its bush dances, its rousing ballads and catchy folksongs sung to the accompaniment of a bush band, it was indeed a most effective dramatic combination, justifying its many revivals in Queensland and throughout Australia. Reviews regularly reported enthusiastic reception:

> A few nights ago, at the All Saints' Hall, a capacity audience would not let the cast leave the stage when the final curtain fell. Four encores of the play's highlights were demanded, and given. Finally, the Bushwhackers Band assembled outside the exit and played the audience out of the hall.

After this resounding success, Brisbane New Theatre presented another Dick Diamond musical. *Under the Coolibah Tree* proved popular with the public, but it never reached the heights of its predecessor. With its simple story of shearers, Indigenous people, river sailors and show people, set on the Darling River 80 miles from Wilcannia, it brought to life the Australia of the 1880s as a rollicking musical with colourful, old-fashioned dialogue.

The premiere took place in All Saint's Hall on 17 March 1955. The performance did not impress the *Courier-Mail* reviewer, perhaps because it was insufficiently rehearsed. But the show gathered pace and played on a total of 21 occasions across many venues in Brisbane; it also toured to Ipswich and Maleny.

It must be noted that there was ambivalence and lack of unanimity within the left movement regarding folklore-inspired art and literature. The recurring celebration of the 1890s as the source of an Australian radical culture was, in fact, at odds with theories of culture discussed in the CPA particularly. While the CPA supported a range of initiatives by alternative groups intent on creating or reviving a radical culture in the 1940s and 1950s, it also strongly exhorted writers to adhere to orthodox socialist realism.

INTERNATIONAL POLITICS

The stand New Theatre took on international political issues mainly continued that of Unity Theatre before the war. However, the geopolitical climate was significantly different. With the fascist threat temporarily dispelled, the latent conflict between the communist and the capitalist worlds took centre stage. This became evident as early as the war's end, when disagreements on German borders split wartime unity. In the ideological tug-of-war between the alleged neo-imperialism of the USA and other capitalist countries, and the alleged threat of communist tyranny, the attitude of groups such as New Theatre was predictable.

The left's wariness of the hidden agenda of US foreign policy was apparent soon after the war's end. *Lion on the Square*, a satirical comedy by Soviet journalist Ilya Ehrenburg, who had lived in Paris for many years, deals with the implications for the French people of Marshall Aid to France. New Theatre staged it in 1949 in their new clubrooms at King Edward's Chambers, in Fortitude Valley. To a small provincial town in southern France comes North American James Low, a smart dealer in junk antiques to be sold back home for a sizeable profit. Mistaken for an important US business observer, Low negotiates a deal with the mayor: food from the people of Jackson, USA, in exchange for the Lion on the Square, a historical relic from the 15th century, symbol of the town's independence. Low's identity is finally exposed, but he warns the townspeople against the real US observers' Marshall Aid plans. The Lion is restored to its pedestal in the Square, and the townspeople declare their determination of maintaining their independence from US economic domination. Although the play has a serious message, it is a rollicking, satirical comedy that treats disclaimers of wartime collaboration and anti-communist hysteria with ironical acuity. The play's topicality ensured a long and successful season.

Winston Churchill's appeal in March 1946 for an Anglo-American fraternal association, to oppose the spread by Russia of 'communist tyranny' in Europe, signalled the beginning of the Cold War. Anti-communism had been evident in Australian politics since World War I, but the beginning of the Cold War initiated a true anti-communist crusade in this country. Communists were accused of being traitors, saboteurs and spies; for the next 10 years, they became the archenemy, apparently the greatest single cause of real or supposed industrial anarchy.

Just after the 1951 referendum, the presentation to Brisbane audiences of Howard Fast's play *Thirty Pieces of Silver*, which exposed the climate of fear and betrayal existing in the contemporary USA during the McCarthy era, was a timely warning to Australians of what could occur in this country unless civil liberties were preserved. The play centres on David Graham, an irresolute, mild-mannered statistician who betrays his wartime friend Leonard Agronsky, a Russian-born Jew and now Secretary to the Department of Commerce. To avoid dismissal or arraignment before a loyalty committee, David makes a false statement swearing to Agronsky's Communist Party membership. His duplicity and lack of principle are finally exposed, causing his marriage to break up.

A Broadway producer dismissed the play as 'impossible', but it had a second chance: after Melbourne New Theatre sent a request for plays, *Thirty Pieces of Silver* came to Australia for its world premiere performance. Following successful seasons in Melbourne, Sydney and Brisbane, it played in many European countries from 1951 to 1953. In 1952, productions were running 'simultaneously in Berlin, Vienna, Budapest, Warsaw, Pilsen and Moscow...with openings in Antwerp and Rome...[and] Canada scheduled for 1953'.

The New Theatre production of Arthur Miller's play *The Crucible* in Brisbane in 1960 was still relevant for Australian audiences because, in this Cold War period, Australians were not immune to political persecution and reckless smearing. The Australian press, with its reports of activities in the USA, undoubtedly promoted an atmosphere where anti-communism flourished.

Colonial struggles, one of the main issues of postwar politics, claimed the attention of radical theatres. In 1954 and 1955, Brisbane New Theatre produced *Strangers in the Land,* a Mona Brand play sympathetic to the Malayan independence movement. When the British administration resumed power in Malaya after the Japanese surrender in 1945, labour militancy and the struggle for independence led by the Malayan Communist Party seriously challenged Great Britain's colonial rule and its economic interests. The rulers instituted a state of emergency; banned all political parties and trade union organisations; and arrested, detained and later banished their leaders. *Strangers in the Land* denounces this ferocious counterinsurgency campaign.

In Brand's play, the planters' attitude is, indeed, less heroic than in the film. Christine Warren has just arrived in Malaya from England to marry Roderick Howard, a planter, and stays with Douglas Streeter and his wife Joyce. Christine discovers, to her dismay, that Rod and Douglas are members of the special constabulary involved in 'bandit extermination' and village burning. She meets John Gifford, a cynical Englishman, and Nan Price and her husband Basil, a planter, who is later ambushed and killed. Douglas and Rod set out to avenge Basil's death. John Gifford, sceptical about Britain's role in the country, reveals to Christine his sympathy with the Malayan nationalists. When Christine's fiancé Rod shoots Seng Lee, the Chinese houseboy who

Bury the Dead, 1950 New Theatre Contact Group playreading at an Enoggera Home. Readers (standing) – **Patsy Robertson** (nee Dickie) and **George Petersen**

● ● ● ● ● ● ● ● ● ● ● ● **Patsy Robertson and George Petersen reading the script of**
● ● ● ● ● ● ● ● ● ● ● ● *Bury the Dead* **at a member's home, Enoggera, Brisbane, 1950.**

is attempting an escape to join the 'terrorists', she decides to leave Malaya, rejecting the coercive attitudes that Rod and his planter friends show towards the local inhabitants.

The play won high praise at a showing by Unity Theatre in London. A Soviet cultural delegation then visiting England attended a performance. Famous Soviet writer Konstantin Simonov, a member of the delegation, was impressed by the play and took several of Mona Brand's works back to Moscow for translation. Brand was subsequently invited to Moscow and learnt of the play's scheduled production in the Soviet Union.

The Brisbane production was very successful. Interestingly, reviews did not criticise the subject matter, addressing only technical deficiencies, such as lack of action on stage and the fact that the Malayan people's struggles were represented only in the character of a houseboy.

Strangers in the Land, Brisbane NT, 1955.

As it had done in the 1930s, Brisbane New Theatre gave support to the campaign for peace. Irwin Shaw's play *Bury the Dead*, written in 1936, had a revival in 1950. First playing in the theatre's clubrooms, it continued to various suburban venues and, later in the year, played at the Albert Hall in a partnership with the Queensland Peace Council. The program notes drew the audience's attention to the play's enduring relevance:

> **Bury the Dead** was written about 1936, between the two 'great' wars; and in common with many of the plays of the period (such as those of Clifford Odets, Elmer Rice and Albert Maltz) possesses a note of violent social protest. It bears most of the virtues and defects that were dominant in the literature of the Thirties and is consequently 'dated', yet the Thirties – with its post-war disillusionment, its depression 'blues', and its fear of a new war – is so similar in many respects to our own contemporary scene, that the play is perhaps more significant now than it was then.

British playwright Leonard Irwin also took an antiwar stance in *The Circling Dove* (1951, 1952). The play's plot involves a secret emergency War Office plan to disperse chronic patients and take over hospital beds in a British general hospital, in the event of a war which, they consider, is threatening the country. Matron Linson's refusal to cooperate and her forced resignation eventually win support from staff and patients, compelling the War Office to cancel the plan. The characters are realistic, and the Matron cuts a fine figure of humanity in her courageous stand against the cold edicts of the British War Office. The lingering, painful death of Ted Branston, a 29-year-old plumber, victim of a World War II air-raid in which he lost both legs, presents a poignant message to those who contemplate and plan a future war.

Queensland playwright Nance Macmillan wrote *Land of Morning Calm* (a.k.a. *Christmas Bridge*), a plea for peace in wartime, which Brisbane New Theatre produced in 1952. All the action of the play takes place on 5 November 1950, at and near the fortress at Kwanai, a town on the river Tuman which marks part of the frontier between Korea and China. The play deals with the attempt by a unit of United Nations soldiers to blow up the bridge over the Tuman River to prevent the arrival of Chinese army support troops. The

United Nations unit consists of four soldiers, two North Americans and two Australians. Attempts by the Koreans to prevent the blasting of the bridge and to warn the Chinese are thwarted, and Marguerite Stern, a US newspaper woman who arrives at the camp, gives a graphic description of the mass slaughter by US troops of Korean civilians – which was finally stopped by the intervention of British troops.

Critics believed that some serious faults marred the play, quite apart from its political stance. New Theatre actor and director Edmund Allison, who had seen London Unity Theatre's production, had urged Sydney's New Theatre never to produce the play. George Petersen, Secretary of Brisbane New Theatre, levelled some serious technical criticisms at the play in a letter to Miriam Hampson, Sydney New Theatre; in particular, he pointed out:

> In November 1950 the Yalu and Tuman rivers were frozen over and the Chinese volunteers actually crossed over the ice. It would therefore he unnecessary to blow up a bridge at that time. Nor could four men carry enough explosives to blow up a bridge of this nature; such bridges would be few and heavily guarded, probably with an anti-aircraft unit. A specialist like Slim [Parker] would be at least a Sergeant and the likelihood of a mixed nationality patrol was very rare.

However, *Land of Morning Calm* had a successful six and a half weeks' season in 1952 with London Unity Theatre. It played in Brisbane, Melbourne, Sydney and Adelaide and at the Youth Carnival for Peace and Friendship in Sydney. In another letter to Hampson, George Petersen subsequently wrote:

> *Land of Morning Calm* played well over three nights with about 300 in the audience. [There was] the usual boycott from the daily press and [the attendance of] two plainclothes coppers on opening night. I hear that Melbourne New Theatre is having trouble with the State authorities over the play. We had no trouble here. In fact we borrowed a revolver for firing blanks from the Police department.

Brisbane New Theatre produced two widely dissimilar plays with a common basis – the need for all people to take responsibility for maintaining peace – against a turbulent background: continuing fears of nuclear proliferation; reports in November 1961 of the Soviet Union's violation of the atmospheric test ban treaty with a series of Arctic test explosions; and an extension of tensions between the Great Powers. *A Most Important Letter* (1962), by Jim Crawford, took as its theme 'the challenge of life throughout the ages to defy Death'. Several historical characters call on the people of today to preserve peace, while contemporary figures – Mrs Brown, a peace activist, her daughter Mary, a scientist, a worker, a general and a financier – are all concerned about the possible effects of a nuclear war. The play opened at the Social Services Hall in Fortitude Valley and played at various local halls in Stones Corner, West End and Enoggera.

The shooting down of the U2 spy flight over Russia, followed by the trial and conviction of US pilot Gary Powers, and the serious rift between Russia and China, openly admitted in 1960, brought the danger of another world conflict very much closer. This is the background for Soviet playwright Konstantin Simonov's play *The Fourth* (1962), the story of a Western newspaper man who abandons his high principles and betrays his friends for status, wealth and power. Ted Frank, a fellow-survivor from a POW camp, seeks his help to stop the flight over Russia of a high-altitude plane which could lead to another, more devastating war. The journalist contrasts his life with the sacrifices made by his ex-POW friends and, finally unable to evade his responsibilities, makes the fateful decision, irrespective of the consequences, to alert the world to the danger of war.

RACISM

Despite being a nation of migrants, Australia is far from having a history of racial tolerance. Racist and xenophobic attitudes were widespread in the 19th century and found frequent expression in the literature. After the war, the exposure of Hitler's racial genocide and the influx of migrants of many nationalities helped to break down Australians' parochial attitudes to some extent, provoked a greater awareness of racism and awakened some recognition of Australia's neglected Aboriginal and Torres Strait Islander people. Public feelings did not change overnight; but writers, artists and the intelligentsia generally began to give the problem the urgent attention it needed.

Combining the dual themes of racial prejudice and worker solidarity, *Tanker Mackay* (a.k.a. *Longitude 49*; 1949, 1953), by US playwright Herb Tank, a seaman during World War II, bases its story on an actual incident in which an officer on board a Liberty ship shoots an African-American seaman dead. In the play, the Mate of US tanker *Mackay*, docked in an oil port in Iran, singles out Brooks, the African-American seaman and delegate, as a communist and troublemaker, shoots him, and claims that Brooks had attacked him with a fire-axe. When Brooks dies, the men unite, forcing the Captain to arrest the Mate for murder. The play was popular with Brisbane audiences for its faithful depiction of working-class life. Brisbane Seamen's Union Secretary, John Connor, sent a circular letter to his members:

> I have read *Tanker Mackay* and am proud to be able to commend my union brother's play to all seamen, to all trade unionists, to all people who in their hearts feel no despair, but hope for the world. There is another America...this America belongs to the common people, who toil and struggle, and in this struggle, make common cause with all men striving for peace and a better world.

ABORIGINAL AND TORRES STRAIT ISLANDER RIGHTS

Brisbane's first theatre, opened by George Croft in Russell Street, South Brisbane, admitted Indigenous people in 1847. Unfortunately, this snippet of historical trivia turns out to be no indication of any special Brisbane open-mindedness; the admission of Aboriginal and Torres Strait Islander people, as well as the fact that improper songs were sung, quickly diminished audiences. Croft sold up within a few months.

In 1931, George Landen Dann's play *In Beauty It Is Finished* created a storm of indignation in the white community for his sympathetic treatment of Aboriginal characters. Throughout both urban and rural society in the 19th century, Aboriginal and Torres Strait Islander people had been subjected to widespread violent treatment, dispossession and extermination. Even so, before the war, no Brisbane theatres had produced a play dealing with the plight of Australian Indigenous people. It seems that the brotherhood and solidarity of the working class, which other political dramas advocated, did not generally extend to their Black brothers and sisters. After the war, however, this became a major focus for New Theatre.

One of the most controversial dramas staged by the Brisbane New Theatre, *Rocket Range* (1948, 1950, 1955), concerned the reaction of Australian Aboriginal people to the white invaders of their tribal hunting grounds. Jim Crawford wrote this one-act play in 1946 when the federal government announced its intention of removing several remote groups of tribal Aboriginal people from Central Australia to make room for a rocket range. The characters in his play are given the names of some of the tribes nearly exterminated in frontier warfare: the Black War waged between 1860 and 1890 against Australia's Indigenous people. Crawford explains in the program:

> The Kalkadoons, Kajabbis and Kamilerois were concerned in a night skirmish with a Native Police detachment on 24 January 1883...at the height of the Black War. A white officer – one Marcus de la Poer-Beresford – was killed in the affray. Later, these tribes were decimated by Native Police, a squatter punitive column led by a white officer named Frederick Urquhart, at a place still known as Battle Mountain, near Cloncurry, Queensland.

The play is set in an Aboriginal encampment at night where they are discussing the intrusion of a white man into their tribal territory. The white man's behaviour is offensive and causes resentment. He has taken a female, Kalkadoon, and is camping near a lagoon at a site forbidden to male members of the tribe. Kalkadoon later returns after being harshly beaten. Kajabbi wants to leave their territory and go to the hills. But, if they leave, warrior Namalka fears that they will suffer starvation like that experienced by the Warrandooks tribe when expelled from their territory.

Gimbin, the tribal elder, favours the adoption of the white man into their totem. They learn that the white man is claiming their territory for the government to set up a rocket range. The white man indignantly refuses their offer to join their totem and is killed, according to custom, as a trespasser on their land. Arriving with a Black tracker, the investigating policeman shoots Namalka as he prepares to throw a spear. The tribe are rounded up, chained and taken off. Only one girl, who has escaped, returns to the campfire to mourn their departure.

The play was entered in the British Drama League Festival in Sydney in 1946. Although the adjudicator, Mr Harvey Adams, gave high praise to the production, decor and theatrical qualities of the play, he criticised the play's content as ideological propaganda and threw it out of the festival, saying:

> I cannot but feel that this play has been chosen for presentation for no other reason than ideological propaganda, and, as such, I have no option but to throw it out of what is designed as a 'theatrical' Festival.

In his summing up of the play's dramatic achievement, Mr Adams awarded half the possible marks for 'the splendid impression left upon the spectators', but violently condemned:

> the spectacle of an Australian policeman, even in the Woop-Woops, wading in like any Chicago gangster and shooting down his defenceless black brother...it is utterly slanderous upon a fine body of men...this, I am afraid, registers no marks, as it fails to advance the Drama.

Jim Crawford pointed out that the scene was far from incredible:

> in fact, not one, but seven tribal Aborigines were shot by a police party in north Western Australia only six years before the play was written, in circumstances similar to those shown on stage.

Rocket Range has played throughout Australia and had a production in Budapest in 1949, by the Australian delegation to the Second Congress of the World Federation of Democratic Youth. Both the Brisbane *Courier-Mail* and the *Sydney Morning Herald* agreed that the production was impressive and memorable and signalled a dramatist of high promise, while *Pertinent* magazine considered that:

> in any other country than Australia, Mr Crawford would be able to make a living writing plays. Its treatment of the Aboriginal and the coming of the white scientist [sic] to the Centre, is arresting and vital.

Despite this high praise, the play was still incurring official proscriptions some 15 years later. In 1961, it was banned from a public play reading at the South Brisbane Municipal Library, sponsored by the Brisbane City Council, on the grounds that it was too political. In protest, Brisbane New Theatre refused to submit a substitute play to the council and did not participate in the Drama Festival staged at this venue a short time later.

Racial discrimination towards Aboriginal people was also the topic for a play by Oriel Gray, *Had We but World Enough*, which was produced for a 10-week season in Brisbane in 1950 and entered by New Theatre into the Jubilee Drama Festival in 1951. This play had topical interest at the time. New Theatre reminded the audience:

> at this very moment, in Brisbane, coloured people living at Moorooka have had their huts burnt down with all their possessions and left to find shelter wherever they may.

In spite of the controversy created by the production of George Landen Dann's *In Beauty It Is Finished* in 1931, Brisbane Repertory Theatre was bold enough to present in 1942 another play by the same author, *Fountains Beyond*, also pleading for an understanding of the plight of Aboriginal people of mixed descent living on the fringes of white society. New Theatre presented the play at the end of 1958.

The central character of *Fountains Beyond* is Vic Filmer, an Aboriginal man regarded as a leader by the local Indigenous people working as boatmen or labourers and living in shacks on the outskirts of a small coastal town. The setting is the Tweed district of northern NSW. Vic is married to Peggy, a pretty but superficial young Aboriginal woman who is attracted to Wally, a young larrikin. The community, led by Vic, opposes a move off the settlement reserve down to the swamp to make way for a proposed new playground. When wealthy ex-sugar farmer Mayor Watson asks Vic to organise a corroboree in aid of a children's playground to provide local colour for visiting English writer Gertrude Harnett, Vic refuses. But unprincipled Wally not only accepts the commission rather than unload a sugar boat, but also seduces Peggy. Forced to an election by the land rights controversy, the mayor wins, and the Aboriginal people are evicted from their land. Vic accidentally kills Peggy, guilty of infidelity with Wally. Suffering a personal tragedy and betrayed by one of his own people, Vic, accompanied by Henry, an old Aboriginal man, sails off in despair with Peggy's dead body to her island tribal homeland.

The Brisbane *Courier-Mail*'s Roger Covell gave the play a sympathetic review:

> Queensland playwright George Landen Dann's *Fountains Beyond* made a welcome local re-appearance in All Saints Hall last night. The New Theatre Club Brisbane...presented it with a good deal of skill and persuasiveness... Producer Ossie Nash showed insight into the play and its message. He received good support from a cast in which Ted Kelk's sensitive Vic Filmer and Ron Fraser's blustering alderman were outstanding. The play has its weaknesses, but it remains possibly the most important play produced in Queensland.

The author was generally acclaimed for the rhythm and beauty of the dialogue and his sympathetic insight into the problems of Aboriginal people.

Brisbane New Theatre premiered a play by Queensland playwright Nance Macmillan, *The Painter*, in 1961. The play is based on the life of painter Albert Namatjira (1902–59), an Aboriginal artist from the Aranda tribe, born at Hermannsburg Lutheran Mission near Alice Springs. Several exhibitions of his landscape paintings occurred from the late 1930s to the 1950s, with the help of Australian artist Rex Battarbee. Nance Macmillan became interested in Namatjira when she saw his first exhibition of paintings in Melbourne in 1938.

The play is set in the Aboriginal camp of Duncan Namiraba (Albert Namatjira) on the Finke River near Alice Springs in Central Australia, where he and his wife Elkalita and other family members (grandson Jimmy and sons Reuben and Nym) have gathered. Reuben and Nym are planning to buy and run a cooperative cattle station, which Namiraba would finance from the money earned from his paintings. Police enter the camp and charge Namiraba with the illegal act of supplying liquor to his son, Reuben, who was then a ward of the state. Police subsequently charge Reuben with disorderly behaviour and resisting arrest and his brother Nym for consuming liquor illegally. Despite support from the white community, including Scott – the artist who first encouraged Namiraba to paint – the play concludes on a despairing note: all three are convicted in the court case which follows. *The Painter* played to packed houses in the Albert Hall on four nights but never travelled to other states.

Set for "FOUNTAINS BE

marquee.

THE other day the New Theatre Club was rehearsing its coming production "Fountains Beyond" in a backyard at Woolloongabba and during the climax of the play there's a struggle for the possession of a gun in the course of which the heroine is shot. They'd no sooner finished the rehearsal than up screeched a car-load of policemen who'd turned out after an urgent call to a shooting tragedy.

These amateur theatre groups must be getting better and better.

A tale of shanties

Queensland playwright George Landen Dann's "Fountains Beyond" made a welcome local re-appearance in All Saints' Hall last night.

The New Theatre Club, Brisbane, which describes itself as "a working class theatre" (whatever that means), presented it with a good deal of skill and persuasiveness.

Dann's play is a sincere and impassioned statement of the plight of a group of aboriginals living in a shanty settlement on the outskirts of a small Queensland coastal town.

This plight emerges in effective dramatic terms through the personal tragedy of an idealistic half-caste, Vic Filmer.

Producer Ossie Nash showed insight into the play and its message.

He received good support from a cast in which Ted Kelk's sensitive Vic Filmer and Ron Fraser's blustering alderman were outstanding.

The play has its weaknesses, but it remains possibly the most important play produced in Queensland.—Roger Covell.

Connie Healy' scrapbook page on Fountains Beyond, Brisbane, 1958.

C. MAIL

ANTISEMITISM

New Theatre produced three plays about antisemitism: one examined its impact on a Jewish family, and the others dealt with its effect in the wider community. The first was *Friday Night at the Schrammer's*, by a gifted young local playwright, Laurence Collinson. This one-act play deals in a light-hearted vein with emerging intergenerational conflict during a Friday night Sabbath in a Jewish family living in Melbourne. Mrs Schrammer observes the traditions and customs of European Jewish communities and accepts the conventional Jewish attitude that women should pursue an exclusively nurturing role in the family. The attitudes of her children, Mark and Sadie, who are trying to be accepted in Australian society, confuse her. Sadie declares herself an atheist, opposes Jewish customs, is interested in scientific rather than domestic achievement and denies her background in a bid for peer acceptance. Mark, striving for independence, also rejects the Jewish emphasis on family life and religion; he is critical of his father Harry's caution about political involvement for change.

Home of the Brave, by US playwright and director Arthur Laments, was a 1940 wartime drama also dealing with antisemitism. The plot revolves around Pete Coen (Coney). As a result of a traumatic shock during war service in an US engineering unit in the Pacific area, Coen suffers amnesia and paralysis. A sympathetic psychiatrist helps him regain his mental and physical health by guiding Coen back through the incidents which led to his breakdown, enabling him to confidently return to civilian life. A review of the Brisbane production was rightly critical of the dubious psychological theories of the basis of racism which underlay the plot.

The theme of *Sky Without Birds*, by Oriel Gray, is antisemitism in a small settlement on the edge of the Nullarbor Plains. Heinrich Schafer, a German Jewish refugee from the horror of a concentration camp, arrives in Koorora to work as a loco-mechanic on the Trans-Continental Railway. He hopes to adjust to a new life and restore his faith in humanity but, even in this isolated community, he finds himself a victim of racial prejudice. However, he makes two friends who both hold a positive view of humanity and show sympathy for him. Violence erupts, but the matter is resolved without police interference. Heinrich's faith in humanity is restored, and he decides to reject isolation and face up to the wider community.

According to the review by Syd Davis in the Queensland *Guardian*, the play was well received by the two nights' audiences: 'who understood and liked the ideas in the drama and forgave any technical shortcomings in the script or the production'. The review went on to say that the play was worthwhile as a literary piece in the library of thoughtful, progressive Australian plays, but that there was a lack of action, that 'essential ingredient of drama which is so often absent from the works of modern playwrights.'

Another timely production with an anti-racist theme was Australian playwright Richard Beynon's *The Shifting Heart*. It is set in Collingwood, an old, run-down working-class suburb of Melbourne, and concerns the isolation and rejection of an Italian family by the Australian community; this results in their son Gino's death in a drunken brawl on Christmas Eve. Sponsored by the Elizabethan Theatre Trust, this play won the Sydney Journalists' Club Competition in 1956 and placed equal third in the London *Observer*'s competition the following year, out of 2,000 entries

FEMINIST THEMES

The 1949 staging of Laurence Collinson's one-act comedy *No Sugar for George*, 'a human and amusing slice of life', was a 'happy justification of New Theatre's policy of staging Australian writers of merit'. Its plot revolves around the failed attempts of an interfering woman to arrange a marriage. Molly, a busybody and scheming matchmaker, introduces her friend's sister Emily, a 'brisk, almost handsome woman' in her mid-forties, to her old friend George Richardson as an eminently desirable husband. But Emily, clearheaded and independent, refuses this 'last chance' to marry a capitalist entrepreneur, who shamelessly exploits the women workers at his factory as he did his former wife at home. George is satirised as a thoroughly objectionable, narrow-minded character who opposes education, dislikes card playing, abhors gambling and disparages tea drinking as an 'unhealthy feature of our national life'. In rejecting the marriage, Emily repudiates conformist attitudes and affirms the right of women to an independent and fulfilling life without the necessity of a marriage partner.

Apart from this early instance, the most militant feminist pronouncement in this postwar period is to be found in *Billets or Badges*. Other plays touching on the question of marriage and the role of women in society did so in a lighthearted, ambiguous fashion. The 1957 production of John Millington Synge's one-act play *The Tinker's Wedding* marked another venture into comedy for New Theatre. The frustration of a tinker couple's attempt to marry and their rejoicing at their escape from matrimony is the theme of the play, which humorously celebrates their simple life of freedom roaming the countryside. New Theatre presented Sean O'Casey's *The End of the Beginning*, also a one-act comedy, at All Saints' Hall and later as its entry in the Third Ipswich Drama Festival in July 1957. Set in the kitchen of an Irish farmhouse, it deals in a hilariously comic fashion with the troubles encountered by Darry Berrill, a farmer who decides to do his wife Lizzie's work in the house, while she ploughs the fields. The play's production in Ipswich was apparently very successful:

> The non-stop riotous behaviour of the two central figures in the play, the farmer [Syd Davis] and his somewhat doubtful help [Les McWilliams], was greatly appreciated by the audience. Although on stage for a brief period only, Gwen McKay, gave a sterling performance as the farmer's wife.

The juxtaposition of feminist themes and comedy is perhaps an interesting reflection of attitudes at the time. Treatment of the role of women in society was frequently comic, depreciating the theme and the issue. Innumerable cartoons published in the press of the time illustrate this.

CULTURAL POLICIES

The Governor's Stables (1953, 1955), by Jim Crawford, is a plea for the establishment of an Australian national theatre, 'against the opposition of commercial interests, in particular, Hollywood films'. It also advocated state-subsidised theatres with cheap seats, to make the theatre readily accessible to all sections of the Australian people. The play is based on historical facts. Under the patronage of Governor Macquarie, Francis Greenway, convicted of forgery and transported to Australia in 1814, became Sydney's first civil architect. He was granted a ticket-of-leave, conditional emancipation in 1817 and, finally, a full pardon in 1819 for his excellent public works and his designs for new buildings. Macquarie gave him unrestricted freedom to design a new government house, including stables which were so grand that they were often mistaken for Government House itself. When this extravagance became known in London, the Colonial Secretary forbade its completion. In the early 1820s, Macquarie's vision of Australia as a nation, not purely as a punishment station, came under scrutiny, and his governorship was investigated. The British Colonial Office removed him to the Isle of Ulva (off Scotland) and cancelled or interfered with many of architect Greenway's projects. Governor Brisbane, Macquarie's successor, finally dismissed Greenway ignominiously in 1822.

Crawford's play, a comedy in three acts, presents in dramatic form the basic historical details outlined above. The scene is then transposed to a modern setting at the Sydney Conservatorium of Music, which is now located in the old Governor's Stables, to a meeting discussing the establishment of an Australian national theatre.

The play won the West Australian Theatre Council's £100 annual prize for an original Australian play. The adjudicator described the play as:

> a comedy in true comedy vein. It employs clever dialogue, unique situations and well-handled satire. The author has struck a distinct note of originality, particularly in the introduction of a theme of olden times on which to base his present-day nation. The characters are well defined.

This commendation shows that the play was eminently stage-worthy; yet, the Australian Playwrights' Advisory Board, which normally organised the distribution of Australian plays, refused to handle *The Governor's Stables* on the grounds that it was propaganda.

Jim Crawford told the Queensland *Guardian*:

> The Board's refusal to handle the play because it is 'propaganda' means that a self-styled advisory body is exercising a political censorship. All plays written with conviction are propaganda for something or other.

Brisbane New Theatre admitted that the play was propaganda, but for desirable objectives which would further the interests of Australian theatre. They eventually produced the play together with similar 'propaganda' for a British national theatre, *The Dark Lady of the Sonnets*, by George Bernard Shaw.

OTHER HISTORICAL PLAYS AND AGIT-PROP SKITS

Another Jim Crawford play, *They Passed This Way*, was a 'phantasy in one act' about Brisbane's origins as a penal colony. It had its premiere at the second annual One Act Play Festival in Ipswich. In his notes on the play, Jim Crawford points out that:

> From 1825 until 1840 Brisbane...was the worst penal station of the British Crown... Captain Patrick Logan was one of the worst commandants at Brisbane at this time... Floggings, suicides and perpetual semi-starvation were the order of the day.

One of Brisbane's historic landmarks, the Observatory, originally a windmill that Captain Logan built in 1829 to grind flour, provides the setting for the play. Unable to function effectively as a windmill, it was converted into a treadmill, worked by convict labour, and a gallows. The play contrasts the modern life of Brisbane residents, walking in the shadow of the windmill, with life in Brisbane's early penal settlement. It denounces the inhumanity of a system that transported prisoners for the most trivial crimes and the brutal punishments prisoners received. The audience is reminded that these 'prisoners of the Crown' were the founding fathers of the city, the men and women who, with their own hands and skills, erected its first buildings.

Anther play inspired by the same interest for stories of the early days of settlement is *The Night of the Ding Dong*. It is a little-known fact of Australian history that, in the 19th century, the colonies' fear of a Russian invasion periodically reached panic proportions. Australian playwright Ralph Petersen wrote a comedy on this subject, *The Night of the Russians*, first produced in Britain to rave notices. Brisbane New Theatre presented it, renamed *The Night of the Ding Dong,* in 1959. Jeff Underhill adapted it for television in 1961.

New Theatre also produced agitprop forms of theatrical activity. Its efforts reached their peak in the 1950s and early 1960s, when they took peace plays, skits and songs of *Reedy River* and other musicals to the suburbs and performed in backyards and private homes. They also presented them in centres outside Brisbane, at various workplaces, down the mines, in May Day processions and for International Women's Day and Communist Party celebrations.

The Courier-Mail Wharfie and *Butcher's Hook* were two of the most notorious of these performances. New Theatre contact group performed Jim Crawford's *The Courier-Mail Wharfie*, also known as *The Judge and the Shipowner*, in 1954 in a roof-top show to wharfie pickets at the WWF hall in Macrossan Street. Workers greeted the scene with great hilarity, responding to the play's attack on the local newspaper. At this time, the *Courier-Mail* used its columns to launch vicious attacks on Brisbane wharfies, depicting them in cartoons and prose as overweight, overpaid, underworked and far too militant.

Many other skits taken to social events in suburban halls and homes came from Jim Crawford's prolific pen. Left-orientated organisations and the trade union movement called on him to provide short items, and he readily obliged. *A Box of Matches* (or *What About it Ned?*) called for the Labor government to introduce price control, a burning issue during the downturn experienced in the economy in 1951–52. *Heil Hanlon* (1948) challenged the anti-picketing legislation enacted during the rail strike in Brisbane; *Forty Hour Wait* (1951) dealt with the effect of broken shifts on tramway-men and their families; *The Remedy* (1961) expounded the theme 'Get Monopoly Off Our Backs' and had a performance as part of the Communist Party's federal election campaign; and *The Good Oil* (1962) was an attack on US control of Australia's petrol distribution industry.

BRISBANE NEW THEATRE'S DEMISE

In 1959, for the first time in the history of New Theatre Australia, Brisbane was the host branch for the 12th National Conference. Roger Milliss' summary of the conference in the national *Spotlight* newsletter was a forewarning of the future of the national organisation. It indicated the precarious situation of many New Theatre branches, with falling membership and audiences, competition from television, soaring costs and financial difficulties. The report of the 1960 conference, held in Melbourne, summarised the work of the theatre over the years with the following statement:

> In the 28 years of its existence the New Theatre movement has endeavoured to be a theatre of the people, dedicated to a drama based on realism and the democratic traditions of Australia.

Despite reports at the conference that all branches had shown signs of consolidation and growth over the last year, the national organisation had disbanded by the end of the 1960s. The only two surviving groups were in Melbourne and Sydney.

Brisbane New Theatre collapsed in 1962. With a smaller population than other capital cities, Brisbane has always faced difficulties in maintaining its amateur theatres without government subsidies. These difficulties were more acute in the case of a left-wing theatre which, in a hostile political climate, depended for financial support entirely on its members and supporters. Enthusiasm and devotion to a good cause could not wholly compensate for the heavy handicaps this peripheral situation in the community caused. The relative longevity of the Brisbane New Theatre in a time of contraction of public interest for theatre may actually be judged surprising.

The advent of television in 1956 had seriously affected film and commercial theatre attendances by 1958. The establishment of a national professional theatre was another factor that exacerbated the situation for Brisbane New Theatre. Perhaps the major cause of the theatre's decline, however, was its loss of direction – occasioned by the external political situation and indicated by a steep decline in membership of the CPA. Confusion among the left in this period not only dampened the ardour and enthusiasm of theatre activists; it also led to internal divisions within New Theatre. To stimulate its decreasing membership and audiences, one faction argued that the theatre should present plays with non-controversial themes, to attract a more middle-class audience, rather than the provocative and daring plays that had been the basis of its repertoire (and the very reason for the theatre's existence).

The final blow was the departure of some of the theatre's leading actors through retirement or transfers to other states. Some of New Theatre's remaining members continued to perform sketches at trade union socials and other left-wing organisations' functions for a little while. Jim Crawford, who continued his writing career until 1970, wrote many of these sketches. The Nindethana Theatre, an Aboriginal theatre in Melbourne, performed one of his last plays in 1972: *The Cattle King* was expanded from an earlier sketch called *The Jackeroo*, In 1973, the ABC used *The Cattle King* as part of a television program entitled *Basically Black*, in which the National Black Theatre featured. By this time, however, Brisbane New Theatre had finally collapsed.

FURTHER READING

Connie Healy Collection, UQFL191, University of Queensland, Fryer Library.

Healy, Connie, *Defiance: Political Theatre in Brisbane 1930–1962*, Brisbane, Boombana Publications, 2000.

George Landen Dann Collection, UQFL65, University of Queensland, Fryer Library.

Jim Crawford Collection, UQFL301, University of Queensland, Fryer Library.

Katharine Susannah Prichard, a founder of the Perth WAC, with son Ric Throssell.

CHAPTER 7
Fomenting Revolution in Perth

Charlie Fox

> Believing that the commercial theatre, if it has any relation to reality, concerns itself in only a small part of life, the Workers' Theatre has set itself the aim of showing Perth a drama which is nearer the interests of the ordinary man and particularly a drama dealing with the social structure from the point of view of the working man or woman.

This was how Maurie Lachberg launched the WAG theatre program in Perth in 1936, with a clarion call for a new form of theatre: new perspectives, styles and topics. For the next five years, a succession of stunning plays followed, such as Perth had never seen. An international movement, emanating from Europe, the USA and the Soviet Union in the 1920s and 1930s, had arrived in Perth – a movement of radical theatre with political plots and avant-garde methods, sets and artwork. WAG was much more than its plays; it introduced the same revolutionary impulse into Perth's art, literary, musical and dance worlds. Layman and Goddard call it a part of the 'renewal of working-class cultural life spearheaded by radical, and in particular, Communist party members'.

For five years, the Guild blazed furiously. It 1941, it flickered out. However, this wasn't the end of radical workers' arts in Perth. The same angry demand for change after World War II, although in a completely different context, inspired the birth of the New Theatre. It operated in Cold War Perth with new plays, new actors and new directors. Mostly unnoticed, it, too, died after several years. Its last play was in 1956.

WORKERS' ART GUILD

The WAG grew out of the Workers' Art Club in May 1935, as the first chapter explained. The drivers were communist novelist Katharine Susannah Prichard (KSP), radical trade unionist Maurie Lachberg and avant-garde theatre director Keith George. Prichard, who had seen radical theatre groups on her trip to Europe and the Soviet Union in 1933, was keen to set up similar bodies in Australia. Her friend and fellow communist, Jean Devanny, had also seen such bodies in Europe and set up the first one in Sydney in 1932. Melbourne playwright and communist Betty Roland, who had lived with KSP in Moscow, set up another in Melbourne, also in 1935.

The Club quickly began to rehearse three plays: the anti-fascist sketch *Who's Who in the Berlin Zoo*, *The Thief*, by KSP, and *A Bed-Time Story*, by Keith George, who became the group's director. However, its only public performance seems to have been at a MAWF meeting in August 1935, where it staged the antiwar play *X=O: A Night of the Trojan War*. Keith George was President of MAWF.

In December that year, the Club, renamed the Workers' Theatre, made its public debut with three new one-act plays in the Princess Theatre, just outside Perth's CBD. The plays were *Captain Pernod's Honour*, set in the 1871 Paris Commune; KSP's *Forward One*, about the exploitation of female Perth shop workers; and *Calpurnia's Claws*, set in Ancient Rome.

In 1936, the group changed its name again and became a WAG. Its members' abilities and interests were wide, so the WAG formed five different sections: drama; literature; dancing; plastic and graphic arts; and music. It also acted as a point of entry for radicals into wider philosophical and political debates. It had its own constitution and headquarters and worked continuously on its public identity.

The WAG was, to an extent, the artistic voice of the West Australian branch of the Communist Party, which had been established in Perth in 1931 in the depths of the Great Depression. By 1935, the party probably had no more than 150 members. In 1938, it had just 200; but, by 1944, membership had increased to 1,500. Before 1939, the WAG was never subject to close control by the CPA, as some of its equivalents in the eastern states apparently were. Bill Mountjoy, the state party Secretary, once said that he knew nothing about theatre – so how could he control its theatrical choices? In fact, Keith George, protected by KSP, controlled the theatre section's agenda. Yet, it did seem to change direction in 1939, when events in Europe caused it to alter its choice of plays. Nevertheless, while the WAG wasn't the creature of the CPA, it moved in the same close circles, taking part in all the CPA's campaigns and those of its fraternal bodies.

From 1933 on, the CPA set up several of those fraternal organisations. KSP had a hand in practically all of them. Already a founding member of the national CPA, she was also the leading figure in the Perth branch. She had established bodies to support unemployed girls and women in 1932, started the Movement Against War (MAW) in 1933 (which became the MAWF in 1934) and was largely responsible for the WAG in 1935 and 1936. With another left-wing activist, Cecelia Shelley, she set up International Women's Day in Perth in 1936 and the Modern Women's Club in 1937. She probably had a hand in forming the Spanish Relief Committee in 1937.

Like all CPA fraternal organisations (or fraternals), the WAG comprised people from a range of backgrounds. Keith George was never a member of the party, but most members were. Although one source describes members as 'bohemians and university students', there were enough working-class members to allow it to claim workers' organisation status. The WAG was both intellectual and activist. Many members were already famous or would be, including KSP and Keith George. Axel Poignant, who did the WAG's photography, was already well known. John Oldham was an architect who built sets, created art and later achieved international success. Maurie Lachberg was a unionist, a working carpenter and actor; later, he marshalled and led Perth's Labour Day marches, riding a white horse. Phyl Harnett, whom the *Daily News* described in 1939 as a 'complete bohemian', became one of Perth's best-known and most accomplished actresses; many years later, she played a cameo role in the movie *Sunday Too Far Away*. Harald Vike, Max Ebert and John Lunghi were artists with national profiles who built sets and drew programs and posters. John Hepworth became a well-known author and journalist. Even Rolf Harris played a couple of parts, late in the piece.

THEATRE

In the early 1930s, the Great Depression and an accompanying entertainment tax killed off Perth's professional theatre, and many of Perth's live theatres became picture theatres. However, by the mid-1930s, as the Depression slowly lifted, amateur theatre blossomed. The WAG, the Repertory Club, the Independent Players and the Shakespeare, Marlowe and Garrick clubs all ran productions in small halls, venturing forth on occasions to Perth's grand old

THE NEW THEATRE IN AUSTRALIA

Report on Perth's staging of *Till The Day I Die*, *The West Australian*, 1936.

VIGOROUS DRAMA.

"Till the Day I Die" Revived.

(By "Socio.")

Clifford Odets's drama, "Till the Day I Die," which the Workers' Art Guild produced for six nights earlier in the year, before it achieved fame at the hands of the Chief Secretary of New South Wales, was revived by the guild at His Majesty's Theatre last night. There have been considerable changes in the large cast, though the central trio of characters remains unchanged, but the producer has not changed his treatment of the play with the new material.

The play takes one into the underground struggle, which, if authorities are to be believed, is still waged between the Nazi State in Germany and the suppressed political faiths. The story is a simple one of grand old-fashioned heroism—old-fashioned in the theatre, but gaining repute again. It is of a Communist worker, fallen into the hands of Nazis, who are doing their best to force

A scene from a rehearsal of Clifford Odets's play "Till the Day I Die." The play will be performed in public tonight.

him to expose his comrades; his abandonment by these comrades for the safety of the movement; and his suicide, after ... convinced the comrades that he ...

... weakening of his resolve under Nazi brutality. Such a story could be heroic and nothing else, and hence is a little silly. That it is not so is due to the exaltation ... for something worth while ... the play "Till...

His Majesty's Theatre. The Repertory Club was the biggest, but its offerings typically were farces, drawing room dramas and comedies. The WAG's theatre group had an audience ripe for the picking.

The WAG's first major play was in 1936. *Till the Day I Die*, by young US playwright Clifford Odets, was a blistering attack on German fascism. Irwin Shaw's famous antiwar play *Bury the Dead* followed. Perth was astounded! The reviews were sensational! The Labor Party's newspaper, the *Westralian Worker*, was ecstatic about *Till the Day I Die*:

> The play was produced and staged entirely by workers and it gave Perth something to think about. Amateur dramatics have to date, been a privilege of the silvertails. Last Friday's performance showed that the workers can not only produce art, which compares favourably with that of the silvertails, but can beat them at their own game.

The *Daily News* reviewer described *Bury the Dead* thus:

> In these days when the theatre is occupied by emasculated plays of escape, it is refreshing and even thrilling to see drama, which attacks current great problems with skill and courage.

The WAG was adventurous and imaginative. It went on to produce socialist realist dramas about the class struggle, such as Odets' famous *Waiting for Lefty*; Albert Maltz's *Private Hicks*, about a soldier who refused to shoot strikers; the German play *Floridsorf*, about the 1934 socialist riots in Vienna; and the theatrical adaptation of Englishman Walter Greenwood's novel *Love on the Dole*. It also produced antiwar satires, like the English *Where's That Bomb?* and *Cannibal Carnival*, an attack on western imperialism.

The WAG was truly internationalist. It staged plays from the USA, Britain, Germany, Australia (Betty Roland's *Are You Ready Comrade?*) and the Soviet Union (*Inga*), along with local plays like KSP's *Women of Spain*, *Forward One* and *Penalty Clause* and Phyl Harnett's *I am Angry*. It also played the classics, staging Ibsen's *Ghosts* in 1937. It even had a children's theatre, which produced *Tommy Tucker*, a play by kids for kids, in 1937.

In 1940, it staged two feminist plays: Clare Booth's *The Women*, a US play that satirised the 'frivolous and meaningless' lives of wealthy North American women; and Olive Popplewell's *This Bondage*, the story of three generations of English suffragists, with an all-women cast. *The Women* was a more important play for the WAG, because it did several new things. Marjorie Berry, who acted in both the WAG and Independent Players, directed the play, and all cast and crew members were women. The WAG 'sponsored' the play, and the performance was 'by arrangement with' the theatrical company

> The Perth *Daily News* review of *Love on the Dole*, 1940.
>
> ## "Love On The Dole"
>
> Brilliant direction of Victor Arnold who recently came to Perth from the Sydney New Theatre League gives a polish not often found in amateur productions to the Workers' Art Guild presentation of "Love on the Dole."
>
> The inadequate audience at the Repertory Theatre last night saw a production marked also for its smooth action, clever mountings, outstanding lighting effects and understanding portrayal of every character.
>
> The settings by Perth artists Harold Vike and John Lunghi were an object lesson in effective simplicity. Reginald Gow and Walter Greenwood's play traces part of the life of a family living in unemployed poverty.
>
> Sally Hardcastle (admirably played by Gwen Duggan) and her fiance Larry Meath (cleverly handled by George Wignall) endeavour to lift themselves from the squalor into which they have been born.
>
> But Larry is killed in a dole riot. Sally "lifts" herself from her environment by becoming "housekeeper" for a loathsome bookmaker. Incidentally she thus gets jobs also for her brother and father.
>
> The play has several light patches. The entire cast does excellently. It includes Ernie Gutteridge, Jean Wilbur, John Douglas, Marjorie Harris, Joyce Goodes, Elizabeth Hamill, Gordon Iles, Frank Percival, Joan Mockeridge, Bruce Harris, Maurice D. Lachberg and Rolph Harris. "Love On the Dole" will be presented again tonight and tomorrow night. Part of the proceeds will be donated to the Free Milk Council.—R.S.

Perth's *Daily News* promotion of the WAG's production of *The Women*, 1940.

FOMENTING REVOLUTION IN PERTH

The Workers Star review of Inga, 1938.

THEATRE

(By "Backseat")

SOCIALIST BIRTH-PANGS

"Inga," a play which has had wide popularity in the Soviet Union—it ran for 250 performances on its first production in 1938 at the Moscow Theatre of the Revolution, and is still widely played—was produced by the Workers' Art Guild at the Assembly Hall last Friday and Saturday.

Concerning itself with the building of a new socialist order rather than the struggle against a still-living capitalist system, it could not hope to speak so directly and tellingly to the people of Perth as it spoke to the people of the Soviet Union. Nevertheless, its vitality can be recognised through the obscurities raised by a different time and a different system.

Socialism is not built in a day. The backward forces conflict with the progressive, old ideas instilled under a different system conflict with the needs of the new order, and out of the hurly-burly of these conflicts the drama of "Inga" is made.

Its components are Inga, woman manager of a clothing factory; Dmitri, chairman of the Factory Committee, who loves her and by whom she is loved; Glafeera, his wife; and all the petty, backward people, who cannot stomach a woman in authority. Out of these elements comes at last Inga's renunciation of Dmitri's too-demanding love for her more vital work as an activist, and the lifting of Glafeera from her backwardness and unhappiness to a sense of the goodness of life in work for the new order.

With twelve scenes, it was not an easy play to produce without drags, but a sense of the essentials in setting enabled the producer (Keith George) to stage it without the expenditure of an unnecessary minute. The speed with which it moved and the almost complete absence of amateur self-consciousness among the actors made it ...nite the unfamiliarity of its ...

EVALUATION

Discussing "Inga" naturally brings up the query: what does this ten-year-old Soviet play contribute to the immediate struggle of the West Australian worker against oppression? Compared with, say "Where's that Bomb?" it seems at a first glance irrelevant to the day by day fight for an hour more or four hours a week less. It cannot even be regarded as a correct picture of socialism in action today, for the Soviet Union moves fast, and the conditions of the first Five Year Plan period are ancient history now.

But on the credit side, through all the conflict and upset pictured in the play, there shows a strong sense of confidence and determination to succeed—its popularity in the Soviet Union ...oves it to have been an accurate reflex of the feeling of the people. It lets up the weaknesses of the times for all the world to see, and then laughs at them. In that you see a confident people.

J. C. Williamson, although it is unclear what this meant. It also used women from practically all of Perth's amateur societies, because it required 40 female actors – and the WAG simply did not have enough. It used frocking and accessories provided by local department stores, because fashionable (and expensive) clothing was necessary to give the play authenticity. And – a first for a WAG play – the program printed advertisements (for the shops which provided the costumes). Advertisements continued to appear in WAG programs afterwards.

The Women was a good, strategic choice and did extremely well. Free publicity in the *Daily News*, which near opening day ran a full-page feature on it, helped. Promotion of the play was clever; the Hollywood film of the play had recently been shown in Perth, but heavily censored. The WAG made sure to advertise its performance as the unexpurgated version. It booked out every night, and the WAG put on two additional shows.

The WAG also entered plays in the annual West Australian Drama Festival, sponsored by the *West Australian* newspaper and held at His Majesty's. The Festival was a big deal in Perth, as the list of patrons shows. It is a who's who of Perth's social and cultural male elite: J. S. Battye, State Librarian and Chancellor of the University of Western Australia (UWA); Talbott Hobbs, former soldier and architect; Walter James, a former Premier; Conrad Charlton, manager of the Perth ABC; H. B. Jackson, chairman of Western Australian Newspapers; and J. J. Poynton, the Lord Mayor of Perth.

The WAG was immediately successful. At the first festival in 1937, in the competition for new scripts, Harnett won with *I am Angry*. In the competition for full-length plays, the WAG won third prize for the German antiwar play, *Hinkemann*, and its *Private Hicks* won first prize in the competition for one-act plays.

The 1939 competition took place after Australia had joined World War II on 3 September. It immediately faced problems. The Repertory Society pulled Ernst Toller's antiwar play, *No More Peace*, because they thought it inappropriate in the circumstances, and the Independent Players pulled their antiwar play because they had run out of actors. That both had chosen critical/social plays for the first time shows just what influence the WAG had on Perth theatre. The WAG's entry, *Blood on the Moon*, staged on 23 September and directed by Phyl Harnett, was an anti-Nazi play examining the impact on a Jewish family in Germany when Hitler seized power.

It was an interesting choice. In August 1939, the CPA dropped its anti-fascist line when the Soviet Union and Germany signed the Molotov–Ribbentrop non-aggression pact. Doubtless acting on instructions, the WAG eschewed such plays for the next two years, except for *Blood on the Moon*. It is difficult to explain why it did *Blood*; perhaps it had been rehearsing for too long to stop. Whatever the reason, the WAG did not produce any more anti-fascist plays until after the German invasion of the Soviet Union in late June 1941. Instead, in late 1939, it produced the USA's anti-capitalist plays, Mark Biltzstein's *The Cradle Will Rock*; Albert Maltz's *Rehearsal*; and John Drinkwater's blank verse anti-war play, *X=O: A Night of the Trojan War*, all at its headquarters at the western end of the city. After this, it staged no anti-fascist or antiwar plays for two more years. We will return to this later.

For most of its life, Keith George was the creative director of the WAG's dramatic section. KSP chose him because of his outstanding record with other Perth theatre groups, and he selected and directed most of the plays until 1938. It was George who introduced avant-garde theatre to Perth. His plays were unique for their time; one of the WAG actors, Poole Johnson, later said that George had a 'genius for production'. He introduced method acting to Perth, inspired in part by Konstantin Stanislavski, one of whose books was in his bookshelves. Poole Johnson later remembered:

> he invoked a performance, he didn't instruct, you see, because acting is purely mental...it comes from within. People worry about the face, why should you worry about the face, why should you worry about expression, because if the thoughts are there the expression will follow.

He also had an eye for talent. He might see somebody on the street who could, he thought, fill a particular role; and he would sign them up on the spot.

He also introduced new forms of set design. The *West Australian*'s theatre critic, Polygon, remarked on the 'adventurous' methods of set design used for *Till the Day I Die* and *Bury the Dead*, observing that the Guild had adopted the style introduced by the Constructivists in the postwar years of the Soviet Union. Ernst Toller's play *Hinkemann* had no set at all, just the bare stage.

George also ran education and training classes, including 'histrionics, fencing and ballet tuition', as well as the histories of language, art, theatre and architecture, all to develop his actors' skills and knowledge. It was certainly an all-round education.

George was expelled from, or left, the WAG in late 1937; other members had apparently grown tired of his autocratic ways. Although he directed a couple of plays in 1938, he finally left early in 1939. Others took over. Howard Smith, a regular WAG actor, produced three plays; Marjorie Berry produced *The Women*; and Phyl Harnett, by now the WAG's Secretary and lead director, directed her first play in the post-George years, Odets' *Awake and Sing*, followed by *Blood on the Moon* and the WAG's last play, *Till the Day I Die*, in October 1941. *Blood on the Moon* was not a success. Polygon was unusually critical, panning its staging, acting and direction and caustically observing that Germany's actual invasion of Poland three weeks before had upstaged it. The Guild proved to be open to criticism, especially from such a powerful reviewer. Advertisements in the local papers revealed that the play had been extensively refashioned, and audiences were promised that the next show would be much better.

In 1940, the WAG arranged for Vic Arnold, the 'organising genius of Sydney's New Theatre League', to come to Perth and take over control of the theatre program. Clearly, the WAG wanted a 'new' Keith George, an experienced and creative hand on the tiller. Arnold produced just two plays, both of which were successes. Polygon paid tribute to his direction of *Love on the Dole*, remarking on how 'smoothly and efficiently' the play moved, and congratulated him on the complex and difficult job of producing KSP's *Penalty Clause*, with its 11 scene changes. However, Arnold decided to return to Sydney in early 1941. The locals were sad to see him go.

Over the life of the WAG, the reviews in the major newspapers were, on the whole, spectacular; however, some reviewers, particularly Polygon – who was an associate member of the Guild – were quick to criticise slip ups in production, some underwhelming acting and directing and, occasionally, a play itself. For example, Polygon disliked *Floridsorf* but still praised the group for choosing it. He wrote in his review: 'It is at least a vitalising change from the usual stage Vienna where fat widows fall in love with seedy aristocratic gigolos'.

Polygon was Paul Hasluck, whose later career as a member of the Liberal Party, a minister in the Menzies government and a Governor-General makes him an unusual candidate to be a supporter of the WAG. But, in the 1920s, he had been the theatre critic for the UWA student newspaper, *Pelican*. He tried his hand at script writing, directing and acting; read widely in the history and techniques of theatre; joined the Repertory Society; and moved sideways in his job at the *West Australian*, from journalism to criticism. Never a socialist, he wanted to build a more rounded, civilised and refined social world in Perth. He despised Perth's conservative cultural insularity and detested what he called the 'politically brassbound and flabbily cosmopolitan' theatre audiences. In truth, he admired the WAG partly because its plays were so confronting.

The most pointed criticism of the WAG plays came from an unexpected source: Backseat, the theatre critic for the local CPA's *Workers' Star*. He criticised the Guild for staging too many plays remote from 'things that touch [workers] here and now' – a critique he kept up for the whole history of the Guild. He also criticised some plays for not having a luminous communist character to lead the subjects to revolution or an active trade union presence, but he was full of praise for a 10-minute play in 1939 about compulsory national registration, writing: 'it is these little agitprops on immediate issues that will make the Guild a social force'.

The WAG's plays weren't just for the paying public. Throughout its life, it staged plays to build membership, raise funds for left-wing causes and support political campaigns. In 1940, the program for *Love on the Dole* notified readers that some plays would in future be staged at the WAG premises in the city for associate members only and then invited people to join. In 1936, the WAG performed *Till the Day I Die* in the Perth Trades Hall, to raise funds for the Labour Women's Organisation. In 1937, 1938 and 1939, it staged events for the Spanish Relief Fund. In 1937, it staged *Private Hicks* at a meeting to welcome Ron Hurd, a member of the International Brigade, on his way home from the Spanish Civil War. In February 1938, *The Secret* played at a big fundraising public meeting where Professor Walter Murdoch, noted feminist Irene Greenwood and other notables spoke. In August 1938, it staged *Women of Spain*, KSP's hymn to the revolutionary women of Republican Spain.

Early in 1939, the WAG left theatres for the backs of trucks, to stage 'street dramatisations' on topics like the housing problem and unemployment for the ALP at the 1939 state election. This was during the united front period of the CPA's journey and happened despite the ALP State Secretary, Percy Trainer, rejecting an offer by the WAG to stage such plays. Local Labor candidates in Perth seats, including the member for West Perth, were more open to the WAG and invited it on board. There was disquiet in the Guild in 1939 over whether it ought to take part in such electioneering, but a majority of the members at a meeting to discuss the matter were keen to continue.

The WAG's relationship with the ALP reached new heights in July and August 1939, when it put on the short sketch *Workers Beware*, a critique of the then federal *Transport Workers Act*, for the 50th anniversary of the Fremantle Lumpers Union. Premier John Wilcox attended. They staged it again at the birthday social of the ALP's Mosman Park branch, to an audience that included John Curtin and his wife. Later, the WAG returned to its roots and staged *I am Angry* for the Modern Women's Fair at the Perth Town Hall, presented a play to celebrate the 'anniversary of Socialism in the Soviet Union' and produced a 10-minute playlet satirising the plans of the government for a compulsory national military register, for a meeting opposing the scheme.

Although the WAG flourished in 1939 and did well in 1940, it faded away in 1941. It did take part in the 1941 Drama Festival, when its actors joined the other major amateur companies to put on *Quiet Night*, by the Melbourne author Dorothy Blewett, which was the only play staged that year. Phyl Harnett produced *Till the Day I Die*, which had been such a success in 1936, in October. This was its last performance.

Who were the audiences for the WAG's plays? A diverse crowd; at the plays and events for left-wing groups, they would have been members and supporters of the CPA, left wingers in the wider labour movement and middle-class supporters of individual campaigns. The Spanish Relief Committee, for example, had supporters from all Perth's social classes. The 'truck tray' offerings in working-class suburbs played to workers and their families. And the WAG often took plays to working-class suburbs and towns. In September 1937, it took *Waiting for Lefty* and *Where's That Bomb?* to the working-class suburb of Midland, then, a week later, to the coal mining town of Collie, 200 km south of Perth. It also staged plays for trade unions and at Trades Hall as part of political campaigns.

Perth historian Dylan Hyde argues that its plays on the theatre circuit were mainly middle class. Given the collapse of professional theatre during the

Great Depression, regular theatregoers would have looked forward to events like the annual Drama Festival, with its social standing. Hasluck suggests that there was a steady audience of about 1,000 over each season. He remarked that theatregoers went to opening nights, as they always had done, 'in black tie and long frock'. Most WAG plays appeared at smaller theatres around the CBD, which certainly would not have had the cachet of His Majesty's.

But where were the workers? Backseat, from the *Workers' Star*, observed that the numbers of workers would need to be 'multiplied ten-fold before the theatre could be regarded as an essential part of working-class life'. Yet, as we have seen, this is not quite true, because the theatre went to the workers, and prices at the bigger theatres were set to attract as wide an audience as possible. Although the best seats at the June 1936 performance of *Till the Day I Die* at His Majesty's were four shillings each, there were seats as low as one shilling. The WA basic wage in 1936 was £3/13/09. For women, it was just above half that. Although many jobs were still part time and intermittent, they got better as time went on. Unemployment, still high in 1936, did not return to pre-Depression levels until the war began, so it might have been possible for workers to spend one shilling to go to a play.

How did audiences receive the big plays? Some did really well. In 1937, *Where's That Bomb?* at the Assembly Hall in Pier Street met with 'rapturous applause stamping and whistles.' Betty Roland's *Are You Ready Comrade?* had already won the 1938 best Australian play award at the Drama Festival when it played to a packed His Majesty's Theatre of 1,400 people on its opening night. In 1939, Phyl Harnett's production at the Assembly Hall of *Awake and Sing* was 'nearly full'. 'Crowded houses...roared with laughter' at *Cannibal Carnival*, at the Unity Theatre in July 1939. *The Women* was a hit, playing to full houses every night.

Historians seem undecided about the WAG theatre group's reception. Terry Craig claims that it, and its individual members, were attacked by 'every Establishment source, from Government House, Parliament, the churches, the Police Force and from the descendants of the best-known founding families' for being communists. Yet, he also claims that WAG members whom he interviewed many years later (along with actors in the Repertory Society, which may have changed things somewhat) didn't remember this. Instead, Craig wrote:

> Without exception they were of the opinion that there was no sharpening of class divisions and no real conflict in Perth other than the odd hiccup

> now and then – 'we were all in it together'. Perth,
> they were quite adamant, was the secure, tolerant,
> confident and egalitarian society...with no more or
> less competition or difference of opinion than is to be
> expected in a democratic society.

Dylan Hyde argues that there was institutional opposition to the WAG from the ALP, The Catholic church and local fascists; more generally, he identifies a middle-class 'loathing of the Guild's propagandist theatre'. Yet, he also writes that the WAG made 'an immediate and stunning impact on Perth, electrifying its audiences', most of whom, he also wrote, were middle class.

The ALP never banned its members from joining the WAG, either nationally or in WA. It did ban its members from joining other political parties and, in the 1920s, it targeted parties to its left. In the 1930s, it also began to ban members from joining what it called CPA fronts; in Perth, this meant the MAW and, later, the MAWF. The peculiar organisation of the WA ALP, which included the entire trade union movement, also meant that the party could banish any affiliated body that elected communists to its leadership. Secretary Percy Trainer summed up its attitude, writing in 1937 when the CPA asked whether it could affiliate:

> The ALP hereby refuses affiliation to the Communist
> Party, and disassociates itself from its policy, methods
> and propaganda. It declares the Communist Party
> to be anti-Labor...in direct conflict with the policy,
> platform and constitution of the ALP.

Although the WAG escaped being banned when the Menzies government banned the CPA in June 1940, it was, nevertheless, under surveillance by Military Intelligence and the Special Branch of the WA Police Force in the first two years of the war. They compiled lists of WAG members, built up character portraits of leaders, seized mail, spied on meetings, plays and other events and seized material in raids on its premises. Intelligence wanted it banned. One report said:

> It is felt that as long as this organisation is deemed
> lawful, Communist and subversive propaganda
> must to a certain degree remain unchecked and it is
> recommended that their activities be curtailed.

Police also raided members' houses during the big raids that preceded the banning of the CPA. KSP's was one, Phyl Harnett's another; but this may have been because they were communists rather than WAG members.

Why was the WAG's theatrical section so successful? Hyde suggests two main reasons. The first credits WA's isolation, which 'led to a highly non-conformist art movement' where 'there were not the same cultural and political constraints on art practice…as elsewhere'. This enabled a thriving modernist movement, which the WAG largely carried. The second is that its titular head was KSP. KSP held an ambiguous place in WA at this time. She was a communist, a famous novelist and the widow of war hero Hugo Throssell, the son of a former conservative premier. She was at the forefront of the WA and Australian literary and cultural establishments and famous in the feminist, labour and peace movements. Her prestige was so great that, in 1934, the *West Australian* published her book *The Real Russia*, the story of her trip to the Soviet Union in 1933, in serial form.

The Perth press also played a part in the WAG's success. It is extraordinary, given its connection to the CPA, that its plays were reviewed, its art shows reported on, its concerts, literary occasions and dances described. It speaks to a certain openness in the press, which was almost completely absent after World War II. Also, as Paul Hasluck noted in his book *Mucking About*, reviewers had a freer hand in newspapers than other journalists; in the 1930s, his editor had a respectful approach to reviewers of high culture, especially music and theatre.

The major reason for the WAG's success, however, was that it arrived in Perth at precisely the right time. Professional theatre had disappeared. Its antiwar plays tapped into a residual pacifism and anti-militarism from World War I. The Spanish Civil War provided a foretaste of what fascism looked like. Events in Europe and the Northern Pacific made it seem inevitable that Australia would be caught up in another war. The plays about capitalism and its consequences surely struck a chord in a population that had just been through the Great Depression.

MUSICAL AND DANCE SECTIONS

Although none of the other sections of the WAG had the success or the profile of the drama team, the music section was busy. It ran lectures on musical appreciation and performance and staged public and 'community' concerts, 'musicales' and 'entertainments' at its clubrooms and in local halls.

Along with the dance section, it ran cabarets – at which its performers read poetry, and its choir sang – for good causes. It ran a recital in 1937, in the Theosophist Society's Arundale Hall, to raise funds for the Spanish Relief Fund; Phyl Harnett read *The Chant for the Mothers of the Slain Militia*, written just a year earlier by Chilean poet Pablo Neruda. A 'speaking chorus' of children recited Australian poet Frank Wilmot's anti-conscription poem *Nursery Rhyme*. One month later, Harnett reprised Neruda's poem in another Spanish Relief Fund concert, with support from 14-year-old John Hepworth and journalist Ray McLintock, who recited their own poems

A choral section began rehearsing in August 1938. In November, it contributed songs from the Soviet Union, to illustrate a talk on Soviet music for a meeting of the Society for Cultural Relations with the Soviet Union. A week later, it performed at another benefit for the Spanish Relief Fund: Harnett again recited poetry, and the radical Oreski Club orchestra, the Oreski String Band, played Spanish and Yugoslav music. This band of Yugoslav migrants played tamburitsas, stringed instruments typical of Balkans folk music. In 1939, the music section ran concerts of working-class music and staged performances by singers like Charles Gordon, who sang songs ranging from 'negro spirituals' to opera and explained their meanings as he went along.

The music section was also educational. In 1937, it offered a lecture and exhibition of Aboriginal dance and music. Roy Wood and Keith George, who was interested in a range of art forms, delivered the lecture, on materials from the Adelaide Conservatorium of Music. The lecture addressed the potential for Aboriginal music to be an inspiration to musicians everywhere; it could become the basis for a genuine Australian musical tradition. After listening to the talks, the musical section resolved to assist in the preservation of Aboriginal music.

ART

The Plastic and Graphic Arts section was also active. Early in its existence, it offered lessons for aspiring artists and hosted visits from well-known practitioners. The Melbourne artist, Ernst Buckmaster, visited in 1936; and Harald Vike taught drawing and painting at the WAG's headquarters as part of his work for the WAG and to democratise and de-mystify the art world.

But the WAG also wanted to take its art to the people. It exhibited the three WAG artists, Vike, Ebert (also known as Herbert McClintock) and Lunghi, in galleries around Perth. Art historians in WA have observed that the WAG was a modernist insurgent in Perth, working against what art historian Janda Gooding called the '19th century pastoral tradition' and the hidebound conservatism of the WA Art Gallery

The next year, the Art section conducted its biggest venture: an exhibition of modern art and a series of lectures, co-sponsored with the Adult Education Board at UWA. It was a sign of the isolation of Perth that the exhibition could find only prints of modernist European art to exhibit, but it did show the work of modernists from Melbourne and Perth. The three featured Perth artists were Vike, Ebert and Lunghi.

The exhibition struck a chord. Art lovers must have been starved of modern art, because the exhibition caused 'considerable interest'. Big crowds attended the lectures, which ranged across a number of issues. The first night, the Board's Art lecturer, Dr Kurt Rogers, lectured on the 'Origins of Modern Art'. On the second night, in a session on 'revolutionary and surrealist art', the three speakers, Harnett, Mrs E. Hamill and Ebert, were all WAG members. Harnett, who was well educated in a range of artistic fields, spoke about art in revolutionary Russia; Mrs Hamill lectured on the history of surrealist art; then Ebert followed on the technical aspects of 'modern art', from cubism to abstraction. The next night, J. J. Thomson, a lecturer in the English Department at UWA, spoke about 'the Science of Appearances'; artist Brian Elliot spoke about 'Imagination in Art'; and Mrs P. Thomson lectured on 'Cautious Criticism'.

This exhibition represented a salvo in an ongoing war between modernist and conservative art, because all the speakers tried to define, demystify and promote modernism and explain scarily incomprehensible schools like Cubism and Surrealism. But the series also introduced the idea of art for the people: Alec King, another young lecturer in the English Department at UWA and a friend of the WAG, proposed that art should be taken out of the galleries and put where the people were. People, he said, 'need art to sleep on, to walk on, to eat beside, on their floors, their walls, in public buildings, in streets'. Perhaps this was the most revolutionary suggestion of all.

The Art section also immersed itself in labour politics. The WAG began a new relationship with the trade unions in 1938 when Harald Vike designed new banners for three unions: the Butchers' Union, the Amalgamated Engineering Union (AEU) and the Amalgamated Society of Carpenters and Joiners. Produced for the 1938 Labour Day march, they were a sensation, beautifully rendered and skilful examples of socialist realism; any sign of Vike's Impressionism was gone. One side of the AEU banner, for example, shows machines of the future being built by engineering tradesmen 'whose skills underpin the well-being of society'. On the other, a heroic, male industrial worker:

> in overalls, virile and alert, stands astride the
> Earth. Spread before him is a blueprint from which
> he is taking a size. His feet are firmly set with
> disdain among the broken munitions of war.

The artistic section also made displays for the annual Labour Day march and other celebrations. In 1939, it produced a range of designs for floats, the displays with which unions advertised their past and present interests; interested unions chose from those on display in the Trades Hall's Unity Theatre. Impressed, *The Westralian Worker* wrote that the WAG had:

> shown the true Labor spirit of co-operation
> in the preparation of a remarkably diversified
> series of designs for floats suitable for inclusion
> in the procession.

Layman and Goddard describe one display adopted by the Amalgamated Engineering Union:

> The Engineers slogan was 'we work for peace' and
> the tableau concerned the threat to world peace
> posed by fascism. CIVILISATION is represented
> by the modern city building atop the truck and the
> panorama of tall buildings around its sides. At the
> rear, civilization is menaced by heavy field artillery
> while three men with rifles stand guard. Around the
> edge, the cityscape has been replaced by a phalanx
> of shells representing the threat of the fascist powers
> to the world.

Keith George directed the display, and Axel Poignant filmed the procession. The armistice between Labor and communists, or at least with the WAG, was working.

LITERARY

The Guild seems to have had three separate and successive literary sections. The first, set up at the beginning, was, according to Vic Arnold later: 'to provide plays written on local subjects of social significance', written collectively by members. One play was an exercise in collective writing about the trials of group settlers, featuring participants in a disastrous scheme to settle families in the great forests of the South West. It was never performed, and the new method of collective writing did not go well; it apparently alarmed the members involved. Nonetheless, it continued.

The literary section was also educational, and the Guild had many experts on hand. In May 1937, KSP lectured on the short story, urging prospective writers to write about the 'real and vital life around them' – as she had done in her novels. In June that year, Keith George spoke to prospective playwrights about different styles in writing plays for stage and radio. Much later, in 1941, the section ran a series of discussions on modern English literature, featuring the works of Aldous Huxley, D. H. Lawrence and T. S. Elliot.

In late 1937, a new literary section formed, in part to write and produce a revue for the Labor Party in an upcoming federal election campaign. Titled *The Workers' Art Guild Presents, A Political Satire, The Lyons Bungles*, it played at the Trades Hall Unity Theatre with the byline: *Vote Labor. Make Curtin Prime Minister.* Entry was one shilling and tuppence, cheap enough to encourage a big attendance. Later that year, the section began another revue on the evils in the catering business, enlisting the help of Cecelia Shelley, the militant Secretary of the Hotel, Club, Caterers, Tea Room & Restaurant Employees Union.

It also produced a series of living newspapers: short, snappy plays like *Hold Your Wheat*, about a 'recent attempt to hold up wheat deliveries'. The living newspapers concept originated in the early days of the Bolshevik Revolution and involved producing 'rapid response' plays that addressed current crises. These were also popular in the USA during the Great Depression, as part of the Roosevelt government's Works Progress Administration employment schemes. Indeed, some of the living newspaper plays came to Australia from the USA. The collective writing method, which the WAG's literary section pioneered, wrote others. It seems that the literature department was now producing plays of its own, not in the small theatres that hosted the theatre group's plays, but in its own rooms in the city. Thus, in November 1940, it produced *Rehearsal, Feed the Sheep* and *Sub Editor's Room*.

Soon after, this literary section broke up. Many members joined another group outside of, but linked to, the WAG, that wrote agitprop plays and also living newspapers, on topics like soldiers' pay, the budget and the beer tax. These played to audiences at a dance hall and, on three WAG river cruises, to about 150 people each time. Arnold wrote:

> [This] writing group is politically conscious, topically minded and submits readily to criticism and discipline. It remains for us to work with this group, to catch up with them and to work out ways of taking the material to the most valuable and receptive audiences.

In early 1941, Arnold wrote that 'our writing machinery for production of agitprop is working better than the Theatrical Department'. This was a bad sign for the WAG; the theatrical department was the public face of the WAG and seemed to be in terminal decline, if the literature section had indeed taken over most of its functions.

The WAG ended its shining career in late 1941. There are several competing explanations given for its demise, including a loss of momentum after Keith George left, the impact of World War II, a change in theatrical direction away from their radical roots, and heavy-handed interference by the local branch of the CPA. Hyde believed that the wartime plays were politically conservative and that the WAG 'became, increasingly an establishment company', with the consequent divisions in the WAG contributing to its decline. However, the list of plays produced in 1940 and 1941 does not support the argument that the WAG's offerings were now conservative. Although none of the 1940 plays was anti-fascist or antiwar, *The Women*, *This Bondage*, *Love on the Dole* and *Penalty Clause* were not conservative. The last play it produced, in 1941, was *Till the Day I Die*, the play with which it introduced itself to the public in 1936.

It is most likely that wartime austerity and repression, the loss of leading members and the conservative political environment contributed to the decline of the theatre. Hyde is right when he argues that the banning of the CPA in June 1940 and the earlier raids on, and arrests of, members, combined with the impact of war, led many members to go underground, put their heads down, join the military or go East. A quick roll call of those we know left the WAG is illustrative of an organisation in crisis. George finally left the Guild in 1939; Vike left for Melbourne in 1941, Harnett for Adelaide in 1943;

Arnold, Hepworth and wife Kathleen, Gordon Burgoyne, Hope Bath and John Hector all left for Sydney in 1940; John and Ray Oldham probably left for Sydney in 1939; and Max Ebert left for the East in 1940. With its leading members gone, and with radical art and culture unlikely to flourish in the new repressive and conservative wartime context, left-wing theatre vanished from Perth for another seven years. It re-emerged as the New Theatre.

NEW THEATRE

The New Theatre, with its headquarters in the rooms of the Modern Women's Club in the city, opened in August 1948 with the slogan: 'a march towards the kind of plays the people want to see – progressive plays and Australian plays'. Two veterans of Australian literature, Dymphna Cusack and Miles Franklin, wrote the first piece, *Call Up Your Ghosts,* a biting satire on the Australian publishing industry. Two young WA writers, Vic Williams and Dorothy Hewitt, accompanied the performance with poetry readings.

Another 11 plays followed, all staged in Perth's small theatres. *Mrs Warren's Profession*, by George Bernard Shaw, and WA author F. B. Vickers' play *Stained Pieces* played in 1949. In 1950, the New Theatre staged Oriel Gray's *Had We but World Enough*, Jim Crawford's two plays, *Miner's Right* and *Rocket Range* and US playwright Elmer Rice's anti-fascist play, *We the People*. In 1951, it staged Perth playwright Ben Kidd's play *Six Hungry Families*. In 1953, it staged two US plays: *Thirty Pieces of Silver*, an attack on McCarthyism in the USA by the US author, writer and communist Howard Fast; and US socialist and former merchant seaman Herb Tank's *Longitude 49*. Dick Diamond's classic musical story of the 1890s shearers' strike, *Reedy River*, played in 1954. The last play, in 1956, was another musical by Dick Diamond, *The Coolibah Tree*, exploring the world of paddle steamers on the Darling River. It is noteworthy that three of these plays were about Aboriginal people: Gray's *Had We but World Enough*; Vickers' *Stained Pieces*; and Crawford's *Rocket Range. Rocket Range* was truly revolutionary as the first Australian play to attempt to present the world through the eyes of Aboriginal and/or Torres Strait Islander people.

The postwar New Theatre was different to the WAG. Like the WAG, it was inspired by KSP, who formed it with left-wing theatrical identities Bob Smith, Harry Leighton and Joan Broomhall. However, it was just a theatrical company; and, based on the longstanding and successful Sydney

New Theatre, it never undertook the revolutionary work in literature, music, art and dancing that the WAG did. It also turned to Australian plays for most of its productions, because both the CPA and its fraternal cultural organisations were going through a radical nationalist phase, a belief that Australian radicalism had its roots in Australian history, particularly its cultural history. This was apparent sometimes in the use of Australian folk traditions, sometimes in opposition to US cultural imperialism. The Perth Theatre opposed, for example, what it called the 'very great menace of the popular Hollywood film'. Indeed, building an Australian theatre became one of the key distinguishing features of Perth's New Theatre. Gone was the bullish revolutionism of the WAG. Art was used less as a weapon and more as a means of building a more authentic Australian culture: the 'art of the people, by the people, for the people'.

A completely new troupe of actors and technical and production staff created the New Theatre's plays. There appear to be no common actors, directors or technical people in the lists of people involved in the two companies, which is surprising, because its first play was staged just seven years after the last WAG play.

The main difference between the WAG and the New Theatre, however, is the press response: in the main, the local press, including the *Westralian Worker*, boycotted the New Theatre; only the *Workers' Star* gave it coverage. Only two plays received reviews, and it is hard to find anything else in the papers – other than in the advertising sections. That prewar openness of the Perth press to radical theatre had disappeared. The usual sources are all but silent on the New Theatre.

The Cold War is the obvious context, manifest in the rapid growth of tensions between the ALP and the Australian Communist Party (previously the CPA). At the federal level, that tension became apparent in 1949, when the Chifley government broke the communist Coal Miners' strike with troops. And, as the Catholic right of the ALP flexed its muscles, the National Executive was busy enforcing rules against joint membership of CPA fraternals, including the Sydney New Theatre. In WA, as Macintyre suggests, the Labor government, Arbitration Court and press led the exclusion of communists from all union posts.

Worse was to come with the election of the Menzies government. Its unsuccessful but damaging attempt to ban the CPA in 1951, the Petrov affair in 1954, the Australian reverberations of the Korean War, the Communist victory in China and the first test of an atomic bomb by the Soviet Union, all built Cold War tension in Australia. So, Macintyre notes, the CPA's postwar ambitions were halted and reversed. The effect on the CPA was disastrous. Its national membership, riding high at 17,000 in 1945, had fallen to 10,000 just five years later.

Unlike the WAG, the New Theatre never had dedicated groups devoted to art, music, dance and literature. It did have a number learning the theatrical ropes: artists doing design; a music group; a discussion group about theatrical issues; a group working on experimental plays; an editorial group producing its journal; and a social group producing the experimental plays and organising outings. It also had its own journal, *New Theatre*, which published five issues in 1950 before winding up. Each issue accompanied a new play, so they included programs and notes on the author and the play. They also covered literary and theatrical issues of many kinds. In one issue, US author Howard Fast wrote about his experience at the anti-communist riots at Peekskill in the USA in 1949, where Paul Robeson was the key speaker. Another advocated for a national theatre, to rescue Australian culture from what the New Theatre regarded as the growing threat from trashy Hollywood films.

Conversely, like the WAG, the New Theatre also played for leftist and good causes. In 1949, it supported the creation of a branch of the Australian Peace Council in Perth, which old friend KSP headed. In 1952, it supported metal workers in the big Galvin's margins strike: entertaining the strikers at meetings, putting on shows for strikers' kids and raising funds. On another occasion, it performed *Five Poor Families*, at the then outer coastal suburb of Coogee, for destitute families forced to camp out because of a housing shortage in Perth. In 1954, it performed *Reedy River* for the Bassendean P&C Association, to raise funds for a school library, and at the Fremantle Town Hall for the Fremantle branch of the Slow Learning Children's Association.

Also like the WAG, the New Theatre entered plays in the new Perth Theatre Council's festivals. There is no record of the first play it entered in 1952, just a reference to an entry. The next year, it performed Tank's *Longitude 49* to a generally good review in the *West Australian* (which probably reviewed it only because it was staged at the festival). The reviewer praised the acting and stage craft but criticised the rude language.

This was the first of only two reviews of its plays. The second was a rather patronising review of *Reedy River*. Fedilio wrote in the *West Australian*:

> *Reedy River* is certainly an entertainment out of the ordinary. In its material presentation it is also a very unsophisticated one... A fairly large audience laughed at its homely jokes and generally gave it a very friendly reception.

On the whole, the *Workers' Star* liked the New Theatre's plays but demanded a stricter adherence to socialist realism. In reviewing Rice's play, which showed how big business used war as a way out of economic crises, it argued that the play did not show 'the action and organisation of the working masses of the USA' nearly enough. It criticised Jim Crawford's play, *Miner's Right*, which dramatised the struggle between mine owners and miners, because it did not show the radical and militant side of miners' actions strongly enough:

> Weaknesses such as these must be overcome if left drama is to use to the full its opportunities, to enrich the political understandings of its audiences and bring them further into activity.

Finally, the New Theatre made no bones about the fact that it took advertisements. There may have been two reasons for this. Firstly, it must have been struggling for funds; secondly, its box-office takings were not big enough to support it by themselves, as they apparently had been for the WAG.

The New Theatre folded in 1956. Limited sources make it difficult to say why, although it is likely that the difficult Cold War political environment proved too much for the theatre and its supporters. However, it would be a shame to regard the New Theatre as simply an epilogue or afterthought to the WAG. Each group represents a remarkable achievement in Western Australian cultural and political life. Neither had the longevity of Sydney's New Theatre; instead, the WAG lit up Perth's cultural scene for seven years with its insurgent politics, while the New Theatre kept radical theatre afloat in unfavourable circumstances for another nine. Together, both groups established a radical tradition; but Perth had to wait another 10 years for the next burst of radical culture to arrive, this time in a very different context: The Sixties!

FURTHER READING

Bolton, Geoffrey, *Paul Hasluck: A Life*, Crawley, UWA Publishing, 2014.

Craig, Terry, 'Radical and Conservative Theatre in Perth in the 1930s: Western Australia between the Wars, 1919–1939', *Studies in Western Australian History*, no. 11, 1990, pp. 106–118.

Fox, Charlie, 'Katharine Susannah Prichard and the Inter-War Peace Movement', in C. Fox, B. Oliver and L. Layman (eds.), *Radical Perth, Militant Fremantle*, Perth, Black Swan Press, 2017.

Gilbert, Helen and Lo, Jacqueline, *Performance and Cosmopolitics: Cross Cultural Transactions in Australasia*, London, Palgrave McMillan, 2009.

Gooding, Janda, *Western Australian Art and Artists, 1900–1950*, Perth, Art Gallery of Western Australia, 1987.

Hasluck, Paul, *Mucking About*, Crawley, UWA Press, 1994.

Hyde, Dylan, '"We Present This Play Not for Your Entertainment but For your Chastening": the Worker's Art Guild, 1935–1942', *Papers in Labour History*, no. 18, 1997, pp. 40–53.

Hyde, Dylan, *Art was their Weapon: the History of the Perth Workers' Art Guild*, Fremantle, Fremantle Press, 2019.

Layman, Lenore, Goddard, Julian, Wise, Wendy and Ho, Robin (eds.), *Organise! Labour: a Visual Record*, Perth, Trades and Labour Council of Western Australia, 1988.

Macintyre, Stuart, *Militant: the Life and Times of Paddy Troy*, Sydney, Allen & Unwin, 1984.

Milner, Lisa, 'The Cultural Front: Left Cultural Activism in the Post War Era', in J. Puccini, E. Smith and M. Worley (eds.), *The Far Left in Australia Since 1945*, Milton, Routledge, 2019.

Throssell, Ric, *Wild Weeds and Wind Flowers: the Life and Letters of Katharine Susannah Prichard*, Melbourne, Angus & Robertson, 1975.

CHAPTER 8

Adelaide New Theatre

Peter D Douglas

BAKER'S COLLECTIVE: 1937-38

John S. Baker was a telegrapher and trade unionist from country South Australia. He came to Adelaide during 1936 in his early twenties. In February 1937, he circulated an advertising pamphlet:

> At 11 Pitt Street, Adelaide, opposite the Methodist Mission, a 'collective' has been formed, where young people suited to the work may receive a free training as performers for an Australian Theatre. The objective is the establishment of a performance company of Australian theatre workers from whose association will be developed a dramatic form expressive of their natures and country. As a business organisation it will, eventually, be managed and owned collectively. At the end of February 1938 the membership of this collective will be doubled to 40, for another years [sic] training. Applicants of any age, for these 20 positions will be considered, mainly for their proficiency in athletics, as instrumentalists and singers, or in the trades of carpentry, electronics and dressmaking.

We know little of Baker or the collective he formed. However, an idea of what he had in mind becomes much clearer when viewed in the light of two series of articles he wrote from October 1937 to May 1938, published in the *South Australian Workers' Weekly Herald*. The 21 articles demonstrated a detailed knowledge of national and international workers' theatre, dating from the October 1917 Russian Revolution. The first two chapters discuss the clear connections between the New Theatre's global development and the October Russian Revolution.

The first series comprised four of Baker's pieces: 'Sit Down Theatre'; 'Elections Theatre'; 'Unionist, Actor, Dramatist'; and 'The Right Theatre is Left'. All were a 'call to arms', urging local theatre companies to begin producing plays that were of national and international political concern to everyday South Australians, rather than staging works that chronicled 'ancient Greece', 'Shakespearian England' or the 'France of Moliére [sic]'.

The second series of articles, 17 in total, was titled *Workers' Theatre of The World*. Each article concerned the history, development and health of leftist theatre in various countries, including the USA, many European nations, China, Mongolia and Australia.

Baker's main political concern, as it was for many at the time, was the rise of fascism. He applauded American New Theatre's 1935 world premiere of Clifford Odets' one-act play *Waiting for Lefty*, about the plight of New York taxi drivers and their vote to strike after company thugs murdered Lefty, the union leader. Baker won even more praise for the company's next production, Odets' full-length *Till the Day I Die*, which directly challenged fascism. Set in Nazi Germany, it centres on an underground group agitating for the restoration of democracy. A member is caught by the Gestapo, interrogated, released, and then falsely identified by his comrades as an informer. Rejected by them, he commits suicide to end his torment and ensure his own fidelity. Both plays were influential in their spread from the USA and saw the transition of workers' theatre companies across the world into New Theatres. Baker described this global movement as a coalition of liberals and militants who had 'organised their forces for the destruction of Fascism'.

Baker's knowledge of the Australian movement was equally comprehensive but not nearly as complimentary. In 1936, Sydney and Melbourne

New Theatres had both mounted *Waiting for Lefty*. Following international precedent, they then announced an intention to stage *Till the Day I Die*.

Baker said of these developments: 'the best of a bad lot playing in Australia at the moment is the New Theatre League of Sydney'; but he then accused them of existing only to 'entertain Sydney's left intelligentsia' by presenting 'old fashioned dramas about Nazi Germany and New York strikes, that, now, are not pointers but pointless.'

As earlier chapters in this volume note, controversy had arisen in 1936 when state authorities banned the Melbourne and Sydney companies from performing *Till the Day I Die*, because the German Consul had lodged an objection. The Sydney production had opened as scheduled before police entered the Pitt Street Theatre in an attempt to halt proceedings. When a young actor, Vic Arnold, stepped forward and asked the audience whether they wanted to see the show, the answer was emphatic: 'Yes!' The performance continued without further interruption. Baker described these events as a 'fiasco', adding: 'by consolidating their position following a fortunate accident these theatre workers learning their policy of self-centredness have taken the lead in the Australian theatre.' The 'fortunate accident' was the broad level of interest and popularity generated for New Theatre in the eastern states by the controversial decision to ban *Till the Day I Die*. This reflected the views of that era; many found the idea of Australian governments obliging a fascist regime distasteful.

The spark for Baker's negativity appears to have been the issue of relevance. Baker clearly thought that, although New Theatre had 'taken the lead in Australian Theatre', unlike certain international counterparts, it also had a tendency towards classist elitism and self-indulgence. He did say a few kind words about the Melbourne ensemble, which had just devised and staged *Thirteen Dead*, a dramatisation of the Wonthaggi mine disaster. The play took the miners' side, saying that the company had blood on its hands; its negligence was the real cause of the explosion and deaths, not some foolish miner with a cigarette. The key for Baker was, most likely, that after the King's Theatre season concluded in July 1937, the production was then taken to Wonthaggi and performed for the mining community.

It wasn't until his penultimate piece in the *Herald* that Baker gave any firm clue as to his own political leaning within the cultural coalition he was advocating. In article 16, he writes:

> **Russian theatre has fought for the Revolution with the workers, struggled with them to overcome**

interventionist, civil warmonger, and counter revolutionary. It has followed, reflected and interpreted the paralleled periods of economic ruin and recovery, industrial, agrarian, cultural and constitutional revolutions. It stands today as the embodiment of the world's greatest theatre.

I interviewed John S. Baker twice by telephone in 1988 at the outset of this research. He remained largely enigmatic about his own political views, the company he formed and the personal associations he made while in Adelaide. There are, however, certain scraps of evidence that might provide some clarity.

Among the bibliographical references Baker listed in his articles are works by Diderot, Mercia, Romaine Rolland and a little-known performance theorist named Enid Rose. These works are grouped together, in this order, within the exclusive personal theatre collection of a woman named Nan Angel Floy Symon, making this the most likely place for Baker to have sourced them – and suggesting a possible association between the two.

Angel Symon was born and grew up in Adelaide at the turn of the 20th century. Her father, Jessiah, was a lawyer who helped frame Australia's Federal Constitution. Angel Symon attended local private schools and finishing academies in Europe before going on to study economics at London University. Throughout the 1920s, she toured Europe, taking in theatre and compiling her extensive performing arts collection. On returning to Australia, she administered a touring theatre company from Melbourne before settling back in Adelaide as a volunteer kindergarten worker and theatre enthusiast. She never married or had any children.

Angel Symon and John Baker were from vastly different backgrounds. Baker grew up in poverty and, during his time in Adelaide, lived in a one-room hovel off Pirie Street. This class divide raises the question: how was it possible for the two even to meet, let alone work together?

A likely link is Angel Symon's cousin, Eric Symon, who came to South Australia to convalesce after being badly injured in World War I, settling on a farm near Murray Bridge. He moved to Adelaide during the Depression and, in the mid-1930s, opened South Australia's first left bookshop: The Anvil, also just off Pirie Street. He soon launched the Left Book Club. In later years, he became a writer of agitprop theatre.

On arrival in Adelaide, a militant trade unionist like Baker would probably have gravitated to the city's only left bookshop, a few doors up the street. It is entirely possible that the two men not only met, but became collaborators, along with Eric's cousin Angel, whose input would have been of great value in the establishment of Baker's left theatre company.

Whatever the case, Baker did confirm, speaking by landline from his home in NSW, that the collective he formed during 1937 staged several productions – including *Waiting for Lefty*, Soviet playwright Tretyakov's *Roar China* and Ernst Toller's *Masses and Man*. He was evasive when asked the name of his company. Regardless, Baker's support for an anti-fascist cultural coalition of the left, and his group's staging of *Waiting for Lefty* as its inaugural production – both New Theatre cornerstones – leaves little doubt that his Collective was very much part of the national and worldwide New Theatre expansion of the time.

Baker also revealed that the ensemble was in existence for about 18 months, probably disbanding shortly after his final article, 'The Right Theatre is Left', appeared in the *Herald* on 6 May 1938. Following this, Baker moved to Sydney. In later years, he became a key figure within the Australian trade union movement.

NTL: 1938-39

On 13 November 1938, roughly six months after John S. Baker had left Adelaide, Eric Symon's Left Book Club convened a meeting at the Adelaide Jewish Club. This meeting oversaw formation of the Left Book Club Theatre. Prominent at this meeting was a leftist theatre enthusiast and practitioner named Hal Pritchard, who had known Baker. The two men had certainly exchanged theory, to mutual benefit, but it is unclear whether or not Pritchard was ever a member of Baker's collective.

The Left Book Club Theatre's first production opened on 29 January 1939. It was an agitprop piece called *Vote No*, obtained from the interstate New Theatre network's script exchange section of the nationally published *Communist Review*. The play's centrepiece was military conscription, a hot topic with World War II looming. Hal Pritchard played the lead character, Billy Hughes. The company's first season consisted of a single performance at a Left Book Club Theatre picnic in Long Gully, 50 miles south of Adelaide.

A month later, the ensemble renamed itself NTL and gave a presentation at the Jewish Club of *Remember Pedrocito*. Melbourne New Theatre also mounted this play, about the rise of fascism in Spain, later that year. Originally, the Adelaide company had scheduled the production to be broadcast over radio, but that did not happen because the radio station in question was accused of espionage and taken off air for sending secret messages to the Germans.

With Communist Party financial assistance, the NTL then relocated from the Jewish Club to a basement below extensive terraces on the city's fringe, at the corner of Hackney Road and North Terrace. The CPA also gifted a snooker table. The venue opened on 29 April 1939 with a piece called *Beer Garden,* performed to celebrate the event.

Tensions between the New Theatre and the Communist Party soon developed over the issue of non-party members using the facility. The CPA withdrew funding. The company looked for another home and moved to an attic on the northwest corner of Hindmarsh Square in the city. After this move, the group continued for another six months with readings and agitprop performances in the new space. By the beginning of 1940, however, it had ceased functioning.

The main reason for the theatre's closing was the CPA's position on the war. When war was first declared, some communists in the company enlisted for military service, consistent with the party's united front anti-fascist policy. In August 1939, following the negotiation of the Hitler–Stalin non-aggression pact, the CPA reversed its support for the war – leaving those who had enlisted high and dry. The CPA was stigmatised, as were affiliated bodies such as the New Theatre, and this ultimately led to the company's demise.

LABOUR YOUTH THEATRE: 1940–42

It was another year before New Theatre activity reignited in South Australia. Vic Arnold, the actor who'd confounded the banning of *Till the Day I Die* at the Sydney opening by securing audience support for the play's continuance, was the agent. In early 1941, NSW sent him to Adelaide with the express purpose of reviving that branch. By May of that year, he had successfully relaunched the South Australian movement, which went on to work at a prolific rate.

Arnold enlisted the help of a prominent young female trade union activist named Marjory Johnston. They secured facilities at Trades Hall and began gathering members, including Hal Pritchard, who had been with NTL. They adopted a new name: Labour Youth Theatre. Probably, they chose to avoid New Theatre to reduce the risk of persecution because of its known connection with the now outlawed Communist Party.

The company published a notice in the Workers' *Weekly Herald* announcing formation of the new youth theatre group. Its objective was to 'produce popular theatre that deals with issues of concern to working people'. The notice also announced that the Labour Youth Theatre was currently in rehearsal for a full-length Russian comedy by Valentine Kateyer [sic] called *Squaring the Circle*. It urged all prospective contributors to contact the group's Secretary, 'Marjory Johnston at Room 35, Trades Hall, Grote Street, Adelaide.'

Squaring the Circle, first performed in the Soviet Union during 1927, focused entirely on the new norms to which young people in particular were exposed as a result of the transition to communism. This focus may have indicated that the Labour Youth Theatre, in keeping with Communist Party policy, was staying well away from any commentary on the war effort. Interestingly, at the same time the Adelaide production was 'playing to large enthusiastic audiences', the Melbourne New Theatre was having a sell-out season of the antiwar *I'd Rather be Left*, as did the Sydney company later that year. That play featured a song that became something of a blue-collar anthem: *There'll Always be a Menzies While There's a BHP*, sung to the tune of *There'll Always be an England*.

Following *Squaring the Circle*, the Labour Youth Theatre produced a repertoire of agitprop pieces. They included *Federal Budget*, *Union Label*, *It's Up to You*, *No Conscription* and *Three Wives*, performed at venues and forums such as the Botanic Park Labour Ring, the State Conference of Labour Women and the Trades and Labour Council building; and for organisations such as the Metal Workers' Union, the Furnishers' Union and the Builders' Labourers' Federation.

However, this concentration on agitprop, a form of theatre more suited to promoting the communist cause and reinforcing an antiwar stance, as the first two chapters discuss, all changed on 22 June 1941. Germany invaded the Soviet Union, and British Prime Minister Churchill declared that same day that the Soviet Union would receive all possible allied support.

On 18 July, the Labour Youth Theatre announced in the *Herald* its intention to revive *Waiting for Lefty*, a play with a strong anti-fascist undertone, indicating a return to the position of renewed support for the war effort. The season spanned 1–3 September 1941 and was applauded enough for an encore performance on 17 September, along with Catherine Duncan's living newspaper-style production, *Soak the Rich*.

Labour Youth Theatre published a notice in the *Herald* on 28 November, confirming its new political and artistic direction: it 'had abandoned agitprop in favour of producing realist drama' and 'is about to begin rehearsals on a full-length play by Clifford Odets called *Till the Day I Die*.' Melbourne and Sydney New Theatres had set the precedent earlier in the month, and Sydney had successfully applied to have the pre-war ban lifted.

Labour Youth Theatre's *Waiting for Lefty* was a success, but they never performed *Till the Day I Die*; and in early 1942, just a matter of weeks later, the company had almost completely disappeared. The attack at Pearl Harbour on 7 December 1941 and the subsequent Japanese invasion of Malaya had brought the war to Australia's northern doorstep. Members of Labour Youth Theatre, including Hal Pritchard, enlisted – depleting the company once again. Labour Youth Theatre gave its last recorded performance, reported in the Labour Ring section of the *Herald* as a 'play about May Day.'

ADELAIDE NEW THEATRE: 1946-60

Towards the end of 1946, employees of the Brompton Gasworks staged a sit-in strike; it lasted 42 days. The sit-in generated a great deal of sympathy for the strikers among the local labour community, which provided both moral and practical support for their cause: organising a strike fund, freely donating food and establishing an entertainment committee. A communal Christmas party and nine different performance groups provided entertainment for affected families during the sit-in. The strike was successful, and this event triggered the re-emergence of workers' theatre in Adelaide.

Just before the strike, a small group of performers had formed an un-named company and rehearsed a repertoire of agitprop plays. The Brompton Gasworks sit-in provided the first opportunity for this ensemble to perform publicly. Participants included a number of actors, such as Marjory Johnston, who'd been with Vic Arnold's Labour Youth Theatre, and others who not only helped found the new company, but also became instrumental in Adelaide New Theatre's future development.

The first of these was Mary Warren. During the war years, Mary was a union organiser in munitions, working alongside Elizabeth Johnston, sister-in-law to Marjory Johnston. Mary and Elizabeth were the first two female union organisers in South Australia to be appointed as representatives to the United Trades and Labour Council.

Shortly after the war, Mary joined a local amateur company called the Adelaide Theatre Group. Here she met Rosemary Smith, who was to become prominent in Adelaide New Theatre. Smith had been involved with the trade union movement and various labour youth organisations, firstly in her hometown of Perth, then in Melbourne from the early 1940s. She was soon acting in productions for the Eureka Youth League Theatre, the youth arm of Melbourne New Theatre.

At the end of the war, Rosemary moved to Adelaide with her family and looked for a leftist drama group to join. Discovering that there was none, she joined the Adelaide Theatre Group, which had a policy of producing new Australian plays. There she met Mary. The two quickly became friends, but they found Group Theatre's lack of any issue-based or political drama frustrating. They decided to branch out on their own.

Marjorie and Elizabeth Johnston were soon on board, along with another Labour Youth Theatre member from the war years, Ron Heiser. Midway through 1946, Mary and Rosemary moved into share accommodation at a subdivided old mansion called Riverside at 20 Fitzroy Terrace, Prospect – an inner-city suburb. These premises became the group's headquarters. At its inaugural meeting, each member contributed £5 for the purchase of sets, props and costumes required for the company's planned production of an agitprop repertoire. The group performed this repertoire at the Gasworkers' sit-in strike.

Encouraged by the results, the group decided early in 1947 to expand and try to popularise its activity with a more ambitious project, in a proper theatre, with a cast beyond its slim membership of five. Through word of mouth, the small ensemble advertised its intention within Adelaide's left network, including the Left Book Club, the Anvil Bookshop, the Trades and Labour Council and the Communist Party. However, in addition to these traditional avenues of support, the group also drew upon a resource which had not previously featured within the Adelaide New Theatre movement's development: university students.

In April 1946, a Socialist Club formed at Adelaide University. A short time later, the Students' Theatre Group appeared. The numbers passing between the two quickly grew, although none of the plays produced could be described as leftist. There were also strong connections between these two university groups and other elements of Adelaide's left network.

One connecting member was Don Porter. In 1947, Don was in the Socialist Club, involved with the Students' Theatre Group, a member of the Left Book Club and a patron of the Anvil Bookshop. He went on to work with Adelaide New Theatre for the duration of its life. However, his first involvement came as a result of the small agitprop group's word of mouth advertisement stating its intention to stage a major production. Porter, along with many other

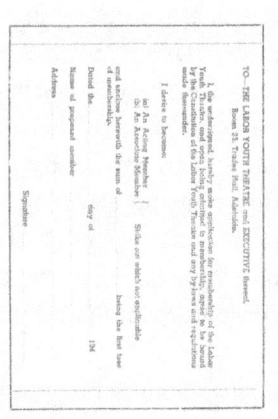 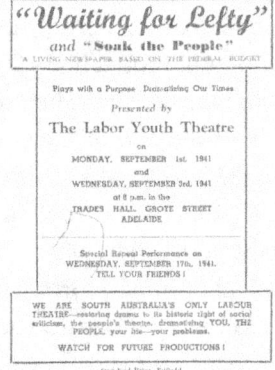

Handbill for Waiting for Lefty, 1941.

theatre enthusiasts from Adelaide University and the broader left network, all turned up at the company's first expanded production meeting early in 1947 and expressed their interest.

The divisive effect of the Cold War fuelled enthusiasm for this new theatrical push. At Adelaide University, the Socialist Club was the frequent subject of jibes and outright abuse which conservative pockets of the student population published in the university newspaper, *On Dit*. Members of left organisations, such as the Socialist Club, viewed this new conservatism as the re-expression of old fascist tendencies and welcomed the opportunity to become involved in a theatrical venture committed to combatting it. After a series of meetings, the newly formed company had selected a play, cast it, negotiated a venue, and organised a rehearsal schedule. The play was the evergreen *Waiting for Lefty*, and the venue, yet again, Trades Hall.

A capacity audience received the show enthusiastically at its one and only July performance. A few days later, a press notice announced a new name for the theatre group, stating that the NTL had mounted the production of *Waiting for Lefty*. Some of the university contingent did not receive the announcement well, objecting to their public association, without consultation, with an organisation with known communist allegiance.

The name remained, however, through the influence of people such as Hal Pritchard, who'd joined the Communist Party during his time with Labour Youth Theatre and had retained membership throughout his time in the army. The new company, still forming, invited Pritchard to become

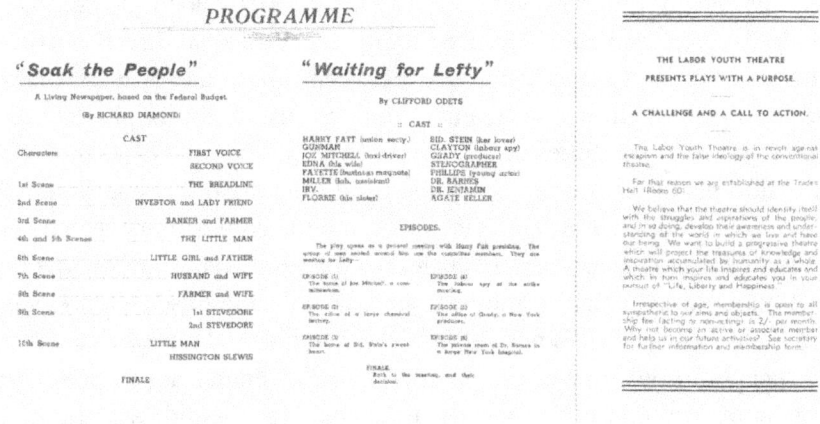

involved and act the character of Joe in *Waiting for Lefty*, the part he played in Labour Youth Theatre's production. Although Pritchard declined the offer for personal reasons, he did work as an adviser on the production and remained peripherally involved with Adelaide New Theatre throughout the remainder of its tenure.

Dispute over adoption of New Theatre as the group's name saw the departure of some, but the effect was negligible. Over the following three years, Adelaide New Theatre was able to consolidate the success *Waiting for Lefty* had begun.

The next production was a social realist play called *Welcome Home*, by Melbourne New Theatre activist Jim Crawford. It addressed the hypocrisy faced by Australian service personnel returning from the war. By 1947, Melbourne New Theatre had also staged another of Crawford's short plays, *Rocket Range*.

Over the next 12 months, Adelaide New Theatre produced three full-length plays which all presented similar commentaries on Cold War developments. The first was Maxwell Anderson's *Winterset*, staged on 1 and 2 March 1948. *Winterset* muses on the fate of a terminally ill mobster who is falling from power and intent on committing one last despicable deed before he dies. Set within the 'lower depths' of a US metropolis, the play presents a bleak commentary on the forces responsible for the collective US psyche's darker side and its quest for power, whatever the cost.

Then, for something completely different, on 9 and 10 April 1948, Adelaide New Theatre staged Aristophanes' comedy *Lysistrata* – another dig at war, but from a completely different perspective. This play expanded the company's appeal by targeting an audience not usually catered for so directly: women. The men in *Lysistrata* started the war between Sparta and Athens, and the women end it through ingenuity and common sense: they simply deny their husbands sex until hostilities cease.

The third play in the series was Auden and Isherwood's *The Ascent of F6*, staged on 28–31 July 1948. This play is a symbolic commentary on the death of the British Empire. Its narrative parodies the English adventure novel and focuses on a group of British mountaineers who decide to scale a previously unassailable peak as a statement of patriotic endeavour. However, in contrast to the successful outcome characteristic of the adventure novel, one by one these men of fortitude perish on the mountain's face – and, with them, the spirit of British colonialism. *The Ascent of F6* may have been intended as the company's own small contribution to the Empire's decline.

All three of these dramas were stylised verse plays, representing a temporary departure from 'slice of life' social realism. The person who directed all three influenced the decision to produce them: Frank Bailey. Bailey was a public servant employed in the Department of Motor Registration. However, he had earlier trained in London as a director at the Royal Academy of Dramatic Art. Back in Adelaide, without opportunities to work in professional theatre, Bailey spent his spare time working with amateur groups. He was renowned locally and had directed many successful productions. Bailey had also worked with Hal Pritchard and Agnes Dobson in the Independent Theatre before the war. On the New Theatre's revival, he supported the company by securing production facilities at the University of Adelaide's conservatorium and helping the group to stage this impressive trio of plays.

On 13 and 14 May 1949, the company returned to a social realist format with a production of Arthur Miller's *All My Sons*. This play exposed the middle-American free enterprise ethic as hypocritical and treacherous. It concerns a patriotic mid-western family which has lost a son in the war. As the narrative unravels, the audience learns that, by selling faulty machinery from his business to the armed forces, the father had not only been complicit in his son's death but had also sealed the fate of many other military personnel.

After *All My Sons*, the company did not stage a major production for almost a year. However, it was by no means idle during this time, initiating a range of activities which further consolidated its place. By June 1948, the company had established the New Theatre Film Society; over the following nine months, it screened a range of international films. Among them were

René Clair's *An Italian Straw Hat*, Basil Wright's *Song of Ceylon*, Edward Porter's *The Great Train Robbery*, Chaplin's *The Tramp* and Pudovkin's *The Mother*. During the same period, Adelaide New Theatre also held regular play readings at the Jewish Club and Riverside. Works included Shakespeare's *As You Like It*, Synge's *Riders to the Sea*, Oriel Gray's *Lawson*, Irwin Shaw's *Bury the Dead*, Ibsen's *A Doll's House* and Molière's *A Physician in Spite of Himself*.

In March 1950, the company announced in the Communist Party newspaper *Tribune* that it was going to stage yet another production of *Waiting for Lefty*. It did so on 28 and 29 March and received a glowing review in the *Tribune*. This also marked the directorial debut of Mary Miller, née Warren, who compiled an impressive list of directing credits with the company over the following eight years. From this historical juncture, the company's artistic, technical and administrative personnel remained relatively consistent, and its theatrical output steadied.

In 1951, the company added another string to its artistic bow by forming a subsidiary ensemble called the Wattle Dance Group. In April of that year, Adelaide New Theatre and the Wattle Dance Group travelled to Sydney and participated in their respective performance competitions at the Youth Carnival for Peace and Friendship. The Wattle Dance Group won third prize over some highly fancied international entries. But Adelaide New Theatre was the dark horse: the surprise winner of the drama competition, coming in ahead of the Sydney and Melbourne companies. The Adelaide group presented the world premiere of *Land of Morning Calm*, set in North Korea. It concerns Australian and US involvement in the military conflict occurring there at the time. Melbourne journalist and short story writer Nance McMillan wrote the play.

Arriving back in Adelaide, the company restaged McMillan's play. In August and September, it presented Oriel Gray's newest work, *Sky Without Birds*, which explores the plight of a New Australian Jew as he settles in a small railway town on the Nullarbor Plain and attempts to come to terms with Australian life. The company rounded off 1952 with a production of Donald Ogden's *How I Wonder*.

In May 1953, Adelaide New Theatre presented a season of one-act plays, including Chekhov's *The Anniversary*, directed by Mary Miller. *Mary's Own Paper*, circulated from the Mary Martin Bookshop, reviewed the show. The original Angry Penguin himself, poet Max Harris, owned and ran the bookshop, edited the paper and was its main critic. His review was positive:

> Such a play demands creative imagination and skill from the producer [director]. Mary Miller has both. The characters were all convincingly represented by a good team of actors. One can only hope to see more Mary Miller productions.

In August, the company produced Oriel Gray's *Had We but World Enough*, which highlights the issue of racial prejudice in an Australian country town. The play concerns the plight of an Aboriginal girl, Lily Palmer, who has been cast as Christ's mother in the local school's Easter nativity production. The decision to have a Black girl playing the Virgin Mary meets with resentment and outright hostility from the white community, and a vigorous public debate ensues. Blaming herself for the conflict, Lily disappears into a stormy night and is found dead next morning at the foot of a collapsed bridge. The community is left to ponder its culpability over what could have been either suicide or a tragic accident. Max Harris also reviewed *Had We but World Enough*:

> So few plays of this calibre can be found in Australia... The producer, Bryce Stewart and his team of sincere actors did a fine job presenting the play in the right way, with simplicity of action and decor. Each of them should receive a twig of the laurel; but the rest goes to Eric Walsh who played the reporter.

By 1954, Adelaide New was staging three to four major productions a year. It was travelling interstate to participate in national New Theatre skills workshops and competitions. It conducted regular New Theatre Club Nights to train its own expanding membership. It was also in the process of forming a music group, which became known as the Bushwhackers Band. The 100th anniversary of Eureka fell in 1954, so the company kicked off the year in nationalistic celebration with a suburban tour of *Lawson*.

Meanwhile, to mark the same event, Melbourne New Theatre writer Dick Diamond had penned *Reedy River*, addressing the problems that a group of shearers working outback faced in the wake of the 1891 shearers' strike. Earlier chapters have explained that the show's unique and outstanding feature was its music, with songs such as *The Ernabella Shore, My Old Black Billy, Banks of the Condamine, Click Go the Shears* and many more, which had not been in popular use since the late 19th century. More than anything, it was the revival of this popular Australian music tradition that helped *Reedy River* achieve its nationwide success. Sydney, Melbourne, Brisbane, Adelaide and Perth New Theatres performed the play to an estimated 500,000 people across metropolitan and country Australia during 1953–54.

After Adelaide New Theatre's suburban tour of *Lawson*, *Reedy River* took up most of 1954. Popular demand brought the show back a number of times. The first Adelaide season opened at the grand old Australia Theatre on Angas Street in the city. New Theatre then remounted it for a number of individual organisations before a return season at Stow Hall on Flinders Street, Adelaide. Restaging *Reedy River* was challenging. Many of the 40-odd actors, singers, dancers and musicians had to be recast for each season, which testifies to the level of performer depth Adelaide New Theatre enjoyed at this time.

Two events in December rounded off activity for that year: another new Australian work, *Home Brew*, by first time Sydney New Theatre writer Joan Clark, explored the Australia-wide housing crisis prevalent at the time; and the Bushwhackers Band and the Wattle Dance Group performed the songs and dances from *Reedy River* at a Christmas concert.

In 1955, Adelaide New Theatre staged two more new Australian musicals. The first was a comedy called *Song of 54*, by Len Dowdle, set in Melbourne and Ballarat during the time of Eureka. The second was Dick Diamond's sequel, *Under the Coolibah Tree*. This production showcased another series of revived, traditional Australian songs. The Bushwhackers Band and the Wattle Dance Group were again at the forefront. As with *Reedy River,* the company toured *Under the Coolibah Tree* through suburban Adelaide and nearby country towns.

One of the Adelaide group's most significant offerings for 1956 was Sydney New Theatre writer Dymphna Cusack's *Pacific Paradise*, which concerned a community of Pacific Islanders whose existence was threatened by hydrogen bomb testing. Clifford Odets' *Golden Boy* followed during March and April, and in June came Jean-Paul Satre's black absurdist comedy *Nekrassov*.

In August, Adelaide New Theatre produced Oriel Gray's *The Torrents*. The play is set in a newspaper office in a goldfield town of the late 19th century. Owners Rufus and Ben Torrent, father and son, have advertised for an assistant and are dumbfounded when an attractive, businesslike young female, Jenny Milford, turns up in reply to Ben's letter of acceptance. Jenny is determined to earn a living in a 'man's way'. She not only succeeds in persuading the Torrents to give her the position; through ingenuity and journalistic skill, she transforms the paper into a much more dynamic concern. She eventually becomes a partner in the business.

Of the writers whom Sydney New Theatre fostered, Oriel Gray was noteworthy as both a pioneer and a contributor to the movement's dramatic literary development. Oriel Gray joined New Theatre in 1938, a communist convert because of the Spanish Civil War. She was the first professional employed to write radio scripts for a Communist Party-sponsored program, and she further developed her skills by participating in New Theatre writers' workshops, writing and acting in revue sketches before composing full-length plays, beginning with *Lawson* in 1944.

Oriel Gray's involvement with the movement also demonstrates the CPA influence asserted within the New Theatre. In 1949, the communist push within the labour movement forced Chifley's federal Labor government to call out the army against striking coal miners. Gray considered the Communist Party tactic divisive and resigned her membership. By 1952, the New Theatre had all but severed its relationship with Oriel Gray, who said of this development: 'the dead hand of the Party came down on New Theatre.' She was not alone. Another New Theatre writer ostracised by the movement for not adhering to Party policy was Betty Roland. After contributing important works such as *War on the Waterfront*, in the late 1930s Roland was labelled a Trotskyist, and New Theatre did not produce another of her plays.

In the case of Oriel Gray, however, although her works were not produced in the eastern states after 1952, in 1953, Adelaide New Theatre contravened the Party line by staging *Had We but World Enough*. In 1954, it produced *Lawson* and, in 1957, it mounted this production of *The Torrents*.

The Torrents is a landmark in the history of Australian theatre but has gone largely unnoticed. Gray wrote the play in 1954 and submitted it to the inaugural Playwrights' Advisory Board of Sydney's playwrights' competition. In 1955, out of more than 200 scripts, *The Torrents* won jointly with Ray Lawler's *The Summer of the Seventeenth Doll*; the latter had a production by the newly formed Elizabethan Theatre Trust and went on to be recognised as a beacon in the development of new Australian drama. However, the Elizabethan Theatre Trust refused to produce *The Torrents*. The play did not have its world premiere until 1957, when Adelaide New Theatre mounted this production, with Mary Miller directing. Gray travelled to Adelaide for the season, which played to 'large enthusiastic audiences'.

Oriel Gray stayed on in Adelaide for a while after her play came down. By all accounts, she'd developed a warm relationship with the company, especially its core members, Mary Miller in particular. Gray returned to Adelaide intermittently to honour these friendships. Over the next 40 years, Gray went on to build an even more distinguished career, not only in theatre, but also as a screenwriter and novelist.

In November 1957, the Adelaide New Theatre staged another new Australian play, *The Day Before Tomorrow*, by Ric Throssell, son of Katharine Susannah Prichard. Like *Pacific Paradise*, *The Day Before Tomorrow* centred on the potential dangers of nuclear armament. The play pictures a stark portion of the earth soon after nuclear holocaust has all but wiped out civilisation. A journalist, his wife and their young daughter are among the few survivors. They shelter in a makeshift hovel, and the fight to survive reduces them to degradation. The daughter, Carol, prostitutes herself in exchange for food, and the parents come to accept the necessity. Eventually, a relief squad arrives – too late to prevent tragedy.

This bleak commentary contrasted starkly with the company's first production of 1958, a satirical review called *Sighs of the Times*, in which 19 performers presented 25 variety acts. These ranged in style from farce routines to song, dance and musical comedy. The sketches had titles like *Slaughter on King William Street*; *TV or Not TV*; *In Which we Strip*; *Hospitals*; *Leave it to the Ghouls*; and *Here we Slip on our Pelvis*. Eric Walsh directed *Sighs of the Times*, which played to near capacity houses. By all accounts, it was politically poignant and hilarious.

In June 1958, Adelaide New Theatre staged Edmund Morris' social realist *The Wooden Dish*, about a poor farming family in the southern USA who must decide whether or not to commit an ageing parent to an old people's home. In September, the company concluded the year's schedule by staging J. B. Priestley's *They Came to a City*.

After this, Adelaide New Theatre's activity and dramatic output declined drastically until 1960, when it ceased altogether. Research suggests that the company mounted only one major production during this time, a devised children's puppet show called *Topsy-Turvy Land* in February 1959. Although the reasons for such a rapid decline are not entirely clear, there were a number of influences.

THE END OF AN ERA

The Soviet Union's invasion of Hungary during 1956 had a profound effect on the CPA. Significant numbers condemned the act as treachery, disavowed the party and resigned, further alienating the CPA and associated organisations such as the New Theatre. Liberals who were otherwise sympathetic with Adelaide New Theatre's outwardly moderate political stance became suspicious and withdrew support – or just left. Others who remained began using pseudonyms, lest association with the New Theatre adversely affect their careers and lives generally. Finally, only the mainstays, people such as Mary Miller, her husband Frank and Don and Rosemary Porter, née Smith, remained.

By the late 1950s, this group no longer had the energy and dedication for the time-consuming, exhausting and thankless grind of producing amateur theatre. In 1960, Frank and Mary Miller took advantage of a job opportunity and moved to Whyalla. With their departure, the remaining meagre contingent also disbanded. Don Porter remained working in theatre; in 1960, he acted in South Australia's first subsidised professional production, Patrick White's *Ham Funeral*. The Elizabethan Theatre Trust produced the play, which the University of Adelaide Theatre Guild performed and John Tasker directed. Rosemary Porter, conversely, disillusioned by having committed so much to Adelaide New Theatre's development, only to see the company dissolve, decided to redirect her energies and devote her time to family life. She never worked in theatre again.

THE COLD WAR BACKLASH

Adelaide New Theatre never featured much in the local mainstream press. Nor did it rate a mention in the main chronicle of South Australian theatre history: *From Colonel Light to the Footlights*. This places a question mark over the group's significance; but those from within company ranks claimed that this was, purely and simply, censorship.

There were plenty of examples of censorship – internationally, nationally and locally – which made it difficult for groups linked to the CPA. In Hollywood, the House Committee on Un-American Activities had been blacklisting known and suspected communists from the film industry from the late 1940s. When the Menzies-led Liberal Party won government in 1949, it immediately outlawed the Communist Party (again). In 1954, Russian defector Vladimir Petrov's claim that communist spies were receiving 'Moscow gold' for working subversively within the labour movement helped return Menzies' government and split the Labor Party, which remained in opposition for the next 18 years.

In 1948, as a previous chapter describes, the *Sydney Morning Herald* ceased sending critics to review New Theatre shows and stopped accepting paid advertisements from the company after a production of Sean O'Casey's *The Star Turns Red* in Sydney. Anti-communist graffiti regularly defaced Melbourne New Theatre posters. In her article *New Theatre Movement Part 1*, Mona Brand said of these occurrences:

> In retrospect, this withdrawal of *Herald* coverage was the first icy blast of the Cold War that was to breathe on the Australian New Theatre movement for the next 12 years.

Nor was the Adelaide branch exempt from this Cold War backlash. During the late 1940s and 1950s, an ASIO agent worked as a subversive operative within the company. The agent was a 58-year-old widowed housewife

Members of the Adelaide Wattle Dance Group, in Sydney, 1951. L-R Dorothy Hodges, Kathleen Shertock, Gwen Uren, Skeet Lawrence, Brenda Kennedy, Fay Ingram, Flo Edmonds. Some of the costumes were sewn by Anne Neil, ASIO spy.

[58]

EVALUATION B2 GRATIS if paraphrased
Copy No. 2   D/1/28   SECRET
                REPORT NO. 4471

Event: 22 October, 1955
Information: 27 October, 1955
Report: 3 November, 1955

SOUTH AUSTRALIA

POLITICAL

ADELAIDE NEW THEATRE

"Welcome Home" Party for Dick DIAMOND

for D. Diamond
on New Theatre S.A.   Remarks: 1.
                               2.
                               3.
                               4.

GRATIS - if paraphrased

A "welcome home" party organised by the Adelaide New Theatre in honour of Richard F. ("Dick") DIAMOND, who has recently returned from the Fifth World Festival of Youth and Students for Peace at Warsaw, was held at the home of Pauline Adrienne ADAMS, 24 Highbury Street, Prospect on Saturday evening 22 October, 1955.

2. **Attendance**:

Approximately 43 persons were present including the following:

John Burnard AYLEN (M)
Anthony Edward BRAN and his wife
Reginald Percival BROWN
Mr. Norman COLLINS and his wife Joyce
John Booker DAWSON (M)
Dorothy HODGES (M)
Brian FISHER
Kevin FISHER (probably Kevin Dominic FISHER)
Dudley Richmond FISHER
Jean Isobel FINGER (M)
Mrs. Pat GLENISTER
Eileen Valerie HOWE (M)
Ivan Lynne Claude HOWE (M)
Lorna HAIGH
Beryl Effie JURY (M)
Roy Talbot JURY (M)
Marjorie Vivian JOHNSTON (M)
Brenda Florence KENNEDY (M)
Trevor LAWRENCE
Mary Patricia MILLER (M)
Rex Albert MUNN (M)
Beatrice MONRO
Frank MUELLER
Freda Bennett ("Anne") NEILL (M)
Judith RUSSELL
Mary Eileen SMALL
Pauline Adrienne ADAMS
Mary WHITE
George Frederick WHITE
Oldrich ZASKOLNY
Yvonne Cynthia GEARY (M)

GRATIS if paraphrased

ASIO surveillance report, 1955.

2. REPORT NO. 4471

David Carson GEARY (M)
Gerald Douglas BORN

3. The guest of honour, Dick DIAMOND, was asked to give some of his impressions of the 5th World Festival of Youth and Students for Peace at Warsaw.

(a) He stated that "whilst travelling through Italy and Austria on our way to Warsaw, we thought that we were the forgotten delegation because no one met the train throughout the journey; but a different story awaited us when we reached Warsaw where we were made very welcome."

(b) "I saw very little of the 'games' as I concentrated mainly on the theatre, which is my main interest."

(c) Dick DIAMOND then talked on his trip through Warsaw, China, Siberia, Moscow and Vienna etc., but stated nothing worthy of note.

(d) To cope with the large number of persons present at this social, the church hall adjacent to Pauline Adrienne ADAM's home had been hired for the evening. A very convivial air prevailed throughout the evening, and the guests wandered backwards and forwards from the church hall to the private house with replenished beer jugs.

4. <u>Sunday Evening Social 23 October, 1955</u>:

A further social to welcome Dick DIAMOND was organised by the Adelaide New Theatre, and held at the home of Peter Kimpton STALLEY, 17 Prescott Terrace, Rose Park. This social was primarily intended for the more intellectual types, and the following persons were among the 19 present:

Peter Kimpton STALLEY (M)
Eric Alfred RUSSELL (Adelaide University)
Dr. John BRAY (lawyer)
Derek Maurice van Abbe (Adelaide University)
Brian Robinson ELLIOTT (Adelaide University)
Sydney Harold LOVIBOND (M)-(Adelaide University)
John Booker DAWSON (M)
Colin BALLANTYNE (photographer and theatrical producer)
Frank MUELLER
Beatrice MONRO
Pauline Adrienne ADAMS (teacher - Education Department)
Jean Edna BLACKBURN (M)-(Teacher at Presbyterian Girls' College)
Gerard ("Dick") BLACKBURN (M)-(C.S.I.R.O.)

5. <u>Invited but did not attend</u>:

Charles JURY (Adelaide University)
Brian MEDLIN

6. This social evening was restricted to a very convivial and informal gathering at which the guest of honour, Dick DIAMOND, discussed his Warsaw visit personally with those present.

named Mrs Roy Neil, of Glenunga in Adelaide's eastern suburbs. She gave her exclusive story to the *Sunday Mail* after being discharged from ASIO because of ill health in 1962. She'd been recruited in 1949 after attending a conference organised by the peace movement; she informed ASIO, through a politically conservative associate, that the whole thing was being run by communists. Within two years of recruitment, Mrs Neil had joined the Communist Party, infiltrated 20 other communist organisations and was regularly reporting to ASIO.

Within Adelaide New Theatre, she worked as a seamstress, making costumes for the Wattle Dance Group, and as an organiser within New Theatre's International Film Society. Along with Elliot Johnston, she was a delegate to an international peace conference in the Soviet Union, where the Kremlin received her as a guest. Mrs Neil also travelled to Canberra as part of a peace conference delegation and had several private meetings with Vladimir Petrov shortly before his defection.

Throughout her eight years as a spy within the Communist Party and Adelaide New Theatre, Mrs Neil was only ever regarded as a hardworking, committed communist. After retirement from ASIO, she returned to being a volunteer church worker and activist within the Women's Liberal Country League.

Some people from other contemporary amateur companies of the time, including Adelaide Repertory, Independent Theatre and Group Theatre, dismissed any notion of the New Theatre suffering at the hands of censorship or being the subject of some conspiratorial subterfuge. Rather, they suggest, the main reason the press and history books ignored New Theatre was to do with competence: the company's shows simply weren't up to scratch and not worth reviewing. All the evidence seems to suggest, however, that Adelaide New Theatre was at least as proficient as its peers.

Reviews the company did receive indicate that it was a more than competent theatrical exponent. During the mid-1950s, Adelaide New Theatre enjoyed great popularity. Its performer depth, extensive membership and audience numbers would have turned other local amateur companies green with envy. The combined runs of *Reedy River* alone used up to 60 different actors, singers, dancers and musicians, not to mention production crew. It's difficult to imagine that the company could have prompted this level of involvement and audience response, or made shows such as *Land of Morning Calm*, *Reedy River*, *Under the Coolibah Tree*, *Sighs of the Times* and *The Torrents* the popular successes they were, if its theatrical abilities had been at all compromised. Conversely, revelation of Adelaide New Theatre's prolific activity, range of achievements, list of credits and popularity suggests the opposite: that the company was an extremely proficient local exponent of amateur theatre, particularly during its final years.

Regardless of whether or not there was any attempt to historically censor Adelaide New Theatre, the main facts concerning its existence are now clear. They offer a positive indication of the company's history and significance, both in South Australia and as part of the national movement.

FURTHER READING

Baker, John, *The Sit-Down Theatre*, Adelaide, Felstead & Ormsby, 1937.

Brand, Mona, 'New Theatre Movement Part 1,' *Theatre Australia*, October, 1978, pp. 13–15.

Brand, Mona, 'New Theatre Movement Part 2: Cold War and After', *Theatre Australia*, November, 1978, pp. 19–20.

Diamond, Lilian, 'New Theatre's First Decade', *New Theatre Review*, 1947–1948, pp. 3–13.

Douglas, Peter, *Origins: a History of the Adelaide New Theatre Movement*, M.A. diss., Adelaide, Flinders University of South Australia, 1991.

Harper, Ken, 'The Useful Theatre', *Meanjin*, vol. 43, 1984, pp. 56–71.

McCredie, Andrew (ed.), *From Colonel Light to the Footlights*, Adelaide, Pagel, 1988.

Moss, Jim, *Sound of Trumpets: History of the South Australian Labour Movement*, Adelaide, Wakefield, 1985.

Rees, Leslie, *A History of Australian Drama Vol. 1: The Making of Australian Drama 1830s to 1960s,* Sydney, Angus & Robertson, 1978.

Samuel, Raphael, McColl, Ewan and Cosgrove, Stuart, *Theatres of the Left 1880–1935: Workers' Theatre Movements in Britain and America*, London, Paul, 1985.

Stourac, Richard and McCreery, Kathleen, *Theatre as a Weapon: Workers' Theatre in the Soviet Union, Germany and Britain 1917–1934*, London, Paul, 1986.

Act 3

Plays with a Purpose

THE NEW THEATRE IN AUSTRALIA

Sydney NT poster for *Till the Day I Die.*

CHAPTER 9

Political Theatre and the State

Phillip Deery and Lisa Milner

New Theatre was political theatre. It was oppositional, contrarian theatre. It was explicitly partisan, socially engaged theatre. New Theatre, therefore, was theatre with a purpose: it sought to challenge power and change the status quo, radicalise its predominantly working-class audiences, inspire more 'progressive' positions and even political action and stand outside mainstream repertory by embracing experimentation and rejecting commercialism. The mission of New Theatre, proclaimed one of its early officials in 1939, lay in fulfilling its 'emotional capacity to stir our conscience, clarify our outlook, and stimulate activity'. Thirteen years later, its newsletter, *Spotlight*, similarly announced:

> our theatre [is] different from other 'Little Theatres'. Where they are confined to problems of 'theatre', we set out to pose or solve problems of life in terms of theatre, to create the illusion of reality.

The genesis of New Theatre in Sydney was the WAC that formed in 1931. Although visual art and writing featured heavily in the WAC's activities initially – including the first exhibition of Soviet art in Australia – the theatre became the main activity after a few years, and 'the drama took over full control'. In Melbourne, the WTG appeared in 1935, emerging from both the Pioneer Players, formed in 1921 by Louis and Hilda Esson, and the WAC, which had its inaugural meeting in 1932 under the auspices of the FSU at the home of Itzhak Gust, a Russian Jewish immigrant. In 1937, it affiliated with the American New Theatre and thereafter became the New Theatre. Brisbane, Perth and Newcastle established theatres in 1936. Also in 1936, the Sydney branch became the NTL, with other branches following. Few of these branches survived longer than 40 years; Sydney is the only remaining branch, with an unbroken record of performances from 1932 to today. Together, however, they all produced over 400 plays by Australian and overseas dramatists. The production of overseas plays underscored the transnational connections of New Theatre. Studies of the USA's New Theatre League and Britain's Unity Theatre have demonstrated that radical theatre sought not only to develop cultural activism locally, but also to embody the broader aims and aspirations of an international working-class theatre movement. New Theatre in Australia was no exception.

CENSORSHIP OF NEW THEATRE: *TILL THE DAY I DIE*

The federal government, under Prime Minister Joseph Lyons, banned performances of Clifford Odets' *Till the Day I Die* (1935) in July 1936, apparently at the request of the German Consul, Dr Rudolf Asmis. The play, written to accompany Odets' *Waiting for Lefty* (1935), ran for one hour. It revolved around the experiences of a member of the underground opposition movement in Germany who, after torture by Nazi officials during a brutal interrogation, committed suicide. This already well-known play had 'caused keen discussion in other countries' before New Theatre adopted it in 1936, five years before London's Unity Theatre.

Queensland, led by the Forgan Smith Labor government, permitted the Brisbane Unity Theatre to stage *Till the Day I Die* and did not interfere with its production; consequently, 'the trouble anticipated by the Brisbane theatre did not eventuate'. Performances eventually went ahead at several theatres in both Brisbane and Ipswich in February 1939.

South of the border, however, the Sydney New Theatre's Secretary, Victor Arnold, presented the play illegally at the Savoy Theatre on 22 July 1936, defying Colonial Secretary Frank Chaffey's prohibition. While they fought the ban, they staged the play every Wednesday night at the New Theatre's regular rooms at 36 Pitt Street and, subsequently, for the next two years. According to the *Australian Quarterly*, attempting to proscribe the play was 'a political error – hundreds have seen it who would otherwise have not heard of it'. Similarly, the left-leaning artist, Rod Shaw, who worked with the New Theatre, remarked that 'more people would have seen the play than normally' because of the ban. New Theatre member Eddie Allison went so far as to claim that the play 'put the New Theatre on the map'. The prohibition lasted

POLITICAL THEATRE AND THE STATE

Will Mahony's cartoon, *Daily News*, 1940.

for five years, until 1941. The Sydney Secretary, Freda Lewis, maintained that the government's decision to remove the ban 'showed the correctness of the theatre's policy' in defying it for so long.

THE MELBOURNE EXPERIENCE

Silencing *Till the Day I Die* was far more effective in Melbourne. The situation there is worth recounting because it highlights the obstacles confronting the emerging WTG – and because the earlier chapters have not detailed the Melbourne experience. The Lyons government lacked powers to ban plays, so it contacted the Country Party Premier of Victoria, Albert Dunstan. Dunstan referred the correspondence to his Chief Secretary, Henry Bailey, who seized the baton. Bailey read the script, thought it 'undesirable' and prohibited all Melbourne performances.

The Council for Civil Liberties convened a protest meeting against the ban on 6 November 1936. The audience of 200 heard several speakers invoke

A cartoon in the Melbourne *Herald* by Alex Gurney.

the right of free speech. L. F. Giblin, Macmahon Ball and Rev. William Bottomley all voiced their concerns. The resourceful and determined new director, Catherine Duncan, encapsulated the WTG's position – 'We are not pamphleteers merely disseminating propaganda' – and announced that WTG would perform the play before or on 11 November in an unlicensed hall without charge. She added that the venue would remain secret until the day before. Like its Sydney counterpart, the WTG sought to exploit a legal loophole whereby free 'private' performances (with a one shilling donation) seemed permissible.

Following press reports of this meeting, the Chief Secretary announced that he would 'use all his powers' to prevent the staging of *Till the Day I Die* in any hall, licensed or unlicensed. He clarified his objection: 'the play offends against good manners' and would cause 'class and national prejudice'. It is arguable that Bailey's objection was less concerned with the play's anti-Nazi theme than with Odets and the WTG being pro-communist. The Victorian Special Branch had the WTG under surveillance from at least as early as 16 August 1936. Several additional protest meetings were called, and the Trades Hall Council pledged its support. William Slater, the former Attorney-General in two state Labor governments, offered to lead a deputation. And, significantly, the Mayor of Collingwood, Laurence Marshall, agreed to a performance – despite the embargo – under the rubric of a charitable concert to aid the Mayor's Fund for the unemployed.

A stormy meeting of the fractious Collingwood Council on 16 November 1936 spelt trouble for this last plan. Several councillors asked the mayor whether reports of the proposed 'illegal' staging of *Till the Day I Die* on 18 November or of 1,500 invitations having already been issued were correct. Correspondence from the town clerk to the mayor was tabled, confirming that the Chief Secretary had banned the play, that the booking fee (paid personally by the mayor) for the hire of the main hall had been returned, and that the mayor must 'clearly understand that in no circumstances will [he] be permitted to use the halls of this city' for the production of the play. In defence, Marshall told councillors that he was 'not a Communist' and – thinking, presumably, of the loophole – reassured them that 'as long as I am mayor, the law will not be broken'.

He did not reassure most councillors. The next day, 17 November, 12 councillors wrote to the town clerk authorising him to 'take any action' he considered necessary to prevent the use of the town hall. The stage was set for a showdown. From 6.30 pm on Wednesday 18 November, a crowd estimated at 'several thousands' assembled outside Collingwood Town Hall. It included 'a large number of artists, journalists, lawyers and students'. Twenty uniformed police and several plainclothes detectives were also in attendance. The mayor and his wife arrived at 7 pm to find all doors locked and bolted. Marshall then tried forcing a window open to admit the crowd. Police stopped him, and he remonstrated: 'I am the Mayor of this city, and you have no...power to prevent my breaking in to my own town hall'. By now, traffic in Hoddle Street was completely blocked. Also blocked was an attempt to perform the play in a nearby vacant allotment. Two thousand people assembled, until police cautioned them, saying that it was an offence. Catherine Duncan mounted the steps of the town hall and proclaimed to a cheering crowd that the WTG would never be censored. That night, a special meeting of the WTG congratulated Marshall on his 'courageous stand', made him a life member and denounced Collingwood councillors for their 'violation' of free expression.

Duncan was undaunted. She told a sympathetic meeting of the Social Science Forum: 'The Collingwood Council, the Government and the censors need not think for one moment that we are going to accept their dictum'. Offers of money and services poured in, circulars were sent to various metropolitan councils seeking an available town hall, and a deputation of three miners from Wonthaggi requested a performance in their town. The WTG was now aiming for an audience of 10,000 for the play. 'We will fight for freedom of expression in Australia,' she continued, 'even if it takes till the day we die'.

Her defiance, and the extensive support for the WTG, withered in the face of resistance. Local councils including Coburg, Fitzroy, St Kilda, South Melbourne and Wonthaggi all refused permission to stage the play. A plan to present the play on the beach at Inverloch to Christmas holiday-makers never materialised. Even the Melbourne Unitarian Church reneged after it was threatened with prosecution under the Health Act if it did not comply with regulations appropriate to 'a place of public entertainment'. The only hope lay with the Brunswick City Council. When it received an application from the WTG for the use of its town hall, members of the council requested a private rehearsal performance for municipal officers and councillors. This occurred on 21 December. Reactions were mixed: one councillor believed that it was undoubtedly a propaganda play, but to suggest that it would cause conflict was 'ridiculous'; another thought that 'there was nothing in it'; while a third remarked: 'If they don't improve on tonight's performance, they won't get an audience for the second performance'. The council then voted 6–3 to permit the use of the hall on 21 February 1937 for the first public performance in

Melbourne of *Till the Day I Die*. This was more than three months after its first scheduling.

Approximately 1,200 people attended this performance. According to a press report, the reaction was one of 'enthusiasm'. In the audience were A. E. Officer and a Mr Bird, who were either State Special Branch or CIB field officers, and they were not enthusiastic. The first play, *Waiting for Lefty*, was 'practically unintelligible to most of the audience', because the cast failed to project their voices. During interval, it was announced that a loud air-conditioning plant was responsible; efforts would be made to overcome the competing noise in the second play. Even so, despite the production of *Till the Day I Die* being 'much better', according to the security report, 'it is doubtful if more than half the audience heard a quarter of what was spoken'. The officers observed that at least 60 percent of the 1,200-strong audience 'comprised foreigners or persons of alien extraction, jews [sic] predominating'. The officers collected (and attached to the report) a leaflet distributed inside the hall relating to the Spanish Civil War and noted the publications sold outside the hall – *Workers' Voice*, *Moscow News* and *Soviet Russia Today*. The play ran every weekend for another 18 months; in the words of a New Theatre stalwart, it meant that 'we became known'.

SYDNEY, 1940: THE FIRST PROSCRIPTION

It was not until 9 September 1939 – a few days after the outbreak of war – that the the passage of the *National Security Act 1939* laid the foundations for national censorship of the New Theatre. An amendment to this legislation, introduced in April 1940, 'made it an offence for people to print for publication, to publish or to have in their possession any paper that bore in any way on the war'. The CPA's *Tribune* was banned in the same month. Because the amendment also covered possession of material, the New Theatre came within its range. The Governor-General's speech at the opening of federal parliament on 17 April made the danger clear enough:

> My Government...is reviewing the provisions of the existing law; it has arranged that Communist newspapers and periodicals shall be submitted to rigid censorship; it proposes to introduce special rules regarding the signing and authorisation of certain pamphlets and other printed matter; in appropriate cases prosecutions will be instituted.

On 24 May 1940, parliament passed Regulation 17B under Statutory Rules 1940 No. 90. The government now had the power to ban CPA papers by placing a notice to that effect in the Commonwealth Government *Gazette*. Initially, nine CPA publications were prohibited. New Theatre did not, then, issue a regular publication that could be banned; but it did publicise its work through the *Workers' Weekly*, *Daily News*, *Tribune*, union organisations and the mainstream press. Then, on 15 June 1940, under Statutory Rules 1940 No. 109, the National Security (Subversive Association) Regulations were introduced. Regulation Three under Statutory Rules 1940 No. 110 outlawed the CPA and nine other organisations. That very night, police raided the CPA headquarters in Sydney, Melbourne and Brisbane, along with the homes of many members, confiscating paperwork, books and other property. According to Stuart Macintyre, there had 'never been a police activity of this kind on the same scale'. Reports state:

> the raids, which were synchronised to begin together, so that organisations in one State could not be warned by those in another, were a sequel to the issue of a proclamation declaring Communist and Fascist organisations to be unlawful.

That night, police also raided the Sydney New Theatre – still at this time performing *Till the Day I Die* – confiscating about 600 play scripts, including some Shakespearean classics. Freda Lewis, New Theatre's Assistant Secretary and Publicity Officer, recalled: 'they took any books that had a red cover...they behaved like Fascists'. After the raid, she announced, disingenuously, in the *Daily Telegraph*: 'We have no communists in our organisation, and we are not connected with the Communist Party in any way'. The raid on a cultural organisation that was not prohibited certainly astonished many in the labour movement who were not connected with the CPA. One was the editor of the WEA's journal, who wrote: 'the seizure of every kind of book, regardless of its nature or contents, has [produced] amazed indignation that such things could happen in Australia'. The story of the raid is often recalled as a defining moment in the history of the Sydney New Theatre.

These raids ensnared numerous other organisations and individuals, prompting widespread protests about infringements of civil liberties. Even the conservative *Sydney Morning Herald* protested, calling on the Menzies government to define precisely both subversive literature and the limits governing the police powers of seizure:

> There is accumulating evidence that the raids...have resulted in an indiscriminate clearance of valuable libraries. Policemen naturally cannot be expected to exercise expert judgment, but it is both disturbing and ludicrous that the instructions under which they have acted are apparently so loose or sweeping as to result in the confiscation of purely classical works... It should be as little the part of the Ministry to emulate Nazi intolerance on this question as it should be the function of the State police to despoil bookshelves of cherished volumes which no person of average intelligence could possibly stigmatise as 'subversive'.

On 3 July 1940, the New Theatre organised a meeting at the Sydney Trades Hall, 'to protest against the raiding of the NTL and the interferences with cultural work'. The speakers were Paul Mortier and Rupert Lockwood from the CPA, Rev. Stuart Watts (recently dismissed as editor of the *Church Standard*), Freda Lewis from New Theatre and 2KY announcer J. K. Morley. Richard Wilson from the Civil Liberties Committee presided. The police report of the meeting noted:

> the general tenor of the speeches was indignation at the raiding of the League's premises and bitter hostility to the government. A militant note was struck throughout.

The raid on the theatre also provoked fresh protests against the four-year-old ban on *Till the Day I Die*. Freda Lewis formed a deputation from New Theatre to meet the NSW Chief Secretary in July 1940. He refused to meet the deputation; his formal response was that the ban would remain because the play 'would have a degrading effect on those who saw it' and 'could do no good'. Lewis, in response, invited him to the play's next performance. We can assume that he did not accept the offer.

Lewis wrote to Prime Minister Menzies on 8 August, seeking that their scripts be returned, or at least preserved. Accordingly, they were returned, along with many other items (reports, leaflets, CPA booklets and eight stage rifle props) on 14 August. A box of detonators, however, was returned instead to its purported owner, the railways. The accompanying letter from a Criminal Investigation Branch investigator notes that his examination of the confiscated plays, which included works by George Bernard Shaw and John Galsworthy:

The *Daily News* report on the 1940 raid.

> does not reveal anything which indicate that such plays are used for and on behalf of the CPA, and, therefore, there seems no legal reason why they should not be returned.

This was despite Menzies' confident declaration the previous night that 'the type of material seized fully justified the steps that have been taken'. The letter also indicated that the confiscated plays by Betty Roland, who had recently left the CPA, 'are ordinary working-class propaganda and cannot be considered as being connected with the Communist Party'.

Although members were not immune from the impact of the raids and the general antipathy to communism, police charged only one New Theatre activist under the National Security Act: Phyllis Johnson served one month in Long Bay Women's Penitentiary. She had joined the CPA in 1937, when she was just 19, and was now a member of the Central Committee. The charge related to her speech at an anti-conscription meeting and the prison sentence to her refusal to agree to a good behaviour bond. Inside Long Bay, Johnson proclaimed: 'let there be no surrender'.

Yet, notwithstanding the raid on the Sydney New Theatre premises, there was no Commonwealth law that declared the NTL illegal.

D. R. B. Mitchell, Inspector of the Sydney CIB office, made strenuous attempts to include the New Theatre in the list of banned organisations – but failed. Nevertheless, New Theatre's Oriel Gray noted:

> the theatre fraction of the party went underground – enjoying every minute of it! The Sydney committee ordained that no fraction meetings should be held on the premises of any organisation that was openly communist. We crowded into a tiny room in a rabbit-warren building in Hunter Street. We arrived in ones and twos (and met afterwards in a pub or coffee shop, all in one merry group)...we were warned to be alert for infiltration by security agents.

The 1940 ban on the CPA took effect in the wake of the Nazi–Soviet non-aggression pact, when a great many disillusioned individuals broke from the Communist Party and New Theatre. One was Betty Roland (who previously went to Russia with Guido Baracchi, a founding member of the CPA); the party expelled her and 'excised' her plays from New Theatre. The Trotskyist Workers' Party/Communist League of Australia was scathing:

> Presumably we are supposed to believe that the same plays [by Roland] previously endorsed and performed by the New Theatre League are now anti-working class. The truth is that the New Theatre League is just another 'stooge' outfit of the 'Communist' party whose puppets dance to the tune called by Miles, Dixon and Sharkey.

The theatre did not cease its activities once the CPA itself was banned, but efforts to silence it continued. One instance was on 20 September 1940, when Freda Lewis took some New Theatre performers to the suburb of Mortdale. She intended to contribute some political sketches to the election meeting of her cousin – Sam Lewis, CPA member, NSW Labor candidate for the federal seat of Barton and, from 1945, President of the Teachers Federation. The police in attendance stopped the performance and took away their loudspeaker. Conversely, New Theatre extended its work to Wollongong, established links with the local ALP and the newly established Trades Hall and formed a (short-lived) New Theatre branch. Lewis spoke at several South Coast meetings and began training interested people. Along with Eddie Allison and Jim Hector, she performed sketches for various union meetings.

Meanwhile, attacks on the organisation continued. The federal Attorney-General, W. M. Hughes, now 78, wrote to the Minister for Information about New Theatre in July 1941. He claimed that it was still:

> disseminating defeatist propaganda by means of
> stage plays at union meetings, street corner meetings
> of the State ALP (a lorry), and at lunch hour meetings
> at factories.

After quoting from a letter by Freda Lewis that listed various New Theatre activities at the time, Hughes recommended:

> one way in which the New Theatre's activities could
> be stopped would be by declaring it an unlawful body
> under the National Security (Subversive Associations)
> regulations.

CIB director H. E. Jones' position typified the attitude of federal and state authorities on the potential impact of left-wing drama of the sort that the New Theatre was promoting: 'Propaganda of this nature is more lasting upon the minds of the public and far easier absorbed than the written word'.

Defiantly, the Sydney New Theatre maintained its normal schedule, producing a mix of Australian, US and British plays on a wide range of topics, uninterrupted, throughout 1940. These included *No Conscription*, an antiwar play based on the writings of Australian author Rupert Lockwood. Catherine Duncan adapted the play, and Vic Arnold produced it. This production saw the NTL face the federal government in a legal censorship case. On 16 April, the Commonwealth censor had suppressed the play in its entirety, as it was being prepared for broadcast by the ALP on their Sydney radio station 2KY. J. R. Hughes, the President of the NSW Labor Council, had complained about this act of prohibition at an anti-conscription meeting at the Sydney Town Hall, attended by 2,000 people, where:

WHY ANTI-NAZI PLAY IS BANNED

NEW Theatre League (Sydney) defied ban of Chief Secretary (late Mr. Frank Chaffey) four years ago and produced "Till The Day I Die," a smashing indictment of Nazi Germany and its methods. Producer Victor Arnold was later fined. Secretary (Miss Freda Lewis) contends that since we are at war, ban should be lifted. Present Chief Secretary Tonking refuses, stating that play emphasises brutality, would degrade audience. PIX here shows "Till The Day I Die," acted by New Theatre League players.

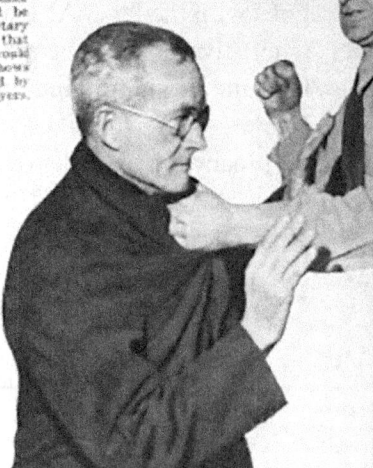

"INTERROGATION" "Don't Hit Me. I was ill the w—— kind for heavens," implores her Storm-Trooper grasps him by throat. To Mr. Tonking, Miss Lewis ing? Spectacle of courage and idealism against heavy odds about

SHADOWS Ernst Taussig, German Communist publishing anti-Nazi literature is central figure. Arrested, beaten, ill-treated in Nazi Brown House, he is shown crouching in cell with ever-present menace of persecutors depicted by Storm-Trooper's shadow on wall.

REVOLT "The First Instinct of a Jew is to run." Disloyal to Nazism, Storm-Trooper Major Duhring, of Jewish descent, is goaded by that taunt by a subordinate, shoots him. Swastika, German symbol of bestiality, always there. Police present at Sydney showing.

Torture "Play An Instrument?" Storm-Trooper softly a "Formerly the violin." Says Brown Shirt, "Put Then with pistol butt, he smashes fingers. Members of E ard, believing he has been forced to disclose comrades' nam

PIX——Page Twenty-six

TORTURER Storm-Trooper gives Nazi salute, travesty of old Roman salutation. Author Odets won fame when his plays, "Till the Day I Die" and "Waiting For Lefty" were produced by Group Theatre, American workers' theatre. He is now one of America's leading playwrights.

THREAT With inevitable Swastika in background, three broken men raise their hands wearily to salute the Fuerrer, in Storm-Trooper Overalons there with Ernst . . . It is ironic that Swastika, emblem of new Germany, has been found in ruins of ancient synagogues.

PLEA Freed, Ernst knows that he cannot endure torture indefinitely. "Take the gun . . . One day more, and I'll stand there like an idiot identifying prisoners." Tilly and brother Karl refuses to shoot him. Odets was recently charged in U.S.A. with being Communist supporter.

SILENCE ". . . . No Peace For an honest worker in the whole world," Ernst tells Tilly, who examines mutilated hand. He appeals to friends to carry on struggle against Hitlerism. To ensure own silence, so that comrades will not be betrayed, he shoots himself.

Pix magazine's spread on *Till the Day I Die* was great publicity for the banned play.

> his announcement was received with 'boos' (presumably for the censor). Eddie Ward, who was one of the speakers at the Town Hall meeting, later asked in the House of Representatives why the play had been banned; a play which, he claimed, was 'purely historical'. Sir Henry Gullett, the acting minister for information, responded by saying that 'it was not usual to give reasons for censorship'.

At Christmas in 1940, Sydney New Theatre put on its first revue, *I'd Rather be Left*. This satirical production, billed as 'a musical burlesque about people, politics, and parasites of this day and age', advanced a clear interpretation of the war as a capitalist one. An internal history recorded that the revue 'mercilessly exposed the Fascist leanings and the profiteering of the leaders of the "Phoney War"'. Sydney New Theatre members believed that this riotous and popular show, which mocked Menzies and Churchill, but not Hitler and Stalin, opened up a completely new medium for performance. James McAuley, one of the writers and, later, a renowned poet and conservative intellectual, played the piano. The play was highly successful and sold out well into the middle of 1941. Many of its songs entered popular culture. One of the most popular ran: 'There'll Always be a Menzies While there's a BHP, for they have drawn their dividends since 1883'. Miriam Hampson recalls:

> the show was a counter to all the talk at the time about helping Hitler go into the Soviet Union...it raised all the political issues of the day, it was funny and beautifully done.

Marie Armstrong wrote that, with this season: 'the ice was broken. The Australian writer of revue and drama had become an essential to the development of the Australian theatre'.

SYDNEY: WORLD WAR II TO THE COLD WAR

After Germany invaded Russia in June 1941, CPA policy underwent a volte-face. It now supported the war enthusiastically. Sydney New Theatre followed suit, as their work with the Council for the Encouragement of Music and the Arts (CEMA) reflects. The model for CEMA (later renamed the Arts

Council of Australia), established in 1943, was the British organisation of the same name. Its objectives were:

> to take the arts to the people – the country people – to encourage amateur groups [and] to provide a field in which artists could support themselves by their art.

With CEMA's support, New Theatre's mobile work began in earnest: it produced plays under primitive conditions but sent scripts and advice to soldiers in the fighting line, which assisted morale.

Despite problems with production and performance space and the resources expended on CEMA touring work, Sydney New Theatre maintained its regular seasons of plays throughout the 1940s; 1944 was an especially busy year, with 10 separate seasons. These included works by Gray, Anton Chekhov, the US dramatist Lillian Hellman and Australia's Katharine Susannah Prichard – indicative of the immense versatility of the group. Between 1940 and 1948, the Sydney branch performed 17 works written by Australian playwrights. In the late 1940s, it toured regional NSW with a mobile unit. Fortified by the success of its earlier mobile work through CEMA and encouraged by similar wartime efforts of the London Unity Theatre, Sydney New Theatre purchased a truck that enabled it to connect with the experiences and hopes of new, non-working-class audiences. Mobile theatre represented a revival of the highly politicised, semi-itinerant agitprop theatre style pioneered in post-revolutionary Russia. During the 1949 coal strike, a concert party travelled to the Newcastle area to entertain the strikebound workers and their families. In Wollongong, it performed for the Port Kembla Workers' Federation Delegates Committee to raise money for the Pensioners' Christmas Dinner Fund. From 1953, *Reedy River*, the most successful of all New Theatre's plays, played in factories, regional localities and country towns. As was the case in the early 1940s, censorship from commercial media organisations plagued the Sydney New Theatre in the late 1940s. While many trade union and communist papers, such as *Workers' Weekly* and *Tribune*, regularly reviewed and advertised its productions, commercial journals were more capricious. The *Sydney Morning Herald*, *Wireless Weekly*, *Home* and *Daily Telegraph* had previously publicised and reviewed productions, but this coverage now ceased. One of the most frequently mentioned aspects of the history of the Australian New Theatre is its exclusion from mainstream Australian newspapers during the Cold War.

New Theatre producer Marie Armstrong recalled that, in 1948:

> we performed a fantastic production of [Sean O'Casey's] *The Star Turns Red*, and one of the hierarchy in the *Herald* came to see it and saw the politics in it. The first edict that came from him was no more reviews, and then later they would not let us advertise, wouldn't take our money. For 12 years we had to fight the *Herald* for the right to advertise.

The ending of the ban, on both reviews and advertisements, occurred when the communist-controlled WWF pointed out to the *Herald* editors that their newsprint had to be transported through the Sydney docks. Not until 1960 did the mainstream Sydney press once again review the New Theatre plays; the first was Arthur Miller's *All My Sons*.

MELBOURNE, 1943-53

In 1937, selling *Moscow News* outside the Brunswick Town Hall aroused the interest of the security services as a sign of disloyalty. Five years later, however, the Soviet Union attracted widespread sympathy and support following Nazi Germany's invasion in June 1941. The USSR became a wartime ally, and the local Communist Party and its 'front' organisations, such as the New Theatre, bathed in the reflected glory of the Red Army. After the Russians defeated the Germans at Stalingrad in February 1943, admiration became adulation. Melburnians donated generously to the 'sheepskins for Russia' campaign, joined the Australian–Soviet Friendship League in unprecedented numbers and eagerly participated in cultural activities at Australia–Soviet House, opened by the Lord Mayor in 1944. This favourable political climate was the all-important context for the successful expansion of cultural activities conducted by New Theatre during the war years.

When the President of Melbourne's New Theatre, Charles McCormack, wrote that '1943 has been a busy year for New Theatre', he was probably understating the range of its activities, the energy of its volunteers, the size of its audiences and the relevance of its plays to contemporary political issues. However, the war itself confronted the New Theatre with new problems to overcome: actors and technicians became soldiers; shift work and overtime in essential industries impeded schedules; and war-induced shortages of materials necessitated improvisation of stage props. Another 'problem' was the insufficient politicisation of its members. A private letter in March 1944 from Lil Diamond to her Sydney counterpart, Alan Herbert, obtained by military intelligence, confirmed this impression. Lil Diamond was a Melbourne New Theatre member and editor of *New Theatre Review* during this period. She was married to Dick Diamond, Secretary of Melbourne Actors Equity, who is perhaps best known for writing *Reedy River*. She judged the political level of CPA members within New Theatre as 'very poor'; they were 'too liberal' in outlook – unlike the more sectarian comrades in Sydney. Few attended branch meetings or classes, which meant that 'they're not getting any stronger politically'.

Despite this perceived deficiency, the security services continued to conduct extensive surveillance of the members, policies and activities of New Theatre – which, it claimed, disseminated 'insidious propaganda'. There are dozens of thick ASIO files, from 1936 to 1970, on individuals in, and all the branches of, the New Theatre. These files, which incorporate intelligence reports inherited from its predecessors, contain innumerable New Theatre publications; production committee notes; lists of the members of the cast and crew of productions, gleaned from the programs; newspaper reviews; detailed reports from informants on meetings, especially national conferences and national schools, including the full names of all those who attended or spoke; phone call intercepts; car registration details; and film surveillance footage of New Theatre meetings. The files provide, by default, a parallel history of the New Theatre. Along with several other left cultural organisations 'judged to be subversive to the security of the Commonwealth' (including the Realist Writers, the Australasian Book Society and the Fellowship of Australian Writers), their activities were a source of concern for successive Australian governments and, therefore, of interest to the various security services. Norma Disher, long associated with the Sydney New Theatre, was convinced that ASIO operatives were 'always around'. ASIO certainly faced 'an immense task' in maintaining surveillance of these organisations, relegating its B1 (Counter-Subversion) Branch field officers to conduct 'Research' into the groups rather than direct investigation of them. Section officers in the early 1950s were too low in numbers and resources to concentrate their main attention on organisations other than the CPA.

The war years and their immediate aftermath, despite shortages and austerity, marked the heyday of Melbourne's New Theatre. With the onset of the Cold War, audiences dwindled, reviews dried up, and improvisation and resourcefulness were severely tested. Increasingly perceived as the 'Communist front' that it increasingly became, the New Theatre battled to stay afloat. The forces of anti-communism were in the ascendant, and 'progressive theatre' became synonymous with disloyalty. Yet, the casual reader of *New Theatre Review* would have found few signs of impending difficulties in its daily survival or its struggle to maintain its identity as a crucible of social and cultural activism. It is true that, by the end of 1948, *New Theatre Review* noted the 'marked decline' in its audiences. And, in July 1949, the *Guardian* newspaper carried an uncharacteristically bleak review of New Theatre's production of Ben Jonson's famous comedy, *Volpone*. While congratulating the players for not losing 'heart and spirit completely', it bemoaned the 'unnervingly small' audience on opening night and challenged 'progressive people' to become more actively involved. But the 'progressive people' were not immune from the rising tide of anti-communism. New Theatre was identified, not unjustifiably, with the CPA, and the party was besieged in 1949. When *Volpone* opened in early July, a general coal strike was crippling the economy. The Chifley Labor government labelled it a communist conspiracy. At the same time, a Victorian Royal Commission into the Communist Party was hearing damning testimony that appeared to confirm communist manipulation; and the party's General Secretary, L. L. Sharkey, was on trial, charged with sedition. These and other events contributed to the corrosive political atmosphere which severely tested the allegiance of theatregoers to committed, left-wing theatre. Thus, the more New Theatre became closely connected to the Communist Party, the more it became vulnerable to political attack and the object of community hostility. The closing play for 1949 was a pre-election revue, *Take It As Read*, featuring 'witty, candid comment on current affairs'. With deliberate irony, the program requested: 'Please Do Not Engage in Subversive Activity'. Less ironic was the fact that none of the actors' real names was listed. Only the *Guardian* reviewed it.

By 1950, the threat of prohibition, rather than the dove of peace, was again circling around the left. Talk of 'subversive activity' infected public debate on the Communist Party Dissolution Bill, which Menzies introduced to the new House of Representatives in April 1950. We will mention only briefly the controversial events of 1950–51: the passage of the bill; the ambivalence of the Labor Party; the High Court challenge; and the defeat of the referendum to ban the CPA. However, it is reasonable to assume that New Theatre felt, at least initially, isolated and on the defensive. In that brief pause in October 1950, when the bill became law, police again conducted raids; the CPA prepared to go underground; New Theatre was – potentially – a 'declared' organisation which had to prove its 'innocence' of communist sympathy; and a siege mentality reigned.

Undoubtedly, this climate of fear and suspicion influenced New Theatre committee members and faithful supporters. However, as with the CPA records, there are few surviving records of New Theatre for this period that enable us to examine responses in any detail. We do have, from 1951, intermittent issues of *Spotlight*, a roneoed (and, understandably, poorly produced) newsletter, which went some way to filling the gap left by the closure of *New Theatre Review* in July 1949. The second issue, published in mid-1951, commented: 'we are now faced with the referendum proposals of Menzies and partners-in-grime'. If the referendum passed, *Spotlight* continued, 'an immediate full-stop to all forms of expression which are in any way hostile to the U.S.–Liberal [sic] policy' would result. It called on opposition from 'a solid front of genuine democrats and patriots' and, 'if we are to survive', a strengthening of ties with the militant trade union movement.

But New Theatre did survive. Indeed, it managed to produce 10 plays in 1950 and 1951, and the repertoire continued to mix Australian with overseas scripts, local with international issues, social comment with political critique. Increasingly, overseas plays came from blacklisted US writers. Three of the most prominent were Albert Maltz, Dalton Trumbo and Howard Fast. Maltz and Trumbo were two of the famed 'Hollywood Ten' who defied the House Committee on Un-American Activities and went to prison in 1950. Maltz's *Peace on Earth* opened on 19 July 1950. With the Damoclean sword of legal proscription hovering, the program identified none of the cast. In an act of solidarity and generosity, Maltz signalled his intention to remit his royalties on *Peace on Earth* back to New Theatre. New Theatre also produced his *Private Hicks*, an anti-draft play, in May 1951. In these early Cold War years, taking a short-term tactical stand meant sacrificing longer-term creative expression. In short, aesthetic concerns were a casualty of ideological objectives. The didactic one-act play *The Nail on the Wall*, which Frank Hardy wrote while awaiting trial on charges of criminal libel, further demonstrates this. Reciprocally, New Theatre was harnessing its resources to mobilise opposition to the legal proceedings over Hardy's novel, *Power Without Glory*. The sole review of Hardy's play, in the *Guardian*, assessed it as 'a straight left to Menzies' jaw'. Because its theme (the impact of government legislation that makes a young communist, Ray Muldoon, an outlaw), paralleled the 'No' case then being waged in the referendum campaign, New Theatre came close to agitprop – minus the mobile trailer.

New Theatre's tactical engagements and political responsiveness had always been apparent, stretching back to *Waiting for Lefty* in 1936 and its struggle over *Till the Day I Die* in 1937. But the theatre – like most communist-influenced or controlled organisations in these years of 'high Stalinism' – had become insular, inward looking, controversial and adrift from the person 'in the street'. By Christmas 1952, New Theatre was as much, if not more, preoccupied with causes than with bringing theatre to 'the people': protesting to the Immigration Minister Harold Holt against the threatened deportation of a Greek Cypriot communist, Jimmy Anastasiou; and protesting to US President Harry Truman against the death sentence imposed on Julius and Ethel Rosenberg. Not until the hugely successful *Reedy River* – which opened in March 1953, drawing on Australian bush and ballad traditions and invoking a romantic radical nationalism – was New Theatre rescued from financial insolvency and political didacticism. This play, by Dick Diamond, not only fulfilled New Theatre's mission to present issues with a radical message; it also used broad themes and rousing songs to attract a wide audience. Hardy observed that *Reedy River* signalled 'a development in our national culture of very great importance', but was also a play 'to which you can take any of your non-Party friends or workmates'. This was true. For a great many Australians, the play rode the crest of a wave of nationalist interest in folk and bush music, and the incorporation of many popular musical numbers in the play added much to its continuing popularity. If long queues in Flinders Street and 'Full House' signs were the criteria for success, New Theatre in Melbourne – a full 16 years after its formation – had at last achieved success. This was a work that brought mainstream audiences to the New Theatre all around the country. It also brought much satisfaction to theatre workers: one member felt that 'to work in a theatre like the New Theatre affords not only great pleasure in the many new friends we meet, but leaves us with the full feeling that it is a job indeed well worth doing and, in the case of *Reedy River*, a job well done'.

CONCLUSION

Although New Theatre continued its commitment to explicitly political theatre, official suspicion of New Theatre waned. With the rise of the new left and social movements that challenged government policy on conscription and the Vietnam War, ASIO had different – and seemingly more threatening

– targets. A letter from Colonel Charles Spry, the director-general of ASIO, to the Prime Minister's Department, dated 5 November 1969, exemplified the changed position:

> participation in New Theatre activities does not necessarily indicate Communist sympathies and, in view of the current ideological confusion within the CPA, the New Theatre can no longer be accurately described as a Communist 'Front' organisation, but it can be said to be under considerable CPA influence.

We have argued that, for much of the 20-year period examined in this chapter, New Theatre was nonetheless burdened by its status as the disseminator of 'insidious propaganda' and its connection, real or perceived, to the CPA. The struggle for artistic expression, especially when challenges to dominant cultural and political values were mounted, confronted major difficulties; but New Theatre remained defiant in the face of such obstacles. It either met or sidestepped efforts by governments, security services, local councils and the conservative press to limit its activities. When its performances were overtly propagandist in message or agitprop in style, political imperatives subsumed aesthetic ambitions, and New Theatre became more vulnerable to attack. When its plays were more congruent with mainstream (and, thus, less explicitly working-class) concerns, as in World War II, or when they tapped into a radical nationalism that revived folk and bush traditions, as with *Reedy River*, it realised its mission of introducing theatre to 'the masses' and was also better insulated from opponents' desire to silence it. Irrespective of the extent to which New Theatre echoed the prevailing communist political line, it remained a significant artistic forum for a generation of writers, directors, performers and countless behind-the-scenes volunteers seeking to refashion society in mid-20th century Australia.

FURTHER READING

Cain, Frank, *The Origins of Political Surveillance in Australia*, Sydney, Angus & Robertson, 1983.

Capp, Fiona, *Writers Defiled: Security Surveillance of Australian Authors and Intellectuals 1920 – 1960*, Melbourne, McPhee Gribble, 1993.

Darby, Robert, 'New Theatre and the State: the Ban on *Till the Day I Die*, 1936–41', *Labour History*, no. 80, 2001, pp. 1–19.

Devanny, Jean, *Point of Departure: the Autobiography of Jean Devanny*, St Lucia: University Press, 1986.

Macintyre, Stuart, *The Reds: the Communist Party of Australia from Origins to Illegality*, Sydney, Allen & Unwin, 1999.

McLaren, John, *Writing in Hope and Fear: Literature as Politics in Postwar Australia*, Melbourne, Cambridge University Press, 1996.

CHAPTER 10

'Them Songs are Dangerous': Anti-fascism, Antisemitism and Jewish Connections

Max Kaiser and Lisa Milner

The scrutiny of censoring bodies has touched several theatrical works in Australia, as authorities attempted to uphold the morality and political correctness of the stage across the decades. One play stands out in the New Theatre's history. Deery and Milner (Chapter 9) recount the furore surrounding *Till the Day I Die*. After months of protests against the Victorian 1936 ban, and attempted illegal stagings, around 1,200 people attended a performance at the Brunswick Town Hall on 21 February 1937. According to A. E. Officer and a Mr Bird, who were either State Special Branch or CIB field officers, at least 60 percent of the audience 'comprised foreigners or persons of alien extraction, jews [sic] predominating'.

The reported composition of the audience at this performance was just one indication of close connections between Jewish communities in Australia and the New Theatre. As other chapters in this volume explain, the New Theatre was a key venue for progressive culture through the middle decades of 20th century Australia. It shared with an emerging Jewish left through the late 1930s and the 1940s many concerns about the evils of war, imperialism and colonialism. However, the major issue joining Australian Jews and the New Theatre was the international fight against fascism. Jewish communities in Australia were united in their abhorrence of the Nazi regime. Through the 1940s, in developments reflecting the emergence of a transnational Jewish anti-fascist left, a Jewish anti-fascist politics became powerful in Australian Jewish communities. It was particularly strong in Melbourne, where the

Jock Levy, here directing the November 1948 production of *The Alchemist*.

major Jewish left organisation, the Jewish Council to Combat Fascism and Anti-Semitism (JCCFAS) was based. The New Theatre produced a slew of anti-fascist and Jewish themed plays through the late 1930s to the 1950s, mostly based on US scripts. We argue in this chapter that, while an international influence was strong, the Australian New Theatre's productions also reflected the impact of Australian Jewish left activists and organisations such as the JCCFAS. This ensured that a critique of antisemitism as intimately linked with fascism was an important part of a broader progressive discourse in Australia.

In this chapter, we firstly give a brief overview of connections between Jewish communities around Australia and the New Theatre, then discuss a selection of New Theatre productions dealing with fascism, antisemitism and Jewish politics through the 1930s, 1940s and 1950s. We then assess plays by three Australian writers associated with the New Theatre that closely reflect themes and politics associated with the Australian Jewish left.

JEWISH COMMUNITIES IN AUSTRALIA AND THE NEW THEATRE

Like radical theatre groups in other English-speaking countries, the Australian New Theatre developed from the dual impulses of providing a theatre for a working-class audience and presenting progressive, radical ideas to that audience. The New Theatre produced works of social realism, or socialist realism, in line with other left-wing theatre groups around the world. Beginning in revolutionary Soviet theory, socialist realism developed from Lenin's 'art is a weapon' dictum, in which art had a directly political purpose: the propelling of society towards communism. Social realist theatre in the West aimed to expose the 'truth' of capitalist society, through the presentation of characters as social types. As the events in Brunswick indicate, the New Theatre was the performative nexus of an anti-fascist, popular front during World War II. Subsequently, the New Theatre played a similar role in the postwar peace movement. From its beginnings, the 'New' has been a politically committed theatre, committed against war, fascism, racism and oppression of all kinds.

Theatrical groups focusing on Jewish history and themes have thrived in emigrant strongholds of Jewish culture. Australia is no exception; there was a thriving Yiddish theatre scene throughout the middle decades of the

20th century, which continues (although nowhere near as prolifically) today. Australian New Theatre branches considered antisemitism a major issue of importance, performing many plays on Jewish themes and coming out in protest against issues such as the Rosenbergs' execution in 1953. There was a supportive Jewish audience from the beginning of radical theatre in Australia – including some who joined the New Theatre movement as actors, directors and writers. The popular front and the rise of many left-wing groups associated with, but not formal arms of, the CPA emerged as a hotbed for cultural activism. Many Jewish immigrants and their children joined groups such as the NTL and the Eureka Youth League, places where young Australian left-wing Jews made a home.

There was quite a crossover between the New Theatre, the CPA and left cultural activist groups in all states, and Jewish identities and themes were always a part of this. Trinidadian-Australian writer Ralph de Boissiere, a member of the left-wing Realist Writers Group (RWG), wrote the anti-colonial musical *Calypso Isle* for the New Theatre. In 1949, the Melbourne New Theatre's journal *New Theatre Review* published *The Man in the Train*, a short story by the German Jewish migrant Walter Kaufmann, de Boissiere's close friend and fellow Melbourne RWG member. The German Jewish writer David Martin, a mentor of Kaufmann, was a member of the CPA and the RWG; he was also a playwright for the New Theatre.

There were many links between Australian Jewish communities and the New Theatre. The *Sydney Jewish News* (1939–73), the *Australian Jewish News* (Melbourne) and the *Australian Jewish Times* (1953–90) would often review New Theatre plays. In Melbourne, the WTG had emerged in 1935 from both the Pioneer Players, formed in 1921 by Louis and Hilda Esson, and the WAC. The WAC had its inaugural meeting in 1932 under the auspices of the FSU at the home of Itzhak Gust, a Polish Jewish member of the CPA and the FSU. The WTG went on to become the NTL's Melbourne branch. Angela O'Brien writes that, in Melbourne: 'Anti-Semitism was always an issue for the theatre both in terms of the plays it imported, and its membership'; and the Melbourne New Theatre 'enjoyed the support of a number of educated Jewish people who had migrated during or after the war years'. *Mother Riba*, for example, played as a special performance for Melbourne Jewish patrons in 1954.

In Sydney, prominent New Theatre figure Jock Levy and his brother Lew helped to form the Eastern Suburbs Jewish branch of the CPA, which established a Jewish Youth Theatre League (JYTL) in 1937. The JYTL presented talks as well as theatre, and its members socialised with New Theatre members. One notable JYTL production among many on Jewish themes was Israel Zangwill's Jewish immigrant drama *The Melting Pot*, which featured Jock Levy in the leading role in 1937. With the threat of Nazism looming, Jock's group had a strong Jewish following, but the JYTL folded in 1940 when it lost its premises. Jock then went to the New Theatre, where he was a leading actor and director for decades. One of the first plays he directed for the New Theatre, in 1940, was Clifford Odets' *Awake and Sing* – the story of a Jewish family in New York.

Other prominent Jewish members of the Sydney New Theatre included the Theatre's long-time Secretary Miriam Hampson (a member of the Aarons family), who had many connections within her Jewish communist community in Sydney and elsewhere. Michael Pate, a Sydney New Theatre member, had also worked in the JYTL. Another of the Sydney WAC and New Theatre personnel, George Paizie, had directed *Israel in the Kitchen* and *The Petrified Forest* for the JYTL in 1939; Jock Levy acted in both these productions.

The JYTL performed *The Yellow Spot*, a.k.a. *Professor Mamlock*, for the Sydney New Theatre on 26 November 1938. This was a powerful play about the situation of Jews in Nazi Germany. The play starred the world-famous Yiddish actor Yankev (Jacob) Waislitz, performing in English, a language he had only started learning on his arrival in Australia three months earlier. Waislitz had come to Australia from South Africa, where he had spent seven months trying to establish a Yiddish theatre. In Melbourne, he went on to be a central figure in the golden age of Yiddish theatre in the 1940s and 1950s.

In the last years of World War II, from 1942 onwards, Jewish and African-American US troops visiting Sydney found their way to the New Theatre rooms near the harbour, where they found a sympathetic group of people with whom to discuss politics and music and work on theatre. After the war, members of the Progressive Jewish Youth of Sydney would often attend New Theatre performances; and, in 1955, the group sponsored a performance of David Berg's *Mother Riba* (discussed below) at the Maccabean Hall in Paddington. In the 1960s, members of the Strathfield Jewish community would make large block bookings for New Theatre plays.

In Adelaide, there were very close connections between the Adelaide Jewish Club and the early radical theatre scene. The Adelaide Jewish Club, founded in the early 1930s, was on the corner of Hyde and Pirie Streets in the city. It soon became a meeting place for some of the senior members of Adelaide's left fraternity. In turn, the sons and daughters of these leftists also began to congregate at the Jewish Club until it became the meeting place of Adelaide's largest left youth organisation, the Labor Youth League. This was an umbrella organisation for a number of groups; one was the Left Book Club Theatre, which changed its name to the NTL in 1939. Subsequently, the Jewish Club regularly hosted plays and readings. In Adelaide, as elsewhere, there was a great crossover of personnel between these groups. Hal Pritchard was a prominent member of the theatre group; his wife Sadie Pritchard's father, Lewis Saunders, was a founding member of the Jewish Club; and Sadie, a historian of the Adelaide Jewish community, was also a member of the Women's International Zionist Organisation.

PLAYS ON JEWISH THEMES

Through the 1930s, 1940s and 1950s, the New Theatre produced many plays addressing antisemitism and fascism. Here is a brief overview of some of the most notable productions.

Blood on the Moon

Paul and Claire Sifton's 1933 play *Blood on the Moon* premiered at the Mayan Theatre in Los Angeles. The play is about the family of a celebrated brain surgeon in Berlin, whose fortune changes in 1933 when his Jewish heritage is discovered. It stands as a rare, early condemnation of Nazi Germany by US writers. Not only was the play a sophisticated treatment of Nazi ideology and the early days of Nazi rule; it was also very prescient. Despite being written just after the Nazis came to power in 1933, the play remained highly relevant through the 1930s and the war period, because it foresaw that the nature of Nazism meant a new world war, extreme political repression and widespread murder. It also highlighted the centrality of antisemitism to the Nazi regime.

The Sydney New Theatre first presented *Blood on the Moon* on 22 July 1939, one of a few plays they produced about fascism and antisemitism between 1936 and the start of World War II. Frederick Hughes directed. The cast included James Allgood, Eddie Allison, Vic Arnold, Jean Blue and Jack

Fegan. New Theatre promoted it as 'a powerful indictment of Fascism and anti-Semitism'. In a program note for the Sydney production, activist Jessie Street urged Australian asylum for 'these persecuted and tortured people'. The play had broad audience appeal, causing the New Theatre to extend its run to 30 July and 6, 13 and 20 August. The first lines were delivered in pitch darkness, and the *Australian Theatre News* found the production:

> one of the most gripping, poignant and intense plays this writer has seen. Almost every word uttered and definitely the climax of every scene reveals the authors' very real understanding of human character, their sympathy with the victims of German Fascism and their complete knowledge of the demands made by intelligent playgoers.

Hugh Carlsson was 'outstanding' as the doctor; Leslie Wiggins, as the younger son Hans, demonstrated a 'splendid piece of hysterical emotion' (one night he cut his finger during the performance and smeared blood over his face for Act 3); and Elsie Dick and Jean Blue were 'natural' in their parts.

In Perth, the WAG presented the play as a 'festival production' for the annual Drama Festival in the Pier Street Assembly Hall on 23 September 1939, soon after the outbreak of war. Phyllis Harnett produced the play. The response was not particularly favourable; the columnist 'Polygon' complained that 'seeing the play was like reading yesterday's newspaper when tomorrow's issue is just going to press.' The WAG revised their production and restaged it on 6 and 7 October that year. The revised production was, by some accounts, a 'tremendous improvement', 'presented with fire and conviction', causing one audience member to respond:

> after seeing that play I realise why we have got to go on fighting Nazism. I knew such things happened in Germany, but you can't quite grasp it till you see it in a play.

When police raided communists' and fellow travellers' homes and businesses in June 1940, they confiscated the script of *Blood on the Moon*, described as 'Communist literature', from the Sydney New Theatre's office. D. R. B. Mitchell, the Inspector, wrote of the 'insidious' propaganda that such stage presentations represented: 'it will be seen that some of the plays they have produced are of an antiwar variety'.

The Melbourne New Theatre produced *Blood on the Moon* in 1943 from 15 June for two weeks at 92 Flinders Street. Hilda Esson and Bob Mathews directed. This was a benefit performance for the Merchant Navy Appeal Fund. The program warned that, while the action of the play was set in Berlin:

> anti-Semitic propaganda and persecution is fostered by fascists the world over, to divert the attention of the people from major issues. *Blood on the Moon* should act as a warning to us in Australia that division of the people by such methods leads only to disaster for the Army of Freedom in its fight against fascism.

The *New Theatre Review* urged readers to remember 'the tortures and the massacres of the Jews throughout the whole of Nazi-occupied Europe', because 'obviously it is the duty of every clear-thinking person to combat this evil by every possible method, at every possible opportunity'.

Renegade

John Hackett Pollock was an Irish pathologist and writer; a friend of W. B. Yeats. He wrote under the pseudonym 'An Philibin' (the Plover) and was a founder of the Gate Theatre in Dublin. The New Theatre staged Pollock's *Renegade* in March 1940 on a double bill with *Where's That Bomb?* The play tells the story of David Berman, a New York rabbi who struggles to know which side to take in a strike. Batya, David's daughter, is a unionist helping to organise the strike against her uncle Morris' factory. Karl, the younger brother, is disdainful of Batya and wants to assimilate to escape being Jewish. The play is an argument for Jewish cooperation with working-class progressive movements as a route to fighting antisemitism, against the option of political quietism and support for reactionary ruling class forces. It is a short but powerful piece which touches on some complex political issues with a deft hand.

Vic Arnold produced the play, with John Sherman as Rabbi Berman and Freda Lewis as his daughter Batya. One report said:

> both plays attracted big and appreciative audiences, and their success indicated that the New Theatre League is destined to provide the kind of working-class intellectual entertainment that for far too long has been denied to a very large section of the would-be play-going Sydney community.

Under the auspices of the Works Committee of the Mortlake Gas Works, the New Theatre took this double-header of *Where's That Bomb?* and *Renegade* to the Memorial Hall at Central Concord on 10 April 1940 in a 'return visit'. The program described the play as 'a strong drama of Jewish life and trade unionism'. The Brisbane New Theatre staged it in December 1940, in the Student Theatre Rooms. Melbourne New Theatre staged it in August 1940. The *Argus* noted:

> as the New Theatre Club prefers to hide the identity of its players it is not possible to hand out individual praise – other than to say that the young lady as Mrs. Berman was outstanding.

Thirty Pieces of Silver

One of several non-Australian Jewish activists to make connections with the Australian New Theatre was US communist writer Howard Fast. His play, *Thirty Pieces of Silver*, is set in Washington DC in 1948. The narrative centres on statistician David Graham, who names his wartime friend, a Russian-born Jew named Agronsky, as a communist. Unlike Judas, he receives no 30 pieces of silver, but loses his government job. Essentially, the play is about a stool pigeon who informs against his friend. *Thirty Pieces of Silver*, like *Renegade* and *Blood on the Moon*, took the form of a social realist domestic drama. In *Thirty Pieces of Silver*, a battle plays out between David and wife Jane over attitudes towards their African-American maid and their friend Agronsky. The play skilfully ties together themes of anti-Black racism, McCarthyist anti-communism and antisemitism.

Branches of the New Theatre staged the play just before and after the September 1951 referendum to ban the CPA. Howard Fast wrote:

> I received a letter from the New Theatre, in Melbourne, saying that they were looking for scripts about the modern scene, and did I have anything they could possibly use? Possibly because Australia was sufficiently distant for me to plunge again, and possibly because the fascination of the theatre is something no writer truly shakes loose from, I rooted out the MS of *Thirty Pieces of Silver*, shook the dust from it, read it through, made some changes, and sent it off to Australia.

Fast, together with 10 others from the Board of Directors of the Anti-Fascist League, had received a prison sentence in June 1950 for refusing to disclose names to the House Committee on Un-American Activities. The CPA's Melbourne newspaper, the *Guardian*, described the play's focus as 'the attack on American democratic liberties':

> Bland suave Mr Fuller, an agent of the US Department of Justice does not like to be called German – that term is far too melodramatic. Fuller carries a briefcase, and dresses unobtrusively. He questions you politely but persistently: 'Do you know a man Agronsky? Is he a Jew? Is he a Communist?' And then suddenly you're on the spot. Will you betray your friend? Will you tell a lie to please Mr Fuller and save your own skin? What would you do if it happened here in Australia?

In a subsequent letter, Fast stated:

> In a certain measure we are being turned into a nation of stool pigeons. Thousands have become professional as well as semi-professional informers for the FBI. The little story told in *Thirty Pieces of Silver* is not a figment of my imagination! I wish to God it were.

Thirty Pieces of Silver had its world premiere in the Melbourne New Theatre on 24 February 1951. With a small, 'competent' cast, it brought in good houses and was a financial success. The Sydney New Theatre season, with John Armstrong directing, then began on 10 March 1951. After these successful runs, Fast did a complete rewrite (basing his new version on criticisms from Australia), after which the play became very popular in Europe. At one point during 1952, Fast recalls: 'productions were running simultaneously in Berlin, Vienna, Budapest, Warsaw, Pilsen and Moscow'. Buoyed by its international success, he wrote to the Sydney New Theatre, encouraged by stories of their Antipodean political activism:

> We were most cheered to read of the struggle being put up in Australia...we are part of a great peace movement whose victory is inevitable. It is cheering to be able to think of this as one faces the insane terror and repression of the Truman-Acheson combine.

Mother Riba

Mother Riba, by US playwright David Berg, had its first Australian performance at the Melbourne New Theatre on 2 July 1954. Seymour, the son of a Jewish family living in a Bronx tenement, is drafted during the Korean War. His mother Riba signs a petition asking the US President to end the Korean War. She develops from a naïve to a politically active woman, joining forces with Mrs Branch, an African-American woman whose son has also been drafted to fight in Korea. Her values start to clash with those of her husband Bennie, who is a social climber trying to impress the successful business owner Frohman, father of his son's girlfriend. *Mother Riba* has strong feminist politics; Bennie tries to restrain Riba within the ideological constrictions of the family, while Riba forges her own path against his oppression. The play's setting in the clothing trade and theme of class and political struggle within the Jewish community would have been highly relevant to a rapidly changing Australian Jewish community. Howard Fast described the work:

> It is a play about man's greatest and finest hope. It is
> a sensitive, fine drama – for me the most important
> post-war drama written in America.

The Sydney New Theatre produced it on 30 July 1955, and it had a reasonable season until 25 September. The CPA paper *Tribune* called it 'a memorable production'.

Friday Night at the Schrammers

and

Traitor Silence

The young gay Jewish communist Laurence Collinson was heavily involved in the New Theatre in Brisbane, including as a set designer, actor and producer. Between 1948 and 1950, Collinson produced for the New Theatre: Arthur Laurents' World War II drama about antisemitism, *Home of the Brave*; Ted Willis' satirical melodrama *God Bless the Guv'nor*; Collinson's own one-act play, *No Sugar for George*; Irwin Shaw's antiwar drama *Bury the Dead*; and Jim Crawford's *Miner's Right*. He also acted in major roles in Oriel Gray's anti-racist play *Had We but World Enough* and Ilya Ehrenburg's *Lion in the Square*.

Collinson wrote a one-act Jewish family drama called *Friday Night at the Schrammers*, which the New Theatre performed in Brisbane in 1948. The play, set in the northern suburbs of Melbourne, deals with family conflict over issues of assimilation, religion, antisemitism and politics. This was a common thread through the US scripts discussed above; all took the form of the social realist domestic drama, with different family members representing different social positions and tendencies. Daughter Sadie is ashamed of being Jewish, because of the antisemitism she suffers at school. Mother Mrs Schrammer struggles with the atheism and new social attitudes of her children. Son Mark is a leftist activist who wants to escape the confines of the family and participate in social change. His Jewishness is not expressed through strict observance; instead, he asks, when challenged about his religious/family

commitments by Mrs Schrammer: 'what are those six million Jews eating tonight? Also the Friday special?' This understanding of Jewish identity as an issue of transnational political solidarity grew from the events of the Holocaust and its memorialisation by Jewish organisations worldwide in this period.

After moving to Melbourne in 1950, Collinson took up some of these same issues in his major theatrical work of this period, *Traitor Silence*, written in 1952 but never performed. It is not known whether he intended the play to be performed by the Melbourne New Theatre or by the drama group (founded by Collinson) of the youth wing of the left-wing JCCFAS. The play still stands as an excellent encapsulation of Jewish anti-fascist politics of this period and political and class tensions within the Jewish community. *Traitor Silence* was a fictionalisation of a controversial event in 1952, when the ABC sponsored an Australian tour of German pianist Walter Gieseking. Gieseking had acted as a kind of cultural ambassador for the Nazi regime, and his tour provoked an outcry from the Jewish community. This issue became yet another conflict point between an activist Jewish left, led by the JCCFAS, and forces of the Jewish right then in the ascendant. The Jewish establishment condemned JCCFAS' protest against Gieseking. Rather than endorsing a public confrontation with Gieseking as a matter of principle, they judged this protest as inviting antisemitism and endangering the respectability of the Jewish community.

Collinson dramatised this whole affair through the character of Simon Goldberger, a young Jewish musician whose star is on the rise. He eventually takes a principled public stand against the tour of the Nazi conductor, Heinrich Schultz. Goldberger, whose father and grandmother are Holocaust survivors, has to make increasingly difficult choices and endanger his own career as the play progresses. Collinson's play was obviously autobiographical, to an extent: he was a young artist who himself became involved in the CPA and the JCCFAS.

One of the play's central themes is the relationship between art and politics. In the first scene, Goldberger is uncertain

Laurence Collinson, photographed in the eary 1950s

about taking a stand; he suggests: 'Music's my job, not politics'. However, as the play develops, he takes a stronger stand, suggesting the important role of cultural figures in legitimating Nazism: '[Schultz's] orchestral baton was as much an instrument of slaughter as any club held by an S.S. man.' As the New Theatre slogan affirmed, art here was conceived as a weapon, either for good or for ill.

The tensions between a Jewish anti-fascist politics and the narrower politics of an ascendant Jewish right come out when Goldberger must choose between speaking at a protest organised by his new friends in the 'anti-fascist league' or do as Matthew Levine, the Jewish establishment leader, wishes – and stay silent. Goldberger's dialogue with Levine is instructive. Levine maligns the Jewish 'radicals' of the 'anti-fascist league', suggesting that he does not 'regard them as true Jews'. This was a strong echo of the rhetoric of contemporary Jewish right leaders. Levine continues, suggesting that his 'main interest is in the good reputation of the Jewish community'. And the best way to maintain this reputation is political quiescence:

> MATTHEW: Mr Goldberger, forgive me for underlining the obvious, but you are no fool. The Jews of this city, of Australia in fact, are a highly respected part of the general community.
>
> SIM: You think silence is the best method of keeping this respect.
>
> MATTHEW: Certainly.
>
> SIM: What about our self-respect?
>
> MATTHEW: The better type of Jew – or should I say rather the better-educated type of Jew – such as yourself, and with your permission, I include myself also – have certain important links to maintain with the non-Jewish community. You probably know that I am rather – well regarded – in the – er – higher circles of the Labour [sic] Party. Others of us have important contacts with the Liberal Party. Such links, which grow stronger every day, are not merely important to

our personal ambitions. The welfare and good name of the Jewish community are to quite a large extent dependent on the quality of this relationship. This relationship must not be jeopardised in any way.

SIM: Your impersonal and objective analysis of the situation is admirable.

Collinson here very effectively skewers the new conservative leadership of the Jewish community, making it clear that they represent their own class interest despite dressing up their claims as representing the community as a whole. He also makes it clear that this political split meant differing attitudes to the memorialisation of the Holocaust. After Levine suggests that the USA has already given Schultz a 'clean sheet' in West Germany's de-nazification process, Sim replies:

SIM: My young teacher friend [from the anti-fascist league] of last night showed me a file of cuttings of all the people the Americans had freed and whitewashed. It was a very long and quite revolting list…a man such as Schultz can be very valuable in the cold war. As a cultural ambassador, as one of the saviours of Europe against the Russian barbarians to quote an American authority in a similar case – he is the equivalent of millions of dollars in propaganda. His past isn't important any longer. But his ideas are currently very useful. That apparently is his new role. That may satisfy you but it doesn't satisfy me. I doubt if it will satisfy the millions who are still suffering from the effects of Nazi 'culture'.

MATTHEW: To be quite honest, I think the atrocities have been much exaggerated.

The Jewish left wanted to further the memory of the Holocaust but connect it with a wider anti-fascist, anti-imperialist political analysis that was critical of US warmongering in particular. Such a narrative did not suit the Jewish right, who wanted the community to fit in quietly as loyal Australian citizens, on board with the Cold War. While Levine's comment here is a caricature, it is certainly indicative of a developing approach to Holocaust memorialisation that was much more conservative.

From our perspective, the anti-racist, anti-fascist and pro-working class struggle orientation of the New Theatre opened up discursive space for the possibility of presenting works such as *Traitor Silence*, and thus the conditions for its writing – despite the fact that it was never produced. In this case, Collinson's experience in the New Theatre combined with the politics of JCCFAS to produce one of the clearest and most powerful cultural expressions of Jewish anti-fascist politics in Australia.

The Shepherd and the Hunter

Hungarian-born Australian Jewish writer David Martin wrote *The Shepherd and the Hunter* in 1946. The play addresses complex issues around Zionism, anti-imperialism and racism. Although it did not directly address fascism and antisemitism, its production in both Sydney and London reflected major themes of Jewish left concern as they intersected with an anti-imperialist, internationalist politics.

David Martin had a very international life before arriving in Australia in 1949. He was born into a Jewish family in Hungary, then grew up and was educated in Germany. He joined the Communist League of Youth when he was 17 and handed out leaflets under the noses of the Brownshirts. He left Germany in 1934 to live variously in Holland, back in Hungary and in Palestine. He volunteered in the Spanish Civil War, then spent time in both London and India.

Our story focuses here on his time in Palestine and the play he wrote about it: *The Shepherd and the Hunter*. The play is an excellent example of the links between left-wing theatre movements in London and in Australia, because it played first in London in 1946 and then in Sydney in 1947. The Sydney production first brought Martin to Australia, where he spent the rest of his life, becoming a very well-known writer and poet. His work with fellow members of the left-wing RWG brought him into contact with other New Theatre writers, including Frank Hardy, Mona Brand and Dorothy Hewett.

We should note here that the dual productions of this play were not David Martin's only transnational political and cultural connections. He moved in Communist Party circles in Palestine, in London and in Australia, where he joined in 1951. He was also part of the burgeoning Jewish anti-fascist left political and cultural movement as the literature editor for *New Life* in the UK and, upon his move to Australia, as a frequent writer for *Unity* magazine; these were, respectively, the premier English-language Jewish left publications of each country.

The Shepherd and the Hunter is a politically complicated and somewhat confused work, which Martin described as 'a call for Jewish–Arab friendship', although this is not always obvious from the text. The main characters are: Jakov Koenig, a member of the right-wing Jewish terrorist group the Irgun; Jakov's wife Malke, a recent arrival and Holocaust survivor; Shura Kutzman, the de facto leader of the right-wing Zionist terrorist cell; and his father Berl Kurtzman, the orange grower. The British blackmail Jakov to inform on his cousin-in-law, Shura Kutzman, and the rest of the group. The play reflected a number of themes of contemporary concern for the Jewish left and, indeed, a wider audience, about grappling with the political consequences of the Holocaust and the choices available to Jews in the pre-state Jewish settlement in Palestine.

Jakov is portrayed as a broken man who used to have dreams of a bettered humanity but now says: 'we have been betrayed too often…hope has become a delusion more deadly than hopelessness'. In a similar vein, another character describes Shura, the hard man leader, as trying to be 'as cruel as history'. Martin's depiction of Shura paints a romantic portrait of a hard and determined resistance leader, while also condemning his extreme right-wing Zionist political ideology. This is clearest in the scene where Shura interrupts a moment between Malke and Leila, a local Arab Palestinian woman. Shura tries to prevent their friendship, yelling at Leila and calling her 'vermin'. Shura says:

> our hearts have been open too long. For hundreds of years they were open for sorrow and persecution. It is time to close our hearts and answer bullet with bullet, blood with blood, terror with terror.

NEW THEATRE
presents

The Shepherd
and the Hunter

A play by
DAVID MA[RTIN]

Sydney's program for The Shepherd and the Hunter.

This sort of ideology is anathema to Shura's father, Berl, who is portrayed as a typical old school Labour Zionist. He regrets deeply that his son did not join him as an orange farmer and that hatred has 'made him blind'. Despite this, Berl is not the moral centre of *The Shepherd and the Hunter*. This is clearest in Berl's confrontation with the foreman of the orange grove towards the end of the play. The foreman wants to hire some local Arab Palestinian labourers, suggesting that there should be no such thing as separate Arab and Jewish plantations. Berl responds forcefully with a recitation of the zero-sum separatist Zionist dogma of 'Hebrew labour': 'Every Arab keeps a Jew out. Every Jew saves another Jew.' Here, Martin is suggesting that it is not only the extremist right-wing that is in the wrong, but Zionism as a whole, which has led to conflict and dispossession in Palestine. We know from Martin's other texts, written contemporaneously, that the foreman's critique accorded with his own politics. Malke, Jakov's newly arrived wife, is sceptical of both Shura's over the top masculinist posturing and Berl's separatism. She asks: 'But separate, how can we live? Such a small country and each by himself?'

The political priorities of the play broadly reflect the international Jewish left and the international communist movement's then current views on the Palestine situation, which the foreign policy imperatives of the Soviet Union largely determined. While disdaining Zionism, they supported the Jewish settlement in Palestine and their battle for independence from the British. The struggle is framed in internationalist, anti-imperialist terms. In *The Shepherd and the Hunter*, this is most obvious in the opening scene: the British soldiers compare the Arabs to the Indians and the Jews to the Irish. However, this anti-imperialist message is somewhat lost in the closing scenes, where the British commander appears as a wise figure of dramatic reconciliation.

Some of the play's subtler politics appear to be lost in its two productions. This was partly due to faults in the script, particularly its ending in the somewhat overwrought death of the anti-hero-cum-hero Shura. *The Shepherd and the Hunter*'s internal confusions were the cause of much angst, both in London and Sydney. In London, there were troubles about the politics of the play, despite healthy takings of £600 for the Unity Theatre. David Martin notes that the producer, Ted Willis, who was himself a prominent left-wing playwright, wanted to rewrite whole scenes. Martin could only prevent this by threatening to leaflet the audience on the first night with handbills proclaiming that the play they were about to see was not his. Martin was successful, but he still had issues with the CPGB, who were worried that the play could be seen as too Zionist and lacking a clear positive message. East End party branch meetings hotly debated the play for being pro-Zionist, and Irgun supporters visited the theatre during the play's run. *The Times* described it, somewhat cautiously, as a play which, while 'set against the tragic background of Palestine', was 'no more political than Sean O'Casey's plays'. Martin wrote, in response to a British *Daily Worker* review, that 'my play is anything but Zionist', accusing the reviewer of libelling both himself and the Unity Theatre cast. The controversy became all the hotter when, just a couple of weeks after the play's run at Unity, Irgun terrorists blew up the British military headquarters at the King David Hotel in Jerusalem, killing 91 people.

In Sydney, Jock Levy directed the play and starred as Shura. The New Theatre had its own reservations about Martin's play; the program included the note:

> the value of the work, however, would have been enhanced had the author indicated a way out of the conflict to a peaceful and constructive future.

In an interview many years later, Jock recalled how horrified they were that the local Zionists loved the New Theatre's production of *The Shepherd and the Hunter*, thinking it very good propaganda for their cause. In a critical review of the play in *Tribune*, Rex Chiplin noted that Levy as Shura 'tended to overact and rant in places' in an effort 'to paint Shura in as black a light as possible'. We can see here how the acting was to an extent straining, if not against the dialogue, then against the narrative arc of the play's structure. In overdoing the villainy of Shura, Levy tried, it seems unsuccessfully, to counteract the implied tragic heroism of Shura's death scene. Levy himself believed that Marxists were opposed to the play's 'naturalism', and that 'Arabs' had as much right to the land as the Jews.

A mainstream review of the Sydney production noted that the play 'presents a highly controversial topic upon which constructive thinking needs to be done'. Rex Chiplin's review in the *Tribune* suggested that the play's message of Jewish–Arab unity was completely lost in the dramatic arc of the narrative. Here, the production compounded the faults in the script with the treatment of the foreman who objects to Berl's Zionist separatism. According to Chiplin, the unity theme had an opportunity to come out more clearly in this scene; but it was 'ruined by faulty casting' of the foreman character. Chiplin suggested:

John Hepworth as a British major in The Shepherd and the Hunter, 1947.

'so weak was the actor portraying the part that the scene became uncomfortably ludicrous.'

After the London and Sydney performances, the play also appeared in Manchester and Bradford. The Dublin Jewish Dramatic Society took it to Ireland. According to Martin, a well-known New York Jewish producer contacted him after the script's publication, wanting to stage it on Broadway. However, this was conditional on changes to the ending, to strengthen the Zionist anti-imperialist message through 'a short speech of fierce defiance… to be flung into the teeth of the British anti-Semites who were hunting down Jewish freedom fighters.' Martin replied that he was willing to 'strengthen the climax' but not to rewrite it. This was for two reasons: firstly, 'it did not suit his style'; secondly, he was 'hoping to apply one day' for British citizenship. *The Shepherd and The Hunter* was an incredibly politically fraught play. Its ambiguities and contradictions created the possibilities for productions to take very different turns.

Sky Without Birds

Australian playwright Oriel Gray had more than 14 theatre scripts produced in almost every capital city of Australia between 1943 and 1960. A multiple award-winning writer, Gray also had works performed on radio and television. Michelle Arrow describes Gray as: 'arguably one of the most important representatives of pre-1960s theatre in Australia'. She was a member of the CPA from 1938 to 1949. She began her connection with the Sydney New Theatre as a chorus girl, usher and actor in 1937, before becoming their first playwright-in-residence in 1942. She wrote a number of plays for the Theatre, including, in 1950, *Sky Without Birds*.

What is striking about *Sky Without Birds* is Gray's transnational analysis of fascism and its intimate tie with antisemitism and racial prejudice. Gray was not Jewish; her knowledge of issues around fascism and antisemitism came through her experience in the CPA and associated milieus, such as the New Theatre. Gray's play reflects an anti-racist, anti-fascist understanding of antisemitism and xenophobia. *Sky Without Birds* is set in the post office of the small remote town of 'Kooroora' in the Nullarbor desert and revolves around the arrival of a German Jewish refugee, Heinrich Schafer, to the town. The play's characters reflect a microcosm of Australian society: Bartley is the reactionary capitalist stirring up trouble; Rick is the kind-hearted and understanding progressive worker; the Major is the conservative stick-in-the-mud; Peter, Bartley's son, is the young man to be won away from reaction; Cruddie is the dangerous, boorish one, spurred on by Bartley. The female characters, Nereira and Peggy, are less clearly social types. Much of the drama focuses on Nereira and Heinrich's love story, leading not to a marriage plot but, reflecting Gray's feminism, to their personal growth.

Sky Without Birds features a transnational rendering of fascism's dangers and its connection with antisemitism, an analysis which was a fundamental tenet of the Jewish left and its allies. Repeatedly throughout the script, Heinrich sees Bartley's intense antisemitism and reactionary politics as reflecting 'the old hatred, the old contempt that they feel for me, but that I feel too, for them!' Nazism here was not regarded as a German cultural or civilisational deficiency; it was an intensification of a reactionary politics that

'THEM SONGS ARE DANGEROUS': ANTI-FASCISM, ANTISEMITISM AND JEWISH CONNECTIONS

also manifested in Australia.

In Gray's clear dramatisation, Bartley's antisemitism is ideological, irrational, and materially motivated. This, too, was an idea central to the contemporary Jewish anti-fascist analysis. The contradictory and irrational workings of antisemitic ideology and the hypocrisy of antisemites is illustrated by this dialogue from Bartley:

> Not a yid! They're the worst, you know. If they're working for you, they're always stirring up trouble, and if you're working for them, they sweat you dry. It's true what's said about them, you know – they count every penny. Every penny. Fancy him being one of them. [He shakes his head sadly and prepares to go.] Well, good afternoon to you both. [He starts out, then pops back.] Dear me – I forgot my change!

Later in the play, Bartley gets Cruddie drunk and riled up and motivated to attack Heinrich. Heinrich says:

> You meant him to come here, didn't you, Mr Bartley? You knew I was here also. You meant there should be trouble and gossip. [Almost wondering] Somehow, you profit from it, as you profit from sharp practices in your little shop.

Radio Repertory — 'Sky without Birds'
A PLAY OF ORIEL GRAY

Oriel Gray, making her initial bow before an A.B.C. audience, is an Australian palywright who has achieved considerable success with stage plays that examine and probe at social issues.

"Sky Without Birds" was written quite recently for the theatre, and has had one production. It will be heard in Radio Repertory on Monday, August 25, at 7.30 p.m. from 2BL and 3LO. The story is set on a small railway settlement on the lonely Nullabor Plains line that links east and west. Here a group of typical Australians are joined by a New Australian loco mechanic, Heinrich Schafer.

Hans is Jewish, young, handsome, introspective, on the defensive all the time. Falling in love with attractive Nerela, who is married, he gets into trouble with the men folk of the settlement. Will he have to leave? And if he does, will it be the enmity of some of the "old" Australians that drives him out, or will it be Nerela's love? It is an ironic situation handled thoughtfully and imaginatively.

There are some good characterisation readily recognisable in our present national melting pot phase, with its frictions and difficulties, and need for human sympathy.

The *Sydney Jewish News* noted *Sky Without Birds*.

Gray here suggests that Bartley's stirring of antisemitism is motivated by a desire to foster division, which will benefit his reactionary capitalist agenda.

Gray's account of the Holocaust also reflected anti-fascist ideas. When Heinrich gives an account of why he did not fight in the last war, he says:

> Even in the later stages of the war, the German army were not conscripting concentration camp prisoners who were being held for offences against the Nazi state. Especially if they were also Jewish. So I missed the last...show.

On first glance, this slightly nonsensical dialogue indicates that even those on the left and even those who wished to highlight the antisemitism of the Nazis misunderstood the Holocaust in this period. They understood the antisemitism of the Nazi regime as simply an additional dimension to its program of murder and political repression, rather than being central to its functioning, as we understand today. Schafer was, therefore, rendered both as an anti-fascist and a Jew. His primary reason for incarceration was his dissident political activism. This leads to the following dialogue between Peggy and the Major:

> MAJOR: No one asked him to come, of course.
>
> PEGGY: No...although we're always saying we need people here, aren't we?
>
> MAJOR: Selected immigrants...that's different. We need a good type...plenty of people who were against them [the Nazis] wouldn't be what I'd call the right types for out here.

This dialogue was an effective rendering of the immigration politics in Australia at the time. Jayne Persian suggests that the Australian Government's mass migration program in the late 1940s was both racially and politically selective, above all based on the potential labour contribution of migrants. 'Balts' were favoured, because they were blue eyed and blonde, with reactionary politics; southern Europeans and Jews were imagined as both racially inferior and communists. The Major's statement echoes groups such as the

Returned and Services League (RSL) of Australia, who tied an anti-communist politics to their antisemitism, attacking Jewish migrants in this period as 'doubtful security risks'. As Phillip Mendes documents, the press and government were in thrall to ideas of 'Judeo-communism'.

One of the central themes of the play is Heinrich's battle with his relationship to the past:

> HEINRICH: That is why I came here. I do not expect to regret anything from my old life...to regret or remember. Just for a moment...gone in a breath...you reminded me of someone I used to know...someone who died a long time ago. Just for a moment, I even asked myself, 'Do the dead return?'
>
> NERIERA: Perhaps they do...in one way or another. Or perhaps they never die.
>
> HEINRICH: They do, I assure you. Everything dies, I have discovered...people, dreams, ideals... Forgive my poor English that it makes such big sounding words. But truly it is a comforting thought...everything dies and one is left with a nice tidy mind and heart, swept clean like an empty attic. No old ties, no obligations.

The play is set up to interrogate this false and unhealthy independence from the world. In *Sky Without Birds'* narrative arc, in order to grow a healthy attachment to people in the world, Heinrich also needs to stop repressing his past. Nereira reproaches Heinrich:

> You left them, not they you. All the time you have been turning your face from the sick world, they have been working and thinking and talking to make it well and beautiful. Now ask them politely if they will have you back among them.

The answer for this alienation from the world was social action. As the play progresses, Heinrich develops a new attitude:

MAJOR: You haven't made yourself exactly small. You've had a lot to say about conditions in the sheds here, I believe – been backing Rick and Rick's always disturbing the peace. Meaning it for the best, of course, but still – apart from that, you've had some very heated arguments with Mr Bartley and made some very wild statements.

HEINRICH: Is it so wild to protest that this beautiful land should be hampered with the old prejudices, the old injustices, the old hatreds which have scarred older countries? Is it so wild – to be angry to see in a little country storekeeper [Bartley] the hypocrisies, the cruelties which were put at the service of the Nazis in my own Germany? If this is to be my country, may I not be jealous for her honour?

Here, the transnational nature of fascism as an intensification of reactionary politics and as intimately connected with racism and antisemitism appears clearly to Heinrich. His anti-fascist politics drive both an active engagement with the world and a coming to terms with his past. Reflecting Australian Jewish anti-fascist left ideas of the time, the memory of the Holocaust brought political consequences and responsibilities in Australia.

The play enjoyed a number of performances in Australia during the 1950s. Sydney New Theatre produced the play first, as the opening work of the very popular Drama Festival of the Youth Carnival for Peace and Friendship in March 1952. Jock Levy directed this piece, with a cast consisting of Laurence Booth, Nan Davies, John Evans, William Flaus, David Futcher, Shirley Keane, Paul Lavelle, Reginald Lye and Tom Posa (who had previously lived in a small town in the Nullarbor) as Heine. As with many New Theatre plays in the Cold War, ASIO attended this production and maintained files on all the performers and crew.

Drama critic Leslie Rees, upon reading the play ('Unfortunately I missed seeing [it]'), wrote: 'once again one notes and appreciates Oriel Gray's direct feeling for the dispossessed, while wishing that she had been able to devise more varied as well as more believable situations and use fewer long speeches'; he did believe that it was sensitively written, but with 'too sluggish a movement towards a resolution'. Another reviewer noted that, while the play received an enthusiastic response from its Festival audience, the actors 'were handicapped by a tendency of the script to rely too much on longish introspective speeches, and not enough on action'. The play closed on 11 May after 23 performances with poor houses. Jock Levy, the director, left the New Theatre because of this play, 'claiming he was opposed to the author's treatment of the Jewish question and had been persuaded to direct the play for heavy-handed political reasons'. Paul Herlinger has suggested that Miriam Hampson was doing the persuading.

Sky Without Birds was produced for radio a number of times in Sydney and Adelaide, in 1952 and 1957. The Adelaide New Theatre produced the play at Plympton Park on 25 September 1952, and then in Stow Hall on 12 and 13 September. Bryce Stewart, the producer, 'made the most of the material at his command', according to one reviewer. The Brisbane New Theatre staged *Sky Without Birds* on 10 October 1952 at All Saints Hall. Syd Davis, in his *Guardian* review of the Brisbane production, believed that the audience 'forgave any technical shortcomings in the script or the production' because they 'understood and liked the ideas in the drama'.

Gray's play reflected a mature reckoning with fascism, antisemitism and the politics of migration and migrant memory. It presented a thoughtful engagement with issues that were then very important for the Australian left. We suggest that *Sky Without Birds* also reflected ideas that were central to the Australian Jewish left, suggesting the Jewish left's influence in a wider left cultural milieu.

CONCLUSION

In 1960, a global wave of public swastika daubings also affected Australia. These attacks seemed to presage a re-emergence of fascist antisemitism. The New Theatre was quick to respond, staging a production of John Hepworth's newly written montage script *Writing on the Wall*. In the play's opening scenes, members of the New Theatre in Melbourne enter their theatre to find it vandalised; large swastikas and antisemitic slogans have been painted around the stage. The characters react with horror, and some with confusion. To educate each other, the actors restage scenes from the past 30 years of New Theatre productions about fascism and antisemitism. The second half of the play was a living newspaper that looked at the large numbers of Nazis in high positions in West Germany.

Writing on the Wall was meant to educate a new generation about the history, and still current dangers, of fascism and antisemitism, but also to celebrate the New Theatre's own proud record of combating these forces. One character says that, despite most people involved in these past productions being non-Jewish and so not understanding antisemitism first-hand, these plays were 'part of our lives – part of what we thought and felt.' Productions such as those this chapter covers made a major impact on the cast, crew and audiences of the New Theatre. In performing overseas and Australian-bred works, the New Theatre was one of the few sites in Australia where Jews and non-Jews together could develop a sophisticated and deeply felt insight into fascism, antisemitism and Jewish politics.

In the opening scene of *The Shepherd and the Hunter*, Martin makes a somewhat self-referential claim. Two British guards are guarding a Jewish prisoner who is singing a Hebrew song of lament. One guard suggests that the singing is harmless, to which the second guard says:

> Them songs are dangerous. They sing and sing and one day – bang, bang – they blow the place sky high with you'n me and all in it. Can't trust 'em.

While Martin was certainly opposed to right-wing Jewish terrorism, he points here towards the great power of cultural production for political and social movements. The power of the ideas that shone through in Jewish and anti-fascist plays in the New Theatre suggest that 'them songs' may still be dangerous.

FURTHER READING

'Collinson, Laurence Henry, ASIO File', National Archives of Australia.

Collinson, Laurence, *Friday Night at the Schrammers*, in G. Branson (ed.), *Australian One-Act Plays*, Adelaide, Rigby, 1962 (1948).

Gardiner, Allan, 'Pushed into the Bourgeois Camp: David Martin and the CPA', *Overland*, no. 142, 1996, pp. 27–30.

Hatherell, William, 'The Brisbane Years of Laurence Collinson', *Queensland Review*, vol. 13, 2006, pp. 1–12.

Kaiser, Max, '"A New and Modern Golden Age of Jewish Culture": Shaping the Cultural Politics of Transnational Jewish Antifascism', *Journal of Modern Jewish Studies*, vol. 17, no. 3, 2017, pp. 287–303.

Martin, David, *My Strange Friend: an Autobiography*, Sydney, Pan Macmillan, 1991.

Martin, David, *The Shepherd and the Hunter*, London, Allan Wingate, 1946.

Mendes, Phillip, 'Constructions of Judeo-Communism and the Unravelling of the Melbourne Jewish Council to Combat Fascism and Anti-Semitism, 1949–1950', *Australian Jewish Historical Society Journal*, vol. 20, no. 1, 2010, pp. 110–122.

Zable, Arnold, *Wanderers and Dreamers: Tales of the David Herman Theatre*, South Melbourne, Hyland House, 1998.

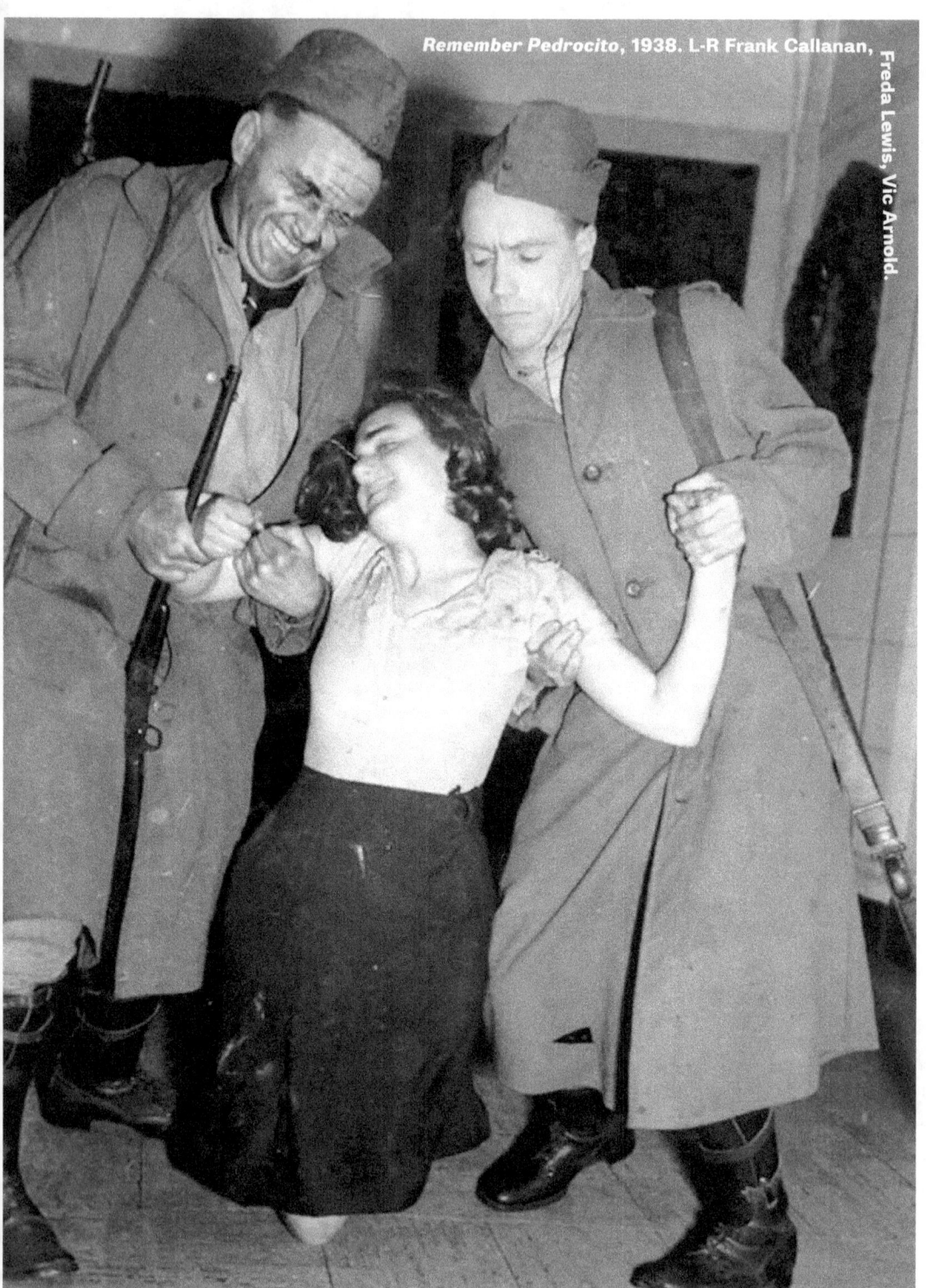

Remember Pedrocito, 1938. L-R Frank Callanan, Freda Lewis, Vic Arnold.

CHAPTER 11

Sydney New Theatre: Give Peace a Chance

Lyn Collingwood

Sydney New Theatre's Constitution lists one of its objectives as producing: 'works that challenge, inspire and encourage people to create a better world for themselves and each other'. The theatre has always embraced this ideal. Its past reputation was founded on its anti-capitalism stance and, even more strongly, its robust opposition to war.

The New supported a multiplicity of local and international pacifist groups, including the League for Peace and Democracy, Women's Commission of International Peace, Australian Peace Council, NSW Peace Council, Peace & Friendship Group, All India Peace Council, Newcastle Anti-Conscription League, Australian People's Disarmament Conference and the Association for International Co-operation and Disarmament. After World War II, as anxiety over nuclear conflict grew, the New raised money to send its delegates to the Bucharest World Festival for Peace, the Stockholm Peace Conference and the Hiroshima Peace Conference. It joined the Five Power Peace Pact campaign, opposed the Vietnam War and the first Gulf War, and supported Chilean Solidarity, Indo-China Solidarity, East Timor independence and the Bring the Frigates Home Coalition. Until 1991, members marched on Hiroshima Day under the New Theatre banner.

Pacifism was a key concern for WAC co-founders, artist George Finey and writer Jean Devanny. The latter was a member of the Communist International Committee for the Struggle Against War, and both sat on the National Committee Against War. Finey's disillusionment was a result of his experiences during four years' service with the New Zealand infantry in World War I.

THE NEW THEATRE IN AUSTRALIA

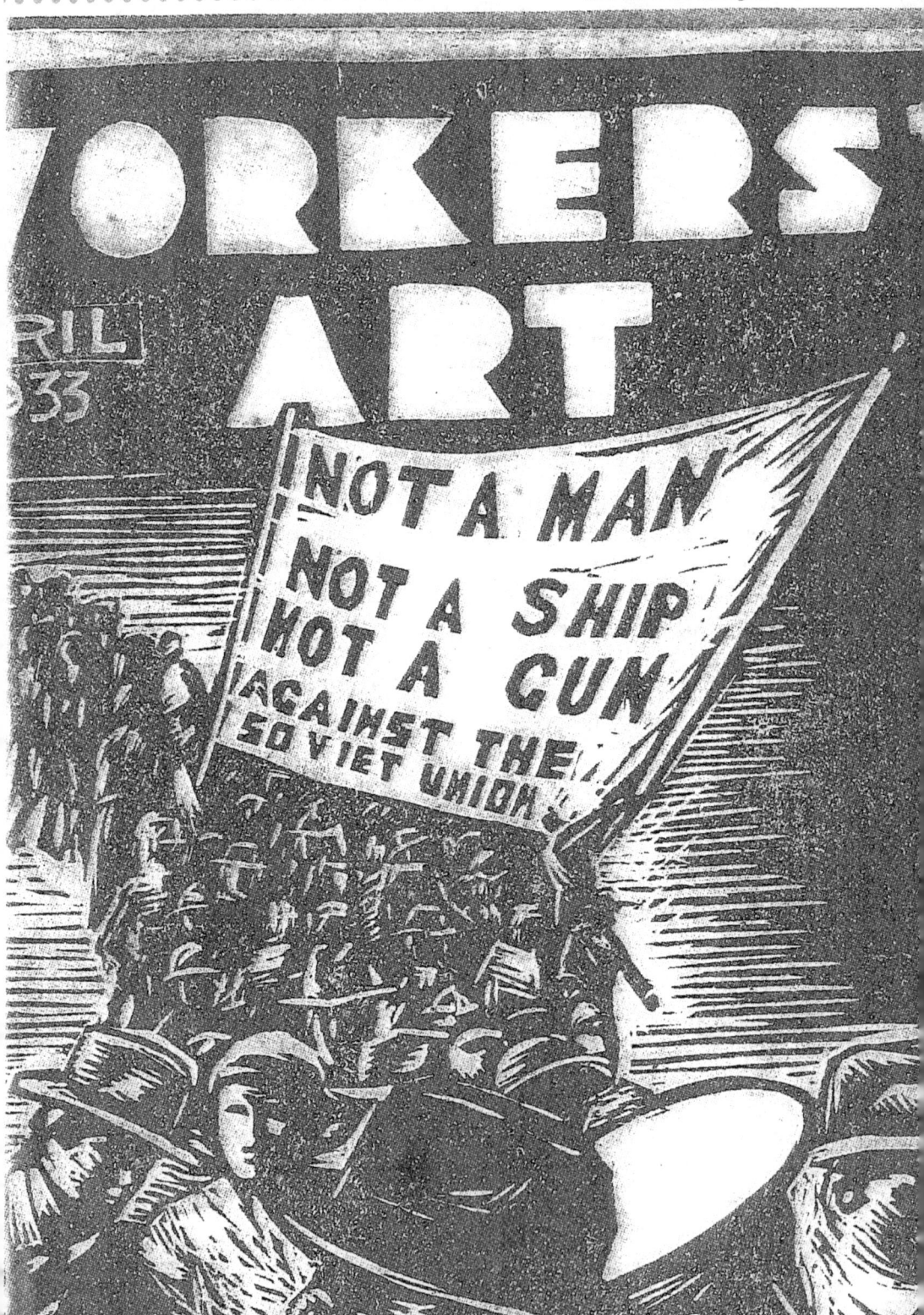

Workers' Art Magazine, 1933.

In April 1933, Finey exhibited his and his art students' linocuts at a conference organised by the Australian League Against Imperialism. Among images of the horror of war were John Harvey's caricatures of Mussolini and Hitler. Later in the year, the WAC was the venue for All-Australia Congress Against War benefit performances of *Lieutenant Pernot's Word of Honour*, set during the 1871 Paris Commune.

Soon after Finey and Devanny resigned from the WAC, its Art and Literature sections folded; the Drama section strengthened. Nelle Rickie, who had been writing propaganda for years, was a core player. Her *Defensive Warfare* played in 1931 for the FSU. In a sketch where young women sit around their flat discussing their vision for a better Australia, Rickie took the lead role:

> Joan: I wouldn't fight in a war, even a war for defence.
>
> Lulu: Are you one of those bloody rebels?

WAC actors participated in outside projects such as *Peace or War* (in aid of the MAWF) at the Railway and Tramway Institute, but, once the drama group was consolidated, most small-scale performances were in the club's own rooms.

Playwrights drew on the impact of World War I long after the conflict was over. In A. A. Milne's *The Boy Comes Home*, a young returned soldier finds that, because he has lost four years of his life, he is now too old to train for a profession. The young man in *The Face*, by US writer Arthur Laurents, has suffered permanent injury and is hidden by his mother out of view. He is an offstage presence whose disfigurement is imagined by the audience from the reaction of a visitor who returns, horrified, to the stage from the wings.

With a cast of 39, Irwin Shaw's *Bury the Dead* was too big for the clubrooms of what was now the NTL, and they staged it at the Conservatorium. Battlefield corpses sewn into hessian shrouds refuse to lie in their graves. One by one, they rise up out of the trenches and, cheated of the lives and loves they should have had, give their reasons for living. Bodies of dead Australian soldiers had been left in Europe where they fell, and the play had a profound effect on audiences. The NTL remounted it at least twice. The 'witch of Kings Cross', Rosaleen Norton, played a prostitute in the original production.

In Miles Malleson's *Black Hell*, staged in 1940, a Siegfried Sassoon-like character comes back from the front a hero but denounces the conflict as madness and says he won't go back to the grinding degradation of trench warfare.

A female version of *Journey's End*, Muriel Box's *Angels of War* concerns women ambulance drivers stationed in France in 1918 who find the glory of service hollow. The play was based on a novel, *Not So Quiet*, based in turn on real-life war diaries. After the armistice, a warning is delivered: 'There can never be another war after this. We've proved how futile and hopeless it is. It can never happen again.' First staged in 1936, the play was revived in 1940 – when the unthinkable had happened. 'Dedicated to the Cause of Peace', the second production toured 10 of the New's regular actresses to suburban venues.

John Drinkwater wrote *X=O* in 1917, while war was still raging in Europe. The NTL staged it in 1937 and revived it more than once. Political cartoonist Les Tanner designed and acted in its 1948 production.

Catherine Duncan won the NTL's 1937 playwriting competition with *The Sword Sung*. Duncan structured the play as a series of World War I scenes. The action shifts between France and Australia. In verse, in the living newspaper style of Ernst Toller, it did not appeal to one reviewer who labelled it didactic harangue. In contrast, powerful acting camouflaged slabs of propaganda in William Kozlenko's *Trumpets of Wrath*, staged for Peace Week 1938.

Betty Roland referenced the divisive conscription debates of World War I in *No! No! or Vote 'No!'*. The agitprop piece urged the audience to respond and to join in singing the finale, its tune 'Old Black Joe':

> Commentator: In 1938 the clouds of war hang overhead again. Only united action can prevail today. What do you want? A free Australia or a country under military dictatorship which is only another name for fascism. Men and women of Australia, answer! DO YOU WANT CONSCRIPTION?
>
> All: Conscription! Conscription! Every man must go. I hear Australian voices calling. No! No! No!

The title hero of *Private Hicks* is a recruit in the US National Guard who refuses to fire on unarmed strikers, throwing down his gun and urging his fellow guardsmen to do the same. The play had several revivals. Its message interpreted as anti-draft, it was seen as relevant when Robert Menzies proposed a National Register of adult males in 1939. In June 1941, NTL Secretary Freda Lewis told a *Private Hicks* audience at interval that the work was an inspiration to young workers to resist conscription. As she spoke, on the other side of the globe, Germany was declaring war on Russia – a turning point in the theatre's attitude to mobilisation.

Private Hicks' author Albert Maltz was later jailed as one of the Hollywood Ten. Sydney New Theatre kept in touch with him for decades.

In 1936, civil war broke out in Spain. The New supported the Republican cause through fundraising, agitprop and mainstage productions, and invitations to speakers – including the Spanish Consul – to address audiences. An Australian who fought in Spain sought refuge in the NTL clubrooms after returning from the conflict frail, bronchial and shell-shocked. Dick Whateley, a drifter who picked up odd jobs, joined the International Brigade after he found himself stranded and broke in France.

In Ramón Sender's *The Secret*, a man is locked up in the Barcelona office of the Chief of Police:

> Prisoner: I am thirsty.
>
> General: Why are you thirsty?
>
> Prisoner: I have been kept for three days without water.
>
> General: Oh well, the same old story. Neither have you been fed, true?
>
> Prisoner: Sardines and raw salt cod.

The Brave and the Blind concerns the 1936 siege of Alcazar by Spanish Government forces. Its author, Michael Blankfort, was a friend of Albert Maltz.

In *Remember Pedrocito* a female civilian sniper is brought into an abandoned house occupied by members of the Spanish Regular Army who finally desert to the Republican cause. The last to leave addresses the girl:

> Juan: All the fighting isn't done with guns, little comrade. If they win, your mother and all the others that are fighting with her, they'll need you to help them make a new Spain, where people can be happy and have enough to eat without stealing, and where men won't be shot for trying to help their brothers.

Bertolt Brecht's *Señora Carrar's Rifles*, Synge's *Riders to the Sea* reimagined in Civil War Spain, was staged in 1939.

Closer to home was the threat from Japan. Betty Roland's agitprop *War on the Waterfront* was written and rehearsed at speed in response to the refusal by wharf labourers to load the *Dalfram* steamer with pig iron destined for Japan – on the grounds that it would be used to make weapons against Manchuria, and then come back to Australia as bullets. Attorney-General 'Pig Iron Bob' Menzies invoked an Act to end the strike. The iron was eventually shipped; but, for every two bins loaded, one fell into Port Kembla harbour.

> Joe: I say, Bill, I wonder where this pig iron's for?
>
> Bill: Hanged if I know.
>
> Joe: Wonder if it's going to Japan?
>
> Bill: Shouldn't be surprised. They're the ones who seem to need it most these days.
>
> Joe: Then they don't get me to load it, by crikey!

The actors who defied a ban on performing *War on the Waterfront* in the Domain were arrested, defended by recent law graduate John Kerr, and fined. Betty Roland's *Workers, Beware* was also about the *Dalfram* affair.

After 1936, when Clifford Odets' *Till the Day I Die* was banned as offensive to a foreign power, the League continued to warn of the threat from Nazism. In *Blood on the Moon*, a Jewish family is destroyed: 'It isn't enough that they should kill us. They must drive us to kill each other'. In *Bessie Bosch*, underground communists work against fascism. The Jewish Youth Theatre League (JYTL) performed Jacob Waislitz's *Yellow Spot* in the NTL clubrooms.

Ignoring a *Sydney Morning Herald* prediction that the two dictatorships would return to diplomatic friendship, the League was caught off guard when Germany signed a non-aggression pact with Russia in August 1939. Its allegiances tested, the NTL management committee settled for a program mostly of repeats, guest productions and plays on workers' issues and resisting conscription. The 'Resist Speed Up' slogan on the 1940 May Day float defied the government's push for productivity.

In *The Patriot and the Fool*, by Sydney writer Cecil Watts, a simple farmhand refuses to be bullied into joining up. *42A And All That* (named for a Regulation in the *National Security Act* which made disloyal or subversive comments on war policies or administration punishable) played on the back of a truck in inner Sydney suburbs. The keynote sketch involved a boss challenging two of his workers. 'Why aren't you men in uniform?... Stick a gun in your hands, that's what we ought to do! Conscription!' The capitalist is told that the men are making what the country needs: steel and munitions.

Catherine Duncan adapted the writings of Australian journalist Rupert Lockwood into a one-act documentary drama, *No Conscription*. The title summed up the message. Like Betty Roland's agitprop *No! No!* it is set during the heated debates of World War I. Clearly, it dealt with current events and not the historical past, so the Chief Secretary banned the piece after a couple of performances at Transport House and 36 Pitt Street.

Veterans of Sydney University revue, including pianist James McAuley, were the stars of *I'd Rather be Left*, which ran for months in 1941. Its political targets were domestic: it parodied Menzies and an Air Raid Precautions lecturer giving advice on how to deal with the bang and smell of bombs.

In June 1941, Germany attacked Russia. NTL members were now free to enlist and to work in munitions factories. The community noticeboard at 36 Pitt Street tracked the progress of the war with maps and news clippings. In a reversal of opposition to speeding up production, the heroes of Bill Brown's *Men Who Speak for Freedom* were miners desperately hurrying to fill an urgent defence order.

One month after the ban on *Till the Day I Die* was lifted, the NTL mounted a fresh production. Other anti-Nazi plays followed.

In Geoffrey Parsons' *According to Plan*, a group of German soldiers, cut off from supplies, fear that Hitler's strategy isn't working:

> We'll all be wiped out. It's only a matter of time before the whole German army will be nothing but an army scattered over a handful of scorched earth.

The Cave, 1943. L-R Jerold Wells, John Gray, Alan Herbert.

According to Plan played at fundraising appeals and for the armed forces. At Randwick barracks, US soldiers rigged up stage lights, dressed the set with straw from their bedding and helped the actors with their makeup. *Counter Attack*, set behind enemy lines where Russians and Germans are trapped in a collapsed building, was taken as far as the Albury army camp. *Tomorrow the World*, examining the long-term impact of Nazi propaganda on German children, travelled to Katoomba, Yaralla Hospital and the Bathurst army camp. A variety show, *Giggle Suits and Overalls*, played at Yaralla and the Ingleburn army camp.

In *The Cave*, Nazis, desperately short of manpower and physicians, offer a Jewish doctor from the ghetto his old hospital back to treat German troops so that they can return to the battlefield. The doctor considers the offer:

> Levi: Naturally in my work, I shall often have occasion to resort to blood transfusion. All healthy Germans, as you know, are at the front. There'll be a shortage of donors. Yet blood will be needed. What do you think, Colonel, may I in case of need use the blood of prisoners-of-war – Czechs, Poles or Serbs?

> Colonel Braunkraft: Why, of course. It is the result that matters. Every stormtrooper must be made fit to go back to the front and fight.
>
> Levi: So in case of necessity one must shut one's eyes to the principle of the purity of German blood.

Winner of two British Drama League awards in 1943, *The Cave* played in hospitals, for War Loan appeals and to the armed forces.

The League's second revue was Oriel Gray's *Marx of Time* (not Karl but the Marx Brothers). It parodied Hitler, Mussolini and Emperor Tojo, who sang to the tune of *The Mikado*'s 'Three Little Maids':

> *Three little men from Mars are we*
>
> *Fascist dictators, as you see*
>
> *Filled to the brim with devilish glee,*
>
> *Three little men from Mars.*

It featured gin-swilling memsahibs who got out of Singapore before it fell to the Japanese:

> *We are the Singapore martyrs*
>
> *Down to our last 12 frocks.*
>
> *Once we were upper stratas,*
>
> *Now we are on the rocks.*
>
> *To say we fled off*
>
> *Is quite absurd.*
>
> *We left ahead of*
>
> *The common herd.*
>
> *It's such a bore, folks,*
>
> *To be at war, folks,*
>
> *So let's make whoopee!*

Oriel Gray also penned *Sur Le Pont*, set in occupied France.

A program note for Edward Chodorov's *Decision*, staged in 1944, forecast a vision of world peace. By mid-1945, Allied victory in Europe was in sight and an optimistic ending had to be hastily written to replace the original in Catherine Duncan's verse play *Sons of the Morning*, set in wartime Crete.

Several works staged immediately after the war concerned domestic problems, particularly the housing shortage. One exception was David Martin's *The Shepherd and the Hunter*, which dealt with escalating conflict abroad.

Jakov and Shura are members of a right-wing Jewish terrorist cell in British mandated Palestine. Jakov's wife Malke, a recent arrival and Holocaust survivor, questions Shura's father Berl, an orange grower:

> Berl: They hate our trees. Every tree gives work to a Jewish hand, every Jewish hand clasps another. And the Arabs want to work in our plantations.
>
> Malke: And can't they work in our plantations?
>
> Berl: Let them work in their own.
>
> Malke: How will it all end? How can there be peace?

The author described his politically complicated work as 'a call for Jewish–Arab friendship'. A mainstream review of the Sydney production noted that the play 'presents a highly controversial topic upon which constructive thinking needs to be done'. *The Shepherd and the Hunter* was performed by London Unity in 1946 and opened Sydney NT's 1947 season.

As the 1940s progressed, fear of nuclear war increased. Revue songs were set to popular tunes, such as 'After the Ball':

> *After the next war's over*
>
> *After we're all blown up*
>
> *No one will push up clover*
>
> *Not even a buttercup.*
>
> *Atom bomb piles are growing*
>
> *They're making them more and more*
>
> *Who cares a fig where we're going*
>
> *After the war.*

The 1949 revue *Pot of Message* highlighted suspicion over the expanding power of the USA in a parody of the Andrews Sisters' hit 'Rum and Coca Cola':

> We have lots of Marshall Aid
>
> But how can it be repaid
>
> There's a catch it's plain to see
>
> We can't get hard currency.
>
> Koka Kola rots your teeth
>
> Even rots your toes beneath
>
> Still we drink it by the can
>
> On the terms of the Marshall Plan.
>
> Drinking tons of Koka Kola
>
> Losing every molar
>
> 'Cause the British Empire's
>
> Working for the Yankee Dollar.

The Marshall Plan, a program providing financial assistance to Western Europe to help them recover from the devastation of World War II, was denounced in 1948 in *The Governor of the Province* as a tool of the USA to rebuild the monopolies that financed Hitler. An argument of the play was that the USSR had rigidly adhered to the terms of the Potsdam Agreement's tripartite military occupation and was standing up to its blustering rival. (Even *Tribune* panned the show, but Jack Fegan received good reviews in the title role, despite once absent-mindedly putting a lit cigarette into the pocket of his uniform.)

As the Cold War heated up, Robert Menzies became a familiar figure in revue:

> I'm atom bomb Menzies
>
> I fall into frenzies
>
> Each time I see anything Red
>
> I look through old piles of my Liberal files
>
> And I even look under the bed.

Hewlett Johnson, the pacifist 'Red' Dean of Canterbury, visited the New in 1950 to watch a performance of *We, The People*. In the same season was Aristophanes' *Lysistrata*, 'a racy record of feminine revolt against war'. The Soviet Union Peace Delegation and Soviet and Indian delegates to a Union of Australian Women Congress were in the opening night audience 13 years later, when it was revived as *Operation Olive Branch*.

The 1950s generated a string of antiwar shows. In Leonard Irwin's *The Circling Dove*, the Matron of an English hospital protests against military plans to evict patients to make way for victims of a third World War. Donald Ogden Stewart's *How I Wonder!* explores the dilemma of reconciling academic freedom with accepting the backing of financiers who support both universities and armament manufacturers. Les Tanner played 'The Mind' and fellow journalist Charles Sriber 'The Body' of the central character, a professor worried about an atomic war and conflicted by his conscience. (A 1951 Jubilee Play competition rejected the work as 'not acceptable'.)

David Berg's *Mother Riba* is a naïve Jewish woman who becomes politically active after her son is drafted. She signs a petition to the US President to end the Korean War. UN soldiers turned saboteurs blow up a North Korean bridge in local writer Nance Macmillan's *Christmas Bridge*. A casting challenge (Caucasians ended up playing African-American, Korean and Chinese characters) on top of an improbable plot meant that the play did poor business.

The Korean War was also the subject of a Shakespearian parody:

> Witches:
>
> > How we love to have a war
> >
> > We've had two, now we want more
> >
> > Atom bombs are so exciting
> >
> > We hate peace and we love fighting.
> >
> > Hubble, bubble, toil and trouble
> >
> > Fire burn and cauldron bubble.
>
> 3rd Witch:
>
> > By the pricking of my thumbs
> >
> > Something wicked this way comes.

1st Witch:

> 'Tis John Foster Dulles to play Macbeth
> To lull us with grim tales of death.

An item in the 1957 revue *TV or Not TV* was 'Leave it to the Ghouls', a variation on a popular women's panel program. It explores the topic: 'Do we need the bomb?' The scientist's contributions are ignored, and the actress and the society hostess make fatuous comments. The military expert is quick to respond:

Brigadier Woodenhead:

> Can kill millions just like that. Terrific timesaver...
> This damned radioactive nonsense! How do we
> know there is such a thing? A bomb is a bomb –
> the important thing is to drop it on the other fellow.

In 1959, *Fission Chips* revue performers waved to May Day crowds from the New Theatre float, its banner: 'Preserve Outer Space for Peace'.

Dymphna Cusack's *Pacific Paradise* dealt with issues close to home – atomic testing by foreign powers in the South Pacific – and proved popular with audiences after opening in December 1955. The UK and the USA had exploded full-scale nuclear devices off Australia's northwest coast in the Monte Bello Islands in 1952. Cusack sent a draft of her script to literary friends, one of whom commented that it would be out of date before she finished it. This prediction proved false. There was a second testing in the Monte Bello Islands in 1956, and bomb trials continued in South Australia until 1963.

Set on a fictitious island, *Pacific Paradise* raised questions about people as guinea pigs; the sovereignty rights of those who refused evacuation orders; and the impact on Australians whose long coastline was threatened by contaminated currents. The BBC turned down this national competition runner-up to *Summer of the Seventeenth Doll* and *The Torrents*, but ABC radio broadcast it. The Mayakovski Theatre in Moscow asked for a copy. Eventually, translated into Russian, it played in the Orenburg Theatre in 1960.

A number of plays dealing with war-related issues featured in the 1960s. In *The Long and the Short and the Tall*, set in Malaya during the Japanese

Mother Courage and Her Children, 1966. L-R Carole Skinner, Patti Asange, Linal Haft, Eric Long.

advance on Singapore, a trapped British patrol has to work out what to do with a captured enemy infantryman. With pungent and authentic dialogue, from fey Welshman to worldly-wise Cockney, Willis Hall's play was a 1962 Arts Council Drama Festival winner.

In *The Wall,* the first drama staged in NT's new premises on St Peters Lane, trapped occupants of Warsaw's Jewish ghetto resist Nazi seizure in 1940. Playwright Millard Lampell was blacklisted when he refused to testify before the House Committee on Un-American Activities.

Alan Seymour's *The One Day of the Year*, examining the myth of Anzac Day, was part of the 1964 season. Brecht's *Mother Courage* played in 1966, with Patti Assange (Julian Assange's step-grandmother) as the lead. *Postmark Zero*, dramatised letters written by German soldiers during the 1942 siege of Stalingrad, marked the stage debut of John Hargreaves. Playwright Alex Buzo was in the crowd scenes in *Macbird!* – its main villain Robert Kennedy, because he had no interest in peace.

In 1965, the New sent a petition to the US consul protesting against aircraft activity above North Vietnam. A desperate search began for theatrical material. Mona Brand, who had lived in Vietnam for two years, sat down with a team to write something that would show Australians that this was a war they shouldn't get involved in. The result was a documentary vaudeville. *On Stage Vietnam* recalled the living newspaper of the 1930s and Joan Littlewood's *Theatre of Fact* and presaged *The Gillies Report*, *Fast Forward* and the *Wharf Revue*.

On Stage Vietnam received good publicity. ABC TV interviewed Roger Milliss, reviews were positive, and excerpts from the show became part of pacifist clergyman Alan Walker's Sunday gatherings. It played at outside venues. Scripts went to Adelaide University's Footlights Club.

In traditional revue style, political lyrics were set to popular tunes. 'The Road to Mandalay' was sung by Madame Bon Bon:

> *Our civilising mission*
>
> *Leaves us little short of bored.*
>
> *If ze cross can't cower ze natives*
>
> *Zen we treat zem to the sword.*
>
> *As we bear ze white man's burden*
>
> *In zis land of teeming sin,*
>
> *We will make zat burden lighter*
>
> *Drinking vermouth double gin.*

A chorus of Vietnamese children sang 'Teddy Bears Picnic':

> *If you go down to the fields today*
>
> *You're sure of a big surprise,*
>
> *If you go down to the fields today*
>
> *You'd better look up the skies,*
>
> *For every plane that ever there was*
>
> *Will come again for certain because*
>
> *Today's the day the Yankees are dropping their candy.*

The birthday ballot determined Australians' conscription into the Vietnam War: marbles with birth dates were drawn out of a barrel, lottery style. Pat Flower wrote a piece for *Exposure 70*, which the parent of a Liberal voter whose son is called up delivers:

> *Somebody's made a boo-boo*
>
> *They've got their marbles mixed.*
>
> *I've tried every wangle, dodge and finangle*
>
> *To get the faux pas fixed.*

Mona Brand's *Vietnam Hocus Pocus* concluded:

> *You put your Tricky Dick in*
>
> *When LBJ drops out*
>
> *He puts a lot more in*
>
> *And he calls it pulling out.*
>
> *He does the hocus pocus*
>
> *Saving face all around*
>
> *And that's what it's all about.*
>
> *In Cambodia we're in*
>
> *When Sihanouk flies out*
>
> *They didn't ask us in*
>
> *But let them try to get us out.*

The Vietnam War galvanised agitprop. Actors, their bodies outlined in chalk on pavements, held up antiwar signs to passers-by. At moratorium gatherings, performers denounced Nixon and portrayed GIs raping Vietnamese women and war veterans begging.

The 1970s began with *The Sunday Walk* by Georges Michel, showing the effect of the Algerian war on metropolitan France. David Campton's *Little Brother, Little Sister*, a macabre fairytale of the aftermath of a nuclear war, was workshopped, as was Jean-Paul Sartre's adaptation of *The Trojan Women* (with a program note warning of the devastation of an atomic war).

On Stage Vietnam, 1968.

Imperialism, David Williamson's satire on US control of Australian resources, was one of the sketches in *It's Time to Boil Billy*; but, like *The Pirates of Pal Mal*, most mainstage ridicule in the Whitlam period targeted domestic affairs.

Meanwhile, agitprop Street Theatre was active in the movement against uranium mining:

> So listen to your conscience
>
> And help the cry go 'round
>
> Act while there is still a chance
>
> And LEAVE IT IN THE GROUND.

The decade closed with John McGrath's *Events While Guarding the Bofors Gun* and Brendan Behan's *Richard's Cork Leg*. The first depicts the absurdity of a disgruntled group of British soldiers guarding an obsolete anti-aircraft weapon in 1954 occupied Berlin. Behan's play ends with a warning on nuclear conflagration.

Oh What a Lovely War, Mate played in 1980. Two years later, John Tasker directed Bill Morrison's *Flying Blind*, a condemnation of the polarising of political thought in Northern Ireland. A review praised the production for reaching 'sublime heights of lunatic terror and comic climax'.

Peter Kemp joined Stafford Sanders and Tom Bridges (authors of 1983's successful *Ron Raygun in the Antipodes*) to devise *At Last! The 1984 Show*. In the 'slick, pacy revue', the US President reassures the public:

> I just want to reiterate clearly and categorically that the purpose of our nuclear weapons stockpile is purely as a deterrent to the Soviet Union. We've spent billions of dollars building these weapons – but we have no intention of ever using them. We only have them to deter the Soviets – to let them know we have them and that we're prepared to use them. But you can be sure we have no intention of using them – unless we do use them. I hope that clears things up.

The following year saw the Great Canadian Theatre Company's *Sandinista!* Its subject is US interference in Nicaragua.

Donald Freed's *The Quartered Man* is set in the US Embassy in Costa Rica: 'There used to be just one superpower...now there are two... the USA and the CIA.'

Also part of the 1989 season was *Sink the Belgrano*, Steven Berkoff's indictment of 'a pack of fakes' whose sinking of the ship led to needless loss of life on both sides in the Falklands War. The satirical take on the backroom deals and cover-ups was reviewed as 'gutsy, powerful boots-and-all theatre'. Thrifty as always, the New sold Maggot Scratcher's wool carpet at the end of the run.

After filing reports to *Pravda* from the site and talking to survivors of the Chernobyl nuclear power station explosion, Russian journalist Vladimir Gubareyev wrote *Sarcophagus*, a 'tomb of radioactivity'. Staged in 1989, the play warns of the dangers inherent in the way nuclear fuels are stored and handled, with no realistic safeguards or solutions for the disposal of radioactive waste:

> *An isolation clinic contains cubicles housing victims of the explosion. Anna (a research scientist) and Vera (a newly qualified doctor) come out of cubicle three.*
>
> Anna: No one will see his face again. A lead coffin and a concrete sarcophagus. It has to be like that because his body is emitting two or three roentgens an hour.

And it will go on doing so for several decades. I'm afraid you can't go in there again.

The light in cubicle eight starts to blink.

Quickly! And wipe away your tears. You must always go into a cubicle with a smile. They're waiting for your smile. Come on, girl.

Lights are blinking in cubicles number eight, number six and number four. The glowing of burning graphite shines brightly on the cyclorama.

The setting for Alex Buzo's *Pacific Union* is San Francisco in 1945, where a conference is drafting a charter for a new organisation to preserve peace and build a better world. Away from the big powers, Australia's Foreign Minister, Bert Evatt, is involved in protracted negotiations 'to create world security, a pacific union of all nations for all time'. The New produced *Pacific Union* in 1998, three years after the script was published to mark the 50th anniversary of the birth of the United Nations.

Productions since the year 2000 include Swedish playwright Lars Norén's *War*, centred on a family living in squalor in an unnamed country ravaged by conflict and ethnic cleansing. Sydney playwright Katie Pollock's *A Quiet Night in Rangoon* is set in Burma during the 2007 Saffron Revolution. Against a background of resistance to the repressive military junta, a travel journalist becomes embroiled in a minefield of political engagement.

Pacifist works that are not mouthpieces for propaganda but focus on individual behaviour have attracted the New's biggest audiences. Twice in recent years, *The Diary of Anne Frank* had sell-out seasons. And R. C. Sherriff's *Journey's End*, based on his own experiences as an officer in World War I, proved the power of authenticity decades after the play's 1928 premiere: 'There's not a man left who was here when I came'.

..., Saturday and Sunday), fifty one weeks of the year, ... attendance per year is estimated at between 5,000 and 7,000.

The average attendance is small and ninety eight per cent of ...ience consists of people who appear to be either Communists, "...travellers", or sympathisers.

This ninety eight per cent includes a large proportion of ... under thirty years of age. In fact, most of them are teen-age ...ly twenties and appear to be members of the Eureka Youth League ... Theatre. These are the people who are noticed attending various ...ist, Liberal or Labor organised meetings, and who always support ...mmunist Party "line" and are quick to take offence at any point ... to the contrary.

It is from this group there appears a particularly vicious apparent ... young thug and the /homo-sexual. The two outstanding features ... homo-sexual habitue of the Theatre is the number and its type. ...is probably more followers of the New Theatre, who are homo-..s, than the number evident at any other legitimate theatre in ... But more important is the type; and he (the female aspect ...ost non-existent) is the most degenerate breed of homo-sexual – ... possessing low intelligence. It has been alleged from a ... source that the Vice Squad has raided the premises occupied ... Eureka Youth League on more than one accasion.

Also included among the ninety eight per cent are the ...ist Party members of trade unions, the militant worker and his ...with, perhaps, a friend who has been persuaded to come and ... a look'. The remaining two per cent comprises intellectuals, ... who find all the movie theatres sold out and the anti-Communists. ...ource)

SECRET

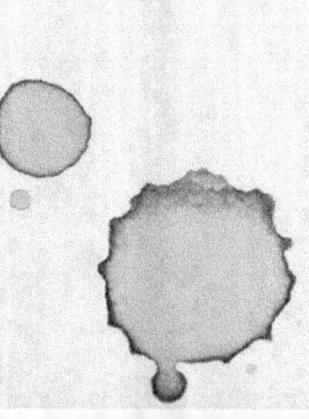

An ASIO agent's assessment of the Sydney New Theatre audience.

CHAPTER 12

Sydney New Theatre: The Fight for Equality

Lyn Collingwood

Since its foundation, Sydney New Theatre has given a voice to victims of discrimination. It has explored marginalisation on the basis of gender, race, class, religion, sexual orientation and identity through drama, revue, music and agitprop, engaging audiences in better understanding the cultures, beliefs and lifestyles of others. The New has opposed colonial oppression and antisemitism and supported the rights of women, Aboriginal and Torres Strait Islander Australians, African Americans and people dealing with social isolation and mental illness. Since 1994, an annual production has been an official Mardi Gras event.

WOMEN

The theatre's championing of women's rights is unsurprising, given the number of relevant organisations with which it has been affiliated: multiple peace groups, the New Housewives' Association, United Association of Women, Australian Women's Charter Movement, Women's International Democratic Federation, Union of Australian Women, Seamen's Women's Committee, the WWF Women's Committee, Women's Abortion Action Campaign and the Older Women's Network. New Theatre members participated in pageants and concerts marking International Women's Day.

Most of the New's administrators (notably Miriam Hampson, who kept it going for 32 years) have been women. Management and production committees have always been egalitarian – and, at a time when women were not allowed in public bars, they drank with the men. The theatre has a history of encouraging female directors, designers and writers, including 'resident' playwrights Pat Flower, Oriel Gray and Mona Brand.

As a volunteer organisation whose performers are unpaid, the New can afford to produce works with big casts. Hundreds of actresses have been given the opportunity to develop their skills, and many performed tour de force roles.

In 1939, Betty Roland played the female lead in her own script *Are You Ready, Comrade?* Dominating the stage in Brecht's *Mother Courage* is the title character, wresting a living from war; buying and selling anything from bread and vodka to bullets and bandages, she is towering, rugged, shrewd, tenacious and earthy. Patti Assange won praise for her performance in 1966, as did Gertraud Ingeborg in the 1998 reprisal. Paul Foster's *Elizabeth 1*, a 'production clean and crisp and right on the mark', opened the 1976 season. A naïve housewife is in nearly every scene in John McGrath's *Yobbo Nowt*, staged in 1981 and 1985. Pam Gems' *Queen Christina*, examining the public and personal life of the Swedish monarch raised as a boy, played in 1990. Director Kevin Jackson and actor Elaine Hudson collaborated again on Alma de Groen's *The Woman in the Window*, its subject the poet Anna Akhmatova, under house arrest in Stalinist Leningrad. Anthony Skuse's production of *Medea* also brought good houses in 2005, and Italian writer Dacia Maraini's *Mary Stuart*, a two-hander for women, toured to the USA, where it won an International New York Fringe Festival award.

INEQUALITY AT HOME

Valerie Wilson directed Bernard Shaw's *Pygmalion* in 1934 (revived two years later). Watching the first dress rehearsal, WAC members interrupted the action with cries of 'encore!' When the bright and witty dialogue transferred from 36 Pitt Street to the 520-seat King's Hall in Hunter Street, critics received it enthusiastically: 'Absolutely splendid!' 'Don't miss it!' The play reaches its climax when the two central characters battle for control:

> Eliza: You want me back only to pick up your slippers and put up with your tempers and fetch and carry for you.
>
> Higgins: I haven't said I wanted you back at all.

Eliza: Oh, indeed. Then what are we talking about?

Higgins: About you, not about me. If you come back I shall treat you just as I have always treated you. I can't change my nature.

Ted Willis' *All Change Here*, staged in 1945 on a set designed by Margaret Olley, explored the fight for equality. London bus conductresses have become self-reliant in wartime and have trouble readjusting to their returning husbands:

Doll: Don't you see? I've altered...you've altered...we can't just pick it up where we dropped it in 1939. We've got to make a new go of it. If we don't, Johnnie, so help me, it's curtains.

Johnnie: Doll...mind what you're saying.

Doll: I'm Doll Paine, see? What I do, I do in my own right. See? I've finished being a 1939 wife. I'm a 1944 woman...get it? We learned a lot in the last few years. The sooner you men get that...the better.

Two other Willis plays were mounted in 1946–47. Women negotiating relationships postwar is a theme in *The Bells Are Ringing*. *What Happens to Love?* tracks the breakdown of a marriage, from the honeymoon to the divorce court.

The intrusion of the 'other woman' further complicates the troubled domesticity of a returned soldier and his wife in Oriel Gray's *My Life Is My Affair*. Reviewers praised the author's 'deep and subtle understanding of human nature' in her depiction of the couple working towards equality and the woman taking responsibility for her own life.

New Theatre produced member Joan Gibson's debut play in 1948. The central character in *The Dangerous Sex* is a contemporary wife and mother. Angry about union objections to women in the workforce and musing on the female lot, she falls asleep and is taken through a historical cavalcade of people (including Florence Nightingale, Mary Wollstonecraft, Fanny Burney and Anna Seward) struggling for emancipation. The play begins in the cave age and ends with a call to arms for gender equality. The wife confronts her husband:

Iris: When this suburb gets a day nursery where I can leave George, and a play centre where Jane and Teddy can wait till their parents come home from work, I will certainly be working in industry, washing up or no washing up. Till then, I'm tied to the housekeeping, and I can't walk out on it.

Bill: Unless of course there's a Depression and out go the men and in go the women, and you have to turn to and keep me.

Iris: You'd better do something about women's wages in the meantime, for your own sake. Keep the likes of you!

In contrast to her feckless husband, it is the wife who holds the family together in *Juno and the Paycock*, which played in 1949 (when Sean O'Casey was waiving royalties for the New) and 1979.

The ultimate in female domestic revolt, Aristophanes' *Lysistrata* was staged in 1950, but it was rumoured to contain 'too much sex', and audiences were small. Ewan MacColl's adaptation as *Operation Olive Branch* garnered mixed reviews in 1963. Opinions ranged from 'fluent and inventive' to 'propaganda platitudes...lacking sparkle'.

INEQUALITY IN THE WORKPLACE

Nelle Rickie was an early WAC mover and shaker. As a foundation member of the CPA and an Australian Theatrical and Amusement Employees Association delegate, Rickie was arguing in 1922 for a reduction in working hours for all women. By 1925, she was lecturing on 'Feminism or the Class War'. A 1933 WAC program of her sketches included *Weights and Measures*, about obstacles to getting the dole. Those applying for food relief had to fill in a 32-question government 'hunger form'. Rationing was inequitable for women, and deserted wives had to answer another 72 questions – including whether their children were legitimate.

Katharine Susannah Prichard's one-act *Forward One*, staged in 1937, deals with the working conditions of female shop assistants. The women, who spend their days dealing with difficult customers and going up and down

Making up for All Change Here, 1945.

ladders to fetch stock, are never allowed to sit down. Worried that they will lose their jobs, they are scared to protest:

The shop is hot and the new shop assistant faints.

Miss Drew: Take her into the packing room…
Supposing a customer should come in.

Vera: Let them come. Let them all come and see what you've done to this girl and Elsie and me. I'll tell them that there are scores of girls in the city in other show rooms who are suffering torture with their backs and feet, just because you and your sort won't let them sit down during business hours, even when there's no business doing. It's sheer brutality.

In Betty Roland's radio play *It Isn't Possible!*, female shoemakers come under pressure to increase production after a time-and-motion man is brought into the factory:

> Seamer: I can't work any faster. 760 pairs a day I do. They're asking 924 small pairs or 859 of large.
>
> Braider: 3,110 they want – for lower pay.
>
> All girls: It isn't possible. We've given everything we've got.

The NTL actors had an hour's rehearsal before the piece was broadcast on the ALP's station 2KY in 1939. Roland's inspiration was a real-life strike in the shoe-sewing rooms of Dunlop Perdriau's factory at Birkenhead Point. Claiming that they were being paid less for more work when new assembly-line methods were introduced, the women stopped work. The dispute ended after the Rubber Workers' Union was threatened with deregistration. In the opinion of Arbitration Court Judge Drake-Brockman, the strikers were a handful of rebels who should realise that they owed something to the community.

The 1941 revue *I'd Rather be Left* parodied Sir Sydney Snow, whose retail business flourished in wartime, largely because he hired women and youths who were paid less than men. In the same year, NTL member Joyce Batterham was one of the organisers of a strike demanding better pay and provisions at the Alexandria Spinning Mills, a major employer of girls and women. Infamous for its poor working conditions, it manufactured military clothing during World War II.

A strike in 1888 at Bryant and May's lucifer match factory in London's East End marked the beginning of the trade union movement. The female workforce laboured in terrible conditions; worst of all was their development of 'phossy jaw' through exposure to phosphorus. Robert Mitchell's *The Match Girls* came from London's Unity Theatre and played in 1948. Reviewers judged it melodramatic, with little scope for subtle emotion, but audiences received it warmly. Standout performers were Dolores Smith as Kate, an intense and formidable figure goaded into action by injustice, and Jean Blue, who conveyed the compassion, fire and resolution of crusading social reformer Annie Besant. Miles Franklin, an opening night regular, found the piece too 'unrelieved' to be a good play but saw it as an unbearable indictment of

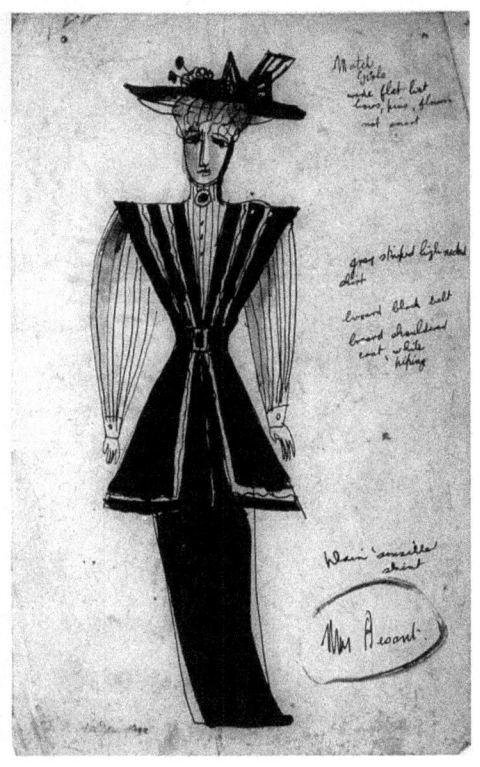

Costume designs for *The Match Girls*, 1948.

a relatively recent system of workers' exploitation. She labelled those who lived off the labour and fearsome conditions of others 'fiends'.

The 1888 strike had a different treatment in 1972. *The Matchgirls*, by Bill Owen with music by Tony Russell, was reviewed as an English *Reedy River* – with pleasant, catchy tunes. The enthusiastic performances received positive reviews and attracted a cross-section of audiences; pocket books of matches were handed out as part of the show's promotion. At the time the show was playing, women process workers working ten-hour days at Sydney's Federal Match Company were negotiating for a 35-hour week. New Theatre revived the musical version in 1981.

Also mounted in 1981, Jean-Claude Grumberg's *The Workroom* is set in a Parisian tailor's atelier, where seamstresses who have survived World War II carry out their tasks in airless and cramped conditions. Like John Tasker's other productions, it was popular with audiences.

In 1998, New Theatre presented Oriel Gray's *The Torrents* as a moved and costumed reading. A female editorial assistant arrives in the newspaper office of an 1890s gold town, to the disquiet of the all-male workforce. *The Torrents* was co-winner, with *Summer of the Seventeenth Doll*, of the 1955 Playwrights' Advisory Board's award for Best Play.

EQUAL PAY

At the time of the WAC's founding, the CPA's monthly paper *The Working Woman* was calling for equal pay for equal work. Before being sacked by the Alexandria Spinning Mills for being pregnant, writer Dorothy Hewett demanded equal pay for women at a Textile Workers' Union meeting. This was in the 1950s, when Mona Brand penned a revue number that became part of the repertoire of Street Theatre (then called Contact). It went to so many workplaces where most employees were women that the NT singers got sick of singing it:

> I dreamed that I had equal pay
>
> And believe me children that ain't hay
>
> When you come to think of what I'm equal to.
>
> I dreamed I owned a Cadillac
>
> And a modest 25-room shack
>
> All paid for from the back pay that came through.

SEX WORK

The limited number of jobs then open to women is touched on in *Pygmalion*:

> Eliza: I'll go and be a teacher.
>
> Higgins: What'll you teach, in heaven's name?
>
> Eliza: What you taught me. I'll teach phonetics.

In 1935, the WAC made the bold decision to stage *Mrs Warren's Profession*. The title character has made her money from prostitution; the printed program noted that it was not a 'nice' play, but 'since when has Shaw been "nice"?' It opened to an overflow house in the Theosophical Society's Savoy Theatre and received good reviews, especially for Cleo Grant's intelligent and sympathetic portrayal of Kitty Warren. 'Bernard Shaw's Slashing Indictment of Modern Moral Humbug' went on to play in the theatre's clubrooms.

The same year saw *Love on the Dole*, a grim piece about unemployment in Manchester, adapted by Ronald Gow from a novel by Walter Greenwood. Central character Sally Hardcastle becomes a kept woman as her only chance to subsist. In the last scene, the locals jeer as she leaves town in a taxi. This exchange between Sally's parents precedes her departure:

> Hardcastle: Haven't Ah worked all me life, body an' soul, t' keep a home for her? Haven't Ah kept meself respectable for her, when God knows Ah've been near driven to drink wi' things. And now me own daughter tells me she's a whore – aye, and proud of it too.
>
> Mrs Hardcastle: Where should we ha' been all these months if it hadn't been for our Sally? It's her money we've lived on since they knocked you off dole, an' well you know it.

The CPA considered *Love on the Dole* a worthy project, and it had revivals in 1936 and 1938 in the clubrooms and outside venues. Benefit performances raised funds for the CPA and the Seamen's Relief Fund.

In 1990, the Australian premiere of Kay Adshead's *Thatcher's Women* revisited sex work as an option for those otherwise unable to secure an income. The play showed the human price of Thatcherism in a divided England. In the north, the economy plummeted with the loss of factory jobs; in the south, it flourished. To pay their bills, women took the train to London's Kings Cross Station to work as prostitutes during school hours.

In the play, police harass and fine three Manchester women who try their luck in the two weeks before Christmas. Sex workers use force to protect their territory:

> Lynda: If she'd have told me to go I would have done. Nobody told me it was her flamin' pitch.
>
> Norah: There's nothing broken anyway.
>
> Lynda: One minute I was standing there minding my

own business, next minute the incredible hulk's on top of me.

Norah: You'll have a fat lip, mind.

Lynda: Vicious cow. I could have the law on her. If I'm marked that's it – I might as well go home now.

Adshead wrote the play after seeing a TV program describing how the English Collective of Prostitutes had increased at Kings Cross with an influx of workers from the north.

NTL member Kathleen Carroll wrote and directed *Office Interlude* in 1944, raising the issue of sexual coercion in the workplace. A girl has had an affair with her married boss, who dies suddenly, leaving her, we surmise, pregnant. The author became a well-known writer of radio serials with Grace Gibson Productions.

FEMINISM

In 1941, core NTL members Freda Lewis, Jean Blue and Hughla Hurley delivered agitprop views on women's issues from the back of a truck to bystanders as far afield as Wollongong and Cessnock. Three decades later, the women's movement was mainstream and strengthening. At a Women's Liberation rally in Martin Place, police pulled up Street Theatre stalwart Graham Richards and fined him for offensive behaviour. In a pro-choice abortion sketch, Richards had played a chauvinist husband pushing a wheelbarrow containing a pâpier-maché phallus, while his fellow performer was a pregnant woman pushing a pram.

Produced during International Women's Year 1975, Steve Gooch's *Female Transport* is set on a female convict ship, carrying six prisoners sentenced to be transported to a life of hard labour in Australia. During the long voyage, the women learn how they have been affected by the male-dominated class system – knowledge which unites and empowers them.

A tough-minded, intelligent, successful woman is the lead in *Just Talk (Apart from the Songs)* by Sydney writer Laurel McGowan, staged in 1985. Its synopsis: 'Girl meets boy. Girl gets bits of boy. Girl finds she can manage without boy'. The comic musical opens with Friday night drinks in the office, both genders singing, 'Gonna score! Gotta score!'

To unsettle audience preconceptions of sexuality and race, *Cloud 9*'s author

Caryl Churchill specified that characters be played across gender and colour. The first act is set in 1879 in 'darkest Africa'; the second 100 years later, in Thatcher's London. With hindsight, we can ridicule our Victorian ancestors' behaviour, but it's more difficult to do the same with our own stereotyping. *Cloud 9* was part of the 1993 season.

Dorothy Hewett's *The Chapel Perilous* played the following year. The author's teenage diaries inspired her to dramatise creative and rebellious Sally Banner's emotional journey from the strictures of her rural community:

> ABC Interviewer: And everyone's talking about Sally Banner's grand slam: first, second and third in the Jindyworobak Poetry Competition. Mrs Banner, I believe Sally was wilder, a live-wire in her university days?
>
> Mother: Well, no more than most really. They were unsettling times. The Americans were here, lacing our daughters' milk shakes with Spanish Fly. It turned their heads. We all worried about our daughters. What decent mother wouldn't? (*aside*) She was a real trollop. She'd lie down anywhere and do it like a dog. It was as if she wanted to punish us for something. Why, what had we done? We only loved and protected her.

A reviewer of the 2017 revival of *The Chapel Perilous* described the work as: 'one for the history books. It strikes a blow for freedom, feminism and absolute fabulousness'.

Women, Power and Culture, a program of new Australian works, was an all-female affair in 2011 – from writers to directors to crew. The playwrights included Katie Pollock, Suzie Miller, Gina Schien, Alana Valentine and Van Badham (whose *Five Feminist Melodramas* was part of the *Art is a Weapon* season in 2007 when the theatre celebrated its 75th birthday). An associated event was a free public forum on progress since the passing of the 1984 *Sex Discrimination Act*. Adele Horin moderated a panel that included Susan Ryan, Jane Caro, Eva Cox, Verity Firth and advocates for Muslim and Aboriginal and Torres Strait Islander women.

Alice Livingstone directed Caryl Churchill's *Top Girls* in 2013. The play examines what it means to be a successful woman in Margaret Thatcher's

ABORIGINAL ACTOR

For the first time in the history of the Australian theatre, an Australian aoriginal—in a leading role—has depicted the life of his people as they really live it. The actor is Mr. George Patten, a leader of the Aborigines Movement, and a strong fighter for aborigine rights.

He appeared in "The Sword Sung," prize-winning play by Catherine Duncan, recently produced by the Melbourne New Theatre Group.

One episode in this interesting and thought-provoking play presents a cross section of aboriginal life. In this particular scene, Mr. Patten took the leading part.

* * * *

The Workers Star report of The Sword Sung, 1939.

Britain. Marlene runs an employment agency: can she be both a career boss and a carer in family life? Aspects of womanhood are examined through historical figures: English explorer Isabella Bird; Japanese courtesan turned Buddhist nun Lady Nijo; Dull Gret, the subject of a Breughel painting; the legendary Pope Joan; and Patient Griselda, the obedient wife in *The Canterbury Tales*. Marlene proposes a toast:

> **Marlene:** We've all come a long way. To our courage and the way we changed our lives and our extraordinary achievements.

In 2016, Livingstone directed Wendy Wasserstein's feminist classic *The Heidi Chronicles*, which tracks a woman's search for political, professional and personal fulfilment over three decades. Reviews were positive for Wasserstein's 'ode to women, their adaptability, difference and struggle'.

INDIGENOUS AUSTRALIANS

George Landen Dann's *Fountains Beyond* in 1942 was the New's first full-length production dealing with the marginalisation of Australian Aboriginal people. When a traditional resting ground is to be flattened to build a children's playground, a man with Aboriginal ancestry is offered work in exchange for his support. The printed program noted: 'The old Australian families are falling away' – a reference, not to the Macarthur-Onslows in white society, but to Aboriginal tribespeople whose way of life was disappearing. 'Blacked up' Caucasians played non-white characters. This was standard practice until fairly recently, reflecting both the composition of the theatre's membership and problems reaching out to the broader community.

In *Rocket Range*, by Brisbane writer Jim Crawford, Central Australians are driven off their tribal grounds to make way for missile testing.

> *Kajabbi brings news that the white man whom he was going to invite to a corroboree has been killing animals and using the initiation ground as a lavatory.*
>
> **Kajabbi:** I asked him what he wanted on our tribal grounds. He said 'This place not tribal ground. This place belong big gubment feller now...belong Prime Minister.'

> Namalka: Gubment feller? Prime Minister? Who're they?
>
> Gimbin: They must be warriors or elders of this rascal's tribe.
>
> Namalka: They can't be warriors. Warriors don't steal tribal territory. Women perhaps – but a tribe's whole territory – no!

Impressively directed by Stanislav Polonski with original music by John Antill, *Rocket Range* played in 1947, its silhouetted actors creating an eerie atmosphere on Cedric Flower's set. Ten years later, the work was revived because of renewed nuclear testing.

Oriel Gray's *Had We but World Enough* dramatises growing tension in a country town after a teacher decides to give an Aboriginal girl the role of the Virgin Mary in a school nativity play. The playwright, a journalist on the local paper and a returned soldier who fought alongside Indigenous servicemen all approve the casting, but others, forced to take sides, find their careers, relationships and social standing threatened.

Mona Brand's *Here Under Heaven* is set during World War II. Amelia Hamilton, the matriarch of a Queensland sheep station, has thrown tribal people off her land but learns that one of her sons, killed in the war, has fathered a daughter with an Indigenous woman. The pregnant wife of another son, missing in action, arrives from Singapore – further challenging her racist views. Amelia is horrified to see that her daughter-in-law is Chinese, but she finally accepts the new family member and her unborn child. *Here Under Heaven* played widely overseas, including in Moscow, Budapest, Prague and Berlin. Italian radio broadcast it as *Famiglia Hamilton*.

In the 1970s, Street Theatre performances highlighting brutality and hypocrisy towards Aboriginal men were so convincing that the public became involved. A revue item probably dates from this period:

> When Phillip sailed into that cove
>
> With his little fleet
>
> It never crossed our mind
>
> That we should be unkind
>
> And send them back because their skins were white.

In 1973, the New contributed to the Free Kevin Gilbert Fund and drew up a petition asking the NSW Justice Minister to drop charges against the Aboriginal artist and playwright.

In the 1988 season, *The Death of Phillip Robertson* shed new light on a Northern Territory Black death in custody. Q&A sessions after the Sunday show involved audience members (including students from Narrabri High). NT members raised money for the Aboriginal National Theatre Trust, distributed leaflets at a Hyde Park Black deaths in custody rally, and placed a Sorry Book in the theatre foyer for signing.

Alana Valentine's *Parramatta Girls* is based on real testimonies. Former inmates of the Parramatta Girls' Training School reunite to face the demons of their shared experiences, the action shifting between the past and the present. The institution operated from 1887 to 1974 and housed delinquent, neglected and juvenile young offenders, including Indigenous girls. They received minimal education; most trained as domestic servants. Many suffered bullying and abuse, and there were frequent riots. The 2011 production included Indigenous actors.

ANTISEMITISM

The banning of Clifford Odets' *Till the Day I Die* in 1936 put the NTL on the map as an opponent of Nazi brutality and an advocate for the Jewish cause. Theatre members socialised with the Gezerd Younger Set and Jewish Youth Theatre League (JYTL) actors. During World War II, Jewish and Black American soldiers were welcomed into the League's clubrooms.

The JYTL brought its production of *The Yellow Spot* to 36 Pitt Street in 1938. Like *Blood on the Moon*, staged the following year, Jacob Waislitz's play deals with Nazi persecution. The 1940 production of *Renegade*, in which a New York rabbi is involved in a confrontation between garment workers and their employers, was a plea for tolerance. The play touches on Social Credit, an economic doctrine criticised as antisemitic because its formulator, C. H. Douglas, asserted that 'international Jewry' controlled major banks.

Jock Levy was a leading actor with the JYTL before joining the NTL, where he made his directing debut with Clifford Odets' *Awake and Sing!* about a poor Jewish family in the Bronx. The printed program for *The Shepherd and the Hunter* (staged in 1947 with Levy as both director and actor, a common practice) noted that the tragedy of the Jewish people and the urgency of their needs 'make a sane approach to Palestine and its associated problems most necessary'.

In 1952, Levy directed Oriel Gray's *Sky Without Birds*, a study of antisemitism in an isolated railway town on the edge of the Nullarbor. Levy was unhappy with the author's treatment of the Jewish question, and reviewers dismissed the script as over-wordy, over-sentimental and containing too much muddled philosophy. In 2007, however, in her introduction to Currency Press' published version, Katharine Brisbane found the play 'satisfying...more penetrating than it might appear on the surface'.

The New's first play at St Peters Lane was *The Wall*, by Millard Lampell, one of the writers blacklisted after refusing to testify before the House Committee on Un-American Activities. The 1963 production marked the 20th anniversary of a real-life event: the failed uprising of Jews who had survived three years of Nazi entrapment behind the wall of the Warsaw ghetto. Although the *Australian Jewish Times* reviewer found the play's message blurred because of technical problems (and the disconcerting Irish brogue of the Polish rabbi), readers of the newspaper supported the show with block bookings.

Ties with the Jewish community strengthened the following year, when the Israeli consul was approached for material on Jewish culture to display in the theatre in association with its production of Arnold Perl's *The World of Sholem Aleichem*. The consul was an opening night guest, reviews and word of mouth reports were good, and the season was extended. Perl's script is a dramatisation of three tales about the absurdities and cruelties of life for Jews in Czarist times. One story, 'The High School', exposes the quota system that prevented Jewish people from receiving an education.

Part of the New's 1987 season was Jean-Claude Grumberg's *Dreyfus in Rehearsal*, set in 1931 Poland. A Yiddish amateur company is rehearsing a play about the Dreyfus Affair. Comedy is a sugar coating for a bitter pill: a reminder of antisemitism in the Dreyfus era and its reawakening in the period leading up to the Holocaust.

AFRICAN AMERICANS

Among the hundreds of scripts in New Theatre's archives is *Scottsboro Newsreel*, a living newspaper agitprop call to arms in support of International Labour Defense (the legal arm of the Communist Party USA) and its advocacy for nine Black youths wrongly convicted of raping two white women while hoboing on a train in Alabama in 1931. No evidence has come to light of any WAC performance of *Scottsboro Newsreel*, but the FSU Dramatic Section did stage something about the 'Scottsboro Boys'.

Publicised as an answer to the idealisation of slave owners in *Gone With the Wind*, Lillian Hellman's *The Little Foxes* was part of the 1944 season. Also set in the USA's Deep South is James Gow and Arnaud d'Usseau's study of racial prejudice, *Deep Are the Roots*. It played in 1947, when lynchings were still happening and miscegenation was a taboo subject.

A young white girl, Genevra, falls in love with the educated but underprivileged African-American playmate of her childhood, to the alarm of her sister:

> Genevra: No, he didn't force me. I asked him to go. We went walking down by the river.
>
> Alice: At night! All alone! Walking!
>
> Genevra: Yes.
>
> Alice: You don't think anybody will believe that? You don't think I can believe it?
>
> Genevra: Why not?
>
> Alice: You're trying to protect him.
>
> Genevra: Of course I am.
>
> Alice: Why? Why should you defend him?
>
> Genevra: Because I like him.
>
> Alice: Nevvy! Nevvy! You couldn't have wanted him to touch you.
>
> Genevra: That's what you're bound to believe, isn't it?
>
> Alice: My God, you must have tried to stop him.
>
> Genevra: Pretty soon you'll be saying something worse. Rape.

Reviews were positive for the quality of the script, production and acting. However, the New had to cut the season short because it couldn't pay the professional royalties, and for years afterwards had trouble acquiring the rights for works from the USA.

The last play mounted in the WWF Hall was *A Raisin in the Sun*, by African-American writer Lorraine Hansberry. In racially segregated Chicago, a Black chauffeur dreams of power as his family struggles to attain the dignity of a decent style of living. NT publicised the play as relevant to other events in 1962: riots in Mississippi, where Black students were trying to gain admission to a white university.

Another Black writer, Ossie Davis, wrote *Purlie Victorious*, a satire on segregation – portrayed as ridiculous because it makes good people, Black and white, do ridiculous things. The title character is a self-appointed coloured preacher scheming to buy a barn to convert to a church.

NT was proud of its long association with US Black singer and actor Paul Robeson who sent his son to school in Russia (believing that Russia treated minorities well, in contrast to his own country, torn apart by racial hatred). In 1941, a pre-show recording of the bass baritone's 'Arise, arise ye who refuse to be born slaves' played before the curtain rose on *Till the Day I Die*. In 1942, audiences listened to Robeson's songs in praise of longshoreman unionist Harry Bridges. In 1958, the New Theatre National Conference sent the famous supporter of universal Black rights greetings for his 60th birthday.

In 1960, Robeson, accompanied by his wife Eslanda, made his first trip to Australia. The NSW Peace Committee for International Co-operation and Disarmament organised a welcoming function in Paddington Town Hall, which NT members attended. But this buzz of excitement was eclipsed when the couple accepted an invitation (extended also to visiting Jamaican-American singer Harry Belafonte) to attend a performance of *All My Sons*. Actress Jean Blue, in civilian life a nursing sister, threatened to resign if she didn't get time off work. At the end of the show, Robeson spoke and sang from the stage before going backstage. He chatted with theatre members and accepted a souvenir recording of *Reedy River*.

Edward Albee's *The Death of Bessie Smith* played in 1971. Injured in a car accident, the singer dies after being driven around trying to find a hospital which will treat her:

> Jack: Ma'am – I got Bessie Smith in that car there –

Nurse: I don't care who you got there, Nigger. You cool your heels!

Christopher Sergil's adaptation of Harper Lee's *To Kill a Mockingbird* was a box-office sell-out in 2014:

> You never really understand a person until you consider things from his point of view. Until you climb inside of his skin and walk around in it.

COLONIALISM

London cab driver Buckley Roberts included parodies of hymns and biblical texts in his *Cannibal Carnival*, a musical satire on 'bringing civilisation to the natives'. An English buccaneer, a policeman and a clergyman, shipwrecked on an island, impose their code of progress, private property and morality. After banning dancing and erecting a Union Jack, a fence and advertising hoardings, they annex the breadfruit and hot dog trees and set the inhabitants to work:

> *An islander, Egbert, is humbugged into giving the strangers most of his food.*
>
> Bumpus: The heathen in his blindness! He doesn't even know the difference between religion and robbery.
>
> Egbert: But I do, white man. When you take bread it is patriotism and religion. When I take bread it is robbery and violence.
>
> Crabbe: He couldn't have put it better if he'd been to Oxford.

The natives develop a concept of unemployment, establish a socialist government, address each other as 'Comrade' and, in the last scene, bundle the bishop and the capitalist into a gigantic cooking pot. *Cannibal Carnival* was a popular show in 1939.

One production the following year was Geoffrey Trease's *Colony*, set in 1936 in a British port in the West Indies where trouble with indentured

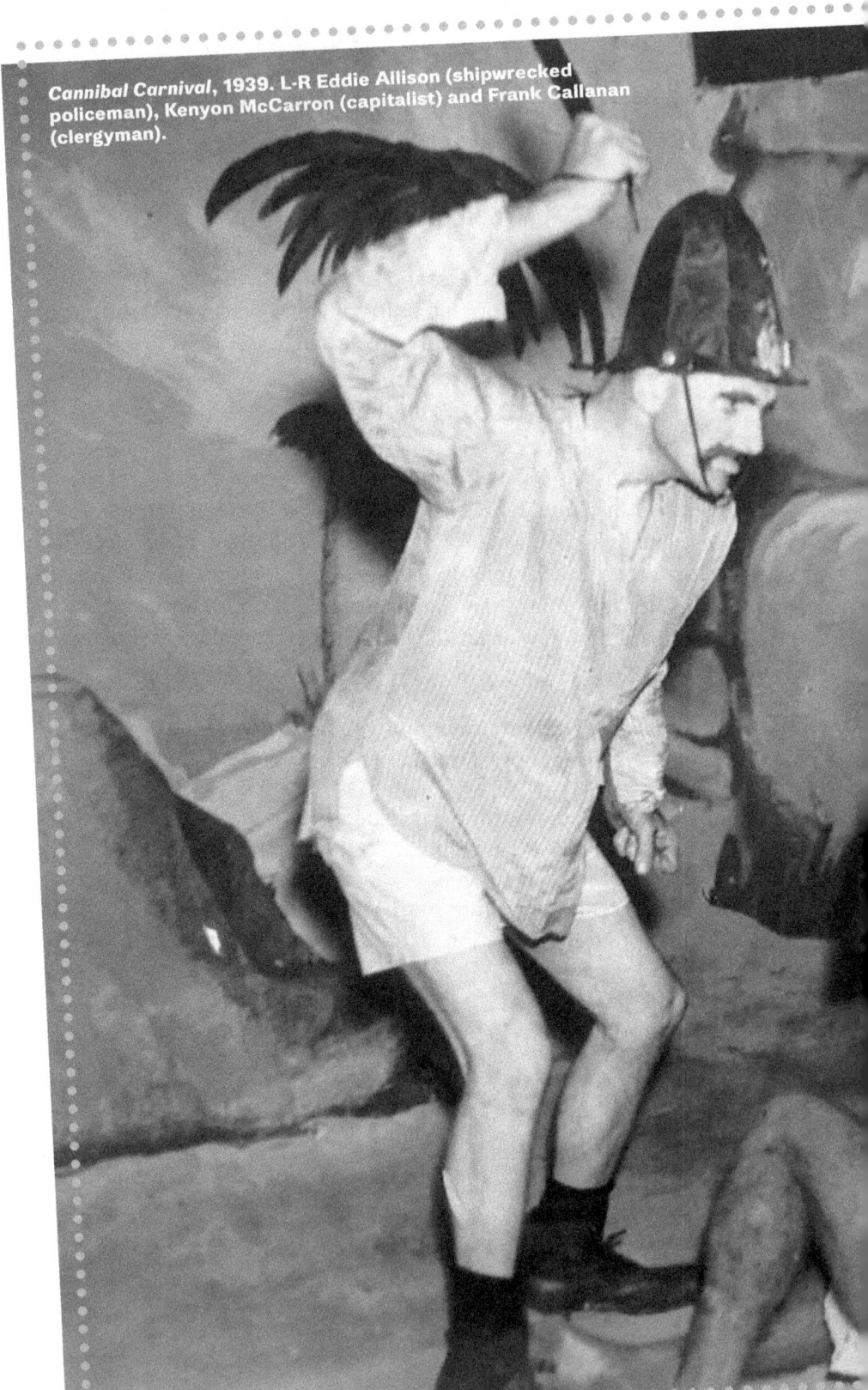

Cannibal Carnival, 1939. L-R Eddie Allison (shipwrecked policeman), Kenyon McCarron (capitalist) and Frank Callanan (clergyman).

labourers expands to a widespread strike. A left-wing British MP visits the governor:

> Lady Munro: I'm so sorry my husband wasn't here. He's...he's at some sort of conference.
>
> Jane: What sort of conference?
>
> Lady Munro: Oh...something to do with the...welfare of the sugar workers.
>
> Jane: So that's what all the trouble's about. *(SFX: Four shots in the distance.)* Rabbit for supper?

Strangers in the Land, by Mona Brand, concerns the struggle for Malayan independence, shown through the eyes of a visiting English girl about to marry a rubber planter. The author wrote the play while living in London, and Unity staged it before it became part of the 1953 Sydney season.

Brand also lived in Vietnam. She had first-hand experience of 'The Not So Quiet American', her target in *No Strings Attached*:

> Doppeldanger: Say! Where's my goddam Scotch?
>
> Mrs Templeton: Oh, hasn't the waiter brought you your drink yet, Mr Doppeldanger?
>
> Doppeldanger: No! And I gave that goddam coolie a half dollar.

In a fictional Far East country, US businesses offload their electrical appliances, cosmetics, Californian oranges and violent films offensive to Buddhists on a country whose real need is for schools and hospitals. Self-interest is disguised as foreign aid, and elections are manipulated with gifts to chosen candidates.

In the 1958 production, a Chinese medical student from Malaya and a university student involved with the Chinese Youth League played minor roles. *No Strings Attached* was translated into German and Russian.

Staged in 1971, *Niugini!* was a program of short plays by members of a creative writing class at the University of Papua New Guinea. Each showed a different aspect of life in the emerging nation.

In John Waiko's *The Unexpected Hawk*, a kiap (white patrol officer) comes to a village 'like a hawk coming to catch a rat' to try to force its inhabitants to amalgamate with others in the district. Leo Hannett's *The Ungrateful Daughter* explores the cultural dilemma of a young Bougainvillean woman being coerced into marrying an Australian by a white couple who have adopted her. Humiliation is *The Old Man's Reward* in Arthur Jawodimbari's play, not the medal he is given by the Australian External Affairs Minister.

In M. Lavori's *Alive*, reviewed as the program's most authentic script, Gombe woos a proud young woman who doesn't want to marry. After sleeping with him, she kills him; she then repents and follows him into land of the dead.

> *Gombe presents Ada with a gift of sweet potatoes, bananas, taro and yams.*
>
> Gombe: I want you to be my wife. Can any man do more to deserve a woman? Haven't I earned you yet?
>
> Ada: Your talk is smoother than pig grease. But once you have married me, won't you treat me like all the rest? I'll be a slave like every other woman in this village.
>
> *He brings out a parcel from his string bag.*
>
> Gombe: I walked five days to find this for you. Twice I was chased by our war-like neighbours. Wear it proudly. It was brought across the sea by the pale-skinned people. On the coast they say it comes from the dead.
>
> *Ada unwraps a bright red piece of calico and lets out a cry of delight.*
>
> ....
>
> *In the underworld, Gombe questions his dead uncle about whether he can go back to the living.*
>
> Gombe: Can the living ever cross the boundary to the land of death?

> Uncle: Once you have crossed the river to the West there is no more return. The order of things must not be upset. Do you want to turn night into day? Day into night? Do you want cassowaries to mate with pigs?

Despite good notices, audiences for *Niugini!* were disappointing, and full body makeup was a costly budget item for the 20 Caucasians playing New Guineans – including Simon Burke, who celebrated his 10th birthday during the run.

Also staged in 1971 was *1971 – A Race Odyssey*, set in a town called Greensville where a green-skinned race persecutes a purple-skinned race. The work was commissioned with an Australia Council for the Arts grant. Bill Noonan, one of its authors, had observed Australians' paternalism during his service in New Guinea in World War II; and Wayne van Heekeren, one of the actors, had first-hand knowledge of racism growing up on a Port Moresby plantation.

Indians, which played in 1982, takes a fresh look at 19th century white US relations with the Indigenous inhabitants. A mix of Wild West Show, vaudeville and circus, Arthur Kopit's play debunks the Hollywood myth of the brave Western hero taming the primitive savage:

> Chief Red Cloud: They made us many promises, more than I can remember. But they never kept but one. They promised to take our land and they took it.

Brian Friel's *Translations*, set in a hedge school in County Donegal in 1833, illustrates military and cultural imperialism. The arrival of English Royal Engineers, authorised to Anglicise the Celtic place names, disrupts life in the quiet rural community. *Translations* was part of the 1997 season.

APARTHEID

Following the 1960 Sharpeville massacre, the theatre sent a telegram to Australian Prime Minister Menzies, urging his government to lodge a protest with the South African Government. A letter to South African Prime Minister Dr Verwoerd called for an end to apartheid and to 'cease the murder of men, women and children'.

In the revue *Exposure 70,* Roger Milliss and Zigurds Richters, armed with binoculars, were cricket commentators on the final no-day's play between England and South Africa:

> It's wonderful weather here today, the tear gas has cleared overnight, not a cloud in the sky, and a slight south-easterly breeze from the demonstrators' end.

Street Theatre joined protesters against the Springboks' tour of Australia in 1971. White footballers, their coach and supporters played in the city with a black ball. Publicity for *The Death of Bessie Smith* drew race relations parallels between 1937 Tennessee and anti-apartheid demonstrations in 1971 Sydney.

Two major works on the apartheid system played in the 1980s. Frank McNamara directed both. *The Jail Diary of Albie Sachs* (adapted by David Edgar from Sachs' *Jail Diary*) is a white South African anti-apartheid protester's description of his detention without charge or trial. The drama won praise for its spare, unsentimental writing, matched by performances direct and free from melodramatics:

> *A cell in Cape Town.*
>
> Albie: I was entering my chambers this morning. I had parked my car and was at the entrance of the building. I felt a hand on my shoulder. There were men in suits all around me. I am detained under the 90-day law. After 90 days I can be arrested for a further 90 days. And then again. Ad infinitum.
>
> *He scratches 1/10/63 on the cell wall.*
>
> It is Tuesday October the first 1963.
>
> *He scratches his initials.*
>
> I am Albert Louis Sachs.
>
> *He scratches a single scratch.*
>
> Day One.

In the distance he hears the chime of a clock. Albie instinctively reaches for his watch, remembers it's been taken by a guard. He listens, the clock strikes 6.

Thank God for that.

'A relentless indictment of police brutality and medical duplicity', *The Biko Inquest*, by British journalists Jon Blair and Norman Fenton, was based on the official transcript of the inquest into the death of Black anti-apartheid activist Steve Biko. While studying medicine at the University of Natal, Biko became involved in organisations promoting his people's rights. Arrested several times for subversion, he died in 1977 in police custody from head injuries.

The 1985 production was well reviewed ('Biko Story Told with Devastating Effect') and David Ritchie's performance as the Biko family's barrister 'outstanding'. The New extended the season.

MENTAL ILLNESS

The New's longest ever straight run was in 1975: Dale Wasserman's *One Flew Over the Cuckoo's Nest* played to full houses for five months, involving understudies and cast changes. There were regular queues hoping for cancellations. The show could have gone on for longer, but there was fear of stagnation and other directors, actors and works missing out.

The Australian premiere of the entertaining and thought-provoking play, which predated the film, dug the theatre out of huge debt. First-class acting and Stanley Walsh's sharp direction won praise; theatre critic Norman Kessell named *Cuckoo's Nest* the best play of the year.

Sunday post-show discussions involving mental health professionals addressed such questions as: Is US society emasculated? Is behavioural therapy justified? Is man free? A doctor defended neurosurgery and electric shock treatment to a near-full house. The New mounted a fresh production of *Cuckoo's Nest* in 2002.

Eccentric sex reformer William Chidley is the subject of *No Room for Dreamers*, by Sydney writer George Hutchinson. A product of childhood repression, Chidley preached his theory on how to attain physical, mental and spiritual health by 'natural coition'. Dressed in a Greek-style tunic, he sold his booklet *The Answer* in Adelaide and Melbourne and in Sydney's Domain.

The New's 'entertaining and thoughtful production' was staged in 1987.

In 1990, Street Theatre devised *Mind Your Head!* for Mental Health Week. Peter Brook's *The Man Who*, inspired by neurologist Oliver Sacks' *The Man Who Mistook His Wife for a Hat*, was part of the 2006 season. Louis Nowra's popular work *Cosi*, staged in 2009, questions whether true madness lies inside or outside a psychiatric hospital.

ON THE FRINGE

Sydney New Theatre's first home was near Circular Quay, the shabby end of town. In the Depression years, its clubrooms were handy for those wanting a free cuppa before making their way to Central to collect their food rations after picking up their dole tickets at Wharf 7. Unemployed WAC members lived on the premises, bunking down at night in the auditorium. Those lucky enough to have jobs helped others who were out of work. All sorts of people drifted in: artists, wharfies, anarchists, Trotskyites – and a down-and-out Peter Finch.

WAC President Jerry Wells was himself near derelict in 1935 when he played the Cardboard Box Man in *Carrion Crow*, winner of that year's Sydney Eisteddfod one-act play award. Impoverished by unemployment, Cockney slum dwellers, like the clever, fearless scavenging bird, rummage through garbage tins at night:

> Rag Woman: Yer ain't got to do nuffink fer a copper ter git yer. They hoccupies their spare time wiv the likes of us. E's nailed me twice, this 'un 'as.

Recent plays dealing with social isolation include the Melbourne Workers' Theatre's *Who's Afraid of the Working Class*, Sam Sejavka's *In Angel Gear* (drivers in neutral or 'angel' gear abandon control and coast downhill) and *The Angry Brigade* – 1970s British urban guerrillas who carried out a series of bombings targeting symbols of the 'class enemy'.

Part of the 2011 *Spare Room* season with guest companies was *Lucky*, a physical theatre piece by Ferenc Alexander Zavaros about a refugee who pays a human trafficker to take him to Australia to join his brother. The ethnically diverse cast of Peter Weiss' *Marat/Sade* performed within a giant metal cage. The 2016 production drew parallels with asylum seekers in offshore detention.

SEXUAL ORIENTATION AND IDENTITY

In the early days of the WAC, the Central Committee of the CPA labelled some of its members 'artistic freaks'; but it was not until the theatre was at St Peters Lane that the first gay man 'came out'. Although there was plenty of male nudity in David Storey's *The Changing Room* in 1976, another 16 years passed before the New put on a play dealing explicitly with sexual identity. This was Peter Kenna's *Furtive Love*, in which the main character struggles to reconcile his homosexuality with his Catholic faith.

In 1994, the theatre officially linked with Mardi Gras and, since then, has produced an annual show dealing with homosexual or cross-gender themes under the Mardi Gras festival umbrella (often with a foyer warning notice: 'contains nudity, drug use, strong language and adult themes'). The first was *The Boys in the Band*, marking the 25th anniversary of Mart Crowley's classic. *The Death of Peter Pan*, by local playwright Barry Lowe, followed – another box-office success appealing to a wide audience

Other Mardi Gras productions include Barry Kramer's *The Destiny of Me*, concerning the early days of the AIDS epidemic. Lee Blessings' *Thief River* follows the half-century relationship of two men from their teenage years growing up in a small Minnesotan town. Joshµa Conkel's 'romp with a serious point', *MilkMilkLemonade*, is about sexual awakening in the rural US Bible Belt. Douglas Carter Beane's *The Little Dog Laughed*, on Hollywood hypocrisy, references another childhood rhyme. Richard Greenberg's baseball play, *Take Me Out*, explores homophobia and racism in sport. Jonathan Hall's *Hardcore* examines the gulf between watching and making gay pornography. A tribute to civil rights pioneers, Jonathan Harvey's *Canary* spans five decades of Gay Liberation activism, and Jon Marans' *The Temperamentals* tells the story of the Mattachine Society, the USA's first gay rights organisation, when 'temperamental' was a code word.

Moises Kaufman's *Gross Indecency: The Three Trials of Oscar Wilde* played in repertory with *The Importance of Being Earnest*, both with an all-male cast. Mark Ravenhill's *Mother Clap's Molly House*, its action moving between a 21st century Bloomsbury loft and an 18th century brothel where boys dress as women, had repeat seasons. Terrence McNally's *Corpus Christi*, which depicts Christ and the Apostles as gay men from Corpus Christi in Texas, drew publicised protest and good houses. Theatre members Gill Falson and Louise Fischer headed teams devising a series of *Funny Business* and *Lemon Delicious* cabarets in the period 1998–2004. Charles

Busch's *Vampire Lesbians of Sodom* complemented Clint Jefferies' *Tango Masculino* in 2007.

Peter Nichols' cheekily titled *Privates on Parade*, based on the British Army Entertainment Company touring Malaya, played in 1989 and again for Mardi Gras in 2014. Other main season works include Canadian playwright Brad Fraser's *Unidentified Human Remains and the True Nature of Love* and Alex Harding's musical *Only Heaven Knows*, set in the gay subculture of 1940s–50s Kings Cross. The relationship between tenor Peter Pears and composer Benjamin Britten is the subject of *Once in a While the Odd Thing Happens*, and sexual orientation and identity viewed through the life of US writer Carson McCullers is a central theme in Alana Valentine's *Singing the Lonely Heart*. Gina Schien's *Relative Comfort* explores lesbian relationships. It played in repertory in 1999 with Brad Fraser's *Poor Superman*, on male homosexual intimacy.

The theatre has participated in Queer Fringe as part of the Sydney Fringe Festival and supported the Gay Solidarity Group and Counteraid. In 2016, the New received the AIDS Council of NSW Arts and Entertainment Award for its ongoing commitment to 'recognising diverse sexualities and genders as an important demographic within the theatre's community and audience'.

THE NEW THEATRE IN AUSTRALIA

CHAPTER 13

No Handmaidens Here: Women, Volunteering and Gender Dynamics

Lisa Milner and Cathy Brigden

Three decades apart, two reports told a worryingly similar story about women's representation in Australian theatre. Both the 1983 and 2012 commissioned reports highlighted the importance of women's contribution to creative leadership but identified ongoing absence and persistent barriers. Commenting on the 2012 report, to which she contributed, Susan Miller sets out an overview in 'Women and Leadership: Theatre' (in *The Encyclopaedia of Women and Leadership in Twentieth Century Australia*). Curiously absent is any mention of the women of the New Theatre. This is striking, because documentation exists about the role of women playwrights in cultural production through their New Theatre works. The playwrights are but one group of women who, through the New Theatre, contributed to theatre leadership.

Women provided both creative and organisational leadership to the various New Theatre branches and were integral to the branches' development and sustenance. In contrast to other gendered spaces in the theatrical, industrial and political spheres, women held these theatres together as directors, producers, performers, writers and designers. They were committee members and held key elected offices. The distinction that Miller draws between creative and organisational leadership – in which 'artistic leadership [is] clearly differentiated from the management and production roles in which women are often well represented, typically as general managers or producers' – was decidedly blurred in the New Theatre. In common with other amateur theatres, the New Theatre primarily relied on volunteers, both front and back of stage, with few

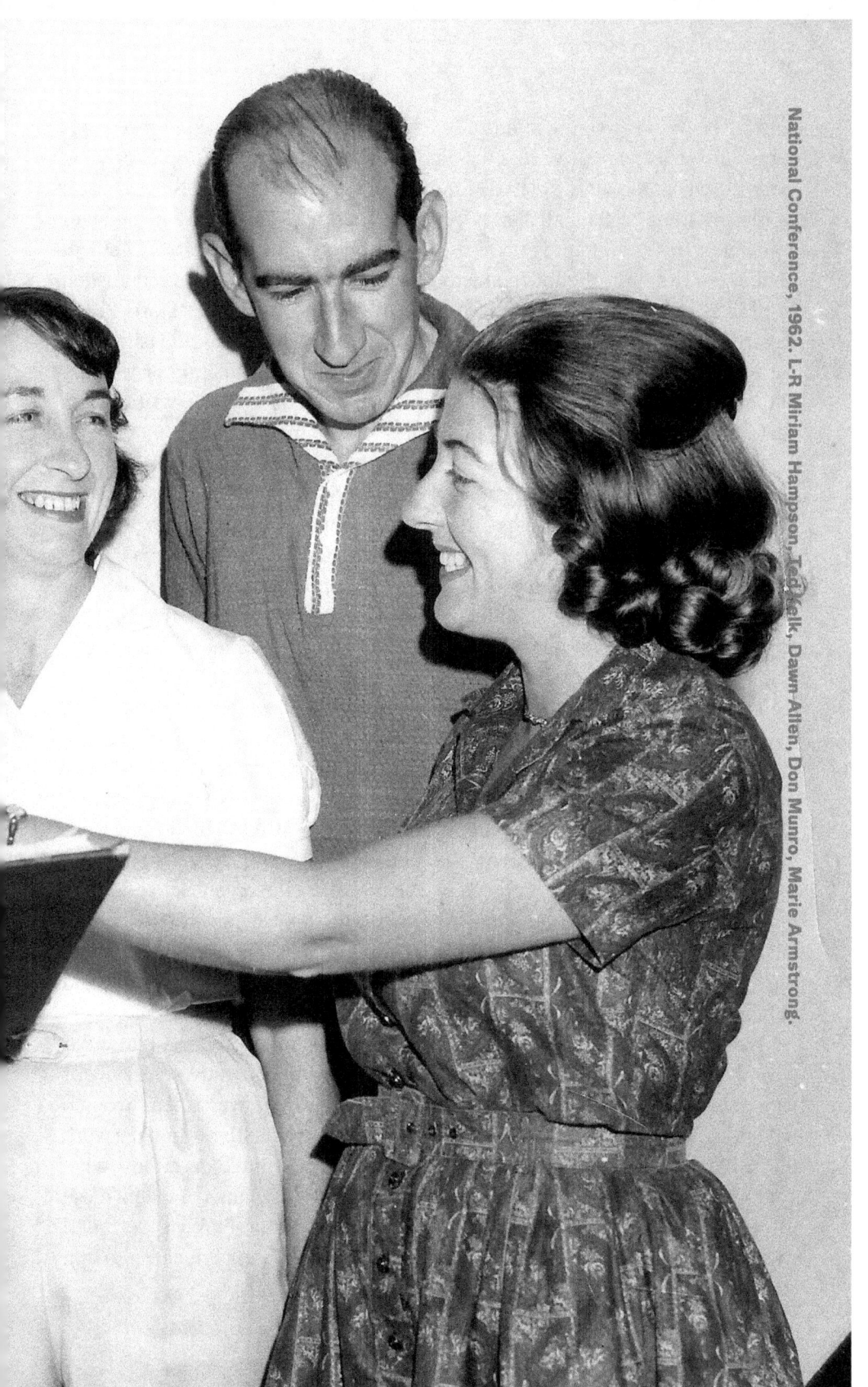

National Conference, 1962. L-R Miriam Hampson, Ted Kelk, Dawn Allen, Don Munro, Marie Armstrong.

paid roles. What is significant, however, is how the women combined roles across this artistic/creative and management divide. These multiple, or what we will call compound, roles distinguished the profile of the New Theatre women. Although the 'all hands on deck' approach is typical in amateur companies, less common is the crossing of the artistic/creative/management divide. For example, the Independent Theatre, which Doris Fitton established in 1932 as a Limited Company, had a company contract stating: 'Doris Fitton has free and unfettered control of all productions'. Rather than focusing on a particular aspect of theatre work, such as performing or directing or writing, numerous women combined performing and directing, script writing and performing, or producing and performing – plus committee work.

In this chapter, we investigate the ways in which women carved out this compound role profile in the New Theatre. The Sydney branch is our illustrative case, but we note that this pattern was not limited to the Sydney women. Selecting the 1930s until the late 1960s as the focal period means that our study includes the time from the theatre's inception to the time when the women's movement began to influence women's participation more generally. Also at this time, new radical social, political and cultural movements drove a new period of volunteerism.

The women who feature in this chapter worked in a variety of roles in the Sydney branch, combining artistic and managerial creative roles and adding to the New Theatre's theatrical output and organisational strength in many ways. The longevity of their contribution is also impressive. For many decades, the theatre dominated their leisure hours, as they juggled their theatre work with home, family life and paid employment. All these women shared a vision of the aims and outcomes of the New Theatre. Both the organisation and the individual women developed out of this work, with the women infusing the organisation with values of community and commitment. Three factors enabled this participation: degree of family/partner support; capacity to juggle paid and volunteer work; and scope for development of personal and political identity.

We focus on selected women with this compound profile in a particular period of the New Theatre's life, rather than providing a broader overview of women's contribution. However, we recognise that there were many women who primarily contributed in one area and also engaged in the voluntary work that all members were expected to undertake. We pose three questions: what volunteer roles did the women take on; how did the women sustain these roles; and what were the organisational gender dynamics? What we found was a distinctive participation pattern shaping women's experiences, arising

Evelyn Docker (standing at right) in O'Flaherty VC workshop.

from the intersection of gender dynamics with volunteering, political and personal activism, and leisure, which provides a contrary picture to the 1983 and 2012 reports.

RESEARCH INTO WOMEN IN THEATRE HISTORY

Many canonical texts of traditionally male-centred Australian theatre history pay scant attention to women – apart from the most well-known performers and writers. In his revised 1978 edition of *The Making of Australian Drama*, Rees added a short chapter on the work of Australian women playwrights of the 1930s to the 1950s, writing patronisingly:

> for the first time in our emerging literature of drama, some such equal treatment [of men and women playwrights] is possible...in Australia women showed quite as much talent as men.

From the mid-1990s, Australian theatre historians began to cover the contributions of women more fully. One of the pioneers of this more detailed research was Susan Pfisterer, whose analysis of Australian women's theatre in her 1997 doctoral thesis built on what she had earlier identified as Australia's 'meagre contribution' to women's theatre studies. Pfisterer focused on the careers of two playwrights, Inez Bensusan (also an actor) and Stella Miles Franklin. While that literature opened up the configuration of Australian theatre history about its female contributors, it continued to focus on performers and writers. The work of women in mainstream theatres has attracted more attention than that of those working in the margins: some recognise that 'mainstream theatre *is* gendered cultural production' (original emphasis). Heckenberg does acknowledge that women ran a large proportion of smaller Australian theatres in the 20th century. Hunt has discussed the changing place of women in Australian cultural history, noting that the emerging trend is to 'recover unknown women cultural producers, outline policies of exclusion, or identify feminine aesthetics'.

Few (female) Australian researchers have highlighted the place of female performers and writers in Australian theatre; few, if any, studies examine the breadth of women's contribution – in this case, their compound roles. These newer theatre histories also overlook women's achievements in other areas of theatre and, as Cockin observes, in:

> theatres of low status and informal organisation, such as travelling players performing often without script on makeshift stages in the open street, [rather] than in the high-status theatres equipped with permanent buildings and [official] patronage.

This literature also focuses primarily on paid work, with little attention given to women undertaking voluntary labour.

Here, debates within labour history about the definition of 'work' and its broadening to include voluntary labour are helpful. Shaping these debates about recognising voluntary action as work and the implications for labour history was the transformative push which Melanie Oppenheimer and Joanne Scott began in the late 1990s. Oppenheimer's work has particularly transformed the scholarly and public debate about volunteering and volunteers, successfully challenging the prevailing definition of work as paid labour and the presumption of volunteer work as the province of middle-class women. Locating voluntary work squarely within the academic study of labour history has driven a new appreciation of its parameters and impact. With the traditional discipline focus on trade unions and political parties, it is timely to remember that they all started through voluntary action and depended on activists volunteering their time and energy to the cause. Oppenheimer reminds us that, of those organisations 'involving people coming together around a specific need or interest for mutual gain', trade unions are 'perhaps one of the largest, original self-help organisations'.

Women's volunteer work is often within women's organisations, and historians examining women's volunteer experiences generally studied these. In mixed-gender organisations, women's participation was often directed to women's committees or sections. This was the case in the ALP, while the CPA's often contested relationship with its women members also included gender-specific activities. Some male-dominated unions sought to include women relatives in women's auxiliaries.

In the leisure literature, research on the intersection of volunteer work with leisure led Stebbins to focus on developing this conceptual space. He asked:

> Is volunteering unpaid, productive work or is it leisure? These two seemingly incompatible conceptualisations figure prominently in the modern debate on the nature of volunteering. Yet, it is possible to see volunteering as both unpaid work and attractive leisure.

Stebbins' particular contribution is his characterisation of the 'serious leisure perspective', in which there are three forms of leisure: serious, casual and project-based leisure. He defines serious leisure as:

> systematic pursuit of an amateur, hobbyist or volunteer activity sufficiently substantial, interesting and fulfilling for the participant to find a (leisure) career there acquiring and expressing a combination of its special skills, knowledge and experience.

Stebbins lists six characteristics of serious leisure: career, perseverance, effort, benefits, unique ethos and social world, and distinctive identity. Our study has found decades-long instances of these characteristics among the New Theatre volunteers. We can extend Stebbins' discussion of volunteering, because these women (and men) clearly engaged in 'political' volunteering, where ideological commitment and conviction drive the nature, frequency and longevity of volunteering. The motivation for this was often (although not always) their values, including a commitment to socialist ideology (associated with membership of the CPA) and the other progressive organisations' aims.

Therefore, labour history debates, set against the cultural history literature highlighting absence of women's experiences and contributions, have broadened the concept of 'work' to encompass volunteering – an activity in turn explored through the concept of serious leisure. This chapter will show that, for New Theatre women, the sense that they were very much part of a community of interests was important to their social worth.

To construct the story of the Sydney New Theatre women, we examined archival records and undertook interviews. Most of the archival records were included in the State Library of NSW's New Theatre collection. The scant organisational records remaining from the 1930s and 1940s made identifying women in the early years of the Sydney New Theatre more difficult. An album of newspaper clippings provided much-needed information about activities and key members. New Theatre playwright Oriel Gray's autobiography gave insights into theatre life. More substantial archival records were available from the early 1950s, including minutes of the management committee, general members' meetings and annual general meetings (still not complete, however) and assorted inward and outward correspondence. On the basis of these combined sources, we focus on the period 1936 to 1969.

In order to build our appreciation of the women's experience and roles, we carried out six semi-structured, audio-recorded interviews with nine participants – seven women and two men, including two married couples. The couple interviews included both partners, which enabled us to collect complementary and divergent memories and to explore how family dynamics shaped the nature and degree of participation. Apart from one interview, we interviewed together, and the interviews ranged from one to three hours. We primarily identified participants through referrals. Among the interviewees were three life members whose experiences dated back to the late 1940s. Most retained some ongoing connection with the theatre, attending performances and, in one case, still volunteering regularly and performing occasionally.

We then examined the patterns of women's involvement, to determine how many women were active in taking on both organisational and creative roles. Our criterion for inclusion was whether they were active in two or more roles: elected committee work, back of house, teaching/workshop, performing, contact work (performances taken out to audiences), writing. On this basis, we estimated that 21 women took on compound roles (see Table). Four of these women – Marie Armstrong, Norma Disher, Betty Millis and Silvia Salisbury – were among our interview participants.

THE SYDNEY NEW THEATRE AND WOMEN

The New Theatre's objectives, especially those concerning freedom, democracy and social justice, underpinned an organisation that differed from other contemporary amateur theatres. Working to meet these objectives, which flowed naturally into the choice of plays and the methods of the theatre's operation, was a key reason for many members' participation. Norma Disher said:

> the inspiration, for me, and I'm sure for many of the members, was the Constitution. It could be described as idealistic, or political, but it was a humanity-orientated social democratic approach to theatre, which I found had purpose. And it was something that I wanted to be part of.

Miriam Hampson believed:

Women in the Sydney New Theatre, 1936-1969

Focus woman	Partner/husband also in N.T.; Other family links	Paid occupation
Audrey Grant [Audrey Ward nee Hill]	Len Grant	Typist C.P.A.
Betty Milliss nee Cole	David Milliss	Clerk and floorwalker at Coles; office work at Bonds factory
Betty Spink		Secretary to Eddie Allison (N.T. member) at Quality Films
Edith (Edie) McLaren		Wigmaker
Eileen Allison nee Bullen	Eddie Allison sister: Pat Bullen	Sales
Elsie Dayne		Hairdresser/wigmaker
Evelyn Docker nee Thomson	Norm Docker brother: Bert, son: Alan, grandson: Einar	Actor
Freda Brown nee Lewis	Bill Brown	C.P.A. functionary
Jean Blue		Actor, nurse
Joan Clarke nee Willmott		Playwright
Kip (Mary Marguerite) Lambert nee McDonald	John Lambert daughter: Jan	
Marie Armstrong nee Stonehouse	John Armstrong	Typist, administrative work for Produce Importers' Committee, Newsletter Printery, Metalworkers Union
Miriam Hampson nee Aarons	Stan Hampson (W.A.C.) niece: June Worth	Biochemist; munitions factory in W.W.II; Secretary of N.T.
Mona Brand	Len Fox	Playwright
Muriel Horton nee Small	Bill Horton	Radio performer
Nan Gow/Vernon nee Davies	Keith Gow; then Howard Vernon	Actor, shearers' cook, window dresser, petrol station attendant
Norma Disher	Bruce Hawkins	Musician librarian at Radio 2SM, Clerk at Miscellaneous Workers Union, clerk at Trade Union Club
Oriel Gray nee Bennett	John Gray	Writer
Pat Flower nee Bullen	Bruce Jiifkins; then Cedric Flower Sister: Eileen Allison	Writer
Shirley Keane nee Roberston	Kim Keane (Melbourne N.T.)	Technical librarian
Silvia Salisbury nee Meech	Tom Salisbury	Clerk in the Department of Air

New Theatre Roles	Years of Membership
Actor, Assistant Secretary, Management committee	1960-1966
Actor, Vice-President, Contact committee, Management committee	1952-2021 Life Member
Actor, Stage Manager, Management committee, Contact committee	1954-1958
Actor, Committee, Social Secretary	1956-1965
Actor, Director, Assistant to director, President, Vice-President, Management committee, British Drama League Festival Adjudicator	1949-1966
Actor, Dancer, Singer, Choreography, Wardrobe, Costume and wig designer	1942-1992 Life Member
Actor, Stage Manager, Assistant secretary	1952-2003 Life Member
Actor, Director, Publicity officer/Assistant secretary, Secretary, Contact committee	1936-1944
Actor, President, Director, Workshop committee	1936-1984 Life Member
Playwright, Management committee	1952-1958
Actor, Front of house, Management committee	1958-1980
Actor, Singer, Dancer, Director, Asssstant director, Stage Manager, Choreographer, Management committee, Contact committee, Secretary of Natonal Federaton	1946-2022 Life Member
Secretary, Assistant secretary, President, Management committee, Contact committee, Production committee, National Federation President	1937-1993 Life Member
Playwright; Assistant Secretary, Contact committee, publicity, play judge	1953-2007 Life Member
Actor, Treasurer	1947-1955
Actor, Costume designer, Contact committee, Workshop leader, Assistant secretary, Director, Assistant director	1949-1991
Wardrobe, Music, Sound designer, Director, Production committee, Workshop committee	1948-current Life Member
Actor, Playwright	1938-1949
Actor, Secretary, Teacher	1944-1977 Life Member
Actor, Director, Teacher	1949-1970
Actor, Singer, Treasurer, Management committee	1951-current Life Member

> in fact, our principles have kept us removed from the sort of amateur theatre that becomes art for art's sake, and depends on the dominance of big personalities; our structure is very democratic.

Because of its links to the CPA, the New Theatre also operated in a charged political environment. Security circles regarded it as a communist front. When the CPA was banned in 1940, police raided the Theatre's office and those of other organisations suspected of posing security risks. They confiscated items like the membership file and hundreds of play scripts. The Theatre assumed that ASIO, after its establishment in 1949, was carrying out increased surveillance, and this later proved to be true. Norma's response about her production committee work – 'Yes, I was. And you can get ASIO to prove it, too!' – echoed Marie's assertion: 'we always suspected there were always people spying on us. We know ASIO was bugging our phones.' While stage names were common in the professional theatre, the branch adopted them to protect people's identities. Norma recalled that they chose to have:

> no names on the program for [*Out of Commission*, Mona Brand's play about the Petrov Commission]. Because the Commission was in operation...we didn't have any names, because it would have been stupid... they were sending ASIO [to the theatre].

Indeed, many of New Theatre's activities appear in theatre members' ASIO files, the release of which revealed the extent of surveillance.

During the war years, in response to the fight against fascism and the entry of the USSR, CPA membership increased. Theatre membership reflected this – and five of our interviewees were party members, illustrating this point. In the postwar years, especially once the Cold War had begun, authorities actively pursued anti-communism, politically and industrially, and subjected such political volunteering to increased scrutiny. The available written records in the 1950s make it clear that the CPA exercised little direct control over the plays and the messages contained therein, but there was nevertheless a CPA presence, to which interviewees alluded. This added a further dimension to theatre members' volunteering, because it broadened their political volunteering to the party and, for others, also included their trade union. Silvia Salisbury explains the structure's democratic nature, which she enjoyed:

Everything that flowed from that was answerable to the General Membership. They made the decisions, or they suggested things to be done. They divided it up into the Management committee, who looked after the paying of the bills and all that sort of thing. And then there was the Production committee, that read the plays, and worked out who was going to be the next director, and what the plays were going to be. A sub-committee of that was play readers. And they were all elected positions, elected from the general membership as who ought to be good.

The Workshop committee was a practical training group:

people who were interested in directing could choose a [one-act] play… We would read the play, the same as the big people on the Production committee would read the play, and see if it was related to the Constitution.

Not everyone appreciated the commitment to democratic process, but most regarded it as important in ensuring inclusive decision making. Miriam Hampson observed:

sometimes this democratic way of work is a little heavy, and sometimes I would agree with anyone who says: 'Oh, but it's stifling.' It can be stifling but I think you have to pay some dues for having something that is run for everyone, and not just the flaring stars.

Hierarchical structures in volunteer organisations are often a barrier to women's involvement. In this case, however, democracy was the overriding feature promoting participation. Commenting on the Sydney New Theatre's establishment in the early 1930s alongside other 'Little Theatres', John Craig wrote: 'looking at the theatrical scene in those days it is interesting to see the amount of artistic production and organising done by women'. The participation of women as elected office bearers was obvious to new members. Tom Salisbury joined the New Theatre in 1947 and recalls:

> I suppose one of the most impressive things I've thought about New Theatre, when I first joined, was that the Secretary, Pat Bullen, the President, Jean Blue, and the [Treasurer], Muriel Small, they were all women. They were all in charge, and they were elected.

Leading members of the Sydney branch of the New Theatre were instrumental in forming the National Federation. They called delegates of the Melbourne branch to a Sydney conference in 1948 and formed New Theatre Australia; other branches soon joined the Federation. The governing body, the National Conference, met twice yearly, and the management committee included branch representatives plus officers. Here, too, women took on key leadership roles, with Miriam Hampson and Marie Armstrong elected President and Secretary in 1957.

The theatre's commitment to broadly socialist ideas extended to performance style. Activities were not limited to theatre spaces; engagement with workers extended into workplaces and public spaces through 'Contact' work, as other chapters in this volume detail. At the forefront of organising, writing and performing contact work were Freda Lewis, Betty Spink, Miriam Hampson, Nan Gow, Mona Brand and Marie Armstrong. New Theatre produced plays and short sketches for unions, CPA branches and other left organisations on current industrial or political issues. They staged performances at workplaces, parks and beaches, next to dole queues and from trucks. One example is Betty Roland's short play, *War on the Waterfront* (about the Port Kembla wharfies' refusal to load pig iron destined for Japan), which played at the Watson's Bay beach (after an initial attempt at the Sydney Domain). In 1959, a Mona Brand song, *Arthur Murray taught me Dancing in a Hurry*, featured at the picket line of the dance instructors locked out by Arthur Murray's Sydney dance studio.

FOCUS WOMEN

For the theatre not only to survive but also to flourish, the work of women was critical. From the outset, women shaped the theatre's direction. By contributing their skills and labour in diverse ways, women enabled the performances to occur regularly and to spread messages. Testament to their contribution is that 11 of the 21 who performed compound roles became honorary life members. For many of these women, their commitment to the

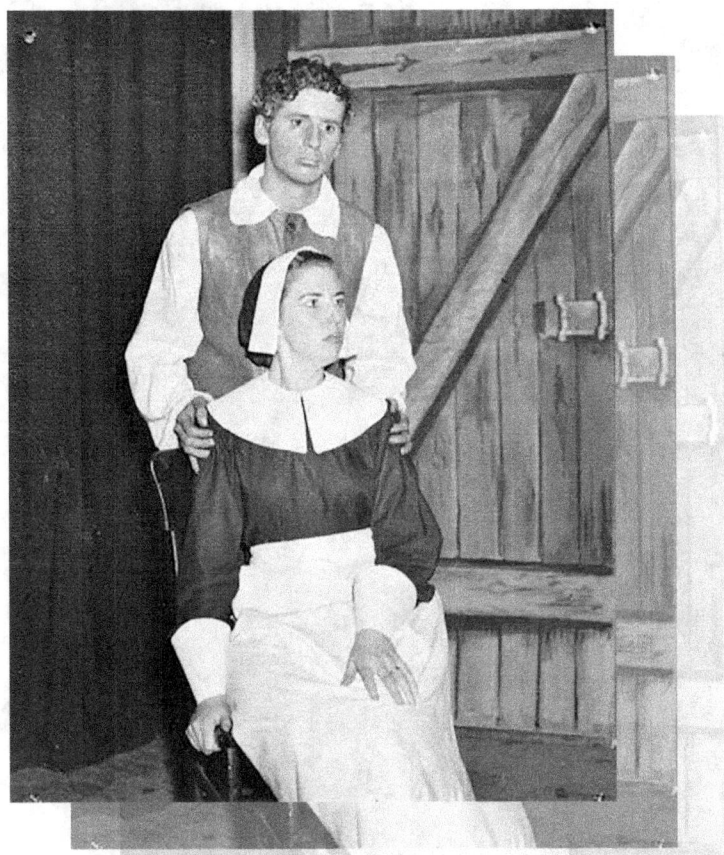

Betty Milliss and Brian Vicary in *The Crucible*, 1958.

New Theatre alongside their male comrades lasted for decades. They were, to use Stebbins' term, 'career volunteers' – or, more specifically, 'career political volunteers'.

We now introduce a selection of women, beginning with women active in the late 1930s and 1940s. Although fewer records document women's roles in the 1940s, the available records reveal these 'compound roles'.

One of the few professional actors, Jean Blue joined the Sydney branch in 1936 and combined acting with directing and organisational leadership. Playing in both stage-based and contact productions, Jean was perhaps best remembered for her parts in Oriel Gray's play *Western Limit* and in the award-winning *Lawson*. President from 1942 until 1948, Jean was a member of the Workshop committee and worked in the Contact unit in the 1930s and 1940s.

Freda Lewis building a set.

In 1936, Freda Lewis, having just turned 17, first attended a performance of Clifford Odets' anti-Nazi resistance play *Till the Day I Die*. Immediately joining the theatre, Freda began selling tickets and calling for donations, a front of house job that normally followed performances. She made her stage debut in 1937, began directing performances the following year, then became a member of the New Theatre Writers Group. Freda was Publicity Officer/Assistant Secretary in 1940 and Secretary in 1941 and 1942. She also engaged in contact work; for example, throughout July 1941, Freda, Jean Blue and Hughla Hurley presented sketches of political issues from a woman's viewpoint at street corners or from the back of trucks. Hughla was a management committee member in 1940 who was then working for the New Theatre full time, concentrating on lunch hour meetings and agitprop.

Miriam Hampson arrived in Sydney with interstate experience from her time as the Melbourne branch's Secretary. She joined the Sydney leadership group as Assistant Secretary in 1943 and was elected Secretary in mid-1950 – a position she retained until 1982. Miriam's role differed from those of the other women as the only ongoing paid role. A private income supplemented her small salary. However, her contribution to the theatre stretched well beyond her secretarial position. She took on multiple roles in the branch and nationally. Many New Theatre members remember Miriam as the Theatre's backbone for decades; one member described her 'very strong personality'.

Norma Disher joined in 1949. A member who was a co-worker at Sydney radio station 2SM soon realised that Norma was a talented dressmaker. When Norma went to the theatre:

> they grabbed me straight away. So, I discovered, then, that there was something there that I could do. I didn't want to act, but I could be helpful.

Until 1985, Norma was more than just 'helpful' as the theatre's chief costume-designer and maker. Later, she spoke eloquently of it as 'my complete vocation'. While she primarily worked on wardrobe, Norma also turned her hand to directing and became a member of the Workshop and then the Production committee:

> the other thing that interested me was Workshop. So shortly after I joined the theatre, I was somehow got to be leading Workshop...and then

Norma Disher, Lisa Milner and Jock Levy, Australian National Maritime Museum, 2003.

> shortly after that, I was elected to the Production committee, so that meant I was involved, all the time I was there I was involved in the Production, choice of plays, discussions.

Marie Armstrong explained how Norma's compound role developed:

> Norma never acted, she was always the wardrobe, but she was always on committee, she was a prominent member, she then directed, she moved into directing through that...It was multi-skilling stuff.

Like others, Marie Armstrong initially came to New Theatre performances and then became more broadly involved. However, as with Norma, performing was not her initial motivation. She drew on her office skills, particularly typing scripts, before being recruited as the Education Sub-committee's Minutes Secretary. For over 50 years, she provided organisational leadership – as a management committee member and as Federation President for a decade – together with directing, contact work, choreography, teaching, acting and some writing. Marie was on a committee of one type or another from 1951 to 1963. She wrote much of the national *Spotlight* magazine and many versions of the New Theatre's history through pamphlets and articles. In 2016, she was still performing, in the annual May Day event.

As is true for many of the women, Mona Brand's association with the New Theatre spanned decades. Starting in 1948 and often referred to as the theatre's 'major dramatist' or 'almost the house playwright', Brand was also a key member of the Contact committee and a performer. Yet, she remains relatively unknown in Australia. Pfisterer has pointed out: 'Australian communist women playwrights have a higher profile elsewhere in the world then they enjoy in Australia'. Joining the Melbourne RWG and the CPA in 1946–47, Mona attended a New Theatre performance the next year. Between 1948 and 1984, the New Theatre produced 17 of her plays and dozens of revue sketches. In 1954, Mona became Assistant Secretary, by that time a paid position. Alongside Milton Moore, she ran the contact shows in 1954 and 1955, writing and performing a great deal of the material. Although she resigned as Assistant Secretary in 1955, when she married Len Fox, Mona continued writing for the theatre, teaching classes, giving lectures in scriptwriting and occasionally working in the office.

Betty Milliss joined the New Theatre in 1952, after her brother had introduced her to a neighbour who was a New Theatre member. She combined acting and leadership roles, joining the management committee 'fairly soon... I was always on Management committee'. Elected Vice-President in 1956 and joining the Contact committee in 1960, Betty recalled: 'most of the people on Management were also involved in some aspect of production, acting, or behind stage'.

Silvia Salisbury's father first took her to see a New Theatre play when she was a teenager. Her love of the works she saw there evolved into a long commitment for her:

> the thing that struck me even as a child was the enthusiasm and commitment they had to plays that were saying something...there was nothing much for working-class people in 1947.

Silvia joined to perform, both acting and singing, but she moved into leadership roles, becoming Treasurer in 1956. Her key contribution was to the Production committee: 'I was Secretary of the Production committee for a long time because they thought it was a good way to learn.'

FACTORS ENABLING THE WOMEN'S COMPOUND ROLES

Three main factors enabled, encouraged and facilitated this degree and type of participation in the New Theatre for women: amount of family support; capacity to juggle paid employment and theatre work; and scope for development of personal and political identity. The women undertaking these compound roles realised that some barriers found in other volunteer settings were either surmountable or absent. Studies of women's participation in trade unions have found that the most common barriers have been lack of family support; either benign or more overt opposition; family responsibilities; timing of meetings, and personal confidence. In this case, family arrangements often created a supportive environment for their involvement, especially when spouses were also involved in the theatre.

Firstly, these women had a high degree of support from family and partners. Couples with shared values found ways around the demands that the theatre schedule posed. The shared experience of the theatre became the backdrop to many romantic and sexual liaisons, as personal relationships developed between members. Silvia married Tom Salisbury in 1955. After 60 years of marriage, she commented on the relationships that were forged, and sometimes faltered, in the New Theatre:

> That was another thing they used to have, all the different marriages in the theatre. We used to call it 'Miriam's Matrimonial Club', because we'd say that Miriam would organise all these things. Well, she didn't, but we all used to call it that, matchmaking... But it was just because you were in contact with each other for so long.

Betty Milliss confirms Silvia's memories:

> There was a point there where we used to call the New Theatre 'Miriam's Happiness Club', because so many people had met in the theatre, and were either living together, or married.

Sixteen of our focus women met their partners (sometimes more than one) at the Theatre. Among those whose spouse was also a New Theatre member were Mona Brand and Len Fox, Betty Cole and David Milliss, Nan Davies and Keith Gow, Freda Lewis and Bill Brown, and Norma Disher and Bruce Hawkins. Others included Eileen and Eddie Allison, Audrey Ward and Len Grant, Oriel Gray (née Bennett) and John Gray, Pat Bullen and Cedric Flower, and Kip and John Lambert.

For many of these women, their individual involvement became a shared activity with their partner in both creative and organisational areas. Theatre couples who raised a family faced the challenge of both partners needing to attend rehearsals, meetings and performances. Caring for children required accommodation: when the management committee was advised in 1960 that Pippa Hood needed child care, they suggested a specific babysitter. It affected how much Betty and David Milliss could do; their joint involvement 'all changed, of course, when we had kids. It was always one or the other of us doing things.' Betty described how she and David worked this out:

> we lived in a very old house [with fellow New Theatre volunteers Barbara and Trevor Finch] ... we lived in one

> flat, and they lived in the other ... With a door in between. And we could open or shut this door. So the four of us, at any time, three of us could be in the theatre, and one person was left at home, looking after all four kids.

Silvia and Tom Salisbury also took turns, with one parent looking after their three children when the other was at the theatre:

> I was lucky Tom being in the theatre, and we would take turns in doing shows... I had to do this play every Thursday, Friday, Saturday, and I'd be leaving early, and Tom would have to look after this newborn baby, and feed him, and look after these... little girls as well. Get them bathed, and into bed, and I don't know how he did it... I remember that was hard going, but Tom was really good.

The second factor was the capacity to juggle paid employment and theatre work. As working-class women, all our focus women (except Miriam, who was paid) needed to work full time to sustain themselves and their households. The demands of full-time, paid employment were then an ever-present consideration for these women. Proximity to the theatre allowed lunchtime volunteering, while others had sympathetic employers. Working for employers and organisations with shared values, like trade unions and other progressive organisations, further assisted; the starkest example is that of Marie and her boss, union leader Laurie Carmichael. Marie explains some of her organising strategies:

> I was doing [Contact work] in lunch hours, I was in charge of it for some time...luckily, the job I had, I was able to use the phone to ring people. That's been a very big advantage with me, that I haven't been in a factory where I didn't [have a phone]. When I was with the metal workers' union, it was understood... Laurie knew it, and other people did... I was on the phone, organising...it was just as well I had a job that I could, because it was really quite a job, all of that...mine was the 'get in the back of a truck, and out there in the lunch break'.

Physical proximity also helped Marie:

> So I was there, down in Sussex Street, for 10 years. And that's when I used to go up to New Theatre at lunchtime, I was central, [near] Market and Sussex [Streets].

Juggling jobs and theatre work was nonetheless a constant struggle, as three of the women explained. Marie described how, in another job, she managed to take part in the performance 250 km away:

> I had a full-time job... Everybody else seemed to have a full-time job... Had to take a day off, wouldn't I? Would I be 'sick'? If they rang Mum to say, how is she? Or, do I tell Mum?... So I had to cover myself at work, and cover myself at home. Can't remember how I swung that so nobody would ring anybody else about me. Nobody knew what I was doing in the family, or at work.

Both Betty and Silvia talked about the effect of after-work rehearsals. Betty recalled what she called the rehearsal 'madness':

> You'd rehearse four nights a week, and Sunday... And you would have rehearsals begin at seven... And depending on the director, sometimes, you wouldn't get out of there till nearly midnight... I was living with my brother and sister-in-law in Mosman, and I used to travel by ferry. And I can remember running down Pitt Street to get the last ferry to Mosman at midnight.

Silvia Salisbury remarked on the fatigue:

> I worked in the public service...night after night, and long rehearsals, you know, and I'd have to really concentrate on what I was doing...it was tough at times, because I'd be having to really keep my eyes open and concentrate... And by about 3.30 in the afternoon, I'd start to come really to and I could do a whole lot of work really quickly. And come five o'clock... and then I'd be all fresh for the rehearsal.

Thirdly, our interviewees identified scope for development of personal and political identity through volunteer work as a strong reason for joining and staying with the New Theatre for years. For many members, personal identity clearly became bound up in loyalty to the organisation and its aims. The distinction between theatre work, political activism/volunteering and leisure was not always clear cut and often blurred, with volunteer labour occurring in settings and organisations that could, and did, combine two or all of these elements. Few distinctions were drawn between work, leisure, political activity and creative activity. Norma Disher's recollection was: 'everybody volunteered completely'. The Workshop committee contributed to Norma's personal development:

> It was a really, really fascinating little episode in my life, and I took it extremely seriously...they needed somebody to lead it, and I finished up leading it for a while. And apart from making costumes and things, it was my first feeling of having an important job to do, you know?... So it was just a memorable sort of situation for me that I'd learnt to open my mouth and say what I thought. I'm still doing it!

The women brought particular skills with them, bolstering their confidence in carving out initial roles. Marie explained that, although typing scripts was her initial contribution, her singing propelled her performance career: 'the next thing, I'm being asked to be in the revue. And they found out I could dance'. Betty had acted in England but was then encouraged to learn the skills of a committee secretary.

Intersecting with this personal development was the political dimension of their theatre work. A number of the women were teenagers when they joined, finding the theatre's political purpose and messages attractive. Volunteering for other theatres could not replicate this. Moreover, membership's political commitment brought with it dangers and risk not experienced elsewhere: stopped performances and security surveillance put jobs and livelihoods at risk. The particular nature of the volunteering means that we can describe them as 'career political volunteers'.

The demands of volunteering did take their toll on some. For two of the scriptwriters, the problem was ensuring sufficient time for their primary contributions to the theatre. Joan Clarke resigned in 1958 because she felt that she was not being given sufficient time to write. She advised:

> When you find a promising writer, get them writing plays and don't expect them to do too many of the many numerous tasks in theatre organisation.

The response was that they needed 'active participation' from all members 'but that time for creative [sic] will always be granted'. Although the theatre relied on Mona Brand's script writing, she had to request one day off for writing in 1955: 'preferably Thursday'. When she married that year, she resigned as Assistant Secretary, prompting the observation that 'the sharing of the typing work, etc. would need to be discussed'.

Contact work brought its own challenges, as Marie recalled:

> things like street theatre rely on the enthusiasm of groups of people, and we have a very high turnover. Any theatre has this problem. People don't always get what they expect when they join a theatre, and there's a lot of discipline and hard work involved in working for the New. There's a lot of fun too, but we take our work seriously and expect total commitment.

Even for someone as committed as Norma, there were limits to her ability to go from one production to another:

> It's amazing, you know, what you can do when you're reasonably young. I was in my thirties then. But you're needed... And so many times working in the theatre, I would, on the Production committee, I'd say, 'well, who's doing the costumes?' and they'd just go [you]...you had to do all the sewing at weekends and night time, you had to work during the day. After I'd finished I would be exhausted, and I wouldn't do the next show... I'd go to other plays, and I'd go to the cinema, and I'd build up my own need, you know, for [external stimulation].

GENDER DYNAMIC

In mixed-gender organisations, gender dynamics frequently reflected gender stereotypes; women often found themselves relegated to 'caring' duties, those that were extensions of their domestic duties such as cooking and cleaning, or segregated into women's committees or auxiliaries. Studies of women and the CPA show that the intersection of class and gender was a common debate, shaping organisational dynamics. The historical period examined here encompasses World War II and the postwar period in Australia, which was a high point in volunteering. One effect of the wartime years was that women were more visible in public life. However, after the war, as the political environment grew more conservative, women were expected to return to the home and contribute to postwar reconstruction by focusing on family and household responsibilities.

In contrast, the New Theatre did not reproduce those gender dynamics embedded in the broader society. The female interviewees, speaking about their experiences, made this clear. The consensus view, often very forcefully expressed, was that no differences existed between the women and the men. Norma was adamant that:

> there was no differentiation between the role of women in the New Theatre as far as I was concerned. I was never, ever, aware, of all those years in the theatre, of any differentiation of gender at all. I never ever was conscious of that, from the point of view of the theatre, or the members themselves. And I think it was due to the fact that people were contributing in a group, and only their ability to contribute was what was needed.

Silvia had the same view – although she had anticipated more traditional gender dynamics:

> the other thing that I liked was they seemed to be so equal, the genders. I mean, you were all just working to get the play on. I can't ever remember there being [any sexism] – and it was good for me, because coming into my teenage years, I expected every organisation to be like that. There was no discrimination because you all had a part.

Marie appreciated the unconscious feeling of gender equality:

> I wasn't conscious of women being LET have a go, it was just they were there already...all I can say was that I fell into an area where I was working with women who were stage managers, and women who had power in the theatre. And it wasn't that I was made aware, 'we're women and we've got this'; they were just there. Because that's what theatre is. It's a mixture of talent, and it doesn't matter what sex, well, if you're lucky it doesn't matter.

However, not all was perfect. Sometimes, certain tasks did appear to be the province of men, such as back of house, and this reaffirmed stereotypical gender roles. Betty Milliss commented in 1958 that: 'women should be able to help on backstage'. Women challenged presumptions that they would clean up and make the coffee. A 1955 management committee discussed sharing the clearing up after functions at people's homes, including who should be doing this work: 'All agreed – also that it was not a job for the women only.' Minutes of a 1959 General Meeting affirm that it was: 'Not necessary to always be a woman' in charge of the coffee. New Theatre neither typically relegated women to minor roles nor excluded them from decision making. This was, therefore, a notable exception to Joanne Scott's observation that, during the interwar period in Australia: 'many voluntary organisations with a mixed sex membership restricted women's opportunities to participate fully through, for example, limiting their involvement to "ladies" committees'.

WHAT CAN WE CONCLUDE?

From the earliest times of the Sydney New Theatre's history, women carved out space in organisational pathways of the theatre. Women's presence in decision-making forums was at times starkly different, with a much higher proportion taking on executive roles than ever seen in the CPA, the ALP or in many mixed-gender trade unions. They actively engaged in sustaining the democratic structure of the theatre, sought office bearing roles, were nominated and elected by their peers. They did not always face competition in elections, but support for women's greater management responsibility is apparent, from both male and female members.

The women delivered creative and organisational leadership at a time when their independence was still challenging societal norms. This was especially the case in the postwar years, when society was actively encouraging women to return to the home. Unlike many women-only organisations or committees in mixed-gender organisations, the New Theatre valued women for their creative contributions in roles more typically undertaken by men: director, producer, writer – and in a range of organisational leadership roles.

At the beginning of this chapter we identified three factors supporting women's career volunteering: the amount of family support; the capacity to juggle paid employment and theatre work; and the scope for developing personal and political identity. Our interviews and research reveal clearly that, for decades, the Sydney New Theatre provided opportunities for its members on a number of levels. Firstly, it offered opportunities for personal development and a heightened sense of personal identity. Secondly, it was a place of creative and political activism for like-minded people. Thirdly, it gave a sense of belonging to an organisation that provided, as Teather explains: 'affective bonds that grow out of shared ideals and aims, affirmed through years of cooperative activities'. Perhaps most importantly for our argument, Sydney New Theatre provided opportunities to combine creative and organisational leadership.

New Theatre abolished or nullified many of the barriers which, literature shows, inhibit women's participation in organisations and management. It enabled confidence, the recognition of women's skills and capabilities and a degree of partner and family support. Although family responsibilities were still concerns and needed to be managed, partner support countered these. A number of women, including many of those interviewed, found that the involvement of partners in the New Theatre sustained their ongoing participation.

In contrast to middle-class women volunteers who may not have been in the paid workforce, this group of working-class volunteers also faced the demands of paid employment. While middle-class women may have juggled caring responsibilities and volunteer work, working-class women also juggled full-time paid work. For some interviewees, their paid employment enabled participation; for others, it was a surmountable barrier. Engaged in serious leisure, these women fit Stebbins' definition of career volunteers: they clearly demonstrated labour and perseverance; they derived a range of benefits and a sense of career; and they experienced, and contributed to, their theatre's ethos and distinctive identity.

The nature of the volunteer work was decidedly a blend of work, activism and leisure. The Sydney branch generally had only one paid worker, plus a multitude of volunteers. A politically motivated organisation, it included activities otherwise constituting leisure or a hobby when undertaken in the guise of amateur dramatics. The women were visible, their participation was substantial, and they also participated in broadening the nature of protest through art.

In their quest to fulfil the New Theatre's objectives, our focus women organised the theatre, developing innovative and resourceful approaches to the institutional norms of theatre of their time, adapting formal and informal strategies and creating new ones. Their leadership and activism were vital to sustaining the success and longevity of this small organisation. While their left-wing origins and their aims led the New Theatre to move away from presenting bourgeois ideas on stage, turning a profit or pandering to the demands of high-billing stars, they still had the conventional problems that any theatre troupe must solve: organising themselves and their work; publicity; staging; and attracting audiences. Sarah Miller recognises that such women theatre workers are often consigned to longstanding historical oblivion:

> [it] can be read in gendered terms to represent women's skills and habits of organisation as performing the function of handmaiden to the arts, rather than artist and creator of cultural meaning and value per se. It may also be a matter of deep cultural conditioning that women in these roles (as well as others) deny or downplay their leadership.

Contrary to Miller's 'handmaiden to the arts' concept, women were at the forefront of the Theatre's leadership.

Rachel Fensham's study of feminist practice within 21st century Australian theatre revealed:

> in spite of 30 years of active feminism in Australia, as well as feminist theatre criticism and practice, the mainstream has only partially absorbed the influence of feminist ideas.

The New Theatre was well ahead of its time. Our research indicates that our focus women's gender did not constrain them from crafting successful volunteering careers in the New Theatre's first four decades. Women and men worked cooperatively together, generally, towards the shared goal of enacting the New Theatre's constitution and aims, on the stage, behind it and in communities.

FURTHER READING

Burgmann, Meredith (ed.), *Dirty Secrets: Our ASIO Files*, Sydney, New South, 2014.

Capp, Fiona, *Writers Defiled: Security Surveillance of Australian Authors and Intellectuals 1920-1960*, Richmond, McPhee Gribble, 1993.

Cockin, Katharine, 'Introduction', in Lizbeth Goodman with Jane de Gay (eds.), *The Routledge Reader in Gender and Performance*, New York, Routledge, 1998, pp. 19-20.

Craig, John, 'We Never Closed: Success of a Political Theatre', *Direction Labor*, vol. 2, 1979, p. 8.

Damousi, Joy, '"The Woman Comrade": Equal or Different?', *Women's History Review*, vol. 2, 1993, pp. 387-394.

Delaney, Anne, 'Red Aesthetics: the Establishment and Development of the Workers' Art Club and New Theatre in Sydney, 1932-1945', *Past Imperfect: University of Sydney Historical Journal*, vol. 1, 1987, pp. 35-54.

Fensham, Rachel, 'Farce or Failure? Feminist Tendencies in Mainstream Australian Theatre', *Theatre Research International*, vol. 26, 2001, pp. 82-93.

Heckenberg, Pamela Payne, 'Women of the Australian Theatre', *Australasian Drama Studies*, vol. 12, 1988, pp. 125-145.

Hunt, Jane, 'Finding a Place for Women in Australian Cultural History: Female Cultural Activism in Sydney, 1900-1940', *Australian Historical Studies*, vol. 36, 2004, pp. 221-237.

Miller, Sarah, 'Women and Leadership: Theatre', *The Encyclopaedia of Women and Leadership in Twentieth Century Australia*, Melbourne, Australian Women's Archives Project, 2014, pp. 1-10.

Oppenheimer, Melanie, 'Voluntary Work and Labour History', *Labour History*, vol. 74, 1998, pp. 1-9.

Oppenheimer, Melanie, *Volunteering: Why We Can't Survive Without It*, Sydney, UNSW Press, 2012.

Rees, Leslie, *The Making of Australian Drama: From the 1830s to the Late 1960s*, rev. edn., Sydney, Angus & Robertson, 1978.

Scott, Joanne, 'Voluntary Work as Work? Some Implications for Labour History', *Labour History*, vol. 74, 1998, p. 15.

Southern Cross University Ethics Approval ECN-15-178.

Stebbins, Robert, *Serious Leisure: a Perspective for our Time*, New Jersey, Transaction, 2007.

Stevens, Joyce, *Taking the Revolution Home: Work among Women in the Communist Party of Australia 1920–1945*, FMelbourne, Sybylla Co-operative Press and Publications, 1987.

Teather, Elizabeth, 'Voluntary Organizations as Agents in the Becoming of Place', *The Canadian Geographer/Le Géographe canadien*, vol. 41, 1997, pp. 226–234.

West, Guida and Blumberg, Rhoda, *Women and Social Protest,* Oxford, Oxford University Press, 1991.

CHAPTER 14

Brave Red Witches: Communist Women and Identity

Susan Bradley-Smith

'Happy Birthday, Brave Red Witch', reads the headline to Dorothy Hewett's 1983 tribute to Katharine Susannah Prichard, written to mark the centenary of her birth. Hewett revered Prichard as a fellow playwright and communist, an exceptional woman who provided a seductive role model:

> I was always fascinated by the idea of her, and thought how wonderful it would be to be a writer and a rebel just like her...'the Red Witch of Darlington'.

Julie Wells notes that Hewett's tribute conjures up just how stimulating the triad of 'communist', 'woman' and 'writer' could be: freedom, glamour and rebellion on the one hand, and the marginalisation from respectability on the other. This chapter explores how that duality affected the work and lives of women dramatists who sought to reconcile their desire to further their careers as theatre practitioners with their political selves.

The willing submission of communist women to the mandates of the party was complicated by the demands of family, motherhood, domesticity, inequality in professional endeavours and duplicity in sexual relationships. The prescribed circumstances of women deeply involved in party life meant that they met these demands in different ways. In this regard, communist women playwrights differed from other women dramatists; their promotion of communist ideals often set them apart from the more common feminist agenda and from their male comrades, in that their concerns were, by necessity, broader.

Sydney performance of Dymphna Cusack's *Pacific Paradise*, 1955.
Set design by David Milliss, costume design by Norma Disher.

The public nature of theatre distinguished playwrights from other communist women writers because they had immediate audiences for their work. Despite their exposure to swifter and more obtuse censorship, both from within and outside the party, the ephemeral nature of performance, compared with the printed word, gave them a greater freedom to express dissent. Often, things were said that might not be said elsewhere. Being a 'Brave Red Witch' was both a blessing and a curse for the careers of these women, whose work dealt with topics presumed to be of universal importance. This period in world history saw the rise of nationalism, and women playwrights who critiqued these developments caused much concern. Katherine Kelly observed that, when Western countries were busy 'defining their identity in terms of differences from one another', playwrights whose writing was interested in 'the destabilizing of womanhood – often portrayed as the domestic anchor, or mother, of nationhood – must have caused profound anxiety'. Creating anxiety in the quest for revolutionary change was indeed the work of the dramatists discussed in this chapter.

THE AUSTRALIAN COMMUNIST WOMAN: POLITICS, MODERNITY AND AESTHETICS

The CPA formed in 1920. Its founding members included Katharine Susannah Prichard and Adela Pankhurst. Both had been involved in the women's suffrage movement, in Australia and overseas, and the peace movement during World War I. Yet, women of the CPA 'did not regard themselves as feminists, no matter how actively they were engaged in women's politics', because, as one member put it: 'sexuality was not seen as a political question [by the party] and it too would somehow come right under socialism'. A shift in this attitude did occur in the 1930s, when women in the CPA began working with other women's organisations, but the fundamental philosophy – that women's exploitation was linked to capitalism rather than sexism – remained. Women's work within the party, therefore, was meant to be devoted to the destruction of capitalism rather than to issues of specific concern to women.

An analysis of modernity will partly explain this devotion. Joy Damousi reveals that, despite the perception that ideas usually associated with modernity have more to do with artistic and literary genres than with political ideologies, modernity did inform socialist views on women. Notions of rationality, efficiency and reason – part of modernity's masculinist discourse – became essential elements of the left-wing rhetoric that the CPA embraced.

Further, the ideas of modernity, infused as they were with the Enlightenment values of truth, reason and universalism, operated within a paradigm of white supremacy. Socialists adopted modernist ideas and framed them within white supremacist notions of progress, reinforcing conventional views of womanhood and the idealisation of separate spheres – that a woman's role is different from a man's. The CPA assumed, for example, that CPA women would undertake the fundraising work for the party rather than be involved in 'masculine' party politics, that is, the real decision making.

Australian women communists were by no means a generic group. Damousi argues that the reasons why women joined the CPA were historically specific and connected with their age, marital status, class, motherhood status, degree of political activism and experience of what was happening in the world around them at the time. They did, however, have one thing in common: 'the promise of a utopian society that realised their desires, hopes and fantasies'. This 'magical' appeal attracted women to the party, and the promise of these dreams being realised helped to keep many committed. More significantly, however, the party provided important social networks that nurtured and delighted many women – including the fun of being involved in the New Theatre. Oriel Gray recalls: 'here we lived, experienced, loved, laughed, fought, argued and then relived it all again'.

Damousi's work on socialist women in Australia shows how the female gender has been constructed within a historical context: those visual, linguistic and ideological constructions marginalised women within male-dominated organisations such as the CPA. Damousi's examination of the CPA's iconography reveals that the images favoured by the party clearly valued male productive labour. There was no place for the representation of feminine values other than the ability to rear children and the auxiliary 'care-giving' roles. The New Theatre logo, for example, depicted an 'assertive young male worker, who is slim and physically attractive'. Given that most participants in the New Theatre were women, it is ironic that a representation of masculinity, with images of 'brotherhood' and 'comradeship', symbolised the theatre. Yet, it worked towards the party's cultural agenda, which sought to accentuate the masculinism of the arts. It aimed to rescue the arts from their traditional effeminate reputation, so that they could play a vital role in educating the masses. The traditional constructions of femininity, even within a professedly radical organisation, make the verbal and visual representations of gender documented in this chapter doubly subversive.

Cultural communism was central to the political projects of the CPA, in both theory and practice, because the party aimed to influence all areas of its members' lives. Sustaining the cultural activities of the party became a primary task for the women whose role was to create a family atmosphere at cultural gatherings. The New Theatres emerged, and the party endorsed their cultural activities, under these conditions. During and after formal meetings of the party, short sketches and plays strengthened camaraderie and lightened the atmosphere, enhancing the enjoyment of the communist experience. Under the auspices of the New Theatres, the role of dramatic entertainment in cultural communism enlarged, and this was important for women. Damousi points out: 'Within the paradigms of Marxism, Communist women used the language of class, difference and equality to create a space for women'. This was within a political discourse that:

> constructed women as a 'problem' to be educated and instructed in communist ideology, in order that they could join their male comrades in the struggle against capitalism.

Examination of the spaces that these women playwrights created is enlightening.

THE NEW THEATRE IN AUSTRALIA: AN OVERVIEW

The phenomenon commonly referred to as the Little Theatre movement was extremely precious to the development of Australian theatre. Even a cursory glance at the foundation and running of theatres will show that women were at the helm of this movement. The standard of work was erratic over the years, but the Little Theatres provided opportunities to local playwrights, theatre practitioners and audiences at a time when the big commercial managements did little Australian work.

The New Theatre movement in Australia shared the higher profile locally written drama and women playwrights enjoyed in the Little Theatres. The movement began in the USA in the late 1920s, inspired by Soviet agitprop groups and responding to the economic climate and rising unemployment. While Hollywood reacted with cheery films, these small theatres, which came to be known as New Theatres, dealt with the serious side of the Depression. They began by staging agitprop pieces in support of selected causes. When the news reached Australia, the Communist Party initiated their own New Theatres. Despite the party backing, many non-aligned people eventually joined the Australian New Theatres. Indeed, the theatres played an important recruiting role for the CPA. Pacifist Joyce Batterham, for instance, recalls that she was 'interested in amateur dramatics and a group of us in Newcastle formed a branch of the NTL. This was quite successful and involved me a lot'. Through her association with the theatre, she 'came to know more trade unionists and more political people'; as a result, she decided to join the CPA in 1937.

The New Theatre's 'anti-box office' emphasis, rather than its overtly political aims, did most for the development of Australian drama. The first New Theatre in Sydney was presenting Australian plays within a year of its creation. New Theatres functioned as a crucible for many women playwrights; Peta Tait suggests that they provided: 'One of the few areas where women... consistently participated in the production process in Australian theatre since the 1930s'. Tait considers it rational that such an organisation should be responsible for the generation of such work and the building of traditions. 'Perhaps it is logical' she says:

> that a theatre organisation affiliated with the labour movement contesting ownership of the means of industrial production would also be more accepting of women struggling to gain access to the material facilities of theatre production.

The important consequence of these enhanced professional environments is measurable not only in output, but in the legacy of the tradition of women's theatre practice.

CRISES OF IDENTITY: NATIONALISM VERSUS INTERNATIONALISM

Being aligned with the New Theatre had its limitations, as well as its freedoms. As Australian attitudes towards the USSR swung between respect and hatred, those who championed communism had to be careful not to offend other sensibilities. On a less public level, many members of the party found themselves questioning their political beliefs as domestic issues became more crucial. Women, particularly, felt cruelly the dilemma of fidelity to a patriotic nationalism or an international idealism. The dramas of New Theatre's women playwrights in Sydney provide unique insights into themes of war and isolation, often presenting a very different case for internationalism from that of their male colleagues.

During the war and its immediate aftermath, the attitudes of the CPA, and those of others towards them, underwent several changes. The German invasion of Russia in June 1941 transformed the party's opposition to the war: it became a 'People's War of Liberation'. As the USSR became an ally, other Australians also had to do a quick rethink; the 'Red Menace' became the 'heroic Red Army'. When the Curtin Labor government assumed office in October 1941, the CPA, banned since 1940, gained confidence. In 1949, however, the conservative Liberal Party won power. Robert Menzies was again Prime Minister. The following year, Australian troops went to Korea to fight an anti-communist war. During the McCarthyist scares and subsequent censorship of this period, the New Theatre continued to nurture Australian drama, but significant events affected the changing fortunes of the Theatre. Mona Brand said that, although people were interested in what the New Theatre was doing, the Cold War atmosphere meant that they were 'afraid to go to the New Theatre, quite afraid'. Nevertheless, the show went on.

This is the historical context for the women playwrights discussed in this chapter. The New Theatre attracted them for reasons that were as diverse as their backgrounds. Their plays testify to the combination of those historical circumstances. The texts I examine here highlight an ambivalence in the arts in Australia: between deviation from what can be classified as nationalistic concerns, and fidelity to what was recognised as an international vision. In certain circumstances, some people thought that these concerns were mutually exclusive; and this worry created most conflict.

FREEDOMS: EXPERIMENTATION AND INTERNATIONAL INFLUENCES

Being involved in an international political movement had its artistic benefits. It is interesting that many women who experimented with dramatic form during this period were involved in the New Theatre, and this association emboldened them. Women, historically more constrained as theatre practitioners than men, were especially responsive to these possibilities. Perhaps for this reason, as Mona Brand points out: 'most of the theatre's satirical writing has been by women'.

Playwright Oriel Gray recalls the impact of international influence on Australian theatre when US soldiers came to the Sydney New Theatre during World War II. They came because 'they were interested in theatre, or they were left-wing, usually both', often bringing with them experiences from prestigious New York theatres. This inspired the theatre to institute new style acting classes; and, during this period, Gray wrote some of her best plays:

> Had we brought other Little Theatre groups into the classes, had they begun to work with us in these, experiments in creative acting and writing, the Actors Studio might have begun in Sydney...something that could have been marvellous and...far reaching just did not happen.

The innovations she encountered at the New Theatre influenced Gray herself to expand her dramatic concerns as a playwright. The stimulating relationship began in 1938; aged 18, she joined the theatre and, subsequently, the CPA. Her autobiography provides some illuminating details on the conflicts of nationalism and internationalism occurring in the theatre at the time. On 23 August 1939, she recalls reading her paper on a Sydney tram; the headline was: 'Russia signs pact with Germany'. She walked into a bewildered theatre that night, where the general reaction was 'that it was some trick of the capitalist press'. They waited around the radio for a denial from the Soviet Union, but the only explanation forthcoming was that the Soviet Union would be willing to sign a non-aggression pact with any nation desiring to live on good terms with it.

Gray was frantic with worry, because the set of values that she had come to believe in had failed her: the Soviet Union was no longer opposed, as she was, to 'cruelty, racism and the naked imperialism of German Fascism'. 'But they can't do it', she said, only to have a male actor shout back at her: 'For Christ's sake, love...do you think you know better than Stalin?' She had no reply. Soon after, on 3 September 1939, she once again clustered around the radio at the theatre to hear Prime Minister Menzies pledge Australia to fight alongside England.

In 1940, the Menzies government banned the CPA. Gray remembers that the 'theatre faction of the party went underground – enjoying every minute of it!' as they crowded in tiny rooms, arriving in ones and twos. Real dilemmas of loyalty emerged in 1940. Gray could accept opposition to the capitalist war; she could even enjoy being 'a romantic convert to Pacifism'; but she was deeply disturbed to find that the antiwar feeling among CPA members was sometimes on the point of being pro-German; which, to her, meant Nazism:

> This feeling was aggravated, or caused perhaps by the tension that developed in Australia as our troops became involved in real fighting. The good-natured acceptance of Left-wing views – 'Ah, they're a bunch of ratbags' was replaced by a real animosity and sometimes violence... In turn, the fundamentally humanist attitude of many Party members degenerated into a 'them or us' viewpoint.

Gray made a stand in the theatre after seeing some newsreels from Dunkirk. She defended the soldiers who had fought against fascism. Her emotional conviction wilted in the face of theoretical arguments from her friends and colleagues. The subject was painful, so she closed it and would not re-open it:

> I had had a frightening glimpse of the No Man's Land lying out there beyond the shelter of unquestioning Party convictions. My marriage, my friendships, theatre, enjoyment of living, even my sister were all contained under that shelter, and Baby, it could be cold outside.

Gray has identified the conflicts that play between nationalism and internationalism in her work:

> While I think that Internationalism should be the overwhelming aim and direction of the human race as a whole, there are times when Nationalism is important, and even essential. My first full-length play *Lawson* was written when Australians were rediscovering the uniqueness of this country, faced with Japanese aggression... Nationalism can be a horrible and destructive force. Love of your own country, a sense of place, of belonging is a necessary thing and has been accepted even in law,

> as progressive Aboriginal legislation has proven...a national dream and conscience is important and a country that loses its legends loses its soul.

Gray believes, and her plays have always argued, that both 'human national aspirations as well as international breadth of vision' are the necessary approaches for universal humanity.

Apart from major productions, the New Theatre held regular workshop nights. They involved, for example, an experienced producer working with inexperienced actors. *Lawson* (1943) emerged from such a workshop. Adapted from the poems and stories of Henry Lawson, the play has an episodic structure whereby various characters meet the eponym and enjoy his anecdotes. The play's original conception and unusual structure earned an enthusiastic critical reception. The *Sydney Morning Herald* declared it to be 'a very entertaining and dramatic experiment with its well-selected material and craftsmanship'. In contrast, it did not convince a later critic, Colin Kenny, who did not see the play performed. Kenny admired Gray's writing style but, from reading the play, was unable to fathom her innovative theatrical visions. He described *Lawson* as 'having some worth, but in a very limited way' and believed that the short episodic structure was 'inclined to become boring'.

DRAMATISING THE PARTY LINE

Katharine Susannah Prichard

Katharine Susannah Prichard regarded the writing of plays as 'a matter of conscience, part of her political duty to things she believed in and the people she cared about'. Completely unsubtle about her dramatic intentions, Prichard aimed to politicise audiences through cultural means. We have already discussed some of Prichard's plays; this section will emphasise her use of the theatre as a vehicle for the dissemination of communist ideology.

Forward One (1937) is an example of this practice. The play's message is about better working conditions – and the role of unions and individuals in attaining those ends. The action takes place in an exclusive frock shop, where the assistants walk out. The girls had never received their entitled rest breaks. When newcomer Phyllis questions Vera about why the union does nothing, Vera explains: 'It's got the sleeping sickness, darling. I never heard it doing anything for shop assistants that would be unpleasant for the shopkeepers'.

Vera decides that the workers must make the union act, that they are 'fools' to put up with it when the law is on their side:

> PHYLLIS: What's the good of it [the law], if everybody breaks it?
>
> VERA: If we could get the girls to stick together and make the union fight for us, you'd see.
>
> ELSIE: We're all so scared of losing our jobs...
>
> PHYLLIS: If women would refuse to buy a dress or a hat, in any shop where the girls aren't allowed to sit down...it would make a difference.
>
> VERA: ...it would be more to the point if we made our union act.
>
> ELSIE: I don't see what's wrong with trying both ways. Get the girls to stick together, stir up the union, and ask the women...to support us.
>
> VERA: Let's do it, girls!

Unionism was an international issue, one of great national importance in the years before World War II. Prichard calls specifically for women to take action, rather than simply watching and supporting the men in the movement to achieve reform. This focus of perspective on women makes the play uniquely bold. First performed by the WTG in Perth in December 1935, *Forward One* had its Sydney premiere at the New Theatre in January 1937.

Another union-based drama, *Solidarity* (1940), attracted the label: 'the first Brechtian play of quality written by an Australian, and it also anticipates later techniques of audience participation'. Prichard was aware of the influence, writing in a note to the producer that the play used a modern technique 'which has been influenced by the Brecht pattern of small scenes played without a break'. The epic structure of the play has a continually shifting focus, with 29 speaking characters, and no one episode leads inevitably to the next. The set was spare and functional, and miners' torches were used for lighting. The play's dramatic interest lies in its presentation of a strike in 11 small scenes. The audience were part of the cast, acting as strike meeting participants, and actors were planted among them to speak particular lines. One critic described *Solidarity* as a propaganda play and assessed it accordingly:

> I am not against using the stage as a propaganda platform, but this is just a bit too much. I have no doubt, given…an imaginative and socialistic producer that the thing could surge along with a great deal of action and excitement – but too much would have to be put into it to get too little out. After all, what does it say?… A play that appeals to a specialised audience is not really a play at all.

Another reviewer who wondered whether the play would be 'doomed to obsolescence' as soon as the question of penalty clauses was settled, nevertheless commended it for its fine qualities; it did: 'score strongly through its human values' because it revealed something of the human situations behind industrial relations. Prichard includes the representation of migrant workers in the play, giving voice to the diversity of the working-class population. It is in keeping with those concepts of brotherhood and solidarity of central concern to communist ideology. Prichard was concerned to reflect those voices accurately, as this extract demonstrates:

> PETE: (*a big Yugoslav miner, awkwardly*) We hear big fall, Charley Luff and me. Charley say 'By Chris'… Got to do the best I can, getting Bob and Charley out… I just about all in. Sorry, I can't do nothing…*comeradan*.
>
> TED: Three cheers for Pete Rogovitch. **Cheers around**.

While Prichard is clearly doing the business expected of her as a communist playwright in *Solidarity*, the play steadfastly ensures that female perspectives within the mining communities are essential to the plot:

> MARTY: I like Bob. I want you to be happy. But I can't help worrying about you having to live like I've done.

The Little Theatre in Australia

AN AUSTRALIAN DRAMA THAT RINGS THE BELL

By L. L. WOOLACOTT

● Superlatives are so easy. Hence my diffidence in proclaiming Oriel Gray, whose latest play is now current at the Sydney New Theatre, as one of the most significant and talented Australian playwrights whose work has so far been produced here.

I THINK I know the work of all of any importance, from David Burn, 1842, to Sumner Locke-Elliott, 1950. At the dingy New Theatre, 167 Castlereagh Street, Miss Gray's three-acter, Had We But World Enough, drives me to superlatives.

It is a tragedy based on the theme of race-discrimination, as practised by Australia's respectables against aborigines.

SO to four superlatives:

(1) Except in the third act, when the abrupt shift of interest to the schoolmaster seems to me slightly out of focus with the rest of the play, I have never witnessed so intensely interesting an Australian drama that fulfils the definition of a great play —a play that is national in sentiment; universal in appeal; and yet belonging intrinsically to no age or country.

(2) The casting was as nearly faultless as I can ever hope to see; for the actors and actresses created the illusion that **nobody was acting.**

(3) The details of production were perfect. I mean that; and I should like to know where the producer, John Armstrong, learned his job. If he is an amateur, then he is also a wizard.

(4) The dialogue does not shimmer on surfaces, like Noel Coward's: it scintillates from depths deeper than any Coward has ever explored.

If play and production are not both superlatively brilliant, then the Button-moulder from Peer Gynt is

Theatre critic Leslie Woolacott on Had We but World Enough.

waiting just around the corner for me. Oriel Gray, whom I don't know, is for me an Australian woman of genius.

IN the issue of The ABC Weekly dated November 19 I committed the truism, "Honest bawdiness will forever be an ingredient of great literature." That brought me several acidulous letters. The most abusive was from a lady in South Australia, who ended thus: "And I notice you put the word 'purity' in inverted commas whenever you use it in your so-called criticisms, and that you praise bawdiness. Don't you believe in purity?"

By a remarkable coincidence, I am able to answer that question through having had this month to attend, among others, two shows on successive nights, one of which demonstrated the wrong attitude to bawdiness, and the other the right attitude.

THE Residuary Legatee, a comedy by Jean Francois Regnard, is being pulled out of its smelly grave, after about two centuries, twice a week at the Independent Theatre, North Sydney.

This nauseous and peurile play should have been allowed to rot undisturbed in its grave. It demonstrates the wrong attitude to bawdiness, and some disgusted members of the audience may be prompted, in consequence, to draw the attention of the proper authorities to it.

Now, I do not believe in any form of censorship, and can give cogent reasons for my belief. Instead, I believe that if qualified critics are given their heads in Australia there would soon be no need for any form of official censorship of the arts.

As for "purity" in the arts, I most emphatically do not believe in it, if the word is taken to mean any form of pietism.

THE other show was Shaw's Overruled, probably his wittiest one-act play. In its preface, Shaw calls a spade a spade, when discussing sexual morality; but in the play he gives the perfect exemplar of how to handle bawdiness on the contemporary stage. The theme is a double-barrelled "affair" between two husbands and two wives who have "sinned" in intention if not in deed, when away on separate holidays. Shaw achieves all the effect he wants, without going into any bedroom details.

Badly as it was acted, and inaudible for the most part, the play was a

Oriel Gray . . . an Australia[n] not afraid of a tragic the[me]

good start for the newly o[rganised] Postal Institute Dramatic [Society,] Sydenham Branch. The sec[ond play] was also a good choice—Je[an-Jac]ques Bernard's Martine. B[ut] watching Martine's mout[h open] throughout two scenes as if [she were] holding a conversation with [herself,] I bolted home. The S[ydenham] Branch's producer must l[earn to] teach his casts that their fi[rst duty] is to make themselves heard.

HERE is a Melbourne item [long] delayed through the holid[ays.]

In December the Tin Alley [Players] were misguided enough to p[resent at] South Yarra T. S. Eliot's pr[etentious] and dreary play, The Fam[ily Re]union. It was, I am told by [com]petent observers, as footling a[s] Murder in the Cathedral. [As a] dramatist, Eliot should joi[n forces] with those two charlatans—[and] Picasso, each of whom h[as tem]porarily abandoned flinging [wet] paint in the public's face i[n lieu] of writing what THEY call [poetry.]

This month the Tin Alley [Players] have redeemed themselves b[y putting] on a good, honest old me[lodrama,] Only An Orphan Girl. The [audience] was invited by the manage[ment to] pelt the players with peanuts[. A good] time was had by all. It's a [pity the] management did not extend [the same] invitation to those who had [suffered] Eliot's Family Reunion.

FOUR hard-working playe[rs from] the University Dramatic [Society] (Brisbane) did their best in D[ecember] to grapple with the mou[nting] difficulties of Tennessee [Williams'] The Glass Menagerie. This [play is] almost Maeterlinckian in its [depend]ence on "atmosphere" rath[er than] plot. As entertainment, [the Bris]bane effort seems to have bee[n rather] a minus quantity.

ELSIE: I'm a miner's daughter, same as you Marty.

MARTY: I didn't say you weren't, did I?

ELSIE: I remember Dad coughing his lungs up with the dust. And Mum slaving day in day out, doing washing and mending to keep things going when we were all little! It makes me mad to think of it.

This female perspective was a defining feature of Prichard's dramatic writing and an important aspect of her political plays.

CATHERINE DUNCAN

Catherine Duncan was another playwright whose work found favour with the New Theatre. In Duncan's case, war provided an opportunity for pointed political comment. In her verse play *The Sword Sung* (1938), the female difference in attitude towards war is removed from the emotional arena and enunciated in political terms. Marion farewells her lover, Michael, as he departs for war:

MICHAEL: I shall come back, Marion.

MARION: Never to me. Someone may come back – a man with rotted limbs, nerves twitching to the tune of rattling guns, a mind twisted by nightmares. Someone may come back, but not the man I know.

MICHAEL: Why do you say these things? I fight for you.

MARION: For me? For an empty catchword phrase that gulls a man with hopes of playing hero; and blinds a woman with the sense of pedestalled importance. If you fought for me you'd stay to fight beside me.

MICHAEL: What do you mean? When King and country call...

> MARION: ...the men who fight against you are my brothers; and every foot of soil in all the world I call my country... Necessity divides us. You must go. I stay. We shall cry 'stop!' to men, to women. See! That is our fight. You might have fought beside us.

Sydney's New Theatre first performed *The Sword Sung* in 1938, indicating the sincerity of the author's political intentions. Michael and Marion are lovers, working through a series of emotions about war, death and love. A verse play in seven episodes, its impact relies on the use of a two-level stage. It incorporates frequent spots and blackouts, giving the atmosphere expressionistic overtones. Non-verbal action and symbolism associated with a creative use of lighting heighten the drama. The finale, for example, is the first time in the play that full lights flood on:

> **We see that the hulk of the troop ship has vanished, and Michael and Marion are standing in a green field at the height of noon.**

Duncan's later play *Sons of the Morning* was adapted for the stage from a radio drama in 1945. In the original 1943 version, a memorial to Gallipoli and a critique of the glorification of death, two valiant Australian soldiers die in a stand against the Germans. Duncan explained: 'It was necessary for us to believe that the sacrifice of so many of our young men was justified'. By 1945, when the tide of the war had turned, and the need was to believe in an optimistic future, she rewrote the play so that only one soldier dies; the other falls in love with a local woman. Duncan's work demonstrates a commitment to communist ideals and the flexible space that women playwrights created within the New Theatre – not only for their critical political voices, but in the very contours of their dramatic expression. In this 'feminine' space, women found room for experiments in content and form that suited their needs for self-expression.

DYMPHNA CUSACK

Despite her long association with the New Theatre and the CPA, Dymphna Cusack never formally joined the party. Her anti-nuclear play *Pacific Paradise*, produced in 1955 at Sydney's New Theatre, has an interesting history. In

London, Independent Television bought the rights and adapted and cast it for television. Yet, although it was scheduled for live broadcast three times, they returned the script unproduced. Independent Television claimed that the play was not broadcast for reasons 'beyond our control'. At the time, England was planning to test bombs in the Pacific. The play went on to international success, however, being translated into Russian, Japanese, Hindi, Spanish and Albanian, and playing in many more countries:

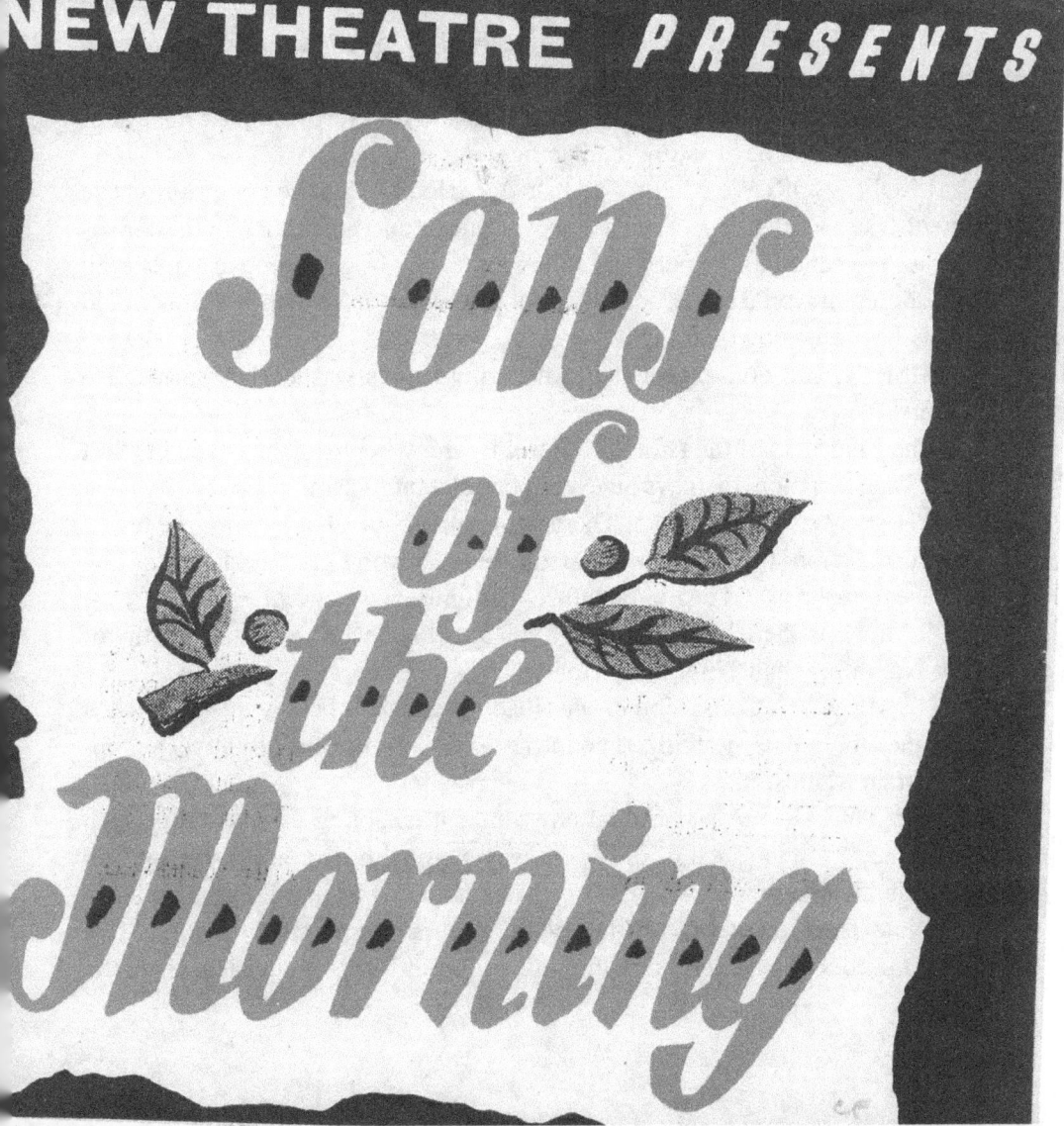

Program for *Sons of the Morning*, 1945. Graphic design by Cedric Flower.

> It is the result of the great success of her two plays no less than that of her novels that Dymphna is – so the Russians say – the most popular contemporary foreign writer in the Soviet Union.

Pacific Paradise primarily concerns the mindless destruction involved in bomb testing in the Pacific. The action takes place on a small island which has been selected for the next test. The inhabitants create dramatic conflict when they refuse to evacuate the island. The press whips up an international scandal, monitoring the islanders as they await certain death. While primarily concerned with peace, the play also attacks racism. Viti, the native wife of Englishman Simon Hoad who owns the island, is supported by her husband when she asks Professor Nicholas, the nuclear physicist in charge of the experiment, why it must be her home which must pay the price of 'progress':

VITI: Why don't you explode your bombs in the North Atlantic instead of coming here and devastating the Pacific?

PROFESSOR: We couldn't do that, Mrs Hoad. Even the countries whose interests are vitally concerned are proving most unco-operative in these matters as a result of all the publicity following the hydrogen bomb test at Bikini. In addition, it would be particularly unpopular with those whose shores would likely be washed by radio-active waters.

SIMON: But you expect me to have my shores washed by radio-active waters?

The Chairman of the Atomic Control Board, who visits the island in a last plea for evacuation, displays an even more blatant racism:

CHAIRMAN: Co-operate. There is no other equivalent site for the test… the current from this area goes directly south. It won't give the Japanese any excuse to make a fuss again, but above all it misses America.

SIMON: Is there any reason why you should consider yourself worthy of survival rather than Tinika and Moluka?

CHAIRMAN: Come, come, Mr Hoad. There can't be any question when it comes to…modern civilized countries against a handful of natives on un-important islands.

The New Theatre was a vital environment, enabling expression of such sentiments. When much of Australia was busy with national concerns, and the federal government was vigorously defending racist immigration policies, the New Theatre's political atmosphere and its communist affiliations fostered the concerned expression of more universal issues – such as racism, the

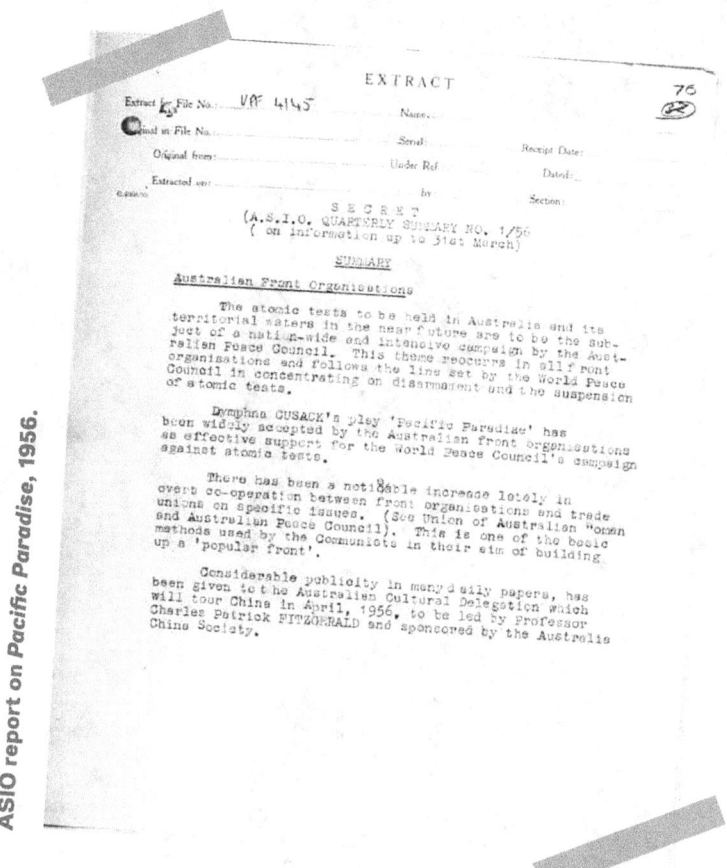

ASIO report on *Pacific Paradise*, 1956.

exploitation of minorities and the destruction of pristine environments for imperial and economic gain.

MONA BRAND

Mona Brand, another New Theatre playwright, lived in Melbourne as a young adult before leaving for London at the height of the Cold War. She then travelled through Hungary to the Soviet Union. She is perhaps better known overseas than in Australia. Brand's association with the New spans more than three decades, during which the New produced over 20 of her plays and revues. Asked whether her political commitment had been an obstacle to her recognition or success, she replied: 'I do think so more as time goes by. I've heard it so often said, "Oh, she writes for New Theatre – full stop"'. Asked to define a New Theatre play, Brand answered:

Here Under Heaven, Sydney NT, 1961. Diane Jan (centre) as Lola, a new arrival from Singapore.

> a New Theatre play either overtly or by implication suggested that there were great weaknesses in capitalism and strengths to be found in socialism… Personally I looked and hoped for a human quality, something that was an affirmation of life.

Brand's play *Here Under Heaven* is an extraordinarily confrontational and powerful play about domestic issues with international ramifications. The action is set on a Queensland property during World War II. The play is about racism, directed against both Aboriginal Australians and migrants. The character of Mrs Hamilton, widow and matriarch, must cope not only with the 'naughty natives' on her property but also her new daughter-in-law, Lola, a Chinese refugee whom her son married while overseas on service. In this exchange, Lola confronts her mother-in-law, whom she has overheard complaining to a neighbour about the humiliation she suffers because her son married an Asian woman. Mrs Hamilton is indignant:

> MRS HAMILTON: …no stranger can possibly understand what this country means to an Australian.
>
> LOLA: Ah, but I thought that I could understand. When I married your son I naturally required a greater knowledge of his country. Therefore I studied carefully the history of Australia. I studied and admired. Here, I said, is a country that even before England gave women the vote, a country that had striven to abolish the great distinction of class, and to give education to the masses of its working people… In Australia, I thought, I shall find culture and broad minds.

Instead, Lola came to a home where inequality was rife. Her mother-in-law is determined to run the Aboriginal people off the property, because they are sick and dying and causing commotion on the riverbanks, 200 yards away from a rich homestead. She declares her intentions to the station manager:

> MRS HAMILTON: They've dared to come and settle on my land!… And you say you won't move them off, but I will!

REYNOLDS: Why do you hate the poor devils like you do? It's wrong. It's bad.

MRS HAMILTON: (*pointing to a painting of a pioneer*) They killed that man. They came in the night, the murderers.

REYNOLDS: But don't forget how he broke up their tribe. He shot them and murdered them too... It was their land before it was his.

MRS HAMILTON: And now it is my land. These are my acres. We've made a home for decent people and I mean to keep it...

REYNOLDS: Well I'm sorry, but I won't turn them out... it would be murder in a drought.

MRS HAMILTON: Let them die.

The play appeared in a period of Australian history when Aboriginal and Torres Strait Islander Australians had no vote. It offers a strident and subversive political voice. Championing land rights, to this day an unresolved issue for the Australian Government, was both progressive and controversial.

A 'significant' professional theatre ultimately rejected the idea of producing *Here Under Heaven*, despite impressive and favourable reviews from an amateur production, on the grounds that: 'there is no colour problem in Australia, *ipso facto* it would be irrelevant to Australia's experience and not worthy of a large commercial production'. Brand's 'irrelevant' play dealt with many issues of importance, as the play's successful international productions and translations testified.

In a period of Australian cultural history when critics of Australian drama were still declaring what was and was not Australian, the New Theatre was also asking bigger questions. New Theatre playwrights wanted their dramas to question what might be the best future for the world. At the end of *Here Under Heaven*, Lola says:

> Perhaps some day when this war is over we might
> be friends. And I do not only mean this war of arms.
> I mean a greater war raging inside each nation,
> between those who desire the death of the world, and
> those who love mankind.

Access to, participation in, and control of the artistic means of production partially defines feminist theatre practice. In this regard, the New Theatres enabled women playwrights to pursue not only their political agenda as communists, but also their personal agenda as women and their professional agenda as practitioners, often espousing feminist ideologies. These interstices worked well for Brand in her experience of the production process for *Here Under Heaven*. Having joined the Communist Party the preceding year, Brand found the professionalism of the New Theatre and its association with her political ideals impressive, but more practical concerns won her over to the theatre. She notes that the director of her play at Melbourne's New Theatre in 1948, Erika Rathgeber, went out of her way to make Brand feel welcome at rehearsals. It was Brand's first production of a full-length play, and this reception was to influence her feeling for the theatre. She was able to make essential script changes, and she insisted that this face-to-face contact taught her fundamental lessons about the craft of theatre writing. Brand feels indebted to Rathgeber's 'complete writer–director consultation' and the chance to workshop her play thoroughly. Such opportunities for professional development were not easily accessed and were, therefore, highly regarded.

Here Under Heaven received favourable reviews, and the run continued as Brand left for England. An edited production of the play later won prizes in the Ballarat South Street competitions, so Brand's anti-racist theme apparently struck a chord in rural communities as well as with the more politically select audiences of the New Theatre. This audience popularity suggests an endorsement of Brand's sentiments; this is interesting, given that race and racism have long been a fraught area for debate. Susan Sheridan points out that Australian women writers have regularly engaged in the political issue of race discussions in their work, but that this is not unproblematic:

> The discursive traditions [of race] are so profoundly
> patriarchal that the position of women writers is
> always contradictory. As well, as white women they

are positioned in racist and colonialist discourse as dominant subjects; the relationship of white Australian women writers to prevailing discourses of nationalism, race and gender is a profoundly ambiguous one.

While acknowledging this, we must also recognise the positive contributions that Brand and other communist women playwrights made to the debates surrounding the issues of race and national identity. Their work adds an extra prism to these complex debates, one that reveals more than it conceals about Australian society.

EXPATRIATE FAME: WORLD STAGES AND OPPORTUNITIES

How is it that many of the women playwrights who feature in this chapter have a higher profile elsewhere in the world than they enjoy in Australia? And why is it that those female dramatists best known internationally – the most translated, the most performed, the most travelled – are communist women? Both these questions can be partially answered by the extraordinary international support network that communism provided for its members. We should not undervalue the benefits of this network when assessing the success of these women dramatists. Introductions to the right people in the right places were crucial in promoting their work and securing productions. It helped, of course, that women like Mona Brand and Dymphna Cusack chose subjects deemed to be universally important, at least by those engaged in the international struggle against the perceived evils and exploitations of capitalism. Regardless, the women playwrights discussed here sought and gained entry into this modernist discourse. They exploited it, not only for communist ideals, but for their own ends: to be successful (women) writers. Brand is an excellent example.

Armed with a letter of introduction from the New Theatre, Brand took advantage of her new-found status as a 'leading playwright' in Australia and tried to peddle *Here Under Heaven* in London. Unity Theatre, a similar enterprise to the New Theatre, was finally discouraging, remarking that 'no British audience would have the slightest interest in anything from Australia'. They asked Brand whether she could perhaps 'set the play in America and turn it into one involving Negroes instead of Aborigines'. She declined. Brand respected the work of the Unity, so she was 'sorry we didn't part on better terms'. She never regretted refusing to change her play. Many years later, she tried to make sense of the situation:

> perhaps part of the trouble was that I was Australian, and in those days even some communists in Britain were inclined to regard those of us from 'down under' as colonials.

Brand did not join the British Communist Party, instead involving herself in peace politics.

In this instance, English empirical attitudes overrode the universal camaraderie of communism, and Brand had no luck. During this period, she wrote two more plays: *Better a Millstone*, which the Sydney New Theatre first produced in 1954, and the unproduced *The Silent People*. As Brand continued to write, her political connections paid off. In 1953, at Jessie Street's suggestion, she went from London to Budapest to attend the World Peace Council Congress. Here, members of the Hungarian Writers Union approached her, wanting her to produce their translated version of *Here Under Heaven*. Reluctantly, Brand had to approve a script change: Lola, after reconciling with her mother-in-law, returns to China to participate in revolutionary struggle. The revised version played the following year.

At the congress, Street introduced Brand to the Secretary of the Soviet Writers Union, who promptly invited Brand to visit, and she did. Through her theatre-going activities in Soviet Europe, she developed an understanding of communist tastes in entertainment, which ranged from interpretations of the classics to contemporary pieces whose themes reflected the interests of most of the Soviet people. During her travels, Brand learnt much about what communism meant, and this influenced her writing.

One feature distinguishing Australian women dramatists involved in the communist movement is that they could hardly be described as working class. Brand says:

> The Communist Party regarded itself as mainly a Party of the working class, but my contacts with workers were almost non-existent when I first joined, and in fact have never been very close since.

So, when the party asked her to become more closely involved in the 'class struggle' in 1954 by mixing with the workers during the waterfront strike of 1954, Brand did:

> I wasn't sure what I was supposed to do apart from mingling. However, this in itself provided some useful hints for dialogue... Most of the time though I found myself doing what women usually find themselves doing – helping to prepare the food.

She wrote a sketch for the workers, at their request, and they performed it at a lunchtime fundraising concert.

Better equipped by her travels in Soviet Europe to associate with the struggles of the workers, as defined by the party, Brand brought home a new sophistication to add to her already well-developed skills as a dramatist. Without the international artistic stimulus of the market that the ideologies of Europe provided, Brand may have been a very different writer. She admits:

> Without the New Theatre there would have been no forum for me at the time I began writing for the stage. Being a member of the New Theatre and the CPA are experiences I'll never regret.

CULTURAL SPACES

Oriel Gray, too, remains grateful for the opportunities extended to her by the Sydney New Theatre:

> We produced some Australian plays...that only the left theatres would consider seriously, and that must always stand to their credit in the history of Australian drama.

Australian women playwrights enjoyed a patronage under the auspices of the New Theatres that was integral to their continuing development, as these examples have demonstrated. Those women who wrote for the New Theatre during this period stretched the boundaries of Australia's theatrical imagination. Their peculiarly introspective nationalism, informed by communist critique and coupled with clearly focused international sincerity, made them unique among Australian dramatists. Julie Wells and others have pointed out that the CPA marginalised women writers. They were creative writers and political activists in a society that often misunderstood or devalued their work – and within a communist party which often viewed literary endeavour with suspicion. In this scenario, the challenges these women dramatists posed, in the way they lived their lives and the dreams and aspirations they expressed while imagining a better way of life for all, must stand as subversive negotiations of feminist spaces.

Rosemary Creswell wrote an Australian short story in the 1980s with a telling message. The scene is a business lunch, where a group of educated, retired professional women are discussing literary women: 'Someone', said Mary, 'said that Dymphna Cusack was supposed to be a successful writer, but I don't know anyone in Australia who's read her'. She goes on to say:

> When I was in Russia everyone was talking about her. But who'd want to read her here? I mean I've read her because I thought I'd better if everyone in Russia was reading her.

It is ironic, and perhaps embarrassing, to note the truth in this scene; but it is nonetheless encouraging to think that, as ongoing research deconstructs Australian theatre history, the possibilities for change are tremendous.

FURTHER READING

Brand, Mona, 'A Writer's 36 Years in Radical Theatre: New Theatre's Formative Years 1932–1955 and their Influence on Australian Drama', in *Australian drama 1920–1955: papers presented to a Conference at the University of New England, Armidale, September 1–4, 1984*, Armidale, NSW, University of New England, Department of Continuing Education, 1986, pp. 1–8.

Brand, Mona, *Enough Blue Sky: the Autobiography of Mona Brand, an Unknown Well-known Playwright*, Sydney, Tawny Pipit Press, 1995.

Creswell, Rosemary, 'Business and Professional Women', in J. Bedford, and R. Creswell, *Colouring In: a Book of Ideologically Unsound Love Stories*, Fitzroy, Penguin, 1986.

Damousi, Joy, *Women Come Rally: Socialism, Communism, and Gender in Australia, 1890–1955*, Melbourne, Oxford University Press, 1994.

Gray, Oriel, *Exit Left: Memoirs of a Scarlet Woman*, Ringwood, Penguin, 1985.

Poole, Gayle, 'A Very Humanitarian Type of Socialism: an Interview with Mona Brand', *Australasian Drama Studies*, no. 21, 1992, pp. 3–22.

Sheridan, Susan, *Along the Faultlines: Sex, Race, and Nation in Australian Women's Writing, 1880s–1930s*, Allen & Unwin, 1995.

Stevens, Joyce, *Taking the Revolution Home: Work Among Women in the Communist Party of Australia, 1920–1945*, Melbourne, Sybylla Co-Operative Press and Publications, 1987.

Tait, Peta, *Converging Realities: Feminism in Australian Theatre*, Paddington, Currency Press, 1994.

Throssell, Ric, 'Paths towards purpose: the Political Plays of Katharine Susannah Prichard and Ric Throssell', in *Australian Drama 1920–1955: Papers Presented to a Conference at the University of New England, Armidale, September 1–4, 1984*, University of New England, Department of Continuing Education, 1986, pp. 28–38.

Wells, Julie, '"Red Witches": Perceptions of Communist Women Writers', in M. Dever, *Wallflowers and Witches: Women and Culture in Australia 1910–1945*, St Lucia, University of Queensland Press, 1994, pp. 150–155.

THE UNHOLY TRINITY

A Common Cause report of a Sydney street corner NT performance, 1940.

Out on the street corners go New Theatre League players to dramatise the election issues. They have been campaigning in this novel fashion in many electorates. The photograph was taken during a street corner performance of a topical sketch in verse called "The Unholy Trinity."

CHAPTER 15

Radical Theatre on the Move in the UK and Australia

Cathy Brigden and Lisa Milner

The 1930s saw the emergence of new radical theatres in Australia and the UK. The Australian New Theatre began life with inspiration from US and British radical theatre groups and evolved from the WACs. In the UK, Unity Theatre (hereafter, Unity) emerged in March 1936, following the amalgamation of the WTM, the Rebel Players and other left theatre groups. It began with one branch in London but soon expanded to 50 branches with 10,000 members, plus 3,000,000 affiliated members in trade unions and other organisations.

Both theatres were membership-based organisations that relied on volunteer labour, front and backstage. Brief forays into professionalism by London and Glasgow aside, they were always amateur in structure. Their stylistic repertoires over the decades were wide and included vaudeville, pantomime, pageant, musical, choral declamation, revue, sketch and agitprop, as well as more conventional dramatic forms such as the three-act play.

Mobile theatre represented a revival of the highly politicised, semi-itinerant agitprop style. There were also film screenings, folk music and dance concerts. One advance was the use of the living newspaper form, a type of critical reportage that incorporated poetry, dance, film, and drama. This style began its life on Soviet stages. US workers' theatre adopted it widely, and the New Theatre and Unity branches embraced it enthusiastically.

Both theatre families desired a permanent theatre space, existing as a 'stage curtain company', although only a few branches achieved it. The London branch was most successful, securing a theatre space (previously a Methodist chapel) in Goldington Street, Camden Town from 1937 until a fire destroyed the building in 1975. Other Unity branches led more peripatetic lives. The most stable Australian branch was in Sydney, though it, too, faced tenancy uncertainty over the years.

For many of the New Theatre and Unity branches, taking performances to audiences, commonly described as 'mobile' work, was both a response to this lack of certainty about theatre space and a political tactic. Both these theatre families had active travelling theatre groups; theatres needed the political desire to undertake mobile work and the capacity to address the practical tasks of getting enough people willing to move around and then transporting the cast and crew to different sites.

In this chapter, we consider three questions: what motivated the mobile work; what forms did it take; and what were the enabling and constraining factors?

TAKING THE SHOW ON THE ROAD

The New Theatre's commitment to broadly socialist ideas extended to their performance style and to its extensive range of performance sites. Theatre members would perform at parks and beaches, next to dole queues and, very often, on the back of flatbed trucks. The Sydney Domain was a common site for living newspaper-type performances, until these were banned during the early years of the war. Their presentations on street corners and in union and trade halls, large factories and workplaces such as railway yards and wharves left an impression long after the applause died away. They feature in a number of CPA members' memoirs.

The mobile work of the Sydney New Theatre branch expanded greatly through their work with CEMA, later the Arts Council of Australia. CEMA, modelled on the British organisation of the same name, stated its objectives as:

> to take the arts to the people – the country people –
> to encourage amateur groups [and] to provide a field
> in which artists could support themselves by their art.

With CEMA's support, New Theatre's mobile work began in earnest. It produced works in military camps, often under the most primitive conditions. It assisted in War Loan rallies and sent scripts and advice to soldiers in advanced areas, to help maintain morale – essential for victory.

In Melbourne, the New Theatre developed a concert party group which toured productions to army camps around Victoria. This mobile group remained active after the war, taking productions to factory gates and street meetings.

Fortified by the success of its wartime work, the Sydney New Theatre purchased a truck in the late 1940s in order 'to extend their agitprop work to new locations'. This enabled them to tour towns in regional NSW, connecting with new audiences' experiences and hopes. During the 1949 coal strike, a concert party travelled to the Newcastle coal mining area north of Sydney to entertain the strikebound workers and their families. At the end of that strike, 10 members of the Sydney New Theatre toured the coalfields to the north and south of Sydney, playing to audiences ranging from 100 to 2,000. They 'were given enthusiastic receptions as they presented plays and sketches dealing with the miners' struggle and the Arbitration Court'.

Reedy River (1953), the most successful of all the New Theatre's plays, was performed in halls, factories and outdoor venues all over Australia. In Wollongong, the Port Kembla Workers' Federation Delegates Committee organised a performance to raise money for the Pensioners' Christmas Dinner Fund. The Melbourne branch presented *Reedy River* at the Melbourne Repatriation Hospital in 1955. They also mounted special performances of this popular play, with proceeds going to striking meat workers of the Butchers' Union. Requests came from factories, rural and regional localities and country towns. One memorable performance was staged as 'drive-in' theatre; the Emerald Progress Association 'built a stage at the end of a football field and the audience drove their cars on to the oval'.

Reinforcing the diversity of performance spaces, the Sydney branch performed for striking miners inside a coal mine at Glen Davis, west of Sydney, in 1952. *The Candy Store*, a US play about the owner of a Bronx store, had been playing to packed audiences in Sydney. The Menzies government decided to close down the shale mine at Glen Davis; the miners had been striking underground for two weeks when the Miners' Federation invited the New Theatre to take *The Candy Store* out to the mine, as Chapter 17 details.

This was literally an underground performance. The New Theatre chartered a bus, and the entire cast of the play travelled up to Glen Davis, a tiny town of 3,000. 'Smuggled into the mine, the actors improvised a stage with a hessian curtain at the junction of five shafts with small, inadequate lamps set on a rickety table.'

The miners used their headlamps to provide the lighting for the play. It was the first time most of the miners had seen a stage play, and they 'wanted more'. After the performance, theatre members helped the stay-in miners to record taped messages to their families on the surface, adding the song that the miners had composed about their strike. After a second performance in the town to the wives and children, the theatre members returned to Sydney the next day, 'tired but convinced we had found the real meaning of art belonging to the people'. 'That's a hard one to beat,' said Marie Armstrong, one of the players down the mine.

Also in 1952, the theatre performed Len Fox's *Stay Down Miner* to another audience of striking miners inside the Hunter Valley's Great Greta coal mine. Fox wrote:

> it was an inspiring experience to stand there in the dark, dimly lit mine, and hear the miners applauding the singing of Henry Lawson's *Freedom on the Wallaby*.

IN PARKS AND FACTORIES

One reason that the New Theatre – in all its branches – has a longstanding place in Australian cultural history is their members' enthusiasm for performing almost everywhere they were asked. This was most pronounced in the labour communities of the cities. Newcastle, for example, performed offsite from as early as 1937; the New Theatre team had a ten-by-six trailer for when they went on the road, taking their shows out to towns including Toronto, Stockton, Kurri Kurri and Cessnock.

In 1956, the Sydney New Theatre staged a performance of *Under the Coolibah Tree* for Katoomba audiences in the Russell Hawke Park, as part of a three-day festival welcoming foreign journalists to the Blue Mountains. The presentation 'was an original and commendable way for the [Katoomba] Chamber of Commerce to seek tourists; and, judging by the audience's reaction, an effective one'.

The Brisbane branch of the New Theatre took their shows on the road as early as 1939, when they toured *Till the Day I Die* to workers at the Booval coal mine on 25 April. The Booval miners proved to be very receptive to New Theatre productions, as their response to Jim Crawford's play *Miner's Right* during the 1948 coal strike showed. Following the presentation to 500 miners and their families, Vic Arnold wrote: 'although *Miner's Right* received a hostile reception from critics on southern dailies, it was enthusiastically received by miners and their families in Queensland and Victoria', including at Booval.

In 1954 and in subsequent years, members of the Brisbane New Theatre toured their production of the popular *Reedy River* to the rural towns of Maleny and Ipswich. Members of the Nambour Amateur Theatrical Society attended the Maleny performance, and 'from that performance came the idea that the Nambour people themselves should stage *Reedy River*' – which they did, a year later, to great acclaim.

Brisbane New Theatre also performed short works and excerpts to visiting Soviet and Chinese trade union delegations at the Brisbane Trades Hall on 12 May 1956. One jolly, unrehearsed item was an impromptu joint rendering of *Sovietland* by the three Soviet unionists and theatre members Val Mald, Jim Petersen, Syd Davis and others. Everyone enjoyed it immensely, especially the Soviet blokes. Val's Russian proved equal to the occasion.

Peter Douglas notes in Chapter 8 that the Adelaide branch of the New Theatre had been active in mobile work from its beginnings: 'everywhere that workers congregate – in the Labor ring at the Botanic Park, at trade union meetings, at social and political gatherings', the group 'presents sketches and short plays on present-day problems'. Rosemary Smith declared that the intention of the group would be to 'bring drama to works and factories...with emergency stages and a minimum of equipment'. Similarly, one aim of Perth New Theatre when it formed was to write sketches and 'take these presentations to factories, union meetings, workers' functions.' They performed *Five Poor Families*, by local Perth author and New Theatre member Benjamin Kidd, at factories during 1955 in support of the 'No' vote for the Campaign for Powers Referendum. They also collected signatures for that campaign.

By the late 1950s, however, support for mobile work and the numbers of those prepared to undertake it were waning. A combination of factors contributed to this decline: loss of transport; community shifts in popular entertainment (particularly the arrival of television); fewer members; and increasing divisions within the CPA (soon to result in a split). Some members did sustain a desire for mobile work, however, and expressed that view at the second National Conference in 1959, when attracting bigger audiences was a major talking point for members from all branches: 'The solution, it was thought, was to take the theatre out to the people, by means of tours [and] contact shows.' And, in the late 1970s, the Sydney New Theatre (by then the only branch in operation) revived the mobile unit:

> Already there is a revival of the old NT practice of taking parts of shows out to the people – to the waterfront and other jobs, workers' clubs, etc. Younger members are responding to this.

This, too, proved unsustainable.

MINERS' HALLS AND SHOP WINDOWS: THE UK EXPERIENCE

The strong influence of the WTM and earlier radical theatre groups existing in the UK meant that Unity and its members were aware of the need to take theatre to the people, as well as attracting people to a physical theatre building.

For many Unity branches, performance locations included parks, schools, outside factory gates and docks, at May Day rallies and public and political meetings (including CPGB and Labour Party conferences), trade union and CPGB congresses, bus depots, mines, and even Hyde Park and the plinth of Nelson's Column in Trafalgar Square. In 1953, Surbiton Unity performed Gadfan Morris' play *Homer's Nod* at a garden fête organised by the local Labour Party, 'where it was seen and appreciated by a large and enthusiastic audience'.

For London Unity (as well as many other branches), claiming space happened alongside making space: once it gained its own place at Goldington Street, from the late 1930s, the mobile work operated in tandem with traditional 'stage curtain company' productions. Originally called the Outside Show Group, the sub-committee's name changed to the Mobile Group. Securing their own transport broadened their range. With old taxis bought for 50 shillings each in 1936 (its first year of operation), a lorry in 1937, and a coach donated by the trade unions in 1938, the London group was equipped to work outside traditional theatres and stages, taking their work to the people.

They undertook three prewar regional tours to the North East, playing at miners' halls and the Newcastle People's Theatre. The members of the Mobile Group were interchangeable with other Unity groups in that branch – 'so that, in time, everybody takes a turn at theatre performances and mobile work'. During the war, Unity's Mobile Group – which included not only play production but orchestras and choirs, 'shop window' productions and other Unity 'extra-mural' performance activities – played a key role:

> The outside work became intermittent but continued and throughout the war Unity presented more than 1,000 such performances, providing a bridge from prewar Unity, as well as continuity through the 1940s, and playing a crucial role in helping Unity to survive.

Odets' *Waiting for Lefty* was a huge success for Unity, both on stages and out on the streets, but:

> it is generally agreed that the finest performance of the 400 times Unity played it were the 11 given in various bus garages during the great bus strike of 1937.

Throughout the five years of what has been described as 'Britain's most protracted industrial dispute', involving 27,000 transport workers, Unity's performances of the play were notable for their impact.

One consequence was the writing of *Busmen*, a living newspaper that emerged from Unity members' experience performing in the garages and depots during the strike. That connection with the day-to-day experiences of the busmen at work and on strike contributed to what Colin Chambers describes as:

> a unique contribution to British drama – an original Living Newspaper on an indigenous dispute written collectively with the help of those who had led the fight and presented in the most challenging theatrical styles of the day.

The Goldington Street mobile unit played to small and large audiences, as many as 1,000 in its time. Zelda Curtis, a member of this unit, recalls: 'We performed anything, anywhere we were wanted: sometimes cabaret, sometimes one-act plays or musicals that we devised, or often we just performed individually.' The mobile groups entertained people further afield. Their contributions to the British local authorities' 'Holidays at Home' campaigns in 1943 alone supplied 50 two-hour programs for parks and halls in Surrey, Essex, Middlesex and Greater London.

Going to the people even included following them underground; performances occurred in tube stations used as shelters during the bombing of London in World War II. Needing to adapt their repertoire to a different type of audience, being entertained by dint of their presence rather than by choice, the Outside Show Group also had to deal with cramped and noisy space:

> Ten minutes at one end of the platform, and finally a show at each end on the lift shafts. Even when these items [sketches, solos, songs and jokes] had to be

London Unity Theatre's mobile truck, c.1954.

done sideways on, with occasional trains roaring through, they went over big, and the crowd was almost as pleased as we were.

Other locations included St Pancras Hospital, the Royal Mint, homeless camps and:

> rest centres in civil defence depots, in parks, barracks and canteens, at Second Front rallies, Aid for Russia meetings, Royal Ordnance hostels for munitions workers, and at the National Fire-fighting Service stations.

The CPGB had been organising Shelter Committees and, through Unity, were the first to arrange entertainments in the shelters; 'mobile groups went to different shelters to sing songs and perform their lighter sketches'. The Unity mobile group also performed in the Tilbury Shelter in Stepney – one of the largest shelters – which eventually held 10,000 East Enders. Factories now working around the clock enjoyed performances on all shifts, including the night shift. Unity took plays:

> direct to the workers on the job. Here artists may present half-an-hour's performance during a midnight break and remain until morning – usually sleeping on the firewatchers' bunks! Or a midday canteen show.

The move to a national society and the establishment of the professional company shifted emphasis away from the mobile group for a time. It re-emerged in 1946 as the 'propaganda arm' of Unity's amateur company. This followed a show at a mass squat the CPGB had organised at Duchess of Bedford House, an empty block of luxury flats in Kensington, 'which marked a return to making links with the audience and with current social and political struggles'.

The mobile group now had a particular labour movement focus, performing plays based on industrial disputes. *Six Men of Dorset*, at the annual celebration of the Tolpuddle Martyrs, was billed as the 'Working Class Event of 1949'. During the 'Hands Off Russia' campaign, the Mobile Group took *Jolly George*, a Ted Willis play about the 1920 refusal of London stevedores to load arms and ammunition on to a Russia-bound ship, to the East End docks. In Harrow: 'we had to put on the house lights to stop the applause and stamping following the final curtain'.

Throughout 1950, *The Docker's Tanner* played at town halls, the Derbyshire Miners Welfare Holiday Camp and the local baths for the Southwark Trades Council. Before *The Match Girls* (about the 1888 Bryant and May strike) went on the road, the play had a successful local run through at Garibaldi's Restaurant (a CPGB watering hole in Theobalds Road, Holborn) in front of an audience of trade union leaders, Unity management committee leaders and fellow Unity members.

The Unity Theatre Federation's Annual Report for 1949 notes that one of their main tasks was to 'encourage mobile work' in the areas that were served by Unity branches. The Chingford group was especially keen on mobile work and moved a resolution that the London Group Committee should meet to discuss the coordination of mobile work, noting:

> mobile work of the highest standard being of the utmost political importance, it is necessary to have a centrally controlled mobile theatre service for the whole of London.

Accordingly, Unity formed a National Committee on the 'special subject' of mobile work, with delegates from the Goldington Street and Chingford branches in London working alongside Merseyside, Birmingham, Aberdeen, Manchester and Cardiff representatives. At Federation meetings, this was a popular topic of discussion.

Despite these successes, questions over the future of the mobile unit continued in the 1950s. In his support of mobile work, Bill Wardman referred to tensions over its role:

> The work that our Mobile Unit is doing cannot in any way be separated from the main tasks of the theatre. We must be absolutely clear about this. If there still remains amongst our Active Membership the idea that the Mobile Unit is an expensive toy to be taken up or discard[ed] as our bank balance rises or falls, let them think again. The facts are that at least half of every Mobile audience has never seen a Unity production before.

Interventions from Unity's General Manager George Leeson led to the dissolution of the mobile unit. However, the CPGB and the labour movement sought to revive it, as the Federation's 1954 breakaway Mobile Conference indicates. This was:

> a healthy affair with discussions that made it very obvious that labour organizations, affiliated or not, definitely want us to continue with mobile work, both musical and straight. The demand is certainly there, only we have fallen down in not being prepared for it, in having to withdraw our forces when we should be expanding.

Ongoing access to transport proved a key factor driving down activity. By the end of 1954, the coach could no longer be repaired or replaced – curtailing the activities of the mobile group considerably. From 1955, bookings for the group were restricted 'to places which can be reached by London Transport'. Apart from a brief revival in the late 1950s 'performing music hall, folk, and skiffle...it had an intermittent life thereafter'.

A similar combination of theatre-based and mobile work operated within the Glasgow branch. When the WTG joined with four other Labour theatrical societies to become the Glasgow Unity Theatre in 1940, a touring group or 'outside show group', initially separate from the 'indoors' company, staged a wide variety of short pieces throughout the Scottish coal field towns. It also performed at 'trade union events, at hospitals, to troops, and at rallies of all kinds.'

A very large pageant, *The Masque of Spain*, played in Glasgow's Scotstoun showground in August 1939 in support of the Spanish Aid Committee. Over 500 performers participated. Glasgow's 1946 tours were booked for coalfield towns, the Ayr Butlin's Camp and the Saltcoats Beach Pavilion, alongside performances in more conventional theatres and halls. Like the London group, Glasgow Unity had purchased several vehicles for their touring group, but loss of transport curtailed their work earlier than in London. By 1948, 'in view of the excessive expenditure on motor vehicles during the year the Buick car to be sold to avoid incurring any further expense'.

In contrast, Manchester Unity Theatre was largely a mobile-based branch and suffered from the lack of a permanent venue. They staged many productions in hired halls and other buildings, but outside work was a feature for this branch. They provided performances in the parks of the city in summertime over a number of years; interestingly, these were paid for by the City Council. Unity in the Parks also played at large parks outside Manchester, Boggart Hole Clough and Platt Fields. *The Engineers' Pound* entertained an audience of 2,000 engineers from a flat-back lorry in Platt Fields in November 1951. With this script, the players 'went out and took the play to the audience – a vast, enthusiastic audience' who proved 'conclusively, if proof were ever needed, the usefulness of a workers' theatre'.

Towards the end of 1954, the theatre members turned their reliance on mobile work to their advantage, assessing that 'the old argument of mobile plays or full-length plays has...been solved by making all our productions mobile'. However, lack of rehearsal space, declining trade union support, fewer requests for performances, loss of key players and declining audiences combined to reduce the mobile work and then the theatre's viability by the mid-1960s.

The parallel experiences of the two theatre families shows the political and practical roles mobility played in their work. The movement of ideas accompanied the physical movement of people. We now return to our three questions about the two theatre movements' use of their mobile work.

THE WHY AND HOW OF MOBILE WORK

Zabala contends that:

> one of the key innovations of the New Theatre was its redefinition of performance space. For the workers' theatres took their productions to the streets, literally.

While the mobile performances were notable feature of the New Theatre work, this claim neglects the continuity of such practices. They had found inspiration in the work of the mobile agitprop companies, founded on the model of the German Red Rockets and exemplified by the Prolet Buehne and the Shock Brigade (or Shock Troupe) of the WLT in New York and Red Megaphone and the self-named WTM in the UK.

A 'propertyless theatre for a propertyless class', the WTM presented 'its distinctive revolutionary messages on what it called "open platform" stages – carts, lorries, steps, on street corners, in parks, at factory gates'. The Rebel Players similarly produced agitprop plays in the open air from the backs of lorries, taking them to the factory gates when there was a strike, or taking part in demonstrations. Here was a whole new audience, a new kind of actor, expressing a new set of ideas in a new form.

Outdoor performances in Manchester had begun very early in the 1920s with the Clarion Players, later called the Red Megaphones, one of the precursors of Unity. A Salford-based group who only performed outdoors, most of their work consisted of songs and short sketches. Drawing upon this rich history as well as the already existing, centuries-old practices of travelling theatre troupes, Unity and the New Theatre did not limit their works to theatre buildings and halls.

Educating the working class and enthusing them to action motivated the work. Joe MacColum was a theatre worker, director of the Left Theatre in Ireland, who went on to work at the London Unity Theatre and, later, in Australian stage and screen works. He directed the Goldington Street branch's mobile unit for a number of years. In 1949, he is reported to have said:

> at the present time, with the effects of devaluation, the coming election and the need for peace, Unity's task was limited to helping the workers to face and tackle their problems and he took it for granted the other groups agreed that mobile units, working-class in content and playing to working-class audiences, was the way to do this.

He went on to discuss how audiences had responded to mobile performances of *Six Men of Dorset* and 'how the trade unions had used it to stimulate union organization'.

Similar motivations can be found in the Australian mobile work. In 1952, one of the leading Brisbane members believed that a New Theatre member could use mobile work:

> as a propagandist, using his [sic] art to encourage his fellows to take a definite action towards a better life... pointing the way to greater strength, a Mobile Group at a factory gate is doing this too... The suggestion has been made that, in order to relate mobile work more closely to the building of theatre audiences, five or six factories be chosen and visited regularly by the Mobile Group.

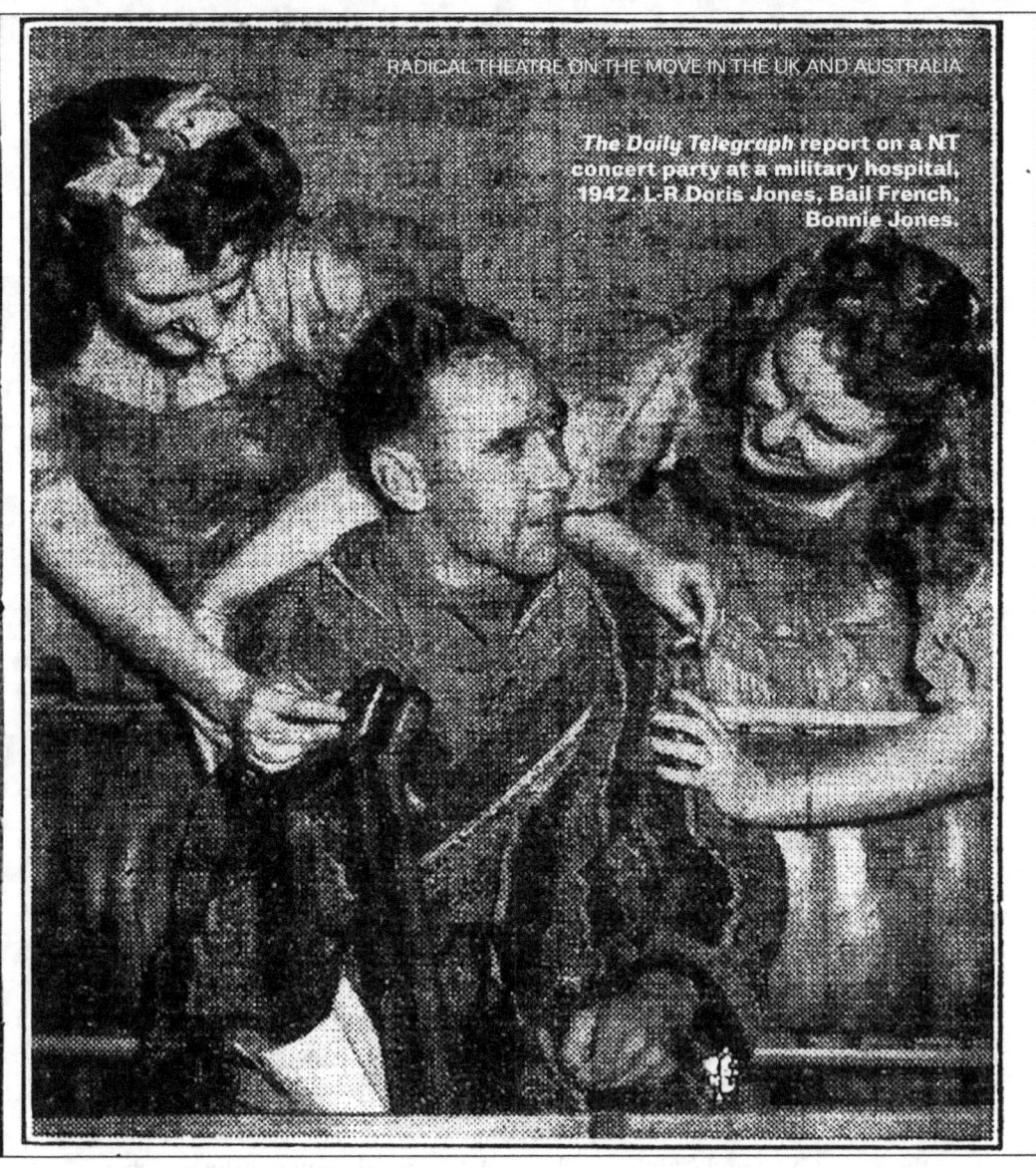

The Daily Telegraph report on a NT concert party at a military hospital, 1942. L-R Doris Jones, Bail French, Bonnie Jones.

Some of the large range of mobile work sites the two theatre movements used had previously seen theatrical action: the street, for example, had long been a place of theatre and of protest. Strikes, street marches, May Day and labour parades in much of the world have long traditions of incorporating theatre, and the mobile work of the New Theatre and Unity was no different.

Some of the theatre sites were private (workplaces, factories or mines), but most were public (streets, parks or hospitals). In particular, the use of traditional 'speakers' corners', including London's Hyde Park and the Domain in Sydney, were radical reclamations of public space. Consequently, this work

Sydney Domain performance of *The Miners Speak*, 1938.

took political and theatrical ideas out of the private theatre halls into the public domain, as well as to novel private places.

Movement was not only domestic. Unity groups regularly travelled to Soviet and European arts festivals to stage performances and enter drama competitions, often winning awards. The Sydney New Theatre performed *Reedy River* at the World Youth Festival in Warsaw in 1955. Particularly for the Australian thespians, such overseas trips were combined with the 'study trips' to the Soviet bloc and China that the CPA bestowed upon worthy members.

This work – this movement – saw the active transformation of places like mines, parks and factory gates into relatable spaces of theatrical performance and political disruption. The two theatre movements' activity overturned the older concept of places as stable and settled. They disrupted not only a previous tradition, but the authorities – who, for example, banned mobile work in the Sydney Domain – to protest against working conditions or censorship.

The street corner or the footpath was no longer merely a place of transport; the performances evoked different meanings in those spaces, facilitated a new kind of social interaction and, temporarily, transformed the relations of power. The travelling body of the street-users, the footpath-users, the park strollers, was transformed into a stationary, thinking, receiving body. The factory gate, traditionally coded in the management's image as a space of movement, was recoded with the performances. Creativity, performativity, play, political ideas: all became parts of that recoding adventure.

In seeing these novel performance sites as spaces of cultural performance, the mobile groups challenged the exclusivity of those sites – the exclusivity of the street corner as a site of individual pedestrian transport, the exclusivity of the factory as a site of production. The results of this mobile work included the creation of theatrical space out of previously non-theatrical places. In many instances, they turned non-social places into social spaces.

The mobile groups mediated and restructured those places in innovative ways, changing their meaning, albeit temporarily, and creating spaces in which politics and culture unfolded. They made new political and cultural spaces, disrupting the earlier naturalised meanings and behaviours of those locations.

The mobile work reached out to spaces and audiences that were otherwise inaccessible for a place-bound theatre troupe. They were inaccessible for many reasons. In the Blitz, ironically, people were sheltering in the Underground – a place of movement rendered immobile by the bombing – and the troupe had to win over a 'captive' audience. There had been no travelling to see the performance, but the performance both came to the people and moved through the space – up and down the platform – to enable the greatest number of people to experience the performances. 'Going to' the people manifested itself in different ways; the performance for the sit-in strikers at Glen Davis was another example of a 'captive' audience, but one who had requested the performance. Performing in workplaces during shifts – by invitation – was another example of positive audience 'captivity'.

ENABLING AND CONSTRAINING FACTORS

Mobility studies place great importance on the transformation of many types of mobility by the coming of the car. Access to motor transport was a key enabling factor. The purchase or donation of private vehicles opened up the ability for the groups to travel to working-class communities and was particularly critical in enabling the theatres to access communities outside metropolitan areas.

The theatres' purchase of cars and trucks indicated the importance of being able to travel across greater distances. The loss of transport had an effect on the capacity of the theatres to sustain the mobile work. When the London Unity

The Story of our MOBILE GROUPS

OFTEN the question is asked: "What part do Mobile Groups play in Unity Theatre"? The answer is: a necessary and integral one.

Three months ago the mobile section was known as the Outside Show Department. Now, within the new theatre organisation, we have, instead, two distinct companies, the Variety and Amazons.

The history of Mobile Groups goes back to before the days of our Britannia Street Theatre to the time when bands of artists performed on the backs of lorries and coal-carts, on the steps of Trafalgar Square, or in any hall open to them. Where are our present mobile theatres?

First, in the factories, where we take shows direct to the workers on the job. Here artists may present half-an-hour's performance during a midday break and remain until morning—usually sleeping on the firewatchers' bunks! Or a mid-day canteen show; but these are obviously more difficult as players themselves are working during the daytime. On one occasion a shop steward in a big London factory told one of the performers that "after such relaxation, production soars up."

Then in the "Holidays at Home" campaigns, organised by the local Borough Councils. Last year the then Outside Show Department supplied fifty two-hour programmes for parks and halls in Surrey, Essex, Middlesex and London.

This year bookings are again coming in and Variety and Amazons are to be kept busy. This sort of work calls for skill and toughness. It is hard work performing on a curtainless, temporary stage and in the open air. Dressing rooms are invariably cramped—often ten to twelve girls will be herded into a tiny space with no overhead covering. And washing facilities may be non-existent.

Again, groups have played a big part in entertaining the Forces. A train has to be taken, perhaps, to the nearest station to some outlandish place, where it is met and company and props piled on to a lorry and taken off to camp. After the show, all concerned sit at a large mess-table and eat a handsome supper—a glorious moment for the tired artists. And so back to London.

These are some of the important ways of getting out to the masses of the people, at the same time helping the theatre financially. Incidentally, has your Trade Union or organisation booked one of our Mobile Shows?

Audrey Hale

Beechwood Rise, Watford, Herts.

---

van/truck could no longer be repaired, this had a direct effect on the capacity of the mobile unit to sustain its program and curtailed its work. There were other factors, but the transport issue was significant in determining where the unit could perform and to whom. Far-flung audiences moved out of range.

The mobile work was a tactic which the two theatres occasionally employed to alleviate the problems they had in securing traditional theatrical space. This was the case when the Melbourne New Theatre had trouble finding a location for *Till the Day I Die*. Generally, however, they rejected the more conventional spatial boundaries of theatre by choice. The mobile work was consciously intended to serve a political and a social function – to get ideas (as a priority) and performances (secondary) in front of people who might not go to a traditional theatre.

The plays and other performances frequently had power relations and dynamics as their topics and themes, in keeping with the radical political philosophy underpinning the theatres' objectives and vision. Travelling to working-class communities and audiences was part of the political agenda espoused by the theatres – not just what was performed, but where it was performed and to whom. The theatres

Unity Theatre Call report on mobile groups, 1944.

did not eschew permanent performing space in a traditional theatre setting; this was important, in terms of having an identifiable place, but it was not essential. The transience of performing space was not an inhibitor in the communication of the theatres' messages. This was politics on the move – the use of mobility as a deliberate political strategy. These mobile actions are examples of theatre companies breaking out of the fairly conventional spaces of theatre performance to produce new spaces of entertainment, artistic reception and political debate.

Certainly, both theatre groups were conscious of the importance of their ability to tour their works as a promotional tactic for their world view. Urry reminds us:

> mobility in general is central to gluing social networks together, while physical travel is especially important in facilitating those face-to-face co-present conversations, to the making of links and social connections, albeit unequal, that endure over time.

The mobile work would certainly have expanded the theatres' social, cultural and political networks. In taking their militant work to these new spaces, they consciously mobilised ideas and emotions and feelings of resistance, struggle, militancy and political activism.

There were both practical and philosophical constraining factors. Mobility was not uncontested, and the branches' mobile work ebbed and flowed and then ceased by the late 1950s. Limited resources, both financial and human, meant that priorities had to be established. Movement became harder when vehicles were no longer available. Analysis of the Unity Theatre Federation minutes from the early 1950s reveals that, outside the London Goldington Street Mobile Unit's work, a lack of suitable material for mobile work was one reason for the demise of the units in most branches of Unity in the UK.

In 1952, reports say that Eric Paice's script *Focus on Germany* and

> the mobile version of **Ragged Trousered Philanthropists** [were] the only other new script[s] used by the Goldington Street Mobile Unit. This [last script] was available but the large male cast did not make it very useful to smaller groups.

Another issue was unions' and other organisations' failure to request mobile work. At the same time, many branches wished to stage more complex plays, requiring more elaborate staging, costumes and props. The vast majority of Unity's mobile work ceased in the mid-1950s.

The introduction of television and the changing leisure patterns of working-class Britons were also influential. London Unity's General Manager, Heinz Bernard, complained: 'a large proportion of their once regular audience now apparently preferred to stay at home and twiddle knobs on their television sets'.

CONCLUSION

Cresswell argues for an approach that is alert to the 'historical conditions that produce specific forms of movement, which are radically different'. In this chapter, it also meant thinking about why the mobile work started in the first place and why it stopped – not only because of the coming of television, but also because of the waning power of the union movement and of working-class solidarity and the growing anti-communism of the Cold War years.

Earlier, place-based communities, like some of the coal mining cultures Unity and the New Theatre visited, had stressed solidarity at a community level. This was on the wane by the 1950s. With the postwar economic boom came higher levels of social and geographical mobility for workers as well, so they were less likely to stay in the city after work for a performance.

We understand from the insights that labour history has brought to the discussions of locality that locality is 'an important site of class conflict, negotiation, and accommodation'. This examination of the mobile practices of Unity and the New Theatre demonstrates their active approach to class mobilisation. These two theatre families coordinated their resources and actions to take their work to the people. They configured this part of their work to being physically mutable – not fixed, but fluid and migratory – and their organisational strategies showed a distinctive and flexible spatiality.

Motivations for mobilising theatre included strengthening civic engagement and persuading adherents to their causes. The theatres expanded the practice and potential for culture and politics – in some cases, contentious politics – by taking their works to places generally excluded from mainstream political discourse. Examination of the innovative spaces and places to which the mobile theatres travelled demonstrates how these could signal different sociopolitical and philosophical assumptions made by Unity and the New Theatre.

They employed mobile work as another form of political and cultural activity, not separate from, but part of, the theatre's broader aims. This work helped the theatre groups to achieve a wider geographic circulation of their plays and political messages through a more interventionist approach. It developed a more widely shared political identity. Unity and the New Theatre pursued universal, as well as local, truths in their work in a presentation of proletarian mobile theatre that offered a particular type of transnational citizenship.

FURTHER READING

Chambers, Colin, *The Story of Unity Theatre*, London, Lawrence and Wishart, 1989.

Enright, Frank, 'The Illustrious Life of Sydney's New Theatre', *Green Left*, 13 April 1994, https://www.greenleft.org.au/content/illustrious-life-sydneys-new-theatre (accessed 18 December 1999).

Fox, Len, 'Stay-down Men Solid: Stir over New Theatre Visit', *Tribune*, 1 December 1952, p. 1.

Grivas, Cecil, 'New Theatre Play in Mine at Glen Davis', *Tribune*, 2 July 1952, p. 7.

Harper, Ken, 'The Useful Theatre: the New Theatre Movement in Sydney and Melbourne 1935–1983', *Meanjin*, vol. 43, no. 1, 1984, pp. 60–61.

Hillel, Angela, *Against the Stream: Melbourne New Theatre 1936–1986*, Melbourne, New Theatre, 1986.

'Jim Crawford: Background to a People's Playwright', *New Theatre Newsletter*, no. 4, 1950, p. 5.

Mortier, Paul, Bullen, Pat and Levy, Jock, *Fifteen Years of Production*, Sydney, New Theatre, 1948.

'New Theatre, Melbourne', *New Theatre National Spotlight*, vol. 8, no. 1, 1960, n.p.

Noakes, Frank, 'New Theatre', *SNOOP: A Magazine of UTS Journalism*, no. 5, 1996, p. 21.

Zabala, Gabriela, 'New Theatre: Unacknowledged and Out of the Mainstream: the Life of a Theatre with a Purpose', *Southerly*, vol. 69, no. 2, 2009, pp. 187–200.

THE NEW THEATRE IN AUSTRALIA

NT float, May Day, Sydney, 1937.

CHAPTER 16

Workers' Struggles on Stage

Cathy Brigden and Lisa Milner

As the New Theatre pursued its ideological and political objectives in advancing working-class culture and activism, it cultivated relationships with union members, trade unions and other organisations committed to advancing social justice. Certain unions placed great importance on creating and sustaining supportive interactions with the New Theatre. The dynamics of these reciprocal dealings have so far received little analysis. This chapter examines the theatre's Sydney branch and its experiences with four trade unions over 30 years. Drawing on theatre and union journals and a set of interviews, we highlight how the theatre used its practice of 'contact' work to take performances to union audiences, how its playwrights created scripts explicitly dealing with union issues and disputes and the various forms union support took.

In 1980, the ACTU Congress, the national peak union key decision-making forum, considered amendments to its Arts and Creative Recreation policy. One proposal highlighted the 'urgent need' to become more involved in art and cultural life, particularly through 'a dramatic improvement in the facilities available in workplaces for the performance and participation in creative and artistic activities'. This prompted a focus on art and working life in the early 1980s. Some delegates would have applauded this as a progressive development; for others, this discussion would have served as a reminder of past relationships between unions and art-based organisations. Specifically, they may have recalled performances of the New Theatre in their workplaces and communities; presentations of contemporary industrial and political issues through revue, skits and songs; the theatre's support when the workers were on strike, and how they engaged in reciprocal fundraising for the theatre.

From the outset, the New Theatre emphasised its labour movement connections. Speaking to Lismore people interested in setting up a branch, Victor Arnold, the Sydney Secretary, said: 'The New Theatre was essentially a part of the labour movement and accordingly deserves the assistance of the trades union movement and Labor supporters'. Few of the numerous works about the New Theatre consider the union/theatre connection. This chapter will shed light on the dynamics of the relationship. We will examine how the theatre used mobility to develop and sustain connections, through what it called 'contact work', and how it made and remade space. 'Contact work' meant taking performances out of formal theatre spaces to workplaces, community halls and outdoor spaces, with the explicit purpose of reaching a broader audience. It was, therefore, quite literally about making closer contact with its audiences in their communities and workplaces. Sometimes called 'mobile work', it was mobile insofar as the performers travelled to audiences rather than having audiences travel to their theatre. With the New Theatre's motto of 'art for the people' and commitment to taking performances to audiences, mobility was a key feature of its practice, building and sustaining its relevance to unions and their members.

In order to reconstruct the relationships between the New Theatre and unions, we analysed the minutes and publications of the Sydney branch, along with the national *Spotlight* newsletter. In order to highlight and explore how trade unions portrayed their ongoing relations with the New Theatre to their members, we selected four union journals: *Common Cause* (Miners' Federation), *Seamen's Journal*, *The Maritime Worker* (WWF) and *The Australian Worker* (Australian Workers Union; AWU). The CPA newspaper *Tribune* was another source that highlighted the reciprocal relationships. Interviews also revealed the myriad ways supportive union officials could assist with the day-to-day theatre activities.

Our four selected union journals profiled the theatre and encouraged attendance, publicised performances and reviewed them. *Common Cause* editor Edgar Ross strongly endorsed the New Theatre–trade union connection. As a CPA Arts Committee executive member in the 1950s and 1960s, Ross exhorted:

> the arts constitute one of the most important spheres of activity in the deep-going ideological struggle between decadent capitalism and the forces making for human liberation.

Maritime Worker published articles clearly written by the New Theatre, making direct entreaties: as 'the only workers' theatre in Sydney, [it] deserves the support of all trade unionists' and:

> a theatre of the people is of great use, and must be used to the utmost by the Labor Movement, along with its own press. It is your theatre! It must have your support.

For the Seamen's members, there was an added connection. Nance Macmillan, one of New Theatre's playwrights, was married to Geoff Wills, a Queensland official. The *Seamen's Journal* pointed this out when Brisbane's New Theatre Club performed her play *The Painter* in 1961.

For the WWF, the Building Workers' Industrial Union and the Seamen's Union, ideological commitment to radical oppositional unionism led, in turn, to their attraction to the New Theatre. Each of these three unions espoused political convictions shared by the most prominent New Theatre members. Shared membership of the CPA was the common ground on which they met and shaped their interactions.

Broader support from other left-wing unions further extended the web of solidarity. At the behest of the Postal Workers' Union, the NSW Labor Council agreed in 1939 to recommend that unions invite a New Theatre speaker to their meetings. The CPA newspaper, *Tribune*, approved:

> The fine work being done by the New Theatre League in producing working-class plays will be brought to the notice of all the trade unions by the Labor Council.

The Boilermakers' Union NSW branch donated £25 to the New Theatre. Under the headline 'Worthwhile Plays', *The Australian Worker* reviewed 'two outstanding working-class plays' – *Renegade*, by J. H. Pollock, and *Where's That Bomb?* by Roger Cullan and Buckley Roberts – claiming:

> both plays attracted big and appreciative audiences, and their success indicated that the New Theatre League is destined to provide the kind of working-class intellectual entertainment that for far too long has been denied to a very large section of the would-be play-going Sydney community.

Wireless Weekly report on Iris Shand, 1940.

Iris Shand, who plays a leading part in the musical comedy, "Off The Leash," now being staged by the New Theatre League.

This reference to would-be playgoers highlights the class divide and the portrayal of the arts as being for more 'highbrow' folk. The New Theatre and unions sought to challenge and break down the barriers to play-going and make theatre accessible and relevant for working-class people. *The Australian Worker* had previously described the audience as the 'real intelligentsia of Sydney... No £500 mink coats and small black moustaches on big fat faces were conspicuous'.

Union–theatre connections encompassed storytelling (performing for trade unions and writing material about trade union disputes and issues), attending stage-based performances and providing meeting, rehearsal or performance space. Miners' Federation women's auxiliaries engaged in fundraising efforts; in 1939, the Richmond Main lodge sold 500 tickets on behalf of the Kurri–Pelaw Main Women's Auxiliary.

Mutual support through reciprocity underlined the union–theatre relationship. Reviewing *Off the Leash*, the *Maritime Worker*'s article approvingly noted:

> As befits a play demanding unionisation of actors, the cast is headed by the Actors' Equity Secretary, Hal Alexander, Equity Committee Member, Iris Shand and Equity Treasurer Hal Eldridge, who is also a member of the Tramways Union.

During a key coal mining strike in 1938, Vic Arnold's expression of solidarity specified:

> we are anxious to be of every possible assistance. Come to our Sunday night production to put your case and fund raise. We will sponsor a program and donate 75% to the [strike] relief fund.

Not only did the New Theatre fundraise; it also performed *The Miner Speaks*, playwright Betty Roland's work, specifically for the strike. As the Sydney branch made arrangements to fundraise for the South Coast miners in Wollongong, they asked the union leaders: 'can you help organise the audience?' When New Theatre Secretary Freda Lewis addressed the AWU NSW branch meeting on the Working-Class Theatre Movement, she invited members to see the banned play *Till the Day I Die* and collected £1 in donations to the theatre.

In September 1940, a group of New Theatre players performed several sketches at the celebrations of the establishment of the Wollongong Trades Hall. Addressing the assembled crowd, Lewis gave her general support to union causes down south of Sydney, including formation of a South Coast branch of the theatre. When the South Coast branch formed, less than two months later, Lewis continued this outreach work, travelling back to Wollongong to train the new group and aiming to create a new theatre–union network. In her work as the New Theatre Secretary, and also through her playwriting, Lewis believed that unions which the New Theatre had assisted – such as the miners – realised what the theatre could mean to them. She urged the group to present plays 'dealing specifically with local issues and adapted to the problems of each union'. She mentioned the success of *The Firing Line*, a drama that she and Jock Hector, a fellow member of the New Theatre Writers Group, had quickly written in 1939. Dealing with the Port Kembla ironworkers' stoppage, the play was a series of exchanges between strikers and 'Big Business Government and Press Magnates'. Lewis and Hector not only performed the play on the Port Kembla ironworkers' site, along with two of the strikers, but also presented a number of short sketches at various localities in the Wollongong and Port Kembla areas. They left a copy of the script there, so that the ironworkers could produce the play for themselves – another example of sharing storytelling.

Progress report on the Sydney NT visit to Port Kembla, 1940.

> **THEATRE**
>
> **N.T.L. at Port Kembla**
>
> Port Kembla strikers laughed and cheered frequently last Friday during the New Theatre League's production of The Firing Line, brilliantly written drama dealing with the ironworkers' stoppage.
>
> N.T.L. players arrived at Port Kembla on Thursday, wrote the play the same night, staged it midday on Friday.
>
> Cast consisted of N.T.L. actors Jock Hector and Freda Lewis, and two of the strikers.
>
> Highlights include brisk dialogue between strikers and a character who appears successively as Big Business Government and Press magnate answering successive phone calls as "Electrolytic Zinc," "North B.H.," "Metal Manufactures," etc.
>
> N.T.L. players left copy of script so that strikers can produce play for themselves.
>
> Another outstanding success is scored by the New Theatre League in its production of the Soviet thriller Showdown..
>
> Showdown is running at New Theatre, 36 Pitt Street, on Sunday nights.

Alerting readers to the power of Betty Roland's *The Miner Speaks*, the *Common Cause* article, 'Our Case in Agitational Play', portrayed how:

> Our message is shot from the stage with lightning-like jabs at reactionary coal owners and governments, leading up to the crisp answer in dramatic exclamations to the question, 'why this strike?' Eight speakers individually and collectively telling of massacre and disease; criminal negligence that cause it; the plight of youths, old men, mothers and wives, and Federation demands.

Roland also wrote *War on the Waterfront* for the WWF during its 'Pig Iron' dispute (protesting the shipping of pig iron to Japan). This was 'an agitprop piece...intended for performance without props, utilising informal venues like the backs of trucks, factory canteens, footpaths' which played in Port Kembla. Katharine Susannah Prichard's work was able 'to socialistically educate many wage-workers'. New Theatre playwright Oriel Gray wrote a 'dramatic presentation on coal' for the Miners' Federation's 1946 function recognising 150 years of coal mining; it accompanied a memorial service for men killed in mines, and a dance-social followed later in the evening. During the protracted 1949 miners' strike, the New Theatre staged Gray's play *Coal*, a history of Australian mining and earlier disputes, outside the theatre. Running as many as six performances each day, on week days and weekends, they toured the coalfields to the north and south of Sydney to entertain and inform audiences ranging from 100 to 2,000. They 'were given enthusiastic receptions' as they presented *Coal*, along with other plays and sketches dealing with the miners' struggle and the Arbitration Court, at community halls and other semi-public spaces at the coalfields. After each performance, unionised miners would give a short talk about the strike.

The Sydney branch's *Spotlight* newsletter showed the variety of performance spaces: at the Tramways Union for its social (September 1953); a nurses' home building site (July 1954); Eveleigh rail yards and the WWF hall (August 1954); outside the Arthur Murray dance studio, for the picket line of striking dancers (August 1959); and a lunchtime meeting at Garden Island (September 1962). The New Theatre travelled to mining communities; in 1939, for example, there were 'several tours' to Cessnock, Wallsend and Kurri.

The New Theatre supported other broad union occasions. For the 1938 Sydney May Day procession, as well as supplying costumes, the New Theatre helped to create the tableaux for the NSW Labor Council's set of floats, depicting Australian labour history. The following year, AEU delegate Bradshaw was full of praise as he informed the Labor Council that:

> These people are among the most sincere members of the Movement... Before the May Day Demonstration they worked all night constructing the floats which made the procession so impressive.

'Full assistance' was the offer for the 1945 40-hour week demonstration and rally. On the 75th anniversary of the first recorded May Day, at Barcaldine (site of the 1891 shearers' strike), the May Day dinner included 'an historic tableau'. During the 1940 federal election, the *Australian Worker* reported that the New Theatre would support the ALP's campaign by performing:

> at public meetings, or in the open streets...a number of playlets putting the issues of the moment in dramatised form before the people.

The 1952 Carnival for Peace and Friendship, initiated by the Eureka Youth League, also brought unions and the New Theatre together in Sydney. The Carnival headquarters were at the International Seamen's Club at 36 Pitt Street, which had previously given the New Theatre space. New Theatre Secretary Miriam Hampson took leave of absence from her theatre work to help organise the Carnival support from trade unions, the peace and youth movements and many other community groups. Members of interstate New Theatre branches met in Sydney for the Carnival, and two branches performed. As well as hosting the Carnival's Drama Festival, the Sydney branch staged Oriel Gray's plays *Lawson* and *Sky Without Birds* (its world premiere), while the Brisbane branch, their trip partly funded by the union members of the Northgate Railway Workshop, presented Leonard Irwin's *The Circling Dove*, a three-act play.

Reciprocity of external solidarity occurred when the New Theatre was under attack, as one example demonstrates. In 1939, after the New Theatre was fined for performing in Sydney's Domain, the Ironworkers'

Melbourne Guardian report on union connections, 1946.

Union sought support from NSW Labor Council affiliates. Addressing fellow delegates, P. O'Neill:

> praised the New Theatre...which...had done much valuable work in dramatising industrial struggles... Whenever there is any effective propaganda of value to the Working Class Movement...we see the mailed fist of Fascism... The action taken against the New Theatre League is an encroachment on our liberties, and must be resisted.

Labor Council Secretary King agreed, claiming that the New Theatre 'had been responsible for wonderful working-class propaganda, and that was why they were being attacked. It was the thin end of the wedge'.

As well as performances going out to audiences, unionists were encouraged and assisted to come to the theatre, as delegates to the Seamen's Union National Conference of Women's Committees discovered. Finishing their conference with a trip to the opening night of *Operation Olive Branch* (Ewan McColl's *Lysistrata* adaptation), the women offered their thanks for being able to attend: 'it was indeed most enjoyable'. There were joint programs: *Trumpets of Wrath* followed an address on the Czechoslovakian crisis by John Chapple, an official with the Australian Railways Union. A 1951 New Theatre document, outlining how members could encourage trade union connections, encouraged speakers to:

> get into your subject by telling them that the New Theatre is run on strict trade union lines. It is the only theatre which elects its own officers and at which the rank and file members demand the right to the fullest reports from all functioning committees.

Attracting audiences to their stage-based performances was complicated; they experienced challenges in maintaining access to dedicated theatre space. In the early days, Wednesdays and Sundays had to be the designated performance days, because premises were shared with the Seamen's Union, which needed them for a weekly Saturday night dance. From 1943 to 1954, there was stability when Angus House at 167 Castlereagh Street housed the Sydney branch. However, Silvia Salisbury recalled: 'we eventually lost being able to have 167 Castlereagh Street, and we had no premises then'.

The WWF came to the theatre's rescue, allowing it to use the union hall. This co-sharing stretched into years. It was vital, but co-existence was not always easy, as Betty Milliss recalled:

> We spent 10 years in the wilderness – rehearsing on one place and playing in the Waterside Workers' Theatre. The Waterside Workers were absolutely marvellous to us. They made their hall available to us for our performances, but it was a very tiny stage and we had to clear it every single week-end. We had to clear the whole set, the props, furniture, everything, into a tiny little loft, and we did that for 10 years.

Silvia Salisbury also spoke of the mixed blessings of the WWF experience:

> And the Waterside Workers let us have their hall for performances. And we used to have our rehearsals in their office space down in Phillip Street, and it was just – it was very nice of them to do it, but it was very cramped and crowded and confined to do that. And to then transfer it at a weekend from rehearsal to performances.

Time was another gift. The New Theatre relied on its members to volunteer their time, and that meant organising lunchtime performances during work time. For Marie Armstrong, her boss' overt approval made a critical difference:

> when I was with the metalworkers' union, it was understood that if I wasn't busy, some of the other secretaries didn't like it, because – but I used the

phone a lot for New Theatre. But Laurie [Carmichael, the national secretary] knew it, and other people did. That meant that I was on the phone, organising, I mean a booking [would] come into the office at the theatre, and then Miriam would sort of say to me, [this is what is needed, can you organise it?] And then I also knew what material we had that would be suitable for whatever we were requested, whether it was peace, or equal pay, or whatever the campaign was, that we had something at our fingertips.

Financial and material support also materialised. The Railways Union Band 'contributed a feast of selections' for a performance of *Bury the Dead*. Silvia further explained that they were:

> always scratching for money… [The Sydney branch Secretary, Miriam Hampson] would ring unions to say 'can you help out on this'…other unions would help financially, if you talked to them… Because [Miriam's] job was during the day in the theatre, she could talk to union people, and say, can you donate something. Or, sometimes it would be…specialised equipment for certain plays.

Vocal supporters among senior union leaders were invaluable for the essential work of promoting the plays. Jim Healy, WWF General Secretary, pronounced in a ringing endorsement that *Reedy River*, the Dick Diamond musical about the 1891 Great Strike, 'must be seen by every Australian worker. It is, in my opinion, easily the best play yet written or produced here in Australia'. Emphatically underscoring its relevance, Healy declared:

> From start to finish, it breathes of the struggle and life of the Australian worker. While it is true the theme flows from the shearing industry and its struggles, nevertheless, the very heart of the problem – that Joe Collins has to face up to in his fight to maintain union organisation in the face of the employers' attack – is the same central problem that the working class of this and other countries had to face in the fight

> for the right to organise and to maintain the trade union structure in which they had struggled through so many bitter years. I am sure that any waterside worker seeing this play will see in it the struggles and problems of the Australian waterfront. It is a play that no Australian worker can afford to miss.

He continued, reinforcing the importance of bringing the work to the members:

> I hope that the New Theatre will be able to so organise its showings that it can be brought down to the waterfront. I am sure that the tunes and the words that go with them will immediately impress themselves on the wharfies' minds, and will be echoed around the waterfront from Thursday Island to Geraldton.

Such lunchtime performances did occur. *Reedy River*, whether the full production or a group of songs, became one of the New Theatre's most popular productions.

The Sydney branch members reinforced the diversity of performance spaces in 1952, when they travelled to Glen Davis, west of Sydney, to support striking Miners' Federation members. An earlier chapter in this volume explains that what marked out this particular experience was not that they performed in the miners' workplace, but where that workplace was: 1,500 feet underground. The men were staging a 'stay-in' strike because of the federal government's decision to close the mine. This was literally an underground performance. The miners had been striking underground for two weeks when the Miners' Federation invited the New Theatre to take *The Candy Store* out to the mine. Solidarity underscored the theatre–union relationship, with the striking men using their headlamps to augment the lighting for the play. After the performance, theatre members helped the stay-in miners to record taped messages to their families on the surface, as well as the song that the miners had composed about their strike. Returning to the surface, the troupe then performed for the townsfolk, including the strikers' wives and children. Six months later, they again performed underground, this time for the Great Greta miners' stay-in strike. Len Fox, partner of New Theatre key playwright Mona Brand, wrote *Stay Down Miner* especially for the occasion. The New

Theatre's dedication to taking art to the people, apparent in their willingness to travel underground, demonstrated the bonds of solidarity between unions and the theatre folk.

The progressive vision of the unions and the New Theatre intersected: unions desired to recruit members beyond the workplace, and the theatre strove to connect directly with its audiences in familiar places. The relationship between union and theatre drove the integration of art and culture into working lives and working-class communities. In today's language of community unionism, union–theatre relations were in, and for, the community. However, alliances were based on a different footing to contemporary community unionism. A political project was afoot. Shared ideology and a shared commitment to radical cultural uplift underpinned and sustained alliances. For the New Theatre, it was about having an avenue that would give voice to their political philosophy – where workers could see legitimacy and advocacy for their struggles.

The dimensions of the mutual support are clear in the theatre's communication of the unions' messages and campaign narratives. Plays, skits, revues and musicals communicated union values, and stories articulated and embodied ideas, beliefs and convictions. The New Theatre gave voice and shape to the stories that passed from member to member within the union, sharing them in public performances with other unions and the broader community.

The support of socialist values and commitment to working-class progress through access to the performing arts was the bridge between the theatre and the unions. Both parties sought ideological congruence; synergies between the unions' identity and ideology and the identity and values of the New Theatre members, who were also workers and union members, underscored the reciprocal relationship. This was particularly true of unions with communist leaderships. The New Theatre certainly opposed capitalism. Its contact work challenged the control of employers over work spaces, including those underground coal mines. Plays written for particular industrial disputes reached members in a different way: audience members could identify and connect with subject matter that spoke to their lived experience.

Unions committed to the cultural development of their members, such as the WWF, used the theatre as part of a broader strategy. The WWF's preparedness to house the theatre was in line with its broader arts policy, which included their Film Unit. Other unions held different views in different branches, as an excerpt from the report 'How Coms Are Infiltrating Cultural Organisations', from the Queensland branch of the AWU, indicates:

Connie Healy's scrapbook page on *Miners Right*, 1949.

New Theatre actors prepare to go down Box Flat mine (Bootal) near Ipswich
Foreground: Ossie NASH
Back row, A Miner,
Actors, Barbara Colley, Gwen McKay, Judy Dillon and Ted Kelk

(Miner's Right Staged by N. Theatre - 1949.

> The objectives of the New Theatre are stated to be to bring a message to the masses through drama. Performances...conclude with a political-culture address by a member of the cast or executive committee, which includes Katharine Susannah Prichard, a member of the Central Executive of the Communist Party. Many of the plays it presents strike an extreme Leftist propagandist note. Associated with the New Theatre venture is Mr. Lloyd Lambie, whose recent election to the presidency of Actors' Equity was disputed by an anti-Communist faction in Equity.

Another radical element of the relationship was the exercising of power in making and remaking space. Every worksite performance transformed an employer's work space into a different space, even if only temporarily. For both the unions and the New Theatre, exercising power over space was critical in their fight for workers' rights and the political messages. When the New Theatre performed at workplaces, they joined with the unions onsite to reclaim the work space for the workers and recast it as educational, political and entertainment space, full of subversive messages. Just like mass meetings and picket lines, the performances were reminders that what was seen as the employer's space during working hours was an artificial construct, able to be unsettled and remade. Although such transformations were transient, every new performance recreated the space. Waterfront performances recast the docks as spaces of resistance and challenged management's control over space. The stay-in strikes were a similar reclaiming of space. A mining company could tunnel underground to create a place for coal extraction and labour power, but theatre could remake that place. At Glen Davis, the union had already subverted the mine spaces from their productive uses; the performance remade it again as a place for storytelling.

A lesson Glen Davis taught was that performances for communities had to resonate with them:

> When we took our play into the Glen Davis mine to the staydown strikers – well, that was the beginning of a new attitude, said a member of New Theatre. Members who had been aloof were inspired by the solidarity, the enthusiasm and interest of the workers.

Writers who went among the staydown miners learnt a lot, too:

> They agree that writing must avoid the slick and sophisticated. Scripts for acting need to be simple, with the parodies based on folk-tunes rather than the more fancy songs. In Great Greta, for instance, a parody of *Old Smokey* went across well, but one on *Much Binding in the Marsh* [a British radio comedy set in a fictional Royal Air Force station] largely missed.

At the outset, we identified the issue that a lack of historical insight into the dynamics of the theatre–union relationship was limiting our understanding of the New Theatre. This analysis of the ideological and value alignment in the relationships forged between these four unions (and others) and the New Theatre's Sydney branch shows reciprocity's mutual benefits. This chapter examined how the theatre used mobility to develop and sustain those union connections through its 'contact work' and how the unions and theatre worked together to subversively make and remake space. This analysis focused on four unions and their journals, mentioning others in passing, and it has found significant relationships; it is a beginning and should be extended to investigate more unions' records. It would be interesting to know more about how more unions considered and debated the relationship internally. It is clear, however, that the unions provided access to audiences, and the New Theatre told the unions' stories and opened cultural avenues embedded with political and industrial messages for working-class people in the 1930s to the 1950s.

FURTHER READING

ACTU, *Arts and Creative Recreation Policy*, Melbourne, ACTU, 1980.

Arrow, Michelle, 'The New Theatre', in T. Irving and R. Cahill (eds.), *Radical Sydney: Places, Portraits and Unruly Episodes*, Sydney, UNSW Press, 2010, pp. 210–215.

Arrow, Michelle, *Upstaged: Australian Women Dramatists in the Limelight at Last*, Strawberry Hills, Currency Press, 2002.

Brand, Mona, 'A Writer's 36 Years in Radical Theatre: New Theatre's Formative Years 1932–1955 and Their Influence on Australian Drama', in *Australian drama 1920–1955: papers presented to a Conference at the University of New England, Armidale, September 1–4, 1984*, Armidale, NSW, University of New England, Department of Continuing Education, 1986, pp. 1–8.

Brand, Mona, *Enough Blue Sky: the Autobiography of Mona Brand, an Unknown Well-known Playwright*, Potts Point, Tawny Pipit Press, 1995.

Darby, Robert, 'New Theatre and the State: the Ban on *Till the Day I Die*, 1936–41', *Labour History*, no. 80, 2001, pp. 1–19.

Delaney, Anne, 'Red Aesthetics: the Establishment and Development of the Workers' Art Club and New Theatre in Sydney, 1932–1945', *Past Imperfect: University of Sydney Historical Journal,* no. 1, 1987, pp. 35–54.

Filewod, Alan and Watt, David, *Workers' Playtime: Theatre and the Labour Movement since 1970*, Sydney, Currency Press, 2001.

Gray, Oriel, *Exit Left: Memoirs of a Scarlet Woman*, Ringwood, Penguin, 1985.

Healy, Connie, *A History of Political Theatre in Brisbane as Part of Working-class Cultural Tradition and Heritage: the Workers' Education Dramatic Society and the Student/Unity/New Theatre (1930–1962)*, M.A. diss., University of Queensland, 1994.

Healy, Connie, *Defiance: Political Theatre in Brisbane, 1930–1962*, Brisbane, Boombana Publications, 2000.

Healy, Connie, 'Radical Theatre', in R. Evans, C. Ferrier and J. Rickertt (eds.), *Radical Brisbane: an Unruly History*, Carlton, Vulgar Press, 2004, pp. 187–192.

Healy, Connie, 'Women in Radical Theatre in Brisbane', paper delivered at the 9th National Labour History Conference, Sydney, 30 June–2 July 2005, http://roughreds.com/twopdf/healy2.pdf (accessed 4 February 2007).

O'Brien, Angela, *The Road Not Taken: Political and Performance Ideologies at Melbourne New Theatre 1935–1960*, Ph.D. diss., Melbourne, Monash University, 1989.

Poynting, Scott, 'The Youth Carnival for Peace and Friendship, March 1952', *Labour History*, no. 56, 1989, pp. 60–68.

Roland, Betty, 'War on the Waterfront – a Banned Play', *Illawarra Unity – Journal of the Illawarra Branch of the Australian Society for the Study of Labour History*, vol. 7, no. 1, 2007, pp. 49–55.

Zabala, Gabriela, 'Voices Unheard: the Representation of Australian Aborigines by Left-wing Playwrights 1940s–1960s', *Australasian Drama Studies*, no. 60, 2012, pp. 42–55.

NT Sydney Candy Store cast preparing to go down the mine, 1952.

CHAPTER 17

The Glen Davis 'Stay-In' Strike: 'Sydney Actors Make History'

Lisa Milner and Cathy Brigden

Scene one: The 1965 Miners' Federation Annual Convention is celebrating the union's 50th Anniversary.

Delegates and other union representatives watch the Sydney New Theatre perform *Come All You Valiant Miners*, a dramatic presentation penned by playwright Mona Brand.

In this multimedia celebration of the history of mining in Australia, revue material, protest and folk songs, slides and segments of films made by the WWF Film Unit mesh with some vaudeville elements.

From the audience, New Theatre member (and New Theatre playwright Oriel Gray's first husband) John Gray proclaims: 'the history isn't over yet', as he describes how the theatre troupe came to perform in an underground mine:

> On June 17 [1952], New Theatre had a call from the Miners' Federation asking if we'd be interested in taking a show to Glen Davis to present to the miners who'd been on a stay-in strike underground for two weeks. You see, the Menzies government had decided to close the shale oil mines, and the miners were resisting. Well, of course, we said yes.

Scene two: The opening night audience is watching the Sydney New Theatre's revue, *What's New*, at its new theatre at 542 King Street, Newtown in September 1973.

Described as 'a fast-moving amalgam' of sketches, songs and scenes chosen from 40 years' stock of over 200 plays and revues, *What's New* moved through:

> fierce social criticism of the depression years, through the anti-fascist challenge of *Till the Day I Die*, the war, the Cold War with McCarthyism, the Menzies period and ASIO, the historic New Theatre performance under ground during the Glen Davis miners' stay-down strike, and to the Vietnam antiwar and anti-conscription struggles.

Alex Robertson, the editor of the Sydney *Tribune*, wrote: 'they made theatre history by staging a full play underground for the stay-in miners at Glen Davis'.

Scene three: Assembled 'friends of the New' attend a celebratory event at The New Theatre, 542 King Street, Newtown, May Day 2015. Veterans of the stage rub shoulders with bright young things looking for their launch into the art form, as the history of the New unfolds in performance, song and discussion.

Not people to shy away from the limelight or disavow their left-wing origins, the organisers have called it 'a special one-off event': *People, Plays and Politics: Reds, Reformers and Ratbags from New Theatre's Past*. Again, performances, slides, videos, music and talks illustrate this celebration of history. One of the presenters is Frank Barnes, a veteran New Theatre director and life member. In his section on the New Theatre's history of street theatre and agitprop, Barnes relates the story of the Glen Davis performances as a highlight of the event. Audience members leaving the celebration receive a 'brief history' of the organisation, written by New Theatre historian Lyn Collingwood, which boasts 'to say that evening's performance was unique is an understatement'.

Given the hundreds of performances by the New Theatre, what was it about this particular 1952 performance that was so remarkable, decades after it took place? Why was it regarded as 'historic'? The answers lie in the New Theatre's philosophy and relationship with its audiences, as well as the relationships built between its Sydney branch and trade unions.

THE STORY BEHIND THE PERFORMANCE

In addition to traditional stage-based performances, the New Theatre branches focused on developing a key aspect of broader community engagement through contact and mobile work which entailed physically taking performances to audiences, rather than relying on people coming to a theatre-based performance. Being mobile enabled contact with people less likely to be regular theatre goers – people who did not normally experience theatre. Consequently, places not traditionally associated with theatrical plays – workplaces, beaches, parks and community halls – became locations for New Theatre performances. Relationships forged with trade unions also attracted audiences, enabling the theatre to disseminate its messages to working men and women. One of these unions was the Miners' Federation. It encouraged members to attend performances and included reviews in *Common Cause*, the union journal.

From this perspective, it becomes clear that, when the New Theatre's Sydney branch accepted the invitation to perform underground at the Glen Davis mine, it was yet another workplace performance. However, a full account shows that it was not just any workplace performance.

In the early 1930s, the federal government committed in principle to partly finance, with the NSW Government, the start-up of a new major oil shale enterprise in the Blue Mountains. With federal, state and private company funds, National Oil Pty Ltd was set up in 1937 to produce petrol from kerosene shale in the isolated Capertee Valley, 80 km northwest of Lithgow. Oil shale mining commenced at Glen Davis the following year, initially with oil production, then petrol by August 1940. For the period from 1939 to 1952, it provided one-fifth of the shale oil produced in Australia. Communist Party journalists described it as a mine 'to which Australia had looked with such hope as the beginning of freedom from the American oil monopolies'. A town grew and, by 1951, Glen Davis had 3,000 residents.

Despite the *Lithgow Mercury* portraying the mine as a 'national asset', there were grave fears for the viability of the mine from 1948. When the federal government announced its closure, the Miners' Federation reacted strongly, declaring:

> to close Glen Davis would be a gross betrayal of
> the national interests, a sell-out to the American oil
> monopolies. It would also make a mockery of promises
> of full employment.

Moreover, Edgar Ross, *Common Cause* editor, commented:

> Glen Davis will be seen as the symbol of resistance of the people to the ruinous policy of the Menzies–Fadden Government in the tradition of the Port Kembla waterside workers' action against the export of pig iron to Japan.

Through early 1951, unions and the NSW Labor Council worked together 'to save this vital industry for the Australian people'. Miners' Federation President, prominent communist Idris Williams, declared: 'Glen Davis is vital to the defence of Australia. We regard the threat to close it as most serious and will plan appropriate action'. Not only members, 'but...all who believe in our country's right to independent development of its resources' needed the intensified campaign. Six months later, he reiterated:

> There are tremendous resources in this valley. If this plant is allowed to close the oil will be lost to future generations. Let us see this industry is saved – for Australia.

More was at stake than just the mine closure. The fate of the town hung on the decision. Spurred on, the union gave an ultimatum: if the closure proceeded, they would not dismantle the machinery. The government was unmoved. The union prepared to uphold its ultimatum.

On 2 June 1952, the Glen Davis stay-in strike began. Not only did 18 men on the afternoon shift ignore the order to start dismantling mine equipment, but they also refused to leave. The next morning, the 32-men-strong morning shift came down to bolster the numbers. For the next 27 days, the 50 men lived underground.

According to Mrs Hall, wife of the Glen Davis Miners Lodge Secretary, a strike had been planned 'for a long time'; as a consequence, the men were well supplied with food and blankets, with a telephone connected to the surface. One local newspaper highlighted the union's experience with the stay-in strategy: 'The strike is similar to a stay under strike staged by 115 miners at Collinsville mine, Queensland who went on strike on May 1'. Indeed, the first stay-in strike lasted three days in 1937 (at the Sunbeam Colliery in Korumburra, Victoria).

At Collinsville, the nine-day stay-in strike set a new Australian record, breaking the previous record of five days set in Newcastle in 1937. The Glen Davis strike created an Australian record for a stay-in mine strike, falling a mere five days short of the world record.

Other unions rallied to the Glen Davis cause. Sixty AWU members at a lunchtime meeting at Balmain's No. 2 wharf expressed full support:

> We ask our union executive immediately to use the union organisation to give every support, financially and otherwise, and to organise collection of food and money and clothing to aid the people of Glen Davis.

Western district coal miners went out on a sympathy strike, and spontaneous strikes spread to all underground and open cut mines. Two weeks later, coal miners stopped work at 61 mines on the southern and western fields, holding aggregate meetings to protest against the proposed closure. Visitors bringing food and money included the Seamen's Union, the Seamen's Women's Auxiliary, the Hotel, Club and Restaurant Workers and the Federated Engine Drivers and Firemen's Association (Kandos branch).

THE CANDY STORE **GOES DOWN A MINE**

At the time of the Glen Davis stay-in strike, *The Candy Store* had been playing to packed audiences in Sydney. US playwright Barnard Rubin wrote *The Candy Story*, and the New Theatre changed its name. Set in Roan's Candy and Cigar Store, the play relates how the Roan family's livelihood was threatened by a nearby franchise. With Pop Roan, the lower-middle-class Bronx candy store owner, as its hero, the play was a great hit in New York, filled with what the *Daily Worker* called 'rugged proletarian humour'. In another review, the newspaper commented that:

> one of the achievements of the play is the presentation of Communists, not as mechanical figures who enter from time to time and whose lives serve as explanatory footnotes to the drama, but as an intricate part of the action, following naturally into the structure of the drama... *The Candy Story* portrays the world as only a Marxist writer can.

NEW THEATRE PRESENTS

By Barnard Rubin

The Candy Store program, designed by Les Tanner.
Glen Davis miner talks with NT members (opp).

The Candy Story played almost continuously from March 1951 to September 1951 in various New York theatres. A Yiddish version played in Los Angeles.

The play travelled internationally to London and Australia. After the Sydney premiere, the Tribune review started with:

> It's encouraging to find such a fine play as *The Candy Store* [sic] coming from America today... [The audience] felt that here was more than a play – here was a reflection of the strength of the progressive forces in America that defy all threats and all attacks.

Sydney received the play well, delivering good houses for the 23 performances with many audience members coming from the union movement.

Then the Miners' Federation invited the New Theatre to take *The Candy Store* out to the mine, arranging for the troupe to go down hundreds of feet underground into the mine and perform for the miners. The unionists were not just asking for entertainment for the strikers – they were asking for working-class support, at the strike site. While there were many precedents for both these requests, never had such a contact show – underground – been attempted.

In a bus covered with left-wing slogans and flags supplied by the Miners' Federation, a full cast rehearsed the show during the five-hour drive. The tour party consisted of

Roland Grivas, Alan Sherring, John Armstrong, Leon Sherman, Sid Miller, Marie Armstrong, Pat Lavelle, Miriam Hampson, David Walesby, Evelyn Docker, Harry Ciddor, Mignon Michell, Cecil 'Cec' Grivas, Neville Swanson and the stage manager, Tom Salisbury. When the bus arrived at the mine, everyone introduced themselves and discussed the strike and the miners' stories around their work. The miners made their case to the Sydneysiders for the viability of the mine. Grivas remembered:

> one of the engineers who gave us a tour 'up top' picked up a piece of shale that had been through the retorts and lit it with a match to show us how rich the shale was in oil, that even after extraction, there was still oil in the shale.

He 'blacked up' for the performance to portray Johnnie, the African-American communist worker (as was common at the time). Cec's subsequent report conveys the preparatory work by the miners that had preceded their arrival:

> on getting down into the mine our technical people consulted with the miners. Then things started to happen. Some of the miners, including 'Tealeaves' King and 'Burlington Bertie', rigged up a makeshift stage at the junction of five mine shafts. A wooden platform was laid down on a section of the floor that had been levelled. Backdrops provided by the miners were set up. Hessian with copper wire hooks strung on to a length of water pipe went up as our curtain. Stage lighting was arranged with miners' lights. We stood back amazed; the set was almost identical with the original.

Cec also spoke of the inspirational effect of the setting and the audience:

> The curtain went up before the most appreciative audience we have had. The show went off without a hitch. The whole atmosphere of the struggle that was going on down here inspired the cast. The play, which

deals with a strike in the USA, came to life in a way that it had never done before. The curtain came down on the last act and the applause almost brought the roof down. The miners gave three cheers for the cast and sang 'For they are jolly good fellows'. The cast replied in the same manner.

Cec advised: 'This was the first time 95 percent of the miners had seen a stage play, and they wanted more'.

The cast presented the miners with £25 they had raised from donations solicited from Sydney *Candy Store* audiences. Using a tape recorder brought from Sydney, the men recorded family messages before adding to the entertainment:

> The boys then suggested that they sing the Glen Davis song composed by one of them. This went on to the tape also, with a dozen husky miners beefing out the words and ending with a bit of impromptu harmony.
>
> Will Glen Davis be a Ghost Town? No! No! No!
>
> Will we let the Yanks turn off our oil? No! No! No!
>
> Will they run us off Glen Davis oil? No! No! No!
>
> Will we let old Truman rule us? No! No! No!
>
> Will we let Bob Menzies rule us? No! No! No!
>
> Farewells were said and we went up the tunnel with the shouts of comradeship from the miners still ringing in our ears.

Afterwards, local families fed the troupe, with catering courtesy of the Women's Auxiliary. The players then assembled at the town hall for a community performance. From statements at the time and interviews with some of the participants decades later, it is clear that the Glen Davis trip not only provided entertainment and working-class support for the striking miners and their families, but also brought a welcome boost in morale for the New

Glen Davis Illustration by Herbert McClintock.

Theatre family at a time when, soon after the defeat of the Labor Chifley government in 1949, there was an anti-communist and anti-left backlash. Cec wrote: 'We felt [as] if we belonged with these people as we saw the unity that was in evidence among them'. Once again, the play was well received. Then the recorded messages were played, the voices of husbands, fathers and sons ringing out above-ground in the hall. The play thus became the basis for a later shared experience for striking families, with wives, children and other family members able to compare their reactions with that of their men. The theatre members returned to Sydney that night 'tired but convinced we had found the real meaning of art belonging to the people'.

The trip left three theatre members, interviewed 63 years later, with indelible memories. Tom Salisbury pulled out photos during his interview. 'It was incredible, June '52', he recalled, recounting how:

> the miners themselves helped us a lot, built all the stage, and got all the lighting. It was a fairly easy play in the way the whole play was more or less set in the Candy shop, so it was just a one-set scene.

Patricia (Pat) Lavelle remembers the trip:

> I was really excited about doing [the play]. I was all for that, the miners, and going down to entertain them. It was terrific, terrific... It was just a magical feeling when you got down there, the light, for one thing. And in no way did I feel claustrophobic, not for a second did I feel any threat. In fact, it never entered my head – I think the experience of going down there [was terrific]. There were the miners bravely going down there, and there was a whole lot of us, and we were going to do something most unusual.

Another of the young women to join the tour, Marie Armstrong, remembers 'a fantastic experience':

> God, that was an incredible experience...we're driven straight to the gates, there are policemen there. And somehow, it had been arranged that we were allowed through...we've got a photograph of people, us running

toward the opening of the mine where we had to get on the trolley.

> The adventure! And fear of not knowing whether the cops were going to arrest you. You didn't know – oh, I mean, you didn't know, it was not, 'oh yes, you're going to be alright, we've arranged for the cops to let [you in]' – none of that. It was like, step by step by step. So there was negotiations that went on at the gate, which we had to just stand back. And I think part of me was hoping it wouldn't happen. Because, you know, we were going down the…mine… So, we get on the trolleys. And we're taken down the tunnels and go and go and go…and we're at a junction where mine shafts met each other. And in the area of the junction there were some boards that had been put up to give us a stage… And there are blokes sitting down in this junction… And I can remember we were all introduced to them, hello, how are you?

Both women remembered the lights. Marie explained:

> there were little lights, just little lights. But when it came ready, of course, the thing was, they all shone their lamps on us… And the fact that they didn't tell us that, that was all planned.

Pat reminisced:

> I'll just never forget it, the light in the mines, from the lamps or whatever it was that they had, casting this beautiful glow. It was lovely, like entering another world, actually, come to think of it. It really was entering another world that you could never otherwise get to. Yes, it was a romantic, very romantic environment.

Pat was, however, unsure about the choice of play and its relevance for the miners:

> Although I know that I thought, 'I can't really see what relevance this play, **The Candy Store**, has to do with these men in this mine'. I thought, 'mm, it's not a fun play. And it's full of words in it, like very New York – [in US accent] 'I'm gonna have a halva shake', and everything'. What's halva?? We'd all had to go through that ourselves, de-Americanise ourselves. So, no, I did think it was a shame I wasn't doing something a bit more entertaining. But no doubt, they thought it was.

The *Tribune* play review would have allayed her concerns. The reviewer observed that:

> These are the ordinary people about whom the play is written. Ordinary, and divided among themselves. But in the quiet little candy store things begin to happen. A right-wing union leader tries to sell out the strike. The Communist is brutally bashed by company goons. The bill collectors close in and bring the store to bankruptcy. The mother breaks under the strain... AND out of it something is born. Something that is perhaps called unity, or struggle, or hope, or perhaps all three. This is a fine play, full of action, full of real meaning for all of us today. Here is socialist realism.

These qualities of unity and struggle lay at the heart of the resistance and stay-in strike and resonated with the folk of Glen Davis. Armstrong recalled their second performance, in the town that night:

> So, then we came back up, and there were no cops to arrest us. And we were told we were going to be taken to the local hall. And that the wives and the families were going to be there to greet us. And somewhere in that process, we were asked, could we do the play again, in the hall, for them. And of course, we said yes, you know. And so, we repeated it. I remember the kids down the front.

Grivas also remembered that 'the whole town must have turned up...the four front rows solid with kids'.

THE OUTCOME

For all the opposition and support it rallied, the Glen Davis mine did not escape its fate, closing in June 1953. A negotiated compensation package at least provided alternative employment and led to an outcome described as 'the best ever obtained by workers in such circumstances'.

Six months later, in December 1952, another New Theatre troupe travelled north to Great Greta in the Hunter Valley to perform underground once again, in support of 32 stay-in miners protesting against dismissal notices. This time, Len Fox, partner of the New Theatre key playwright, Mona Brand, wrote *Stay Down Miner* specifically for the audience. Fox later wrote:

> Soon, New Theatre players were singing and acting in the dimly-lit gathering place 300 yards in. The miners grouped around, barely visible in the faint light. You could see their eyes sparkling as Menzies and Fadden were burlesqued, and as three sinister 'security snoopers' sang their little ditty. (The ditty was given a touch of reality by the fact that a phone call had just come in to the mine to say that the police were prowling outside.) The New Theatre program concluded with the sketch, written by a member of the Realist Writers' Group, showing the miner and his wife denying Menzies and the bosses, and singing 'Let's all stand united and fight till we win'. Then some of the miners sang their songs, and as we left they told us of messages of support from all over New South Wales and from other States. They're solid as a rock.

The Glen Davis performance was both a typical and unusual experience. Obviously, the location was unusual; but, in many other ways, it was typical of countless New Theatre performances: a workplace setting, a provocative script, worksite and community-based performances. It typified union and New Theatre engagement, utilising contact work to connect with working-class audiences. Moreover, both groups thought the performance nothing out of the ordinary, at the time: there was just the same mention, along with other performances, in the branch Committee of Management minutes. A small article appeared in one issue of *Common Cause*, and a photo of the troupe the following week. It was also not the only time when the troupe performed underground, as the Great Greta performance shows.

The contact work of the New Theatre was, we argue, an early example of site-specific performance. More recent location, or site-specific, theatre in Australia – including some Melbourne performances of the 1970s and 1980s – has been the subject of analysis. Paul Davies described these later works as:

> fashioning various and subtle new experiences for their audiences (compared to more traditional theatrical presentations). The organising principles were: containerisation, authenticity (of space and place), complicity (of audience and actors) in the occupation of that place, and mobility (of stage or audience, or both).

He did not mention the earlier site-specific performances by the New Theatre's Melbourne branch, nor the Glen Davis precedent for these Melbourne works.

What is it about the repeated acts of remembering the Glen Davis performance that make us claim it as notable? It is certainly an activist notion of theatre-and-politics, the acts of remembering Glen Davis; it reinforces, through New Theatre history, the agency of those players who chose to go down the mine. The players were linking themselves to something larger than the play, or the stage: as political activists, they were increasing the ability of theatre to function as activism. New Theatre members and historians, in continuing to highlight the underground performance event, sustain the link of the New Theatre with that form of political activism. They also allow new generations and audiences to imagine change in contemporary political contexts. Discussing the importance of theatrical and carnivalesque contributions to political activism in his book *Tactical Performance*, Larry Bogard reminds us of the crucial importance of sociohistorical and institutional memory to collective action. Repeating and reinforcing the memories of the stay-in strike cement this performance as a continuing part of public space and the narrative of political protest. The retellings are shared representations, making up our collective memory of Australian workers – to twist Benedict Anderson's idea, they make up an imagined community of the working nation. Here, musing on issues of collective memory that these retellings draw from and create, we can make connections with Emile Durkheim's ideas of the 'conscience collective' and 'collective effervescence'. Durkheim believed that the group memory of a social movement, or the creation of a text or symbol of memory, was important in the creation and maintenance of collective sentiments, such as those born out of union membership and strike activism:

> Without symbols, social sentiments could only have a precarious existence. Though very strong as long as [people] are together and influence each other reciprocally, they exist only in the form of recollections after the assembly has ended, and when left to themselves, these become feebler and feebler, for since the group is no longer present and active, individual temperaments easily regain the upper hand.

The New Theatre writers analysed the effects of this location work. One lesson from Glen Davis was that performances for communities had to resonate with them:

> When we took our play into the Glen Davis mine to the staydown strikers – well, that was the beginning of a new attitude, said a member of New Theatre. Members who had been aloof were inspired by the solidarity, the enthusiasm and interest of the workers. Writers who went among the staydown miners learnt a lot, too. They agree that writing must avoid the slick and sophisticated. Scripts for acting need to be simple.

Another notable element of the underground performance was the exercise of power –particularly the making and remaking of space. At Glen Davis, the union had already subverted the mine space from its productive use to one of industrial resistance, and the performance remade it again as a theatrical site. Every worksite performance – factory floor, dockside, shopfront or underground – transformed an employer's work space into a different space, even if only temporarily. We suggest that the Glen Davis performances have been remembered so powerfully because they were fairly extreme instances of creating theatre spaces – place of doing theatre, as well as showing and looking at the play and the players. It was a particularly novel engagement with place. It was a re-imagining of the place of that convergence of mine shafts, hundreds of feet underground, a novel form of contestation of place. For even a short time, this act of underground performance was a political, and cultural, contestation of place, a refusal, even if temporary, of the dominant understanding of that mine, in which the boundaries of work and culture were refused.

This is also a memory of a deliberate alignment of a cultural practice – the play's performance underground – with a political practice – the stay-in strike. Gay McAuley notes that this memory works through successive generations:

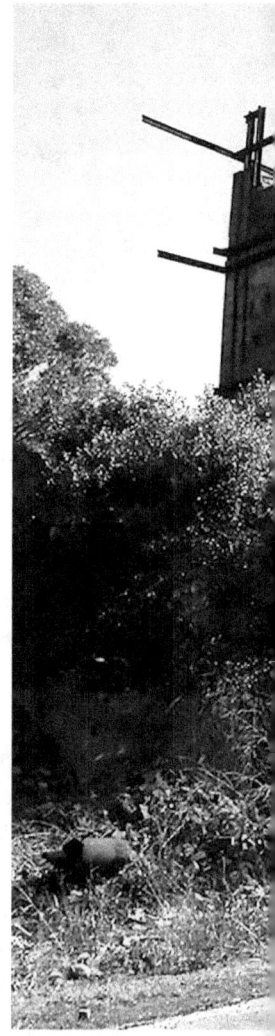

> Knowledge suppressed in one generation can emerge as story telling in a subsequent generation, and because the stories are associated with specific places, so they begin to share in the persistence of place rather than the short lifespan of individual men and women.

The historians and friends of the New Theatre have worked to keep the memory of the Glen Davis events alive.

For the New Theatre, the unions provided access to the audiences sought; for the unions, the Theatre opened up cultural avenues embedded with political and industrial messages for working-class people. The theatre's mobility, the equal involvement of women and men (at a time when women were not permitted to work underground) and a working-class, trade union-based play came together for this working-class, trade union audience – and then kept inserting itself into the remembered history of the New Theatre.

FURTHER READING

Bogard, Larry, 'Introduction', *Tactical Performance: Serious Play and Social Movements*, London, Routledge, 2016.

Davies, Paul, 'Dramatic Tales Stir the Suburb: Melbourne's Location Theatre Movement, 1979–1990', *Australasian Drama Studies*, no. 64, 2014, pp. 39–70.

Davies, Paul, 'Location Theatre and Some Community Encounters of the Third Kind', in Richard Fotheringham (ed.), *Community Theatre in Australia*, Paddington, Currency Press, 1992, pp. 133–140.

Durkheim, Emile, *The Elementary Forms of the Religious Life*, translated by Joseph Ward Swain, London, Allen & Unwin, 1915, p. 231.

The site of the Glen Davis shale mine – a ghost town now.

Fensham, Rachel, 'Location, Location, Location: Australian Theatre on Safari', *Meanjin*, vol. 50, nos. 2-3, 1991, pp. 241-251.

McAuley, Gay, 'Remembering and Forgetting: Place and Performance in the Memory Process', in Gay McAuley (ed.), *Unstable Ground: Performance and the Politics of Place*, Bruxelles, P. I. E. Peter Lang, 2006.

Ross, Edgar, *A History of the Miners' Federation of Australia*, Sydney, ACSEF, 1970.

CHAPTER 18

A 'Great Antiwar Play'

Lisa Milner

BURY THE DEAD ON THE WORLD STAGE

With its compelling story of dead soldiers refusing to be buried as a protest against war, Irwin Shaw's 1936 experimental play *Bury the Dead* achieved instant success on the New York stage. Mainstream and little theatres in the USA took it up eagerly; radical and left-wing theatres throughout the world have staged it most often. In Australia, Great Britain, India, South Africa and Canada, it resonated with audiences. At an early British performance, members of the audience had to be treated for shock.

Shaw drew his inspiration from the horrors of World War I and the Spanish Civil War, and the play's antiwar message and experimental style proved popular with Depression-era audiences fearing another world war. Its relevance has not diminished since that era. It remains a successful tool for moral protest and social commentary to the present day, in many translations and many nations. The forms of production have varied. This chapter explores the continuing attractiveness of *Bury the Dead* as an antiwar drama across a variety of historical, cultural, political and production contexts from 1936 to 2018. It interrogates the play's relevance for theatres in disparate times and places. Drawing on archival research and interviews, it contributes to research on antiwar drama and on the broader literature that seeks to understand left-wing theatre throughout the English-speaking world. Focusing on the play's Australian productions in New Theatre branches, the chapter also provides a comprehensive production history of the work in this country.

Plays aiming to promote peace and oppose war date from the times of Aristophanes and Euripides; but *Bury the Dead* was described in 2004 as 'possibly to this day the single most celebrated antiwar play'. There is a substantial

'The Marching Dead' by Philip Senior.

body of scholarship on radical and left-wing theatre in the USA in the 1930s, and also on antiwar drama, but there is little specific literature about *Bury the Dead*. Its compelling story of dead soldiers refusing to be buried as a protest against war was right for the times when it was first performed on Broadway in 1936. Canada and Australia rapidly imported the play, within months of its first performance, and it continues to be highly mobile and popular today. It is a play that crossed boundaries. Radical theatre groups, colleges and universities, amateur and professional organisations performed it, often translated and adapted. The category of antiwar plays is not large, but they will continue to be produced while wars persist, and *Bury the Dead*'s popularity continues.

IT STARTED IN THE U.S.

It is necessary to set the scene for Shaw's play. Melosh writes: 'most historians since 1945 have overlooked, misinterpreted, or under-estimated the intensity and breadth of antiwar feeling between the World Wars'. The period saw a flowering of US peace organisations from a wide range of sensibilities: conservative, socialist, communist, religious and women's organisations thrived. One particularly active group was the American Student Union; thousands of young men in colleges and universities, at risk of being sent to war, were considering their beliefs. When Japan invaded Manchuria in 1931, a new urgency entered the peace movement. By 1936, with the outbreak of the Spanish Civil War and heightened tensions elsewhere in the world, many left-wing supporters, including the young Irwin Shaw, moved to an anti-fascist stance.

In this period, while antiwar sentiment strengthened as the threat of fascism became more widespread, forms of political protest also flowered in the US theatre. Tensions between ideologically motivated work and box-office success meant that there was no uniform approach. In her study of US political theatre, Ilka Saal examines this topic, noting Theatre Union works that consciously integrated dialectics with the populism of melodrama. Charles Walker and others established Theatre Union, New York's first professional workers' theatre group, in 1933. It was 'not simply looking for socially-conscious scripts but for good plays with a revolutionary point of view'.

New York stages hosted a number of antiwar plays with varying political and aesthetic approaches in the early 1930s. In 1931, the Theatre Guild produced Julian Lee's translation of Austrian playwright Hans Chlumberg's 1930 work *Miracle at Verdun*. It focuses on a group of German and French soldiers who rise from their war graves, 20 years after the war's beginning, and return to their former lives. Disgusted at the unwelcome response they get from their family and friends, they return to their graves. Presenting the play, with its many scene changes and a triple-screen sound film accompaniment, turned out to be 'a costly flop', with audiences 'not strongly attracted to the pessimistic view of war' and 'its insistence upon an unpalatable theme'.

In *Men Must Fight*, by Reginald Lawrence and S. K. Lauren, the USA is at war with Uruguay in the near future. Disputes over pacifism tear a loyal US family apart. The following year, Theatre Union staged *Peace on Earth*, by George Sklar and Albert Maltz, as its opening production. With a large cast (29 actors took on 73 speaking parts), the realistic drama shows the conversion of a liberal professor to antiwar, pro-worker militancy; it highlights the profit motive as a cause of war. Mainstream reviewers thought that it smacked too much of propaganda. In the Theatre Guild's *If This Be Treason*, by John Haynes Holmes and Reginald Lawrence, a newly elected, pacifist US President urges the Japanese Government not to declare war. Himelstein regards Robert Sherwood's play *Idiot's Delight*, with its 'realistic, but not yet hopeless vision of the coming war' as 'the first successful antiwar play of the decade'. It received the Pulitzer Prize soon after the Theatre Guild opened its 300-performance run. The Group Theatre's only musical, as well as 'the only Group play that turned away from naturalism in all its elements', Paul Green and Kurt Weil's *Johnny Johnson*, featured a hopeful young soldier who tries to stop the next war – and temporarily succeeds. And the last of the pre-World War II antiwar plays, *The Ghost of Yankee Doodle*, by Sidney Howard, presents the efforts of a pacifist family to keep their beliefs intact amid the opportunity to sell arms to Japan.

These organisations maintained a network of connections through shared scripts, members and interests; another in this network was the League of Workers' Theatres, established in 1931 and becoming the NTL in 1935, changing its focus from class struggle to antiwar and anti-fascism. Describing itself as 'America's only anti-fascist, progressive federation of theatres', the organisation was active until 1942. It did much to foster workers', left-wing and 'little' theatre groups throughout the USA. The NTL had rapidly embraced popular front politics, and their choice of plays and activities reflected the need to unite people of many classes. While they worked closely with peace groups, not all NTL plays were antiwar; their most prominent works used theatre for political awareness and change in a number of areas. These works include the strike play *Waiting for Lefty*, by Clifford Odets; the German agitprop work *Tempo Tempo*, which critiqued the speed of capitalist industry; and the militant opera *The Cradle Will Rock*, by Marc Blitzstein, which rose to some prominence after winning an NTL play competition. Of the many plays associated with the NTL, the antiwar work *Bury the Dead* is one of the few still produced.

In 1935, in conjunction with the American League Against War and Fascism, NTL held a contest for antiwar and anti-fascist plays. The first prize of $125 was a strong inducement for entrants. One was a young Brooklyn writer, Irwin Shaw. Just 23 years old, 'left-leaning' Shaw had been writing for radio for a couple of years, including scripts for *Dick Tracy*. He had an offer from the Group Theatre to stage his one-act play, *Bury the Dead*, but not immediately. Harold Clurman, from the Group Theatre (which later produced Shaw's works) suggests that Shaw wanted 'an immediate production'. His play missed the contest's deadline; but the NTL's Ben Irwin was thrilled with the play and offered to help fund its performance as an NTL benefit.

Shaw's play had also enthused Theatre Union writer George Sklar. In 1935, Theatre Union were producing Brecht's antiwar play *The Mother*, but it had been widely rejected by critics as being too emotionally distant; after it was 'keelhauled by even the left-wing press', it was replaced in December by *Let Freedom Ring* (adapted by Albert Bein from the Grace Lumpkin novel *To Make My Bread*), to which audiences turned 'with something like relief' for 10 weeks. While this last work was still playing, Sklar brought *Bury the Dead* to Theatre Union. They were immediately enthusiastic and began rehearsing it.

Bury the Dead presents the story of six soldiers, killed on a battlefield, who refuse to be buried. Within an episodic structure of many short scenes in one long act, the play presents the arguments of their fellow soldiers, their army leaders, their priests and rabbis and their womenfolk that they should lie down and be buried, but they refuse. Of all the antiwar plays produced in this period, it is the only one not to explicitly reference World War I, being 'a play about the war that is to begin tomorrow night'. It also passes over specific arguments against the profiteering nature of war; its 'vague but powerful suggestion that outraged nature will tolerate war no longer' was to play a large part in the work's longevity. Shaw humanises the dead soldiers, referring to their lives before they went to war and their reasons for protesting against war. While it is clear that the origins of the resurrected soldiers lie in *Miracle at Verdun*, Shaw's dead soldiers do not return to the grave, as Chlumberg's do; rather, they stride out into the world of the living 'like men who have business that must be attended to in the not too pressing future'. *Bury the Dead* has earned the descriptions 'poetic, expressionist' and 'bitterly absurdist'. A later study of antiwar dramas found that *Bury the Dead* 'was the one play critics of varied political persuasions agreed had an undiluted antiwar impact'.

The Let Freedom Ring Company mounted the first production of *Bury the Dead* on 14 and 15 March 1936 at the 46th Street Theatre. Writing in the communist journal *New Masses*, drama critic Stanley Burnshaw praised Shaw for contributing:

> to the antiwar movement its most moving one-act drama. But this was something more than precise embodiment of a protest. **Bury the Dead** provided two satisfactions for which people have been hungering: poetry and passion... Shaw remakes the Chlumberg device of despair into a passionate song of hope.

The second night was standing room only. After the instant success of those first performances, whetting appetites, the Theatre made a few changes. Producer Alex Yokel was happy to fund the play's move on to Broadway with enhanced production qualities. After a last-minute change of venue from the Fulton Theatre, the play opened at the Ethel Barrymore Theatre on 18 April. It was performed by the same members of the Let Freedom Ring Company, who renamed themselves the Actor's Repertory Company. *Prelude*, by J. Edward Shugrue and John O'Shaughnessy, accompanied the play. There were 97 performances in its first commercial run.

Reviews of the Broadway season were, like the first two-night tryout, very positive. The *Partisan Review* acclaimed it as 'an immediate sensation'. One mainstream reviewer, Robert Garland, wrote:

> nobody has seen fit to deny that Mr. Shaw's is one of the most stirring plays ever fashioned by an American, even at the same time it is one of the most dramatically denunciatory of the antiwar, anti-munition makers, anti-jingo dramas.

More of the same was to come: 'the simplicity and honesty of Shaw's approach make it a forceful pacifist cry as well as effective theatre'. Others praised its innovative style:

Publicity for the New York production of *Bury the Dead*.

ALIVE AS TODAY'S HEADLINES!!

BURY THE DEAD

IRWIN SHAW'S STARTLING ANTI WAR PLAY

John Mason Brown, N. Y. Post: "Bury the Dead is the most moving and eloquent diatribe against the inanities of war which our theatre has yet known. Compared to it Mr. Sherwood's 'Idiot's Delight' in spite of all its manifest excellences stands in about the same relationship that Harry Richman does to Hamlet."

Brooks Atkinson, N. Y. Times: "A shattering bit of theatre magic that burrows under the skin of argument into the raw flesh of sensation."

Robert Garland, N. Y. World-Telegram: Irwin Shaw has uttered a protest against war which says in one scene what Miracle in Verdun failed to say in seven."

Arrange for an **XMAS** Production Immediately!

Write to the
NEW THEATRE LEAGUE, 132 West 43rd St., New York
ROYALTIES $25 PERFORMANCE
RANDOM HOUSE EDITION $1.00
Write for free 1939-1940 play catalogue

248

Mr Shaw's grimly imaginative rebellion against warfare is a shattering bit of theatre magic that burrows under the skin of argument into the raw flesh of sensation.

It packs into its long one act more cold contempt for battles and generals and the dim complacency of man than a hundred tracts issued violently by the societies against war and fascism.

Garland wrote:

Other men, other plays, have told of war's futility and horror and venality of cause. But no play, in my memory, has spoken with such well-directed vehemence.

There were comparisons with *Miracle of Verdun*; Bergun Evans later wrote:

> Shaw's play was more sombre in its tone, his dead more passionate in their regrets, and the suggestion of hope in its conclusion, however vague and romantic, more exciting.

There were some hesitations. Arthur Pollock wrote that the play:

> has a nice idea, but its author writes it in pretty commonplace fashion. You will hear only flat talk at the Ethel Barrymore, where his play is now to be seen, and you will not always admire the dramatist's resources. But it is really a good notion.

While Brooks Atkinson praised the play as 'the most tormenting war play of the year', he also wrote in the *New York Times*:

> If *Miracle at Verdun* had never been written, the primary assumption of *Bury the Dead* might be a more devastating stroke of imagination in the contemporary theatre.

That month, knowing that they had a hit on their hands, NTL published the text of the play in their journal *New Theatre*. The play's success and speedy publication was timely: the Spanish Civil War would soon erupt; fascism continued to rise in Germany; and political events were drawing closer to the outbreak of world war. According to Irwin, with his emphasis on attracting students:

> This play should not only harrow those who witness it: it should affect their lives. That is frankly its purpose. If it can draw new masses of people into the militant struggle being waged against the forces of militarism by such organizations as the American League Against War and Fascism and the American Student Union, it will have fulfilled the prime aim of its young author. *Bury the Dead* should stir two particular classes of people

to action: the students, and all those who depend on their own labor, manual or otherwise, for their living. Their lives and labor will be forfeit in the next war. To the American students and the American workers of all classes and professions, who will be uniting in antiwar strikes and demonstrations throughout the country this month, New Theatre brings Irwin Shaw's play, in the hope that it will be acted, seen and read by hundreds of thousands in the coming months.

The publication of the script was a boon. Just one month after it premiered, a large audience of 1,200 people attended a Hollywood reading of the play by Frederick March and his wife, Florence Eldridge. At the Hollywood Women's Club after the reading, 'the crowd heatedly discussed domestic issues, fascism, the Ethiopian conflict, and the possibility of a European war'. The pro-communist Hollywood Anti-Nazi League organised the event, which attracted high-profile pacifists, including James Cagney and Groucho Marx.

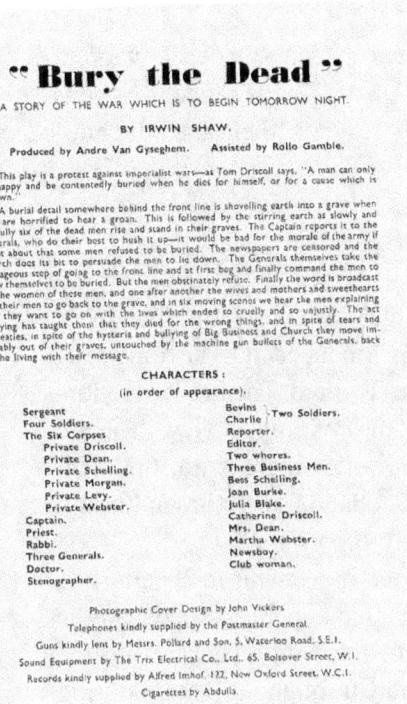

London Unity Theatre program.

Screenwriter Donald Ogden Stewart led the discussion after the reading. 'Thank God', Stewart said to the crowd, 'that that play has been written'. The Hollywood event advantaged this new, and stylistically experimental, work of social engagement, bringing it widespread media attention. 'All the stars', recalled Clurman, 'were burning to finance it and play in it'.

Requests for the play soon spread. NTL had affiliations from 31 theatres across the USA, many connected to trade unions, others community or 'little' theatres. While the earlier success of *Waiting for Lefty* had spurred many of these groups to continue their work, many had not announced their plans for the coming season because they were awaiting the release of the rights to *Bury the Dead*, which they knew would prove to be as big a success as *Lefty*. Then, in July that year, New Theatre announced:

> All amateur and New Theatre groups, and summer theatres should be interested in hearing that production rights to Irwin Shaw's *Bury the Dead* are now available for almost every community.

Through their established network, NTL had a ready-made network of venues to promote Shaw's play throughout the USA. A wide range of groups performed it, particularly college and university troupes: their antiwar sentiment was high, and the cast size was large.

TRANSNATIONAL REACH

Bury the Dead broadened its reach outside the USA, firstly in September 1936, when the Montreal New Theatre Group produced it. The following month, David Pressman staged the play at the Toronto Theatre of Action. Other Canadian theatres followed, including the Winnipeg New Theatre and Vancouver's Progressive Arts Players. The following month, the NTL claimed: 'from all over the world – England, Scotland, Australia and South America – come requests for production rights to *Bury the Dead*'.

As in North America and Australia, the peace movement in Britain was strong in the 1930s, with over 50 peace organisations operating between the wars; peace plays were in demand. Branches of the Unity Theatre and the Left Book Club Theatre Group performed the play throughout Britain during 1938 and 1939, with success; the London Unity Theatre staged a popular six-week run. Unity wrote that the play: 'discussed the problem of war in its very widest aspects in a way which the established playwright had so far feared to attempt'.

In Australia, the antiwar movement also flourished. There were local branches of the MAWF, World Disarmament Movement, Women's International League of Peace and Freedom, the Australian Union of Democratic Control for the Avoidance of War, the International Peace Campaign, the League of Nations Union, the Women's Service Guild, the Women's Christian Temperance Union, the ALP's Antiwar Committee, the United Christian Peace Movement and the Peace Pledge Union. Australian left-wing cultural organisations established in the early 1930s under the influence of the CPA followed British and US models and included theatre groups.

Although New Theatre branches in Australia produced classical plays, contemporary industrial and political situations were often the inspiration for scripts. In some periods, antiwar plays were popular. Producing overseas plays underscored the transnational connections of Australia's New Theatre. Studies of the US New Theatre League and Britain's Unity Theatre have demonstrated that radical theatre sought to develop cultural activism locally and also to embody the broader aims and aspirations of an international working-class theatre movement. The Australian groups were no exception – and these were the only Australian theatres to stage *Bury the Dead*.

The first theatre to stage *Bury the Dead* outside North America was the Perth WAG, with Keith George producing a 10-night season in November 1936. A local critic wrote in the mainstream press:

> as an example of a significant movement in contemporary drama, besides the strong interest of its subject, the manner of its staging, and the enthusiasm of its acting, it is well worth seeing.

Even the conservative *Australian Women's Weekly* gave the unusual work some column inches, branding the play 'virile and provocative' and the performance of one of the actors, Phyllis Harnett, as 'outstanding'. One of the Perth group's founders, writer Katharine Susannah Prichard, had a history of correspondence with NTL's Irwin Shaw; the play probably found its way to Perth through this.

Sydney NT had received the script in early November 1936 (probably through a request from the Sydney Secretary Vic Arnold). They evaluated it highly: 'a short play of an extraordinary type and is perhaps the finest that has come to Australia'. However, they did not produce it until 21 and 22 April 1937, with Jerold Wells directing. It was a big project, in preparation for months and financed through performances and donations. A public subscription list – not unlike a modern-day crowdfunding project – was opened, and 'the value of the play itself is considered to give full justification to this policy'. The Sydney Conservatorium was the venue, because the cast of 40 was unable to fit on to the NT's own modest stage at 36 Pitt Street. Among the cast were author Kylie Tennant and 'the witch of Kings Cross', Rosaleen Norton. Word of this play and its popular Stateside presentations had spread through Sydney's left-wing and artistic circles, and *Workers' Weekly* forecast that the production would be 'the most important theatrical event in Sydney for a long time'.

The presentation achieved 'notable success'. It 'excited a good deal of discussion' and was 'probably the most remarkable and compelling play seen in Australia'. NT historian Lyn Collingwood records: 'at the end of the play audience members were so moved that they stood on their seats and threw their hats in the air'. The play was the reason why: 'by its production the NT still further increased its prestige'. Arrow believes that the performances of

Ian Smith, Assistant Director in Perth, with model stage.

the work, coming soon after *Waiting for Lefty* and *Till the Day I Die*, 'further consolidated Sydney NT's growing reputation for politically progressive, deeply affecting theatre'. Sydney NT publicists argued for the work's wider circulation, claiming it as 'a drama that cries out to be produced everywhere in a war-clouded world' and declaiming that 'such a play should be a property of the whole working class'. A critic from the respected *Australian Quarterly* agreed that it was 'a very effective stage production' and concluded: 'in short, the production is among the best Sydney has seen.' NT Member Simon Bracegirdle believed that it was an 'enormously impressive play', noting that it was 'antiwar, not specifically anti-fascist' – an important distinction, given the politics of the time. For another member, Oriel Gray, the plays the NT had been performing up to now were:

> passionate in their political sincerity, but poor stuff compared to *Bury the Dead*...[it was] like no drama we had ever seen or imagined.

NT staged a second 1937 season in September. Cutting and pasting from the US *New Theatre* editorial of the previous year, in an indication of internationalist sentiment (which was CPA and popular front policy at the time), the playbill added its hope that:

> this play should not only harrow those who witness it; it should affect their lives. That is frankly its purpose. If it can draw new masses of people into the militant struggle being waged against the forces of militarism by such organisations as the Movement against War and Fascism, and the World Peace Committee, it will have fulfilled the prime aim of its young author. In view of the tragic poignancy of war, its utter waste and destruction of all ideals, we, as individuals, and as a progressive cultural organisation, strenuously support the struggle for world peace. That is why we have thrown everything we possess into the production.

A wide range of journals reviewed the play. The *Anglican Church Standard* judged it: 'an unusually powerful exposure of the waste and bestiality of war and the hollowness of much that calls itself "patriotism"':

> In Sydney, for example, no organisation is doing more for the cause of peace than the New Theatre... the message of the play as we saw it, that both Church and State are blind to the hellishness and futility of war.

The author noted that war rewards 'the sordid trade interests of a favoured few'.

A benefit performance on 9 April 1938 was a fundraiser for the Women's Commission of International Peace Campaign. One critic noted: 'the acting, admirably varied in expression for the different characters and the degree of their relationship, uniformly reached a high level'. Another reviewer found Freda Lewis' performance 'a notable success' that 'excited a good deal of discussion'. Sydney NT produced a final season in February and March 1939.

The Brisbane Unity Theatre performed *Bury the Dead* on 3 and 4 March 1938 at the Princess Theatre, in conjunction with the Queensland Council of International Peace Campaign, staging it under their slogan: 'Peace, Freedom and Cultural Progress'. One writer reported:

> the Unity players take their work seriously, and the cast of about 50 players has turned up in full strength at rehearsals and worked for hours on end to ensure a successful production.

A critic believed that 'the play was redeemed by the production' and wrote that 'it is strong propaganda, strong drama'. Another called it 'a most arresting and convincing play, strongly pacifist in its propaganda value'.

The Brisbane group, like others, participated in a transnational flow of play scripts and ideas, both theatrical and political. Unity had affiliated with the NTL very early, in 1939, and also took British Unity Theatre scripts for production. Patricia Allen of the Brisbane group wrote to Ben Irwin in New York to report they had 'found that American plays are on the whole more popular than are British', and that this had been borne out with the success of Shaw's work in Brisbane. Group affiliations to the NTL, subscriptions to the *New Theatre* journal and personal networks facilitated the transnational movement of scripts from the USA to Australian radical theatre branches.

Brisbane Unity revived the play on 25 March 1950. The program reminded its audience of its historical significance, as well as its essential timelessness:

Poster for the Sydney 1937 production of *Bury the Dead*.

> ***Bury the Dead*** was written about 1936, between the two 'great' wars, and in common with many of the plays of the period (such as those of Clifford Odets, Elmer Rice and Albert Maltz) possesses a note of violent social protest. It bears most of the virtues and defects that were dominant in the literature of the Thirties and is consequently 'dated', yet the Thirties – with its post-war disillusionment, its depression 'blues', and its fear of a new war – is so similar in many respects to our own contemporary scene, that the play is perhaps more significant now than it was then.

The Newcastle NT staged *Bury the Dead* in July 1938. For this two-night season, Sydney's Jerold Wells travelled up to direct. Newcastle theatre-lovers received advance notice of 'this striking play' from September 1937. Joyce Batterham, a member of the Newcastle NT, recalled:

> I think our most successful play was ***Bury the Dead*** by Irwin Shaw. When we had some money together we brought Jerold Wells up from Sydney NT and paid him very little to be our producer. For this production we hired the old Lyrique Theatre for two nights and it was very successful.

Norman Clark and Joseph Smith of the Newcastle NT had travelled to Sydney to see a performance there and returned home to recommend it to their group. Pointing to an important reason for the play's persistence, Clark believed that:

> when it actually springs to life on the legitimate stage, [*Bury the Dead*] becomes one of the most vivid portrayals of life in the abstract.

Wells inspired the Novocastrian players to rehearse five nights a week. The play was so eagerly awaited that even a rehearsal was reviewed, and by a mainstream journalist:

> There is a large cast in this play, and as many as 30 may be present. Yet night after night there is a tense,

hushed atmosphere as these scenes are run through, and not infrequently there is a spontaneous burst of applause from the onlookers at the end. Scenes that will sustain such a test as this are of no ordinary merit.

The performance was congratulated in the mainstream media: 'the production of the play makes it clear that it has been rehearsed for weeks, and the lighting and technical effects are outstanding'.

Melbourne NT was next to take up *Bury the Dead*. Sydney New Theatre member Eddie Allison believed that 'in Melbourne they were more go-ahead in the working-class art stuff than we were in Sydney'; the Melbourne group speedily organised a reading in 1937, under writer-director Catherine Duncan's direction, at Judge Beeby's home. The reading was a fundraiser for of the International Peace Campaign, of which Beeby was the patron. The NT performed the play on 12 and 14 November 1938 at the Apollo Theatre. One reviewer approved, writing in the *Age*:

> Frankly propagandist, the play should nevertheless be welcomed by the serious-minded theatre-goer, for out of the propagandist element emerge a body of characters whose individuality is sharply defined in a few lines, together with situations of real dramatic value and a macabre atmosphere that grips the audience.

The *Argus* reviewer believed that:

> it has a vitality of emotion and a fierce intensity that make it one of the most significant of modern dramas. It is splendid antiwar propaganda (of which we could do with more), and it is excellent theatre.

As in Sydney, this was a play that inspired some audience members to join the Theatre. Dot Thompson recalled:

> the first play I saw was *Bury the Dead* which impressed me absolutely and I thought this is the most fantastic thing I have ever seen. So I went along and joined.

Thompson, who went on to become the Melbourne President, believed that the play 'vividly portrayed what life was about, in contrast to the drawing room comedies in the commercial theatre'.

Like Brisbane, the Melbourne New Theatre revived *Bury the Dead* in 1950, the year in which the Australian Peace Congress was held. Angela Hillel writes: 'attitudes to the left were so hostile during this period that actors' names are not recorded on the program'. Significantly, the reviewer for the Melbourne communist journal, the *Guardian*, noted:

> it is not dated; indeed we would rather wish it were not so topical in the sense that its message were no longer needed, but with atomaniacs around and Menzies beating the war drum, it's a timely revival.

The Melbourne group later staged it in May 1980, 'in an effort to revive the company's flagging spirits', at a time when the group was dwindling.

RESURRECTION AND TRANSFORMATION

A more recent Australian performance was in 2014, when Brenda Logan directed the CemeNTworx production for Darwin Community Arts. With a long association with the play, having studied it in drama school, Logan selected it because it 'seemed very relevant to the topics of the moment'. She drew the cast of 14 people from a multicultural group and says:

> we didn't treat it as an old play. We decided it was going to be set in any war in any time. It's absolutely relevant to today.

Logan's comment responds directly to Randy Gener's understanding of how theatre's cultural meanings are 'reinforced, ritualized, and naturalized by revival, repetition and performance'. Alpha Capaque, one of the Darwin performers, recalls:

> I remember thinking 'what a strange concept'...but so compelling in its simplicity. We always think about the sacrifices of a soldier when they serve, but we often forget the sacrifice of those left behind to pick up the pieces...it was gut-wrenching and disappointing

when you realise that every single day, someone somewhere would be feeling the effects of a war they never asked for.

CemeNTworx's experience, particularly because of Logan's long association with the work, points to the play's enduring appeal and continued currency. Since it was first performed, the large cast size of *Bury the Dead* has meant that the work has attracted more attention from student and amateur, rather than than professional, groups. Through the interest of successive generations of university and college staff and students, such as Logan, it continues to be popular in college and school programs.

Alongside English-language productions have been translations to other languages. In 1936, one Canadian reader of the play immediately applied to translate it into Polish for the Experimental Theatre of Warsaw, writing that 'such a play should be a property of the whole working class'. A Hungarian translation was performed in the same year, and a Yiddish version in South Africa in 1938, when German director Leo Kerz visited the creatively productive Jewish community of Johannesburg. Fabio Coen translated it into Italian in 1945. A collection of Broadway scripts included it. There have been performances in Portuguese, Slovenian, Finnish, Hebrew, German, Italian and Turkish. For their first production in 1973, the Jana Natya Manch theatre group in New Delhi staged a Bangla version of Shaw's play, *Mrityur Atit*, a number of times during the Durga Puja festival. Audiences received it 'with great enthusiasm'.

Adaptations of the play into a rich listing of genres, media and modes of performance have expanded its reach, beginning in 1937, when Cornell University ran a radio broadcast of the play. In 1963, Italian actor and puppeteer Otello Sarzi staged a version of *Seppellire i Morti* for puppets. Broadcast readings of excerpted scenes appeared particularly in the decade following the play's first performances. In the UK, the BBC broadcast a radio adaptation in 1965, and Irish state Radio Éireann produced another. Egypt Cultural Radio produced another adaptation, a significant resurrection given the political and cultural situation in that nation at the time. Other restaging work has moved further from the original; in 1971, a musical adaptation appeared on Broadway. *Step Lively, Boy!* by Vinnette Carroll and Micki Grant featured a multiracial cast. Ten years later, a further adaptation of *Step Lively Boy!* expanded one act into two, calling it *The Boogie-Woogie Rumble of a Dream Deferred*. And, in a most unusual turn, the National Technical Institute for the Deaf's dance company adapted *Bury the Dead* for a dance performance in 1984. A more recent musical adaptation is the 2015 Italian *Diglielo a Tutti* at the Teatro di Milano, with Paolo Barillari directing. The show acknowledged its debt to Shaw's work, with the 'clear and unambiguous' message to 'stop the war everywhere'.

We can see how restaging and resetting the play has brought fresh resonances to new audiences. In 2005, Canadian group Artists against War staged an international simultaneous reading of the play as a protest against the conflict in Iraq, a revival of the play that spanned continents: theatre groups in the USA, Singapore and elsewhere took part. In turn, the Subversive Theatre of Buffalo took up this revival for a performance; they believed that, even in 2005, the play 'delivers a chilling and powerful indictment against war that seems all too relevant to issues in the world today'. With its continued performances in the education sector and its translations and adaptations, the play remains attractive and relevant to contemporary audiences, not only in the nation of its origin. Recent revivals and adaptations have often chosen to double up roles, drastically reducing cast numbers.

Smiley has written that *Bury the Dead* 'stands as one of the most effectively persuasive antiwar plays of its length ever written.' Since its first productions in New York in 1936, the play has served as a tool for moral protest and social commentary. Shaw's biographer wrote: 'Shaw's play was more than a drama now; it was an international symbol of the peace movement'. This chapter contends that three reasons can account for the play's continuing life. Firstly, Shaw's deliberate moves to set his work in an unnamed war – knowing that there will always be wars – and to cast his characters as men and women whose pleasures and pains are still wholly recognisable in a number of cultural contexts allow the play to keep its relevance. Next, the inclusion of the US college and university sector in the antiwar movement of the 1930s has allowed generations of the academe to maintain the work's circulation to the present time. And, lastly, as we can see with the discussion of adaptations and reinventions, relocating the play into different contexts has continued the work's popularity. Because *Bury the Dead* does not refer to any specific war or battlefield, as do other 1930s antiwar plays, it keeps its relevance; one reviewer of a 2008 production wrote that 'the angry, searing pacifist drama feels as up-to-date and urgent as an incoming text message'.

FURTHER READING

Arrow, Michelle, *Upstaged: Australian Women Dramatists in the Limelight at Last*, Sydney, Currency Press, 2002.

Denning, Michael, *The Cultural Front: the Laboring of American Culture in the Twentieth Century*, London, Verso, 1997.

Goldstein, Malcolm, *The Political Stage: American Drama and Theater of the Great Depression*, New York, Oxford University Press, 1974.

Himelstein, Morgan, *Drama was a Weapon: the Left-Wing Theatre in New York, 1929–1941*, Westport, Greenwood Press, 1976.

Mally, Lynne, 'Inside a Communist Front: a Post-Cold War Analysis of the New Theatre League', *American Communist History*, vol. 6, no. 1, 2007, pp. 70–78.

McDermott, Douglas, 'The Theatre Nobody Knows: Workers' Theatre in America, 1926–1942', *Theatre Survey*, vol. 6, no. 1, 1965, pp. 65–82.

Saal, Ilka, *New Deal Theater: the Vernacular Tradition in American Political Theater*, New York, Palgrave Macmillan, 2007.

Shaw, Irwin, *Bury the Dead*, New York, Random House, 1936.

Williams, Jay, *Stage Left*, New York, Charles Scribner, 1974.

Encore

**A Musical as Warm as
a Handshake**

Melbourne, 1960

Programme

Melbourne, 1960

REEDY

by Dick Diamond
With acknowledgment to JOSEPH FURPHY AND GEORGE FARWELL

ACT 1   Scene 1:   Night. A bullocky's camp on Brodie's run, near Reedy River township.
         Scene 2:   Next morning. Reedy River pub.

ACT 2   Following day. Outside the Shearer's hut on Brodie's run.

ACT 3   Scene 1:   A few days later. The night of the dance at Reedy River Schoolhouse.
         Scene 2:   On the track to the pub.
         Scene 3:   Reedy River pub.

THE ACTION TAKES PLACE IN THE EARLY 1890's

A NEW THEATRE PRODUCTION Directed by Patrick Barnett

ORCHESTRA - Overture - Arranged and orchestrated by Adrian Bartak

Piano	Janet Laurie
Violins	Victoria Blank and Jonathan Hicks
Cellos	Margaret Goding and Janet Spink
Oboe	Adrian Bartak
Flute	Vivienne Spink
Clarinet	John Laurie
Bassoon	Philip Smith
Percussion	Hymie Slade
Piano Accompaniment	Leah Healy and Margaret Smith

CHOREOGRAPHY - Rae Dowdle   **MUSICAL ADVISER** - Nancy Laurie
STAGE MANAGER - Pauline Bulter   **COSTUME DESIGNER** - Nicki Munro
SET DESIGN - Vane   **SET CONSTRUCTION** - George Cunningham
PROPS - Len Harper - Frank Butson
COSTUMES - Kath Hawkins, Rose Stone, Moina Hall, Beverly Cunningham, Eileen Edson.

New Theatre wishes to thank the many friends who have assisted in various ways with this production.

RIVER

CHARACTERS
(in order of appearance)

DIXON	Bullock Driver	Ocker Hall
ALF	" "	Mick Hurley
BILL	Shearer	Jim Buchanan
THOMO	"	Don Munro
NUGGET	"	Stephen Gray
IRISH	"	Len Dowdle
BLUE	"	Ron Northrope
JOE COLLINS	Bush Worker	Don Duffy
MARY	His wife	Tracy Tombs
BRODIE	A Squatter	Frank Bren
GLOVER	Brodie's Rouseabout	Bernie Hurley
BOB THE SWAGGIE		Neville Lloyd
ROSE	(Barmaid at Reedy River Pub)	Rivka Pile
MISS ANDREWS	Schoolteacher	Loretta Garvey
ELDERLY CHARACTER		Frank Butson
WIDGEEGOWEERA JOE	Farmer	John Mitchell
JIM		Cliff Ball

SINGERS   Betty McAllister, Barbara Lloyd, Merle Lamb, Ken Mooney, Bert Gibson.

DANCERS   Wendy Hoy, Coralie Fahey, Valerie Hunter.

BUSH BAND Bert Cameron, Mouth Organ, Don Hall, Accordian. Bert Thompson, Mandolin. Cliff Ball, Banjo. Wal Lotocki, Guitar. Anthony Lamb, Bush Bass. Jim Buchanan, Lagerphone.

Melbourne, 1956.

Sydney, 1953 or 1954.

Brisbane

Garth Gifford, Brisbane

Bob Burns, Brisbane

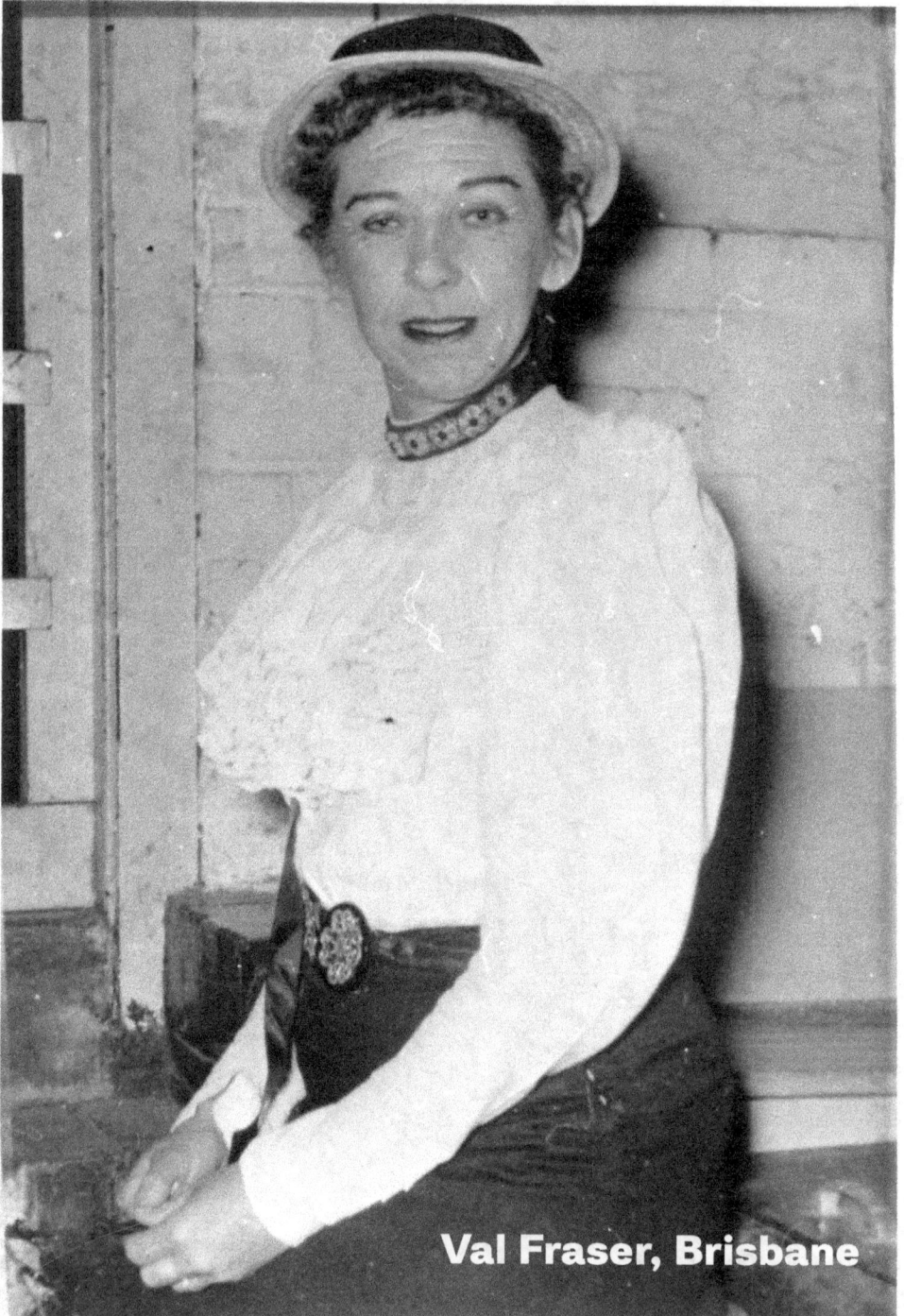

Bob the Swaggie, sketch by Herbert McClintock, 1963

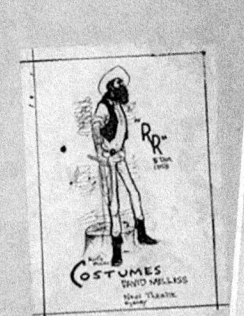

Costume designs by David Milliss.

Sydney
c. 1870.

Sydney.
December 1870.

JOE

ALSO DANCER
NO LEGGINGS

ADD LEGGINGS

SAME COLOUR TROUSERS AT ALL TIMES.

MARY

Alec Robertson and June Cairns as Joe and Mary, Sydney, 1953

Sydney: Marty O'Neill, Jim Dempsey, Michael Adam Smith, 1988

Melbourne, 1953.

Sydney, 2002

A Musical as Warm as a Handshake

Lisa Milner

By far the most successful performance for the Australian New Theatre was Dick Diamond's musical *Reedy River*. It showed at all of the New Theatre sites, elsewhere in Australia and overseas. The work originated in Melbourne, as O'Brien explains in Chapter 3. The indomitable Dot Thompson coordinated its launch into the world; at the end of 1952, she approached Dick Diamond to write the script after earlier submitted scripts proved unsuitable. Diamond acknowledged the role played by John Gray, a New Theatre actor and director who first interested him in the idea of producing a musical from some Australian folk songs that he had collected.

The music came mostly from these, although Diamond and Miles Maxwell wrote two new songs. A 16-year-old musician, Chris Kempster, a founding member of the Sydney-based Bushwhackers, set Henry Lawson's poem *Reedy River* to music for the title tune. Doreen Bridges wrote the music for *The Ballad of 1891*, for which Helen Palmer had written the lyrics in 1950. Unity Dancers, the Margaret Walker Dancers, the Wattle Dance Group and other troupes took on the choreography. Thompson said that the work:

> has been successful because it is Australian in character, is entertaining and expresses a struggle easily recognised through typical characters. The way in which Joe shows his mates how to build the union after the 1891 strike is an object lesson for many people today.

It opened in Melbourne in March 1953, with the Flinders Street theatre packed to capacity every night for weeks. A small orchestra led by Miles

Maxwell provided the music. O'Brien's chapter relates its popularity. The Melbourne group revived it and also organised extensive tours to country areas. Katharine Susannah Prichard was 'thrilled' by the Melbourne production:

> [It] gives an old form a new and Australian significance. It is in the genre of musical comedy but comedy with a purpose. Who ever heard of such a thing? The purpose is to preserve democratic traditions of our people in a story of true love and adventure around the Shearers' Strike, with extracts from literature, poetry, songs and dances of the period. An authentic atmosphere has been achieved. The zest and gaiety of the players creates a delightful entertainment; but I was thrilled, most of all, by the Australianity of the production.

Lyn Collingwood notes, earlier in this book, that the Sydney New Theatre was desperately looking for funds to rent new premises at the end of 1953, but 'a month later, the smash hit *Reedy River* turned everything around'. The Bushwhackers, with John Meredith, Cecil Grivas, Alex Hood, Harry Kay, Chris Kempster and Stan Arthur, inspired by the 1950s folk music revival, were founded in 1952; Sydney NT invited them to perform in the new musical in Sydney. One of the cast members, Silvia Salisbury, recalled:

> the opening night of *Reedy River* was abuzz with excitement, not nerves, for we knew we had a success on our hands. The foyer was decorated with the wonderful reproductions of the Holterman photos of the goldfields of the 1870s whose negatives on glass had recently been discovered. The usual run of a show at New Theatre in those days was 8–10 weeks but *Reedy River,* with its theme and songs, struck such a chord in the people who came to see it, and the strength of 'word-of-mouth' publicity, that the season was extended to nine months with changes of cast and extra performances added.

The Sydney New Theatre performed it not only in the city, but also in suburban and regional NSW venues. They have revived it many times since, at least up to 2002. Sydney New Theatre Secretary Miriam Hampson used to say, 'when in doubt, do *Reedy River*'. Norma Disher said that Diamond had produced 'this experience that brought in our shearers and it was loaded with wonderful tunes that everybody could sing – this incredible bush music'. The music was, indeed, widely popular; people would learn the songs and come again and again to join in the singing. When the 1969 Sydney revival was about to begin, producer and original cast member John Thompson said:

> I was a bit worried at first about how it would go over today with young people who'd never seen it before. But the response has been staggering. People have literally been flocking to get in it, and we just couldn't fit them all in the cast. I think its charm and simplicity and freshness are going to make a big impact, just as it did in 1953.

Elsewhere, New Theatre branches had similar successes with this work, which generally played to capacity audiences. Popular demand enabled revivals, and theatres made great financial returns: Brisbane in 1954 through to 1960, Perth in 1954, Newcastle in 1954–57. In Adelaide, Douglas writes that the first season opened at the grand old Australia Theatre on Angas Street. It was then remounted for a number of individual organisations before a return season, staged at Stow Hall on Flinders Street. One of the original cast members, Rex Munn, still remembered the words of his songs by heart when Jo White, the director of the 2002 revival, asked him to a rehearsal.

June Grivas wrote an ode to the success of the musical:

> *Some people they like Homer, others they like Shaw*
>
> *And others like the 'classics', I could name 'em by the score.*
>
> *Some people they like 'epics' crammed full of blood and lust*
>
> *While others go quite drooly over Marilyn Monroe's bust.*
>
> *But me, I like the stories of Australia land*
>
> *Of the pioneers, the shearers and the gallant Eureka Band.*
>
> *I'm not the only one, there's at least 10 million more*
>
> *So just give us **Reedy River** and the Eumerella Shore.*

In Wollongong, the Port Kembla Workers' Federation Delegates Committee organised a performance to raise money for the Pensioners' Christmas Dinner Fund. The performance at the Granville RSL Hall attracted calls for three encores. The Melbourne branch presented *Reedy River* at the Melbourne Repatriation Hospital in 1955. They also had special performances of this popular play as benefits for striking meat workers of the Butchers' Union. Requests came from factories, rural and regional localities and country towns. In one memorable performance, the Emerald Progress Association staged a 'drive-in' theatre experience; they 'built a stage at the end of a football field and the audience drove their cars on to the oval'. When the Chinese Classical Opera Company visited Australia in December 1956, Brisbane New Theatre combined with other groups in presenting a cultural program. New Theatre's contribution was a presentation from *Reedy River* for the Peking cast at the 4BH Studio Auditorium in Adelaide Street. Many theatres outside the New Theatre family, including Cairns, Darwin, Mullumbimby and Wollombi, have staged the musical. It has also appeared at the National Folk Festival and in schools and halls throughout Australia.

Audiences through the decades greeted the play's depiction of the 1981 shearers' strike, with both union and personal ramifications, with enthusiasm. It not only fulfilled New Theatre's mission to present issues with a radical message; it also used broad themes and rousing songs to attract a wide audience. The bush ballads and poems, which leading folk musicians and bush bands in the 1950s set to music, were popular. Many songs had not been in general use since the 1890s. Douglas notes, in Chapter 8 in this volume: 'more than anything, it was the revival of this popular Australian music tradition which helped *Reedy River* achieve its nationwide success'. Writer Miles Franklin was moved by the 'rousing old choruses of my infancy – I'd forgotten how good those old tunes were'. The success of the musical was just one element influencing the establishment of the Bush Music Club in 1954.

On his Diaphon recording of numbers from the Sydney show, Ken Hannam, Diaphon's Managing Director, said: 'In *Reedy River* you will meet living people, squatters, barmaids, country schoolmarms, shearers, and, of course the eternal lovers'. Peter Hamilton, founder of Wattle Records and Wattle Films, also recorded audio and film versions of some of the songs. And there have been many editions of the *'Reedy River' Song Book*.

In Australia, over 500,000 people have seen *Reedy River*, and it has long been credited with bringing mainstream audiences to the New's theatres. However, there were hitches along the way. Ashfield Council banned New

Theatre's first production in the 1950s. 'They banned it not because of the material itself, but because New Theatre was staging it,' says Lyn Collingwood. And the Wollongong branch of the Arts Council refused to sponsor a production of the play because of its subject matter.

Overseas, London's Unity Theatre hailed *Reedy River* as 'the perfect people's musical'. Its use of the lagerphone, 'a remarkable instrument consisting of a broomstick loosely covered with beer-bottle tops, agitated by a toothed wooden bow' impressed London audiences. Acclaimed singer and political activist Paul Robeson went home from his 1960 visit to Australia with a souvenir record of *Reedy River*.

The Sydney New Theatre performed *Reedy River* at the World Youth Festival in Warsaw in 1955, after raising funds to send Diamond; one performance of songs from the play was at the wharf, with NT friends farewelling Diamond on the *Neptunia*. It was staged in London, at the Unity Theatre and the Little Theatre Club, and in Montreal. Radio Warsaw has broadcast it in Polish and Radio Moscow in Russian.

FURTHER READING

Diamond, Dick, *Reedy River*, Richmond, Heinemann Educational Australia, 1970.

Diamond, Dick, *Reedy River: the Australian Bush Musical*, Sydney, Currency Press, 1988.

Acronyms and Abbreviations

ABC	Australian Broadcasting Commission
ACDM	Australian Culture Defence Movement
ACTU	Australian Council of Trade Unions
AEU	Amalgamated Engineering Union
Agitprop	agitational propaganda
ALP	Australian Labor Party
APG	Australian Performing Group
ARU	Australian Railways Union
ASIO	Australian Security Intelligence Organisation
AWU	Australian Workers Union
BUP	Bristol Unity Players (UK)
CEMA	Council for the Encouragement of Music and the Arts (Australia)
CIB	Commonwealth Investigation Branch
CPA	Communist Party of Australia
CPGB	Communist Party of Great Britain
FSU	Friends of the Soviet Union (Australia)
ILP	Independent Labour Party
IWW	Industrial Workers of the World
JCCFAS	Jewish Council to Combat Fascism and Antisemitism
JYTL	Jewish Youth Theatre League (Australia)
KSP	Katharine Susannah Prichard

MAWF	Movement Against War and Fascism
NT	New Theatre
NTL	New Theatre League
RSL	Returned and Services League
RWG	Realist Writers Group
UWA	University of Western Australia
UWM	United Worker's Movement
WAC	Workers' Arts Club
WAG	Workers' Art Guild
WAT	Workers' Art Theatre
WATG	Workers' Art Theatre Group
WDL	Workers' Drama League
WEA	Workers' Educational Association
WIR	Workers International Relief
WLT	Workers' Laboratory Theatre (USA)
WTG	Workers' Theatre Group
WTM	Workers' Theatre Movement (UK)
WWF	Waterside Workers' Federation

ABBREVIATIONS

NAA	National Archives of Australia
NLA	National Library of Australia
NT	New Theatre, Sydney
SLNSW	State Library of NSW

Image Credits

Every effort has been made to trace copyright holders, but the publisher welcomes contact from anyone with a query.

All artists are unknown unless otherwise stated. All sources given as from a collection are reproduced with permission from the owner of the collection.

Facing p. 1   Reproduced with the permission of NT

p. 3   Reproduced with the permission of NT.
p. 12   *Unity Theatre Handbook*, THM/9/4/6/3, Unity Theatre Records, Victoria and Albert Museum
p. 23   Bristol Unity Players' Club Archives, Modern Records Centre, University of Warwick
p. 35   Box 13, Unity Theatre Records, Working Class Movement Library, Salford
p. 40   Reproduced with the permission of Special Collections Research Center, Syracuse University Libraries.
p. 46   United Automobile Workers of America, District 65 Photographs Collection, Tamiment Library, New York University
p. 60   James Cook University Special Collections, NQID 13768
p. 64   *The Labor Daily,* 29 July 1932, p. 10
p. 72   A467, SF42_149, NAA
p. 77   ML MSS 6244, SLNSW. Reproduced with the permission of NT.
p. 78   *Tribune,* 18 January 1950, p. 5. Reproduced with the permission of the Search Foundation.

p. 94   Reproduced with the permission of Angela O'Brien and the Australian Performing Arts Collection, Arts Centre Melbourne.
p. 104 Reproduced with the permission of Angela O'Brien and the Australian Performing Arts Collection, Arts Centre Melbourne.
p. 106 Reproduced with the permission of Angela O'Brien and the Australian Performing Arts Collection, Arts Centre Melbourne.
p. 108 Reproduced with the permission of Angela O'Brien and the Australian Performing Arts Collection, Arts Centre Melbourne.
p. 110 Reproduced with the permission of Angela O'Brien and the Australian Performing Arts Collection, Arts Centre Melbourne.
p. 127 ML MSS 6244, SLNSW. Reproduced with the permission of NT.
p. 130 ML MSS 6244, SLNSW. Reproduced with the permission of NT.
p. 133 Australian performing arts programs and ephemera collection, 6775285, NAA
p. 138 ML MSS 6244, SLNSW. Reproduced with the permission of NT.
p. 146 ML MSS 6244, SLNSW. Reproduced with the permission of NT.
p. 154 *The Newcastle Sun*, 3 May 1937, p. 6
p. 156 *ABC Weekly*, 29 July 1944, p. 25
p. 164 Leaflet from the collection of Vera Deacon. Reproduced, with permission from Ross Edmonds, from *In Storm and Struggle: a History of the Communist Party in Newcastle 1920–1940*, Newcastle, self-published, 1991, p. 111.
p. 168 *Newcastle Morning Herald and Miners' Advocate*, 2 July 1938, p. 14
p. 177 ML MSS 6244, SLNSW. Reproduced with the permission of NT.
p. 178 Connie Healy Collection, Box 8, Folder 3, Acc071201, UQFL191, Fryer Library, The University of Queensland Library
p. 184 Connie Healy Collection, Box 9, Folder 3, Acc071201, UQFL191, Fryer Library, The University of Queensland Library
p. 189 Connie Healy Collection, UQFL478, Box 8, Folder 6, Acc071201, UQFL191 Fryer Library, The University of Queensland Library
p. 190 Connie Healy Collection, UQFL478, Box 8, Folder 6, Acc071201, UQFL191 Fryer Library, The University of Queensland Library
p. 200 Connie Healy Collection, Box 4, Folder 15, Acc960922, UQFL191 Fryer Library, The University of Queensland Library
p. 210 Collection of Karen Throssell
p. 214 *The West Australian*, 12 December 1936, p. 17
p. 215 *The Daily News*, 2 August 1940, p. 3

IMAGE CREDITS

p. 216   *The Daily News,* 23 April 1940, p. 9
p. 217   *The Workers' Star*, 24 June 1938, p. 4
p. 236   *The Advertiser*, 29 July 1948, p. 6
p. 244   Performing Arts Collection, Adelaide Festival Centre
p. 253   Collection of Lynne Shertock Roper
p. 254   6119, 4674, NAA
p. 260   Reproduced with the permission of NT.
p. 263   *Daily News*, 23 July 1940, p. 6
p. 264   New Theatre records, 2001.040.496, Arts Centre Melbourne, Performing Arts Collection Research Centre
p. 271   *Daily News*, 17 June 1940, p. 2
p. 274   *Pix*, 7 September 1940, pp. 26–27
p. 286   Collection of Brett Levy
p. 298   Collection of Graham Willett
p. 304   Reproduced with the permission of NT.
p. 307   Reproduced with the permission of NT.
p. 309   *The Sydney Jewish News,* 22 August 1952, p. 4
p. 316   Reproduced with the permission of NT.
p. 318   Reproduced with the permission of NT.
p. 324   Reproduced with the permission of NT.
p. 330   Reproduced with the permission of NT.
p. 333   Reproduced with the permission of NT.
p. 336   A6122, 411, NAA
p. 341   Reproduced with the permission of NT.
p. 343   Reproduced with the permission of NT.
p. 348   *The Workers' Star*, 25 August 1939, p. 4
p. 356   Reproduced with the permission of NT.
p. 366   Reproduced with the permission of NT.
p. 366   Reproduced with the permission of NT.
p. 371   Reproduced with the permission of NT.
p. 381   Reproduced with the permission of NT.
p. 382   Reproduced with the permission of NT.
p. 384   Collection of Lisa Milner
p. 400   Reproduced with the permission of NT.
p. 412   *ABC Weekly*, 28 October 1950, p. 30
p. 415   Reproduced with the permission of NT.
p. 417   A6119, 315, NAA
p. 418   Harold Ciddor. Reproduced with the permission of NT.

p. 428   ML MSS 6455, SLNSW. Reproduced with the permission of NT.
p. 436   Hayes Peoples History: Unity Theatre – Mobile Unit – 1954 (The People's Theatre) ourhistory-hayes.blogspot.comp. 443   *The Daily Telegraph*, 24 October 1942, p. 7
p. 444   Reproduced with the permission of NT.
p. 446   *Unity Theatre Call*, No 5, June 1944, p. 4
p. 450   Reproduced with the permission of NT.
p. 454   *Wireless Weekly*, 26 October 1940, p. 17
p.456   Reproduced with the permission of NT.
p. 459   A6122, 417, NAA
p. 464   Connie Healy Collection, Parcel 1, Acc090403, Acc071201, UQFL191, Fryer Library, The University of Queensland Library
p. 468   Reproduced with the permission of NT.
p. 474   Reproduced with the permission of NT.
p. 475   Reproduced with the permission of NT.
p. 478   Herbert McClintock. Reproduced with the permission of NT.
p. 487   Collection of Lisa Milner
p. 490   Artist Philip Senior; reproduced with his permission.
p. 496   New Theatre League Records, Manuscripts and Archives Division, The New York Public Library, Astor, Lenox and Tilden Foundations
p. 498   *Bury the Dead* program, THM/9/4/6/10, Unity Theatre Records, Victoria and Albert Museum
p. 502   ML MSS6244, Box 50, SLNSW. Reproduced with the permission of NT.
p. 505   Reproduced with the permission of NT.
p. 514   Collection of Judy Pile
p. 516   Collection of Judy Pile
p. 518   Collection of Ruth Taylor
p. 519   Bushwackers collection of photographs, nla.obj-147277526, NLA
p. 519   Bushwackers collection of photographs #PIC/8080/5, NLA
p. 520   Connie Healy Collection, Box 4, Folder 14, Acc960922, UQFL191, Fryer Library, The University of Queensland Library
p. 522   Connie Healy Collection, Box 4, Folder 14, Acc960922, UQFL191, Fryer Library, The University of Queensland Library
p. 523   Connie Healy Collection, Box 4, Folder 14, Acc960922, UQFL191, Fryer Library, The University of Queensland Library
p. 524   Connie Healy Collection, Box 4, Folder 14, Acc960922, UQFL191, Fryer Library, The University of Queensland Library

IMAGE CREDITS

p. 525 'Bob the Swaggie', sketch by Herbert McClintock 1963. Reproduced with the permission of NT.
p. 526 XD 843/nos. 1–26, David Milliss Collection of Papers, SLNSW
p. 528 Reproduced with the permission of NT.
p. 529 Reproduced with the permission of NT.
p. 530 Reproduced with the permission of NT.
p. 531 Angela O'Brien and the Australian Performing Arts Collection, Arts Centre Melbourne
p. 532 Reproduced with the permission of NT.

Index

1971 – A Race Odyssey (revue)	360
2KY (radio station)	76, 270, 273, 342
2SM (radio station)	383
42A And All That (NT Writers Group)	323
7:84 Theatre Company	146
Aarons, Eric	71
Aarons, Laurence	71
Abbey Theatre	48
ABC Weekly (newspaper)	138
Aboriginal National Theatre Trust	142
Aboriginal-Australian Fellowship	142
Aborigine Progressive Association	142
Aborigines League	111
According to Plan (Parsons)	323, 324
Account of the Labour and Socialist Movement, An (Bale)	30
Actor Prepares, An (book)	100
Actor's Repertory Company	495
Actors Studio	407
Actors' Equity	455, 465
ACTU Congress	450
Adams, Harvey	197
Adding Machine (Rice)	20

Adelaide Conservatorium of Music	225
Adelaide Jewish Club	239, 290, 291
Adelaide Repertory	256
Adelaide Theatre Group	242, 243
Adelaide University Students' Theatre Group	243
Adelaide University's Footlights Club	331
Adelaide Wattle Dance Group	**253**
Adshead, Kay	345, 346
Adult Education Board at UWA	226
Advertiser (Adelaide)	**236**
Advocate, The (Noah)	134
'After the Ball' (song)	326
Aftershocks (1998 film)	160
Age, The (newspaper)	119, 120, 507
Agreement of the Peoples, An (Slater)	30
AIDS Council of NSW Arts and Entertainment Award	365
Akhmatova, Anna	338
Albee, Edward	354
Albert Hall, Brisbane	179, 192
Alchemist, The (Johnson)	**286-287**
Alexander, Hal	455
Alive (Lavori)	359
All Change Here (Willis)	33, 339, **341**
All God's Chillun Got Wings (O'Neill)	33
All India Peace Council	317
All Live Colour Revue (revue)	124
All My Sons (Miller)	143, 246, 278, 354
All Ordinaries (revue)	152
All Saint's Hall, Brisbane	186, 199, 204, 313
All-Australia Congress Against War	319
Allen, Dawn	175, 177, **368-369**
Allen, John	27

INDEX

Allgood, James	291
Allison, Eddie	193, 262, 273, 291, **356-357**, 376, 388, 507
Allison, Eileen née Bullen	376, 388
Amalgamated Engineering Union [AEU]	226, 227
Amalgamated Society of Carpenters and Joiners	226
America Hurrah! (van Itallie)	123, 143, 144
American Group Theatre	96, 100
American Laboratory Theatre	39
American League Against War and Fascism	494, 497
American Student Union	497
Anastasiou, Jimmy	282
And I Still Call Home Australia (revue)	149
Anderson, Benedict	484
Anderson, Maxwell	245
Andrews Sisters	327
Angels of War (Box)	77, 160, **164**, 165, 172, 320
Anglican Church Standard (newspaper)	503
Angry Brigade, The (Graham)	152, 363
Anniversary, The (Chekhov)	247
Answer, The (booklet)	362
Anti-Fascist League	295
Antill, John	350
Anvil, The (bookshop)	238, 243
Apollo Theatre, Melbourne	100
Arbeitertheaterbund	22
Are You Ready, Comrade? (Roland)	56, 75, 215, 222, 338
Arent, Arthur	43
Argus, The (newspaper)	98, 100, 102, 294, 507
'Arise, arise ye who refuse to be born slaves' (song)	354
Aristocrats (Pogodin)	**12**

Aristophanes	328, 340, 487
Arms and the Man (Shaw)	132, 159, 173
Armstrong, Don Marie	**368-369**
Armstrong, John	297, 376, 476
Armstrong, Marie née Stonehouse	6, 150, 276, 278, 375-377, 380, 386, 389-391, 392, 394, 432, 460, 476, 480-482
Arnold, Victor (Vic)	57, 67, 78, 83, 112, 129, 132, 136, 157, 171, 219, 228-230, 240, 242, 262, 273, 291, 293, **316**, 432, 452, 455, 501
Arnstein, Marc	99
Arrow, Michelle	308
'Arthur Murray taught me Dancing in a Hurry' (song)	380
Arthur, Stan	534
Artists against War	510
Arts Council, UK	32
Arts Council Drama Festival	330
Arts Council of Australia	277, 430
Arundale Hall	225
As You Like It (Shakespeare)	247
Ascent of F6, The (Auden & Isherwood)	**236**, 246
Ashmore-Smith, Stan	146
Asmis, Rudolf	262
Assange, Julian	330
Assange, Patti	**330**, 338
Assassins (Sondheim)	151
Assembly Hall, Perth	222
Association for International Co-operation and Disarmament	317
At Last! The 1984 Show (revue)	334
Atkinson, Brooks	497

Auden, W.H.	246
Australasian Book Society	279
Australasian Post, The (newspaper)	54, 116
Australasian Society of Patriots	175
Australia Theatre, Adelaide	249
Australian Broadcasting Commission [ABC]	100, 329, 331
Australian Carnival of Youth for Peace and Friendship	141
Australian Communist Party [ACP]	49, 96, 231
Australian Council of Trade Unions	142
Australian Culture Defence Movement (ACDM)	139
Australian Education Union [AEU]	457
Australian Elizabethan Theatre Trust	118
Australian Jewish News (newspaper)	289
Australian Jewish Times (newspaper)	289
Australian Labor Party [ALP]	73, 101, 172, 223, 231, 273, 280, 342, 373, 394, 457, 500
Australian League Against Imperialism	319
Australian Left News (journal)	67, 157, 162, 171
Australian Peace Congress	115, 508
Australian Peace Council	141, 232, 317
Australian People's Disarmament Conference	317
Australian Performing Group [APG]	122, 123, 124
Australian Playwrights' Advisory Board	205
Australian Quarterly (journal)	85, 262, 503
Australian Railways Union [ARU]	156, 157, 158, 159, 175, 459
Australian Seamen's Union	**127**, 128
Australian Security Intelligence Organisation [ASIO]	5, 67, 69, 70, 71, 78, 82, 83, 140, 144, **253**, **254-255**, 256, 279, 282, 312, **336**, 377, **417**, 470

Australian Theatre News (newspaper)	292
Australian Theatrical and Amusement Employees Association	340
Australian Union of Democratic Control for the Avoidance of War	500
Australian Women's Charter Movement	337
Australian Women's Weekly (journal)	501
Australian Worker (newspaper)	452, 453, 455, 457
Australian Workers Union [AWU]	452, 455, 463, 473
Australian–Soviet Friendship League	278
Australian–Soviet Friendship Society	139
Australia-Russia & Affiliates Friendship Society	151
Awake and Sing (Odets)	31, 57, 219, 222, 290, 351
Babes in the Wood (pantomime)	27
Bacchae, The (Euripides)	147
"Backseat" (critic)	220, 222
Badger, Joseph	182
Badham, Van	346
Bailey, Frank	246
Bailey, Henry	263, 266
Bainbridge, John	113
Baker, John S.	234, 236, 237, 238, 239
Bale, Samuel	30
Ball, Macmahon	266
'Ballad of 1891, The' (song)	530
'Ballad, The' (song)	183
Bandler, Faith	142
Bandler, Hans	142
'Banks of the Condamine' (song)	248
Baracchi, Guido	75, 99, 272
Barbusse, Henri	62
Barclay, Aubrey	68
Barillari, Paolo	510

Barker, John	32
Barnard, Eileen	160, 174
Barnard, John	144
Barnard, Ken	159, 160, 172
Barnes, Frank	470
Barnett, Patrick	142
Barrachi, Guido	50, 96
Basically Black (TV)	208
Basshe, Emjo	36
Bath, Hope	230
Battarbee, Rex	199
Batterham, Joyce	86, 158, 342, 405, 505
Battye, J. S.	217
BBC (radio station)	509
Beane, Douglas Carter	364
Beasley, Jack	69, 70, 85
Beauty It Is Finished (Dann)	57
Bed-Time Story, A (George)	212
Beeby, Judge	507
Beer Garden	240
Beethoven, Ludwig van	136
Behan, Brendan	176, 333
Bein, Albert	494
Belafonte, Harry	354
Bell, James Wallace	163, 173
Bellbird (TV)	76
Bells Are Ringing, The (Willis)	339
Belvoir Downstairs	150
Bengal, Ben	26, 45, 100
Benny Hill Show, The (TV)	129
Bensusan, Inez	372
Bentley, Derek	139
Berg, David	290, 297, 328

Berkoff, Steven 124, 334
Bernard, Heinz 448
Berry, Marjorie 215, 219
Besant, Annie 342
Bessant, Bob 62, 70
Bessant, George 65
Bessie Bosch (Nikl) 322
Beste, Vernon 25, 26
Better a Millstone (Brand) 139, 424
Beynon, Richard 203
BHP 159
Bickerdike, Jack 135
Biggest Thief in Town, The (Trumbo) 120
Biko Inquest, The (Blair & Fenton) 362
Biko, Steve 362
Billets or Badges (Crawford) 182, **184-185**, 203
Biltzstein, Mark 218
Bird, Mr 268, 285
Birthday of a Miner (Martin) 137
Black Hell (Malleson) 320
Black Magic (living newspaper) 33
Blair, Jon 362
Blake, Ben 37
Blake, J. D. 69
Blake, William 152
Blankfort, Michael 132, 321
Blessings, Lee 364
Blewett, Dorothy 221
Blitzstein, Marc 494
Blood Knot (Fugard) 123
Blood on the Moon (Sifton & Sifton) 218, 219, 291, 292, 293, 294, 322, 351
Blue Blouse movement, USSR 21, 37, 44

Blue, Jean	**138**, 291, 292, 342, 346, 354, 376, 380, 381, 383
Boardman, Len	181
Bogard, Larry	484
Boilermakers' Union	453
Boissiere, Ralph de	289
Bond, Edward	124
Bonn, John E.	37
Bonner, Vera	115
Boogie-Woogie Rumble of a Dream Deferred, The (Carroll & Grant)	509
Booth, Clare	215
Booth, Laurence	312
Bootman, Bram	27
Born Loser, The (Young)	142
Borovansky Ballet Company	113
Botanic Park Labour Ring, Adelaide	241
Bottomley, William	266
Boutmy, Loretta	**78**
Bowers, Raymond	116
Box of Matches, A (Crawford)	207
Box, Muriel	165, 320
Box, Sydney	99, 160, 165, 168
Boy Comes Home, The (Milne)	319
Boys in the Band, The (Crowley)	143, 364
Bracegirdle, Simon	71, 75, 503
Brand, Mona	4, 6, 81, 82, 84, 86, 116, 122, 136, 139, 140, 142-144, 148-150, 176, 188-189, 253, 303, 331, 332, 338, 344, 350, 358, 376, 377, 380, 386, 388, 392, 406, 417, 420-425, 462, 469
Brave and the Blind, The (Blankfort)	132, **133**, 321

Brecht, Bertolt	2, 124, 159, 160, 170, 171, 322, 330, 410
Brenton, Howard	124
Brereton, Laurie	147
Bride of Gospel Place, The (Esson)	49
Bridges, Doreen	530
Bridges, Harry	354
Bridges, Tom	148, 334
Brighouse, Harold	19
Bring Me My Bow (Box)	99, 165, **168**, 169, 172
Bring the Frigates Home Coalition	150, 317
Brisbane City Council	198
Brisbane Courier-Mail (newspaper)	197, 199
Brisbane Repertory Theatre	57, 198
Brisbane Seamen's Union	195
Brisbane Trades Hall	433
Brisbane, Katharine	143, 352
Bristol Aid to Russia Council	30
Bristol Royal Theatre Appeal	30
Bristol Unity Players [BUP]	29-31
Bristol Workers' Theatre	22
British Colonial Office	205
British Drama League Festival	197
British Patriots' Propaganda association	25
Britten, Benjamin	365
Britten, Doris	159
Brockway, A. Fenner	170
Brook, Peter	14, 363
Brooks, H.	120
Broomhall, Joan	230
Brown Pelican (Sklar)	148
Brown, Bill	323, 376, 388

INDEX

Brown, Freda née Lewis	132, 263, 269, 270, 272, 273, 293, **316**, 321, 346, 376, 380, **382**, 383, 388, 455-456, 504
Brown, Paul	160
Browne, Lindsey	143
Brunswick City Council	267
Brunswick Town Hall	285
Bucklow, Jeb	113
Buckmaster, Ernst	225
Builders' Labourers' Federation [BLF]	241
Building a Character (book)	100
Building Workers' Industrial Union [BWIU]	**184-185**, 453
Bull, Hilda	49
Bullen, Pat	71, 83, 376, 380, 388
Bulletin (journal)	48
Bulls See Red, The (BUP)	29
Burgoyne, Gordon	230
Burney, Fanny	339
Burns, Bob	523
Burnshaw, Stanley B	495
Burst of Summer (Gray)	80
Bury the Dead (Shaw)	2, 27, 30, 56, 100, 102, 115, 160, 169, 175, **189**, 192, 214, 219, 247, 297, 319, 461, 487, 489-**496**, 497, **498-499**, 500-501, **502**, 503-504, **505**, 506-511
Busch, Charles	364
Bush Music Club	536
Bushwhackers Band	4, 186, 248, 249, 530, 534
Busmen (living newspaper)	27, 435
Buster (Willis)	31, 33
Butcher's Hook (Brand)	5, 207

Butchers' Union	226, 431, 536
Butterworth, Jez	152
Buzo, Alex	151, 330, 335
Cabaret (Kander & Ebb)	151
Cagney, James	498
Cairns, June	528
Call Up Your Ghosts (Cusack & Franklin)	230
Callaghan, John	57
Callanan, Frank	**316, 356-357**
Calpurnia's Claws	212
Calypso Isle (de Boissiere)	289
Campbell, Sandra	150
Campton, David	332
Can You Hear Their Voices? (Flanagan)	43
Canary (Harvey)	364
Candy Store, The (Rubin) AKA The Candy Story	431, 462, 467, **468**, 473, **474**, 475, 482
Cannibal Carnival (Hodge)	25, 53, 83, 103, 215, 222, 355, **356-357**
Canterbury, Dean of	141
Capaque, Alpha	508
Capek, Josef	20
Capek, Karel	20
Captain Pernod's Honour	212
Care Australia	150
Carlsson, Hugh	292
Carmichael, Laurie	389, 461
Carnival for Peace and Friendship	457
Caro, Jane	346
Carrion Crow (Hines & King)	363
Carroll, Kathleen	346
Carroll, Vinnette	509
Carter, Huntley	21

Casson, Lewis	20, 26
Castlereagh Hotel, Sydney	135
Catherina, St Kilda	120
Cattle King, The (Crawford)	208
Cave, The (Galitzsky)	**324**, 325
Caviar for Breakfast (Roland)	75
Council for the Encouragement of Music and the Arts [CEMA]	277, 430
CemeNTworx	508, 509
Central Hall, Melbourne	100
Centre 63, Melbourne	121
Cessnock Eagle (newspaper)	166
Chaffey, Frank	262
Chamberlain, Neville	69
Chambers, Colin	435
Changing Room, The (Storey)	364
Chant for the Mothers of the Slain Militia, The (poem)	225
Chapel Perilous, The (Hewett)	346
Chaplin, Charlie	247
Chapple, John	459
Charles, Jack	123
Charlton, Bill	147
Charlton, Conrad	217
Chekhov, Anton	48, 124, 277
Cherry Orchard, The (Chekhov)	150
Cherry, Wal	120
Cheryl Crawford	39
Chidley, William	362
Chifley, Ben	137, 280
Children of Hiroshima (1952 film)	138
China (radio play)	99
Chinese Classical Opera Company	536

Chiplin, Rex	306
Chlumberg, Hans	492, 494, 495
Chodorov, Edward	326
Christmas Bridge (Macmillan) SEE *Land of Morning Calm* (Macmillan)	
Church Standard (newspaper)	270
Churchill, Caryl	346
Churchill, Winston	187, 241, 276
Ciddor, Harry	476
Cindie (novel)	70
Circling Dove, The (Irwin)	192, 328, 457
Civic Repertory Theatre, NY	41
Civil Liberties Committee	270
Clair, René	247
Clarion (newspaper)	20
Clarion League	20
Clarion Players, Manchester	31, 442
Clark, Norman	159, 165, 168, 169, 172, 173, 174, 505
Clarke, Joan née Willmot	249, 376, 391
Clerks Union	160
Clewlow, Frank D.	100
'Click Go the Shears' (song)	248
Cloud 9 (Churchill)	346
Clurman, Harold	39, 41, 494
Coal (Gray)	457
Coen, Fabio	509
Coldicutt, Ken	113
Cole, Toby	45
Colley, Barbara	182
Collingwood Town Hall	267
Collingwood, Lyn	6, 7, 470, 501, 534, 537
Collins, Joe	183

Collinson, Laurence	202, 203, 297, **298**, 299, 300
Colony (Trease)	28, 103, 134, 136, 355
Come All You Valiant Miners (Brand)	469
Coming Our Way (revue)	**110**, 111
Common Cause (newspaper)	**428**, 452, 457, 471, 472, 484
Commonwealth Government Gazette	269
Commonwealth Investigation Branch	**72**, 78
Communist International [Comintern]	16, 17, 21, 38, 48, 61, 65, 77, 100
Communist International Committee for the Struggle Against War	317
Communist League of Australia	272
Communist Party Dissolution Bill, 1950	115, 280
Communist Party of Australia [CPA]	5, 13, 15, 17, 18, 48, 50, 54, 58, 61-64, 66-71, 74-87, 97, 101, 102, 115-118, 121, 125, 128, 129, 132, 135-136, 174, 186, 208, 212, 213, 218, 220-221, 223-224, 229, 231, 240, 243, 244, 250-252, 256, 268-271, 276, 279, 280, 281, 283, 289, 295, 299, 308, 340, 344, 345, 364, 373-377, 386, 393, 394, 402-408, 414, 422, 425, 426, 430, 433, 444, 452, 453, 465, 500, 503
Communist Party of Great Britain [CPGB]	22, 75, 306, 424, 434, 438, 439, 440
Communist Party of the Soviet Union	85
Communist Party of USA [CPUSA]	36, 352
Communist Review (newspaper)	66, 75, 116, 135, 239
Community Arts Foundation	123
Conkel, Joshua	364

Connor, John	195
Constable, William "Bill"	101, 113
Contemporary Artists group	113
Conway, Sid	144
Corpus Christi (McNally)	364
Corrie, Joe	173
Corry, Percy	174
Cosgrove, Stuart	34, 38
Cosi (Nowra)	363
Costello, Joseph	176
Council for Civil Liberties	263
Council for the Encouragement of Music and the Arts [CEMA]	276
Counihan, Noel	99, 101
Counter Attack (Stevenson & Stevenson)	324
Counteraid	365
Courier-Mail (newspaper)	57, 186, 207
Courier-Mail Wharfie AKA The Judge and the Shipowner, The (Crawford)	207
Covell, Roger	199
Cox, Eva	346
Cradle Will Rock, The (Blitzstein)	218, 494
Craig, Christopher	139
Craig, John	379
Craig, Terry	222
Crawford, Jim	52-55, 58, 123, 181-183, 194, 196-197, 204-208, 230, 233, 245, 297, 349, 432
Crawford, Pat	53
Creswell, Rosemary	426
Criminal Investigation Branch [CIB]	271, 272, 285
Cripps, Sir Stafford	29
Croft, George	195

Crossroads Theatre	150
Crowley, Mart	364
Crucible, The (Miller)	188, **381**
CUB Non-Fiction Award	149
Cullan, Roger	453
Cupid Rampant (Corry)	174
Current Book Distributors	76
Curtin, John	221, 406
Curtis, Zelda	435
Cusack, Dymphna	6, 119, 138, 230, 249, 329, **400-401**, 414, 416, 423, 426,
d'Usseau, Arnaud	353
Daily News (newspaper)	213, 214, 216, **263**, 269, **271**
Daily Telegraph (newspaper)	138, 269, **443**
Daily Worker (newspaper)	306, 473
Dalton, Leo	169, 170
Damousi, Joy	402, 403, 404
Dangerous Sex, The (Gibson)	339
Dann, George Landen	111, 195, 198, 199, 349
Dark Lady of the Sonnets (Shaw)	173, 205
Darwin Community Arts	508
Davies, Paul	484
Davis, Ossie	354
Davis, Syd	85, 202, 204, 313, 433
Day Before Tomorrow, The (Throssell)	251
Dayne, Elsie	376
Dead Timber (Esson)	49
Deans, Joyce	158, 159, 164, 165, 169, 173
Death of Bessie Smith, The (Albee)	354, 361
Death of Peter Pan, The (Lowe)	364
Death of Phillip Robertson, The (Tomlinson)	149, 351

Decision (Chodorov)	326
Deep Are the Roots (Gow & d'Usseau)	353
Defensive Warfare (Rickie)	319
Democratic Rights Council	140
Dempsey, Jim	529
Denis, Michel St	26
Destiny of Me, The (Kramer)	364
Devanny, Jean	6, 13, 17, 50, **60**-62, 70, 128, 129, 149, 212, 317, 319
Devil's Business, The (Brockway)	170
Diamond, Dick	4, 97, 103, 122, 183, 186, 230, 248, 249, 279, 282, 461, 530
Diamond, Lilian	97, 98, 103, 108, 279
Diary of Anne Frank, The (Goodrich & Hackett)	151, 335
Dick Tracy (radio series)	494
Dick, Elsie	292
Diderot, Denis	238
Dimitrov, George	16
Disher, Norma	73, 279, 375, 377, 383, **384-385**, 386, 388, 391, 392, **400-401**, 535
Disorderly Women, The (Bowen)	147
Distant Point (Afinogenev)	30, 32
Dobell, William	150
Dobson, Agnes	246
Docker, Alan	376
Docker, Bert	376
Docker, Einar	376
Docker, Evelyn née Thomson	**371**, 376, 476
Docker, Norm	143, 376
Docker's Tanner, The (Martin)	439

Doll's House, A (Ibsen)	247
Douglas, Peter	433
Dowdle, Len	122, 249
Drake-Brockman, Judge	342
Dreyfus in Rehearsal (Grumberg)	352
Drinkwater, John	19, 132, 218, 320
Drovers, The (Esson)	111
Dublin Jewish Dramatic Society	307
Duncan, Catherine	82, 96, 97, 100, 241, 266, 267, 273, 320, 323, 326, 413, 414, 507
Dundee Red Front Troupe	22
Dunstan, Albert	263
Durkheim, Emile	485
Eastman, Max	66
Ebert AKA Herbert McClintock	213, 225, 226, 230
Edgar, David	361
Edinburgh Festival	33
Edmonds, Flo	**253**
Edmonds, Ross	163
Egypt Cultural Radio (radio station)	509
Ehrenburg, Ilya	187, 297
Einstein, Albert	62
Eisenstein, Sergei	22
Eldridge, Florence	498
Eldridge, Hal	455
Elizabeth 1 (Foster)	338
Elizabethan Theatre Trust	203, 250, 252
Elliot, Brian	226
Elliot, T. S.	228
Elliott, Sumner Locke	136
Emerald Progress Association	431, 536
Emissary, The (Rickie)	132

Encyclopaedia of Women and Leadership in Twentieth Century Australia, The (book)	366
End of the Beginning, The (O'Casey)	204
Enemy of the People, An (Ibsen)	86, 160, 174
Engineers' Pound, The	441
English Collective of Prostitutes	346
Enough Blue Sky (Brand)	150
Enright, Nick	148, 150
Enron (Prebble)	152
'Ernabella Shore, The' (song)	248
Esson, Hilda	50, 59, 97, 100, 111, 112, 261, 289, 293
Esson, Hugh	97, 102, 103
Esson, Louis	13, 48, 49, 50, 97, 111, 261, 289
Eternal Song, The (Arnstein)	99
Eureka Youth League	120, 289, 457
Eureka Youth League Theatre	243
Euripides	487
Evans, Bergun	497
Evans, John	312
Events While Guarding the Bofors Gun (McGrath)	146, 333
Everybody's Magazine (magazine)	27
Experimental Theatre of Warsaw	509
Exposure 70 (revue)	332, 361
Fabian Society	19
Face, The (Laurents)	319
Fairbairn, Olga	175
Fairfax, Warwick	143
Falson, Gill	364
Farwell, George	114, 180, 183
Fast Forward (TV)	331

Fast, Howard	140, 187, 230, 232, 281, 294-295, 297
Fay Ingram	**253**
Federal Council for Aboriginal Advancement	142
Federal Theatre Project, USA	43
Federated Clerks Union	84
Federated Engine Drivers and Firemen's Association	473
"Fedilio" (critic)	232
Feed the Sheep (Williams)	228
Feet of Daniel Mannix, The (Oakey)	147
Fegan, Jack	291, 327
Feiffer, Jules	146
Fellowship of Australian Writers	279
Female Transport (Gooch)	147, 346
Fensham, Rachel	395
Fenton, Norman	362
Festival and Conference of Workers' Theatres	39
Finch, Barbara	388
Finch, Peter	363
Finch, Trevor	388
Finey, George	62, 128, 129, 317, 319
Firing Line, The (Lewis & Hector)	456
First Class Women (Enright)	150
Firth, Verity	346
Fischer, Louise	364
Fission Chips (revue)	120, 329
Fitton, Doris	370
Five Feminist Melodramas (Van Badham)	346
Five Poor Families (Kidd)	232, 433
Five Power Peace Pact campaign	317
Flanagan, Hallie	43
Flaus, William	312

Flinders Street theatre, Melbourne   102, 108, 113, 118, 120, 530
Floridsorf (Wolf)   215, 220
Flower, Cedric   350, 388, **415**
Flower, Pat   79, 332, 338
Flying Blind (Morrison)   333
Focus on Germany (Paice)   447
For Services Rendered (Maughan)   174
Forty Hour Wait (Crawford)   207
Forward One (Prichard)   212, 215, 340, 409, 410
Forward to a Peoples Theatre (leaflet)   72
Foster, John Cameron   129
Foster, Paul   146, 338
Fountains Beyond (Dann)   111, **130-131, 200-201,** 198, 199, 349

Four Women (van Itallie)   147
Fourth, The (Simonov)   194
Fox, Len   135, 136, 376, 388, 432, 462, 483

Frank, Bruno   132
Franklin, Miles   135, 230, 342, 536
Franklin, Stella Miles   372
Fraser, Brad   365
Fraser, Ron   **178**, 199
Fraser, Val   524
Free Kevin Gilbert Fund   351
Freed, Donald   334
Freedom on the Wallaby (song)   432
Fremantle Lumpers Union   221
French, Bail   **443**
Frey, Margaret   113
Friday Night at the Schrammers (Collinson)   202, 297
Friday the Thirteenth (Morgan)   146
Friel, Brian   360

Friends of America Hurrah	143
Friends of the Soviet Union [FSU]	96, 102, 128, 261
Frisch, Max	176
From Colonel Light to the Footlights (book)	252
Fry's Chocolate Company	29
Fugard, Athol	123
Furnishers' Union	241
Furphy, Joseph	48, 183
Furtive Love (Kenna)	364
Futcher, David	312
Gabrielson, Frank	170
Galsworthy, John	19, 20, 48, 49, 271
Garibaldi's Restaurant	439
Garland, Robert	495, 496
Garnett, Pat	122
Garrick Theatre (London)	33
Garson, Barbara	122, 144
Gas (Kaiser)	20
Gate Theatre, Dublin	293
Gay Solidarity Group	365
Gems, Pam	338
Gener, Randy	508
George, Keith	56, 212, 213, 218, 219, 225, 227-229, 501
German Communist Party [KPD]	62
Ghost of Yankee Doodle, The (Howard)	493
Ghosts (Ibsen)	215
Giblin, L. F.	266
Gibson, Joan	339
Gibson, Ralph	96
Gieseking, Walter	299
Gietzelt, Arthur	148
Gifford, Garth	511

Gifford, Mary-Anne	151
Giggle Suits and Overalls (variety show)	324
Gilbert, Kevin	142
Gillies Report, The (TV)	331
Glasgow players	31
Glasgow Workers' Theatre Group	31
Glen Davis mine	469-477, **478-479**, 480-**487**
Glengarry Glen Ross (Mamet)	153
God Bless the Guv'nor (Willis)	33, 84, 85, 297
Gold, Michael	36
Golden Boy (Odets)	32, 249
Goldstein, Malcolm	36
Gollancz, Victor	26
Gone With the Wind (1939 film)	353
Gooch, Steve	124, 147, 346
Good Hope, The (Heijermans)	182
Good Oil, The (Crawford)	207
Gooding, Janda	226
Gorbals Story, The (McLeish)	32, 33
Gordon, Charles	225
Gorky, Maxim	62, 99
Gould, L. H.	82, 83
Government Regrets, The (Box)	160, 165
Governor Brisbane	205
Governor Macquarie	204, 205
Governor's Stables, The (Crawford)	204, 205
Gow, James	353
Gow, Keith	74, 376, 388
Gow, Nan AKA Nan Vernon née Davies	312, 376, 380, 388
Gow, Ronald	345
Grace Gibson Productions	346
Graham, James	152

Grand United Order of Oddfellows	134
Grant, Cleo	132, 345
Grant, Len	376, 388
Grant, Micki	509
Granville-Barker, Harley	19, 152
Gray, Grayce	**138**
Gray, John	115, 135, **324**, 376, 388, 469, 530
Gray, Oriel	6, 76-**77**, 79-81, 84, 118, 135, 138-139, 176, 198, 202, 230, 247-251, 272, 277, 297, 308, 312, 325, 338-339, 344, 350, 352, 374, 376, 381, 388, 403, 407-409, 425, 457, 469, 503
Gray, Owen	111, 313
Great American Theatre Company	124
Great Canadian Theatre Company	334
Great International Uranium Show, The (Street Theatre)	146
Great Train Robbery, The (1903 film)	247
Green, Paul	493
Greenberg, Richard	364
Greenway, Francis	204, 205
Greenwich Red Blouses	22
Greenwood, Irene	220
Greenwood, Walter	215, 345
Grivas, Cecil 'Cec'	476, 480, 534
Grivas, June	535
Grivas, Roland	476, 483
Groen, Alma de	338
Gross Indecency: The Three Trials of Oscar Wilde (book)	364
Group Theatre, The	39, 41, 256

Grumberg, Jean-Claude	343, 352
Guardian (CPA newspaper)	101, 116, 120, 202, 205, 280-281, 295, 313, **459**, 508
Gubaryev, Vladimir	124, 334
Gullett, Henry	276
Gurney, Alex	**264-265**
Gust, Itzhak	261, 289
Guthrie, Tyrone	26
Guthrie, Woody	176
Gyseghem, André van	24, 27
Hackney People's Players	22
Hackney Red Radio	22
Had We but World Enough (Gray)	**78**, 79, 139, 198, 230, 248, 250, 297, 350, **412**
Haddy, Harry	132
Haft, Linal	**330**
Hair (MacDermot/Ragni/Rado)	143
Hales, Doris	160, 172, 173
Hales, Harry	160
Hall, Jonathan	364
Hall, Mrs	472
Ham Funeral (White)	252
Hamill, E.	226
Hamilton, Famiglia	350
Hamilton, Peter	536
Hampson, Miriam née Aarons	83, 84, 137, 145, 148, 193, 276, 290, 313, 337, **368-369**, 375, 376, 379, 380, 383, 457, 461, 476, 535
Hampson, Stan	376
Hampton, Christopher	124
Hannam, Ken	536

Hannett, Leo	359
Hansberry, Lorraine	354
Hanson, Raymond	139
Hardcore (Hall)	364
Harding, Alex	365
Hardy, Frank	74, 143, 281, 282, 303
Hargreaves, John	330
Harnett, Phyllis 'Phyl'	170, 213, 215, 217-219, 221, 222, 224-226, 229, 292, 501
Harold Park Hotel	150
Harper, Ken	79, 85
Harrington, Pat	166, 167
Harris, Eve	113
Harris, Max	247, 248
Harris, Rolf	213
Harrison, Eris	7
Harvest in the North (Hodson)	27
Harvey, John	319
Harvey, Jonathan	364
Hasluck, Paul SEE "Polygon" (critic)	
Hawkins, Bruce	388
Healy, Connie	**200-201, 464**
Healy, Jim	143, 461, 462
Hector, Jim	273
Hector, Jock	456
Hector, John	230
Heffron, Bob	142
Heidi Chronicles, The (Wasssertein)	349
Heijermans, Herman	182
Heil Hanlon (Crawford)	207
Heiser, Ron	243
Hellman, Lilian	57

Hellman, Lillian 277, 353
Henderson, Marian 145
Hepworth, John 120, 213, 225, 230, **307**, 313

Hepworth, Kathleen 230
Herbert, Alan 279, **324**
Here Comes Kisch! (Brand) 148
Here Under Heaven (Brand) 350, **418-419**, 420-424
Herlinger, Paul 313
Hewers of Coal (Corrie) 173, 182
Hewett, Dorothy 151, 230, 303, 344, 346, 398

Hickey, Tom 156
Hill, Bill 84
Hill, John 33
Hill, Pat **78**
Hillel, Angela 508
Hinkemann (Toller) 56, 217, 219
Hiroshima Peace Conference 317
His Majesty's Theatre, Perth 214, 217, 222
Hitler, Adolf 27, 276, 319, 325, 327
Hobbs, Talbott 217
Hodge, Herbert 25, 103
Hodges, Dorothy **253**
Hold the Line or The Land of Teletap (Brand) 144
Hold Your Wheat (living newspaper) 228
Hollywood Anti-Nazi League 498
Hollywood Women's Club 498
Holmes, John Haynes 493
Holt, Harold 142, 282
Home and Daily Telegraph (journal) 277
Home Brew (Clark) 249
Home of the Brave (Laments) 202, 297

Home of the Brave, The (Gabrielson & Lesan)	132, 170
Homer's Nod (Morris)	434
Hood, Alex	534
Hood, Pippa	388
Hoover, J. Edgar	144
Hopes, Bill	150
Hoppla! We Live (Toller)	132
Horin, Adele	346
Hornibrook, Dorothy	160
Hornibrook, Tom	159, 160
Horton, Bill	376
Horton, Muriel née Small	27, 136, 319, 325, 376, 380
Hotel, Club and Restaurant Workers	473
Hotel, Club, Caterers, Tea Room & Restaurant Employees Union	228
House Committee on Un-American Activities	176, 252, 281, 295, 330, 352
How He Lied to Her Husband (Shaw)	19, 132
How I Wonder! (Stewart)	247, 328
Howard, John	152
Howard, Sidney	493
Howard's End (revue)	152
"HTH" (critic)	57
Hudson, Elaine	338
Huelin, Frank	96, 99
Hughes, Billy	57, 147
Hughes, Frederick	291
Hughes, J. R.	273
Hughes, Jack	83
Hughes, Langston	99
Hughes, W. M.	273
Hungarian Writers Union	424

Hurd, Ron	220
Hurley, Hughla	346, 383
Hutchinson, George	362
Hutchinson's Trust	19
Huxley, Aldous	228
Hyde, Dylan	221, 223, 229
I Am Angry (Hartnett)	170, 215, 217, 221
I'd Rather be Left (revue)	103, 276, 323, 342
'I've Got a Lovely Bunch of Coconuts' (song)	140
Ibsen, Henrik	19, 48
Idiot's Delight (Sherwood)	493
If There Weren't any Blacks You'd Have to Invent Them (Speight)	123
If This Be Treason (Holmes & Lawrence)	493
Independent Labour Party, UK [ILP]	20, 22
Imperial Tobacco	29
Imperialism (Williamson)	333
Importance of Being Earnest, The (Wilde)	364
In Angel Gear (Sejavka)	363
In Beauty It Is Finished (Dann)	195, 198
Independent Players, Perth	218
Independent Television, UK	415 [ITV]
Independent Theatre	136, 246, 256, 370
Indians (Kopit)	360
Inga (Glebov)	215, **217**
Ingeborg, Gertraud	338
Insect Play (Capek)	20, 58
International Bureau of Revolutionary Writers	66
International Film Society	256
International Labour Defense	96, 352
International Labour Party	161
International New Theatre Movement	96

International New York Fringe Festival	338
International Peace Campaign	162, 500, 507
International Seamen's Club	134
International Theatre (magazine)	99
International Workers of the World [IWW]	20, 36
International Workers' Theatre Movement	22
International Workers' Theatre Olympiad	24
Into the Woods (Sondheim & Lapine)	151
Ipswich Drama Festival	204
Iron Cove Theatre	150
Ironworkers' Union	457
Irwin, Ben	173, 494
Irwin, Leonard	192, 328, 457
Isherwood, Christopher	246
Israel in the Kitchen (Elstein)	290
It Isn't Possible! (Roland)	342
It's Time to Boil Billy (revue)	333
It's tough for us Boongs in Australia Today (revue)	123
It's Up to You	241
Italian Straw Hat, An (1928 film)	247
Itallie, Jean-Claude van	143, 147
Ivanova, Vik	7
Jack Charles is Up and Fighting (revue)	123
Jackeroo, The (Crawford)	208
Jackson, H. B.	217
Jackson, Kevin	152, 338
Jail Diary of Albie Sachs, The (Edgar & Sachs)	361
James, Walter	217
Jan, Diane	**418-419**
Jana Natya Manch theatre group, New Delhi	509
Janshewsky, Edward	132, 134

Jawodimbari, Arthur	359
Jefferies, Clint	365
Jerusalem (Butterworth)	152
Jewish Club, Adelaide	239, 240
Jewish Council to Combat Fascism and Antisemitism [JCCFAS]	288, 299, 300
Jewish Institute Players	31
Jewish Youth Theatre League [JYTL]	289, 290, 322, 351
Johnny Johnson (Green & Weill)	493
Johnson, Hewlett	328
Johnson, Lyndon B.	144
Johnson, Phyllis	271
Johnson, Poole	218
Johnston, Elizabeth	242, 243
Johnston, Elliot	256
Johnston, Marjory	240, 241, 242
Jolly George (Willis)	438
Jones, Bonnie	**443**
Jones, Doris	**443**
Jones, H. E.	273
Jonson, Ben	280
Journalists' Clarion, The (newspaper)	149
Journey's End (Sherriff)	320, 335
Judge and the Shipowner AKA The Courier-Mail Wharfie, The (Crawford)	207
Judgment Day (Rice)	164, 167, 172, 173
Juliffe, Bill	113
Juno and the Paycock (O'Casey)	32, 340
Just Talk (Apart from the Songs) (McGowan)	346
Kafka, Franz	148
Kahn, Otto	36
Kataev, Valentine	241
Kaufman, Moises	364

INDEX

Kaufmann, Walter	289
Kay, Harry	534
Keane, Kim	82, 97
Keane, Maurie	148
Keane, Shirley	312
Kelk, Ted	199, **368-369**
Kelley, Alan	150
Kelly, Katherine	402
Kemp, Peter	334
Kempster, Chris	530, 534
Keneally, Tom	176
Kenna, Peter	364
Kennedy, Brenda	**253**
Kennedy, John F.	122, 144
Kennedy, Robert	144, 330
Kenny, Colin	409
Kerr, John	322
Kershaw, Angela	66
Kerz, Leo	509
Kessell, Norman	362
Kharkov Congress	65, 66
Khrushchev, Nikita	118
Kidd, Ben	230
Kidd, Benjamin	433
Kincaid, John	32
Kindertransport (Samuels)	150
King David Hotel, Jerusalem	306
King Edward's Chambers, Fortitude Valley	187
King, Alec	226
Kings Theatre, Melbourne	98
Kippax, Harry	143
Kisch, Egon	17, 56, 148, 149
Kline, Herbert	44

Kollwitz, Kathe	62
Koornang School, Warrandyte	111
Kopit, Arthur	360
Kozlenko, William	320
Kramer, Barry	364
Kruger, Stefan	151
La Mama, New York	146
Labor Daily, The (newspaper)	**64**
Labor Youth League	291
Labour Co-operative Societies	20
Labour Party, UK	20, 29, 434
Labour Women's Organisation	220
Labour Youth Theatre	240, 241, 242, 244, 245
Labour's Cavalcade (Ross)	156, 157
Lachberg, Maurie	209, 212, 213
Laird o' Torwatletie, The (McLellan)	33
Lalor of Eureka (Rees)	135
Lambert, Jan	376
Lambert, John	376, 388
Lambert, Mary Marguerite "Kip" née McDonald	376, 388
Lambie, Lloyd	465
Laments, Arthur	202
Lampell, Millard	176, 330, 352
Land of Morning Calm (Macmillan) AKA *Christmas Bridge*	81, 192, 247, 256, 328
Landmarks of Liberty	30
Lang, J. T.	146
Langelaar, Sonya	158
Lauren, S. K.	493
Laurents, Arthur	297, 319
Lavelle, Patricia (Pat)	476, 480, 481
Lavelle, Paul	312

Lavori, M.	359
Lawler, Ray	76, 118, 250
Lawrence, D. H.	228
Lawrence, Reginald	493
Lawrence, Skeet	**253**
Lawson (Gray)	**106-107**, 111, 247, 248, 249, 250, 381, 408, 409, 457
Lawson, Henry	48, 183, 432, 530
Lawson, John Howard	36
League for Peace and Democracy	68, 101, 317
League of Nations at Geneva, The (Ross)	156
League of Nations Union	500
League of Workers' Theatres, USA	38, 493
Lee, Harper	355
Lee, Julian	492
Leeson, George	440
Left Book Club	26, 42, 67, 157, 238, 239, 243
Left Book Club Theatre Group	56, 239, 291, 500
Left Book Club Theatre Guild	26
Left Theatre in Ireland	442
Leighton, Harry	230
Lenin, V.I.	288
Lesan, David	170
Let Freedom Ring (Bein)	494
Let Freedom Ring Company, NY	495
Let Him Have (1991 film)	139
Let's Be Offensive (revue)	135, **108-109**
Levy, Jock	5, 289, 290, 306, 312, 313, **286-287, 384-385**
Levy, Lew	289
Lewis, Jeannie	145
Lewis, Sam	272

Lieutenant Pernot's Word of Honour	319
Lindesay, Vane "Blue"	113
Lindsay, Jack	25
Lion on the Square (Ehrenburg)	187, 297
Lithgow Mercury (newspaper)	471
Little Brother, Little Sister (Campton)	332
Little Dog Laughed, The (Beane)	364
Little Foxes, The (Hellman)	353
Little Green Bundle, The (Brecht)	173
Little Shop of Horrors (Menken & Ashman)	151
Little Theatre	33
Littlewood, Joan	148, 331
Littlewood, John	113
Living Newspaper Unit, USA	43
Livingstone, Alice	346, 349, 351, 352
Lockwood, Rupert	136, 270, 273, 323
Logan, Brenda	508, 509
Logan, Chris	173
Logan, Patrick	206
London Labour Dramatic Federation	20
London University	238
Long and the Short and the Tall, The (Hall)	121, 329
Long Bay Women's Penitentiary	271
Long, Eric	**330**
Longitude 49 (Tank) AKA *Tanker McKay*	138, 195, 230, 232
Longworth Institute	169
Longworth, William	175
Love on the Dole (Gow & Greenwood)	166, 167, **215**, 219, 220, 229, 345
Lowe, Barry	364
Lowenstein, Wendy	75, 86
Lower Depths (Gorky)	33
Lucky (Zavaros)	363

Lumpkin, Grace	494
Lunghi, John	213, 225, 226
Lye, Reg	129
Lye, Reginald	312
Lyons Bungles, The (revue)	228
Lyons, Joseph	262
Lyric Theatre	169, 175
Lyrique Theatre, Newcastle	505
Lysistrata (Aristophanes)	245, 246, 328, 340, 459
Macbird! (Garson)	122, 123, 144, 330
Maccabean Hall, Paddington	290
MacColl, Ewan	340, 459
MacColum, Joe	442
Macintyre, Stuart	231, 269
Mackay, Gwen	**178**
Macky, Stewart	48
Macmillan, Nance	192, 199, 328, 453
Mad Before Midday (Davis)	151
Magnificence (Brenton)	124
Mahony, Will	263
Major Barbara (Shaw)	132
Major Operation (Barker)	32
Making of Australian Drama, The (book)	372
Malayan Communist Party	188
Mald, Val	433
Malleson, Miles	20, 26, 120, 320
Maltz, Albert	24, 45, 98, 99, 163, 169, 174, 181, 192, 215, 218, 281, 321, 493, 505
Mamet, David	153
Man from Mukinupin, The (Hewett)	151
Man in the Train, The (story)	289
Man of Destiny (Shaw)	19

Man Who Mistook His Wife for a Hat, The (book)	363
Man Who, The (Brook)	363
Manchester Unity Theatre Bulletin (journal)	**35**
Manchester, Elsa	20
Mannix, Daniel	147
Manson, Charles	147
Maraini, Dacia	338
Marans, Jon	364
Marat/Sade (Weiss)	363
March, Frederick	498
Margaret Walker Dancers	530
Maritime Worker (newspaper)	452, 453, 455
Marshall, Alan	66, 82, 83, 97
Marshall, Herbert	24, 26
Marshall, Laurence	266, 267
Martin, David	289, 300, 305, 306, 307, 326
Marvellous Melbourne (Hibberd)	123
Marvin, Mark	44
Marx Brothers	325
Marx of Time (Gray)	76, **77**, 325
Marx, Groucho	498
Marx, Karl	15, 56, 136, 325
Mary Martin Bookshop	247
Mary Stuart (Maraini)	338
Mary's Own Paper (newsletter)	247
Masonic Club	135
Masque of Spain, The (pageant)	440
Masses (journal)	66
Masses and Man (Toller)	20, 50, 239
Masses Stage and Film Guild	20
Match Girls, The (Mitchell)	342, 343, 439

Matchgirls, The (Owen & Russell) — 343
Mathews, Bob — 20, 99, 108, 112, 113, 293
Mattachine Society — 364
Maugham, Jack — 50, 99
Maugham, W. Somerset — 100, 174
Maxwell, Miles — 530, 534
May Day Through the Ages (Ross) — 156
Mayakovski Theatre, Moscow — 329
Mayakovsky, Vladimir — 22
Mayan Theatre, Los Angeles — 291
McAuley, Gay — 486
McAuley, James — 276, 323
McCarron, Kenyon — **356-357**
McCleish, Robert — 32
McClelland, Doug — 145
McClintock, Herbert — 478-479, 525
McCormack, Charles — 278
McCreery, Kathleen — 14
McCullers, Carson — 365
McGowan, Laurel — 346
McGrath, John — 15, 146, 149, 333, 338
McKay, Gwen — 181, 204
McLaren, Edith (Edie) — 376
McLintock, Ray — 225
McMahon, Gregan — 48, 49
McMillan, Nance — 81, 247
McNally, Terrence — 364
McNamara, Frank — 361
McWilliams, Les — 204
Medea (Euripides) — 338
Meerut (sketch) — 24
Melbourne Actors Equity — 279
Melbourne Herald (newspaper) — **264-265**

Melbourne National Gallery School	101
Melbourne Repatriation Hospital	431, 536
Melbourne Repertory Club	48
Melbourne Unitarian Church	267
Melbourne University Dramatic Society	97
Melbourne University Labour Club	99
Melbourne Workers' Theatre	20, 363
Mellords, Charles	160
Mellords, Elsie	160
Melting Pot, The (Zangwill)	290
Memorial Hall, Central Concord	294
Men Must Fight (Lawrence & Lauren)	493
Men Should Weep (Stewart)	32
Men Who Marched Away (pageant)	162
Men Who Speak for Freedom (Brown)	323
Mendes, Phillip	311
Menzies, Robert	18, 82, 115, 116, 135, 142, 174, 270, 271, 276, 280, 281, 321, 322, 323, 327, 360, 406, 407, 469, 470, 472, 508
Merchant Navy Appeal Fund	293
Mercia, Paul	238
Meredith, John	534
Message of the March Wind (Morris)	19
Metalworkers Union	241, 376
Method Acting (book)	99
Metro-Vickers Trial, The (attrib. Bert Thompson & WAT)	54
Meyerhold, Vsevolod	22
Michel, Georges	332
Michell, Mignon	476
Middleby, Bob	160
Middleby, Melba	160

Midsummer Night's Dream, A (Shakespeare) 150
Mikado, The (Gilbert & Sullivan) 144, 325
Milano, Teatro di 510
Miles, J. B. 70
Militant (newspaper) 129
MilkMilkLemonade (Conkel) 364
Miller, Arthur 86, 176, 188, 246, 278
Miller, Frank 252
Miller, Mary née Warren 242, 243, 247, 248, 250, 251, 252

Miller, Sid 476
Miller, Susan 366
Miller, Suzie 346
Millis, Betty née Cole 143, 375, 376, **381**, 387, 388, 390, 391, 394, 460

Milliss, David 376, 388, **400-401**, 526
Milliss, Roger 142, 149, 207, 331, 361
Mills, June 84
Milne, A. A. 319
Milner, Lisa 158, **384-385**
Mind Your Head! (Street Theatre) 363
Miner's Right (Crawford) 181, 230, 233, 297, 432, **464**

Miners Speak, The (Roland) 75, **444**, 455, 457
Miners' Federation 181, 431, 455, 457, 462, 469, 471, 475

Miners' Federation of Great Britain 137
Miners' Hall, Booval 181
Ministry of Fuel, UK 33
Miracle at Verdun (Chlumberg) 492, 494, 497
Mitchell, D. R. B. 272, 292
Mitchell, Robert 342
Mock Beggar, The (BUP) 29
Modern Women's Club, Perth 213, 230

Modern Women's Fair	221
Modjeska, Drusilla	13, 17, 18, 50
Molière	33, 247
Montreal New Theatre Group	500
Moore, William	49
Morgan, Kevin Barry	146
Morley, J. K.	270
Morris, Edmund	251
Morris, Gadfan	434
Morris, William	18, 31
Morrison, Bill	333
Mortier, Paul	83, 84, 270
Moscow News (newspaper)	268, 278
Moscow Olympic Games, 1980	148
Moscow Trial of the Metro-Vickers Workers, The (attrib. Thompson & WAT)	54
Mossop, Cliff	132
Most Important Letter, A (Crawford)	194
Mother (film)	247
Mother Clap's Molly House (Ravenshill)	364
Mother Courage (Brecht)	**330**, 338
Mother Riba (Berg)	116, 289, 290, 297, 328
Mother, The (Brecht)	173, 494
Motor Show, The (Gooch)	124
Mountjoy, Bill	212
Movement Against War and Fascism [MAWF]	17, 56, 68, 97, 212, 223, 319, 500, 503
Mrs Warren's Profession (Shaw)	19, 132, 230, 344
Much Binding in the Marsh (radio play)	466
Mucking About (Hasluck)	224
Mumba Jumba and the Bunyip (O'Shaughnessy & Humphries)	142
Mundey, Jack	145
Munn, Rex	535

Munro, Don	88, 119
Murdoch, Walter	220
Murnane, Miss	53, 54
Murray, Arthur	380
Murray, F. G.	140
My Life Is My Affair (Gray)	339
'My Old Black Billy' (song)	248
Nail on the Wall, The (Hardy)	74, 281
Namatjira, Albert	199
Nambour Amateur Theatrical Society	432, 433
Narrow Road to the Deep North (Bond)	124
Nash, Ossie	181, 199
Nasty Piece of Work, A (Parsons)	151
National Association for Clarion Dramatic Clubs	20
National Black Theatre	208
National Committee Against War	317
National Conference and Spartakiade	38
National Council of Labour Colleges	21
National Drama League Festival	27
National Folk Festival	536
National Gallery Art School	99
National Institute of Dramatic Art [NIDA]	119
National Maritime Museum	384-385
National New Theatre movement, UK	114
National Security Act, 1939	101, 135, 268, 271
National Technical Institute for the Deaf	509
National Unemployed Workers Movement, UK	22
Neil, Anne	**253**, 256
Nekrassov (Sartre)	249
Neruda, Pablo	225
New Directions series	151

New Guard 132
New Housewives' Association 337
New Life (journal) 303
New Masses (journal) 36, 44, 100, 495
New Playwrights Theatre (USA) 20, 36
New Theatre (journal) 26, 39, **40**, 44, 66, 100, 232, 497, 504

New Theatre Adelaide 61, 71, 72, 78, 118, 158, 235-257, 433

New Theatre Australia (federation) 115, 118, 207, 380
New Theatre Brisbane 53, 61, 118, 179-209, 294, 432, 433, 453, 457, 511, 523-524, 536

New Theatre Club Melbourne 51, 96, 97, 102
New Theatre Film Society 246
New Theatre League Newcastle 61, 86, 154-**177**, 405, 505,
New Theatre League USA 1, 18, 26, 27, 30, 38, 42, 44, 45, 124, 169, 236, 261, 262, 493

New Theatre Management Committee 79
New Theatre Melbourne 6, 17, 33, 49, 54, 61, 69, 71, 74- 76, 82, 88, 93-126, 135, 158, 188, 193, 208, 239, 241- 243, 430, 446, 484, 507, 508

New Theatre National Conference 82
New Theatre Perth 61, 118, 158, 210-234, 433,

New Theatre playwriting competition 149
New Theatre Review (journal) 112, 114, 115, 279, 280, 281, 289, 293

New Theatre Singers 113

New Theatre Sydney	1, 3-7, 17, 50, 61, 63, 67, 71, 74, 86, 97-153, 157, 158, 160, 163, 165, 193, 208, 219, 231, 233, 237, 241, 242, 290, 317-365, 380, 417, **418-419**, 424, 425, 430- 432, 433, 457, 466, 467, **468**, 501, 503-505, 507, 528, 529, 534, 535
New Theatre UK	24, 28
New Theatre Writers Group	383, 456
New Theatre's First Decade (book)	98
New York Times (newspaper)	497
Newcastle Anti-Conscription League	317
Newcastle City Hall	162
Newcastle Morning Herald & Miners' Advocate (newspaper)	174, 175
Newcastle People's Theatre	20, 434
Newcastle Stadium Theatre	176
Newcastle Trades Hall Council	155
Newcastle Workers' Club	160
Newcastle Workers' Educational Association	155, 159, 172
Newsboy (Shock Troupe)	38
Newtown New Theatre	**146, 147**
Newtown Prom (revue)	145
Nichols, Peter	365
Night of the Big Blitz, The (Barker)	32
Night of the Ding Dong, The (Petersen) AKA *The Night of the Russians, The*	120, **178**, 206
Nightingale, Florence	339
Nimrod Theatre Company	148
Nindethana Theatre, Melbourne	208
Niugini! (revue)	358, 360
Nixon, Richard	332

No Conscription (Duncan & Lockwood)	136, 241, 273, 323
No More Peace (Toller)	218
No Room for Dreamers (Hutchinson)	362
No Strings Attached (Brand)	358
No Sugar for George (Collinson)	203, 297
No! No! (Roland) SEE *Vote 'No!'* (Roland)	
Noah, Robert	134
Noonan, Bill	360
Norén, Lars	335
Northern Territory Council for Aboriginal Rights	142
Northern Territory Council for Civil Liberties	149
Northgate Railway Workshop	457
Norton, Rosaleen	319, 501
Not So Quiet (novel)	165, 320
Now is the Day (pageant)	30
Nowra, Louis	363
NSW Labor Council	273, 453
NSW Peace Committee for International Co-operation and Disarmament	354
NSW Peace Council	317
Nupkins Awakened or the Tables Turned (Morris)	31
Nursery Rhyme (poem)	225
O'Brien, Angela	2, 289
O'Casey, Sean	26, 28, 136, 176, 204, 253, 278, 306, 340
O'Connell, Elin	177
O'Dea, Ernie	140, 141
O'Flaherty VC (Shaw)	**371**
O'Neill, Eugene	50, 63, 74
O'Neill, Marty	529
O'Neill, P.	459

O'Shaughnessy, John	495
O'Sullivan, Tim	132
Oakley, Barry	147
Objects and Principles (constitution)	68
Observer, London (newspaper)	203
Odets, Clifford	41, 45, 57, 77, 96, 157, 192, 214, 236, 242, 249, 262, 266, 290, 322, 351, 383, 493, 505
Off the Leash (revue)	455
Office Interlude (Carroll)	346
Officer, A. E.	268, 285
Oh What a Lovely War, Mate (Littlewood & Enright)	148, 333
'Old Black Joe' (song)	320
Old Centennial Hall, Brisbane	181
Old Man's Reward, The (Jawodimbari)	359
'Old Smokey' (song)	466
Old Vic Company	144
Older Women's Network	337
Oldham, John	213, 230
Oldham, Ray	230
Olivier, Laurence	144
Olley, Margaret	339
Olympic Games, Melbourne, 1956	119
On Dit (Student paper)	244
On Guard for Spain (Lindsay)	25, 29, 31
On Stage Vietnam (Brand & Garnett)	2, 122, 123, 142, 331, **333**
On the Rocks (Shaw)	19, 132
On the Skids	103
Once in a While the Odd Thing Happens (Godfrey)	365
One Day of the Year, The (Seymour)	330

One Flew Over the Cuckoo's Nest (Wasserman) — 124, 145, 362
Only Heaven Knows (Harding) — 365
Operation Olive Branch (MacColl) — 328, 340, 459
Oppenheimer, Melanie — 373
Optimistic Tragedy (Vishnevsky) — 32
Ordinary Man, The (Leonov) — 115
Orenburg Theatre — 329
Oreski Club orchestra — 225
Oreski String Band — 225
Organ Factory, Clifton Hill, Melbourne — 88, 124
Out of Commission (Brand) — 140, 377
Over to You (Slater) — 30
Owen, Bill — 343
Pacific Paradise (Cusack) — 119, 138, 249, 251, 329, **400-401**, 414, 416, **417**
Pacific Union (Buzo) — 151, 335
Page, Malcolm — 27
Paice, Eric — 447
Painter, The (Macmillan) — 199, 453
Painters and Dockers Union — 84
Paizie, George — 290
Palmer, Helen — 183, 530
Palmer, Nettie — 183
Palmer, Vance — 48, 50, 114, 183
Pandora's Garden (Sharp) — 151
Pankhurst, Adela — 402
Panorama (Uys) — 151
Parker, Lionel — 138
Parramatta Girls (Valentine) — 351
Parsons, Geoffrey — 323
Partisan Review (journal) — 495
Passos, John Dos — 36

Pate, Michael	290
Paterson Strike Pageant (pageant)	34
Paterson, Banjo	56
Patriot and the Fool, The (Watts)	323
Patten, George	101
Peace & Friendship Group	317
Peace on Earth (Sklar & Maltz)	115, 281, 493
Peace or War	319
Peace Pledge Union	500
Pears, Peter	365
Pelican (student newspaper)	220
Penalty Clause (Prichard)	215, 219, 229
People's Art Club	129
People's Court, The (Griffith)	30
People's Theatre Building Conference	31
Perl, Arnold	352
Persian, Jayne	310
Perth Daily News (newspaper)	**215, 216,** 217
Perth Theatre Council	232
Perth Town Hall	221
Perth Trades Hall	220
Perth Workers' Theatre	212
Petersen, George	**189**, 193
Petersen, Jim	433
Peterson, Ralph	120
Petrified Forest, The (Sherwood)	290
Petrov Royal Commission	140, 377
Petrov, Vladimir	116, 137, 231, 252, 256
Pfisterer, Susan	372
Phillips Café, Sydney	135
Physician in Spite of Himself, A (Moliere)	247
Pier Street Assembly Hall, Perth	292
Pioneer Players, Melbourne	1, 48, 49, 50, 97, 261, 289

Pirates of Pal Mal, The (Brand & Upton)	333
Piscator, Erwin	22
Pitt Street Theatre, Sydney	237
Pix (journal)	**274-275**
Plant in the Sun, A (Bengal)	26, 27, 100
Planter's Wife, The (1952 film)	116
Playwrights' Advisory Board	76, 118, 119, 250, 344
Plebs League	21
Poignant, Axel	213, 227
Pollock, Arthur	497
Pollock, J. H.	453
Pollock, John Hackett	293
Pollock, Katie	335, 346
Polonski, Stanislav	350
"Polygon" (critic) AKA Paul Hasluck	219, 220, 292
Poor Superman (Fraser)	365
Popplewell, Olive	215
Port Kembla Workers' Federation Delegates Committee	277, 431, 536
Porter, Don	243, 252
Porter, Edward	247
Porter, Rosemary née Smith	242, 243, 252, 433
Portrait of an Artist (Kelley)	150
Posa, Tom	312
Postal Workers' Union	453
Postmark Zero (Nemiroff)	330
Pot of Message (revue)	73, 327
Power Without Glory (novel)	281
Powers, Gary	194
Poynton, J. J.	217
Pram Factory, Carlton	123
Pravda (newspaper)	334
Prebble, Lucy	152

Prelude (Shugrue & O'Shaughnessy)	495
Press the Point (revue)	140
Pressman, David	500
Price of Coal, The (Brighouse)	19
Prichard, Katharine Susannah [KSP]	13, 49, 56, 99, 120, **210**, 212, 213, 215, 218, 224, 228, 232, 245, 251, 277, 340, 398, 402, 409, 410, 411, 413, 457, 465, 501, 534
Priestley, J. B.	251
Princess Theatre, Brisbane	57, 504
Princess Theatre, Perth	212
Pritchard, Hal	239, 240, 242, 244, 246, 291
Pritchard, Sadie	291
Private Hicks (Maltz)	24, 98, 160, 169, 181, 215, 217, 220, 281, 321
Privates on Parade (Nichols)	365
Professor Mamlock (Wolf)	160, 172, 173
Progressive Arts Players, Vancouver	500
Progressive Jewish Youth of Sydney	290
Prolet Buehne, Germany	441
Prolet Buehne, USA	37
Proletarian Players	179
Proletariat (journal)	50
Pudovkin, Vsevolod	247
Purlie Victorious (Davis)	354
Pygmalion (Shaw)	19, 70, 129, 132, 338, 344
Quartered Man, The (Freed)	334
Queen Christina (Gems)	338
Queen Street Theatre, Melbourne	103, 108
Queensland Council of International Peace Campaign	504

Queensland Peace Council	192
Queensland Shearers' Union	180
Quiet Night (Blewett)	221
Quiet Night in Rangoon, A (Pollock)	335
Radio Éireann (radio station)	509
Radio Moscow (radio station)	537
Radio Warsaw (radio station)	537
Radioactive Horror Show, The (Romeril)	146
Ragged Cap, The (Brecht)	160, 170, 171
Ragged Trousered Philanthropists (Thomas)	21, 22, 51, 57, 132, 134, 179, 447
Railway and Tramway Institute, Sydney	319
Railways Union Band	461
Raisin in the Sun, A (Hansberry)	354
Ramsay, Bill	31
Rathgeber, Erika	113, 422
Rationalist Society	134
Ravenhill, Mark	364
Real Russia, The (Prichard)	224
Realist Film Unit	112
Realist Writers Group [RWG]	279, 289, 303, 386, 483
Rebel Players	429
Rebel Players, Manchester	429, 441
Red Megaphone, Manchester	132, 441, 442
Red Radio	24
Red Rockets Group, Germany	441
Red Stage, The (journal)	**23**
Reed, Jack	36
Reed, John	156

Reedy River (Diamond)	4, 7, 115- 120, 122, 135, 175, 176, 183, 206, 230, 232-233, 248, 249, 256, 277, 279, 282, 343, 354, 431-433, 444, 461-462, **514-532**, 533-537
Rees, Leslie	79, 114, 135, 312
Rehearsal (Maltz)	31, 99, 163, 174, 181, 218, 228
Relative Comfort (Schien)	365
Remedy, The (Crawford)	207
Remember Pedrocito (Boynton)	57, 132, 162, 173, 239, **316**, 321
Renegade (Pollock)	103, 293, 294, 351, 453
Repertory Club, Perth	213
Repertory Society, Perth	218, 220, 222
Repertory Theatre, Melbourne	49
Returned and Services League of Australia [RSL]	311
Revolt of the Beavers, The (Lantz & Lantz)	30
Reynolds News (newspaper)	27
Ribush, Dolia	100
Rice, Elmer	20, 43, 167, 192, 230, 233, 505
Richard's Cork Leg (Behan)	333
Richards, Graham	346
Richters, Zigurds	361
Rickie, Nelle	6, 132, 319, 340
Ride on Stranger (Tennant)	52
Riders to the Sea (Synge)	247, 322
Rifles (Carrar)	45
Rights of Man, The (book)	146
Ringbolter, The (Hardy)	143
Ritchie, David	362
'Road to Mandalay, The' (song)	331

Roar China (Tretyakov)	239
Roberts, Barbara	159, 161, 164, 173
Roberts, Buckley	25, 355, 453
Robertson, Alec	528
Robertson, Alex	470
Robertson, Patsy	**189**
Robeson, Eslanda	354
Robeson, Paul	26, 27, 100, 232, 354, 537
Robinson, Eileen	132
Robinson, Roland	139
Robson, John	175, 177
Robson, Phyllis	175
Rocket Range (Crawford)	123, 196, 197, 230, 245, 349
Rocket That Jack Built, The (Dowdle)	121
Rocky Rogue Show, The (revue)	124
Rogers, Kurt	226
Roland, Betty	4, 56, 66, 74, 75, 84, 96, 212, 215, 222, 250, 271, 272, 320, 322, 323, 338, 342, 380, 455, 457
Rolland, Romaine	238
Romeril, John	14, 146
Ron Raygun in the Antipodes (Sanders & Bridges)	148, 334
Rooney, Vic	176
Roosevelt, Franklin Delano	43
Rose, Bartholomew	152
Rose, Enid	238
Rosenberg, Ethel	116, 282,
Rosenberg, Julius	116, 282, 289
Ross, Edgar	452, 472
Ross, Lloyd	100, 155, **156**
Roving Red Revue Company, Brisbane	52, 56, 179

Rowan, Des	169
Roxy Theatre, Hamilton	175, 176
Royal Academy of Dramatic Art, UK	246
Royal Commission into Soviet Espionage	116
RTP Players	134
Rubber Workers' Union	342
Rubin, Barnard	473
'Rum and Coca Cola' (song)	327
Runciman, Sara	7
Ruskin, John	19
Russell, Tony	343
Russian Association of Proletarian Writers [RAPP]	66
Russian Question, The (book)	115
Rusty Bugles (Elliott)	136
Ryan, Susan	346
Saal, Ilka	492
Sabotage (Willis)	108
Sacco, Nicola	134
Sachs, Albie	361
Sacks, Oliver	363
Sacred Place, The (Esson)	49
Saint Joan (Shaw)	128
Salisbury, Silvia	375, 377, 379, 387, 388, 389, 390, 460, 461, 534
Salisbury, Tom	379, 388, 389, 476, 480
Samuel, Raphael	18, 20, 21
Samuels, Diane	150
Sandanista! (Great American Theatre Company)	124, 149, 334
Sanders, Stafford	148, 334
Sandhog (Robinson & Salt)	142
Sane Democracy League	68
Sane Democracy League Notes (journal)	68

Sarcophagus (Gubareyev)	124, 334
Sartre, Jean-Paul	249, 332
Sarzi, Otello	509
Sassoon, Siegfried	320
Saunders, Lewis	291
Savage Heart, The (Summons)	149
Savage, Mavis	175
Savages (Hampton)	124
Savoy Theatre, Sydney	262
Schien, Gina	346, 365
Scott, Joanne	373, 394
Scottish People's Theatre	32
Scottsboro (Shock Troupe)	39
Scottsboro Newsreel (living newspaper)	352, 353
Sea, Shakespeare by the	150
Seamen's Journal (newspaper)	452, 453
Seamen's Relief Fund	345
Seamen's Union	84, 138, 453, 459, 460, 473
Seamen's Women's Auxiliary	473
Seamen's Women's Committee	337
Search Foundation	7
Searle, Arthur	161
Season of Celebration (novelette)	99
Second Congress of Soviets, The (Ross)	156
Second Congress of the World Federation of Democratic Youth, Budapest	197
Secret, The (Sender)	132, 162, 321
Sejavka, Sam	363
Sender, Ramón	132, 321
Senior, Philip	**490-491**
Señora Carrar's Rifles (Brecht)	45, 162, 171, 322
Sergil, Christopher	355

Serpent, The (van Itallie)	144
Set, Gezerd Younger	351
Seward, Anna	339
Sex Discrimination Act, 1984	346
Seymour, Alan	330
Shakespeare, William	2, 20, 124, 150
Shand, Iris	**454**, 455
Sharkey, L. L.	272, 280
Shaw, George Bernard	19, 20, 48, 49, 50, 62, 63, 70, 132, 159, 173, 205, 230, 271, 344
Shaw, Irwin	30, 45, 100, 115, 169, 192, 214, 247, 297, 319, 338, 345, 487, 501
Shaw, Rod	262
Shelley, Cecelia	213, 228
Shepherd and the Hunter, The (Martin)	300, **304**, 305, 306, **307**, 314, 326, 351
Sheridan, Susan	422
Sherman, John	293
Sherman, Leon	476
Sherriff, R. C.	335
Sherring, Alan	476
Shertock, Kathleen	**253**
Sherwood, Robert	493
Shifting Heart, The (Beynon)	203
Shock Brigade AKA Shock Troupe, NY	38, 441
Shugrue, J. Edward	495
Sifton, Claire	45, 291
Sifton, Paul	36, 45, 291
Sighs of the Times (revue)	251, 256
Silent People, The (Brand)	424
Simonov, Konstantin	115, 189, 194
Sinclair, Upton	20, 36, 50, 62

Singing Jailbirds, The (Sinclair)	20, 21, 36
Singing the Lonely Heart (Valentine)	365
Sink the Belgrano (Berkoff)	124, 334
Six Hungry Families (Kidd)	230
Six Men of Dorset (Malleson & Brooks)	20, 120, 438, 442
Sixty Miler (Smail/Weeks/Foster)	129
Skinner, Carole	**330**
Sklar, George	148, 493, 494
Skuse, Anthony	338
Sky Without Birds (Gray)	80, 202, 247, 308, **309**, 311, 313, 352, 457
Slater, Montagu	30
Slater, William	266
Slickers Ltd (Hammer)	57, 132
Sloane, Honey	129
Slow Learning Children's Association	232
Smail, Jock	129
Smash and Grab (BUP)	29
Smith, Bob	230
Smith, Christian Jollie	149
Smith, Dolores	342
Smith, Forgan	262
Smith, Helen Z.	165
Smith, Howard	219
Smith, Ian	**502**
Smith, Joseph	159, 166, 173, 505
Smith, Joshua	150
Smith, Michael Adam	529
Smith's Weekly (journal)	52
Snow, Sydney	342
Soak the Rich (living newspaper)	103, 241
Socialist League, UK	29, 31
Socialist Theatre Movement	20

Society for Cultural Relations with the Soviet Union	225
Solidarity (Prichard)	410, 411
Song of 54 (Dowdle)	122, 249
Song of Ceylon (1934 film)	247
Song of Spain (Hughes)	98
'Song of the Bends' (song)	142
Song of Tomorrow (Kincaid)	32
Sons of the Morning (Duncan)	326, 414, **415**
Sons of the South (Farwell)	180
Soul of Man Under Socialism, The (book)	19
South Australian Workers' Weekly Herald	236, 237, 239
South Brisbane Municipal Library	198
South Maitland Recorder (newspaper)	166
Soviet Russia Today (journal)	268
Soviet Writers Union	424
'Sovietland' (song)	433
Soviets Today (journal)	128
Spanish Aid Committee	440
Spanish Relief Committee	56, 132, 213, 221
Spanish Relief Fund	162, 220, 225
Spanish Village (de Vega)	33, 112, 113
Spender, Sir Percy	140
Spink, Betty	376, 380
Spotlight (journal)	117, 118, 149, 207, 261, 281, 386, 457
Spry, Charles	283
Squaring the Circle (Kataev)	57, 241
Sriber, Charles	328
Stacy, Enid	19
Stained Pieces (Vickers)	230
Stalin, Josef	118, 276
Stanislavski, Konstantin	26, 39, 100, 112, 117, 218

Staples, Justice — 150
Star Turns Red, The (O'Casey) — 28, 136, 253, 278
Starched Aprons (Stewart) — 32, 33
State Conference of Labour Women, SA — 241
State Library of NSW — 374
Stay Down Miner (Fox) — 432, 462, 483
Step Lively, Boy! (Carroll & Grant) — 509
Stevenson, Philip — 45, 99
Stewart, Bryce — 248, 313
Stewart, Donald Ogden — 247, 328, 499
Stewart, Ena Lamont — 32
Stockholm Peace Conference — 317
Stone, Janey — 7
Stop Laughing, This is Serious! (revue) — 152
Storey, David — 364
Stourac, Richard — 14
Stow Hall, Adelaide — 249
Strangers in the Land (Brand) — 81, 82, 83, 116, 188, **190-191**, 358
Strasberg, Lee — 39
Street Theatre — 146, 363
Street, Jessie — 292, 424
Strike (Gold) — 36
Student Theatre Group, Brisbane — 57
Student Theatre Rooms, Brisbane — 179, 294
Sub Editor's Room (Rees) — 228
Subversive Theatre of Buffalo — 510
Summer of the Seventeenth Doll (Lawler) — 76, 118, 119, 250, 329, 344
Summons, John — 149
Sumner, John — 119
Sunday Mail (newspaper) — 256
Sunday Too Far Away (1975 film) — 213

Sunday Walk, The (Michel)	332
Sur Le Pont (Gray)	325
Sutherland, Doug	148
Swanson, Neville	476
Sweeney Todd (Sondheim & Wheeler)	151
Sword Sung, The (Duncan)	100, 101, 320, **348**, 413, 414
Sydney Conservatorium	139, 205, 319, 501
Sydney Eisteddfod	163, 165
Sydney Fringe Festival	365
Sydney Jewish News (newspaper)	289, **309**
Sydney Journalists' Club Competition	203
Sydney Mardi Gras	337, 364
Sydney Morning Herald (newspaper)	136, 143, 197, 253, 269, 277, 278, 323
Sydney Repertory Theatre Society	48
Sydney Town Hall	273
Sydney Trades Hall	270
Sydney Tribune (newspaper)	470
Sydney University Labour Club	129
Symon, Eric	238, 239
Symon, Jessiah	238
Symon, Nan Angel Floy aka Angel	238, 239
Symphony in Illusion (Bell)	163, 173
Synge, John Millington	203
Tactical Performance (Bogard)	484
Tait, Peta	405
Take It As Read (revue)	280
Take Me Out (Greenberg)	364
Tango Masculino (Jeffries)	365
Tank, Herb	138, 195, 230
Tanker Mackay (Tank) SEE *Longitude 49* (Tank)	
Tanner, Les	320, 328, 474

Tasker, John	143, 252, 333, 343
Teale, Leonard	139
'Teddy Bears Picnic' (song)	331
Telegraph Union	84
Telephonic Communications (Interception) Act	144
Temperamentals, The (Marans)	364
Tempo Tempo (Proletbuehne)	494
Ten Days that Shook the World (Reed)	156
Ten Years of New Theatre (book)	103
Tennant, Kylie	52, 501
Thatcher, Margaret	346
Thatcher's Women (Adshead)	345
Theatre Guild	43, 492, 493
Theatre of Fact (Littlewood)	331
Theatre Union	492, 494
Theatres and Public Halls Act	135, 143
Theosophical Society	225, 344
'There'll Always be a Menzies While There's a BHP' (song)	241, 276
They Came to a City (Priestley)	251
They Passed This Way (Crawford)	206
Thief River (Blessings)	364
Thief, The (Prichard)	212
Thirteen Dead (Melbourne Writer's Group)	82, 97, 98, 99, 237
Thirty Pieces of Silver (Fast)	140, 187, 188, 230, 294, 295, 297
This Bondage (Popplewell)	215, 229
Thomas, Tom	21, 22
Thompson, Dorothy "Dot"	6, 88, 100, 102, **104-105**, 115, 117, 123, 124, 507, 508, 530,
Thompson, John	535
Thomson, J. J.	226

Thomson, P.	226
Thorndike, Sybil	20, 128
'Three Little Maids' (song)	325
Three Wives	241
Throssell, Hugo	224
Throssell, Ric	**210**, 251
Tickner, Bob	148
Till the Day I Die (Odets)	2, 31-32, 56, 57, 77, 78, 96, 98, 158, **214**, 219- 222, 229, 236, 237, 240, 242, 257, **260**, 262-273, **274-275**, 276, 282, 285, 322, 323, 351, 354, 383, 432, 446, 455, 470, 503
Time is Not Yet Ripe, The (Esson)	49
Times, London (newspaper)	27
Tinker's Wedding, The (Synge)	203
Tivoli Theatre	52
To Kill a Mockingbird (Sergil & Lee)	355
To Make My Bread (novel)	494
Tojo, Emperor	325
Toller, Ernst	20, 50, 56, 63, 132, 218, 219, 239, 320
Tom Paine (Foster)	146
Tomlinson, John	149
Tommy Tucker	215
Tomorrow the World (Gow & D'Ussau)	324
Top Girls (Churchill)	346
Topsy-Turvy Land (puppet show)	251
Toronto Theatre of Action	500
Torrents, The (Gray)	76, 80, 118, 119, 249, 250, 256, 329, 344
Touch of Silk, The (Roland)	74
Trades and Labour Council	243

Trades Hall Council	266
Trainer, Percy	221, 223
Traitor Silence (Collinson)	297, 299, 300
Tramp, The (1915 film)	247
Tramways Union	455, 457
Tranby Co-operative College	142
Transit (Stevenson)	99
Translations (Friel)	360
Transport Players	31
Trease, Geoffrey	28, 134, 355
Tressall, Robert	134
Tretyakov, Sergei	63
Trial by Falsehood (Paise & Bland)	116
Tribune (newspaper)	142, 247, 268, 269, 277, 297, 306, 327, 452, 453, 475, 482
Trojan Women, The (Sartre)	332
Trotskyist Workers' Party	272
Truman, Harry	282
Trumbo, Dalton	120, 281
Trumpets of Wrath (Kozlenko)	320, 459
Tuckett, Angela	19, 28
Tuckett, Joan	28, 29, 30, 31
Turnbull, Clive	114
TV or Not TV (revue)	329
Twelve Thousand (Frank)	132
Two Hoots (Searle)	161
Two Ronnies, The (TV)	129
Under The Coolibah Tree (Diamond) AKA *The Coolibah Tree*	119, 186, 230, 249, 256, 432
Underhill, Jeff	206
Unemployed Workers' Movement	52
Unexpected Hawk, The (Waiko)	359
Ungrateful Daughter, The (Hannett)	359

Unidentified Human Remains and the True Nature of Love (Fraser)	365
Union Label (Lawrence)	241
Union of Australian Women	328, 337
Union Theatre Repertory Company	118, 119, 120
United Association of Women	337
United Auto Workers District 65 Drama Club, USA	46-47
United Christian Peace Movement	500
United Trades and Labour Council	242
United Worker's Movement [UWM]	54
Unity (Journal)	303
Unity Dance Group	113, 115, 530
Unity Mobile Group	434, **436-437**, 439, **446**
Unity Outside Show Group	434, 435, **436-437**
Unity Singers	115
Unity Theatre Brisbane	58, 158, 179, 186, 189, 262, 504
Unity Theatre Bristol	28-31, 45
Unity Theatre England	1, 18, 100, 504
Unity Theatre Federation	447
Unity Theatre Glasgow	31-33, 440
Unity Theatre London	8, **12**, 24-28, 31, 33, 34, 99, 106, 112, 114, 116, 124, 132, 134, 183, 193, 262, 277, 305, 306, 326, 342, 358, 423, 429, 430, 434-440, 442, 443, 444, 445, 446, 448, 449, 500, 537
Unity Theatre Manchester	440, 441, 442
Unity Theatre Perth	222, 227
University Labour Club	50
University of Adelaide	246, 252
University of Queensland Radical Club	179

University of Sydney	157
University of Western Australia [UWA]	217
Upton, John	149
Uren, Gwen	**253**
Uren, Tom	148
Uys, Pieter-Dirk	151
Valentine, Alana	346, 351, 365
Vampire Lesbians of Sodom (Busch)	365
van Heekeren, Wayne	360
Vanzetti in the Death Cell aka Vanzetti in the Death House (monologue)	99, 134
Vanzetti, Bartolomeo	134
Vasser Experimental Theatre, USA	43
Vega, Lope de	112
Venetian Twins, The (Goldoni)	151
Vernon, Howard	376
Vernon, Nan SEE Gow, Nan	
Verwoerd, Dr	360
Verwoerd, Hendrik	142
Vestey Brothers	142
Vicary, Brian	**381**
Vickers, F. B.	230
Victoria League	175
Victorian Arts Centre Performing Arts Museum	88
Victorian Drama League One Act Play Festival	120
Victorian Royal Commission into the Communist Party	280
Vietnam Hocus Pocus (Brand)	332
Vike, Harald	213, 225, 226, 229
Village Wooing, The (Shaw)	163, 173
Volpone (Jonson)	280
Vote No! AKA No! No! (Roland)	57, 75, 239, 320, 323

Voysey Inheritance, The (Granville-Barker)	152
Waiko, John	359
Waislitz, Jacob (Yankev)	290, 322, 351
Waiting for Lefty (Odets)	24, 25, 29, 31, 41, 42, 56, 57, 63, 72, **94-95**, 96, 98, 114, 157, 158, 159, 160, 163, 165, 169, 181, 215, 221, 236, 237, 239, 241, 242, **244, 245,** 247, 262, 268, 282, 435, 493, 499, 503
Waiting for Rupert Murdoch (Upton)	149
Walesby, David	476
Walker, Alan	331
Walker, Charles	492
Walker, David	17, 18
Wall, The (Lampell)	176, 330, 352
Walsh, Eric	248
Walshe, Christina	21
War (Norén)	335
War and Peace (Tolstoy)	144
War on the Waterfront (Roland)	4, 67, 75, 250, 322, 380, 457
Ward, Audrey AKA Audrey Grant née Hill	376, 388
Ward, Eddie	276
Ward, Russel	**130-131**
Wardman, Bill	439
Warner, James	150
Wasserman, Dale	362
Wasserstein, Wendy	349
Waterloo Creek (Milliss)	149
Waterside Workers' Federation [WWF]	4, 5, 137, 141, 278, 337, 453, 457, 460, 461, 463
Waterside Workers' Federation Cultural Committee	128

Waterside Workers' Federation Film Unit	463, 469
Waterside Workers' Federation Hall	354
Waterside Workers' Theatre	460
Watt, Alan	83
Wattle Dance Group	247, 249, 256, 530
Wattle Films	536
Wattle Records	536
Watts, Cecil	323
Watts, Stuart	270
We, The People (Rice)	230, 328
Weeks, Wally	129
Weigel, Helene	171
Weil, Kurt	493
Weiss, Peter	363
Welcome Home (Crawford)	111, 245
Wells, Jerold	83, 129, **130-131**, 160, 164, 165, 167, **324**, 363, 501, 505
Wells, Julie	398, 426
West Australian (newspaper)	**214**, 217, 219, 220, 224, 232
West Australian Drama Festival	56, 217
West Australian Theatre Council	205
Western Limit (Gray)	381
Westralian Worker (newspaper)	214, 227, 231
Wharf Revue (revue)	331
What Happens to Love? (Willis)	33, 339
What's New (revue)	145, 470
Whateley, Dick	321
Where's That Bomb? (Cullan)	25, 31, 56, 99, 103, 134, 181, 215, 221, 222, 293, 294, 453
White House Murder Case, The (Feiffer)	146
White Justice (ballet)	**110**, 111

White, Jo	535
White, Patrick	82, 252
Whitlam, Gough	333
Who's Afraid of the Working Class (Melbourne Workers' Theatre)	363
Who's Who in the Berlin Zoo (Red Megaphones)	57, 132, 212
Whole World Over, The (Siminov)	115
Wiggins, Leslie	292
Wilcox, John	221
Wilde, Oscar	19
Williams, Idris	472
Williams, Vic	230
Williamson, David	333
Williamson, J. C.	217
Willis Hall	330
Willis, Eric	143
Willis, Ted	31, 33, 84, 99, 107, 297, 305, 339, 438
Wills, Geoff	453
Wilmot, Frank	225
Wilson, Lily	159
Wilson, Richard	270
Wilson, Valerie	338
Winnipeg New Theatre	500
Winterset (Anderson)	245
Wireless Weekly (journal)	277, **454**
Wisdom of Children, The (Tolstoy)	29
Wolf, Friedrich	160, 172
Wollstonecraft, Mary	339
Woman in the Window, The (de Groen)	338
Woman Tamer, The (Esson)	49
Women of Spain (Prichard)	56, 99, 215, 220
Women, The (Booth)	215, **216**, 219, 222, 229

Women's Abortion Action Campaign	337
Women's Auxiliary of the Miners' Federation	173
Women's Christian Temperance Union	500
Women's Commission of International Peace	317, 504
Women's International Democratic Federation	337
Women's International League of Peace and Freedom	500
Women's International Zionist Organisation	291
Women's Liberal Country League	256
Women's Service Guild	500
Wood, Roy	225
Wooden Dish, The (Morris)	251
Woolacott, Leslie	**412**
Workers Dramatic Council USA	36, 37
Workers International Relief [WIR]	50, 62
Workers, Beware (Roland)	221, 322
Workers' Art (journal)	66, **318**
Workers' Art Club [WAC]	1, 50, 54, 60, 66, 70, 99, 128, 129, 132, 134, 212, 261, 289, 317, 319, 338, 353, 364, 376, 429
Workers' Art Club, Melbourne	1, 50, 52, 65, 96
Workers' Art Club, Sydney	1, 6, 19, 61, 62, 63, **64**, 65, **127**, 155
Workers' Art Guild [WAG]	56, 209, 212, 213, 215, 216, 218, 220, 221, 222, 223, 228, 229, 231, 233, 292
Workers' Art Guild, Perth	99, **216**, 501
Workers' Art Theatre Group [WATG]	57, 132
Workers' Drama League, USA [WDL]	36
Workers' Educational Association [WEA]	21, 30, 58, 156, 159, 169, 170, 269
Workers' International Relief Conference	128

Workers' Laboratory Theatre, NY [WLT]	36, 38, 441
Workers' Sports Federation	65
Workers' Star (newspaper)	**217**, 220, 222, 231, 233, **348**
Workers' Theatre Group [WTG]	1, 28, 261, 263, 266, 267
Workers' Theatre Group, Melbourne	96, 289
Workers' Theatre Group, Perth	410
Workers' Theatre Movement, UK [WTM]	19, 20, 21, 22, **23**, 24, 31, 429, 434, 441
Workers' Theatre, USA (journal)	38
Workers' Voice (newspaper)	97, 98, 268
Workers' Weekly (newspaper)	162, 164, 167, 269, 277, 501
Workers' Weekly Herald (newspaper)	241, 242
Workhorse	103
Working Men's College, Melbourne	99
Working Woman, The (journal)	344
Workroom, The (Grumberg)	343
Works Committee of the Mortlake Gas Works	294
Works Progress Administration, USA	43, 228
World Disarmament Movement	500
World of Sholem Aleichem, The (Perl)	352
World Festival for Peace, Bucharest	317
World Peace Committee	503
World Peace Council Congress	424
World Youth Festival	444, 537
Worth, June	376
Wright, Basil	247
Writers' Association	129
Writers' League	129
Writing on the Wall (Hepworth)	120, 313
X=O: A Night of the Trojan War (Drinkwater)	132, 212, 218, 320

Yeats, W. B.	48, 293
Yellow Spot AKA Professor Mamlock, The (Waislitz)	290, 322, 351
Yobbo Nowt (McGrath)	149, 150, 338
Yokel, Alex	495
Young Communist League, GB	22, 29
Young, D. R.	170
Young, David	142
Youth Carnival for Peace and Friendship, Sydney	193, 247, 312
Youth Theatre of Action	97
Zangwill, Israel	290
Zavaros, Ferenc Alexander	363
Zenith theatre, Chatswood	150
Zetkin, Clara	62
Zhdanov, Andrei	61, 117

ABOUT INTERVENTIONS

Interventions is an independent, not-for-profit, incorporated publisher. We publish left-wing, radical and socialist books by Australian authors. We welcome books which for political or financial reasons are unlikely to be accepted by commercial publishers. Our books cover a wide range of topics including labour history, left-wing politics, radical cultural themes, socialism and Marxism, memoirs, and works about resistance to racism, sexism and all other forms of oppression.

At Interventions we believe radical ideas matter. We want our books to be part of the development of a critical and engaged Australian left.

By highlighting alternative voices, especially those that have been pushed to the margins, we hope to contribute to a greater insight and awareness of the injustices that exist in society, and the many efforts at the grassroots to right these wrongs.

We welcome publishing proposals. If you are interested in submitting a proposal please check out the information for authors on our website https://interventions.org.au/forauthors. If you think your proposal fits our guidelines please follow the submission process outlined there. Please note we are not currently publishing poetry or fiction.

Interventions has no independent source of income and is committed to keeping prices accessible. As bookshops and warehouses close around the world, our future hangs in the balance. By supporting us you will help us keep radical ideas alive and accessible to all. If you would like to support radical publishing in Australia please consider supporting our Patreon. Visit patreon.com/interventions to donate a small amount each month and get some great rewards.

Website: https://interventions.org.au/

Contact us: info@interventions.org.au or use the contact form on the website.

ABOUT THIS BOOK

The Interventions editor and production project manager for this book was Janey Stone with support from Lisa Milner. Simon Strong created the index. Apart from the contributors the following people assisted with proof reading: Roby Aiken, Phillip Deery, Alex Ettling, Kathy Gibbings, Lenore Layman, Bobbie Oliver, Carrolline Rhodes, Sarah Runciman, Karen Throssell and Phillip Whitefield.

This book was copy edited by Eris Harrison of Effective Editing.

This book was designed and laid out by Viktoria Ivanova. Viktoria is a communication designer in Melbourne. She is a book publishing fiend, runs Spark Publishing Inc (for art-centric left books) and also designs for Victorian Socialists.

Passionate Friends
Mary Fullerton, Mabel Singleton and Miles Franklin
Sylvia Martin

'A fascinating portrait of friendship, love, desire, politics and art - and the blurry, shape-shifting lines between them. I relished this book, rich in scholarship and full of heart.'

Clare Wright, author of *The Forgotten Rebels of Eureka* and *You Daughters of Freedom*

Mary Fullerton (1868 - 1946) and Mabel Singleton (1877 - 1965) met in Melbourne as suffrage and peach activists in Vida Goldstein's Women's Political Association. They remained together for 35 years as loving friends, raising Mabel's son born in 1911. Through her literary friendship with Miles Franklin (1879 - 1954), Mary Fullerton's last two volumes of poetry were published in the 1940s.

Rescued from near destruction, a box of Mary's manuscripts eventually made its way to the Mitchell Library. It contained poems she never sent to Mabel. These poignant poems trace a love story that sheds light on how women of the early twentieth century may have understood their love for each other.

MORE FROM INTERVENTIONS

Radical Perth, Militant Fremantle
Edited by Charlie Fox, Alexis Vassiley, Bobbie Oliver, and Lenore Layman

Radical Perth, Militant Fremantle tells 34 fascinating stories of radical moments In the cities' past, from as long ago as the 1890s and as recent as Occupy: the revolutionary theatre of the Workers Art Guild; the riot of unemployed workers outside the Treasury building; rock concerts inside St Georges Cathedral; bodgies and widgies cutting up the dance floor at the Scarborough Beach Snake Pit; the Point Peron women's peace camp, and many more.

MORE FROM INTERVENTIONS

The Crime of Not Knowing Your Crime: Ric Throssell Against ASIO
By Karen Throssell
With a contextual essay by Phil Deery

"'Through entwined poetry and prose, Karen Throssell illuminates ASIO's persecution of her extraordinary family. In the post 9/11 era, too many Australians have forgotten what happened in the Cold War. That's why this story matters."

Jeff Sparrow, writer and broadcaster

My grandmother was one of Australia's greatest novelists, my grandfather won the Victoria Cross for gallantry and my father was hounded all his life as a spy.

This is a three generational story. It's about my life; it's about my father, Ric; it's about my grandparents, the writer Katharine Susannah Prichard and the war hero Hugo Throssell.

It's a study of the psychology of spies and those obsess about them, a narrative of guilt and innocence told through poetry, prose and historical documents.

MORE FROM INTERVENTIONS

www.ingramcontent.com/pod-product-compliance
Lightning Source LLC
Chambersburg PA
CBHW071950290426
44109CB00018B/1980